exotic
tropical
fishes

Dr. Herbert R. Axelrod

Dr. Cliff W. Emmens

Dr. Duncan Sculthorpe

Mr. William Vorderwinkler

Mr. Neal Pronek

Dr. Warren E. Burgess

Distributed in the UNITED STATES by T.F.H. Publications, Inc., One T.F.H. Plaza, Neptune City, NJ 07753; in CANADA to the Pet Trade by H & L Pet Supplies Inc., 27 Kingston Crescent, Kitchener, Ontario N2B 2T6; Rolf C. Hagen Ltd., 3225 Sartelon Street, Montreal 382 Quebec; in CANADA to the Book Trade by Macmillan of Canada (A Division of Canada Publishing Corporation), 164 Commander Boulevard, Agincourt, Ontario M1S 3C7; in ENGLAND by T.F.H. Publications Limited, Cliveden House/Priors Way/Bray, Maidenhead, Berkshire SL6 2HP, England; in AUSTRALIA AND THE SOUTH PACIFIC by T.F.H. (Australia) Pty. Ltd., Box 149, Brookvale 2100 N.S.W., Australia; in NEW ZEALAND by Ross Haines & Son, Ltd., 18 Monmouth Street, Grey Lynn, Auckland 2, New Zealand; in SINGAPORE AND MALAYSIA by MPH Distributors (S) Pte., Ltd., 601 Sims Drive, #03/07/21, Singapore 1438; in the PHILIPPINES by Bio-Research, 5 Lippay Street, San Lorenzo Village, Makati Rizal; in SOUTH AFRICA by Multipet Pty. Ltd., 30 Turners Avenue, Durban 4001. Published by T.F.H. Publications, Inc. Manufactured in the United States of America by T.F.H. Publications, Inc.

TABLE OF CONTENTS

EXOTIC AQUARIUM PLANTS

RAISING TROPICAL FISHES COMMERCIALLY

EXOTIC TROPICAL FISHES

The Fishes are listed in Alphabetical Order and the pages are folioed with the code letter F-.

AQUARIUM MANAGEMENT

Twenty-ninth Edition
© 1988 by T.F.H. Publications, Inc.
Previous copyrights: © 1962, © 1963, © 1964, © 1965, © 1966, © 1967,
© 1968, © 1969, © 1971, © 1972, © 1973,. © 1974, © 1976, © 1977, © 1981,
© 1985

Using the basic tools of the aquarium hobby, you can create a panorama of natural underwater beauty right in your own livingroom. Photo by Van Raam.

1

Principles of Aquarium Management

by Dr. C. W. Emmens

The Tank: Correct selection of a fish tank is the first step in successful aquarium keeping. The rectangular glass tank, either made wholly of glass or with a metal frame and glass sides and a bottom of glass, slate or other material, is by far the best vessel. The tank will usually contain sand or gravel, plants, and decorative rocks or other ornaments, although it is generally felt best to confine the decoration to natural looking substances. The chief decoration of a furnished fresh-water aquarium is the plants. These often contribute more to the attractiveness of the tank than do the fishes themselves.

The tank is usually between five and fifty gallons in capacity; favorite sizes are $24'' \times 12'' \times 12''$ or $24'' \times 12'' \times 16''$, which holds fifteen and twenty gallons respectively. Smaller tanks cannot house a decorative selection of the common aquatic plants, nor many fishes or any large fishes, while bigger tanks are expensive and somewhat more difficult to service. However, tropical fishes can be housed in smaller tanks than cold-water fishes,

The shape of the tank is very important. A standard rectangular tank (below) has a comfortable surface to volume ratio for proper gaseous exchange. The tall tanks (opposite) are ideal for vertically oriented species (*Pterophyllum*, etc.) but will support fewer fishes than one of the same volume but with a larger surface area. Photo courtesy Chris Clear; photo below by G. Steven Dow.

because they can be crowded more and because many of them do not grow so large. Even a 3 or 5 gallon tank can, therefore, contain a selection of the smaller tropicals. With the larger tropicals, a 15 gallon tank might comfortably contain a dozen 3 inch barbs, but only 4 or 5 goldfish of similar size, and only a single pair of fancy goldfish such as Orandas of the same size.

Fishes and Plants: Fishes breathe oxygen and exhale carbon dioxide and thus in total they use up oxygen and foul the water with carbon dioxide and excrement. Plants also breathe oxygen, but in sufficiently bright light they manufacture sugar from carbon dioxide taken from their surroundings, whether air or water, and they release oxygen. They also absorb dissolved salts and use these together with carbon dioxide, in building up complex organic compounds. Animal excrement, usually known as "mulm" is only available to them after it has been broken down by fungi or bacteria and made soluble. Thus plants, in adequate light, tend to restore oxygen to the environment and to remove the waste products of animals. In poor light or in darkness, they deplete the water or air of oxygen just as do fishes.

From these facts grew the concept of a balanced aquarium, with the waste products of the fishes absorbed by the plants, and the oxygen necessary for the fishes provided by the action of the plants in light. This idea must be modified in practice, but the basic principle is nevertheless sound, and a well-planted tank with adequate illumination will usually stay clear and sweet for months or years with little attention.

Aquaria should be as shallow as possible, since the surface of water exposed to the air is the most important factor in determining the number of fish they can safely hold. However, a very shallow tank is an eyesore, and a compromise is always made between biological and artistic requirements. Many prefer a "double cube" type of construction, with the tank twice as long as it is wide and high, i.e. 24″ × 12″ × 12″ as quoted above. This tank is still rather shallow for the full growth of plants and looks better if the height is somewhat increased, so that a common variation is 24″ × 12″ × 14″ or even 24″ × 12″ × 16″. Such tanks can hold no more fishes than the first-mentioned, they merely look nicer.

To compute the gallon capacity of a tank, multiply the length, width and height in inches together and divide by 231, thus:

$$\frac{18 \times 8 \times 10}{231} = \frac{1440}{231} = 6.2 \text{ gallons}$$

This refers to the actual volume of the tank, and if allowance is to be made for a 1-inch air space on top and 1½ inches of sand at the bottom, the actual water volume is only about ¾ of the calculated volume in this instance. This does not matter when considering fish capacity, however, as we then use the surface area, as explained more fully below.

Fish Capacity: Mention has just been made of the balanced aquarium, and of the reciprocal actions of plants and animals. It was believed until recently, that the exchange of carbon dioxide and oxygen between fish and plants, taking place directly through the water, was more important than is really the case. With plants in a good light, and in a crowded tank, this interaction may matter considerably, and the tank is often in a poor state at night. With a tank not unduly crowded, either with fish or plants, the exchange of gases between the air and water is more important than any other factor. This is why the surface area of the tank counts for so much, and why, in practically all circumstances, the influence of plants may be ignored when thinking of fish capacity.

In addition to surface area, surface movement and the circulation of water within a tank are important, and that is why an aerated tank can hold more fish than a still tank. The fact that the movements of the water in aeration are produced by air bubbles is usually of little consequence, and is an example of getting the right result for the wrong reason. The old idea behind aeration was to increase the contact of air and water

This is a large tank. As such it can comfortably hold many fish, but its fish-holding capacity would be increased still further by the use of mechanical aids. Photo by G. J. M. Timmerman.

The fish capacity of a tank can be increased by the use of air stones (right). With ganged valves the filter and air stone(s) can be operated from a single pump. The valves can also be used to control the amount of bubbles released by a stone (below). Photo of air stone by Laurence E. Perkins.

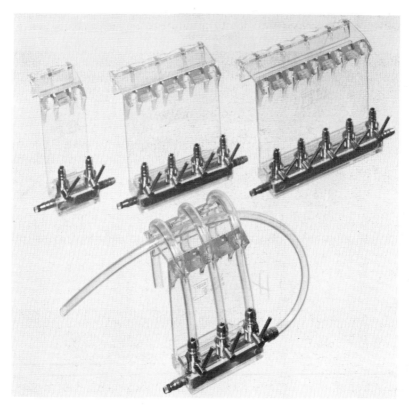

and to "force" oxygen into the water by sending fine bubbles coursing briskly up through the tank. Unless a very heavy spray of very fine bubbles is used, however, the surface of water exposed to air in the bubbles is small and unimportant, and the movement caused at the tank surface is all important.

When we calculate fish capacity by surface area, we may also modify this by including the effects of temperature, water movement and various other factors. The warmer the water, the lower the solubility of oxygen, and the lower the fish capacity. However, the following estimates are based on an average temperature of about 75°F. (for tropical fishes) without aeration. They are also based on the assumption that young fish and small fish, even though adult, use more oxygen per gram or ounce of body weight than do larger fish. This is in line with such scanty experimental reports as are available and also with general experience. The estimates are not based on the "gallon" or "inch of fish" rules, which give various figures for the number of inches of fish per gallon which may be placed in tanks, because this type of computation is clearly wrong and is not in line either with the practice or experience of observant aquarists. It is assumed that, age and activity apart, the same volume or weight of fish uses about the same amount of oxygen per minute whether it comprises a hundred small fishes or one big fish. However, small fish are usually more active and young fish are still rapidly growing. Therefore they consume more oxygen, weight-for-weight, and allowance is made for this to the extent that one ounce of ½-inch fishes is allowed 5 times the oxygen consumption of one ounce of 2½-inch fishes, and at a 6-inch size, each ounce of fish is allowed rather less oxygen than the 2½-inchers. The base-line is the 2½-inch tropical fish, which is allowed 20 square inches of surface area. Fat fishes of the same length are likely to use more oxygen than slimmer fishes, but this fact is fortunately minimized by the greater activity and therefore greater oxygen need of the slimmer, minnow-like types. Estimates should be divided by 3 for cold-water fish and by 6 for fancy goldfish varieties. The 20-square-inch basis for a 2½-inch fish is intended to permit further growth and good health. The fishes would not be expected to show distress if their numbers were doubled, but they would not flourish so well. The estimates are approximate and could be misleading in special cases, but from experience of their application it is felt that they are a much better guide than other common recommendations. One major alteration to the rule applies to the Anabantids (see below) which, when the labyrinth is developed, require only half the surface area per fish otherwise recommended. (The labyrinth is present in all but the very young fry.) It is also well known that Barbs are in need of more air surface than Tetras of the same size.

Body length of fishes in inches.	No. of fish per sq. foot (144 sq. ins.) of surface area.	Sq. ins. per fish.
$\frac{1}{2}$	180	0.8
$\frac{3}{4}$	100	1.4
1	55	2.6
$1\frac{1}{2}$	20	6.6
2	12	12.5
$2\frac{1}{2}$	7	20
3	5	30
4	2	65
5	1	120
6	1	180

The body length excludes the tail fin.

Example 1.

In a 15-gallon tank, with a surface area of 288 square inches, the following fishes are to be housed:

    8 Tetras   each about $1\frac{1}{2}$ inches long
  10 Tetras   each about 2 inches long
    6 Barbs   each about 2 inches long
    6 Gouramis each about $2\frac{1}{2}$ inches long
    2 Cichlids   each about 3 inches long

Are they likely to be overcrowded, or can even more be added?
We have:

        8 fishes at $1\frac{1}{2}$ inches need $6.6 \times 8 = 52$ sq. inches
     16 fishes at 2 inches need $12.5 \times 16 = 200$ sq. inches
      6 fishes at $2\frac{1}{2}$ inches need $20 \times 6 = 120$ sq. inches
  6 Gouramis at $2\frac{1}{2}$ inches need $10 \times 6 = 60$ sq. inches
      2 fishes at 3 inches need $30 \times 2 = 60$ sq. inches
                            Total $= 492$ sq. inches

CONCLUSION: *The fishes are crowded, and cannot be expected to be at their best. Certainly no more should be added, and it would be best to omit a few, especially the Barbs.*

Example 2.

What size of tank should be used to house 100 fry at present $\frac{1}{2}$-inch in length, with room to grow them to $\frac{3}{4}$-inch before moving them again?

It is the final size of fry that matters, hence the tank must have a surface area of 100×1.4 sq. in. or 1 sq. foot approx. If they were to reach one inch, then an area of 260 sq. in. or approx. 2 sq. feet would be needed, i.e. a 15-gallon tank.

Factors Affecting Fish Capacity: The best way to increase fish capacity is water movement, usually supplied by aeration. This can double the safety margin, so that up to twice the fish population can be kept in a well aerated tank, but only if the tank is also well planted and kept clean, or if the water is given frequent partial changes to eliminate the accumulation of waste materials. Water movement tends to stir up waste material and aid its more rapid solution in the water, thus adequate provision for purification is needed.

Factors which reduce fish capacity are the presence of waste materials, more especially unconsumed food or dead fish and plant material, less so actual excretory products of the fishes. All these substances use oxygen as they decompose, reduce that available to the fishes and cause excess CO_2 production. Another factor is the presence of invertebrate animal life, other than air-breathers. Colonial sponges or polyps, an excess of unconsumed living worms or crustacea may make conditions dangerous for fishes. A final important factor is temperature. Oxygen dissolves more readily the cooler the water, so that at 50°F., a gallon of water can hold about 1.8 cubic inches of oxygen (or the oxygen from about 9 cubic inches of air) whereas at 80°F. it holds only 1.3 cubic inches, about 25% less. In the average tank, an oxygen content around 0.7 cubic inches per gallon is quite adequate for the fishes; some fishes can take down to about 0.3 cubic inches without severe distress. However, at a higher temperature the fishes become considerably more active and their rate of consumption of oxygen rises, with the result that the fish capacity of the tank falls quite rapidly with increased temperature. In tropical tanks, which do not usually experience a wide temperature variation, this is not likely to matter much, but the cold water tank which undergoes a considerable rise, as on a hotter day than usual, may show severe symptoms.

The question of balance in a fish tank is therefore a relative affair, and not as pictured by the average aquarist. The greatest "adjustors" are the fishes themselves, which can vary their respiratory rate about 10-fold, and thus cope with a wide range of oxygen availability. This does not mean, however, that they can live in a tenth of the normal oxygen concentration as the rate at which the gills can take it from the water falls sharply with the decrease in concentration, so that the average fish is in distress when a 50% fall occurs, as shown above. That is why some fishes, particularly those used to running water or the open sea, cannot stand ordinary aquarium life, as the oxygen content even at best is below their tolerance.

Aquarium Water: Water from the faucet *may be* perfectly satisfactory for the aquarium immediately after it is drawn, but often it is not. It is likely to contain free chlorine, especially in city areas, and it is possibly under sufficient pressure to contain an excess of other dissolved gases. It may be of the wrong salinity or hardness, and it may be too acid or too alkaline. However, in most districts tap water is satisfactory after standing for a day or two, a process called "conditioning." This allows for gas exchange between the water and the air, which may be hastened by aeration or by boiling and cooling again, followed by brisk aeration.

Chlorinated water may be rendered safe by the addition of one grain per gallon of sodium thiosulphate (the "hypo" of photographers), *but this does not guarantee its suitability in other ways.* Distilled water or even filtered melted snow may be used; if so, some salts should best be added for the comfort of most fishes, particularly live-bearers. A suitable addition to distilled water would be:

3 teaspoons (¾ oz.) of common salt
1 teaspoon (¼ oz.) of potassium sulphate
1 teaspoon (¼ oz.) of magnesium sulphate
per 10 gallons of distilled or snow water.

Rain water may need similar treatment, but it is dangerous to use in towns, for on the way down it collects a lot of dirt and harmful chemicals from the air and may be poisonous. Snow is less liable to be polluted, even in towns.

Hard water contains dissolved salts which are largely absent from soft water. Very soft water may have salts added as for distilled water, whereas normally hard water doesn't need them. Typical analyses of sea water, hard water, and soft water, in percentages of various important salts are as follows:

	Sodium Chloride	Potassium Sulphate	Magnesium sulphate	Calcium carbonate etc.	Total
Sea water	2.8	0.14	0.66	0.10	3.7
Hard water	0.005	0.007	0.007	0.015	0.034
Soft water	0.004	0.000	0.000	0.002	0.006

Hard water is usually alkaline, soft water is usually neutral to acid in reaction. Acidity and alkalinity are measured on a scale which goes from 0 to 14, called the *pH scale.* pH does not stand for "percentage hydrogen," as is often stated, but represents the logarithm of the concentration of hydrogen ions per litre of water. This is a convenient method of expressing the state of affairs in chemistry, but need not worry aquarists further. Neutral water has a pH of 7, acid water has a pH of less than 7 while alkaline water has a pH of more than 7. Strong acids are down in the 1-2 region, strong alkalis up in the 12-13 region. A weak acid like carbonic acid (dissolved carbon dioxide), at full strength, has a pH of about 4, and a weak alkali like sodium bicarbonate has a pH of about 9, and this is approximately the range of pH seen in natural waters. Few fishes can stand this entire range, but most can be happy anywhere between 6 and 8, and many do not show distress when well beyond these limits. Most aquarium plants flourish best at a slightly alkaline pH, in particular the *Cryptocoryne* species which will often rapidly die off in acid water. There was a period of emphasis on pH in fish keeping, when pH differences of 0.1 or 0.2 were thought to matter, but a commonsense view of the problem is now more usual, and few worry about the pH value of ordinary, successfully-maintained tanks. When breeding, pH may matter more, as the germ cells or fertilized eggs and fry, do not necessarily tolerate as wide a range as the adults, but very little is known in detail on this question. The pH of a tank usually rises during the day, as carbonic acid gas is removed by the plants and falls at night when both plants and animals produce it. The extent to which this affects pH readings depends on the degree of aeration, the atmosphere in the room, and the fish and plant density. In a crowded tank in a rather foul room, such as an exhibition tank at a crowded indoor show, the pH may fall alarmingly in a few hours to values of 5.5 or lower.

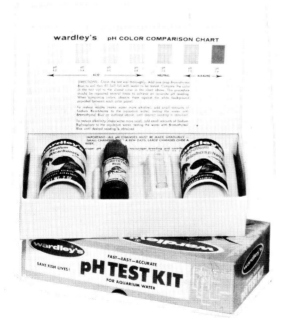

A pH test kit is almost a must for aquarists. Many problems are often solved by checking the pH and adjusting the water to suit the fishes.

To measure pH, chemicals called indicators may be used. These are added drop-wise to a small sample of aquarium water, and change color according to the pH. Thus, the commonly-used bromthymol blue is yellow when at a mildly acid pH, green when neutral, and blue when alkaline, covering a useful range of about pH 6.0 to 7.6. For sufficiently accurate work color charts are supplied in steps of 0.2 or 0.3. A newer departure is the comparator paper which is dipped straight into the tank and compared with a chart afterwards. These are not always reliable after long storage.

To adjust pH, when really necessary, acid and alkaline sodium phosphates are best, but sodium bicarbonate may be used on the alkaline side instead. Such adjustments must be made with care, along the following lines:

Make a solution of sodium monohydrogen phosphate (Na_2HPO_4, the alkaline phosphate) at a concentration of 1 in 100 (1 gram per 100 ml. or $1\frac{1}{2}$ oz. per gallon approx.) and a similar solution of the dihydrogen phosphate (NaH_2PO_4, the acid phosphate). When mixed in equal quantities, these two solutions make up a *buffer* solution, with a pH of 6.9 approx. and a capacity for holding its pH against the addition of other salts. Such a buffer solution may be used for holding an aquarium pH steady, but its capacity is not unlimited and the salts are gradually broken down. If so used, not more than about 1 part in 20 of the mixture should be added to aquarium water, which should first be brought to pH 7.0.

To bring a tank to neutral pH or any other desired pH, a sample of the water, a definite quantity such as 1 pint, should be withdrawn. If the pH is too low, i.e. the water is too acid, the alkaline phosphate solution described above is added in small amounts with frequent testing until the desired effect is obtained. Then, by simple proportion, the amount to be added to the whole tank is determined. This addition should be made with constant stirring. If the pH is too high, the acid phosphate solution is used in the same manner. When making such adjustments, do not forget to calculate as accurately as possible the true water volume, making allowance for space occupied by sand, rocks etc. and for the top level in the tank. Lastly, do not make drastic alterations in pH all at once. Steps of more than about 0.5 per day are to be avoided, and for complete safety it is probably best to make adjustments in steps of not more than 0.2-0.3 at a time. We don't actually know for certain what the safe limits are.

Changing Water: When the earlier aquarists syphoned off detritus and mulm, they usually filtered the water and returned as much as possible to the tank. As a result, the water gradually acquired a rich, wine color and a limpid clarity which is very attractive. It is surprising how yellow or even reddish the water can become without causing comment, unless a sample is compared with fresh, colorless water, when the difference is very obvious.

This "aged" water was supposed to have become more suited to the fishes than fresher, although not necessarily completely new, water. The idea was that fishes make water in which they live more suitable for themselves and even poisonous to other fishes, particularly to different species. There seems to be little foundation for this belief, and it is certain that the same water, kept long enough, becomes poisonous to all fishes, even in the presence of growing plants. Danger to other fishes may well be the result of their inability to take a sudden exposure to water to which the permanent inhabitants have become gradually accustomed, as it has become steadily charged with waste products. However, the question is not settled and would repay more study. It has even been suggested that some "animal protein" factor is involved, but this is again very doubtful. Both expectation and experience now concur in advising a steady change-over of tank water. This may not need to be very much, usually 10-20% per week or fortnight is sufficient, but in crowded, badly illuminated tanks, a change of 20-30% per cent per week may be a decided advantage. Even in winter, when the gas content of fresh tap water is highest, the danger of such a volume of replacement is negligible, but if preferred, it may be left to stand a day or two before use. Of course, the new water must be at the right temperature: never rely on the heater to take care of sudden additions of cold water to a warm tank, as even if the fish escape immediate chilling in the cold stream, the overall temperature after mixing may have fallen dangerously.

Cloudy Water: Water may become cloudy for a number of reasons, some of which demand a complete change with conditioned water. The most potentially dangerous condition is green cloudiness due to the presence of green algae. It is usually brought on by too much light in the presence of organic materials in solution. It is fundamentally healthy water, but it spoils the appearance of the tank and is usually not desired, except when raising fry. If it becomes very thick there is a danger that the rapidly growing algae might suddenly die off and foul the water. The first warning sign of this imminent catastrophe is a slight yellowing of the water, which then rapidly turns foetid and is very dangerous to the fishes. The aquarium water should be changed in its entirety without delay, using even fresh tap water at the right temperature rather than taking the risk of leaving the fishes as they are. A store of spare "aged" water is commonly kept by experienced aquarists for just such an emergency.

Cleanliness, moderate light, no over-crowding of tanks, and the presence of plenty of higher plants, especially floating plants, helps to prevent the appearance of green cloudiness. When a tank receives only, or almost only, electric illumination it practically never develops green water, mainly because it does not receive excessive total illumination. Acidity of the water makes for cleanliness, but not for good plant growth, so that both the algae and higher plants are discouraged together. It is often said that a partial or near-complete change of water only serves to stimulate further algal growth; however, this does not always occur, and green water may be cured immediately by syphoning it off—along with any debris in the tank—and replacing it with fresh conditioned water.

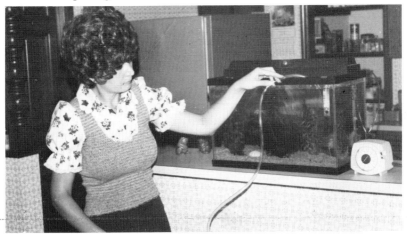

A periodic change of part of the water in your tank is highly recommended. Old water can be siphoned off with a tube as shown. Photo by G. Steven Dow.

Another type of cloudy water, grey cloudiness, may be due to infusoria, bacteria, fungi or just dirt. It often follows on the setting up of a tank, sometimes because the sand was not washed thoroughly, but often because there is a burst of animal life which gets going ahead of the algae. This cloudiness usually disappears in a few days, whether caused by dirt or infusoria, and is not dangerous. Bacterial or fungal cloudiness is a bad sign, usually seen in established tanks which are "going bad." It may be caused by excessive decaying matter, usually dry food, but sometimes by a dead fish, by insufficient light, by overcrowding, or by the use of unsuitable gravel or rock which provide niches and crannies where excreta and food are caught and decay. While attention must be paid to the root causes such as overcrowding, grey cloudiness may often be temporarily corrected by brisk aeration or by the addition of disinfectants and antibiotics. Another effective method with both grey and green cloudiness is to place one or two large fresh water mussels in the tank for a few days. These will clear water when a filter will not.

Removal of Mulm and Algae: In the course of replacing some of the water at intervals of one or two weeks as recommended, it is easy to syphon off much of the mulm from the bottom of the tank. A convenient way to do this is with a glass tube of from ¼ to ½-inch in diameter, slightly shorter than the aquarium depth if it is left straight, or a little longer if the top is given an angle bend. Both are methods for preventing the rubber tubing which is attached to the glass tube from kinking. The end of the glass tube which will be immersed in the water should be softened by heat and then gently pressed on to a flat surface, holding the tube upright, so that the entrance is slightly constricted, to prevent pebbles, snails and so forth from getting into the tube and clogging it further up. Any foreign matter which enters the tube will be small enough to pass readily through. The rubber tubing should reach for 2 or 3 feet below the water level, so as to give a convenient head of pressure.

A syphon is started by sucking the end of the rubber tubing with the glass tube immersed, or, if preferred, by filling it with water by dipping it in the tank. With a little practice, it is possible to start the syphon without getting a mouth full of water. The rate of flow is controlled by

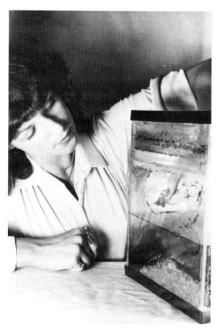

Algal growth, mineral deposits, and other material can usually be scraped off the sides of an aquarium with a simple razor blade or one of the long-handled scrapers commercially available. Photo by Dr. Herbert R. Axelrod.

pinching the rubber tubing, and the syphon is then run gently over the aquarium bottom like a vacuum cleaner. The end of the glass tube may also be poked well into the sand, sucking up sample "bores" to see if all is well, and that underneath the surface the sand is not becoming foul and grey with bacteria. If it is, it is wise to go on syphoning the sand away until the foul patch is removed, and to replace it with fresh sand afterwards. With experience, it is possible to remove much of the bottom of a tank, leaving the plants practically undisturbed, and to replace it by running clean dry sand down a funnel under the surface of the water. If the sand is wet, it sticks and must be washed into the tank, or it may be put in by hand and the plants afterwards well brushed to remove sand grains. The foul sand may be washed, dried off, and left in the sun to be used again.

The base of the syphon may alternatively be flared out like a small funnel, and this if plunged into the sand, does not lift much or any of the actual sand, but it draws out other matter and helps considerably in preventing the major operation just described. However, a well-set-up tank does not often develop serious sand trouble.

There are a number of aquarium gadgets on the market for the mechanical removal of mulm and other materials. The most popular is the filter, dealt with in detail later, but there are also little "vacuum cleaners" available for use with an air pump instead of the simple syphon just described. They may be very efficient in clearing the mulm and clarifying the water, but their use does not involve the removal of some of the water, and so this should still be done even though little or no visible mulm remains to be syphoned off.

Green algae will cause not only green water, but some types will coat the inside of the glass if there is too much light. They may be removed with a scraper, essentially a razor blade on a convenient handle, or more easily, with steel or nylon wool. Wrap a small ball of the wool around the end of a stick and rub the glass over with moderate pressure or use a pad with the hand or fingers immersed in the tank. It usually takes only a couple of minutes to clean a large tank thoroughly. When removing algae at the base of the tank, be careful not to get sand caught in the wool, as it may scratch the glass.

Under electric illumination, blue-green algae are more likely to be a nuisance, settling not only on the glass, but also on the plants. They may be scraped from the glass as usual, but to remove them from the plants is almost impossible. Cut down the light and hope that the algae disappear, or remove all fishes, snails, etc. and treat with 1 part per million copper sulphate (crystalline) for a few hours, afterwards removing nearly all of the water before introducing fishes again.

Light: Indoor aquaria rarely receives ideal natural illumination, which is daylight coming from directly overhead. If they get sufficient daylight, they usually receive it through a window to one side or at the back. This is satisfactory for most fishes and does not cause undue disturbance to plant growth as long as the tank doesn't get too much oblique light. If it does, the eventual result will be plants growing at an angle or at least with leaves unevenly developed, and fishes swimming at an angle, particularly the barbs and some of the characins, which seem to be very sensitive to the direction of lighting.

Large tanks can stand quite a bit of direct sunlight and if it can be arranged so that this falls more on the back and sides and not much on the front glass, the former will become coated with a lush growth of algae, while the latter can be kept clear with only an occasional wiping with steel wool or nylon staple. The algae will act as an automatic light screen and usually provide a very pleasant-looking background to the other plants, giving a look of maturity and depth to the tank, and providing food for the live-bearing fishes. Care must be taken to avoid overheating the tank, and it must be recalled that the tank goes on absorbing heat even when the algal coat has formed. A heat-preventing screen should be made of white reflecting material on the face towards the sun, behind the tank, but not against it. A sheet of glass painted white is excellent, but may still admit too much light.

The tall, thin plant bunched at center background is Hair Grass, *Eleocharis acicularis.* This deep tank must necessarily receive a good amount of light to allow the plants to grow. Photo by Timmerman.

When sufficient light to keep plants growing is not available or desirable, life-like artificial plants can be used to decorate an aquarium. Photo by Dr. Herbert R. Axelrod.

The prime necessity is adequate light for the plants, as quite dull illumination is sufficient for most fishes. Plants function and flourish only in good light, and many of them need bright light for much of the day to grow properly. Even light of sufficient intensity for comfortable reading may be quite useless for them. The various species of *Cryptocoryne* and *Sagittaria* can take less illumination than the rest, and should be used whenever there is any doubt. At the other extreme, plants like *Cabomba* and *Myriophyllum* grow stringy and drab and die off if not in bright light and become a menace instead of an ornament and a help in the tank. Only actively growing plants, and that means adequately illuminated plants, are an asset to the aquarium.

The light utilized by plants in photosynthesis is at the red end of the spectrum, and the growing habit of tinting the back and sides of tanks blue is to be avoided when oblique natural light of borderline intensity will be employed. A significant amount of the useful rays can be removed in this manner, but are not removed, of course, when the light comes from overhead and not through the glass. Winter daylight in most parts of the world is not adequate for indoor tanks, and should be supplemented with electric lighting.

When there is an excess of light, such as to cause a blanket of green algae over the glass and even the plants and rocks as well, it can always be cut down by shading. This shading is best applied to the windows admitting the light, as heat absorption which is likely to accompany the excessive light is avoided as explained above. If it must be applied to the tank, use white or light surfaces so as to reflect as much heat as possible and not to absorb it.

Many different styles of lights are available. Fluorescent lamps such as this one save on energy bills by using less electricity than a comparable incandescent. The bulb and other parts of the lamp are protected from the water by a glass or plastic cover.

Artificial Light: Artificial light must be bright and close overhead. The light in an ordinary room is very inadequate, even if the tank sits underneath the source of light. Ordinary electric light bulbs may be used, but fluorescent lighting has the advantage of causing little additional heat. For all practical purposes, artificial light now means electric light, but both gaslight and pressure lamps can be successfully adopted for aquarium lighting. Oil lanterns do not give a bright enough light to be practicable. Whichever is the choice, it is usual to enclose the overhead tank lights in a reflector. This increases the light thrown into the tank and also prevents dazzle. A reflector decreases the life of the bulbs, because they get hotter when hooded over, so that aquarium top-lights need replacements rather frequently.

Overhead lighting may be towards the front or back of the tank, and the general direction of plant growth will differ in the two circumstances. The tank with front lighting also has a gloomy back and gives an impression of depth and spaciousness, but the plants at the back may not flourish too well after a period. The tank with back lighting has a fine background growth of plants and looks generally lighter and therefore rather less spacious and intriguing, and the fishes are transilluminated when they swim to the front. This gives an effect which depends on the fish, some look very pleasant and others lose effectiveness. On the whole back lighting seems to be the less popular, but it is a good idea to use it routinely and to pull the lights forward for exhibition purposes.

With ordinary bulbs, whether frosted or plain, and a reflector of average efficiency, the following are the requirements of various tanks; assuming no help from even weak daylight: —

Tank Capacity	Usual Depth	Wattage for a 10-hour day
5 gals.	9 ins.	40
15 gals.	12 ins.	60
30 gals.	15 ins.	75
45 gals.	18 ins.	100
80 gals.	21 ins.	120
120 gals.	24 ins.	150

The figures in the last column show the wattage to employ assuming 10 hours per day of illumination. Thus, a 40-watt bulb turned on for 10 hours over a 5-gallon tank is satisfactory, giving 0.4 kilowatt-hours per day.

The difference in plant depth is not doubled because the tank depth is doubled. Plants right down on the sand will be perhaps at about double the distance, but not the average plant leaf, which will often be able to reach just as near the bulb whatever the tank depth. In addition, the use of a reflector modifies the inverse square law and focuses the light into a beam or band projecting it down into the tank and not allowing it to spread out as much as the light from a naked bulb. It also so happens that, even without an overhead reflector, the internal reflection from the inner faces of the glass prevents the escape of much of the light and aids the illumination of the deeper parts of the tank. Thus no simple physical laws apply in calculating the above figures and those recommended are a mixture of theory and experiment—mostly the latter.

While it would give about the same result to illuminate a 15-gallon tank with 120 watts for 5 hours instead of with 60 watts for 10 hours, it is best to use the weaker light and a longer period, since the fishes do better that way. If, on the other hand, it is desired to illuminate for a longer period, then 40 watts for 15 hours would be quite in order.

Fry are sometimes given prolonged or constant lighting to keep them feeding and growing, and this is practiced without obvious harm. In a fry-raising tank it would probably be a good idea to run at a higher total of kilowatt-hours per day, as the fry are very actively consuming oxygen and producing waste, and the plants need to be in their best form. A 30 to 50% increase seems to be in order.

Fluorescent Lighting: Fluorescent lighting often looks very attractive, but not all types of fluorescent tubes are suitable. Some give too much light at the blue end of the spectrum and do not benefit the plants. It is therefore best to use those which copy natural daylight most closely, but this does not mean that so-called "daylight" tubes are necessarily the best. In the Mazda series, the "warm-white" tubes are better, and give more yellow-to-red light than the "daylight." Reports indicate that, if "daylight" tubes are used, they must be switched on for longer periods.

Fluorescent lighting is more expensive to install, but cheaper to run; and the cost of replacements plus initial installation probably makes it rather more expensive all told, but there can hardly be much in it. Each watt of fluorescent lighting gives a little over three times the actual light given by one watt of tungsten filament lighting, so that the figures in the above table should be divided by 3 for fluorescent tubes.

Temperature: Fishes are usually able to stand the temperature variations of their natural surroundings and not much more. If a fish comes from a seasonally variable environment, in which it may stew in summer or freeze in winter, then like the common carp, it can stand these extremes, but it cannot usually stand a *sudden* change from one to the other. If it comes from rock-pools of the sea-shore, like the goby, it may stew in an exposed small pool and then be flushed out by an incoming tide at a temperature 20-30°F. below that of the pool. The goby can stand this, too. If, like the majority of marine fishes, it comes from a very constant environment, and can move about so that even the slow changes in temperature can be avoided if not to its liking, it is likely to be very touchy about the temperature of its surroundings and to be inadaptable.

Fresh water aquarium fishes usually come from fairly still waters which may undergo fairly wide changes in temperature but which do not change suddenly. When these waters are tropical, their temperature does not drop below 65-70°F., but it may rise to 90°F., and so most tropical fishes can stand this range. In the aquarium, they are less happy at the extremes of their natural tolerance than in the wild and so it is usual to try to keep them within a range of say, 72-80°F., with as short a period as possible beyond.

The *sudden* exposure to a downward change in temperature of more than 2-3°F. is likely to cause shock, followed by disease. Slow changes, taking hours or days, may cover 5-10°F. The usual symptoms of chill are a very characteristic slow, weaving motion like slow-motion swimming without getting anywhere, often called "shimmies," and perhaps the development of a disease called "white spot" or "ich." Ich is caused by an organism frequently present in the water, but which does not usually gain a hold in healthy fishes. The condition and its cure are described later. Heat shock is also known, but is not usually seen, even when fishes are suddenly warmed, as when chilled in transport and placed in a warm tank. The signs are gasping respiration, surface hugging and sometimes lack of balance, so that the fish turns slowly on to its side, plunges to

To protect your tropical fishes from cold temperatures a heater is necessary. It must be adequate enough to heat the tank to the proper temperature easily. A thermostatic control is very useful. Photo by Dr. Herbert R. Axelrod.

an upright position, and then repeats the process. The respiratory signs may occur in fishes which simply lack oxygen, whereas after too sudden an increase in temperature they will sometimes occur even in the presence of sufficient oxygen.

The above applies to adult fishes. Their eggs and fry are often much tougher, and can stand a greater variability and a wider range of temperature than their parents. As the young fishes grow up, this tolerance is gradually lost. It also applies to involuntary changes which the fishes cannot avoid. In a pool or a tank, the water may show quite large differences in temperature from top to bottom. Fishes swim from one layer to another in these conditions without harm, probably because they do not stay long at any one fixed temperature, and can tolerate short bouts of immersion in hotter or colder strata. A day-to-night fluctuation in average temperature of 5-7°F. is also safe for most freshwater fishes, but not for many marine or estuarine types. A fluctuation of 10-15°F. is dangerous, and a common cause of unexplained trouble.

Since fluorescent lamps operate at only about 100°F., they do not heat the surface of the water as do filament lamps, and this is a great advantage in hot weather. Another advantage is the spread of light given by the long fluorescent tubes, with resultant even illumination and absence of glare.

Temperature Control: As with lighting, electricity is so much more general and satisfactory for heating aquaria than any other method, that gas and oil represent nothing more than auxiliary emergency measures, except when electric current is not available. In fish rooms or houses, steam or hot water may be used. Electric heating has all the advantages—it may be left almost indefinitely without attention, it is clean, odorless and usually cheap, and most important, it does not have to be applied to the bottom of the tank and thus heat the roots of plants.

The heating capacity of an aquarium heater depends upon its consumption of current; the higher the wattage, the more heat produced. Commonly produced heaters rate at 12½, 25, 37½ 50, 75, 125, 150, 175, 200 and 250 watts, but other series are available at 10, 20, 30, 40, 50, 75 and 100 watts, so that it is possible to obtain a ready-made heater of almost any wattage required. This is important when different tanks are to be heated by separate heaters but all controlled by one thermostat. If higher wattages are necessary, more than one heater should be used.

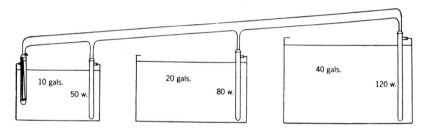

These tanks, each one of a different volume and equipped with a heater, are controlled by a single thermostat.

The heat loss from a heated tank depends mainly on the radiating, conducting and evaporating surfaces of the tank, and on the difference between the tank and air temperatures. Other things being equal, a small tank requires more heat per gallon (more watts per gallon) than a large tank, because it loses heat more rapidly. In theory, we should expect the heat loss to be proportional to the surface area and this is roughly borne out in practice, and holds over a useful range of tank sizes. The rate of heat loss from similar tanks, other things being equal, is also approximately proportional to the square of the air-water temperature difference, thus it takes about four times as much heating to keep a 10°F. difference as a 5°F. difference from the tank's surroundings. This is because the greatest part of the heat loss does not occur by radiation, which follows a different law, but by convection and, in uncovered tanks, by evaporation. With low differences in temperature between tanks and their surroundings, the rate of heat loss follows much more nearly a square law than anything else, although this is not the relationship to be expected at greater temperature differences.

A covered 15-gallon (24 inches) tank requires about 4 watts per gallon, a total of 60 watts, to keep it at 20°F. above room temperature. In actual practice a thermostat would be included to cut off the heat at a predetermined point to allow for fluctuations in the room temperature.

The wattage required per gallon for tanks of the same general shape but of different size, all to be kept at 20°F. above their surroundings is given by:

$$\text{Watts per gallon} = \frac{4 \times L_{15}}{L_x}$$

where L_{15} = the length of the 15-gallon tank (usually 24 inches)

L_x = the length of any other tank.

Thus a 3-gallon tank, of 14-inch length, requires not 4 watts per gallon, but $4 \times \dfrac{24}{14}$, or 6.9 watts/gal., a total of 21 watts approx. for the tank to be held 20°F. above its surroundings.

The wattage required per gallon for the *same* tank, or others nearly identical with it, at different temperatures is biven by:

$$\text{Watts per gallon} = 4 \times \left[\frac{T}{20} \right]^2$$

where T is the temperature difference required.

Thus a 15-gallon tank to be held at 8°F. above its surroundings requires $4 \times \left[\dfrac{8}{20} \right]^2$, or 0.64 watts/gallon, a total of 9.6 watts.

These formulae may be combined, so that the requirements for similar shaped tanks may be predicted. Tanks which are reasonably alike behave much the same, and almost no rectangular tanks likely to be used by the aquarist will differ enough to matter.

$$\text{Watts per gallon} = 4 \times \frac{L_{15}}{L_x} \times \left[\frac{T}{20} \right]^2$$

where the symbols have the meanings defined above.

From the above we may deduce the wattage of heaters required under different conditions, and the relative heater capacities required when one tank acts as a control to the rest, some or all of which are of different gallon capacities.

The following table gives the information for a maximum rise of 20°F. above air temperature, but not more. The heating capacity needed for greater or lesser differences can be worked out as above. The tanks are assumed to be double cubes—i.e., a 15-gallon tank measures 24″ × 12″ × 12″, covered by a sheet of glass. The last column of the table is of particular importance. Being calculated for a 20°F. rise, it covers all normal requirements, and is therefore a column of the heater wattages to be recommended for different sized tanks, which while being adequate, make it unlikely that the fishes will be "cooked" even if the heater remains on when it should be switched off—either through a thermostatic fault or forgetfulness.

Tank length (inches)	Gallon Capacity	Watts per Gallon	Total Watts
10	1.1	9.6	10.5
12	1.9	8.0	15
14	3.0	6.9	21
16	4.5	6.0	27
18	6.3	5.3	33
20	8.7	4.8	42
22	11.5	4.4	51
24	15	4.0	60
26	19	3.7	70
28	24	3.4	82
30	30	3.2	96
32	35	3.0	105
34	42	2.8	117
36	50	2.65	136
42	80	2.3	183
48	120	2.0	240

Heaters and Thermostats: Electric heaters are usually of glass exterior, and may be totally submersible or so constructed that their tops must not be placed under the water. Metal heaters are less fragile than glass ones, but are somewhat likely to cause water poisoning unless of first class manufacture. They cannot be used in marine tanks unless made of stainless steel or other guaranteed rust-resistant metal.

Internally, the heater is essentially a heating coil, wound on a ceramic or Pyrex glass form. This may be surrounded by a layer of fine sand, asbestos, or left bare, inside the outer tube, which is sealed with a rubber bung or cap through which pass insulated wires. Submergible heaters are watertight, others are not and must stand vertically in the tanks with their tops out of water. The resistance wire, usually of thin Nichrome or similar alloy, heats up as does an electric radiator element, and it is therefore necessary to make sure that the lower part of the upright type of heater is immersed in water, or it will burn out and tanks should never be allowed to fall below ⅔ full when the heater is in use. Care should also be taken not to leave heaters on when emptying tanks, or to plug in a dry heater, or, worse still, to plunge it into water if it does get hot when dry. Even Pyrex glass may not stand up to that treatment, and soda glass certainly will crack and shatter.

Totally submergible heaters are popular, as they are not conspicuous and also because of the belief that they heat more efficiently. This is not correct, as whether the heater stands upright or lies along the sand, it causes a current of hot water to rise to the top of the tank and does not heat the water uniformly. The heater should not be buried in the sand; if it is, it may fuse and it may also kill the neighboring plants. As an alternative to the use of conventional heaters, plastic-covered cable is available which may be laid along the base of the tank.

Although a low wattage heater may be safely used without controlling its output, it is usual and much safer to include a thermostat in the circuit. The almost universal type in aquaria is the bimetallic strip, of two types of metal which expand at different rates with a rise in temperature, and so it bends as the temperature changes. The strip carries the electric current, but at the critical temperature the strip breaks contact with one of the terminals in the instrument and the current ceases to flow. As the tank cools again, contact is established, and the current flows once more. The temperature controlled by such a thermostat should remain within about 2°F. of that desired; much greater accuracy is not necessary and causes frequent action of the thermostat and tends to burn it out. A good thermostat should have a magnetic "make," which means that the strip, once it gets near to completing the circuit, is snapped over into position by a small magnet, which does not allow sparking or arcing. The contacts should be of silver or similar metal to prevent excessive wear, and there should be a condenser or capacitor to prevent radio interference.

The thermostat is sometimes submergible, but more often it is not, and is clipped on to the side of the tank. It has a glass body, with the works inside it, and a control, which consists usually of a small adjustable screw with a non-conducting portion so that the operator can alter the setting of the bimetallic strip, and hence the temperature of the tank. Often a pilot light is included which indicates when the thermostat is operating. There are more expensive models in which the thermostat proper is outside the tank, and a temperature "feeler" is placed in the tank like a submersible heater. Combination models of thermostat-plus-heater are also on offer, and seem to be satisfactory. However, they can only be used in a single tank and hence each combination must be repeated for every additional tank if such a set-up is used.

The wattage of a thermostat is the number of watts it can safely control. A usual figure is 500-watts, but anything between 100 and 2,000 is available. A 500-watt thermostat may be used in conjunction with heaters totalling not more than 500 watts. It will often have a multiple plug, allowing several heaters to be plugged directly into it in parallel. Two 100-watt heaters in parallel will mean a current producing 200 watts through the thermostat, and so on, but it must be noted that two 100-watt heaters in series means only 50 watts through the thermostat, and an output of 25 watts per heater. The normal way of heating several tanks is to plug in suitable heaters to a thermostat placed in the smallest tank if there is any size difference. This is because the smallest volume of water most rapidly loses and gains heat from its surroundings, and if a large tank housed the thermostat a small one might fluctuate too much. This arrangement also has the effect of controlling the temperature of the larger tanks remarkable accurately, and although such an extremely even temperature is not usually desirable, it is better than the alternative of widely varying small tanks. The tanks which are all controlled by the same thermostat must be in reasonably similar situations if it is required that they shall be uniform in temperature. Otherwise, some will be hotter than others, although all may be within a reasonable range. Differences may be offset by the use of varying wattage in the heaters.

Aeration: Something has been said earlier about the relationship between plants and fishes, and between oxygen and carbon-dioxide (O_2 and CO_2) content of the water and its effect on fishes. It has been pointed out that the CO_2 content of the water is usually of more significance in an aquarium than is the O_2 content. Fishes suffering from CO_2 excess gasp at the surface and show exaggerated gill movements, whereas it is alleged that fishes suffering merely from an O_2 deficiency lie quietly on the bottom. If this is true, the usual symptoms seen in a crowded or foul tank certainly indicate a CO_2 excess. This is relieved by aeration, which should always be used when a tank has other than a minimal population of fishes.

Aeration does not force air or oxygen into solution in the water and under usual conditions, not much oxygen is absorbed from the bubbles themselves; they merely serve to remove the excess CO_2 from the water. Accounts of the rate at which aeration of different types brings about the solution of oxygen from the air into water differ. The general conclusion seems to be that it is not as efficient as we have been led to believe, some investigators finding that only very brisk bubbling from several aerating stones at once will bring a tank up to 75% saturation within 30 minutes.

The normal rate of aeration is a mild trickle from one stone and was found to be ineffective in causing 75% saturation even within several hours. The rate at which carbon dioxide is "blown off" is probably quite small, but the fact remains that quite mild aeration about doubles the fish capacity of a tank, and although brisk, boiling aeration might quadruple it or even much more, as far as air content is concerned, other factors would in any case prevent us from trying to crowd our tanks so much.

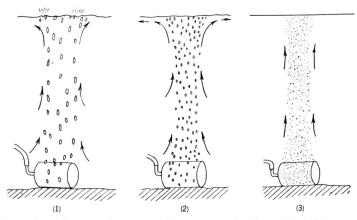

Large bubbles (1) do not stir the water as effectively as the smaller bubbles in (2). A very fine spray (3) is also less effective than one of medium size.

The usual method of aeration is to force air through a porous "stone" at the bottom of the tank; such a stone may be made of various substances from fused glass or natural minerals to leather or felt washers on a metal head. Carborundum stones give about the finest bubbles, but also need the most powerful air pressure, so that only the larger sized pumps are satisfactory for their use. All stones tend to clog, especially when used at a low pressure and should occasionally be removed, baked and replaced. When they are first used or re-used, it is advisable to pass a brisk jet of air through them for a few hours, and when this is turned down a fine spray of bubbles is usually the result.

Experience shows that with bubbles of an average diameter of about 1/25th of an inch or less, an aerating stone delivering 2 cubic inches of air per minute is adequate in a 15-gallon tank. This observation is really of great interest, for it demonstrates the fact that adequate aeration does not work by simple bubble-water interchange, since the surface of the bubbles exposed to the water at any one moment is only about 12 square inches, assuming a bubble diameter of 1/25th inch and a period of 4 seconds for a bubble to travel from bottom to top of the tank. A good stone can give bubbles of less than 1/100th inch in diameter, when the surface exposed by the bubbles is much greater, as not only is it greater per cubic inch of air, but also the bubbles take longer to reach the surface. With 1/100th inch bubbles, which take some 10-15 seconds to travel up through the water, the area exposed is some 120-180 square inches and begins to be an effective factor in gas exchange. With such fine bubbles, the water looks quite cloudy over the stone, for at any one moment something up to one million are suspended in the water. When the bubble diameter is 1/25th inch, a mere 2,000 odd are seen at once. However, such very fine bubbles do not move the water much and do not disturb the surface of the water. They thus cause surface interchange to be little affected, and the effects of very fine subdivision of the same volume of air may not be as good as rather coarser subdivision. It is the opinion of some experts that a bubble diameter of about 1/30th inch is the best.

Deep tanks gain relatively more from aeration than do shallower tanks, for not only are they more in need of it, but since the bubbles take longer to rise to the surface they cause more effective stirring of the water and a brisker surface interchange.

Air Pumps: The usual aerator is an electric pump. These are usually designed to deliver from about 10 to 200 cubic inches of air per minute, and thus to operate from a few to a hundred stones. The electrical consumption of the most powerful is quite small, no more than 30 or 40 watts, while the smaller pumps take as little as 3 watts and thus cost next to nothing to run.

Pumps may be of single or multi-cylinder type or operated by a vibrating diaphragm. The latter are the cheapest to run and are often preferred to the older cylinder pumps. They do not require oiling and are reasonably silent. They must be placed above the level of water in any tank they supply, or water may run back into the pump. On the other hand, they do not reverse, as do some pumps of conventional design, and so cannot actively suck the water into themselves.

Filters: In a filter, an air pump is used to shift water from the tank into a smaller container, or from the container back into the tank, the other part of the water-lift being by syphon. A simple filter may be constructed from a plastic container by boring a set of small holes in the base and clipping it on to the side of the tank. Water is then pumped into the container, passes through a bed of glass wool, nylon staple, charcoal, or other material and out again into the tank. If water is pumped from the filter back to the tank, the same design can be used, when water will pass up through the holes in the bottom and through the filter. This, however, tends to raise the filtering medium and the water passes more beside it than through it, and so the direction of flow is reversed by sucking water from the bottom of the filter, dispensing with a pierced base, and syphoning water from the tank into the top of the filter.

A more usual type of filter is placed outside the tank, clipped on to the side or even on a separate stand. The syphon which carries aquarium water into the filter is provided with a "starter," which consists of a small rubber ball which, when compressed, starts the filter without the operator having to suck at the tube, or to remove it and fill it with water.

It is common practice to place activated charcoal or "coals" at the base of the filter, then a layer of glass wool, through which the water first passes. The glass wool removes any grosser debris or particles, and the activated charcoal absorbs small impurities and also actively soaks up some dissolved material as well as actual suspended matter. Both should be replaced at least once a week, and when this is done, the filter rarely gives trouble. The water intake may be placed at a distance from the filter—perhaps in a front corner with the sand so sloped that waste matter tends to collect there and to be transported to the filter. Many filters have adjustable intake syphons to cope with differing aquarium depths and other dimensions. Others have more than one chamber, so that the water first passes through a charcoal bed and then separately through a glass wool bed, and perhaps a bed of crystals designed to adjust the pH. Filtration is also aeration, as the water is constantly streaming into and out of the filter. In a filtered tank, it may be unnecessary to aerate in addition by any other means, unless with the object of stirring up and removing the mulm.

A recent development in filtration is to use the sand at the base of the tank as the filter bed. This somewhat revolutionary idea seems to work very well and is particularly successful in marine tanks. The airlift is connected at the base to an undersand grid, or system of tubes running through the sand. Water is drawn into the sand over much of the base of the tank and sucked up through it into a collecting tube by the airlift, and then discharged back into the tank. It need never be raised above the surface of the tank. It is a curious fact that certain plants do not flourish if an undersand filter is used permanently. It should be left off for about half of each day.

A large tank properly cared for with healthy flourishing fishes and plants can make an owner very proud.

2

Keeping Fishes Healthy

Setting Up A Tank: A good start is essential in the keeping of healthy fishes and for this the first consideration is the location of the fish tank. The control of plant growth and the suppression of green water or other unwanted algae is much easier if the tank receives only artificial light. Drafty locations must be avoided, and so must the tops of radiators, which heat the sand and cause the plants to wilt, and can overheat the tank far too easily. Thus, the popular window location over a radiator is not to be commended.

The second consideration is the furnishing of the tank with sand or gravel, rocks and plants. The purpose of the sand is to hold down rooted plants and to provide decoration. A sand which is fine packs tightly and prevents plant roots from penetrating, it also promotes the growth of anaerobic bacteria—those which thrive in oxygen-free surroundings and which turn the sand grey or black. If it is too coarse, the plants get little grip, and ride free, and unconsumed food and other detritus gets down into the sand and is not easily removed.

These facts show that the best type of medium is a fairly coarse sand, preferably with a variable grain size for pleasant appearance. It should be laid deep enough to provide adequate root-space for the plants provided, so that in all but the smallest tanks, 2 inches of sand at the back and less in front is about right, but it may be banked up much more than this if desired for decorative effects. Since a great depth of sand is likely sooner or later to become foul, it is best to avoid it, or to pack the deeper areas with rock beneath the sand.

The placing of deep sand at the back automatically provides for three things. First, it looks pleasant, giving the aquarium base a gentle forward slope which best exhibits the content. Secondly, it provides for the largest plants to be sited at the back, where they are usually required. Thirdly, it encourages the mulm to collect towards the front of the tank, where it is easily removed.

Sand must be very thoroughly washed before use. Even if supplied as "washed," it will normally require some further washing. Really dirty sand may need 20 or 30 swirlings in fresh buckets of water, or half an hour's thorough hosing in a shallow container. Failure to do this may cause cloudy water for weeks, or more serious trouble.

The size and type of gravel selected depend upon the type of fishes kept, the plants to be anchored, and whether an undergravel filter is used. Photo by Glen S. Axelrod.

European aquarists sometimes use peat, loam or earth beneath the sand, or in pockets of rock, to nourish the plants. General experience is, however, that such materials sooner or later cause trouble; either they get stirred up and make a mess of the water, or they turn bad and have to be removed. If one is interested primarily in growing fine plants it is possible to take care and to use these substances, but they are hardly to be recommended for the amateur. The plant growth that results is from the material supplied beneath the sand, and the plants may not, therefore, be performing their essential function of removing much of the waste products of the fishes as well as they otherwise would. This is a point which hasn't been clarified, and further research and observation is needed.

As a rule the fishes are more colourful in an aquarium with dark, even black, gravel on the bottom.

Stones and Rocks: The placement and choice of stones and rocks in the tank is a matter for personal taste, *except* when they are used for shelter or for breeding. There are various theories about the relationship between stones and the sand they lie in and about the direction of rock strata, which may influence judges in shows when furnished aquaria are being considered, but they are of little practical importance.

Ornaments, such as treasure chests, divers, sea shells and mermaids are popular but hardly natural looking. It is again a matter of personal

When rift lake fishes such as this *Pseudotropheus zebra* are kept, the tank is usually set up with a maze of rocks and stones, and without plants. Photo by G. Marcuse.

choice. Sea shells or shell grit (sometimes used instead of sand) are in place in the marine tank, but will make a freshwater tank too alkaline, even if their appearance can be tolerated.

Only hard, insoluble rocks must be used in an aquarium. Rocks with a soluble salt content may kill fishes and plants in a few weeks.

Planting: A tank should be set up with young, healthy-looking plants which have been disinfected or quarantined before use. If you wish to use them immediately, a rapid wash in salt water (six teaspoons to the gallon) or sea water of not more than 15 seconds duration followed by a thorough wash in fresh water will probably rid them of most parasites. If possible, they should preferably be left for 2 or 3 days in a solution of potassium permanganate at a strength of 1/5th grain to the gallon (3 parts per million). A longer period should not be used or degeneration may set in.

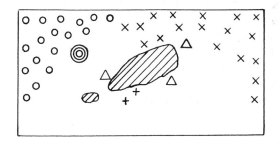

A possible planting arrangement for a 15- to 25-gallon tank.
x,o   *Vallisneria* or other tall plants in groups.
△   Shorter bushy plants, such as *Cryptocorynes*.
◎   A single, striking plant, such as an Amazon sword plant.
▱▱   Rocks.

It is best to make a diagram of the desired planting scheme before going about the job, or it may turn out very different from that hoped for by the inexperienced. Those shown here will give the general idea. The higher-growing and larger plants look best at the back and sides, particularly the long, grass-like plants and the long-stemmed plants like *Cabomba, Myriophyllum,* and *Anacharis.* Then, perhaps in relationship to rocks or stones, may come groups of other plants, such as *Cryptocoryne, Echinodorus* or *Ludwigia.* These are best placed in groups of one type, not mixed up. Some of the smaller grasses or dwarf varieties of other plants may be used in front but it is customary to leave a free swimming-space in the center front. A particularly fine plant, such as an *Echinodorus,* is often used as a center-piece in the larger tanks.

First place about 1½ inches of level sand in the tank, and smooth it back and to the sides in the desired formation, placing any rocks or stones in position at this stage. Next place a large cup or jar in the front of the tank and gently pour water into it, so that it slowly overflows and fills the tank for a depth of 6 to 8 inches, which is most convenient for planting. Meanwhile keep the plants wet, a short period of drying may kill or set them back severely. Cut back the roots of all plants to a length of 1-2 inches, according to size, and anchor them by pushing them into the sand about an inch forward of their eventual site, then drag them backwards or sideways through the sand into their final position. This makes a slight mess of the arrangements, but is easier than trying to push them into place in the usual way with sticks or tongs. It is useless to worry about spreading the roots nicely, as they decay and are replaced by new growth in most cases.

Some plants, like the grasses and *Cryptocorynes,* have a crown above the roots, and must be carefully planted so as to leave the crown exposed, or they may wither and die. Others may be thrust into the sand with less care, but it is best not to submerge too much of the stem and leaves, or these may decay and foul the tank. Leave small spaces between plants, about ½-1 inch at least with grasses and tall, thin plants, and much more with bushy plants, so as to budget for subsequent filling-out by growth and the striking of new plants. A typical 15-gallon tank, with a floor area of 2 square feet, will need about 3 dozen back and side plants, and a dozen central plants.

Planting sticks, long sticks with a notch in the end, and perhaps a sharp, chisel-like blade at the other end, are useful for second thoughts when the rest of the plants are in place, and for resetting plants which have floated up before becoming firmly rooted.

Planting trays are sometimes used. These are flat trays, usually of such dimensions that 2 or 3 of them fill the base of the tank. They are an advantage when it is required to empty the tank frequently, as for exhibition or breeding purposes, but require careful camouflage if they are not to be too obvious. Smaller trays may be used with advantage, if set unobtrusively in the sand or behind rocks, and may house prize plants ·or varieties needing particular care, or which are wanted from time to time in different tanks. It is best to use trays made of bakelite, plastic, china or earthenware, not of metal, however well coated, except with enamel.

When planting is complete the tank should be filled. If the recommended 6-8 inches of water is already present, and the tank is new, leave it for a day and then complete the filling, just in case of leaks.

Filling after planting must be done gently, so as not to disturb the sand. Continue to pour into a jar up to 10 or 12 inches, but if the tank is deeper than this, the rest can be poured in from a few inches above the water level as long as the inflowing water creates a mass of bubbles, which break its force and prevent it from sweeping down on to the bottom. Fill to about 1 inch from the top—the tank usually looks best if the waterline is just hidden under the top of the frame.

It is best not to fill a new tank and then empty it again before planting, to clean it or test for leaks. This may result in springing a leak when the tank is emptied, which then becomes apparent on refilling. It also helps to cause more cement to be pushed out from between the frame and the glass than is desirable, if the tank has not fully hardened. It is generally unwise to empty completely any new tank within a few months of first filling it, particularly a large tank.

Accessories: Every independently heated tank should have a thermometer. There are various types, some floating and some fixed, and most of them liable to be out as much as 5°F. either way. They should be checked at say, 70° and 80° against a standard mercury thermometer. Your local druggist will probably be prepared to do this for you if you have no reliable thermometer of your own. The clock-type thermometers, which have a circular dial and a moving pointer and may be fitted with a rubber suction cap so that their face is fastened to the glass, are as reliable as

A thermometer is a must. It is necessary to keep tabs on the temperature of your tank to see that it does not get too hot or too cold. The new digital thermometers, such as the one shown here, have become very popular.

the cheaper conventional types, but are liable to stick and should be gently tapped before a reading is taken. A great advantage of this pattern is that it can be fastened to the front glass of batteries of tanks so that the pointer is upright at the desired temperature and any departure of 1°F. or more from this is immediately seen.

There is often a considerable top-to-bottom temperature difference in tropical tanks. This is no cause for worry, as it mimics conditions in nature, where the heat of the sun frequently raises the top water well above the lower strata and the fishes just stay down.

Lighting other than daylight is supplied from on top as already indicated. Side lighting may give interesting effects, but it causes many fishes to swim lop-sidedly and may eventually upset them. Also the plants will grow towards the light and may look very odd when obliquely illuminated for any length of time.

In addition to the cover afforded by a reflector, the top of the aquarium is best completely enclosed in some fashion. Glass is popular, and necessary when light must enter through the cover. Otherwise, any material which is water-resistant may be used, and some of the synthetic hardboards have the advantage that they are good insulators, better than glass, yet do not encourage condensation. This helps to prevent the rusting which practically always occurs when covers are used on iron-framed tanks.

Covers serve a number of purposes. They prevent fishes from jumping out and prevent other creatures, from beetles to cats, from getting in. They also help to keep the tank warmer and to prevent rapid evaporation. A tight-fitting cover which encloses about 1 inch of air-space does not suffocate the fishes, which obtain plenty of oxygen from the air enclosed, even if the cover is really airtight, and it usually isn't. The removal of the cover or part of it once or more a day for feeding admits enough fresh air.

A cover is convenient if made in two pieces, so that either a strip along the front or a corner-piece can be lifted for feeding or servicing without removing the whole. However it is best raised a small fraction of an inch by placing a cork or other material at intervals along the frame, or by slipping split rubber tubing or a suitable size of rubber buffering as used in car upholstery along the inner edges of the top frame. Alternatively, the cover may be lowered beneath the frame by suspending it from specially-made clips which may be purchased from most dealers. This scheme has the advantage that any condensation or splashes drip back without touching the frame, and that the cover is again not completely tight. It has the disadvantage that the cover cannot easily be made of more than one piece for easy feeding. Either method prevents much of the rusting and of the dripping from condensation that otherwise occurs with some types of tank. Rusting is unsightly and eventually damages the tank, and drips may contain poisonous material dissolved from paint, solder or the metal of the tank frame. All contact of metal and water, except stainless steel or monel metal with welded or silver soldered joints, must be avoided, whether direct, by drips from condensation or by aeration splash. Even chrome or nickel-plate heaters may develop flaws which lead to electrolysis and the stripping of the plating, with possibly disastrous effects, and should be carefully watched.

Plant Varieties: A very large number of varieties of water plants is now available to the aquarist. Some of these are shown in the accompanying illustrations, but an entire section is devoted to them.

For present purposes, these plants may be divided into the rooted plants, which are placed in the sand or gravel, the rootless plants, which may, nevertheless, be anchored in the sand, and the floating plants, which have roots hanging freely down into the water.

Full covers for an aquarium serve a number of purposes such as keeping the fishes in the tank and unwanted objects out.

An unidentified species of Amazon Swordplant, of the genus *Echinodorus*. Sculthorpe photo.

Among the rooted plants, the various grass-like plants such as *Vallisneria, Sagittaria* and *Eleocharis* may be obtained in many forms, from giants with strap-like leaves which may grow many feet in length, to tiny dwarf varieties only an inch or so in height. Such plants reproduce by runners which lie along the surface of the sand or a little beneath it, and put out buds at frequent intervals. They put forth surface flowers, which unfortunately wither in the reflector of the usual tank, but which may look very attractive in a tank with daylight illumination and no top cover. The larger types of grass-like plant are usually placed at the back and sides of the tank.

Other rooted plants form fine center-pieces, or plants which may be arranged in clumps to good effect. Center-pieces include the Amazon Sword Plant (*Echinodorus* species) the Madagascar Sword Plant, and the Madagascar Lace Plant (*Aponogeton fenestralis*), a much-prized beauty which is still highly priced in most parts of the world. The Amazon Sword Plant reproduces by runners which ride up into the water. New plants occuring on these runners may be carefully broken off and planted separately, when they have produced sufficient roots to look ready for it. The *Aponogetons* have bulbs, which may bud off new ones, or may be propagated from seeds from surface flowers.

Sagittaria and *Vallisneria* are often confused with one another because of their similar appearance. This is *Sagittaria graminea*. Photo by R. Zukal.

A beautiful broad-leaved species of *Aponogeton*. Photo by R. Zukal.

Ludwigia mullerti, which will develop roots when anchored in the sand. Timmerman photo.

Water Sprite. *Ceratopteris thalictroides*, is a remarkably versatile plant. Sculthorpe photo.

Hygrophila polysperma, a fast grower. Sculthorpe photo.

Extremely fine-leaved plants, such as this *Myriophyllum verticillatum*, are often used in spawning tanks to receive the eggs of egg-scatterers. In decorative aquaria, care must be taken to make sure that the plant's leaves do not become choked by settlings. Photo by Sculthorpe.

Still further rooted plants which may be used as center-pieces in smaller tanks or for side decoration in others include various species of *Crypto-coryne*, which also propagate by runners. These are slow growing plants which look very decorative and can thrive with weaker lighting than most others. Some, such as *C. becketti, C. willisi* and *C. cordata* grow only a few inches high, while others such as *C. griffithi* or *C. ciliata* grow nearly a foot in height. The various varieties of water fern (*Ceratopteris*) are in contrast fast-growing and need frequent attention. *Hygrophila, Myri-ophyllum* and *Ambulia* are fine-looking when planted in bunches, and will strike roots from odd pieces thrust into the sand. *Cabomba* is another very attractive rooted plant which needs rather more light than most, but will also root from pieces pushed into the sand. *Ludwigia* is a bog-plant, with attractive red undersides to the leaf in one variety, which survives well completely immersed. *Anacharis or Elodea* is a cultivated variety of the Canadian Water Weed, which also puts out roots all over the place and grows very rapidly. It is more popular in cold-water tanks than in the tropical aquarium.

Rootless plants include *Ceratophyllum* (Hornwort) and *Nitella,* which grow in profusion in a good light and may be artificially anchored in branches with fine effect. These are both particularly useful plants for spawning, or for providing a hiding place for young livebearers.

Floating plants may also be used to give refuge for young fishes or to cut down the amount of light entering the surface of the water. *Salvinia* has fairly large, hairy leaves which are green in ordinary conditions but turn red in bright sunlight, and long hairy roots. It does best out of doors, but will propagate in a good indoor light. *Lemna* (Duckweed) is a smaller, green, floating plant with a single root which propagates rapidly in all normal circumstances and can be a nuisance. *Riccia* (Crystalwort) floats beneath the surface of the water, and together with *Lemna* is a favorite food for some fishes. It also provides perhaps the best cover for new born live bearers, but does not flourish in poor light.

The rootless Hornwort, *Ceratophyllum demersum.* Hornwort is, like *Myriophyllum,* useful in spawning tanks. Hornwort will not anchor itself into the sand, but it grows well if the lighting is bright enough. Photo by Sculthorpe.

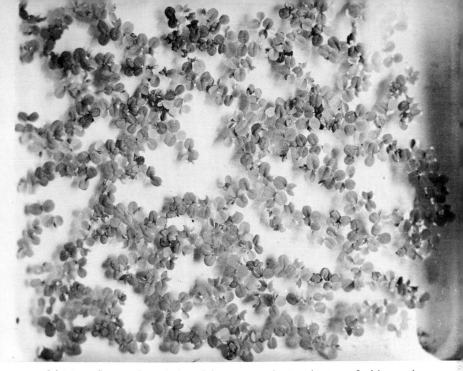

Salvinia is a floating plant which trails long roots under it in the water. Sculthorpe photo.

Nitella is widely used as a refuge for baby livebearers, but it must be very thickly planted in order to be of such use. Timmerman photo.

Introducing the Fishes: After a tank has been set up with the plants in place it is best left for several days before fishes are placed in it. During this period, there is a chance to check that all is well, that no leaks have started and that the temperature control is satisfactory. Nothing is more disheartening than to set up a tank and place the fishes in it and then have to dismantle everything hurriedly and find an emergency home for them. This rest period also allows the plants to become settled in and to start functioning, which they will do fully only after a week or two; more important, it also gives some of the most troublesome fish diseases and parasites a chance to die off if they have been introduced by accident to the tank. This is particularly important with the parasite known as Ich or "White Spot" which does not live long without the presence of fishes, and which is the most widespread of all tropical fish troubles.

New fishes must be acclimated to a new tank slowly. They should be placed in the tank as shown until the temperature of the water in the bag and in the tank equalize. Exchanging some of the water from time to time also helps. Photo by Judy Ronay.

Look over all new fishes very carefully before placing them in the tank. If they seem alright, there is no reason why they should not all be put into the new tank together, taking special care not to chill them or to subject them to a large pH change. The best way to avoid this is to float the plastic bag or jar, in which they have probably arrived, in the water in the new tank until they are at about the same temperature and then gradually mix the waters together. Do not overstock the tank; it is much better to understock it for the first few weeks. Once the tank has a fish population, do not introduce new fishes without quarantine, unless you know for certain that they have been in a disease-free tank for at least a week and know for certain that they have not been chilled on their way to you or subjected to any other risks. If they have travelled for more than a few hours, you can rarely know this. Otherwise, they should be given two weeks quarantine in a special tank, even if they look perfectly well. It is impossible for the owner of only a single community tank to do this, but at least he may as well realize that he takes a risk every time he introduces strangers to the tank and may think twice about adding any fishes which are in any way subject to suspicion. The same applies to new plants. The new fishes can be floated in the main tank in a jar or bowl of generous size, care being taken to see that they are given enough room and air surface, and that they don't jump into the tank.

If you have no spare isolation tank, and have other fishes already in a tank to which you have decided to introduce new ones, probably the best think to do is absolutely nothing, except to keep a close watch on all the inhabitants for several weeks, and be ready to give immediate treatment for any malady which may turn up. It will do no harm, however, to dose the tank with 10 mg. per gallon of Chloromycetin or Tetracycline. These will take care of a good many possible diseases before they have a chance to get started on the other fishes.

If, after all, a new fish does develop disease, don't always blame the previous owner or the dealer. Disease may be present in your tank and the new fish may have caught it from your own stock, which may not be showing it actively. Or the new fish may have been weakened in transit, and fall sick after its arrival. Subsequently, the whole tank may be affected, as it is quite common for a latent disease to start up on a new rampage once it has been given a start by the presence of a susceptible host. From him, it can spread back to the rest in heightened form.

Handling Fishes: The best advice about handling fishes is *don't*, unless necessary! Nets for catching adult fishes in small tanks should be as large as possible, and not very deep. They should not come to a point anywhere, either like a dunce's cap, or have pointed corners, but instead should be gently rounded so as to give a minimum risk of injury to the fishes. They may be made of mosquito netting or other suitable fabric, with reasonably wide pores so as to offer small resistance to the water. Nylon is becoming popular, as it dries with a shake and lasts for a long time without rotting. It is also worthwhile to make or purchase nets with stainless steel frames, as the fabric does not then rot at the edges so readily, or become impregnated with rust. Nets for catching fry should be quite shallow, so that they do not cause the fry to "ball up," but when in use they must be carefully watched as fry usually jump.

If your fishes have the common habit of rushing to the top of the tank to be fed, they may often be caught practically all together with a single well-directed sweep of the net. If you fail at the first attempt it is not usually so easy to repeat the maneuver with any success, so try again later. Most fishes can otherwise be caught without much fuss if you are not in a hurry, but once the necessary self-control is lost a tank is easily wrecked. It is a good idea to try stealth first—gently approach the fish with a good-sized net and try to slip it under the fish and lift it cleanly out without causing any panic. If this, or your patience fails, you may chase more actively, usually with little success. When this stage is reached, it is best to stop and try again in a few minutes; but if you are in a great hurry, then place the net at one end, well ballooned out into the darkest part of the tank, and chase the fishes into it with a free hand or another net. Then, unless you want to remove the lot, lift the net and rest it on the frame of the tank with the fishes in water but still trapped. Finally, remove the specimens wanted with a small tumbler or cup. Never actually handle small fishes if you can avoid it. Large fishes, including goldfishes, are often best caught and removed gently by hand, if possible, as they struggle in a net and may injure themselves more that way than if gently handled. If you are not in a hurry, it often pays to wait until the tank has been in darkness for about half an hour, when if the lights are switched on, the great majority of fishes will remain stationary in the water for a few minutes. During this period they may be located and netted out without fuss as long as they are not alarmed by sudden and violent movements.

Do not move fishes any more than is absolutely necessary, particularly when they have been established in one tank for a long time. Sometimes a transfer to an apparently perfectly suitable tank with water from the same original source is fatal. This does not mean that most fishes cannot be safely moved—they can—but don't do it unnecessarily, just to try the look of them here and there in different tanks. Remember also that it is quite difficult to catch a fish without doing it some slight injury, and that all such abrasions are likely to be the site of an infection which may spread not only on the individual but also throughout a whole tank.

When the tank is finally established and seems to be a happily running concern, you must still be vigilant. Take a purposeful look at your tank at least once a day—for instance, when you feed the fishes. Even after much experience the aquarist may miss the early signs of trouble if he doesn't look carefully for specific symptoms. He must learn to look at the component parts of the set-up and to notice anything that may spell trouble so that corrective action may be taken at the most effective stage.

Points to remember are:

The *smell* of a healthy tank is earthy and pleasant. Look for the cause of any departure from this.

The *plants* should be of good color and not decaying in part or whole. Remove any large decaying leaves, stems or roots and test the pH if decay continues.

The *water* should be clear, or very mildly green, its surface should be clean and without a film of dust, oily material or bacteria.

The *sand* should be clean, loose and not grey below the surface. If it is disturbed no bubbles should rise from it.

The *fishes* should look alert and well, with fins clear and held away from the body. "Clamped" fins or peculiar swimming motions mean impending trouble. The fishes should have no strings of excreta hanging from them.

The *corners* of the tank and hidden crannies should be searched for dead fish or sick fish hiding away.

The *temperature* should be checked as a daily routine in tropical tanks.

Foods and Feeding: A lot of work remains to be done before we can be very certain about the food requirements of fishes. Some of the laboratory animals used in scientific research, such as the guinea pig and the rat have been intensively studied in this regard, yet there are still many problems about their vitamin and mineral requirements. We do not know for certain which of the known vitamins are required by fishes, or whether there are unknown vitamins not yet discovered which are needed by them. We can guess that those of the B group are almost certainly needed, as they are of primary importance to most higher organisms, but it is quite possible that the rest do not matter. We know little about the detailed protein, fat or carbohydrate needs of fishes; although it is sometimes stated that they cannot digest fat, even this belief would seem mistaken and their natural foods, such as plankton, often abound in fat. Presumably they need a balanced intake much like our own, as they must build up a very similar body structure, but we know none of the finer details.

These possibilities do not matter much so long as we can supply natural food to the fishes. Too often we cannot, and then it is desirable to supply as near a copy as we can, or to substitute foods which have been shown by experience to produce satisfactory results.

Natural Foods: Nearly all fry feed on plankton which consists of single-celled organisms (infusoria), the young stages of insects, crustacea, worms and other water creatures. Very small fish fry such as those of the Anabantids (Labyrinthine fishes) consume small single-celled algae or infusoria, later eating large single-celled or multi-celled creatures.

When the fishes grow up, their diet is more varied in nature, but many show a preference for an animal or vegetable diet. Animal diets are preferred by Characins (Tetras), Cyprinodonts (Surface minnows) and many of the larger fishes, which eat insects, worms, crustacea, snails and other fishes. Vegetable diets are preferred by many Poecilids (Livebearers), by the *Scatophagus* tribe, and by odd members of the Tetras and Gouramis, such as the Kissing Gourami and *Metynnis* and *Leporinus* species. Almost all fishes will accustom themselves to an unusual diet in time, but some will only eat live foods. These are fortunately rarities, but include *Badis badis*, *Belonesox* and some of the sticklebacks. Even these are said to eat fish roe with training.

Live Food: An occasional feeding with live food is necessary to ensure the health of fishes, and necessary for breeding many species. It is therefore very desirable to feed live foods as often as possible, and at least once a week. Live foods are not absolutely essential for all species, but they are aways desirable and breeding is unlikely without them except in the live-bearers and a few hardy egg-layers. The appearance and growth-rate of fishes reared entirely on such prepared foods as are at present

Hemiodus quadrimaculatus vorderwinkleri is an interesting South American Characin which likes to nibble on plants, as do its close relatives within the genus *Leporinus*. Photo by Dr. Herbert R. Axelrod.

Common earthworms are an excellent food for fishes. They can be served whole to larger fishes and chopped for the smaller ones. Photo by P. Imgrund.

available leaves much to be desired in the great majority of cases. On the other hand, entirely live diets are quite unnecessary except in the few instances where the fishes won't eat prepared food. Half and half of live food and prepared food often seems to give as good a result as all live food and if an attempt to feed only live food results in reduced rations, fish on prepared food may do better.

Earthworms: The earthworm is a fine fish-food, given whole to the big ones, chopped to the smaller ones, and shredded to the very small ones. Special shredders may be purchased; they resemble a pair of small gramophone records and the worm is placed between them, after which they are rubbed across each other with a brisk rotary motion with worm puree as the result. If you are sensitive, the worms can be killed immediately before use by plunging them into hot water. Unfortunately, fishes seem to prefer them uncooked. Earth-worms may be stored in leaf-mould, in urban shrub boxes or window boxes, or may be coaxed from the lawn by pouring a solution of potassium permanganate at a strength of about $\frac{1}{4}$ grain per gallon on to the surface. They emerge in a few minutes. Avoid the dung worm, which is yellow and smelly and not good for fishes.

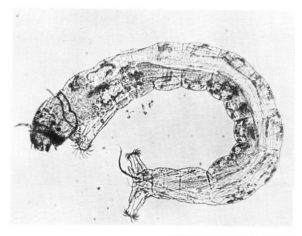

Larva of the blood-worm, *Chironomus*. Photo by Dr. J. Knaack.

Mosquito larvae, excellent fish food, with breathing tubes extended. Photo by Dr. J. Knaack.

A glass worm larva; notice the feathery appendage at the tail end. Photo by Dr. J. Knaack.

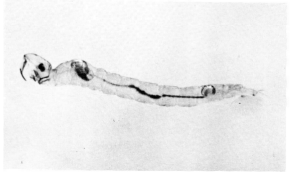

M—52.00

Insect Larvae: Insect larvae are another fine live food. Those of various species of mosquitoes and gnats may be netted by the thousands in warm weather from stagnant water. They may also be cultivated by leaving suitable receptacles in the garden, but avoid increasing the adult mosquito population if you do this. In cultivation it is important to have smelly stagnant and dirty water, as clean water offers little food and does not attract the female mosquito.

The female mosquito lays egg rafts, small sooty-looking floating masses of up to 300 eggs, which hatch out into a swarm of minute "wrigglers." Typical species develop through the next 8 or 9 days before hatching and offer, during this period, a nice range of sizes of fish food. The larvae grow steadily and moult several times, finally turning into pupae, which are comma-shaped and soon hatch into adults. The larvae and pupae are air-breathers, and may be fed freely to the fishes without fear of crowding them out, but with the possibility of them hatching into adults if given in excess.

When collecting larvae or pupae, it is best to catch them as cleanly as possible with a fine net, and then, if necessary to sort them for size by letting them wriggle down through a sieve or series of sieves made from various meshes of wire screening. If they are stored in a refrigerator they keep longer without metamorphosis and also keep sweeter. It is advisable to wash catches thoroughly and to feed the bigger ones only to fish large enough to clean them up quickly. Care must of course be taken to exclude any sizeable insect larvae, such as those of the dragon-fly, which are likely to escape being eaten and to grow to dangerous proportions.

Chironomus larvae, or "blood-worms," are rather similar, but are blood-red. Their parents are also gnats and so the creatures are not really worms. They stay down in the water more than any other gnat or mosquito larvae, and must be separated from mud after collection. This is best done by sieving as with the others, choosing a mesh so that the mud escapes and the larvae are retained. *Chaoborus* larvae (glass worms) are like blood-less *Chironomus* larvae but are found in cold weather, and swim freely in the water. Sometimes they may be collected in quantity, and keep well in crowded conditions.

Daphnia: This is a small crustacean about the size of a flea, and appears in warm, but not hot weather, in stagnant pools. It may be almost colorless, green or red, depending on the variety and also on the food. The red ones have haemoglobin, the same blood pigment as humans. Different species also vary considerably in size.

When really plentiful, *Daphniae* occur in large clouds and may be netted out in thick clumps; so thick that an improperly shaped net will ball them up together and injure them. The right net is fairly shallow and does not come to a point, but is rounded in section. The fleas will suffocate if not given fair room in transporting them, and should also be kept cool.

Daphnia is regarded by many as the very best food for fishes. It is not actually very good food value, as it has a high water content and a hard tough shell, and fishes fed exclusively on it do not thrive as a rule. It should be used in moderation for most tropical fishes, but may be fed more liberally to goldfish. It is available in dried form, but is rather expensive this way, except for the fact that the dried eggs in the bodies of the females will often hatch out and can be used to start a live *Daphnia* culture. These are the winter eggs, which normally last over winter and hatch out the following spring.

The artificial cultivation of *Daphnia* is possible if large pools are available, and on a worthwhile scale even in tubs or old tanks. *Daphnia* normally lives on unicellular algae and other organisms, and it is these which must be supplied in bulk. They are cultured by enriching the water in the pool or tub with decaying vegetable matter or manure. Sheep manure is said to be the best. An appropriate pool would be, say 5 × 10 feet in area and 2 feet deep, and after seeding it liberally with refuse and waiting for it to turn cloudy or green, the *Daphniae* are introduced and should breed well. Such a pool might yield enough *Daphnia* for a regular feeding two or three times a week to several hundred small fishes, but don't expect too much. Such pools are smelly, and yeast or wheat flower may be used indoors as the source of nourishment. If kept well aerated, these have little or no smell.

Other Crustacea: *Moina, Cyclops, Diaptomus* and other less important Crustacea are found as are *Daphnia* and can also be cultivated. They are not usually so abundant, nor are they as palatable to all fishes, but they are small and easily cultivated and are welcome to growing fry. *Cyclops* unfortunately seem to be a feeder on the unhatched eggs of tropicals and should be excluded from breeding tanks at the initial stage.

Gammarus pulex and *Asellus aquaticus* are two common, shrimp-like large crustaceans. They are both ½-¾″ in length and both can be cultured in similar conditions to those needed for *Daphnia*. They are caught in the roots of plants and rushes and often occur in streams. They are eagerly taken by the larger fishes and their younger stages are eaten by smaller species. They have also the advantage that they survive for an appreciable period in salt water and so may be fed to marine fishes. Uneaten specimens—and it is surprising how long *Gammarus*, in particular, sometimes manages to escape—are excellent scavengers.

Daphnia longispinna, a valuable food. Knaack photo.

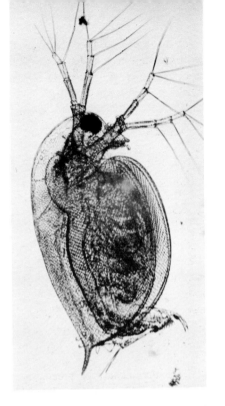

Gammarus.

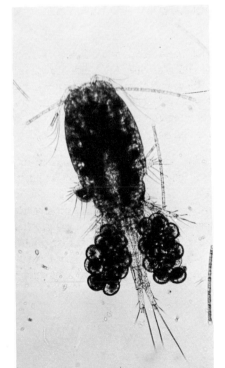

Asellus aquaticus.

A female *Cyclops,* with eggs. Knaack photo.

M—55.00

The brine shrimp, *Artemia salina* (or *salens*), is also a crustacean, but it merits a heading to itself. It is a live food of growing importance, in more senses of the word than one, as without it thousands of young fishes would never reach maturity. The genus *Artemia* is composed of small shrimps which live in very salt water, such as the Great Salt Lake in Utah, and whose eggs can withstand drying up completely for many years. Hence it is very important, for these eggs are now collected commercially and made available to aquarists all over the world. They can be stored for over a decade if necessary, as long as they are kept dry and at an even temperature. More remarkable still, they can be dried out again, even after they have become moist, and they still will retain their hatching capacity.

The eggs look like a fine brown powder and are very minute. About the smallest pinch you can take contains several hundred, and it is customary to hatch many thousands at a time. They are not used until they are hatched—it is the living young shrimp that are of importance in feeding baby fishes, and even adults of the smaller species. There are two main methods of hatching, in shallow pans

Brine shrimp nauplii as they appear under high magnification.

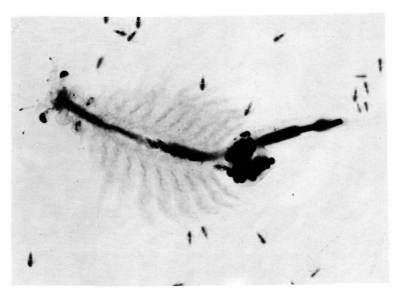

An adult female brine shrimp surrounded by nauplii.

or in deep culture with aeration. San Francisco eggs may be hatched by either method, but Utah eggs seem to yield a higher proportion of young in aerated water.

The following directions are based on the recommendations of the Wardley Brine Shrimp Company, producers of brine shrimp eggs: The eggs hatch only in *salt* water, but oddly enough they hatch more quickly and more evenly in weaker salt water than is needed by the adults. They thrive beautifully in sea water, although the adults do not. Thus, for hatching, use 6 heaped tablespoons of salt to a gallon of tap water (approximately 6 ounces to the gallon, or a $3\frac{1}{2}\%$ salt solution). The eggs will float on the surface and should be sprinkled onto the water and left there, using not more than 1 teaspoon of eggs per 2 gallons of water in shallow vessels. The eggs will hatch in about a day at temperatures of over 70°F., but they will take a week or more at less than 65°F. Even at 70°F. some of the eggs will take a couple of days to hatch out. If more eggs than recommended above are used, relatively fewer will hatch.

The empty egg shells will continue to float if undisturbed, whereas the shrimp swim in the body of the water with a jerky motion. They also collect in the lightest part of the vessel and will congregate so thickly that they will suffocate in a spot that is really bright in contrast to the rest. They may be siphoned off, free of egg shells if the last few teaspoons of water are left behind, and drained on an old handkerchief or other cloth. They should then be rinsed in fresh water, to avoid introducing gradual doses of unwanted salt into the fresh-water tank, and fed with an eye dropper or by rinsing the cloth in the tank. The hatching water may be used repeatedly as many as six times, replacing evaporated water with fresh tap water, as the salt doesn't evaporate.

By the alternative method of hatching, one-gallon jars, or even larger vessels, are two thirds filled with the same salt water as above and subjected to brisk aeration. One or two teaspoons of eggs may then be used per gallon, and the eggs are whirled around in the water until they hatch. To collect the shrimp, the aeration is turned off and the eggs allowed to settle; this they usually do partly on the bottom and partly on the top. The shrimp may then be siphoned off with little or no egg shells. There are also special outfits on the market for the deep hatching of brine shrimp, with convenient taps for running off from the base of the culture vessels.

Brine shrimp grow to about $\frac{1}{2}$ inch in length and are a meaty meal at that stage. They need a different brine from that used in hatching, so that newly hatched shrimp should be transferred within a day or two to a brine made by taking a breakfast cup (10 to 12 ounces) of salt, 2 heaped tablespoons (2 ounces) of Epsom salts, and 1 table-spoon of baking soda to a gallon of tap water. This brine is about twice the strength of sea water and much more alkaline.

The young shrimp (*nauplii*) feed naturally on algae, etc., but bak-er's yeast may be substituted—about $\frac{1}{4}$ teaspoon per gallon, well stirred up. Into a gallon of brine plus yeast, preferably in a shallow tub or tray, put just a few shrimp—not more than a few hundred, unless you intend to use them only partially grown, in which case thousands can be reared. Feed yeast again when the brine clears, which may be in a day or a week, according to temperature and the number of shrimp. Cover to prevent too much evaporation. The shrimp reach maturity in about 6 weeks, sooner if kept really warm, and they will feed on yeast throughout the period and reproduce readily. Thus, the culture, if undisturbed, will soon contain both young and older shrimps, but do not expect it to yield an indefinite supply—you will still need to buy more eggs. Siphon off and wash the adults as you would the young before using them.

Tubificid Worms: The mud worm or sludge worm, *Tubifex rivulorum* and other similar *Tubifex* or *Limnodrilus* species are excellent food, but they are found in very dirty surroundings and must be carefully washed before use. These worms absorb waste material from slow-moving polluted streams, being rarely found in quantity in stagnant water. They live at the bottom or sides of streams and wave their tails in the water, retiring promptly into a tube in the mud when disturbed. They are reddish in colour and vary from thread-like creatures an inch or two long to solid worms three or four inches in length. They may establish themselves in an aquarium and be hard to eliminate (*Corydoras* and Goldfish will do it), and whether they are regarded as an acquisition or a nuisance depends on the beholder.

Collecting *Tubifex* is usually a filthy task. If they are present in worthwhile amounts they will be seen as a reddish wriggling carpet or in separate red patches, which jerk into the mud when a shadow or footfall disturbs them. Dig well under the mud where a patch was seen—or if you are lucky it will be so thick that even when retracted it is still visible—and put mud and all into a large bucket. When the bucket is nearly full, leave it until lack of oxygen forces the worms to collect at the surface, when they may be removed, with some mud still adhering to them. If they must be left for long, run a gentle drip of water into the bucket or they will die and be useless. Most of the worms can be removed within a day or two, and must be well washed under a brisk

Tubifex worms must be carefully cleaned before being given to the fishes. Photo by C. Emmens.

stream of water to remove the residual mud, when they will aggregate into balls and may be stored for a long time, even a month, if placed in large vessels of water under a constant drip from a tap or hose, with a suitable overflow arrangement. They also store well in a refrigerator if placed in containers with no water at all, preferably air-tight. Stored masses should ocasionally be stirred up and washed more briskly, to remove the dead and feces, and should not be fed to fishes for at least the first day.

White Worms: White worms (*Enchytrae*) are relatives of *Tubifex* and of earthworms. They are small worms about an inch in length, which are commonly found in cool, moist surroundings where there is plenty of humus or other decaying matter for them to use as food. The underside of dustbins when on soil is a favorite spot; but the worms are practically never collected from such sites now, as they may be purchased from dealers to start a culture. The common variety is *Enchytraeus albidus*. White worms may be cultured in wooden boxes of rich soil, with added humus and oatmeal. These are stored in cool places such as cellars, and further oatmeal, mashed potatoes, cheese, bread and milk or a variety of other things that will suggest themselves are placed on the soil or into small holes in it, at intervals of a few days. The whole is tightly covered, preferably by a sheet of glass in contact with the top of the soil, mainly to exclude ants and other predators (even mice), but also to keep the soil in a damp state—not wet, just damp. When needed, the worms may be scraped off the glass or collected from the food pockets. A culture usually needs about 6 weeks start before harvesting commences.

On a smaller scale, the worms may be cultured between milk-soaked crusts of bread, stored in tightly covered tins or other vessels. It is advisable to boil the milk and to pour it on the crusts while hot, as this helps to sterilize them and to prevent early souring of the culture. This method nevertheless requires frequent sub-culturing, as the bread slices rapidly go sour and moldy.

There is usually little trouble in separating White worms from their food, but if it is encountered, place the mass of half-cleaned worms on a rather hot surface, and they will rapidly crawl to the top. These worms may be inadvisable as a frequent food, as they are said to cause fatty degeneration of the reproductive organs.

Microworms: A group of minute Nematode worms of the genus *Anguillula,* supplies the familiar vinegar eel, *A. aceti,* and the paste eel, *A. glutinus.* Another, *A. silusiae,* is found in soil and it is assumed that this is the species usually called the Microworm. It is a very small live-bearing worm, at a maximum about 1/10th of an inch long, with young very much smaller.

A Microworm culture; the worms are feeding on a piece of bread soaked in milk.
Photo by Robert F. Gannon.

The Microworm is easy to culture. This is best done in shallow vessels with tight covers. In the base of each vessel is placed about an $\frac{1}{8}$th inch layer of any of the quick-cooking powdered breakfast oatmeals or wheat-meals. The use of wheat germ is said to give superior results to other meals. The meal is moistened with about its own volume of water and is then inoculated with a little baker's yeast, and some Microworms. The yeast may be omitted if unavailable. Growth is rapid and the worms form a seething mass in a few days. If small pieces of wood, water-soaked beforehand, are placed criss-cross over the meal so that the top ones are clear of it, the worms crawl up and collect free of cereal on the top-most pieces. If the sides of the vessel are roughened, as can be done with plastic containers, the worms will crawl up them and can be scraped off. It is not usually worth while to feed cultures once established, but best to keep a series going so that worms are always ready for use. Each culture will last for up to 2 weeks, and the worms thrive best in warmth up to 80°F.

Microworms withstand desiccation, so that dried-up culture can be re-started merely by wetting it.

Grindal Worms: Another White worm, intermediate in size between the usual one and the Microworm, was first cultivated by Mrs. Morten Grindal, a Swedish aquarist, whose name has become attached to the worm. It was isolated from ordinary White worm cultures, and prefers more heat than the usual *Enchytrae*. It is at most $\frac{1}{2}$ inch in length and slimmer in proportion than White worms.

Cultures are maintained as with White worms, except for a higher temperature—70°F. or a little more seems best. Growth is very rapid.

Infusoria: It is still common practice to advocate the use of cultures of infusoria for newly-hatched fishes, despite the fact that newer methods of fry feeding make these practically obsolete.

Infusoria are any minute living creature in water, usually needing a microscope for identification. The term includes plants and animals. A "culture" may be started with suitable pond water, or from a previous culture. The best method is to boil up some lettuce or other vegetable matter in a pint or two of water, allow it to cool and then inoculate with the infusoria-containing material. Even if left to itself, the culture will start up, but not necessarily with the desired types of infusoria. Aeration is advisable, as it both increases the yield and keeps down smell. A medium light is also best, too strong a light may result in an excess of green algae.

Infusoria pills may be purchased, which are merely placed in water and result, or should result, in a rich culture of organisms within a few days. The culture will usually need feeding with vegetable infusion as described above. Water from a flower-vase is often rich in infusoria.

Prepared Foods: The term *prepared food* is used to denote any non-living food made up by the aquarist or bought ready-made for the consumption of his fishes. There is a wide variety of satisfactory commercial preparations on the market, some of which may be used as a staple food with the addition of such live food as proves possible from time to time. A good deal of rubbish is talked about the need of variety in food, but this is only needed in our present state of knowledge because any single food may be lacking in some factor or another which may, if we are lucky, be supplied by a different food. Otherwise, there is nothing against supposing that an unvaried constant diet could prove as completely satisfactory for fishes as it does in the laboratory for many animals. The better foods have the higher protein content.

If you make up your own dry food, which is likely to be much cheaper than buying it if you keep a large number of fishes, there is no need to make the complex cookery exercise out of it that many books advise. Take about equal parts by volume of shredded dry shrimp, liver meal and a fairly finely divided breakfast cereal—preferably one made from wheat germ, and mix thoroughly. The best particle size to select depends on the size of your fishes. If you want to feed very small ones, then select a very fine grade of shrimp and cereal. It is not usually necessary to add any salt or other mineral to the mixture.

A food for large-scale feeding, recommended by the late Myron Gordon is made from:

Liver of beef	5 lbs.
Pablum or Ceravim ...	14 lbs.
Shrimp shell meal	6 lbs.
Shrimp meat shredded ...	3 lbs.
Spinach	3 lbs.

The raw beef liver is cut into 2-inch pieces and boiled for 15 minutes and removed, but the same water used for boiling the other ingredients up, meanwhile the boiled liver is ground or chopped and returned to the mixture for a further 15-minute boiling. The paste is dried and ground for storage.

Finer grades of prepared food for fry feeding may be made from coarser supplies by grinding them in a pepper mill, or crushing them between flat tiles and then sieving carefully. Such food for young fishes may preferably contain more animal material, and may be made from 100% dried shrimp or crab.

A feeding ring may be floated on the surface of the water when using dried food. This is a small ring of hollow glass or plastic which confines the food to a portion of the tank and makes it easier to remove unconsumed portions.

Most fishes like the various baby foods, or porridge, made as for human consumption, but preferably with a little dried shrimp mixed in with it. Serve it in small soggy lumps, but expect to have to clear up the tank afterwards unless you gauge the fishes' appetite very precisely.

Various non-spiced canned foods are much appreciated, such as canned crab or lobster, fish roe or canned spinach. The cold-water fishes, mostly heavy eaters, are particularly fond of chopped up canned foods of this description.

Egg in various forms is also good for fishes—as an omelette, or boiled and chopped up, or poured into boiling water and beaten as it solidifies. Meat is readily taken, particularly minced heart or liver, but this should only occasionally be fed, as it seems to produce intestinal troubles if used much, resulting in thin fish and fouled tanks. Large fishes may be fed almost anything from the kitchen that is not spiced or oily—the latter because the oil spreads as a film over the water rather than because it is indigestible or otherwise harmful, but any food must be fresh and suitably sized.

How to Feed: Most tropical fish should be fed frequently. The warmer the water, up to about 80°F., the better the appetite of the fishes. Thus, Goldfish need almost no feeding in the depth of winter, and in normal cold weather should be fed only 2 or 3 times a week. In summer, however, twice daily is not too often. Tropicals are never so torpid as the cold-water varieties at the lower end of their temperature range, but have in general only poor appetites at below 70°F. At 75°F. they are good eaters, and should be preferably lightly fed 2-3 times daily, and at 80°F. they are ravenous and will eat practically as often as you give it to them. Even so, they will not starve if fed only once per day or even every other day, particularly if fed on live food, but it is difficult to gauge the amount to give if it is given too seldom.

The feeding of prepared food requires careful handling, and the tendency of the beginner is to give far too much at a time. It is therefore very important indeed that the following rule be strictly adhered to at all times. It is a rule originally stated by Innes:

Feed only enough prepared food at one time so that practically ALL of it is consumed within 5 minutes.

Then syphon off any that remains.

An aquarist can go round his tanks dumping in the right amounts of dry food without looking to see the result only after very long experience. Each time you feed, see that the fishes eat it, see that they are well and alert and eating normally. Feed dry foods slowly and give time to them to swell up with water inside the fishes before offering too much. Some aquarists soak food first, but the fishes do not eat so readily when this is done. Feed little and often whenever this is possible. It comes as rather a surprise to most to hear that one ounce of prepared food such as wheat-germ and shrimp mixture will last 100 average tropical aquarium fishes for about two weeks with no other feeding at 75°F.

As long as they are usually well fed, adult tropical fishes can be starved without trouble for several days. Even starvation for a couple of weeks is feasible, as long as the temperature is about 70°F. Cold-water fishes can take starvation easier as long as they too are reasonably cool—say below 60°F. Longer periods may be survived, but the tropicals at least will be pretty thin at the end of them. The importance of this is that, in a normal vacation of not more than 2 weeks, it is possible to forget adult fishes but not young fry. This may be preferable to getting a friend to feed them, unless he is also an aquarium keeper. Other people far too often make mistakes in fish keeping, the most common being gross over-feeding and pollution. If a non-fancier must be asked to undertake the task, it is vitally necessary to give him a few lessons or

Among the most practical of all commercially available prepared fish-foods are the freeze-dried foods invented by Dr. Herbert R. Axelrod in 1966. Freeze-dried foods don't have to be refrigerated, and the cooking and freeze-drying processes to which they have been subjected during preparation kill nearly all of the harmful organisms that might have been contained in the foods.

to make up separate packages of food, one per feeding, with strict instructions not to supplement them with anything else whatever. The only food which can be given in mild excess to tide the fishes over a period is mosquito larvae. These do not consume dissolved oxygen to any appreciable extent and will survive some time if uneaten before turning into pupae and then adults. A tight cover over the tank will prevent the escape of any that manage to reach maturity.

3
Diseases and Parasites

Fishes suffer from a series of diseases resembling those of higher animals, but those about which we know most and can often successfully treat are the external diseases, with symptoms visible to the aquarist. Until recently, very few effective treatments were available; but the cheapening of antibiotics for veterinary use and the discovery of some other methods of cure for a few of the common diseases have now made their treatment much more feasible. Even so, prevention is much the best, and well-kept fishes don't often fall prey to obvious disease.

Various conditions will be taken in approximate order of importance to the tropical fish-keeper, not classified by symptoms or by the nature of their causative organisms. Some of the most important diseases of tropical fishes are caused by protozoa, tiny one-celled animals which parasitize the skin or gills, or in some cases penetrate further. This is in contrast to say, human diseases, the majority of which are caused by bacteria. Antibiotics such as penicillin are not effective against most protozoa, hence they are not much used in fish medicine. The so-called wide spectrum antibiotics like aureomycin or chloromycetin, however, are spectacularly successful in most instances and are used less than they might be only because of availability and cost.

Black Ruby Barbs, *Puntius nigrofasciatus*, catch white spot easily, but it doesn't seem to bother them much, unless the attack is unusually severe. Photo by G. J. M. Timmerman.

White Spot: White Spot, "Ich," or Ichthyophthiriasis, was until recently the commonest scourge of tropical fishes, but has recently been rivalled by Velvet disease, described below. It can attack cold water fishes. It is caused by a protozoon which imbeds itself in the skin of the fish and causes a small white blister to form. This blister enlarges in a few days and then bursts, the parasite drops to the bottom of the tank and forms a cyst which then produces up to 2,000 young in its interior. These become free swimming and start the cycle once more. At 70°-80°F. the whole process takes only 8 or 10 days, but at lower temperatures it may last many weeks.

The symptoms of white spot are, at first, the fish scrubbing itself on plants and other suitable objects, then visible white spots which grow to about 1/25 of an inch across. These are usually first visible on the fins, later and in heavy attacks, all over the body. Some species are more susceptible than others, but susceptibility varies with condition and past history. The Guppy (*Lebistes recticulatus*), Head and Tail Light fish (*Hemmigrammus ocellifer*) and Ruby Barb (*Puntius nigrofasciatus*) are examples of particularly susceptible fishes, but whereas the Guppy dies without showing many spots, the Ruby Barb can be covered with them and seem none the worse.

White spot is very catching and every care must be taken not to infect other tanks. It is fortunately only transferred by wet objects and does not live in the completely dry state. It may, however, be transferred on plants, even if they are washed. All nets and other implements must be thoroughly washed in hot water or disinfectant after use in the affected tank, and splashing scrupulously avoided. The hands should also be washed after handling the affected tank. Attacks are brought on by direct infection from a case of the disease, or by chilling a tank which has organisms present in dormant form. As the *Ichthyophthirius* parasite can occur in tap water in certain areas, although not when it is heavily chlorinated, white spot can seem to come on spontaneously with no apparent cause. However, to show the disease, a fish usually has either to be attacked fairly heavily by masses of parasites or to be in poor health, when it may succumb to a light attack.

It is stated that the free-living stage must find a host within a few days or perish. A tank bare of fishes should therefore cure itself of white spot quite rapidly so that if all fishes are removed for treatment, the tank itself should need no disinfection. Unfortunately, the experiences of many aquarists lead us to believe that something may be wrong with this story, for white spot disease does not behave so obligingly and is extremely difficult to eradicate completely without thorough disinfection of tanks, plants and fishes.

Hyphessobrycon scholzei infested with *Ichthyophthirius*. The first spots are usually detected in the clear fins. Photo by R. Zukal.

The disease is susceptible to treatment in the free-living stage, while existing spots on the fish are resistant to most forms of therapy. There are two worthwhile relatively cheap treatments; by quinine or by methylene blue. To hurry the process up, any treatment may as well be at a temperature of 78°-80°F., which is quite harmless to the fishes and quickens the life cycle of the parasite and thus hastens a cure. The following treatments are effective:

QUININE: This drug is best given as the hydrochloride, which is acid and soluble, but the less soluble sulphate may be used. The dose needed is 2 grains per gallon (30 mg. per liter or 1 in 30,000.) It is dissolved in a liberal quantity of water and added to the tank in three successive lots, each of one third of the total dose, at about 12 hour intervals. An alternative and perhaps rather less reliable method is to give the total in 4 or 5 doses spread over 4 or 5 days. If later seen to be necesssary, the treatment may be once repeated, but only once, without change of water.

Most plants will survive this treatment, but may not survive a repeat dose. The tank may therefore be disinfected as a whole, taking care to stir the dose well into the water each time it is given. Do not expect the white spot to disappear immediately from the fishes, but look out for any new ones developing after about 3 to 4 days. This should nòt occur, for all free-swimming parasites should be dead and thus unable to produce new spots. However, some new ones may well be seen during the first few days, as existing parasites in the skin may continue to develop and produce visible spots later. All sign of the disease should go within 8 to 10 days, if they haven't, give a repeat treatment. This treatment usually cures completely at the first attempt, and has no obvious ill effects on the fishes.

When a cure has been achieved, do not move fishes from the tank and preferably do not change much of the water, as the quinine gradually disappears. A new attack may be started up by too much of a change. Moving what seem to be cured fishes from the affected tank to another within 3 or 4 weeks is quite often followed by an outbreak in the new tank, showing that the treatment may not always rapidly eradicate every parasite, even though the fishes seem cured. When left for about a month from the start of the treatment, the fishes seem then to be really free.

METHYLENE BLUE: Add 5 drops per gallon of a 5% solution of medical quality methylene blue. The treatment may be repeated after a day or two, even several times, but in such amounts the dye is hard on plants, and stains even rockwork and sand semi-permanently. The same eventual precautions must be taken in respect of moving the fishes as with quinine. Methylene blue is not a favorite cure, as although it is harmless and effective, the water is so deeply colored that little is visible, and even the course of the cure may be hard to observe.

ANTIBIOTICS: White spot may be cured without risk to plants or fishes by aureomycin, tetracycline or chloromycetin. The minimum adequate dosage is 50 mg./gallon, twice this dose is preferable and harmless. The best antibiotic to use, for aesthetic reasons, is chloromycetin, which is colorless and undetectable in the tank. However, the tank may go briefly cloudy, but this should soon clear up.

The antibiotic should be dissolved in a pint of warm water and stirred gently into the tank. Aureomycin froths if stirred vigorously, particularly in warm water. Antibiotic-containing veterinary preparations may be used in a tank, but the excipient (diluting material used to give bulk) may cause very cloudy water—usually filtered off quite easily. After treatment with aureomycin or tetracycline, the water may turn yellow or brown in color and thus need gradual changes until it is clear. The brown coloration is not harmful, merely unsightly.

A number of other diseases so closely resemble white spot that they are often mistaken for it. This does not matter as long as the same treatment is effective, but sometimes it is not. There is a newer variety of white spot which has a more yellowish appearance and is resistant to quinine treatment; it is therefore important to notice the presence of this parasite and not to treat with quinine. The other treatments seem effective.

The most important disease sometimes confused with white spot in the early stages, when it is most important to treat effectively without delay, is however, velvet disease, now to be described. With the exception of antibiotics and methylene blue, often avoided because of its bad effect on planted or decorated tanks, the two diseases are not cured by the same agents and it is particularly necessary to tell them apart.

Velvet or Rust disease: With this disease, the skin of the fish looks as if it has been dusted with golden or yellowish powder, which on close inspection is seen to be gently moving. At the beginning there will be a few dots of yellow, later the fish may be covered with them. The difference from white spot is that the spots are *yellower, smaller* and *move*. This disease is fatal to young fishes and must be treated immediately it is seen. Adults often carry it without showing distress, but if they are used for breeding the fry will succumb to the disease.

The cause of the disease is another protozoa, a dinoflagellate called *Oodinium limneticum*. It attaches itself to the fishes by its whip-like longer flagellum (swimming organ) and then grows more deeply into the fish by pushing out pseudopodia. A cyst is formed which remains on the skin, and from it up to about 200 new free-swimming parasites may be released. Treatment may be as follows:

METHYLENE BLUE—as for ich, but up to double the quantity. Not, therefore, the treatment of choice in a planted tank, particularly as a cure takes 1-2 weeks, even at 75°-80°F.

ACRIFLAVINE: (Trypaflavine) may be used, but too long a contact sterilizes fishes for a period of up to several months. The appropriate quantity is up to 4 ml. (one teaspoon) of a 1 in 500 solution per gallon (2 mg. per liter, or 2 ppm.) preferably together with up to one teaspoon of salt per gallon, which hastens a cure, and with a raised temperature of up to 80°F. Repeat after one week.

COPPER: Copper salts such as copper sulfate, are rapidly toxic to velvet, but also to fishes, and a balance has to be struck where the one is killed without the other. This is best done by placing copper gauze or even copper pennies into the tank. About a square inch per gallon of copper gauze is best suspended by a wire or string so that it is easily removed. As the amount of copper dissolved depends on water conditions, the fishes must now be watched carefully day by day. As the copper treatment becomes effective, the parasites leave the fish and may be seen swimming in the water, after which they die. When the fishes are clear of infection, remove the gauze and leave them in the same water for at least a week. Then change the water gradually. Do not introduce new fishes to the copper-treated water, as it may kill them. If during treatment the fishes cease feeding, start to gasp at the surface or show any other distressing symptoms, remove the copper at once and change part of the water.

ANTIBIOTICS: are successful against velvet, and may be used as for white spot. Chloromycetin is a particularly safe and effective cure.

COMBINATION CURES of say, copper plus acriflavine may be used in combatting this resistant and dangerous disease. After any cure has apparently been successful, keep watch for a recurrence, since velvet is very hard to eradicate completely.

White Clouds, *Tanichthys albonubes*, are very susceptible to velvet if kept at high temperatures for too long. Timmerman photo.

Fungus: Various fungi of the genera *Saprolegnia* and *Achyle* attack fishes which have been wounded or are in a poor state of resistance. The spores of such fungi are universal and cannot be eradicated, as they float into the tank from the air. The affected fish appears to have whitish fuzzy areas which may be like a slimy surfacing only, or have a brush of fungus filaments projecting from them. If not treated, the fungus may spread and destroy much of the tissues of the fish, finally causing death. The disease therefore has to be treated as it occurs, and is not to be regarded as infectious in the ordinary sense of the word, so that a fish while under treatment may be returned to a community tank. Treatment may be as follows.

MALACHITE GREEN or BRILLIANT GREEN (zinc free): The affected fishes are taken from the tank and immersed for 30 seconds *only* in a solution of dye at 4 grains per gallon (60 mg. per liter or 1 in 15,000), and the fish is replaced in its tank. The fungus is colored by the dye and usually disappears by the next day. If not, repeat treatments may be given.

The older treatment for fungus is the progressive salt treatment, which must be given in a bare receptable. It is usually effective, but is much more trouble. With the fishes in the bare tank, salt is added gradually over a day or two (best to add a solution of salt in water, not the dry salt), or marine water is added. A final concentration of about 0.5% is usually advocated; some fish can take more. This may be achieved by adding a small volume of water containing a level teaspoon of salt for every gallon in the tank at intervals of a few hours until five teaspoons have been added. When a cure occurs, gradually reduce the salt concentration.

Fungus on the *eye* is dangerous, and may be given special treatment by touching with a brush dipped in a 1% solution of silver nitrate, followed by a 1% solution of potassium dichromate. A red precipitate forms which restricts the silver nitrate to the outside of the eye.

Mouth Fungus: This is a condition attacking the mouths of tropicals, which looks like fungus, but is confined to the mouth. It is caused by a bacterium, *Chondrococcus columnaris*. It is a killer, and once it breaks out in a tank it is liable to spread very rapidly. The characteristic appearance is a white line around the lips of the fish, and when this is seen, do not delay treatment.

The disease is cured by penicillin, 40,000-100,000 units per gallon (about 10-25 units per milliliter), or by the wide spectrum antibiotics in the doses advised for white spot. Penicillin is particularly harmless and easy to use, and may be placed in the tank and left. It does not deteriorate very rapidly and there is no need for repeated, frequent dosage. If a cure is not effected, the dosage may safely be increased to 200,000 units per gallon. At this strength, it is clearly more economical to remove the affected fishes and treat in a small receptacle, in which a cure may be expected within 4 or 5 days.

Fin Congestion and Tail Rot: These are also bacterial diseases, characterized by ragged, opaque-looking fins and tail, and even by blood streaks in the fin substance. They are prone to affect fry if they are overcrowded, and may attack adult fishes too.

The treatment is better conditions, aeration, combined with 15,000 units of penicillin per gallon. This need usually be given only once, but if further treatment is needed, proceed as for mouth fungus, with up to 200,000 units per gallon, or use a wide-spectrum antibiotic.

Hyphessobrycon heterorhabdus with an open wound which has been attacked by a fungus. Photo by R. Zukal.

Haplochromis burtoni which has a bad case of fin and tail rot. Photo by R. Zukal.

Dropsy: "Dropsy" occurs in two forms—a general swelling of a fish which may become severe enough to cause the protrusion of scales, so that the fish looks like a porcupine fish, or a local or general, protrusion of scales without body swelling. Only the former is true dropsy, the latter merely resembles it, and a cure is not known.

This fish is dropsical; notice the swollen body and angled scales. Photo by Helmert.

More than one cause of dropsy seems to exist, and at least one form is caused by a virus. Treatment is really empirical, and because chloromycetin is active against some virus diseases it has been tried, sometimes with apparently good results.

Treatment may be as follows:

CHLOROMYCETIN, 50-100 mg./gallon, with the fishes kept cool rather than hot, say 65°F., or even 60°F. where they can stand it. This limits multiplication of the virus.

para-CHLOROPHENOXETHOL should be given at a dose of 200 ml. of a 1.0% stock solution per gallon gradually added over 24 hours.

In severe cases of dropsy, surgical treatment by puncture of the fish and attempted withdrawal of the fluid has been advocated, but it is a rather heroic procedure in the hands of any but an expert.

Exophthalmia (pop-eye): This appears to be of bacterial origin, sometimes perhaps following an injury, and particularly affects Angel-fish. It is also stated that it may be caused by gas-bubbles behind the eye. The progressive salt treatment as applied for fungus may help to reduce pressure, but no specific treatment is known.

Ichthyophonus: *Ichthyophonus* is caused by a fungus-like organism (*I. hoferi* and others) which attacks the fish internally, starting with infected food and water taken into the stomach. From this organ the parasites penetrate into the blood and reproduce all over the body. The disease cannot usefully be treated therefore by the common external baths.

The disease is manifest as multiple cysts containing yellow, brown or black granules, which sometimes break the surface of the body and may be ulcerated. The ovary is commonly attacked and sterility results. Other symptoms will depend on the sites of worst attack, and signs of liver, circulatory or other disease may be seen.

Treatment was ineffective until fairly recently, when the following cure has been suggested by I. M. Rankin:

para-CHLOROPHENOXETHOL in an 0.1% solution is added as for dropsy, and effects a cure in about four days. Soaking of dry food in a 1% solution and feeding may also be tried.

Swim bladder disease: Sometimes a fish hops about in the water at an angle, rather than swims, and may eventually become completely incapacitated by the condition. It may float helplessly on the surface, belly-up; or be unable to rise from the bottom. The condition is said to be caused by chilling, as during transport, or may arise without obvious cause. It is due to inability of the swim-bladder to control its air content, so that the fish is too light, too heavy, or ill-balanced. The condition is rarely fatal unless extreme and no effective treatment is known.

Skin slime: A slimy condition of the skin, often with faded colors and clamped fins, may be caused by a variety of infections. Common ones are *Cyclochaeta domerguei, Chilodon cyprini* or *C. hexastichus,* and *Costia necatrix.* All are protozoa. Treatment is best with *quinine hydrochloride* as for white spot.

Tuberculosis: This disease causes thinness and emaciation, and may be due to a variety of organisms of which some may actually be related to human tuberculosis. There is, however, no chance of infection. There is no known cure. Two light yellow spots on the caudal peduncle of Tetras is a symptom of tuberculosis.

Neon tetra disease: Neons affected by this disease show fading of the blue-green line and eventually lose the color almost entirely. The disease is not confined to this species and may affect glowlights or other tetras. The disease has been ascribed to various organisms, usually sporozoa, either *Glugea* or *Plistophora,* and has no known cure.

Flukes: The commonest flukes, which may attack both cold-water and tropical fishes, are monogenetic; they have only one host and do not require snails or some other creature as an intermediate host. That is why they thrive in aquaria, whereas the digenetic flukes, requiring an intermediate host, usually do not. These flukes, or flatworms, can be a considerable bother and are responsible for many deaths, particularly in fry. They infect the skin and gills, holding on by an organ on the head known as the haptor, which has hooks.

When attacked by flukes, fishes may dash around and scrub themselves, eventually ceasing through sheer exhaustion. They are hard to get rid of, and several treatments of fair to good efficiency are the best that can be offered.

Gyrodactylus can be seen on the gills, fins or skin with a hand lens, as little waving white threads. It lives all the year round in both cold and tropical tanks, and bears living young. The following treatments may be tried.

Dactylogyrus (left) and *Gyrodactylus* are two aquarium pests that can cause much trouble.

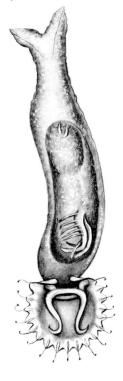

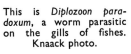

This is *Diplozoon paradoxum*, a worm parasitic on the gills of fishes. Knaack photo.

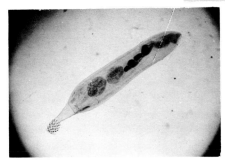

The Scratcher Worm, *Echinorhynchus nodulosus*, showing the haptor by which it makes its holdfast. Knaack photo.

DISINFECTION: Place the fish in ¼ teaspoon of one of the non-poisonous phenolic disinfectants per gallon. The British preparation "Dettol" is excellent. They should stay in this bath for 10 minutes, at a maximum, but treatment may be repeated a day later.

Dactylogyrus affects only the gills, but looks much the same on inspection with the hand lens. It may be differentiated from *Gyrodactylus* by having 4 head organs instead of 2. It is a much tougher brute, and the above treatment has no effect on it. Luckily it is more seasonal, at any rate in cold water tanks, and lays eggs. It is usual for any outbreak to be confined to early summer.

The best available cure is *potassium permanganate,* 2 parts per million approx. This is 1/6th grain per gallon, or 2 mg. per liter. The fishes should be left in for several hours, and in fact can stand twice the concentration without severe distress. The whole aquarium may be treated, and at least half the water syphoned off from the bottom to remove flukes which have let go and sunk down.

Other treatments recommended for flukes of undefined species are a bath for 20 seconds in 1 part of glacial acetic acid in 500 of water, repeated in 3 days; or 20 drops of formaldehyde per gallon for 5 to 10 minutes or until exhaustion.

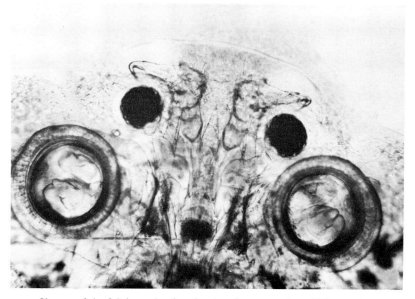
Closeup of the fish louse *Argulus*, showing the rasping discs. Helmert photo.

Fish lice and anchor worm: These are larger parasites rather than diseases, and they burrow into the flesh of the fishes. Both are rare in tanks. Gold-fishs sometimes bring them in from ponds, where they often abound. The fish Louse (*Argulus*) is about 3/16th of an inch in size and looks like a mite or smaller spider. It is flat and colorless and clings to the fish, biting its way into the flesh. The Anchor Worm digs in with a large foot, from which it gets its name, with a thread-like body up to $\frac{1}{2}$ inch long hanging free. Both may be treated with the permanganate treatment as for *Dactylogyrus*.

Shimmies: This condition is usually caused by chilling, or by foul conditions, and is a very characteristic "swimming on the spot." The fish swims without getting anywhere. Treatment is by heat, up to 85°F., and improvement in general conditions. Livebearers are most frequently affected.

WEIGHTS AND MEASURES

It is much the best to get solutions of drugs made up professionally. These often need diluting for use, and the following tables give sufficiently accurate indications for doing so. The table of weights is only for common salt solutions, not other substances.

Fluid Measures

Home Measure (fluid)	U.S. Fluid Measure	Metric System
1 drop (eye dropper)	1/160 fluid oz	1/20 c.c. (or ml.)
1 teaspoon	1/8 fluid oz.	4 c.c.
1 dessertspoon	1/3 fluid oz.	10 c.c.
1 tablespoon	2/3 fluid oz.	20 c.c.
1 teacup	6 fluid oz.	180 c.c.
1 breakfast cup	10 fluid oz.	295 c.c.
1 pint	16 fluid oz.	480 c.c.

Table for Salt Solutions

Home Measure (salt)	Weight (Apoth.)	Metric Weight
1 level teaspoon	75 grains	5 grams
1 heaped teaspoon	125 grains	8 grams
1 level dessertspoon	150 grains	10 grams
1 heaped dessertspoon	250 grains	16 grams
1 level tablespoon	300 grains	20 grams
1 heaped tablespoon	500 grains	33 grams
1 teacup	7 oz.	220 grams
1 breakfast cup	12 oz.	370 grams

When thinking in percentages or parts per million, it is much easier to use the Metric System. One cubic centimeter (1 c.c.) or millilitre (1 ml.) of water weighs 1 gram. A 1% salt solution is therefore 1 gram of salt in 100 ml. of water approx. To make a gallon of 1% salt solution we must know that one gallon equals $3\frac{1}{2}$ liters approximately, or 3500 ml. and so we need 35 grams of salt. This is best measured as 7 level teaspoons of salt to the gallon. A British gallon is $4\frac{1}{2}$ liters.

STOCK SOLUTIONS

The aquarist with many tanks is wise to keep by him stocks of all the commonly needed drugs and salts, preferably ready made up for use. A suitable drug store would be:

Substance	Concentration	Stock Quantity
Quinine hydrochloride	10 grains/fl. oz.	20 fl. oz.
Methylene blue	5% (23 gr/fl. oz)	10 fl. oz.
Brilliant green	5% (23 gr/fl. oz)	10 fl. oz.
Potassium permanganate	1 grain/fl. oz.	10 fl. oz.
Penicillin	—	1 million units
Chloromycetin	—	10 capsules, 250 mg.

Modern preparations of penicillin are available in soluble tablet form, while a capsule of chloromycetin or any other similar antibiotic must preferably be opened and the contents dissolved in a little water before adding to the aquarium.

4
Breeding Fishes

The sexes in fishes are always separate, and in the few cases in which it has been studied, sex determination is genetic and determined by the spermatozoa, as in most other vertebrates; but unlike most other vertebrates, the genetic sex may sometimes alter spontaneously, particularly in live-bearers. When this occurs, the transformation is apparently always from female to male. Winge, who has studied the Guppy extensively, has shown that it is possible to swing sex determination from one pair of chromosomes to another, which indicates that this mechanism in the livebearers is in a primitive state.

Fertilization usually takes place at the moment of spawning. Fish spermatozoa do not live long once they have been ejected into the water. Some aquarium fishes are community spawners, an outstanding example being *Rasbora heteromorpha,* but the majority of species will spawn in single pairs, even though in Nature they may spawn communally. The livebearing fishes were thought to have true internal fertilization, but this is more doubtful since in some instances it has apparently been shown that the male does not place sperm in the oviduct, but merely shoots packets of them in the right general direction through the water.

The fertilized eggs usually hatch rapidly. Those of many Characins hatch within 24 hours at about 75°-80°F., most Barbs within 40 hours, Goldfish in about 3 days at 80°F. but as long as a week at 60°F. Many species of Cyprinodonts lay eggs which take 10-14 days to hatch, while some of those of this group may take several months, as in the *Cynolebias* and *Nothobranchius* genera. The young are usually very small, and require careful and special feeding. Typical numbers of eggs per spawning are 100-1,000 in aquarium species, most of which should be fertile. Livebearers drop anything from half a dozen to 200 young, the latter only from older females.

Livebearers: The livebearing fishes (*Poeciliidae*) breed naturally in the aquarium without special attention, as long as they are well fed and cared for. The only problem is saving the young from being eaten by their parents. A deficiency of either light or warmth can arrest reproduction completely; as also can acid water. Within the temperature range 68°-80°F., the only influence of heat is to shorten the period of gestation, and season has no effect other than through light.

A pair of Wagtail Platies, typical livebearers. The male is the lower fish. Photo by Dr. Herbert R. Axelrod.

A pair of Glowlight Tetras, representative egglayers. The female is the heavier fish, at left. Timmerman photo.

The differentiation of sexes is easy, fortunately, in most fishes of this family. The males characteristically possess a *gonopodium*, an organ of copulation which is formed from the modified anal fin. There is often a large difference in the size of the sexes, males being the smaller. This is particularly obvious in the Guppy, in which the male is also colored and may have long and variously-shaped decorative fins, while the female is drab. (Recent strains of Guppy have quite colorful females, however.)

The males of *Poecilia vivipara*, *Quintana atrizona*, *Phallichthys amates*, *Pseudoxiphophorus bimaculatus*, *Heterandria formosa* and *Gambusia affinis* are much smaller than the females, while in most other aquarium livebearer species the male is usually the smaller fish. In the Swordtails, Platys and Mollies, both sexes show a variety of colors and are about the same size. *Xiphophorus variatus* however, has uncoloured females.

Much more is known about the inheritance of color and color variations in the Platys, Swordtails and Guppies than any other species, with the result that strains have been established in some of them for the early recognition of sex in the newly dropped young. This is done by color linkage, so that before the gonopodium develops it is still possible to tell the males from the females, all of one sex being a particular color or spotted with black.

Although male Guppies, *Poecilia reticulata*, have smaller bodies than females, the greatly enlarged tail in modern fancy strains makes the over-all length of the sexes almost equal. Photo by M.F. Roberts.

Male livebearers are easily recognized by their modified anal fin or gonopodium and the often much larger dorsal or caudal fins than the females. The dorsal fin of this male Molly is especially attractive. Photo by R. Zukal.

Fertilization and development: Young livebearing females can be fertilized at a very early stage if mature males are present, in the case of Platys, some eight days or so after birth. Even when they are fertilized very early, the females do not bear young for many weeks, and Guppies, Platys and Swordtails may be expected to drop their first brood not earlier than 10-12 weeks. Males take no notice of whether a female is already gravid or even about to drop young, but pay court to all and sundry, including other immature males. They hover around the female or chase her about the tank, often with a spreading of fins and, particularly in the Swordtails, a backward swimming motion which is very characteristic. The female seems indifferent to all of this, and the male simply darts in and ejects his sperm when the chance presents itself. The sperm are stored in the female reproductive tract and fertilize successive crops of eggs for the next 5 or 6 months. If fertilization continues to occur, as it does in a mixed tank, the new sperm certainly fertilize some of the eggs, but the extent to which the first, original insemination can be superseded by later ones has never been fully worked out.

In the Guppy, Platy, Swordtail, Mollie and *Gambusia,* successive crops of eggs occur in batches so that one lot of young all of the same age is produced, followed about a month later by another batch. At an average temperature of about 75°F., the actual development of the young from the time of fertilization to birth is about 24 days, while the brood interval is about 30 days. The extra week is taken up by the development of the next crop of eggs prior to their actually being fertilized. Most livebearers produce young at about 22 day intervals when kept near to 80°F. and in a bright light. At 68°F. and still in a bright light, the interval lengthens to some 35 days or more. In a dull light it also lengthens, and as remarked above, cool conditions plus dullness will stop reproduction.

In *Heterandria* and *Poecilistes* and some of their relatives, the eggs ripen and are fertilized at much more frequent intervals, batches being produced every few days, and young being born at similar intervals, so that there are always young at different stages present in the mother and a few are dropped at a time.

The young fishes are nourished during development by their mother and there are various methods in different species by which they receive nourishment. They possess a yolk-sac, a bag containing nourishment present in the egg when fertilization takes place, and use up the food stored within it. The maternal nourishment is usually provided by a *placenta,* an organ in which the blood of the mother and young is very closely mingled without actual mixing, which in some of these fishes is part of the foetal pericardium, the membrane surrounding the heart. The young fishes develop in a folded position, head to tail, and are born with this fold still present. They may sink to the bottom for a short period, but are usually able to fend for themselves either immediately or within a couple of hours. A batch varies in size of fish according to the age of the mother and its own numbers; large broods will contain young fishes half the size of smaller broods. However, an average length for the newly born Swordtail or Platy would be about $\frac{1}{4}$ inch. The first brood from a young female may number only six, later broods may rise to 200. Mollies, however, rarely exceed 30 or 40 and a typical Swordtail, Guppy or Platy birth is around 60 to 80.

The pregnant mother swells unmistakably in most livebearers, sometimes less obviously in Swordtails, and also presents the "gravid spot," which is a dark spot near the base of the anal fin caused by the stretching of the peritoneal wall. Moving the mother, particularly in Mollies, is likely to cause premature birth. She is best moved either early or very late, so that the young are in no danger, or so ready for birth that they come to no harm. The young swim towards the light and if the tank is heavily stocked with fine-leaved plants, they will swarm into them and be safe from cannibalism.

Breeding traps are used to rescue the young from cannibalistic parents or other fishes in the tank. They can be simple or relatively complex (as the one shown here). Photo courtesy Penn-Plax.

Breeding Traps: The oldest breeding trap for saving young livebearers was a cut-off funnel in a jar; the mother could not swim through the small hole, but the young could escape and survive. Such an arrangement does not suit many females, who dash around and injure themselves, and it is more frequently the practice to use a small aquarium with a cage suspended in it with walls of such material that the young can escape but the mother cannot. A cage or barrier of glass rods or plastic material is satisfactory, but tedious to make and rather expensive to buy. Perhaps the most satisfactory arrangement is a screen of mosquito netting on a stainless steel or wooden frame, which can be wedged across the darkest part of the tank so as to confine the female to one end while allowing the young to pass to the lighted end. Even a loose-fitting dividing glass is fairly good, as the young seem to find the slots at the edges quite rapidly and make their way past.

However, most breeders seem to prefer the more natural method of plants in abundance to provide shelter for the young, with removal of the mother at the earliest chance. If the mother is supplied with more live food than she can eat she is unlikely to account for many of her own young, so mosquito larvae or Daphniae are added. If the young have to be moved, syphon them off as gently as possible or, better still, ladle them out with a soup ladle or teacup. Do not use a net. Mollies will usually not eat their young unless they are very hungry, so that a well-fed tank of this species has young present in plenty without further precautions.

In a heavily planted tank, babies of this pair of Blue Platies would be able to escape being eaten. Photo by Dr. Herbert R. Axelrod.

The best sheltering plants are masses of *Salvinia, Myriophyllum, Ambulia, Nitella,* or coarse algae. They allow the young to dive in for protection but are too dense for the adult to follow with any ease. Young born prematurely may still have a visible bulge formed by the yolk-sac and will be small. They are often poor swimmers and are likely to die off rapidly. Sometimes the addition of a little salt to the water helps, about a teaspoon to the gallon, making roughly a 0.1% solution, or even more. Young Mollies or Guppies are quite happy in a 1% salt solution and if bred from marine-acclimatized parents, can take a 3% solution.

Feeding: Livebearer young are quite large and can be fed dry or other prepared food straight away. If they are given only prepared food, growth may be poor, but a mixture of live and dry food is quite satisfactory. A few feeds of live food much affect the subsequent growth-rate of young livebearers, and this early feeding of live food is therefore important for good development. Suitable first live foods are microworms, newly hatched brine shrimp, shredded earthworm, sifted *Daphniae,* newly hatched mosquito wrigglers or shredded white worms. Sifted *Daphniae* are those which have been passed through a large mesh to exclude the larger sizes. However if adult *Daphniae* are used in reasonable numbers—not so as to overcrowd the tank and compete seriously for oxygen—their young are a continual source of food. Suitable dry foods include any fine powdered food, such as dried shrimp finely ground, fine cereals, and liver or egg powder.

Modern strains of Hi-Fin Swordtails are valued for their flowing fins and brilliant colors. The male is the top fish. Photo by R. Zukal.

The small livebearer *Heterandria formosa* (male at left) drops young a few at a time instead of all at once. Photo by J. Kassanyi.

One of the more recent livebearers that has gained sudden popularity is *Xenotoca eiseni*. Photo by Ed Keys.

They should be fed several times daily, and kept at not lower than 75°F. Young livebearing fishes can take high temperatures and thrive in them. They do well with their bellies full, and should go around looking like a fish stuck on to a small football for the first few weeks. They will not overeat, even though it may look like it. If much dry food is used, and of course it must be suitably small in size, scavengers should be present. Snails are the easiest to install, but *Corydoras* will not eat the young fishes as long as they have left-overs to clear up.

A week or so later larger live foods and coarser dry foods can be fed, although the smaller sizes will still be eaten. Tubifex worms, larger larvae of various species and medium sized *Daphnia* are now suitable. The young of Mollies should be fed up to 6 or 8 times a day when this is possible.

Purity of strains: There are many color and other strains of Platys, Swordtails and Mollies. The first two species cross readily and it is doubtful whether the great majority of so-called Platys and Swords are pure species at all, but are instead hybrids of one type or another.

Some of the hereditary factors (genes) concerned in the size, color or configuration of these fishes have been studied in detail, while others have not. Some characters are clear-cut, present or absent, whereas others are the result of the combined action of several genes and exist in all sorts of grades and shades. Thus red and green in the Swordtail are mutually incompatible colors—typically a fish is either red or it is green, and excellent examples of both may be produced by the same parents in the same brood. Moreover the redness of the red or the greenness of the green is not necessarily affected by the fact that it has come from a parent of another color. It may be affected by other factors, some genetic and some environmental, and it may be true that a really good red Swordtail can only be bred from red stock, because only then could factors tending to intensify the redness be properly concentrated and observed. However, this is all conjecture, and observation on the point is needed.

In general, therefore, fine specimens and really worthwhile strains, whether for color or other features, must be kept separate. The fishes themselves do not distinguish between differences of that sort, and any Platy will mate with any other Platy of opposite sex.

Hybrids and General Breeding: Platys and Swordtails mate together readily and most hybrids are fertile. Other species, such as the Mollie and Guppy, do not produce hybrids nearly so readily, and it is with Platy-Swordtail crosses that the aquarist is mainly concerned.

When placed with a mixture of Platys and Swordtails, a fish tends to mate only with its own kind, but if it has no choice, it will mate with the other species. Thus, for hybridizing, it is best to place a mature male of one species with developing young of the other, whereupon the females will be impregnated by the adult male before their brothers have a chance. These young males are also removed as they become detectable, as they will interfere later on if left.

A female Half-Beak, *Dermogenys pusillus*, delivering young. Although the Half-Beak is a livebearer, it could not crossbreed with a livebearer of the family Poeciliidae, because it is not at all closely related. Photo by G. J. M. Timmerman.

This beautiful male Guppy is the result of selective breeding and good aquarium conditions; good fish are not developed overnight. Photo by Dr. Herbert R. Axelrod.

First-cross hybrids of the Platy-Swordtail varieties are large, fine-looking fishes. They are much more uniform than later generations, and if they come from a mating of fairly pure lines of parents, they will be very uniform. They usually grow bigger than either parent, exhibiting a phenomenon called "hybrid vigor," seen in many such crosses. They are deep bodied, with short swords in the males. When mated back to either parent stock, fish of any desired degree of Platy or Swordtail "blood" can be produced.

If livebearers are being bred for particular qualities and colors, they must therefore be separated very early from potential sources of crossbreeding. The scheme will vary according to circumstances, but if an adult male of the desired type is not placed with the young so as to catch the females early, they must be separated off as soon as it is possible to tell their sex, and a careful watch kept for the development of male characters in any of them. By this method, the stock can be housed in two tanks, one with males and the other with females and undeveloped males.

As soon as those young which are of the best quality can be selected, the rest are discarded and the desired matings are made. Sometimes the best parents are not the best lookers, and a fine strain of fishes may have grandparents of only second-rate appearance. It is thus best to keep several pairs, and to progeny-test them—i.e. keep them and their offspring until you can see which line of fishes you want, and then go on breeding from the parents, discarding the others of the same generation.

EGG SCATTERERS

The class of egg-scatterers includes the majority of aquarium fishes— the *Characidae*, *Cyprinidae* and *Cyprinodontidae*. Most of them lay adhesive eggs which stick to plants, and some lay non-adhesive eggs which fall to the bottom. Nearly all eat their eggs if they are given a chance. A typical spawning routine is a chase of the female by the male, accompanied by spasms of egg-laying and simultaneous fertilization. Activity may continue for from an hour to several days, but a few hours at a time is the more general rule.

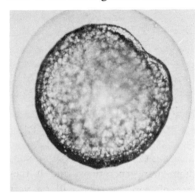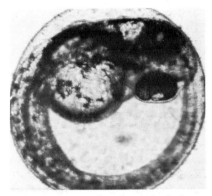

At left, a fish egg recently laid. At right, the same egg, about ready to hatch. Both photos by Dr. J. Knaack.

When the eggs of an egg-laying fish have been deposited, the problems of the breeder may be regarded as just having started, for the eggs must be preserved from predators and disease, must hatch, and the young must then be protected, fed and raised. It is very unusual for any young of an egg-scattering species to survive in a community tank, and somewhat unusual for them to survive if left only with their parents, except in some Cyprindonts. The care of the eggs and young usually includes special preparations for spawning and removal of the parents at an appropriate early stage.

It is therefore necessary to describe a number of general principles which are fairly clearly established and to indicate how improvements may be made in the future, and above all to recommend an experimental approach by all concerned. Perhaps the best general advice is that few species turn out to be as particular in the conditions they demand for successful spawning as most people think and that cleanliness, healthy fish and proper feeding are often more important than pH, temperatures, light and shade. The most important factor in some cases is, however, the hardness of the water. Soft water is sometimes essential for success and it is rarely other than an advantage.

Telling Sex: The majority of the egg scatterers have distinguishable sexes, even out of the breeding time, while nearly all can be told apart quite easily as the female fills with roe. Details of the various ways in which sex can be told are given when discussing individual fishes. When these do not help as much as they might, it pays to remember that the male is often the slimmer and rather smaller fish and is often more brightly colored. In the *Characidae* he usually has minute hooks on the lower part of the anal fin. These may sometimes be seen as a marking on the fin, or they may actually catch in a fine net and leave him hanging from the mesh. In the *Cyprinidae,* the breeding males often develop small white pearly dots on some part or other, as on the gill-covers of goldfish. Most of the Barbs have color differences between the sexes and are very easy to sex for that reason. In the *Cyprinodontidae,* color differences are again the rule, which once more makes matters fairly easy as long as you are certain that some of each sex are present. The technique for breeding these fishes differs from that usual for egg-scatterers and they will be dealt with separately.

A pair of spawning Tiger Barbs, *Capoeta tetrazona,* depositing eggs in some plants. Photo by R. Zukal.

A pair of Pearl Danios, of the family Cyprinidae. The female (distended with roe) is the upper fish. Photo by G. J. M. Timmerman.

One of the newer longfin varieties of the common Zebra Danio, *Brachydanio rerio.* Photo of some spawning action by Jaroslav Elias.

Preparation for Spawning: The egg-scatterers are best bred in specially prepared tanks, using no sand, no plants and specially treated water. The importance of the latter varies with the species, but it is never a mistake to use it with fresh water aquarium varieties. Sand is substituted by *peat,* plants by *nylon mops* or other readily disinfected material, and the tank water should be *soft* and *acid* in pH. These factors are the key to successful fish breeding in the great majority of cases.

The peat for lining the tank should be used whether nylon mops are employed or not, as it catches stray eggs and also gives an opaque base to the tank, which is much the best for many fishes. It is never used new, but must be prepared by soaking in water for some time before use. It is often possible to use peat from the set-up employed in preparing the water to be used in the tank. The nylon mops may be bought commercially or made from nylon wool. They may be sterilized in hot water and used again and again.

The water should be softened and acidified in a suitable filter system in a tank or reservoir set aside for the purpose. The filter contains an ion-exchange resin, such as Zeocarb 225 (Permutit Co.) which removes hardness from the water and substitutes sodium for heavier metals. The "Down-under" Filter and Water Softener may be recommended. In districts with very hard water, the amount of sodium salts left in the water may, be excessive and these may in turn be removed by a suitable resin, which leaves the water equivalent to distilled water, except for sterility. Distilled water may of course be used from the start, but it is expensive and must be *glass* distilled, or it may contain a harmful amount of copper. If it is used, a small amount of sodium chloride should be added, about one teaspoon per 10 gallons.

It is not usually feasible to include enough peat in such a filter to acidify the water with the so-called "humic" acids that seem so beneficial to fishes. Instead it is best to layer the base of the tank with about an inch of previously washed peat and gradually to replace the peat as it is used in the spawning tanks. The resultant water is then soft and acid, a suitable pH is 6.0 to 6.5, and of an amber color. Too long a soaking in peat will give it a very brown appearance, but this does not matter as long as the pH is correct.

The measurement of pH has already been discussed. Hardness may be measured with one of the several commercial testing kits, which give full instructions to the purchaser. A reliable method is by noting the point at which a standard soap solution produces suds. The solution is added dropwise to a measured amount of water, and the bottle shaken at frequent intervals, the end-point being when suds occur. A formula for converting drops of standard solution to parts per million hardness is given by the supplier. Another method is to use a titrating solution which causes a color change as the end-point is reached, as in the BDH "versenate" kit, which gives very accurate readings.

The size of tank depends largely on the size of the fishes to be spawned. Most small fishes to a 2 inch size can be spawned in 3 to 5 gallon tanks, with a mop or two weighted down in the centre of the tank, which is lined by about ¼ inch of *used* peat.

The medium barbs, like *Puntius conchonius* or *P. ticto,* should have rather larger, say 6-8 gallon tanks, otherwise similarly arranged. This size is suitable for the *Danios,* although those which scatter non-adhesive eggs require a different set-up. Only really large fishes like the Goldfish require big tanks.

A dividing glass, with rubber-covered edges, is useful for some varieties. This is used for separating the fishes before spawning is required. Adequate illumination must be provided, and many fishes like a well lit spawning area. It is now the custom of some European aquarists to use a spotlight, illuminating only an area of the tank over the mops, in which the fishes will come and spawn. Tanks should also have individual temperature control as it will sometimes be necessary to raise or lower it to produce the required results.

Tanks prepared for fishes which normally lay their eggs on floating weeds, such as the Panchax group, are similar to those above, but the nylon mop is floated by cork floats.

Spawning: If the fishes are kept at an average temperature of 75°F., the majority will spawn without a further rise in temperature. All that is necessary is to place a full female and a male into the tank with as little disturbance as possible. The pair of fishes placed in the breeding tank must be ready to spawn. For this they are best conditioned for a week or so beforehand with live food, but many species do not require this as an imperative procedure. The female should be full of spawn, bulging, but not left too long, or the eggs may not be fertile and she may become egg bound and die. A thin female will sometimes spawn but usually gives few eggs, for if she has a normal quota, she won't be thin. The male should look pert and well-colored. He may pale off on being moved, but should rapidly regain his form, even within a few minutes. Young males may not fertilize all of the eggs and young females will not give a very large number of eggs, but there is no reason otherwise why they should not be spawned. Spawn early and spawn regularly for the best results. Often, a female will be ready every 10-14 days or even more frequently.

The fishes may spawn immediately, or they may wait for several days. It is best to watch the whole process and to take them out as soon as spawning is over, for they must be removed as soon as possible or there

This spawning pair of Black Ruby Barbs is releasing its eggs in a plant thicket. Photo by A. Van den Nieuwenhuizen.

may be few eggs left uneaten. Even flooding the tank with live food does not always prevent egg-eating, although it may help. However, the use of peat helps to preserve more eggs than would otherwise be saved as they fall into the peat and are less readily eaten, but those on the mops are still in danger. Spawning may take from an hour or two to a couple of days, but the shorter period is fortunately more typical.

If the fishes do not spawn within a few hours, they may do so early the next morning, so be up within two hours of dawn, or cover the tank so that it will stay dark and daylight may be admitted at your convenience. Alternatively, place the glass divider in position with one fish on each side of it and let them contemplate each other for a spell. This often helps, so much that some breeders use the device regularly for a few hours or days before allowing the pair to come together.

If they have not spawned within two days, gradually raise the temperature by 4° or 5°F. This often stimulates spawning quite promptly, but wait for another day or so if nothing happens. If spawning has still not occurred within 3 or 4 days, it is usually best to remove the pair, separate them, or place them in a large community tank, and try again a few days later. If they are kept in the spawning tank for more than 2 days, they should be given live food in moderation.

Variations on the above procedure include the routine placing of breeders in the tank after dark, to induce spawning next morning, placing the female in about half a day ahead of the male, and placing two males with one female. This is thought to increase the percentage of fertilized eggs, but it is a rather doubtful procedure, as the males often spend more time chasing each other than in chasing the female.

The spawning action varies with species. Most of them indulge in the typical chase of the female by the male, but some start with the reverse procedure, and the female chases the male. This is often seen in *Hemigrammus ocellifer* (Head and Tail light fish) and in *Puntius tetrazona* ("Sumatra" Barb). Finally, however, it is the male who chases, and he takes up a position beside the female in or over the spawning mops and with a quivering motion the eggs and milt are released. Some species have spectacular habits at the moment of spawning. The Glowlight Tetra (*Hemigrammus erythrozonus*) pair does a complete barrel-roll, the Giant Danio (*Danio malabaricus*) female whirls around several times in a horizontal plane, the female *Rasbora heteromorpha* loops the loop vertically, depositing her eggs on the underside of flat-leaved plants as she does so (and thus cannot be spawned by the mop technique).

The female *Rasbora heteromorpha* will attach her eggs to the underside of a leaf. Photo by Ruda Zukal.

The Zebra Fish, *Brachydanio rerio* (female at right), lays non-adhesive eggs; special traps may be used to protect the eggs from hungry parents. Photo by R. Zukal.

The above account covers many of the egg-scatterers which lay adhesive eggs. A few lay non-adhesive eggs, outstanding amongst which is *Brachydania rerio* (Zebra fish). With this fish, and with the related fishes, *B. nigrofasciatus* (Spotted Danio) and *B. albolineatus* (Pearl Danio) it is necessary to catch the eggs to prevent their being eaten. This used to be done by covering the bottom with small marbles or pebbles, sometimes interlaced with plants, or by means of a grid of glass rods or other material which allows the eggs to fall beneath and prevent the parents from following. Fairly shallow water, not above 6 inches, is also to be recommended as it prevents the adults from having too long a time in which to chase and eat the falling eggs, as they tend to spawn near to the surface. Now, a peat-strewn tank is all that is necessary, as the eggs fall into the peat, which is stirred up a little as the fishes swim, and remain uneaten.

Copeina arnoldi lays adhesive eggs above the water line, and should be given a sheet of sanded glass or similar material projecting several inches into the air, and slanting at an angle of about 45°. The fishes leap into the air and deposit the eggs some 2 inches above the top of the water; these are guarded by the male from some distance off, and at frequent intervals he dashes over and splashes them with water. Luckily for him, they hatch in about 24 hours.

The Bloodfin (*Aphyocharax rubripinnis*) also leaps out of the water when spawning, but the eggs fall back into the water and, being non-adhesive, sink to the bottom as with *Brachydanios*. The Croaking Tetra (*Mimagoniates inequalis*) was a puzzle to breeders for a long time until it was found that a normally appearing courtship is not followed immediately by egg laying. This occurs a day or so later, in the absence of the male, when the female deposits fertile eggs singly on the leaves of plants. This fish gets its name from the noise made by males.

A number of fishes are community breeders; spawning in nature in large groups of mixed sexes. This happens with some of the Barbs, such as *P. conchonius* and *P. ticto,* but they are also able to spawn in pairs if put to it. Some of the *Rasbora* are much more choosy, and very rarely spawn except in communities. *Rasbora heteromorpha* will spawn fairly readily when at least 8 or 12 fishes are present, and very readily in communities of larger size, when unfortunately the eggs are nearly all consumed on the spot by the onlookers. The best results so far have been reported with the smaller groups, placed in planted tanks so that their habit of depositing eggs on the underside of growing plants can be practiced. Breeders are removed as soon as activity ceases, or as soon as the eggs are being eaten by any of the fishes present.

Aphyocharax anisitsi, the Bloodfin, leaps out of the water during the act of spawning. Three females with swollen abdomens are at the top, with two slender males below. Photo by M. Chvojka.

The Anabantids build bubble nests with their mouths; usually the male builds the nest and guards the young on its own. The eggs are floated in the bubble nest until they hatch, and the fry remain in the nest for some time after this. The male is usually fierce at this stage, and may kill the female if she remains in the tank. The Cichlids usually lay eggs onto rocks or plant leaves, and both parents take care of them and of the young. The eggs are fanned, and when the young hatch out they are mouthed about and even moved from place to place, and are finally shepherded around in a flock with watchful, savage parents on guard all the time.

Telling Sex: Both Anabantids and Cichlids show well-marked sex differences in the adult, but some are very difficult to tell, in particular the Angel and Pompadour. Apart from color differences, the males tend to have longer and more pointed dorsal and anal fins. In the breeding season they are brilliant, and even out of the breeding season they are usually brave. An Anabantid female full of roe is usually very plump, but Cichlids show little or nothing.

As he begins to be ready for breeding, the male Anabantid blows bubbles, sticky with secretion, at the surface of the water. It is easy to see how this has evolved from the habit of these labyrinth fishes of breathing air at the surface of foul water; their air-breathing habits enable them to inhabit it and surface nests are an advantage. The chosen site is often under a leaf or floating plant, or at the edge of a mass of duckweed or algae.

The Cichlids like to choose their own mates, and may kill one selected for them. It is therefore best to keep young fishes together until some pair off and can be separated for breeding. The other method is to introduce pairs to each other and watch, and to be prepared to remove one of the pair before it is injured or even killed. The loser is not always the female.

Suitable Tanks: There is no need for disinfected or bare tanks when breeding these fishes, and since the fry of Anabantids are small and need the finest live food at the start, they are best supplied with this by the presence of mulm and decaying material in the spawning tank. This can, however, be supplied after hatching if a clean tank is used, so it does not seriously matter. The Cichlids young are quite large, so the tank can be clean or dirty, and the parents will keep the eggs spotless whichever is the case. If Cichlids eggs are to be hatched in the absence of the parents however, they must be removed to a very clean tank and particular care taken of them.

The male *Apistogramma ramirezi* (right) is smaller and more colorful than the female and has much longer dorsal spines. Photo by R. Zukal.

Like other Gouramis, the Dwarf Gourami, *Colisa lalia,* builds a surface nest of bubbles and water plants. The male is at the bottom. Photo by R. Zukal.

The eggs of this pair of Paradise Fish are suspended in the water as the female starts to drift toward the bottom. Photo by Milan Chvojka.

Both families should be supplied with large tanks for spawning, the Anabantids because they are in need of infusorial food in plenty, and because they usually produce many young, and the Cichlids because they are usually big fishes. For the Anabantids, the tank should be well planted and not too deep, up to 10 inches at most, and preferably tightly covered to protect the surface nest. Most Cichlids tear up plants at mating time, so it is superfluous to have them present, but it doesn't matter, at any rate to the fishes. Both like a temperature around 80°F. and many species will not spawn at much below it. Even if the Cichlids are given no plants, there should be a good layer of sand, as this is used in nest-making.

Anabantids Courtship and Spawning: When the male Anabantid's nest is ready, spreading a few inches across the water with a central depth of perhaps half an inch if he is a big fish, the female may be introduced. The male is often bad-tempered, particularly the male Siamese fighter (*Betta splendens*) and he must be watched to see that all goes well. The female is often bullied, but should not be removed again unless she is really badly treated.

The male will eventually persuade or drive the female below the bubble nest, circling her with a display of erect fins, and distended gill-covers in the case of Fighters. The female responds with a "submissive" behavior pattern, which inhibits the male from attacking her further.

As they swim below the nest, the male encircles the female in an embrace in which his head meets his tail and they sink slowly downwards, with the release of a number of eggs. The male then dives down and catches them, placing them in the bubble nest with his mouth. Further embraces and spawning follow at intervals for perhaps several hours. An interesting variation of the above occurs when the female remains in a corner of the tank and the male remains under the nest, and she dashes up at intervals to indulge in the nuptial embrace. As soon as it is over, she rushes back to her corner until the next time.

When spawning is over, the male takes complete charge and the female may be removed, particularly if he is too fierce. Otherwise her presence is said to make him take better care of the eggs. He continues to blow bubbles and to restore any falling eggs to the nest, but subsequent behavior varies with species. The male should remain with the nest until the eggs hatch, as he performs a useful function in keeping them afloat and healthy. With most, it is best to remove the male at hatching, which occurs 2-3 days after spawning, and even the best of fathers is likely to start eating the young at the end of the first week.

The male *Betta splendens* leaves the female in order to retrieve the eggs as they sink; he mouths the eggs and puts them into the nest. Photo by New York Zoological Society.

In comparison to the male, the female Blue Gularis is very drab. Timmerman photo.

CYPRINODONTS

The so-called killifishes, or Cyprinodonts, include the various types of "Panchax" or *Aphyosemion* (top-minnows), the Argentine Pearl Fishes (*Cynolebias* species) and other related fishes which lay eggs taking some time to hatch. The panchax group and some of the *Aphyosemion* spawn at the surface on to nylon mops, and are allowed to do this for up to about 10 days at a stretch, when the parents, or the mops, are removed to another tank. Hatching occurs at 12-14 days or longer, and the young must be sorted for size or will eat one another. Each female lays up to 20 eggs per day, and it is common practice to mate one male with two females.

Other *Aphyosemions* and the rest of the group spawn into peat at the bottom of the tank. The *Aphyosemion* eggs will hatch out if left long enough, but may be collected together with the peat and dried out for a period before being replaced in soft prepared water, when most of the eggs will hatch out all together and give an even batch of fry. This technique is very useful and prevents the difficulties of sorting otherwise encountered. The best period for drying varies with species from 2 or 3 weeks to 4 weeks, but most should be dried for the shorter period. It is essential not to dry completely, or the eggs are killed, but drying should be carried to an advanced stage for best results, so that the peat feels like tobacco.

In *Aphyosemion bivittatum* the female has the darker body pattern but the male has brighter fin coloration. Above, two males threaten each other by flaring the fins; notice the black line on the anal fin. Below, a male (right) and brightly marked female. Photos by R. Zukal.

A male (left) and female *Cynopoecilus ladigesi* burrowing into the peat bottom of their aquarium to lay and fertilize eggs. The eggs must be partially dried before they will hatch. Photo by Dr. Walter Foersch.

The *Cynolebias, Nothobranchius* and other species which naturally undergo a period of drying are also treated in the same manner but need an even longer period of treatment. It is usual to allow spawning for about a month, followed by drying for about 6 weeks with the *Nothobranchius* species and 10 or 12 weeks for the *Cynolebias* species, at a minimum. When the peat containing the eggs is replaced in water, a little added dry food may help hatching due to the increased bacterial action. **Incubation of the Eggs:** The great majority of fish eggs hatch in one day or rather less at 75°-80°F. It is best to keep the temperature at the same level as when spawning occurred. The same is true of young fry. There are many reports of Characin eggs taking 2 to 3 days to hatch, and while some are undoubtedly correct, it still remains true that the majority of young are hatched within the first day. They are often hard to see and it may be 2 or 3 days before they hang on to the side of the tank, and become easier to see, and thus it is simple to get the impression that they have not hatched out for longer than is the case.

After spawning is complete, eggs should be sought in the tank. They may be attached to the mops and also be in the peat on the bottom, appearing like small glass beads, usually very small indeed. They should remain clear, and the development of the embryo should be watched to check that all is well. Infertile eggs quickly become opaque and fungussed, looking like a powder-puff, with white filaments of fungus sprouting in all directions. Fertile eggs lying next to a mass of fungus-covered infertiles may be attacked, but usually remain unaffected.

If you cannot see the eggs, don't despair, as they are hard to see, particularly when peat is used. Once you have observed those of a particular species, it will be much. easier to see them the next time.

Hatching: When the eggs hatch, the young fry still have a yolk-sac, containing the remains of the nourishment in the egg. They live on this for a short time, sometimes only one or two days, sometimes as long as 5 days, before taking other food. For the first 12 to 24 hours they often remain still at the bottom of the tank, in the peat, and in some species they take flea-like hops up into the water, sinking back again afterwards. In practically all species they then attach themselves to the glass or to mops or plants (if present) hanging motionless for a further one or two days, still not feeding. They may also hang under the surface film of the water, and frequently start on the glass and then transfer to the surface film. Finally, the yolk-sac is absorbed and they swim freely in the water, hugging the bottom in daylight and spreading all over the tank at night, or in the dark.

At the stage when the fry cling to the glass, it is easy to see them in the right light, which is preferably from behind or the side. They cling head-upward, and are visible as a little glass splinter with a fat tummy (the yolk-sac) and two very large eyes. Watch the yolk-sac go down, for when it does the time to feed is near. In the later, free-swimming stage, they are less easily seen, and at night is the best time. Use a torch or a hand-lamp and send a beam across the tank from one side, and the fry will be seen swimming in mid-water. They may be counted with fair accuracy at this stage, or at the clinging stage before it. The best way to count is to choose a typical section of the tank and count it fairly carefully, then multiply by the relative sizes of section to tank as a whole. It is good practice to make this count, so as to check what is happening later on and to estimate food requirements.

Eggs of *Cynolebias ladigesi*, after removal from the peat moss. Photo by Dr. Walter Foersch.

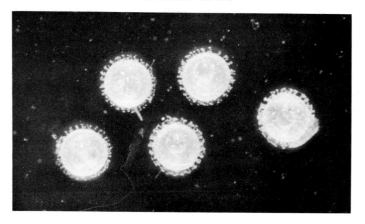

EGG-GUARDING FISHES

Anabantid and Cichlid fishes take care of their eggs and of their young. The extent of this care differs with different species, and is most fully developed in the Cichlids. Linked with this development is a strong tendency to a savage disposition towards other fishes, of the same or different species.

Cichlid Courtship and Spawning: An established pair of Cichlids may be left to their own devices, and sooner or later they will probably spawn. It is only when trying out new pairs that the aquarist must exercise care and be ready to remove one or other. If spawning has taken place and anything goes wrong, or if all of the young are suddenly removed, the pair are likely to quarrel, as if they suspected each other of disposing of the young.

Courtship in the Cichlids is worth watching for its own sake. At first, approaches are made with spreading fins and the body quivers, but soon the fishes take each other by the mouth and start to wrestle. They roll over and over, twisting and tugging vigorously, and woe betide anyone who tires unduly quickly. For this reason, some attempt at matching size when introducing new pairs to each other is often made, but there are many very unequal-sized pairs which get along quite well.

The pair will finally start to clear a place for spawning, and it is given a very thorough cleaning, sometimes for several days. Large stones are favorite spots, but in their absence a patch of the glass side of the tank may be cleaned. Light-colored objects are said to be preferred, and so marble or other light-colored stone is often offered. As spawning approaches, a breeding tube appears from the vent of both sexes. When it is first visible it means that spawning will occur soon, and within a day or two the tube lengthens to perhaps $\frac{1}{3}$ or $\frac{1}{2}$ an inch, and spawning takes place.

The female deposits a few eggs at a time on the chosen surface and is followed by the male who inseminates them, They are often laid row upon row, until in the course of several hours up to 2,000 may be deposited and fertilized. From then on, a constant guard is maintained, and the eggs are frequently fanned and inspected. Opinions differ as to whether the primary function of this fanning is aeration or the prevention of disease. Aeration seems most likely as the fishes also clean the eggs, and eat any which become fungussed. The incubation period lasts 3 to 4 days and at this period the parents dig pits in the sand. Often several pits are dug, and as the young hatch they are moved to one of them. Both parents participate in this, often dashing from the spawning area to the sand-pit in lightning dashes, one with a mouthful of young being transferred, the other to take up the vacated position. Transfers from pit

A pair of Cichlids guarding their fry. Marcuse photo.

to pit then continue until the young are free-swimming, which may not be for another 3 or 4 days. Each time they are moved to a new pit, they are mouthed over and spat into the pit. Since the object of the move can hardly be to guard them, as the parents could presumably do this without shifting them around, it has again been suggested that the process is one of cleaning. Moving them from one pit to another is thought to ensure that every one is well mouthed and cleaned, but there is no evidence that this is necessary, and we do not know why the frequent moves are made.

During this period, the young live on the yolk-sac, looking at first like a mass of quivering jelly, which gradually resolves into wriggling and hopping individuals which finally swim up into the water. The parents guard them carefully and herd them together, spitting any which stray too far back into the swarm. They are quite large, and should now be fed small live food. The parents will continue to guard them for weeks if allowed to do so, but during this period they will not lay further eggs. If frequent breeding is desired, the young should be removed, or the eggs hatched artificially from the start.

The danger signal has been flashed and these young mouthbreeders hurry back to the safety of the parent's mouth. Photo by Milan Chvojka.

The Angel Fish (*Pterophyllum*) lay their eggs on large plant leaves. Alternatively, they will accept upright slate or opaque glass bars or rods, or even the aquarium glass itself. They do not dig pits, but move the young from one leaf to another until they are free-swimming, when they guard them as usual. They are particularly liable to eat their spawn, so it is commercial practice to remove the leaf or rod on which it has been deposited to a clean tank with a gentle trickle of aeration to replace the parents' fanning. Five drops of 5% Methylene Blue per gallon are added to inhibit fungus growth on the eggs.

Some Cichlids have moved a stage further in the care of their young, and retain the eggs and fry in the mouth for several weeks. During this time, the parent that guards the young starves, and gets very thin, and as he or she has a large head to begin with, assumes a very emaciated appearance. The young swim out to feed, but return to the parental mouth if alarmed and only learn to fend for themselves when they get too large for all of them to get back again.

OTHER TYPES OF FISH

Various other aquarium fishes are bred, some very occasionally and others with regularity. Details are given under the various species later in the text, but a few general remarks will be made here.

The *Corydoras* of various species (South American Armoured Catfishes) breed well in captivity, particularly *C. aeneus* and *C. paleatus*. They breed best in communities and lay eggs on plants, or on the glass, and do not harm either them or the young. The eggs hatch in 3 or 4 days and the young feed heavily on live or prepared food from the start. In *C. paleatus*, courtship is brief with the males swimming over the females. Finally, with a male underneath, a male and female take up a crossed position and the female swims up with 4 eggs clasped in her ventral fins. These she deposits on a leaf or elsewhere, and the process is repeated. It is not yet clear where the eggs are fertilized; some observers allege that the female takes sperm into her mouth and sprays it over the eggs, but others deny this. In *C. aeneus*, it is also said that the male spreads sperm on the glass, and that the female follows and lays her eggs.

Corydoras aeneus is now bred and produced regularly in the aquarium. Their spawning antics are fascinating to watch. If fed as a scavenger for too long, these little armored Catfishes lose the desire and ability to reproduce. Photo by R. Zukal.

A male Stickleback, *Gasterosteus aculeatus*, guarding its nest. Photo by Gunter Senfft.

Polycentropsis schomburgki lays its eggs on the underside of large leaves. The male is the darker fish. Photo by R. Zukal.

Although Kuhli Loaches (in this case *Acanthophthalmus myersi*) often spawn "accidentally" in hidden corners of the aquarium, hormone treatments are required to make them spawn "on demand." Photo by Viktor Datschkevitch.

Loaches of various species have also been known to breed in the aquarium, but never to order. *Acanthophthalmus kuhli* (Malayan Loach) is thought by some to be a livebearer, but this is not true. Their eggs are green.

Some of the Nandids are easy to breed. Buchanan's Pygmy Perch (*Badis badis*) spawns rather like Cichilds, and guards the young for a time, and so do the leaf fishes (*Polycentrus schomburgki* and *Monocirrhus polyacanthus*). *Polycentropsis abbreviata*, on the other hand, builds a bubble nest. The male guards the young as in the Anabantids. Other nest-builders include the Sunfishes (*Centrarchidae*). The male of the Pygmy Sunfish (*Elassoma evergladei*) builds a nest at the bottom of the tank and guards the eggs, and so does the male of various Sticklebacks (*Gasterosteidae*). The male Bumble Bee Fish (*Brachygobius xanthozonus*) also guards the young, but does not build a nest.

With all of these fishes it is merely necessary to have them in a tank together, except perhaps the *Corydoras*, with which orthodox spawning techniques may be used. Naturally, if you wish to breed them, you will provide plenty of shelter, place only the desired species in the tank and feed plenty of live food.

In *Oryzias javanicus* the eggs remain in a cluster at the female's vent until they are brushed off on foliage. Photo by Gunter Senfft.

Lepomis gibbosus, a native American Sunfish, gets very scrappy at breeding time. Photo by Dr. Herbert R. Axelrod.

The male White Cloud (bottom fish) is much brighter than the female, with more red in the fins. It is also more slender, as its abdomen does not fill with eggs like that of the female. Photo by R. Zukal.

In the Medaka, or Rice Fish (*Oryzias latipes*) pairing takes place as usual in the egg-scatterers, the eggs stick to the female's vent in a cluster, later to be brushed off at random onto plants. This is one of the few fishes which, although it does not take care of its young, doesn't eat them either. The White Cloud Mountain Minnow (*Tanichthys albonubes*) is fairly safe with its parents also. Some of the pencil fishes (*Poecilobrycon*) guard the area in which eggs have been laid, although this is not the general habit in the Characins, to which they belong.

Raising Fry: Before the advent of microworms and brine shrimp, and before the use of artificial preparations to replace infusoria, the feeding of young fry was a much more difficult task than it now is. In the opinion of the authors, it is now very rarely necessary to prepare infusoria at all, as these may be substituted by egg-yolk suspensions, live yeast, or the young of the microworm together with the material in which it thrives. In addition, many species of fish produce fry which can eat adult microworm or newly hatched brine shrimp straight away, and do not need infusoria or substitutes for them. It is usually safe to feed a mixture of microworm and the culture medium, in moderate quantities, which between them rarely fail to provide adequate nourishment even for the smallest fry. The size of the fry is furthermore not always the deciding factor, so much as their willingness or capacity to eat certain types of food.

It is always easy to check whether fry are eating, particularly with brine shrimp, because their bellies become red and swollen. With microworm they become milky and swollen. Sometimes it will be noted that only some of the batch are able to take the food offered. Either microworm or brine shrimp is a completely satisfactory food and either alone is sufficient for the first few weeks of life without any other food, as long as it is eaten.

FOOD SIZES

Grade 1 (suitable as a start for all fry but livebearers and some of the larger fry such as Cichlids): One-celled algae, baker's yeast, some infusoria, infusions made by shaking a small piece of the yolk of a hard-boiled egg in a little water vigorously, microworm culture medium containing young, some parts of very finely ground foods. The algae and infusoria may be fed as green water, which is a great help for many Anabantid fry at the start. Microworm culture medium has the advantage of containing moving food, which may be necessary for some types of fry. The movement may be simulated with foods like yeast or egg suspension by gentle aeration, not vigorous enough to swirl the fry around.

Grade 2 (suitable for many fry as a start, and for others within a week): Microworms, newly hatched brine shrimp, larger infusoria, newly hatched *Daphniae,* finely ground dry food, finely shredded tubifex or other worms. Gentle aeration helps to keep foods moving and prevents even live food such as microworms from collecting too readily at the bottom of the tank. If any appreciable amount of dry or shredded food is used, aeration is essential and the introduction of small snails should be considered.

Grade 3 (suitable for all fry at 2-4 weeks and for newly born livebearers): All grade 2 foods, plus large size *Daphniae,* small mosquito larvae, Grindal worms, chopped white worms, chopped Tubifex or other worms, "fine" grades of dry food.

Grade 4 (suitable for half-grown and adult fishes): All grade 3 foods, plus fully grown *Daphniae,* mosquito larvae, white worms, tubifex, chopped earth worms, ordinary grades of dry food. It is still possible to feed microworm and newly hatched brine shrimp to small adult fishes, but they need a generous allowance.

Infusorial Feeding: Although we have stated that infusoria are rarely necessary for feeding fry, sometimes they are needed either because the fry are very small or because other foods are not available. The need for a continuous supply of live food or of moving suspended food particles in the early days of the life of the fry may be supplied by drip feeding. Many successful breeders never use it, but some feel happier if they supply it.

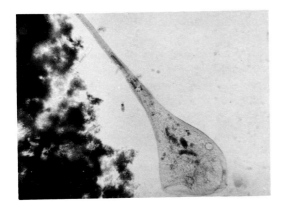

The Trumpet Animalicule, *Stentor*. Photo by Dr. J. Knaack.

This common aquarium rotifer is busy at straining in its food. Photo by Dr. J. Knaack.

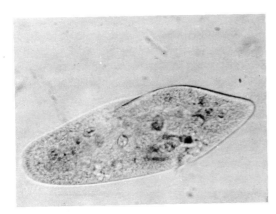

Slipper Animalicule, *Paramecium caudatum*. Photo by Dr. J. Knaack.

When a spawning is planned and infusoria are to be used, a culture should be on the way, in case it is needed. But if it doesn't come along well, use an egg or yeast suspension instead. To feed by drip, it is necessary to syphon the culture very slowly over into the tank. It is not usually necessary to supply a drain for overflow, as not all that much water will be run in.

The main difficulty in drip feeding is to get a slow enough drip, but this is achieved very easily by means of the device illustrated. A 1/16th inch internal diameter glass tube is bent as shown and inserted into a cork or other float. This diameter tubing fills itself by capillary action and will drip at 1 drop per minute (3 ml. per hour) or faster, as long as the delivery end of the tubing is bent upwards. If it faces downwards a minimum speed of about 40 drops per minute is the best it can do, and that is too fast for most cultures. The rate is controlled by raising or lowering the tube in the float, and very slow drip rates are best prevented from stopping because of surface tension effects by slipping a piece of tubular tape, wick or shoelace over the dripping end. A 1/16th inch syphon is also self-starting and can be used in the tank as an overflow drip of similar design.

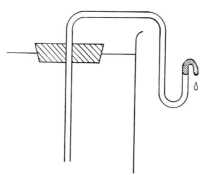

A controllable slow drip feed.

An alternative drip feed is a wick, or piece of cloth, but this may filter off too much of the culture, leaving behind a rich medium and delivering a thin one. Actively feeding fry will eat continuously at the rate of several small infusoria per minute, so a tank of say, 200 fry needs a delivery of some 60,000 organisms per hour. A rich culture may supply 1 or 2 hundred very small organisms per drop, hence a drip rate of about 300 per hour or five per minute might be right, but only experience and rough counting of both culture and fry numbers can suffice as a guide.

The number of infusoria needed per day can be dumped into the tank in two or more doses and will not over-populate the tank while being eaten, as long as the fry are not extremely overcrowded. That is why drip feeding is rarely necessary, but the dumping has to be done with reasonable foresight and careful checks on the condition of the tank. Watch the fry, see that they are eating and estimate even if only roughly the proper amount of culture to feed. Not very much is needed at the start, but the rate at which the fry require food is always increasing as they grow and so larger amounts must be supplied.

Later Feeding: After a start has been made if necessary on a Grade 1 food, try after a few days to substitute a Grade 2 food. Give some and watch what happens with a hand lens. See if it is taken and try to estimate if all the fry are taking it. If not, keep both foods up together for a day or two, and so make the change-over gradually. Do exactly the same when attempting to move from any food to any other food of larger size, and do not starve your smaller fishes. Runts are produced by neglecting this point.

By this method, most if not all of the fry can be brought along as an even batch. The exception is with Goldfish, amongst which so variable a spawning may result that all sorts of fry sizes and quality may be encountered despite the most careful feeding. But with tropicals, which breed true, 1% of runts is as much as should be expected. The rest will vary in size a bit, but should now show the enormous variation so often seen, to the extent that the largest fry finally eat the smallest and so even things up a bit. This is due to inadequate or inappropriate feeding, or both, and can be avoided.

As the fry grow, even if they have been raised entirely on live food for the first few weeks, it is quite in order to start substituting a proportion of dry food. Keep to live food all the time if you can, but do not starve them by trying to supply live food when there isn't enough available. As with full-grown fishes, fry after the first few weeks do very well on about 50% of live food and quite well on only 25 to 30% if really necessary.

Growth: Very young fry tolerate surprising degrees of crowding. Even at ½ an inch in length the fry of many species can be kept at some 30 to 40 to the gallon. An outstanding exception is the Goldfish, in which fry need good space after the first few weeks for adequate growth, and must be sorted out fairly early. The fry of nearly all tropicals can if necessary be kept in the small 3 to 5 gallon breeding tank advocated here for the first 4 to 6 weeks unless the spawning is over 250 per tank, when they will do better if given more room after the first 4 weeks. Experimentation will determine the fish capacity of tanks to be used in later stages of fry raising, and remember that *it is never a fault to give more room than necessary.*

INDEX

notes

notes

notes

A GUIDE TO
AQUARIUM PLANTS
AND THEIR CULTIVATION

BY C. D. SCULTHORPE

All photos by the author unless specifically credited otherwise.

The cultivation and arrangement of aquarium plants can be an intensely interesting hobby.

INTRODUCTION

The interest in aquatic plants has undoubtedly increased over the last fifty years to the extent that aquarists not only regard them as necessary adjuncts to the decorative aquarium but also cultivate them for their own attraction and biological peculiarities. The reason for this growing interest is two-fold; firstly, the importation of exotic marsh and water plants has, as a result of more frequent collecting trips throughout every continent, brought desirable new and often very rare species into commercial supply in America and western Europe and hence into the hands of aquarium plant connoisseurs. Secondly, since Dr. James W. Atz first pointed out the balanced aquarium myth, most aquarists have abandoned the naive assumption that the purpose of a few specimens of *Elodea* and *Vallisneria* in an aquarium is to establish the gaseous exchanges which complement those of the fishes' respiration. Consequently plants have been regarded more as objects with which to decorate the aquarium, creating not only a pleasant visual effect, but also a more natural habitat for the fishes. Of course the basic principle of the complementary respiratory exchanges of fishes and plants within a container is sound, but was long ago grossly exaggerated in the idea of the balanced aquarium, and just how erroneous these early ideas were will be established

Imagination and artistic ability are required in arranging aquarium plants.

when the results of physiological experiments into aeration in aquaria and into oxygen output and carbon dioxide intake of water plants, such as are at present being carried out at the Water Pollution Research Board's laboratories in Hertfordshire, England, become known.

Despite the new enthusiasm shown in aquarium plant culture, there are still many aquarists who make little attempt to lay out rockwork and plants in imaginative designs or to cultivate and propagate their plants. These two aspects of plant culture are quite distinct. The layout of an aquarium is largely determined by the aquarist's imagination, patience, and concepts of pleasing visual effects. In creating an attractive design the important theme is one of contrast, between high and low, light and shade, erect and horizontal, entire leaves and dissected leaves, smooth leaves and ruffled leaves and so on. In an aquascape created by the imaginative aquarist the illusion of depth, the interest at all levels of the water, and the apparently natural growth of the plants will be conspicuous features. Though improvements in aquarium layout usually accrue from practice and experience, aquascaping is an individual ability and no hard and fast rules exist to discipline the beginner. The other aspect of aquarium plant culture, the actual propagation and manipulation of the plants, deserves a more comprehensive discussion. Two natural methods of reproduction, sexual and vegetative, occur amongst plants. Sexual reproduction may involve the formation, dispersal, and germination of seeds, as in the flowering plants, or the union of sex cells formed by a separate plant body derived from minute spores, as in the ferns and other flowerless plants. The first type of sexual reproduction is mentioned later in relation to the propagation of the rarer flowering aquatic plants. The second type is referred to in the section devoted to the interesting aquarium plants which belong to the lower groups of the plant kingdom. Natural methods of vegetative propagation are discussed throughout wherever they are relevant to the needs of the aquarist. I shall now discuss the manipulation of some familiar aquarium species.

The Madagascar lace plant, *Aponogeton fenestralis*, in bloom. One separate bloomstalk is partially obscured. Photo by Pronek.

By *manipulation* is usually understood the direct, *gardening methods*, for example pruning, which are employed to improve the appearance of underwater foliage. Of these methods, we may first distinguish the cutting back of premature floating leaves which tend to replace the submerged leaves in vigorous specimens of *Aponogeton, Echinodorus, Nymphaea* and other large heterophyllous plants. This is usually progressive pruning designed solely to impair the vigor of the plant, thus delaying the climax of its life cycle.

Manipulative pruning of species of aquarium plants used as cuttings often yields the finest bushes of foliage in the underwater scene. The principle of this pruning is that removal of the stem apex eliminates the inhibition of the dormant axillary buds by hormones from the apical bud. This principle is an important feature of the growth habit of many terrestrial plants, though the precise details of the physico-chemical mechanism whereby the inhibition is maintained or removed are unknown. Some species, such as *Hygrophila*

A bushy group of specimens of
Hygrophila polysperma.

polysperma, have a branching habit without removal of the apical bud, and lateral shoots develop freely once the plant is established. Extremely accommodating as regards compost, temperature, and pH value of the water, this post-war introduction from India is the only truly aquatic species of its genus. A very popular plant with aquarists, its bushy habit renders it useful for masking the sides and corners of tanks, and its bright, but pale, green leaves in pairs along the stems contrast with the fine-leaved bushy species of *Cabomba*, *Ambulia*, and *Myriophyllum*. The beautiful rich green sprays of the related giant species *Nomaphila stricta* are, with their bold lanceolate leaves, more strikingly handsome but less easy to trim to the desired shape.

A popular species equally decorative and equally accommodating as *Hygrophila polysperma* is *Cardamine lyrata*, whose stems branch freely if the apical buds are nipped from time to time. Its fast-growing but delicate stems bear rounded lobed leaves of a brilliant fresh green; these leaves adjust themselves so that they are exposed to the maximum light intensity and the plant thus forms a fine bush which looks admirable in front of tall, dark rock formations. Another round-leaved species superficially similar to *Cardamine lyrata* is *Lysimachia nummularia*, a plant frequently inhabiting moist garden soil, but easily acclimatised to submerged life in cold water or tropical aquaria. Like *Hygrophila* and *Cardamine*, it readily forms adventitious roots from the lower nodes and after removal of the apical buds soon forms a dense bush of rich green foliage. *Bacopa caroliniana* is a familiar round- to oval-leaved aquarium plant which was known in England for a while, due to a dealer's error, as *Macuillamia rotundifolia*. Its stout fleshy ridged stem is extremely buoyant and roots develop slowly from the nodes; despite these disadvantages this unusual species is often seen in aquaria. It is a difficult plant to model for it is easily twisted out of shape, and it does not branch as freely as other species planted as cuttings. Its stems and leaves are unusually hairy and out of water the plant has a pronounced fragrance. A fourth, and rare, round-leaved species is *Micranthemum orbiculatum* whose thin, frail-looking stems bear tiny, round, slightly folded leaves which quickly respond to the direction of light.

Lysimachia nummularia, acclimatised to submerged life.

Specimens of *Micranthemum orbiculatum.*

Cardamine lyrata, showing the rounded lobed leaves.

The stout stems and fleshy leaves of *Bacopa caroliniana.*

Production of bushes of foliage is also possible with fine-leaved species by nipping out apical buds. The three main genera of aquarium plants with dissected leaves, *Myriophyllum*, *Cabomba* and *Ambulia*, all respond to this treatment by growing many lateral shoots. There are many species of *Myriophyllum* native to the United States and to the countries of western Europe; a less common species suitable for tropical aquaria is *M. elatinoides*, with whorls of delicate shining green leaves divided into hair-like segments. All the species of *Cabomba* commonly available to aquarists are suited to water at all temperatures from 50°F. to about 80°F. The two most frequent species are *Cabomba caroliniana* and *C. aquatica*, the former being distinguished by the formation of *narrow* floating leaves prior to the flowering phase. Its pretty white flowers are insect-pollinated and develop into small fruits borne downwards in the water within the dying remains of the petals. A rosy-hued variety of *C. caroliniana* is sometimes available, as is *C. furcata*, a species which has the leaves set closely together on the stems. The leaves of *Limnophila sessiliflora*, known also as *Ambulia sessiliflora*, are more finely divided than those of the *Cabombas* and are whorled, not paired.

The tropical milfoil, *Myriophyllum elatinoides*.

Cabomba caroliniana **var.** *paucipartita.*

The water wisteria, *Synnema triflorum,* introduced to aquarists in 1954, is a splendid fast-growing species with a wide range of leaf shape from entire, smooth-margined, oval leaves to deeply divided, toothed leaves superficially resembling those of the Indian fern, *Ceratopteris thalictroides.* The leaves are borne close together on the stout erect stem and from their axils arise lateral shoots; these are encouraged by removal of the apical bud and the plant very quickly forms a luxuriant bush of bright green foliage. The species tolerates a wide range of water conditions and will thrive in a compost of barren gravel, sand, or any of the sand/soil mixtures.

P-10.00

Water wisteria, *Synnema triflorum*. Photo by Tropicarium Frankfurt.

Limnophila sessiliflora, loosely planted in gravel.

The dwarf Japanese rush, *Acorus gramineus* var. *pusillus*.

Sagittaria subulata forma *pusilla*.

Acorus gramineus.

Of course, there are a few species used by aquarists which grow naturally in a habit which displays their foliage to remarkable advantage. Well-known examples are species of *Sagittaria*, such as *S. latifolia*, and *S. subulata*, both of which spread their long fleshy leaves from the crown in a conspicuous manner quite unlike the habit of species of *Vallisneria*, with which they are often confused by novices. *Acorus gramineus var. pusillus*, the dwarf rush, and *Acorus gramineus*, and its variegated form, are even better examples. Their narrow flattened tapering leaves spread out in the form of a fan as they mature and are replaced by younger ones. The fan arises from the almost horizontal rhizome and the dwarf habit, unusual appearance, and shallow root run, all contribute towards the value of these species in the foreground of an aquarium, where they require nothing of the manipulation necessary to control the more rampant species of aquarium plants.

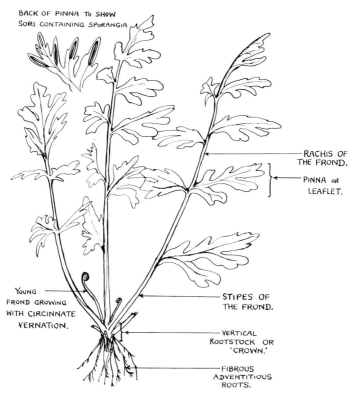

BACK OF PINNA TO SHOW
SORI CONTAINING SPORANGIA

RACHIS OF
THE FROND.

PINNA OR
LEAFLET.

YOUNG
FROND GROWING
WITH CIRCINNATE
VERNATION.

STIPES OF
THE FROND.

VERTICAL
ROOTSTOCK OR
"CROWN."

FIBROUS
ADVENTITIOUS
ROOTS.

A typical flowerless aquatic plant and its details. (*Ceratopteris* species).

FLOWERLESS AQUATIC PLANTS

Most aquarium plants are prevented from flowering by the culture methods used to maintain their decorative submerged foliage. Even so, they have the ability to flower and set seed. A few of the most interesting and attractive plants used by aquarists never produce flowers, and they belong to groups lower in the plant kingdom which reproduce, not by flowers, but by inconspicuous spores. The methods the plant uses to produce and disperse these spores are often complicated, and only visible under the microscope; since they are of special interest they need not concern us here, for these plants rarely reproduce themselves sexually, even in nature. Instead, as is characteristic of almost all water plants, they multiply vegetatively, either by baby plants produced viviparously on the parent, or by fragmentation, which in floating species often occurs at a prodigious rate.

Ceratopteris thalictroides (from *keras* and *pteris*, the Greek words meaning *horn* and *fern*), the Indian fern or water sprite, is a popular aquarium plant which may be grown floating or submerged. Indigenous to tropical America, Asia, the East Indies, and China, it grows in stagnant pools, rooted in the mud, and is often collected as fresh food. A French botanist distinguishes two varieties; one from Sumatra with finely dissected fronds, the other from tropical America as far north as Florida with broad, only slightly indented fronds. This distinction is not really justified as the shape of frond produced depends on the age of the plant and the depth of water in which it is growing. Fronds which are mature or from deep water are twice divided, while fronds which are juvenile or from shallower water are usually smaller, broader and less divided, with oblong pinnae. Fronds of all sizes and shapes may often occur on one good plant. Only sterile fronds are produced by rooted submerged plants, the pinnae unfolding as the fleshy quadrangular stem grows

A mature specimen of *C. thalictroides*, showing circinnate vernation and fine division of the fronds.

P-15.00

from the crown, at first horizontally and then straightening up to the light. Floating specimens have profuse branching roots, with dense root-hairs, while the sterile fronds recline on the surface, forming a rosette of up to thirty inches in diameter. Erect fertile fronds may be produced from the crown to a height of two feet; they are finely divided, with linear segments bearing longitudinal lines of sporangia, which contain the spores. In aquaria, fertile fronds are uncommon, but the plants readily produce viviparous youngsters at the notches of the fronds. These are best detached and floated at the surface until they have strong enough roots to be planted. The bright yellowish-green fronds of *Ceratopteris thalictroides* are unlike any other aquarium plant and contrast excellently with the dark green foliage of many species of *Cryptocoryne*.

Young specimens of the Indian fern, *Ceratopteris thalictroides*.

The floating fern, *Ceratopteris cornuta*, resembles the Indian fern in its suitability for tropical tanks and its viviparity. Its fleshy deep green fronds are only slightly indented, and the luxuriant rosettes this plant forms on the surface make a pretty sight on the tropical pool. Its profuse roots not only give shade to the aquarium but also give protection to fish fry. The reason for the not uncommon, sudden decline of a well-established, thriving colony of *Ceratopteris* plants in an aquarium is unknown.

The floating fern, *Ceratopteris cornuta;* mature plants and youngsters produced viviparously.

This photograph compares the roots of *Ceratopteris cornuta* (left) with the submerged leaflets of *Salvinia auriculata* (right).

Surface view of the large form of *Salvinia auriculata* showing the double row of floating leaves and the submerged leaflets; note that the two halves of each floating leaf, covered with the water-repellent hairs, are inclined at an angle to each other.

The rapid spread of *Ceratopteris* is characteristic of two other genera of water ferns, *Salvinia* and *Azolla*. The first of these, which was dedicated to Antonio Mario Salvini, a Florentine professor of the seventeenth century, is a cosmopolitan genus inhabiting lakes, pools, and stagnant ditches. From the horizontal stem of the large form of *Salvinia auriculata* arise two rows of rounded pea-green surface leaves, clothed beneath with brownish hairs, the upper surfaces glistening with a dense covering of curious looped white hairs which repel any drops of water falling on the plant. Beneath each pair of leaves hangs a cluster of finely branched, rust-colored submerged *leaflets*; these are not roots as is often thought. The small form of *S. auriculata* has leaves $\frac{1}{4}''$ long, but is otherwise very similar. Once introduced to an aquarium, these plants soon cover the surface by rapid vegetative multiplication and they need rigorous control. They thrive under the bright lights of an aquarium hood or the diffuse light of a tropical pool, and though preferring warm water, may be acclimatised to cold water.

Species of *Azolla* (from the Greek *a*—without, and *zoe*—life, alluding to the rapidity with which the plant dries up), are just as adapted to the floating habit as *Salvinia*, their covering of short hairs imprisoning air and preventing them from being submerged. *Azolla nilotica*, a much-branched species, grows to six inches long and, with *Salvinia* and *Ceratopteris*, is important as a constituent of the sudd, the dense floating masses of vegetation which block slow-moving rivers in flat open country, for example the Nile and the Ganges. *Azolla mexicana* is a smaller purplish species from the irrigation ditches of Mexico and the southern United States. The two most widely distributed species are the smallest and the two most well-known to aquarists. These are *Azolla caroliniana* and *Azolla filiculoides* which have, in the last seventy years, demonstrated the efficiency of their vegetative reproduction and dispersal by spreading all over Europe from their origin in western North America, Central and South America. Both seem to have been introduced into Europe via botanic gardens. *A. caroliniana* reached Europe in 1872, spreading through France by 1879, to England in 1883, and to Italy in 1886. It is rare in England, *A. filiculoides* being confused with it.

A surface-covering, smaller form of *Salvinia auriculata*.

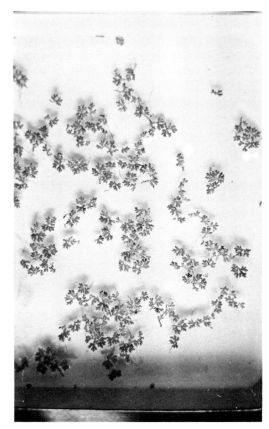

The tiny fronds of *Azolla filicu-loides*.

Azolla filiculoides was introduced to France by a Bordeaux botanist in 1879 and 1880. In England in 1888, a teacher is said to have procured some from Glasgow and put it in a ditch at a village on the Norfolk Broads. Heavy floods in August 1912 carried it up the main rivers and spread it all over the Broads. Now locally common in England, particularly in the warmer humid counties of the south-east and south-west, it is prevented from spreading to the north-west by hard winter frosts.

Identical to the naked eye, both species have a branched stem with thin pendulous roots and overlapping leaves above in two rows alternating right and left. Each leaf has two lobes; the upper floats and possesses chlorophyll and a symbiotic blue-green alga, while the lower is submerged and colorless. The hairs on the upper surface of the leaves of *A. filiculoides* are unicellular, while those of *A. caroliniana* are bicellular. The overall bluish-green tint of the two species becomes purplish-red in strong sunlight, particularly in late summer. The plants grow by fragmentation and rapid spreading, until the whole aquarium or pool surface is covered by the tufted mass.

While the fern *Azolla* appears more like a leafy liverwort, another flowerless aquarium plant, *Riccia*, actually is a liverwort. The plant is a simple flat thallus which branches dichotomously. *Riccia fluitans*, a cosmopolitan species dedicated to Ricci, an Italian botanist, is common in aquaria, bright green tangled masses floating just beneath the surface. It is just as attractive when pegged to the gravel and allowed to grow into a dense carpet.

Ricciocarpus natans is a related floating species which is much rarer, but like *Riccia* species, is found in ponds and ditches rich in mineral and organic matter. It is quite similar to the common duckweed, having lobed thalli about $\frac{1}{5}''$ diameter, each lobe being bright green and bearing shaggy purple scales beneath.

Larger, tufted fronds of *Azolla filiculoides* which have attained maturity and assumed autumnal colorations.

The freshwater moss, *Fontinalis antipyretica*, is another attractive aquarium plant, growing naturally in rapid hill streams. Its specific name alludes to its water-holding capacity and its supposed use in bandaging burns; its common name is willow moss. In general appearance it is very similar to its terrestrial relatives, with its thin, wiry, brownish stems clothed with alternate triangular leaves of a deep translucent green. Underwater it forms thickets, and is useful as a spawning and decorative plant, but is only suitable for coldwater aquaria. A finer leaved species, light green in color, *Fontinalis gracilis*, is suitable for warm water.

The underwater willow moss, *Fontinalis antipyretica.*

Among the dwarf plants so popular nowadays in front of rocks in an aquarium waterscape are species of the genus *Marsilea*. These ferns from shallow waters and mud flats in temperate and tropical regions of the world are named in honor of an eighteenth-century Italian botanist, Fernando Conte Marsigli. In growth habit *Marsilea* has rhizomes creeping in the mud or sand, sending up erect stalks, alternately on each side, which bear four pinnae rather like a four-leaved clover. The pinnae unfold from the coiled bud when the stalk reaches its prescribed height, which varies from one to five inches. Many species are available to the aquarist; *M. quadrifolia*, from Central Europe and Japan, *M. drummondii*, from Australia, *M. vestita*, from the Pacific coast of America, and *M. mucronata*, from the high plains, Rocky Mountains and south-western states, are probably the most common. Being amphibious

This dwarf species of four-leaved clover, *Marsilea hirsuta*, is an admirable foreground plant, contrasting with the strata of the rockwork.

plants, they all show a distressing tendency to form floating and aerial leaves; these may be prevented by judicious pruning and planting in water of more than six inches depth.

Very closely related to *Marsilea* is the peculiarly named tropical fern *Regnellidium sp.*, of similar habit but usually larger and with leaves of only two light green pinnae. It may be rooted, or floating with the rhizome just beneath the surface, the roots hanging below. When *Marsilea* and *Regnellidium* are grown as marsh plants they form spores within stony bean-shaped sporocarps borne singly near the base of the leaf stalks. Mature sporocarps germinate readily in water if they are first cracked. They imbibe water and after a few minutes a strange worm-like structure emerges and slowly swells until it disintegrates, releasing the spores.

Another relative of *Marsilea* is similar to hair grass; this is *Pilularia globulifera*, the pillwort, from temperate regions of Europe. A plant of shallow pond margins, its slender creeping rhizome may be rooted or free-floating. Narrow cylindrical leaves grow alternately from each side of the rhizome to three or four inches tall. They are fresh green and circinnately coiled like those of *Marsilea*. A common but easily overlooked plant of Great Britain and the U.S.A., it is more frequent in the west than in the east. It may be gathered wild and used as a dwarf carpet plant in the coldwater aquarium.

In the spring of 1957 a beautiful aquatic fern arrived from the tropical waters of Indonesia; it is an as yet unidentified species of *Gymnopteris*. From its stout green rhizome, clothed in rust-colored hairs, arise rich shining green stalkless fronds with conspicuous anastomosing veins. The fronds may grow to a height of twelve inches, and they have the tapering spear-like shape of an ox-tongue. Spores are borne on the reverse side, and young viviparous plants sometimes occur on old fronds. The rhizome is maintained above the gravel surface by the symmetrical growth of the brown roots. This lovely plant thrives as a foreground specimen in the tropical aquarium.

The last flowerless aquarium plants of interest are not true ferns; they are the strange plants of the genus *Isoëtes* (from the Greek, *isos*—equal, and *etos*—year, referring to the evergreen nature of the plants). Known popularly as the quillworts, they inhabit the stony beds of bleak, barren, mountain lakes in the cold and temperate regions of the world. *Isoëtes lacustris*, native to northern Europe, has a tuft of spikey green leaves, with transverse white markings, and profuse roots growing from a stout rootstock. The leaves usually bear spores in cavities on the inside of the wide leaf base. When

The Indonesian water fern, *Gymnopteris* species; a mature specimen showing several viviparous plants proliferated on the reverse side, and at the tip of the fronds.

*This plant has recently been identified as *Microsorium pteropus*.

Another specimen of *Gymnopteris sp.* with the fronds spread out to show their alternate arrangement on the rhizome; also two independent young plants.

planted in small groups, this handsome species has a striking appearance in a coldwater aquarium. Other species, such as *I. garnierii*, introduced into France from the Sudan in 1947, and *I. bolanderii*, native to the southern United States, are suitable for warm water.

None of the species of aquatic ferns, mosses, and liverworts just described are demanding in their culture requirements. All thrive under a wide range of light intensities though the floating species enjoy the higher intensities more than the submerged species. Gravel, coarse sand, or a sand/soil mixture suits all the rooted species, sand giving a closer root hold to *Marsilea* and *Pilularia* which sometimes tend to be disturbed by bottom-feeding fishes. *Isoëtes, Pilularia,* and to a certain extent *Fontinalis,* coming from lakes and streams poor in dissolved salts, are lime-hating and must be given non-calcareous gravel or sand, and rather acid water.

The unidentified species of *Echinodorus* with narrow tapering leaves.

LARGE TROPICAL AQUATIC PLANTS

Gone are the days when Amazon swordplants were rarities in aquaria. Many of the thirty or so species of *Echinodorus*, from the American continent, such as the Amazon swordplant, *E. paniculatus*, and the chain swordplant, *E. grisebachii*, have variable growth forms. All species of *Echinodorus*, however, produce bushes of bold foliage, and are therefore eminently suitable as centerpieces and specimen plants. Their leaf stalks are short and they will not produce floating and aerial leaves unless the light intensity is too high. Most species are now commercially plentiful, including the unusual *E. berteroi*, the cellophane plant, which grows through a series of leaf forms, and *E. tenellus*, the pigmy chain swordplant, still erroneously shown in some aquarium books as *Sagittaria microfolia*.

A few species are still rare, and have not been introduced to some European countries. *Echinodorus martii*, the ruffled swordplant from Brazil, with its spectacular furled strap-shaped leaves up to eighteen inches tall, and *E. muricatus*, the Amazon spearplant from tropical America, with its large spear-shaped leaves, are examples of such plants. Two new species were, however, introduced in 1959; they are as yet unidentified. The first one resembles *E. muricatus* in general habit and in leaf structure. The mature leaves are oval to heart-shaped, pointed at the tip, brilliant light green in color, and set at a conspicuously horizontal attitude. When young they are bronze and the five prominent veins are bright red. The stout leaf stalks bear the blades to an overall height of up to fifteen inches. New leaves are produced about once a fortnight under good light, and the plant soon grows into a magnificent bush.

The second species is lower growing, and its leaves are duller green, narrower and tapering, and short-stalked, so that the plant has a more spreading habit. The leaves have a conspicuous mid-rib and net veins which are rust-colored when young. It is a faster growing species than the first, but does not produce runners as do so many species of *Echinodorus*. The self-fertilizing flowers produce clusters of seeds which may be germinated in submerged shallow dishes and grown in sandy soil in small pots.

The water orchid is a rare specimen plant; it is often erroneously named *Spiranthes odorata*, a species which will not survive under water. The form usually grown in aquaria is probably a variety of *Spiranthes latifolia*, a bog species readily adaptable to continued submerged growth. From the fleshy tuberous roots, essential for the plant's survival, grow spreading emerald green lanceolate leaves. Growth is slow, but if the plant is in shallow water under bright light it will produce an aerial stem bearing pale yellow flowers.

The   unidentified   Peruvian   species   of   *Echinodorus*   with   spade-shaped leaves.

Spiranthes latifolia, an underwater orchid, to show the
spreading leaves and short,,but
stout, roots.

The so-called "African Water Orchid".

P-28.00

In 1958, a few specimens of a new aquatic plant arrived from the tropical waters of the French Cameroons. Discovered by Herbert R. Axelrod, they were of distinctive appearance and grew submerged in, and exposed by, slow-moving streams. They have not yet flowered and so identification has not been possible; so far there is only a collector's report, and the few specimens are known as "African Water Orchids." They are well-established cuttings with tough, wiry, red roots; the spray of thick bright green tapering leaves, which seem to ensheath each other, is extremely attractive. In the tropical aquarium the plant is very slow-growing; a specimen of mine has taken eight months to produce two new leaves.

Two very rare species of *Barclaya* were introduced at the same time; both come from Thailand and belong to the same family as *Cabomba* and the water lilies, the *Nymphaeaceae*. *Barclaya longifolia* forms a bush of tapering wavy leaves which are prettily veined, and olive to mid-brown in color. *B. motleyi*, the other species, produces spreading leathery leaves, about three inches wide, whose young pinkish-red color matures to a shade of coppery brown.

The genus *Aponogeton* has been much exploited by aquarists, and most of the available species have erect undulating and twisting foliage arising from a tuberous rootstock. Contrary to popular opinion, *A. crispus* is not synonymous with *A. undulatus*; it is a distinct and uncommon species originating in Ceylon and India. *A. cordatus* is also uncommon, coming from south-east Asia and therefore, with *A. undulatus*, producing the undivided flower spike of Asian species which contrasts with the 'U'-shaped, double flower spike of African species such as *A. ulvaceus*. *A. crispus* may be recognized when young by its short petioles which bear the narrow lanceolate leaves in an erect attitude; when mature the species has narrower leaves than either *A. undulatus* or *A. cordatus*. The leaves of *A. undulatus* are smoothly undulating and of a conspicuous bronze-green tint whereas those of *A. cordatus*, the loveliest species of the three, are very closely crinkled at the margins, deep rich green in color, and though not fully translucent, they show the longitudinal and transverse veins as a molded lattice. *A. natans* quickly forms floating leaves though its submerged foliage of broad, bright yellowish-green, slightly wavy leaves may be maintained by ruthless cutting of the leaves which push towards the surface.

The species of *Aponogeton* about which most has been written is of course *A. fenestralis*, the Madagascar lace plant. The oblong leaves, which may attain a length of eight to ten inches, are borne on slender brittle petioles arising from a tuberous rootstock and are at first reddish-bronze, later assuming a deep green hue. The blade of each leaf consists of seven parallel veins joined transversely by short minor veins, forming a regular lace-like network with almost no cellular tissue. Though of fragile appearance, these

Aponogeton undulatus, whose leaves are smoothly undulating, rather than crinkled.

A beautiful specimen of *Aponogeton cordatus*, the crinkled leaves responding to the direction of the light and showing the vein network in detailed relief.

P-30.00

The deeply crinkled leaves of
Aponogeton crispus, from India
and Ceylon.

Aponogeton natans, with its
broad, slightly waved leaves.

The magnificently furled and
twisted foliage of *Aponogeton
ulvaceus*.

Cryptocoryne nevillii, sometimes offered commercially as *C. beckettii*.

skeletal blades are comparatively tough and strong. The species produces an aerial inflorescence which consists of a twin spike bearing the white flowers. On numerous occasions *A. fenestralis* has been found to produce submerged inflorescences, as frequently happens in the hardy pool species *A. distachyus*, the Cape water hawthorn. Self-fertilisation occurs before the inflorescence opens and seedlings slowly develop while still attached to the bud. The lace plant occurs in Madagascar between 325 feet and 3000 feet above sea level, rooted in non-calcareous sand in the crevices between stones in semi-shaded slow-moving water.

The submerged leaves of species of *Aponogeton* show an interesting structural series. Those of *A. natans* and *A. distachyus* are the least translucent and have the least conspicuous veins; those of *A. crispus*, *A. undulatus*, and *A. cordatus* are more translucent with the veins in relief, whilst *A. ulvaceus* has fully translucent foliage. In the rare Madagascan species *A. bernierianus* the cellular interstices of the leaf partially degenerate but the lace network is not as fully apparent as in the related *A. fenestralis*.

There is considerable confusion over names in the genus *Cryptocoryne*, too. That usually offered for sale as *C. cordata*, with elongated, tapering, olive to bronze leaves is really *C. beckettii*; the commercial species of that name, with pointed smooth bright green leaves is the small growth form of *C. nevillii*. *C. haerteliana* was a temporary name derived from the surname of the German who imported the then unknown plants at the end of the 'thirties. Later they were identified as plants of *C. affinis*, the correct name which dates from 1893. The plant offered as *C. willisii* very closely resembles the species *C. undulata*. The true *C. cordata* is a rare and only occasionally imported plant. It is a dark green species growing to about twelve inches tall with rounded, mottled leaves resembling those of *C. griffithii*. A distinctive species of comparatively recent introduction from Thailand is *C. balansae*, whose spreading leaves are bright shining green, with a deeply crinkled surface. Of an equally bright shade of green are the leaves of *C. djambi;* they are broad, pointed and with recurved basal lobes.

A delightful Sinhalese species, *C. thwaitesii*, is little known to aquarists; it is a most desirable plant for the connoisseur. Discovered by Kendrick Thwaites, a director of the Peradenyia botanic garden from 1857 to 1880, it is a slow-growing species with finely-serrated, delicately marked leaves up to two and a half inches long, and dark green in color. In deep water its leaves tend to lengthen and become tinted with yellow and brown. This rare species produces very few stolons, and its lilac and blue aroid inflorescence has been seen by only one or two people.

During the second half of the nineteenth century the Italian explorer Odoardo Beccari brought to Europe many extensive collections of tropical Asiatic plants, amongst which was *Cryptocoryne longicauda*, from Borneo.

This photograph shows the variation in leaf shape amongst young imported specimens of the true *Cryptocoryne cordata*.

P-33.00

The Siamese species *Cryptocoryne balansae.*

This is a large handsome species, growing to a height of 16 inches, with broad rich green leaves borne on sturdy stalks. The shape of the leaf varies, a feature common to most species of *Cryptocoryne*, but the surface is nearly always deeply crinkled and the margin is waved. Specimens grow well in dim electric light and should not be exposed to direct sunlight; they must be given ample space in which to spread their foliage.

C. versteegii is one of the only two species of *Cryptocoryne* at present known to occur in New Guinea, where G. M. Versteeg discovered it in 1907 on the Lorentz River. It is a dwarf plant suitable for the aquarium foreground where its rigid triangular green leaves make a conspicuous display. The upper surface is glossy and is never mottled with areas of anthocyanin pigmentation. The rate of growth of this species is variable; there are numerous reports of it never producing a new leaf for many months. When conditions suit it, however, subterranean stolons are formed in abundance and its inflorescence is not uncommon.

Introduced to European aquarists in 1954 by an Amsterdam importer, *Cryptocoryne lutea* seems to be a variable species broadly resembling *C. beckettii,* though it does not usually reach a comparable size. It also differs in having shorter and broader leaves which do not usually curl back and which may be slightly ribbed at their margins. It lacks the distinctive olive-green hue of *C. beckettii. C. ciliata* is one of the large and fairly common species which grow consistently when submerged in tropical aquaria. The tapering pale green leaves are usually gently furled and borne erect on stout stalks to an overall height of 15 to 20 inches.

Professor H. C. D. de Wit of the University of Agriculture at Wageningen has described a newly introduced species as *Cryptocoryne wendtii*. This is another low-growing plant; each leaf bears a striking resemblance to a spear-head, being broadly lanceolate but having an abrupt straight base. Varying in color from pale green to bronze, the upper surface is frequently striated and the margins of the leaf are delicately lobed. This species is already in experimental use in Professor de Wit's laboratories and should soon be readily available from commercial growers.

The beautifully colored inflorescences of species of *Cryptocoryne* are seldom formed when the plants are growing submerged; for some species to bloom is rare indeed, whatever the growth conditions. Plants seem to bloom more readily if they are rooted in a rich compost of about 3 parts leaf mould, 2 parts peat, and 1 part coarse sand contained in closed tanks or glass jars and kept at a temperature of 75°F. At first the plants should be just submerged, the water level being gradually reduced until the foliage is growing in humid air at a temperature of 68°F. to 70°F. Some species such as *C. longicauda* and *C. retrospiralis* are unfortunately less amenable to this treatment and must be kept partially submerged.

This specimen of the rare *Cryptocoryne thwaitesii* has the lanceolate to ovate leaves which usually develop when the species is grown under water for any length of time.

C. retrospiralis is an unusually slender species with wavy mid-green leaves only an eighth to a quarter of an inch wide. Other *Cryptocoryne* have been introduced but most of them are unidentified and not in supply. One species, probably from Indonesia, has attractive tapering and undulating leaves, about an inch across at their widest point. When young they are a bright yellowish-green, but within a couple of weeks the color has passed through olive to rich brown. The newest introduction is a very beautiful species with oval to spade-shaped leaves, reddish with dark brown markings above, and mahogany red underneath. This superb specimen plant, which grows to a height of 15 inches or more, has been described as *Cryptocoryne blassii*, a name dedicated to the very successful grower of *Cryptocoryne*, Herr Blass at Munich.

An unusual aroid introduced to Europe in 1950 by a Frenchman is native to Colombia and thrives in an aquarium temperature of 60°F. to 80°F. When transplanted it does not lose any leaves as *Cryptocoryne* often does and during the course of a year it forms many clusters of leaves. Known by the majestić title of *Stenospermation popayanense var. aquatica*, the plant slightly resembles *Cryptocoryne ciliata* and its firm lanceolate pointed leaves have conspicuous veins. The flowers are surrounded by a typically aroid spathe, pure white in color.

Even more exploited than the *Aponogetonaceae*, the *Araceae* have yielded all the species of *Cryptocoryne*, *Anubias*, *Acorus*, *Stenospermation* and *Pistia* which may be used in aquaria. About two years ago, two species of another aroid genus, *Lagenandra*, appeared in commercial supply in England. One of them, *Lagenandra ovata*, had been previously cultivated in aquaria as *Aglaonema simplex* until it was correctly identified. Both the species of *Lagenandra* are indigenous to the coastal regions of south India and Ceylon, where they grow in brackish water as well as in fresh water. Leaves are continuously produced along the creeping rootstock and there is consequently a fine display of young and mature foliage in all levels of water. Each leaf emerges from the sheath of the preceding one and the unrolling blade is borne on a stout petiole. Mature leaves have blades of about nine to ten inches length, and an approximate overall length of sixteen to eighteen inches. *Lagenandra ovata* has dark green petioles which bear lighter green blades with rather wavy margins. *L. lancifolia* is one of the half dozen or so species of aquatic plants which have variegated foliage; its dark green blades have a marginal silver band and are borne on reddish petioles.

All the plants discussed make superb specimens in decorative aquaria, but as most of them are bog species, they must be given a rich non-calcareous soil. They are most conveniently grown in a compost of garden soil, peat moss and sand confined within a small plant-pot and covered with gravel to prevent clouding of the water. Species of *Aponogeton* appreciate more sand

Two of the less common aquarium *Cryptocoryne* species; *C. djambi* (left) and *C. retrospiralis* (ríght).

An unidentified species of *Cryptocoryne* from Indonesia.

A non-variegated form of *Lagenandra lancifolia*, showing the undulating margin and prominent mid-rib of the leaves, and showing a young leaf emerging from its sheath.

An excellent specimen of *Lagenandra lancifolia*, showing the silver marginal variegation and conspicuous mid-rib.

A young specimen of *Lagenandra ovata*, previously known as *Aglaonema simplex*.

and less humus. Plants may be propagated by division of the rootstock, or by germination of fertile seed as mentioned for *Echinodorus*. Young seedlings of *Lagenandra*, and young plants from the stolons of *Cryptocoryne* and *Stenospermation* should be grown as bog plants in a peaty soil at a temperature of 65°F. to 72°F. With some of the less vigorous species of *Cryptocoryne*, such as *C. thwaitesii*, care is needed to avoid removing stoloniferous young plants from the parent plant before they are sufficiently robust. Some aroids such as the *Lagenandra* and *Cryptocoryne* species prefer the more shaded sites in the aquarium and so contrast with species of *Aponogeton*, which must be bathed in bright overhead light and must be given ample room if they are to display their undulating foliage. The tendency of species of *Echinodorus* and *Aponogeton* to produce floating leaves is discouraged by pruning, a process which sets back the life-cycle and at the same time discourages the formation of flowers. Of course, some species such as *Aponogeton cordatus* retain their submerged foliage more easily than others and still flower even when drastically pruned. Some species mentioned may lose a few leaves after transplanting, but when once established they produce leaves throughout the year, rarely showing any annual rest period and indeed often flowering out of their natural season.

FLOWERING PLANTS WITH A FLOATING HABIT

Floating plants are put to various uses by aquarists: when distributed evenly over the surface of the water, they reduce the intensity of light reaching the submerged plants; in masses they are of use to many spawning fishes, and they provide a sheltered habitat for fry; they have a decorative value; and for such fishes as *Leporinus* they are food. Their use results primarily from their habits of growth; some species are small and much-branched, forming a dense network of vegetation, while others have conspicuous aerial foliage and profuse submerged roots. In an earlier section I discussed species of the genera *Ceratopteris, Salvinia, Azolla, Riccia,* and *Ricciocarpus,* all of which had floating habits; now I shall consider six genera of flowering plants.

Bladderworts, of the genus *Utricularia,* when not in flower live completely submerged just below the surface of the water; the plants are rootless and have branched axes bearing finely-divided segments from which arise small utricles, or bladders. The usual botanical concepts of stem, root and leaf are of little value in describing species of *Utricularia;* some authors have regarded the whole plant body as a root system, while others have tried to differentiate between stems and leaves, interpreting the bladders as modified leaflets. Whichever interpretation is accepted, the structure is certainly anomalous, and shows the plasticity so characteristic of aquatic plants. The family *Lentibulariaceae,* to which the bladderworts belong, contains mainly marsh plants and Goebel suggested in 1891 that the aquatic *Utricularias* are descendants of the marsh forms which have become more and more involved in aquatic life. Species such as *U. minor* and *U. intermedia* are capable of producing terrestrial forms, though these do not flower.

Each bladder has a thin translucent wall, usually two cells thick, and is filled with water and bubbles of air; several long multicellular bristles surround the truncated entrance, from which a colorless flexible valve slopes into the cavity of the bladder. There is no doubt that minute animals, particularly crustaceans such as *Daphnia spp., Cypris spp.,* and *Cyclops spp.,* are trapped within the bladders, where they die slowly, possibly by asphyxiation; bacterial decay reduces the bodies to a soluble form, appearing as a murky fluid which is probably absorbed by the hair-like glands in the lining wall of the bladders. Their ability to trap newly hatched fry is unquestionable.

In shallow water some species of *Utricularia* form "earth-shoots" which have sparse segments; these anchor the plant very firmly in the mud or sand. Another modification, known as an "air-shoot," is produced by *U. vulgaris* and *U. neglecta:* it seems to be a reduced inflorescence, thread-like, white, and bearing stomata through which gaseous exchange occurs between the atmosphere and the internal tissues.

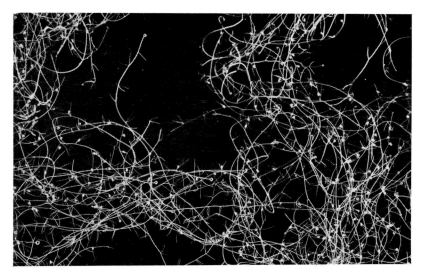

Utricularia species. Photo by Timmerman.

The yellow flowers of most species of *Utricularia* are borne on an aerial shoot, which is maintained erect by a whorl of much-divided segments just beneath the water surface. Bladderworts reproduce vegetatively by fragmentation and, in species inhabiting temperate regions, by turions, or "winter buds." In *Utricularia vulgaris*, for example, the apical region of each shoot forms, between August and November, a tight cluster of sturdy reduced leaves which is covered by a layer of mucilage. Such turions may remain attached to the parent plant throughout the winter, or they may break off and rise to the surface where the foliage opens and growth recommences in the early spring. In natural conditions turions are only formed in the fall but they can be induced at any other time of the year by conditions of poor nutrition.

Many species are suitable for tropical aquaria, such as *Utricularia exoleta* from Asia and tropical Australia, but several of those occurring naturally in peat pools in temperate regions of America and Europe, such as *U. vulgaris*, *U. minor*, *U. intermedia* and *U. neglecta*, are easily acclimatised to warmer water. Some of the genuine tropical species occur in very curious habitats; a man named Gardner, who travelled in Brazil in the 1840's, reported that *U. nelumbifolia* only grew in the water which collected in the leaves of a large *Tillandsia* occurring on a dry rocky part of the Organ Mountains. In a report on the Botany of the Roraima Expedition of 1884, Im Thurn and Oliver described *U. humboldtii* floating in the leaf axils of a great *Bromeliad*, *Brocchinia cordylinoides*, and bearing inflorescences some three or four feet high and clothed in "splendidly large violet flowers."

Pistia stratiotes, showing the leaves spread out with the plant under bright illumination.

Few aquatic plants have caused serious economic problems; two which do possess this singular distinction* are well-known floating species, *Pistia stratiotes*, the African water lettuce, and *Eichornia crassipes*, the water hyacinth or devil's lilac. *Pistia stratiotes* forms rosettes of pale green spatulate leaves whose upper and lower surfaces are covered with minute water-repellent hairs. Over seventy per cent of the volume of each leaf is occupied by air, and when the plant is free-floating, a spongy air-filled tissue develops near the base of the leaf; this tissue, which seems to give the plant extra buoyancy, is not formed when the rosettes are stranded on mud. In the bottom of a groove at the tip of each leaf is a small pore through which drops of water are actively extruded, usually in the early morning. Such water pores are also to be found at the apices of the leaves of most species of *Eichornia*. During periods of bright illumination the leaves of *Pistia* spread out almost horizontally, from which position they move vertically, closing together, during the night.

*There has come into recent prominence a third candidate for such distinction: *Salvinia auriculata* has been stimulated into an explosive phase of reproduction by conditions associated with the rising flood waters of the Zambesi.

Pistia stratiotes reproduces itself vegetatively by proliferating young rosettes, each of which is borne away from the parent by a cylindrical fleshy stolon just beneath the water surface. When such reproduction occurs rapidly, the rosettes stolons and profuse white roots become entangled and form a surface network which rapidly colonizes creeks, backwaters and shallow river margins. As a result *Pistia* often constitutes a great hindrance on the rivers of equatorial Africa, such as the Ogowé and the tributaries of the Congo. In her book "Travels in West Africa," published in 1897, M. H. Kingsley wrote, "It is very like a nicely grown cabbage lettuce, and it is very charming when you look down a creek full of it, for the beautiful tender green makes a perfect picture against the dark forest that rises from the banks of the creek. If you are in a canoe, it gives you little apprehension to know you have got to go through it, but if you are in a small steam launch, every atom of pleasure in its beauty goes, the moment you lay eye on the thing. You dash

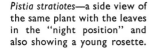

Pistia stratiotes—a side view of the same plant with the leaves in the "night position" and also showing a young rosette.

Pistia stratiotes—a side view of the root system.

into it as fast as you can go, with a sort of geyser of lettuces flying up from the screw; but not for long, for this interesting vegetable grows after the manner of couch-grass . . . and winds those roots round your propeller."

The vegetative reproduction of species of *Eichornia* is very similar to that of *Pistia stratiotes*; young rosettes arise from the leaf axils of the parent and are borne out along the water surface by stout stolons. The two most frequent species, *Eichornia crassipes* and *E. azurea*, are native to the swamps and water meadows of Brazil but have been introduced to many other countries during the last hundred and fifty years. First introduced to the Old World about 1829, *E. crassipes* had become a serious hindrance on the waterways of Java and Singapore sixty years later; in 1896, after high winds and storms had swept Florida, it blocked the St. John's River for twenty-five miles, although it was only six years before that it had been accidentally introduced there. It also flourished in Australia and Cambodia, causing similar problems for local industries which used the inland waterways for transport. It has now spread over the African continent, colonizing the headwaters and upper reaches of the River Nile.

The size and shape of the leaves of *Eichornia crassipes* vary at different stages of development and in different external conditions; this feature of the plant habit is known as heterophylly. Young leaves are very slender and have small circular blades; in succeeding leaves the relative proportions of the blade and stalk change, until the mature form with its ragged transparent sheath, swollen air-filled stalk, and thin orbicular blade is attained. The anatomy of the leaves suggests that the blade and stalk are not equivalent to the lamina·and petiole of the leaves of other aquatic plants such as *Nymphaea spp.* and *Nuphar spp.*: they probably correspond only to the petiole, the tip of which becomes flattened and widened to produce the blade. Bright light and a low temperature seem to induce more prominently swollen, air-filled tissue in the stalk than do high temperatures and poor illumination. The swelling is considerably reduced in leaves formed while a plant is stranded on mud, or on marshy ground.

Eichornia crassipes—the parent plant with a young rosette borne on a horizontal stolon.

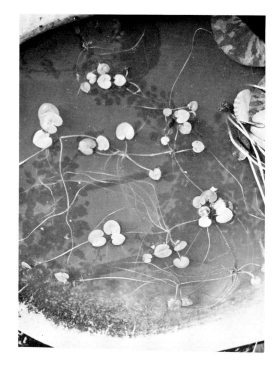

Hydrocharis morsus-ranae—an overhead view of various plants on the surface of a pool in summer.

As aquarium plants, both *Eichornia crassipes* and *Pistia stratiotes* flourish in a humid atmosphere and with natural illumination, but do not grow very satisfactorily in artificial light. Their range of temperature tolerance is from about 65°F. to 85° or 90°F., though these are not absolute limits. *Eichornia crassipes* produces a short-lived aerial spike of large clawed flowers, violet blue in color and often speckled with yellow. *E. azurea* is distinguished by its erect oval leaves and sessile pale blue flowers. After its introduction to Singapore, *E. crassipes* was cultivated by the Chinese who sold its flowers in the streets. *Pistia stratiotes* produces insignificant flowers from which develop berries containing large numbers of minute seeds. It is also cultivated in China for hog food, though it must first be chopped and boiled.

The roots of both *Eichornia* and *Pistia* form convenient natural spawning mops; those of *Pistia stratiotes* are usually white or brown, while mature roots of *Eichornia crassipes* bear dense rows of lateral roots, in all of which there develops a purplish-magenta pigment.

The family *Hydrocharitaceae*, whose members are all aquatic, contains three genera of floating plants known to aquarists: *Hydrocharis*, *Limnobium* and *Stratiotes*. The frog-bit, *Hydrocharis morsus-ranae*, forms a rosette of bronzed, pale green leaves, from the base of which hang long unbranched roots densely clothed with root-hairs. From the nodes of long slender stolons which grow horizontally, just below the surface of the water, from each parent rosette, young rosettes arise throughout the summer. In autumn, or during adverse conditions, these stolons form terminal turions, each of which is enclosed by two scale leaves. When these turions break off, they usually sink to the substratum where they remain dormant until the following spring: the centre of gravity of each turion is in the basal stalked end and so they remain morphologically upright. A minimum limiting intensity of light, especially at the yellow and red end of the spectrum, is required for germination to occur; then the bud scales open, the young leaves develop air-filled lacunae and the growing plant rises to the surface.

The aerial male and female flowers of the frog-bit are borne on the same plant, though at different nodes; the female flowers are solitary whereas the male flowers arise in groups of two or three enclosed within a spathe. Whether male or female, each flower has three obovate white petals which are marked with yellow at their base, and which usually appear ragged and crumpled. Flowers only appear if the plants are brightly illuminated almost daily throughout late spring and early summer.

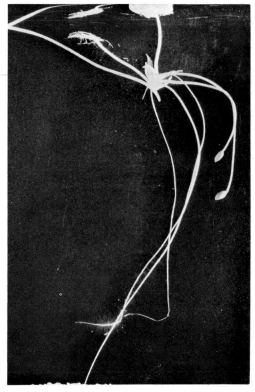

Hydrocharis morsus-ranae—a side view of a plant in autumn, bearing stolons with terminal turions.

Hydrocharis   morsus-ranae—turions in various stages of development.

Hydrocharis morsus-ranae is a widespread inhabitant of pools, small lakes and stagnant water; though it grows more successfully in cold water, it can be acclimatised to a tropical aquarium. A more suitable species for warm water is the American frog-bit, *Limnobium stoloniferum*—also known as *Trianea bogotensis*—which differs from *Hydrocharis* in the structure of its leaves, which are thick fleshy and cordate in shape.

Stratiotes aloides, the water soldier or water aloe, is a curious semi-floating species whose affinities with *Hydrocharis morsus-ranae* are revealed by the similar structure and arrangement of its flowers. The petals are larger and, in England at least, the fruit is rarely, if ever, produced. The species occurs all over Europe and north-west Asia; in the northern regions the plants are female while in the south they are nearly all male. A few hermaphrodite plants have been recorded from time to time, but this is to be expected since the flowers of most members of the family *Hydrocharitaceae* have rudimentary male and female organs.

The stiff, but brittle, leaves of the water soldier sometimes grow as long as twenty inches and are usually covered with small spines, particularly at their margins. The young leaves of the offsets which are produced in the autumn are a bright rich green in color, though this becomes dark and brown as the plant matures. Each plant forms only a few roots, but these are fast-growing, increasing at an average rate of two and a half to three inches per twenty-four hours, and short-lived, and are quickly replaced by new ones. That plants are often unbalanced when any of these roots are experimentally destroyed suggests that their function is primarily to maintain the equilibrium of the surface rosette.

Stratiotes aloides—a mature specimen in early summer.

The famous rising and sinking of *Stratiotes aloides* was thought by the first observers to occur twice within each year; it is now known that the plant rises in the spring, flowers during the early summer, and in late summer sinks back to the bottom of the water, where it forms offsets. The mechanism of these movements is probably a chemical one; during the summer an incrustation of crystalline calcium carbonate is deposited on the aerial leaves by the evaporation of a very dilute solution of that compound which seems to be secreted on the leaf surface by certain cells. This process, together with the waterlogging of old decaying leaves in late summer, increases the specific gravity of the plant, and it sinks. Whilst the plant is submerged, the calcium carbonate is slowly redissolved in the water, and in spring the rapid growth of young succulent leaves probably decreases the specific gravity of the plant, which then floats up to the surface.

Though rather a large species for a cold water aquarium, the water soldier is a fascinating plant for the outdoor pool, and there is commercially available a smaller variety, growing to about six inches in diameter, which flourishes in a tropical aquarium, though it does not show the same regular cycle of movements.

Trapa natans, the water chestnut, is an equally curious species with a floating habit. It occurs in many European localities, and in Siberia, the Caucasus and the Far East, but is rarely in commercial supply. It is now extinct in many places where fossil deposits have shown that it once occurred, for example Belgium, Holland, Sweden, the lowlands of Switzerland, and Scotland. It is an annual species, developing from a dark brown sculptured nut, the horns of which seem to anchor the young seedling in the substratum. When the nut germinates, the first structure to emerge is the hypocotyl, which bears the two rudimentary shoots and the root. One of the two shoots is dormant, while the other grows upwards, producing small narrow leaves which quickly die and are replaced by adventitious roots. At the surface this shoot forms a symmetrical rosette of triangular serrated green leaves; these have glossy, waxed, upper surfaces and dilated petioles. The root does not respond to the force of gravity and grows upwards at an angle of about 45 degrees to the vertical; it later produces many lateral roots which soon grow downward to the substratum. Though occurring naturally in temperate as well as tropical regions of the world, this species thrives in tropical aquaria.

Trapa natans—a side view to show the horned nut, hypo-cotyl bearing the developing and dormant shoots, the pri-mary root and its lateral roots.

A thicket of hair grass, *Eleocharis acicularis*.

DWARF AQUARIUM PLANTS

There is a considerable demand from aquarists for low-growing and dwarf species suitable for the foreground of an aquarium. I have already mentioned aquatic ferns of the genera *Marsilea*, *Gymnopteris*, *Pilularia* and fern allies such as *Isoëtes spp.*, and these, together with dwarf aroids of the genus *Cryptocoryne*, and miscellaneous plants such as *Spiranthes latifolia*, have growth habits which render them useful to the aquarist. There is a number of other genera containing species with a striking appearance and a rosette or branching form of growth, all of which are admirable plants for cultivating in front of strata rockwork.

Hair grass, *Eleocharis acicularis*, forms thickets of very narrow cylindrical leaves and grows to a height of about five to eight inches. New plants are produced at the nodes of slender stolons which creep along, or just below, the surface of the substratum; the species spreads very rapidly in clear water and a fine compost. When first planted in an aquarium, it should be given a sandy compost, in which the sparse frail roots can easily anchor themselves, for in a coarse gravel medium it is apt to be uprooted by bottom-feeding fishes. The predominantly vertical growth of the plant gives it great value in relieving the horizontal lines of rock strata.

The Argentinian species *Elodea callitrichoides.*

Elodea callitrichoides and *E. minor* are both sub-tropical species which thrive in tropical aquaria under a wide range of light intensities. *E. callitrichoides* will grow to a height of twelve or more inches, but if the apical bud of each stem is removed lateral branches readily develop and the plant can be induced to form a dense bush. Native to the Argentine, *E. callitrichoides* is distinguished from the widespread species of temperate regions, *E. canadensis*, the Canadian water weed or water thyme, by its paler green, twisted leaves, each of which has a bright red or brownish base. It may also be distinguished during the flowering phase; both *E. canadensis* and *E. callitrichoides* have inconspicuous male and female flowers on separate plants but whereas the male flowers of *E. canadensis* break away from the tubular spathes borne in the leaf axils and rise to the surface, those of *E. callitrichoides* are carried up to the surface, solitarily, on thread-like stalks. The female flowers of both species are borne up to the surface solitarily by an elongated floral tube; at the surface the flower opens and exposes its three receptive stigmas. Pollination is effected by the buoyant pollen grains, liberated by the explosive rupture of the male flowers, floating by chance on to these stigmas.

P-52.00

Elodea minor is a much smaller species, though it has a similar growth habit to that of *E. callitrichoides*; the pale green fragile stems bear tiny narrow yellowish-green leaves which are recurved, similar to those of *Lagarosiphon major*, a species also known, erroneously, as *Elodea crispa*. Unlike those of other species of *Elodea*, the leaves of *E. minor* are not arranged in whorls on the stem. Both *E. minor* and *E. callitrichoides* grow very quickly in any compost of sand or gravel, producing adventitious roots from the lower nodes of the stems once they have become established.

A foreground plant of unusual appearance which, though it grows naturally in peat bogs and acidic soils in the cooler regions of Europe and Africa, is adaptable to water at a temperature of 55° to 75°F. is *Hydrocotyle vulgaris*, the pennywort. A creeping rhizome produces from each node one simple leaf, consisting of a horizontal, slightly lobed lamina borne on a slender petiole. The length of the petiole is extremely variable; when the plant is only partially submerged the petiole may be as short as one inch, but in an aquarium the petioles tend to elongate, and unless this tendency is controlled by

Elodea minor.

Hydrocotyle vulgaris, the European pennywort.

The dwarf lily *Nuphar pumilum*.

judicious pruning the plant loses its attraction. Flowers are formed in the leaf axils when the species is growing out of water or only partially submerged; these are inconspicuous and develop into bilobed fruits, which are about two millimeters in diameter. Another pennywort, *Hydrocotyle verticillata*, occurring in the Atlantic Coast regions of North America, is very similar in structure to *H. vulgaris* and is equally useful in aquaria.

Most species of the genera *Nymphaea*, *Nymphoides* and *Nuphar*, all usually known as water lilies, are too large for either cold-water or tropical aquaria, but there is one species *Nuphar pumilum*, also known as *N. minimum*, which is sufficiently small to be useful in the foreground of an aquarium. Growing from a stout rootstock, the leaves spread out so that their blades are exposed to the maximum illumination; the edges of the leaves are often furled and the color is a rich translucent green. This plant has a wide temperature range and often grows only slowly, reaching a height of four to six inches after about a year.

Samolus floribundus, known as water rose, is another dwarf plant which withstands a similarly wide range of temperatures. It produces compact rosettes of oval, pale green leaves which are prominently veined; flowers are only formed when the plants are growing in boggy soil, with most of their foliage out of the water. They grow profusely in a compost of sand or gravel and reproduce themselves under water by offsets arising close to the crown of the parent rosettes.

Samolus floribundus, the water rose.

A young specimen of *Lobelia cardinalis var. cardinalis.*

Maturing fruits of *Cabomba caroliniana*, with floating leaves to the right.

Lobelia dortmanna, the water lobelia, is a curious plant of Europe and parts of America, inhabiting the shallow margins of lakes with soft, rather acid water. From the short vertical stem there arise stout linear dark green leaves which bend horizontally at the tip; each leaf contains two large longitudinal air canals which give the plant buoyancy. The profuse simple white roots are frequently spirally coiled. Under natural illumination, the species flowers in early summer, producing from each rosette a single scaly aerial stem bearing several bell-shaped flowers which vary in color from a very pale pink to a rich lilac. A related plant, known by the horticultural name of *Lobelia cardinalis var. cardinalis*, and originating in South Carolina, is more suitable for tropical aquaria, *L. dortmanna* being acclimatised to water temperatures above 65°F. only with difficulty. This plant has stout stems bearing oblong to lanceolate leaves and readily forms axillary branches after the removal of the apical buds. When grown in aquaria these two water lobelias should be rooted in a sandy medium and they thrive in any intensity of artificial light which, however, does not encourage the formation of flowers.

The water lobelia, *Lobelia dortmanna*, showing the relative proportions of the shoot and root systems.

A grove of *Vallisneria spiralis;* highly decorative effects can be achieved with these plants.

SUB-TROPICAL AND TEMPERATE PLANTS

Several plants cultivated in tropical aquaria occur naturally, not in the tropics, but in sub-tropical and temperate regions, and their ability to grow in water at temperatures from 50° to 80°F. seems to be due to the fact that they have a much more extensive range of temperature tolerance than do genuine tropical species. The aquarist is able to acclimatise them to almost any desired range of water temperature; such species are exemplified by some of the most well-known aquarium plants, *Vallisneria spiralis*, *Egeria densa*, *Lagarosiphon major*, and a few species of the genus *Myriophyllum*.

The genus *Vallisneria*, which belongs to the *Hydrocharitaceae*, contains four plants of use to the aquarist; two of these are distinct species, while the other two are horticultural varieties of one of the species. *Vallisneria gigantea* is native to the Philippines and New Guinea and has linear leaves growing to over a yard in length, brilliant translucent green in color and sometimes gently undulated. Its size restricts its use to large aquaria and tropical pools, but it has a wide temperature range, from about 55° to 80°F. *Vallisneria spiralis*, and its two varieties, are smaller plants from temperate waters in every continent and they thrive equally well in cold-water and tropical aquaria. All three have linear tapering leaves produced from the short vertical stem, or crown, and reproduce vegetatively by runners above the surface of the substratum which form young plants at the nodes. The leaves of *V. spiralis forma tortifolia* are spirally twisted while those of *V. spiralis forma rubriformis* are suffused with a reddish anthocyanin pigment, which sometimes slowly disappears under artificial light and is more successfully maintained when the plants are grown in natural illumination and in water at a temperature lower than 70°F.

The pollination mechanism of *Vallisneria spiralis* is an elaboration of that of *Elodea canadensis*. Male and female flowers are borne on separate plants; the solitary female flowers grow up to the surface on the elongated stalks of their spathes. Hundreds of male flowers, each containing two stamens and a small bubble of air, are formed within a spathe near the crown of the plant. When the spathe breaks open, the flowers are released to the surface where each one is ruptured. A man named Scott, the Director of the Calcutta Botanic Gardens, in 1869 reported "seeing under a noonday sun the innumerable florets freed from their spathes and ascending like tiny air-globules till they reach the surface of the water, where the calyx quickly bursts—the two larger and opposite sepals, reflex, forming tiny rudders, with the third and smaller recurved as a miniature sail, conjointly facilitating in an admirable manner the florets' mission to those of the emerging females."

The twisted form *V. spiralis forma tortifolia.*

Vallisneria gigantea, male spathe close to crown. Note also runners from parent plant.

P-60.00

Egeria densa, aquarium grown.

The heavy female flowers depress the surface film and the males are blown to them, sliding down the slope and rubbing the sticky pollen from the dehiscing stamens on to the stigmas. The developing fruit then sinks through the water, partly due to its own weight and partly to the spiral contraction of the stalk.

The members of the *Hydrocharitaceae* thus show an interesting range of floral structure. Most of the genera have unisexual flowers, but it is only in *Hydrocharis* and *Limnobium* that both sexes occur on the same plant. These two genera, together with *Stratiotes*, have conspicuous aerial flowers pollinated by insects. Other genera such as *Elodea* and *Vallisneria* have male and female flowers on separate plants and effect pollination at the water surface; in a related marine genus, *Halophila*, pollination takes place under water. Only in *Ottelia* do hermaphrodite flowers occur regularly; one species of this genus, *Ottelia ulvaefolia* is occasionally available to aquarists. It comes from

Egeria densa, pool grown.

Madagascar and tropical areas of Africa and has translucent furled leaves similar to those of *Aponogeton ulvaceus* but with conspicuous carmine-tinted veins. It is a fragile plant though it has a temperature range of 65° to 90°F. and will grow in fine sand or gravel.

Egeria densa, also referred to as *Elodea densa*, is an Argentinian species which adapts itself to tropical or cold-water aquaria, or to ornamental pools. Luxuriance of foliage is encouraged by natural illumination; in a tropical aquarium under artificial light the stems grow very rapidly and the leaves are smaller and paler green. Whereas the leaves of *Egeria densa* are arranged on the stem in whorls of four, those of *Lagarosiphon major*, previously known as *Elodea crispa*, are not whorled and usually bear short stiff hairs. Although it grows in North Africa in water at a temperature of 75° to 85°F., *Lagarosiphon major* is not as easily acclimatised to warm water as is *Egeria densa*.

A large number of species and varieties of *Ludwigia* is known to aquarists. *Ludwigia natans*, originating from the temperate regions of Europe, Asia and North America, is a fast-growing species with a temperature range of 60° to 80°F. Its stout stems bear oval bright green leaves in pairs and it forms branched adventitious roots from the lower nodes. The solitary greenish flowers are formed in the leaf axils only when the plant is growing out of water, in damp soil. This species, and the related *L. arcuata*, are easily propagated by cuttings. *L. arcuata* is a less common species with slender stems bearing very narrow tapering leaves of a bronze-green color, and with a more restricted temperature range.

There are three genera of aquatic plants, with a bushy growth habit and divided leaves, occurring naturally in the cool waters of Europe and North America, yet possessing the ability to grow in water at higher temperatures. The genus *Hottonia* contains two species, *H. palustris*, the water violet, and *H. inflata*, a North American plant, which resemble each other in structure, culture requirements and tolerance of temperatures from about 50° to 70°F. The whorled pale green leaves of *H. palustris* are divided into narrow linear flattened segments, and from the apex of the shoot axillary inflorescences grow up into the air under natural illumination in early summer. Each inflorescence bears whitish-pink or lilac flowers and is kept erect by a symmetrical whorl of large leaves just below the water surface. The species does

Lagarosiphon major.

Ludwigia mullertii hort.

not produce any perennating organs; young branches arise from the base of the inflorescence and develop into new plants in the following spring. Both species of *Hottonia* will grow as floating plants or rooted in a sandy, loamy compost.

The hornwort, *Ceratophyllum demersum*, is an interesting pool or aquarium plant of unusual appearance, though the plumes of foliage are rarely as luxuriant in an aquarium as they are out-of-doors when the plant receives sunlight. The species does not form roots and, unless it is desired as a floating plant, should just be anchored in the aquarium gravel. Although the plant is brittle, young bright green leaves are hardened by a covering of cutin. In natural habitats, flowering and pollination frequently occur but fruits rarely develop, as they require a water temperature of 80° to 90°F. to attain maturity, and the plant reproduces mainly by fragmentation and by the production, in late summer, of dense shoot apices which remain dormant throughout the winter.

P-64.00

Two species of water milfoil, *Myriophyllum verticillatum* and *M. spicatum*, are widely distributed throughout Europe and North America and will thrive in aquaria at temperatures of less than 70° F. From the rhizomes of both species there arise erect branching stems, bearing whorls of finely divided leaves, each with about fifteen to thirty segments, and in the summer months aerial spikes carrying male and female flowers, which are wind-pollinated. The leaves of *M. verticillatum* are a deep rich green in color and are arranged in whorls of four whereas those of *M. spicatum* are bronze green and are arranged in whorls of three or five. Towards the end of summer *M. verticillatum* forms club-shaped dark green turions at the apices of axillary branches. The leaves which constitute these turions are small and contain a high concentration of starch and other food reserves; in the spring the turions germinate, forming young plants anchored in the substratum by adventitious spirally-coiled roots. Although naturally perennating organs, turions are formed by the plant in conditions of reduced light intensity, lowered temperature, and reduced supplies of soluble nutrients.

Ludwigia arcuata.

M. verticillatum—stages in development of turions; specimen on extreme left showing sleep movement.

The hornwort, *Ceratophyllum demersum*.

The water violet, *Hottonia palustris*.

Myriophyllum verticillatum.

A Brazilian species of *Myriophyllum*, *M. proserpinacoides*—the parrot's feather—has become naturalized in parts of North America and is one of the most beautiful aquatic plants. Its growth habit is really semi-aquatic as even when it is rooted its stems grow upward to produce whorls of finely divided bluish-green leaves above the water. The leaves show diurnal movements, opening out in bright light and then closing up tightly round the shoot apex as the light fades; this habit is also shown by *Synnema triflorum*, *Limnophila sessiliflora*, *Nomaphila stricta* and young plants of *Myriophyllum verticillatum*. As a result of its producing aerial foliage the parrot's feather is more suitable for the tropical or warm pool than for aquaria.

A common feature of aquatic plants is the tendency to produce pigmented foliage under certain conditions. The pigment is usually red or purple and, except in numerous horticultural varieties of water lily of the genera *Nymphaea* and *Nuphar*, seems to be formed only in the superficial tissues of the leaves and

Myriophyllum spicatum.

Myriophyllum proserpinacoides —specimen showing the aerial leaves in the night position.

stems. Species which often develop such pigment include *Bacopa caroliniana*, *Cabomba caroliniana*, *Azolla caroliniana* and *A. filiculoides*, several species of *Cryptocoryne* and *Echinodorus*, *Hydrocharis morsus-ranae*, *Vallisneria spiralis*, several species of *Ludwigia*, and *Myriophyllum spicatum*. There is evidence, though it is sparse, that pigment formation is more conspicuous in plants grown in water at a temperature lower than is normal, and subject to intense illumination, but a systematic investigation of the chemistry of these particular pigments and their distribution in aquatic plants is needed.

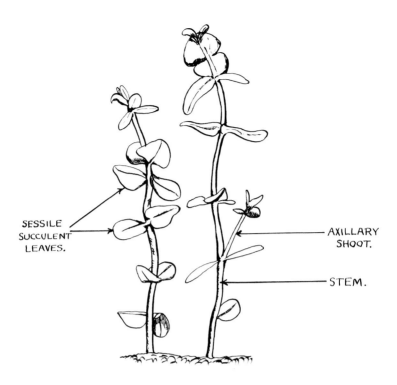

An example of a fleshy-leaved plant propagated by cuttings. (A *Bacopa* species.)

How To Grow Aquarium Plants

The difficulties experienced by many aquarists in cultivating plants are worsened by there being few clear-cut rules or techniques. This is partly because of inadequate experimental data on the influence of physical and chemical factors on the growth of different species and partly because the cultivation of aquatic plants is still based, to some extent, on the myths and misconceptions of the early aquarists. I have mentioned, previously, techniques of cultivation relevant to the particular species which I described, but it may be useful to discuss these techniques more fully. This survey is not free from imperfections, nor does it present any basically new techniques or ideas, but it does attempt to dispel some of the uncritical, and often fantastic, notions which, if their prevalence in the aquarium literature is any criterion, still influence aquarists.

The structure of a species determines the method of planting. Species which are obtained as cuttings, e.g., species of *Hygrophila*, *Cabomba*,

Limnophila, Ludwigia, Hottonia, Myriophyllum, Ceratophyllum, Cardamine, Lysimachia, Bacopa, Synnema, Elodea, Egeria, and *Lagarosiphon,* should be planted in the following way:—

   (i)   The leaves should be stripped from the lowermost nodes.

   (ii)   The shoots should be loosely tied in groups.

   (iii)   Each group should be pressed into the gravel, or anchored on the surface of the gravel by attaching a pebble or a piece of lead foil.

A cutting plant with leaves composed of petiole and lamina, and showing palmate venation. (A *Cardamine* species.)

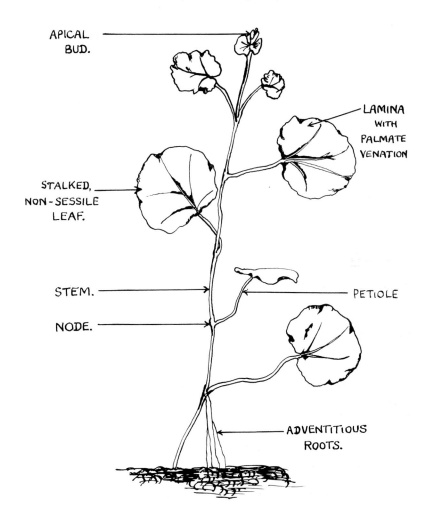

APICAL BUD.

LAMINA WITH PALMATE VENATION

STALKED, NON-SESSILE LEAF.

STEM.

PETIOLE

NODE.

ADVENTITIOUS ROOTS.

Two dwarf foreground plants showing contrasting root systems: *Spiranthes latifolia* (left) with fleshy tuberous roots, and an unidentified species of *Cryptocoryne*, with golden brown foliage arising from a horizontal rhizome bearing fibrous roots.

Species of *Fontinalis* may be gathered from their natural habitats with the wiry stems already attached to water-worn stones.

Species which are obtained as intact plants should be established as follows:—

(i) Species of *Marsilea, Regnellidium, Pilularia, Acorus,* and *Hydrocotyle* should have all their roots covered and their creeping rhizomes just beneath the surface of the gravel.

(ii) Species of *Gymnopteris* should also have their roots buried, but their rhizomes creeping over the gravel.

(iii) Species of *Sagittaria, Vallisneria, Ceratopteris,* and *Lagenandra* should have their roots buried and their short swollen stems, or "crowns," just above the surface of the gravel.

(iv) Species of *Isoëtes, Aponogeton, Nymphaea,* and *Nuphar* should have their stout, tuberous, or corm-like, root-stocks just covered by the gravel.

(v) Species of *Echinodorus, Spiranthes, Barclaya, Cryptocoryne, Lobelia,* and *Samolus* should have all their roots buried and the leaf bases at, or just above, the surface of the gravel.

Most aquarium plants have fragile organs, especially genuine aquatic species, the stems and leaves of which possess few strengthening elements and much spongy air-filled tissue, and care is needed in using wooden or metal planting sticks. Planting by hand, being less severe, is to be preferred.

Cryptocorynes, like the *Cryptocoryne ciliata* pictured here, should have their leaf bases about even with the surface of the gravel.

The texture of the rooting medium and the nature of the root system affect the efficiency of the planting method. For a species to become speedily established it is essential that it should have the most suitable rooting medium, particularly if the aquarium contains disturbing bottom-feeding fishes.

(i) Many species have deep vigorous root systems and grow well in fine or coarse gravel or very coarse sand.

(ii) Cuttings which have no adventitious roots require a fine gravel, which packs round and weighs down the plant better, and facilitates the anchorage of young roots more than does coarse gravel.

(iii) A fine densely-packing gravel is also useful for very buoyant species, such as *Lobelia dortmanna*.

(iv) Species which have shallow root systems, e.g., *Eleocharis acicularis*, require a medium to coarse sand.

Roots are never formed by a few species, such as *Ceratophyllum demersum*, and are not induced to form by administering to the plant hormones of the beta-indolyl carboxylic acid series.

Plants with good root systems, such as these *Luronium natans*, do better if their planting medium is fairly loose. Note also the stolons, the linear submerged leaves on the two plants to the left and the floating leaves on the second plant from the right.

The flowerpot in which this *Heteranthera zosteraefolia* is planted makes it easier to handle the plant.

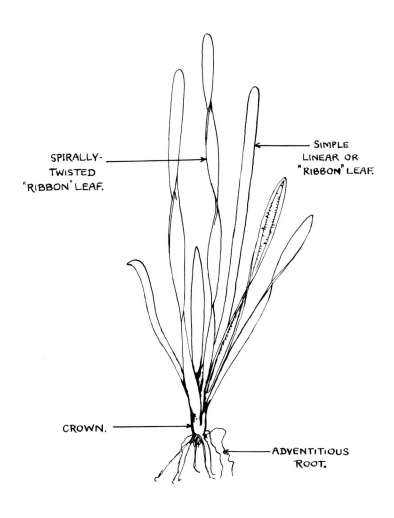

SPIRALLY-
TWISTED
"RIBBON" LEAF.

SIMPLE
LINEAR OR
"RIBBON" LEAF.

CROWN.

ADVENTITIOUS
ROOT.

A linear-leaved rooted plant. (E.g., *Sagittaria* or *Vallisneria* species.)

The possible advantages and disadvantages of mixing peat or soil with sand or gravel in the rooting medium have been debated at unnecessary length in the literature and I mention only these points:—

(i) It is not fully known which substances different species absorb from the substratum in which they are rooted and which substances they absorb from the surrounding water. From observations of the thin permeable epidermis of the stems and leaves and the poorly developed roots several pioneer plant physiologists assumed that aquatic plants absorbed all the necessary inorganic and organic substances directly from the surrounding water. There is no reason to suppose that all species require the same proportions of the different substances or that they all absorb similar relative amounts from the water and the substratum. It is reasonable to assume that aquarium plants which are bog species, growing naturally in rich organic soils, will benefit from the addition of loam to their rooting medium.

(ii) To sterilise loam before using it in an aquarium destroys its value by killing most, if not all, of the microscopic bacteria, protozoa, and fungi which convert the organic debris in the soil into a form which can be absorbed by the plants' root hairs.

(iii) Peat alone is a useless addition since it contains no substances of great value to the plants. It will reduce the pH value of the water and if mixed with soil it will create a more open, and less dense, compost.

(iv) Sterilised gravel is not completely devoid of inorganic salts useful to the plants.

(v) The decaying leaves and fæces which accumulate in the gravel probably supply many of the substances required by the plants.

(vi) An extensive layer of loam beneath the gravel of a large aquarium creates more problems than benefits. Since an undergravel filter cannot then be used, water does not circulate through the rooting medium, which therefore becomes foul and soon needs cleaning out. An undergravel filter normally causes water to circulate through the interstices of the gravel, removing noxious gases, such as hydrogen sulphide, which are by-products of bacterial action, and it incidentally draws the organic debris down to the roots of the plants.

(vii) Loam may be given to specimen plants grown in pots or to plants which are cultivated in separate aquaria, without causing serious problems.

Of the many other factors affecting the growth of aquatic plants, the pH value of the water, light intensity, and water movement are often discussed. As many species which are cultivated in nurseries and dealers' aquaria thrive in waters of a wide pH range it may be concluded that the hydrogen ion concentration of the water is not, for them, of prime importance. But the aquarist must not expect plants from temperate waters of extreme pH value either to acclimatise themselves to, or reach the climax of their life cycle in, aquarium water of opposite pH value. For example, specimens of *Lobelia dortmanna* obtained from lakes in which the water may be pH 4 to pH 5 rarely thrive in aquarium water of pH greater than 7.

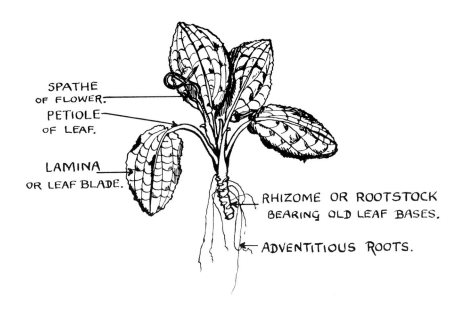

SPATHE OF FLOWER.
PETIOLE OF LEAF.
LAMINA OR LEAF BLADE.
RHIZOME OR ROOTSTOCK BEARING OLD LEAF BASES.
ADVENTITIOUS ROOTS.

Diagram of an aroid, species. (E.g., *Cryptocoryne* species.)

With an aquarium containing a variety of species of plants the aquarist attempts to provide an intensity of light which will be conducive to the growth of all the species but which, in fact, may not be the optimum for any one of them. In providing his plants with natural or artificial illumination the aquarist is involved in a conflict between:—

 (i) the different optimum intensities of light for different species, and
 (ii) the unknown intensity of light which will ensure healthy growth of the majority of species, and
 (iii) the rampant growth of filamentous and free-swimming green algæ, colonial blue-green algæ, and diatoms which occurs in intense illumination, and
 (iv) the etiolation of fast-growing species, such as *Egeria densa* and *Lagarosiphon major*, which occurs in poor illumination.

It is important to remember that the intensity of light decreases with increasing depth of water, because of reflection from the water surface and absorption by particles in suspension. Floating plants and vigorous submerged plants usually require the brightest illumination. Few species reach the climax of their life cycle, the flowering phase, without some natural illumination.

It has been said that circulation of the water in aquaria is beneficial to plants which occur naturally in flowing waters. Examples of such plants are species of the genera *Myriophyllum, Ceratophyllum, Hottonia, Cabomba, Limnophila* and *Ceratopteris*, all of which have dissected leaves, and *Aponogeton*. Since the character of their foliage does not change in still water, movement of the aquarium water should not be considered essential for their successful cultivation.

Many aquatic plants, especially species of *Cryptocoryne*, lose some or all of their leaves soon after they have been introduced to an aquarium. The cause of this frequently reported phenomenon is not really known but it has been vaguely suggested that the mechanical shock of transplantation, a difference in water temperature or pH value, or chilling prior to planting could be responsible.

Often confused with forms of *Elodea*, this is *Potamogeton densus*.

Techniques used for the maintenance of aquarium plants are of three types:—
  (i) The trimming of plants.
  (ii) Methods for vegetative propagation.
  (iii) Methods for propagation by seed.
Trimming the foliage of aquatic plants is desirable for:—
  (i) Tidiness, but it should not be indiscriminate cutting; rather should it be a systematic removal of old or deformed leaves and shoots.
  (ii) The stimulation of branching, by removing the apical bud of a shoot, so partially eliminating the inhibition of growth of the axillary buds.
  (iii) The prevention of the floating habit in species which are desired for the decorative value of their juvenile, submerged foliage.
Vegetative propagation may be accomplished by two principal methods:—
  (i) By taking cuttings from established plants and by dividing root-stocks.
  (ii) By cultivating natural reproductive structures produced by the plant.

Dormant apices of the horn-wort.

Turions and dormant apices of species such as *Myriophyllum verticillatum*, *Ceratophyllum demersum*, *Utricularia vulgaris*, and *Hydrocharis morsus-ranae*, may be collected from wild habitats, ornamental pools or cold-water aquaria later in the year and induced to germinate in water at a temperature of 50°F. to 55°F. Offsets produced by rosette plants, e.g. *Samolus flori-bundus*, may be detached from their parents and grown in a sandy compost in shallow water. Young plants produced by stoloniferous species, e.g., *Cryptocoryne spp.* and *Vallisneria spp.*, may similarly be detached from their parents and grown in the recommended compost. Plants produced viviparously by *Ceratopteris thalictroides* should be carefully removed from

Echinodorus cordifolius is a strongly rooted aquatic.

the parent frond and allowed to float until they have developed strong root systems. Fronds of *Gymnopteris spp.* which are bearing young plants should be left intact and pegged down horizontally on the surface of the gravel, so that the offspring may take root without being disturbed. It is important in cultivating rare and slow-growing species, such as *Cryptocoryne thwaitesii,* that stolons and offsets should not be detached from the parent until the young plants are sturdy and almost independent.

Potamogeton gayi (left) and *Potamogeton octandrus.*

Propagation by seed is often a long and tedious procedure. The difficulties of obtaining seeds from flowering aquatic plants are several:—

(i) Sexual reproduction is remarkably uncommon in truly aquatic species, particularly those living in deep water, although they are capable of developing the necessary organs.

(ii) With dioecious species, there may not be available in the aquarium both male and female plants.

(iii) Natural methods of pollination, by insects, wind, etc., will probably not occur in aquaria, though they probably will occur in outdoor pools.

(iv) Artificial pollination is not easily accomplished with the small delicate flowers of many species and with the heterostylic condition of a species such as *Hottonia palustris*.

(v) Even if pollination and fertilisation are successful the seeds may not mature.

Aquarium plants are encouraged to flower by raising the temperature of the water, by allowing them sunlight during the later stages of growth, and by refraining from pruning those species which naturally form mature floating or aerial leaves. Flowers may not be formed even after the aquarist has made all these three adjustments, or they may arise without him making any of them. Seeds are often formed by self-fertilising species of *Echinodorus*, and by species of *Lagenandra*, *Aponogeton* and *Ottelia* and they should be cultivated in the way I outlined earlier in this survey. If the aquarist is lucky enough to have male and female flowers produced simultaneously by a species which has hydrophilous pollination, e.g., *Vallisneria spiralis*, he may also get seeds produced.

Few hybrid aquarium plants have ever been obtained, though over three dozen natural hybrids occur in the pondweed genus, *Potamogeton*. The rarity of inter-specific hybrids amongst aquatic plants is mainly due to:—

(i) The practical difficulties of effecting pollination and fertilisation which were mentioned above.

(ii) The species having different flowering seasons or structurally different flowers which hinder or prevent cross-pollination.

(iii) The species possessing some physiological incompatibility mechanism which prevents cross-fertilisation.

(iv) The hybrid embryo being inviable or later infertile.

Since those species in which sexual reproduction is rare usually propagate themselves rapidly by vegetative reproduction the need for the aquarist to attempt to propagate them by seed is questionable.

The
Nomenclature of Aquatic Plants

The following list, which is arranged in alphabetical order, gives the current scientific names of the aquatic plants described in this book, together with any synonyms or incorrect names by which the plants are still known.

Current scientific name.	Other names.
Acorus gramineus Solander.	
Acorus gramineus var. *pusillus* (Siebold) Engler.	**A. pusillus.*
Aponogeton bernierianus (Decaisne) Hooker.	
Aponogeton cordatus Jumelle.	
Aponogeton crispus Thunberg.	
Aponogeton distachyus Thunberg.	
Aponogeton fenestralis (Poiret) Hooker.	
Aponogeton natans (L.) Engler et Krause.	
Aponogeton ulvaceus Baker.	
Aponogeton undulatus Roxburgh.	
Azolla caroliniana Willdenow.	†*A. microphylla* Kaulfuss.
Azolla filiculoides Lamarck.	†*A. magellanica* Willdenow.
Azolla mexicana Presl.	
Bacopa caroliniana (Walt.) Robinson.	†*B. amplexicaulis* (Pursh) Wettstein.
Bacopa monnieri (L.) Wettstein.	†*B. minor* hort.
Barclaya longifolia Wallich.	
Barclaya motleyi Hooker.	
Cabomba aquatica Aublet.	†*Nectris aquatica* Willdenow.
Cabomba caroliniana A. Gray.	†*C. viridiflora* hort.
Cabomba furcata Schultes.	
Cardamine lyrata Bunge.	†*Nasturtium japonicum* hort.
Ceratophyllum demersum L.	
Ceratopteris cornuta (Beauvois) Leprieur.	
Ceratopteris thalictroides (L.) Brongniart.	
Cryptocoryne affinis N.E. Brown ex Hooker.	**C. haerteliana* Jacobsen ex Millkuhn.
Cryptocoryne balansae Gagnepain.	**C. somphongsii.*
Cryptocoryne beckettii Thwaites ex Trimen.	**C. cordata.*
Cryptocoryne blassii de Wit.	
Cryptocoryne ciliata (Roxb.) Fischer ex Wydler.	
Cryptocoryne cordata Griffith.	

Cryptocoryne djambi (this name has not yet been
  confirmed.)
Cryptocoryne griffithii Schott.
Cryptocoryne longicauda Beccari et Engler.
Cryptocoryne lutea Alston.
Cryptocoryne nevillii Trimen.   *C. beckettii.*
Cryptocoryne retrospiralis (Roxb.) Fischer ex
  Wydler.
Cryptocoryne thwaitesii Schott.
Cryptocoryne versteegii Engler.
Cryptocoryne wendtii de Wit.
Cryptocoryne willisii Engler ex Baum.
Echinodorus berteroi (Sprengel) Fassett.   †*E. rostratus* (Nuttall)
                                                      Engelmann.
Echinodorus cordifolius (L.) Grisebach.   *E. radicans.*
Echinodorus grisebachii Small.   †*E. intermedius* Micheli.
Echinodorus martii Micheli.   †*E. leopoldina* hort.
Echinodorus muricatus Grisebach.   †*E. macrophyllus var. murica-*
                                                      tus Micheli.

Echinodorus paniculatus Micheli.
Echinodorus tenellus (Martius) Buchenau.   *Sagittaria microfolia.*
Egeria densa Planchon.   †*Elodea densa* Caspary.
Eichornia azurea (Swartz) Kunth.
Eichornia crassipes (Martius) Solms-Laubach.   †*E. speciosa* Kunth.
Eleocharis acicularis (L.) Roemer et Schultes.   †*Scirpus acicularis* L.
Elodea callitrichoides (Richard) Caspary   †*Anacharis callitrichoides*
                                                      Richard.
Elodea canadensis Michaux.   †*Anacharis alsinastrum*
                                                      Babington.

Elodea minor Farwell.
Fontinalis antipyretica L.
Fontinalis antipyretica L. forma *gracilis* Schimp. *F. gracilis.*
Heteranthera zosteraefolia Martius.
Hottonia inflata L.
Hottonia palustris L.
Hydrocharis morsus-ranae L.
Hydrocotyle verticillata Thunberg.
Hydrocotyle vulgaris L.
Hygrophila polysperma T. Anderson.   *Hydrophilia; Onagraria.*
Isoëtes bolanderii Engelmann.
Isoëtes garnierii A. Chevalier.
Isoëtes lacustris L.

Lagarosiphon major (Ridley) C. E. Moss. \
Lagenandra lancifolia (Schott) Thwaites. \
Lagenandra ovata (L.) Thwaites. \
Limnobium stoloniferum (Meyer) Grisebach. \
Limnophila heterophylla Bentham.

Limnophila sessiliflora (Vahl) Blume. \
Lobelia cardinalis L. var. *cardinalis*. \
Lobelia dortmanna L. \
Ludwigia arcuata Walter. \
Ludwigia natans Elliott. \
Lysimachia nummularia L. \
Marsilea drummondii A. Brown. \
Marsilea mucronata A. Brown. \
Marsilea quadrifolia L. \
Marseilea hirsuta R. Brown. \
Marsilea vestita A. Brown. \
Micranthemum orbiculatum Michaux.

Myriophyllum elatinoides Gaudichaud. \
Myriophyllum proserpinacoides Gillies. \
Myriophyllum spicatum L. \
Myriophyllum verticillatum L. \
Nomaphila stricta (Vahl) Nees. \
Nuphar pumilum (Timm) de Candolle. \
Ottelia ulvaefolia Buchenau.

Pilularia globulifera L. \
Pistia stratiotes L. \
Riccia fluitans L. \
Ricciocarpus natans (L.) Corda. \
Sagittaria latifolia Willdenow. \
Sagittaria subulata (L.) Buchenau forma
subulata. \
Sagittaria subulata (L.) Buchenau forma *pusilla*. \
Salvinia auriculata Aublet (large form) \
Salvinia auriculata Aublet (small form). \
Samolus floribundus Humboldt, Bonpland et
Kunth. \
Stenospermation popayanense Schott var.
aquatica. \
Stratiotes aloides L.

★Elodea crispa hort.

†*Trianea bogotensis* Karsten. \
†*Ambulia heterophylla*
Bentham. \
†*Ambulia Baumii* Engler. \
★*L. cardinalis* var. *cryptofolia*.

†*L. mullertii* hort.

†*M. umbrosum* (Walter)
Blake.

†*M. brasiliense* Cambessedes.

★*Hygrophila stricta*. \
†*N. minimum* Spenner. \
†*Damasonium ulvaefolium*
Planchon.

†*Riccia natans* L. \
★*S. sinensis*. \
†*S. natans* Michaux.

†*S. lorata* (Chapman) Small. \
★*S. brasiliensis*. \
★*S. natans; S. auriculata*. \
†*S. parviflorus* Rafinesque.

Synnema triflorum (Roxb. ex Nees) O. Kuntze.

Trapa natans L.

Utricularia exoleta R. Brown.   †*U. gibba* L.

Utricularia intermedia L.

Utricularia minor L.

Utricularia neglecta L.

Utricularia vulgaris L.

Vallisneria gigantea Graebner.

Vallisneria spiralis L.

Vallisneria spiralis L. forma *rubriformis*.

Vallisneria spiralis L. forma *tortifolia*.   **V. spiralis* var. *torta;* var. *torsada;* var. *tortuosa* hort.

†denotes a legitimate synonym.
*denotes an erroneous horticultural or trade name.

GLOSSARY

Adventitious root: a root which develops from the node of a stem or similar organ, such as a rhizome, stolon, or runner; see illustrations on pp. 71, 74, 76, 78.

Apical bud: the principal growing point of the stem; see illustration on p. 71.

Axillary bud: a bud, capable of developing into a lateral shoot, present in the angle between a leaf and the stem on which it is borne; see illustration on p. 70.

Dichotomous: dividing into two equal branches.

Dioecious: having male or female flowers on separate plants.

Etiolation: the formation of weak, spindly foliage deficient in chlorophyll; usually occurs in light of too low an intensity.

Heterophyllous: having leaves of different forms on the one plant.

Heterostylic: having flowers which differ in the relative length of their styles and stamens, such that any one flower is very rarely, if ever, self-pollinated.

Hydrophilous pollination: the transference of pollen from the anthers of the stamens to the stigmas on the surface of the water or under water.

Hypocotyl: that part of the stem of a seedling below the cotyledons.

Lamina: that part of a leaf which is flattened, to a greater or lesser degree, as the 'leaf-blade'; see illustrations on pp. 71, 78.

Node: that part of the stem from which one or more leaves arise; see illustration on p. 71.

Petiole: the stalk of a leaf; see illustrations on pp. 71, 78.

Physiological incompatibility: the existence of some chemical or physical factor in the reproductive organs of a plant which prevents fertilisation.

Pinna: a part of the leaf of a fern, corresponding to a leaflet in some flowering plants; see illustration on p. 14.

Rachis: the continuation of the stipes in a fern leaf which is divided, as, for example, in the illustration on p. 14.

Rhizome: a stem growing more or less horizontally near the surface of the soil or gravel, and sometimes appearing above it.

Rootstock: a very short, but often thick, stem growing vertically at or just above the surface of the soil or gravel; often referred to as the 'crown' of the plant; see illustrations on pp. 14, 76, 78.

Runner: a horizontal stem growing just above the surface of the soil or gravel and rooting at its nodes; see illustration on p. 60.

Sessile: a term used to describe a leaf which has no petiole; for example, the leaves shown in the illustrations on pp. 70, 76.

Stipes: the stalk of a fern leaf; corresponding to the petiole in flowering plants; see illustration on p. 14.

Stolon: a horizontal stem growing just beneath the surface of the soil or gravel, as in numerous species of *Cryptocoryne*.

Stomata: minute pores in the surface of leaves and herbaceous stems through which exchange of gases with the atmosphere occurs.

Thallus: the body of a plant which is not differentiated into stem, root and leaf.

Turion: a modified bud, the leaves of which contain abundant storage reserves, by means of which the plant survives winter and renews its growth in spring.

Venation: the arrangement of veins in a leaf; see illustration on p. 71.

Vernation: the manner in which a leaf, or the parts of a leaf, are rolled up in the bud; also applied to the manner in which the frond of a fern unrolls; see illustration on p. 14.

Viviparous: bearing young plants on vegetative organs, such as leaves.

Whorl: a group of more than two organs of the same kind, for example leaves, arising at the same level.

notes

INDEX

notes

notes

RAISING TROPICAL FISHES
COMMERCIALLY

TABLE OF CONTENTS

These cartons of live tropical fish are being stamped for shipment from Florida to customers up north; tropical fish are now the biggest individual item of air transport from Florida.

INTRODUCTION

The breeding of tropical fish on a commercial basis is being done today all over the world. While Russia does not have a tropical fish industry as we know it there are at least two tropical fish stores in Leningrad, three in Moscow, and perhaps others in the rest of the country. The proprietors of these establishments must, by virtue of the system under which they live, conduct their businesses after normal working hours, as they perform other duties for the State during the day. The vast majority of the fish sold in these shops are produced in Russia by hobbyists. In Hungary, also, the state has not yet nationalized pet shops.

Florida, in the United States, is by far the major tropical fish producing area. Other large and important breeding centers are to be found in East and West Germany, Hong Kong, Singapore, California, England, Holland, Denmark and Belgium.

With the tremendous strides being made in air transport, tropical fish are today available to anyone at nearly any point. The risk of loss in transport has virtually disappeared. Superior methods of packaging and insulating shipments bring the fish to their destination in fine and robust health, which is a welcome change from the conditions existing just a few shorts years ago.

The scope of the tropical fish industry (which a few facts and figures will reveal) immediately indicates that it is far from a small endeavor.

Tropical fish are the largest single air freight item from the state of Florida. In an average week between 5 and 6 thousand boxes containing an average of 175 individual fish per unit are shipped. This means that better than 1 million fish are produced and sold in Florida each week. 50 million fish each year is a conservative total. This does not include goldfish and this is *just* from Florida.

In the Tampa area alone there are 27 individuals who do nothing but raise various types of egg-laying and livebearing fish to supply the fish farmers with items they do not, or cannot, raise in sufficient quantity. These people, in the most part, derive their entire income from this work. They never ship fish, but devote all of their energies to supplying the various shippers in their neighborhood. In all instances their production is specialized. Guy Mollet raises Bettas; Jim Parker raises Bettas and Blood-Red Tuxedo swords; Bud Goddard raises Angelfish and Tiger Barbs; Jack Dias raises Black Tetras, Albino *Pristella* and Bleeding Heart Platies. This illustrates further the magnitude of the industry. In other parts of the United States this type of supplementary breeding also is being done, although in most instances by advanced hobbyists. The demand for good quality fish has never been satisfied. It apparently never will.

There are many smaller, private breeders throughout the world. This is Hiroshi Azuma, breeder of many rare fishes, shown at work in his breeding facility. Photo by H. Azuma.

SETTING UP THE HATCHERY

You will learn in the following pages how tropical fish are bred commercially.

It is absolutely essential before any such venture is started that you have a complete understanding of what is involved. It would be extremely foolhardy for any individual to invest any amount of money in equipment before knowing whether or not he can accomplish satisfactory results. This can be learned by breeding a few species on a small scale, keeping accurate records of your results. Only then can a valid conclusion be reached.

FOOD REQUIREMENTS

In order to raise healthy fish fast they must be fed an adequate and varied diet. Most large hatcheries mix their own dry foods and wet mashes, though commercial diets are usually better. Live foods are fed once or twice every day. Fish are fed a minimum of three times each day. Feeding less often will give poor results, whereas feeding more often will further reduce cannibalism and increase rate of growth.

Dry food is fed first, usually the first thing each morning. The amount of food used depends upon the amount of fish in the raising container. It should all be eaten in less than five minutes. The food is scattered over the surface of the container. It should *not* be delicately dropped into one corner. When the dry food is in a small area the larger fish crowd out the smaller ones and they are deprived of an equal share.

Commercially prepared dry foods are sifted into three sizes:—

(*a*) A dry powder for tiny fish.

(*b*) A medium-small grind for larger fish and full grown fish such as small Tetras, Danios, etc.

(*c*) A large coarse grind for breeding stock and young of fish that will grow to a large size such as *C. meeki, C. severum, P. scalare*, etc.

Fish meal is the basic ingredient of commercial dry foods. Various supplementary foods in dehydrated form such as shrimp meal, crab meal, blood meal, salmon egg meal, pablum, clam meal, beef meal, *Daphnia*, and fish roe are added. The important things are variety, balance and high protein.

Live food is fed several hours after the dry food, by which time the dry food should have been consumed. If it is not all eaten the fish are being overfed.

The very best and safest live food is brine shrimp. The tiny newly hatched nauplii are essential for breeding success. The danger of introducing harmful enemies such as *Hydra*, insect larvae, leeches, etc., is eliminated, since brine shrimp are free of fresh-water parasites. Frozen brine shrimp are especially valuable for adult fishes.

Daphnia is a live food that is cultured by all large fish hatcheries. It can be screened and separated into various sizes for feeding different sized fish. With a bit of care most of the dangerous pests that are introduced with *Daphnia* can be removed. Newly hatched brine shrimp can be raised to maturity in about 25 days if you have the skill and ability to do it. This can be used instead of *Daphnia*.

Daphnia is usually raised outdoors in large dirt pools without running water. The pool must be allowed to develop a goodly amount of protozoan life before *Daphnia* can be raised. Sheep manure and cotton-seed meal are the usual fertilizing agents. As the water clears additional amounts of fertilizer must be added or the culture will disappear.

Cyclops and rotifers are other smaller forms of live food that can be raised in the same manner as *Daphnia*.

Brine shrimp are the most important item in the diet of the baby fishes; here brine shrimp eggs are being hatched by the million.

Tubifex worms can be raised, but this is difficult and seldom practical. These can be collected in fair quantities in most places and stored for a considerable length of time. It is best to leave their collection to specialists.

Mosquito and gnat larvae (wigglers) are superior live foods presenting a dilemma for each user to work out for himself. If overfed you have just raised yourself a batch of mosquitoes!!

Fish eat fish, and baby fish are wonderful foods. Prolific fish such as the Blue Gourami, Red Paradise, Guppy, etc., are raised for food in many places.

White worms, *Drosophila*, bloodworms, *Chironomus* (midge larvae), glass worms, *Gammarus*, micro-worms, fairy shrimp, pond and ramshorn snails, meal worms, and earthworms are other forms of live foods that are used. They are available intermittently, and the attendant difficulties in rearing them in quantity make their use at times impractical.

WET MASHES AND COOKED FOODS

All of these can be prepared in quantity and frozen until needed. The following are all excellent fresh cooked foods. They can be fed singly or in combination with each other: chicken, turkey, fish, beef liver, muscle meats, fish roe, minced clam, boiled shrimp, lobster and crab.

Hatcheries all prepare a pastelike cooked mash. There is no best formula, although there are many different formulae. After cooking, the material is rendered pastelike with a blender. The mash is stiffened to the required consistency by the addition of dry food. It should be packaged in individual units each equivalent to a day's supply and frozen.

The basic ingredient of such a mash is quick cooking oatmeal. To this is added shrimp, liver, spinach, and/or egg yolk. Ingredients can be purchased already cooked and simply combined. The strained and chopped baby foods are perfect.

WATER AND WATER TREATMENT

Before you can breed fish you must be able to keep them alive and healthy. This is a great deal more complicated than most people realize.

You must research your fish. It is essential that you learn as much as possible about the fishes' natural habitat. This information will give you the knowledge to be able to offer the fish:

  (*a*) the correct temperature range.
  (*b*) the proper water composition.
  (*c*) its natural foods.
  (*d*) correct amounts of light.

All of the large successful hatcheries bring water from various locales for mixing and coloring the available natural waters. This is done to enable them to breed a large variety of fish, which would be impossible if they were limited to one fixed type of water.

Deep-well waters are almost sterile, as the lack of light inhibits bacterial and protozoan growth. Not so with river, pond and swamp waters. Exposed water must be treated before it can be used. Prolonged storage in the dark will help purify the water, but this isn't practical. Boiling the water is one safe method to kill off most of the undesirable life. Another method is to use chlorine water followed in about an hour's time by treatment with sodium thiosulphate (one grain to each gallon of water). This will not alter the pH or hardness of the water to any appreciable extent.

Local water departments will supply accurate and correct analysis of your water without charge at any time. In addition, most water departments for a small fee will analyze any water you might bring them. This is very important. There is no excuse for blind groping when the information is easily available.

If your breeding stock is raised in water radically different from the water in which they are to breed, results will be very disappointing. The vast majority of egg-layers come from soft waters on the acid side. When these fish are kept in alkaline water and not bred the eggs nearest the vent apparently calcify, making it impossible for the fish to reproduce. Such fish are not necessarily useless as breeding stock, for these calcified eggs can be stripped by hand with a gentle downward pressure. In a matter of weeks the fish can be bred. This isn't a technique that everyone can manage easily, but it can be done successfully with a bit of practice.

For good results, it is essential that fish be *reared* and *bred* in the same water. If you are aware of the type of water these fish will be kept in when offered for sale to the consumer, they can be gradually acclimatized to this type of water. Healthy fish have remarkable tolerance to pH and hardness changes.

There are many types of good water softening apparatus available today, and unless you are fortunate enough to have soft water from your tap, such an investment is almost a necessity. Water can be permanently demineralized with little difficulty, but I have never found a practical method to permanently acidify water. All of the recommended methods will acidify water, but, within 24 hours, the pH is back to where it started.

Fish have a remarkable tolerance to wide temperature ranges. The danger is sharp fluctuations in temperature. An Angel fish will live happily at 60° and also at 90°, but only if the change is made gradually. The higher the temperature the higher the metabolism. Fish require more food, more room and more oxygen at higher temperatures. The body processes slow down as the temperature is lowered. If it is too low growth will be inhibited. A happy medium is desired. A temperature range between 72° and 76° will give excellent results. When breeding the temperature is raised. A practical and simple method of doing this automatically is to store breeding stock in the tanks closest to the floor and the breeding tanks high. Since heat rises, the breeding tanks will be 5° to 10° warmer at all times.

PREVENTION AND TREATMENT OF DISEASE

Prevention is the key. If you meticulously adhere to certain basic rules you will be rarely troubled with disease. Briefly, these are the most important steps in preventing disease:

1. Nets and hands must be *wet* before a fish is handled.
2. A net is used *one* time in *one* container, and then it is sterilized before being used again. Potassium permanganate solutions and super-saturated copper solutions are used for sterilization purposes in most commercial establishments. Nets must, of course, be thoroughly washed before re-use.
3. Temperature control must be adequate. Nothing causes disease faster than rapid temperature changes. This is just as important up as down. The secret is constant thermostatically controlled heating equipment.
4. All new fish must be isolated. Three weeks is a minimum safe period to be certain the new stock is healthy before mixing them with other breeding stock.
5. Wild caught live foods such as cyclops, *Daphnia*, tubificid worms, glass worms, etc., must be watched carefully, particularly if they are to be used with young fish. Hydra, water tigers, water boatmen, etc., are almost always introduced in this fashion, that is, with live food.

In order to treat a sick fish it is mandatory that you be aware of what malady affects the fish. The use of a microscope is not essential, but it is at times a very useful tool.

A quick synopsis of the accepted commercial treatments is given below.

ICH (*Ichthyopthirius*). Success is often measured by rapidity in catching the disease. If it first becomes apparent by the time the fish are already dead and dying it is difficult to check and cure, but if observed early enough it can be cured without any loss at all. Mercurochrome in a regular commercial solution of 2% is very effective, but this must not be used on fish being raised for breeding stock or for your current breeders, as you can cause sterility with this treatment. When using mercurochrome the proper dosage is 2 drops to each gallon of water. If your water needs changing, siphon it down and add fresh water before treatment starts. Do not move the fish unless it is absolutely necessary. In addition to the mercurochrome use one teaspoonful of Epsom salts to each three gallons of water.

Malachite green, in most cases, just as effective as Mercurochrome, and will not sterilize your fish. A solution made of 5 grams of malachite green in a quart of distilled water is used. Put one drop to each gallon of affected water. This solution must be kept refrigerated or it will soon lose its potency.

Methylene blue and quinine, both of which are frequently mentioned as cures, are, in the writer's opinion, worthless in comparison with the above.

VELVET. Of all the common ailments velvet is the most difficult to diagnose. It is often confused with ich. The velvet granules are considerably smaller than ich, and unless you have unusually sharp eyes they will appear as a velvety coat on the fish's body.

Acriflavine and copper sulphate are the accepted and most successful treatments. To use copper sulphate obtain some of the chemical commonly known as "bluestone" and dissolve two heaping tablespoonsful in a pint of water. This will not completely dissolve, but will give you a super-saturated solution to work with. Use care in handling copper, for an overdose will be fatal. Use one drop to every 5 gallons of water. If the fish are not improved within 24 hours repeat the dose. This is the absolute maximum that can safely be employed.

Acriflavine can also kill fish and should not be overdosed. This is the same dye that the European chemists refer to as "trypaflavine." Two-grain tablets can be purchased. A stock solution is made by dissolving 8 tablets in a pint of hot distilled water. Ten drops to the gallon will give excellent results. Store in a dark bottle out of the sun and the solution will keep its strength for a long time.

These Pearl Gouramis are beautiful, but the species is easily bruised. Timmerman photo.

C - 10.00

NEON TETRA DISEASE. Using commercial formaldehyde, 2 drops to the gallon, will cure Tetras in a matter of hours.

MOUTH FUNGUS, TAIL ROT, INFECTED WOUNDS, BADLY BRUISED FISH. Are all best treated with "Tetracycline Hydrochloride." Unfortunately, this is a very expensive drug. 250 mg. to 5 gallons is a minimum daily dosage, and double this amount is advised.

Neons are not the only Tetras that contract Neon Tetra disease; these Pristellas are also susceptible.

Two other invaluable medications are methylene blue and Epsom salts. The former is a most effective and safe germicidal agent. The latter stimulates the secretion of body slime on fish. In reasonable doses, neither can harm fish, and these are best used in combination with the drugs mentioned specifically to treat the various common diseases.

Any observant person will in time be able to recognize trouble even if he is 50 feet from the afflicted aquarium. Sick fish do not act in their normal manner. Each species is different, but by observation you will unconsciously recognize that something is wrong by the fish's behavior. You must immediately discover what is wrong and try to correct it.

HOW TO BREED FISH

BREEDING STOCK. Adult fish should be avoided and purchased only when no other stock is available. Your potential breeders should be raised in the same water in which they will be spawned. When your fish are of an age to attempt breeding, sexes should be separated. By keeping them isolated in this manner a larger yield will result. However, this can be a dangerous practice unless your breeders are being used on a prearranged schedule. If mature egg-layers are kept by themselves, and not bred often enough, many will become eggbound.

SETTING UP. All breeding establishments set up a minimum of 10 tanks of a specific species at a time and more often a set-up will consist of 75 to 100 tanks of the item to be bred. Disregarding for the moment the more difficult fish, an average of 8 spawns out of every ten set up is considered fair. The really fine breeders, often achieve a fertile spawn in every tank set up.

The obvious point, of course, is that fish which are not properly conditioned and ready to breed should never be utilized.

Most fish will spawn within 24 hours. Some fish (Lemon Tetras, Black Ruby Barbs, etc.) will not start spawning until 48 to 72 hours have elapsed. With the exception of fish that are permanently set up (Scalare, Ramirezi, Kribensis, Bumble Bees, etc.) all breeding attempts will be abandoned after 5 days without result. Fish are never fed while set up.

REMOVE BREEDERS. The majority of spawns will occur in the first hours of the new day. There is never a mad rush to remove the parents, for even the worst egg-eaters will not eat their eggs until spawning is completed. This is not a matter of a few minutes, but often many hours. If spawning commences at daybreak the parents should not be removed for at least 4 hours. A 5-inch net with an ⅛th-inch mesh should be used so that the net itself will hold the parents but will allow all of the eggs to slip through. After the parent fish are captured and before they are completely removed from the spawning tank the net should be sharply struck on the side of the aquarium to dislodge any eggs that may have adhered.

BREEDING EQUIPMENT AND RACKS. There are no hard and fast rules in so far as constructing racks are concerned. As the tanks must be moved on and off the rack frequently the ease with which this can be accomplished should be kept in mind. Angle iron cut to shape and bolted together makes the most practical rack. Bolting, not welding, is suggested, because if it becomes necessary to move your installation it can then easily be accomplished by removing a few bolts. If possible the breeding rack should be in the

Economics dictates that every available inch of space be put to productive use. These concrete vats are built on what would otherwise be non-productive floor space.

center of the room. Utilize the floor by building completely around the perimeter of the room a series of concrete vats. Size is dependent on the amount of fish they are to be used to hold or raise. Breeding stock can be kept in these vats, but it is more practical to use them for rearing young and raising new breeders. The actual current breeders should be in glass-fronted containers where they can be constantly observed. Large wooden casks are to be had for a fraction of their worth from importers of Spanish olives. These hold about 200 gallons and are ideal containers for treating, holding and ageing water.

An electric water pump to facilitate the moving of water is most important.

The roof of the breeding room should be modified to allow for an ample amount of natural sunlight. The cost of skylights can be repaid quickly by utilizing the light to raise aquatic plants in your concrete vats. There is always a ready market for fine aquatic plants. As a tremendous amount of water must be used, be aware of the need for adequate floor drains. Drains are simple to install during construction, but very troublesome when an after-thought.

Although tanks used in a hatchery need not be fancy, they must be sturdy and built for years of rugged use. These tanks have seen a lot of service.

Breed your fish in ample-sized aquariums. An over-sized container will help, but an under-sized restrictive container will inhibit breeding efforts. Containers smaller than eight gallons are seldom used. The use of stainless steel tanks is wise, though plain galvanized aquariums may be used. A well made aquarium is a sound investment. A bargain aquarium invariably costs three times what you think you are saving. It will fail you when it is most needed. Before purchasing your aquariums be sure to have a complete written understanding of your guaranties with the seller. It is further suggested that the seller make you aware of just what will be charged for such repairs as replacing broken glass and stopping leaks.

The breeding room should be kept as close to a sterile condition as possible. Visitors should be discouraged. Cleanliness is essential.

COMMERCIAL BREEDING TECHNIQUES

Zebra Fish (*B. rerio*) **and Pearl Danio** (*B. albolineatus*)

Since these fish can be handled in an identical manner we will discuss them together as group spawners that drop non-adhesive eggs. They are best spawned in a breeding trap. As many as six trios (2 females-1 male) are placed in the spawning trap, depending upon the size of the trap. The best results are obtained when the breeders are covered with no more than 1 inch of water. Fifteen to twenty set-ups are worked at the same time. The breeders are left in the breeding traps until the young start the free-swimming stage. This is usually the fourth day after the fish have been set up. The fry should be fed with infusoria often and copiously. After three days the fry are removed to larger vats for raising. If the weather is warm enough fry can be put outdoors directly into concrete or dirt pools for raising. These fish can stand an outside temperature as low as 30°F. when grown and acclimated, but the babies will succumb if the temperature is below 60°F. when they are put outside. The breeders often injure themselves in the confined traps while breeding. It is advisable to medicate them with sodium sulfathiozole and Epsom salts after removal from the breeding trap. Zebra Fish are voracious egg eaters if given the opportunity.

If allowed to spawn in deep water, adult Pearl Danios will almost always eat many of their eggs before they drop to the safety of the bottom. Photo by R. Zukal.

Danio malabaricus, the Giant Danio, lays adhesive eggs. For this reason they are usually spawned in thick mats of mosses or similar plants to keep the parents from reaching the eggs.

Giant Danio (*D. malabaricus*)

Unlike their smaller cousins described above, Giant Danios have adhesive eggs. This makes spawning traps impractical. Giant Danios are bad egg-eaters and a thick spawning medium must be utilized. The most common *egg receiver* is Spanish Moss, which is placed thickly and completely over the bottom of the spawning tank. A single pair is set up in each aquarium. Breeders are 3 to 4 inches in length and a large aquarium should be used (10 to 15 gallons). A well conditioned pair will throw 600 to 1,000 eggs. They grow fast. The secret of raising quantity is to give the young plenty of room.

Three Spot or Blue Gourami (*Trichogaster trichopterus*)

This is a hardy fish and will withstand temperatures as low as 55°. The adults are better able to withstand cold than the youngsters. The fish will spawn naturally in a dirt pool, but no production can be achieved this way.

The standard procedure is to set up about 30 pairs at a time each pair in 8 gallon aquaria. Water should be 4-inch depth. They spawn prolifically in water on the hard and alkaline side. A few Water Hyacinths (or similar floating plants) should be put in each tank. This helps anchor the bubble nest. The tank should be empty of all foreign matter except for the floating plant. There does not have to be a wild rush to remove parents after spawning, because this fish seldom will eat its young. Two days after the fry are free-swimming the parents can be removed. This fish is extremely prolific and it is usual to hatch more than 1,000 fry from a spawn. The parents can be bred again within 2 weeks. If the fry are to be raised indoors the problem will be to feed the young sufficient food, and yet keep the container clean. Most Blue Gouramis raised commercially are bred from April through July and, depending on the size of the vats or pools available, taken outside and released when 6 or 8 days old. They are harvested in the Fall before extreme cold weather sets in and held inside for sale throughout the winter months. The fish does not command a high price, so it is impractical to attempt to supplement stocks by indoor raising.

Opaline or Cosby Gourami are handled in a manner identical to the above, but as this is a higher-bred strain of *T. trichopterus* yields are smaller and the percentage of successful spawns will be lower.

Pearl Gourami (*Trichogaster leeri*) are handled in a similar manner, with the following exceptions. The fish is extremely soft-bodied and unusually susceptible to fungus. They must be handled with extreme care. Since they will not trap it is dangerous to attempt to raise them in an outside dirt pool. It is more practical to raise them in large concrete vats where they can be safely caught with nets.

The Pearl Gourami is almost as simple to breed as the common Blue Gourami, but the fish are more susceptible to fungus at all stages.

Siamese Fighting Fish (*Betta splendens*)

This is one of the most simple egg-layers to breed. The ability to raise a majority of the spawn is the difficult part. The fish breeds simply in a small container. A one-gallon tank is sufficient. Water level should be no more than 3 inches. The female must be given a hiding place and this can be done with clean aquatic plants, pieces of slate or other rocks. The male will, in most instances, kill the female unless precautions are taken. Remove the female immediately upon completion of spawning. The male will then repair the nest and return the young that fall through. It is safe to keep the male with the young for 48 hours after the babies are free-swimming. The young are fed heavily with infusoria and after another 48 hours are moved to a larger rearing tank or vat. At this time various spawns can be combined.

If you are to raise *Bettas* successfully they must get adequate food . . . often

A nest-tending male Betta; eggs are visible under the nest.

and plentifully. If the male is removed from the spawn prematurely the young will drown. All Labyrinth Fish grow unequally. While this is true to some extent with most fish it is more pronounced in this family. As the *Bettas* grow, the males, which will be obvious by their longer fins, are removed and placed in individual pint jars. They are raised in isolation or they will tear each other's fins apart. *Bettas* should be raised on live food only, because it is difficult to feed dry foods in a confined space without fouling the water and losing the fish. Brine shrimp, tubificid worms, and *Daphnia* are the best foods. It should take no more than 5 months to raise a male *Betta* to maturity. If it takes longer the fault lies in the diet.

Bettas can survive in terribly foul water by utilizing their labyrinth chambers. However, to raise good males the water must be changed at least one time before sale and oftener if possible. A percentage of all jars should be changed each week. If this is done methodically it can be accomplished without undue labor, but if it is allowed to accumulate there will never be sufficient empty jars to move a quantity into clean water at the same time. The technique is simple. The entire jar is poured (including the fish) through a 3-inch net and then the fish is dumped into a shallow pan. When the pan contains 25 to 50 fish they are netted out individually and placed into clean jars.The dirty jars are then cleaned and filled with proper water. They are then ready for next week's changes.

Rainbow Pumilus Gourami *(Trichopsis pumilus)*

This is a recent introduction and a most delightful fish. It has no bad habits and is easily raised. The fully grown Pumilus is barely 1½ inches. They should be spawned like *Betta splendens*, the exception being that the male is not aggressive and will not injure the female. The *Pumilus* nest is considerably smaller than a *Betta* nest and seldom as large as a nickel. The nest is invariably built in a corner of the tank; as it is small, the metal corners of the tank can obscure it from view, so you must check carefully. *Pumilus* is a prolific but slow-growing fish.

Angel Fish *(P. scalare)*

This is certainly one of the very best fish for the small breeder to produce. Spawns are large and the young, if properly fed, can be of saleable size in 8 weeks. Most important, there is always a ready market for the fish.

Once a compatible pair is obtained they can be expected to produce some 25 spawns per year which should yield some 5,000 to 10,000 saleable fry.

When selecting breeders it makes little sense to attempt to short cut and purchase a so called "mated pair". Invariably what you will obtain will be a proven pair BUT the hitch is that the fish are rapidly approaching the end of their productive life as breeders. The only practical approach is to purchase young, medium-sized fish and grow them to maturity together in a large tank.

In this maturing aquarium is usually a piece of slate, but any number of other types of inert material can be used, such as colored rigid plastic tubing or sheeting, rocks, a large Amazon Sword Plant of the broad leaf variety or a sheet of ground glass or other opaque glass. When the fish have attained sexual maturity they will pair off by themselves. The trick is to be able to single out the pair from the group. This can be done with a bit of practice.

It is perhaps more common with Angel Fish than any other Cichlid for two females to pair off. This necessitates accurate records of spawns so that if infertile eggs are obtained three consecutive times the pair (?) can be discarded.

An aquarium of 10-gallon capacity is ideal for Angels. In the Tampa, Florida area an aquarium designed by Joseph Cooley has found much favor. The advantage is that the height and the shape makes for easily arranged spawning batteries.

The breeding tank will contain an air stone, a piece of slate, suitable water and nothing else.

Success in breeding Angel Fish is more dependent on food than any other single factor. Variety is the secret. The very best foods are, in order:—

> Baby Guppies (first feed the Guppies heavily with dry food)
> Tubifex Worms
> Mosquito Larvae
> Water Boatmen
> Earthworms (chopped and cleaned)
> *Daphnia*
> White Worms

The eggs should always be removed from the breeding tank on the slate upon which they were laid. They should be placed in one-gallon aquariums containing water identical to that in the breeding tank. A moderate stream of air from an airstone should be played against the slate, which should be slanted. This is important to prevent an accumulation of detritus on the eggs. The water should be colored with methylene blue to prevent excessive bacterial activity.

When the babies are free-swimming they must be fed infusoria. After they have been fed for four days they can be removed to larger quarters for raising. At this point they are able to take newly hatched brine shrimp. Feed a little at time until you are sure they able are to take it, and then keep food in front of them constantly. They will grow very fast.

Breeders that consistently throw a percentage of malformed young should be destroyed.

Fancy Angel Fish (veiltails, black lace, all-blacks and the various combinations of these) are handled indentically. However, you will find much larger percentages of runts in these spawns. These are not necessarily bad or weak

Although Angel Fish will lay eggs on large leaves and the glass sides of the aquarium, it is more convenient to use a piece of slate or plastic which can be removed from the aquarium when it is covered with eggs.

fish and generally are the more desirable specimens since they rarely eat their spawn. At 30 days of age all of the smallest fish should be removed and raised separately. They will quickly put on normal growth when they no longer have to compete with their larger brothers and sisters for the available food.

Large Cichlids. Unfortunately this group of fish has fallen into disfavor and most of the staple sellers of years gone by are no longer called for by the buyers. Several items, however, are consistent sellers.

Astronatus ocellatus (Oscars) are huge fish, and full-grown fish are seldom seen outside of breeding establishments. They are extremely long lived and very hardy.

The writer at one time owned two breeding pairs. At the time of disposal one pair was 14 years old and the other pair 8 years old. Both were still producing young in normal quantities. These fish are extremely difficult to pair and must be allowed to pair themselves. As it takes a minimum of two years to raise a breeder, and the breeders need enormous amounts of space, it isn't a task to be lightly undertaken. In addition, the fish require copious amounts of live food (such as small goldfish, ghost shrimp, crawfish and bait fish) and this is not always easily available. When the fish are finally old enough to breed they must be paired. Unless watched closely, incompatible fish will kill each other, and then two years of work is finished.

These Oscars, *Astronotus ocellatus,* just ate a large number of recently laid eggs. Like many other cichlids, eggs or young should not be left in the aquarium with their parents. Photo by H. Rofe.

If you are still interested, and haven't given up the idea of breeding Oscars by this time, look at the other side of the story. A proven pair is like a money machine. If properly fed and conditioned they will breed continually. An average of 25 spawns per pair per year is not unusual and this should yield at least $3,000.00 at 25¢ per baby.

C. severum is another large Cichlid, although not quite so huge as Oscars. They will produce almost as many as Oscars in number of young, but, unlike Oscars, there is a task to sell all of the *Severum* that a good pair will produce.

C. festivum, C. meeki, A. pulcher, C. biocellatum, C. nigrofasciatum, are all bred and sold in limited quantities.

Geophagus braziliensis is the only member of the genus easily bred. It is a beautiful fish and relatively new. It sells very well.

Tilapia (mouthbreeders) sell as novelty items, but the demand is lessening as the novelty wears off.

Symphysodon discus and other *"Discus"* *species* are unquestionably the most desirable of all tropical fish from a strictly commercial outlook. The very finest professional and amateur breeders have devoted many years to breeding this fish. Many times it has appeared that a breakthrough was at hand, but this has not happened to date. In checking back over the years without exception all of the people who have bred "Discus" have subsequently given up in frustration.

Cichlasoma meeki, the Firemouth, spawns easily and is a popular seller in pet shops.

Aequidens curviceps is an uncommon but very pretty little South American Cichlid that is fairly easy to spawn.

Dwarf Cichlids are much more popular than ever before. They do not have any of the objectionable habits of their larger brethren. They are all very hardy fish. Temperature plays an important part in breeding this group. *A. ramirezi* will spawn best at 90° and none will breed easily at less than 80°. Small tanks are adequate; slate bottoms are best and they should be covered with a half-inch of well washed gravel. Broken flower pots make ideal spawn-

Kribensis are very colorful African Cichlids which spawn readily when given up-turned flower pots or similar dark caves. The egg laying occurs upside-down.

ing mediums and enough should be put into the breeding tank to give the fish room to hide. Young can be raised with the parents, although most breeders will remove the parents and raise the young in the breeding tanks. Some of the new Dwarf Cichlids from Africa, such as *Julidochromis*, *Lamprologus*, *Tropheus*, *Nannochromis*, and *Pelmatochromis* species, are among the prettiest of all tropical fish. If specimens can be obtained it will be found worthwhile to breed these, as prices will always be high.

A new bright yellow Ramirezi is now available from one of the largest hatcheries.

C - 24.00

Pseudotropheus lanisticola and other Mbunas from Lake Malawi are mouthbrooders, holding the eggs and young in the mouth. Here the female swallows sperm from the male to fertilize the eggs in her mouth. Photo by Ken Lucas, Steinhart Aquarium.

Rams are among the most popular of all Dwarf Cichlids.

Halfbeaks—*Dermogenys pusillus*. This unique livebearer is bred with great success as follows: A large (3′ x 3′ x 1′) shallow aquarium or wooden vat should be employed. A 1-inch square wooden rod is cut to the length of the opposite corner and when floated in the vat will divide the container into two equal triangles. One half is left completely bare and the other half is thickly filled with Hornwort. The advantage of Hornwort over most other floating plants is that it will resist decay for a long period of time even in dim light. Fifteen female and 5 male Halfbeaks are placed into the vat for breeding purposes. Live food should be in front of the breeders at all times, for these fish are extremely cannibalistic. The combination of adequate hiding space and ample food ensures success. Breeding occurs at any hour and continually. Babies should be individually captured and removed. Thirty to forty young daily is the average yield. Be alert for the inevitable introduction of dangerous aquatic insect enemies with live food. If these get to be a problem the best and easiest cure is to re-make the entire set-up.

The Halfbeak *Nomorhamphus celebensis* is a new and spectacular import that commands a high price. Photo by H. J. Richter.

Not too long ago the White Cloud was looked down upon as "the poor man's Neon";
today White Clouds are more expensive than young Neons.

White Clouds—*Tanichthys albonubes.* While extremely easily bred this fish
is often in short supply. The outstanding advantage this fish possesses is the
fact that it will eat neither its eggs nor its young. This is a decided advantage
to a breeder who cannot always be with his fish when success demands his
presence. There are many ways to breed this fish but the two methods
described below yield the greatest results. The writer personally favors the
first.

(*a*) Two trios are placed in a 7-gallon tank bare except for a fair-sized
clump of Spanish Moss. The aquarium should be checked daily
until the first young are observed. The breeders are removed 24
hours after and tested for 10 days before being set up again. At this
point the young must be given infusoria. They are very small when
hatched, so they should be fed on this for at least one week. At
that point a bit of brine shrimp is added, but the infusoria must be
continued. As eggs are laid over a period of days, new young will
hatch days after the first are observed.

(*b*) Larger quantities of breeders are kept in concrete vats or large
wooden vats. The container is heavily stocked with plants and
usually is old and mulm-filled to insure a ready stock of infusoria.
White Cloud babies come to the surface and stay the first few days
of their free-swimming life so it is a simple matter to remove them
with a small net and rear them separately.

White Clouds do best in hard, alkaline water. Best method to sex is by body
shape; if the females aren't quickly apparent they are not yet ready to breed.
Males have longer and more colorful dorsal fins.

C - 27.00

The black fins of the male *Puntius nigrofasciatus* readily distinguish it from the pale female. Photo by R. Zukal.

Puntius (Barbus) Species. All of these fish are bred in an identical manner. The size of the breeders determines the size of the container. While not as fussy as Characins in so far as water is concerned, they do best in soft, slightly acid water. This group has a tendency to get eggbound, and care must be taken to see that breeders are bred frequently or left together so that the females may rid themselves of eggs. Spanish Moss "skeletons" are the best spawning medium, but any similar sterile material will work. Commercial breeders do not like to use plants, the reason being that plants are carriers of enemies. Synthetic fibers are now being used with wonderful success.

Tanks should be bare except for the spawning medium. Spawning starts an hour after daylight, and breeders should be removed as soon as they are finished. The newborn young are relatively large, and after a few days on infusoria are ready to take brine shrimp. After three days on brine shrimp they should be removed to a larger container for raising. *Puntius* as a group require a great deal of oxygen and cannot be crowded. They are susceptible to *Oodinium* (particularly *P. oligolepis* and *P. nigrofasciatus*). A copper sponge placed in the raising container will eliminate this trouble.

Unless you have a large or varied outlet for sales it is impractical to breed the more exotic varieties. The best commercial *Puntius* in order of importance are *tetrazona*, *titteya*, *everetti*, *nigrofasciatus* and *schuberti*. Two very good though difficult *Puntius* are *hexazona* and *lineatus*. The largest and most prolific spawners are *everetti*, *lateristriga*, *filamentosus*, and *arulius*. Two of the most dramatic are the seldom seen Africans, *candens* and *hulstaerti*. These are found in such extremely acid water that it is doubtful they will ever be adjusted to normal water conditions. I wouldn't advise wasting time with them, although the returns would be very high if successful. *Gelius* is a lovely small fish with not much demand. *Oligolepis* is very pretty but grows very, very slowly and only large specimens are in demand. Other Africans such as *callipterus, holotaenia, usumbarae,* and *viviparus* are not pretty enough to be of lasting interest. Not much has been done with *schwanenfeldi* and the specimens available have all been expensive. It is a pretty fish but grows very large. No mention has been made of *conchonius* or *ticto,* because these will breed by themselves in dirt pools and are tremendously prolific. They sell at low prices. It would be of little practical use to breed these where space is limited.

Rasbora Species: The most popular *Rasbora* is *heteromorpha,* the "Harlequin". Unfortunately, this fish until now has never been bred in a practical manner. It is very common in its native Malaya and large quantities of imported specimens make it available at reasonable prices. This fish can be bred in pairs or in community schools. The best method is 3 females and 2 males. The species most commonly and easily bred is *trilineata,* the Scissortail. This is a larger than the average *Rasbora* and very prolific. A good spawning will yield 500 young. The fish supposedly grows to 8 inches in length, but I have never seen a fish larger than 4 inches and the average breeders are $2\frac{1}{2}$ to 3 inches in length. They are a soft bodied fish and great care must be taken in handling them, as they bruise and fungus very easily. Other varieties of *Rasbora,* such as *maculata, pauciperforata, dorsiocellata,* and *borapentensis* are bred commercially but in very limited numbers. *Trilineata* should be bred in large aquaria for best results. The water should be on the acid side and soft. Spanish Moss is an ideal medium. If spawning hasn't been accomplished in 48 hours chances are that they will not spawn. It is impractical to leave them set up for longer periods. They grow fast and are omnivorous. If fed properly the young will be saleable in 90 days.

The Tiger Barb is the most commonly seen Barb and certainly the one most often spawned by aquarists.

Although not colorful, *Rasbora trilineata* is hardy and prolific. It is moderately popular in the hobby.

Not many *Rasbora maculata* are bred in commercial quantity, for if the fish is not attractively displayed in the dealer's tanks it will rarely sell.

C - 30.00

Undoubtedly *Rasbora heteromorpha* is the most popular *Rasbora*; it is colorful, hardy, cheap, and not too difficult to spawn.

Catfish: Any and all Catfish of suitable aquarium size can be sold with little effort. Even the most bizarre and rare types can be sold easily, as this entire group holds great interest for advanced hobbyists and owners of family community tanks. Tremendous quantities of the more easily obtainable types are imported. The various South American collectors ship in excess of 8 million wild caught specimens each year. The only catfish that are bred commercially are *Callichthys, Hoplosternum thoracatum, Corydoras,* mostly *aeneus* and *hastatus,* and one variety of African Glass Catfish.

Callichthys and *Hoplosternum* are bred in an identical manner. They require large quarters that should have a minimum of 350 square inches of surface. Water depth should be 5 inches. Water should be slightly alkaline and medium soft. These fish are bubblenest builders and must have something floating to anchor the nest and eggs. I have seen and used the following egg anchorers successfully and they will all work: a 6-inch square of polystyrene, an aluminum pie plate, a piece of wood and various floating plants. The parents guard the nest and young and are not interested in eating either eggs or progeny. They spawn prolifically but are not easy to induce to spawn. Breeders are 4 to 7 inches long and the young grow rapidly. The female is invariably larger than the male. The young can immediately take brine shrimp.

C - 31.00

Corydoras are bred as follows: It is most important that the breeders be large enough and old enough. The aquarium should be of at least 10-gallon capacity. The bottom should be covered with well washed gravel. A few clean *Cryptocoryne* plants will give the breeders more security. Breeders should be placed in the spawning tank at night, and, if in condition, will spawn the following morning. If spawning is not accomplished in 48 hours, change breeders. Eggs will be placed on the plant leaves or sides of the aquarium and will number two to three hundred. While it is true the parents do not show any further interest in the eggs and usually will not eat them, it is best to remove the parents immediately after spawning. After this is done add methylene blue to the tank. Raise the young in the breeding tank. The eggs hatch in five days and the yield is never more than 30 or 40% of the eggs laid.

Why there is such a consistent number of infertile eggs has never been satisfactorily explained. The young are large enough to take brine shrimp and micro-worms immediately. 7.4 pH and medium soft brown water yield best results. The newest development in *Corydoras* is an albino *Corydoras paleatus* which is being bred in very limited quantities in Belgium, where the sport developed. As this is an unusually attractive color variety it is hoped that it will not be long before this fish is available all over the world.

Plecostomus have never been commercially produced, although they are being tried by advanced aquarists all the time. The available quantity is low, and supply hasn't approximated 25% of the demand for several years. This

Some Catfish get too large for small tanks; their popularity is consequently restricted.

Corydoras burgessi, a beautiful new import that is representative of the many new catfishes reaching the market today. Photo by Dr. W. E. Burgess.

Corydoras paleatus are now more often seen in Europe than the United States, but they are still bred commercially in this country.

fish presents a real challenge and would be very worthwhile if it could be bred. I witnessed a successful spawn of *plecostomus* several years ago. The fish spawned inside a large piece of drain pipe in a concrete vat. An additional hint from the writer's own collecting experience is that *plecostomus* spawn in holes in the mud banks of rivers, streams and creeks. Large specimens are extremely plentiful in nature.

Characins (Tetras). The most important factor in breeding Tetras is to grow and condition your breeders properly. If correctly handled any common member of this family can be spawned every three weeks. If time and space permits best results will be realized by keeping the sexes separate. The danger, of course, is in not utilizing your egg-filled females often enough. This will cause an eggbound vent and makes subsequent breeding attempts difficult and sometimes impossible. The size of the breeding container necessarily depends on the size and number of breeders to be used. Characins, more than any other group, can successfully be bred by utilizing more than one pair at a time. When group spawnings are attempted the usual ratio used is 2 males for every 3 females. The danger of eggs being eaten is greatly increased in group spawnings and constant vigil must be employed to prevent a large loss through negligence. The most widely employed spawning mediums used are Spanish Moss, knitting yarns and fine-leaved plants such as Hornwort or *Cabomba*. Live plants are being used in large commercial establishments less frequently as despite all precautions, they will carry undesirable organisms into the spawning tanks.

Thayeria boehlkei, one of the Penguins, is commonly seen in aquarium shops but is not bred in quantity. This is true of many other marginally popular Tetras.

The GTO, a long-finned Black Tetra variety popular in recent years. Long-finned mutants occur in many different species of fish and are almost always popular.

The water used for Tetras depends upon the fish although the vast majority prefer a soft, light brown water of 6.4 to 6.8 pH. You must research your chosen fish to best determine the characteristics of the natural conditions where it is found in the wild. The pH figures given above would yield poor results with Rummy-nose Tetras and Bleeding Heart Tetras, as these fish require *extremely* acid water. The exact opposite type of water (hard and alkaline) is preferred by Bloodfins and Swordtail Characins. This group should be of particular interest to those of us who have limited space available.

Tetras in most instances are small, and large quantities can be raised in a comparatively small area. At this writing the most popular Characins commercially produced are:

Black Tetra (*Gymnocorymbus ternetzi*)
Head and Tail Lights (*H. ocellifer*)
Serpae (*H. serpae*)
Serpae Minor (*H. callistus*)
Pristella (*Pristella riddlei*)
Albino Pristella
Blind Cave Fish (*Anoptichthys jordani*)
Penguins (*Thayeria obliqua*)
Von Rio (*H. flammeus*)
Lemon Tetra (*H. pulchripinnis*)
Glo Lights (*H. gracilis*)
Bloodfins (*A. rubripinnis*)
Rosaceus (*H. rosaceus*)

All of the above can be sold easily and in good volume. This list most certainly shouldn't imply restrictions as to the variety bred as there are many others that can profitably be bred and sold.

Neons, Pencil Fish, *Metynnis*, Hatchet Fish, *Anostomus*, *Leporinus* and *Chilodus* are impractical to breed either because of difficulty in propagating or the extremely low prices for imported specimens. All are available in large quantities from foreign exporters of tropical fish.

Cyprinodonts: This group can only be described in broad language as the variety of reproductive habits they employ would easily make a full length book. The group is tremendously fertile, but few species are given to large spawnings. The most commercial Cyprinodonts are:

> Flag Fish (*Jordanella floridae*)
> Fundulus (*Fundulus chrysotus*)
> Fire Killies (*Nothobranchius* species)
> Medaka (*Oryzias latipes*)
> Panchax Lineatus (*A. lineatus*)
> Lyretails (*A. australe*)
> Panchax Chaperi (*E. chaperi*)

This is a most interesting family of fishes and will give a devotee much delight in accomplishment. The suspense attendant to a six-month delay in hatching *Nothobranchius rachovi* makes any of Hollywood's suspense-dramas tame by comparison.

There apparently is a very steady demand for all varieties of "Panchax." This group would be a worthwhile specialty for any small breeder.

Breeding of the *Nothobranchius* species is best done intensively, on a small scale. This beautiful fish is *Nothobranchius rachovi*.

Easy breeders, these *Epiplatys chaperi* are old favorites.

Flag Fish are colorful natives of American waters, but their scrappiness holds down their appeal to the fish-buying public.

RAISING LIVEBEARERS IN OUTSIDE POOLS

The size of this type of business is best illustrated by the accompanying aerial photograph. The dirt pool method of propagating tropical fish is of comparatively recent origin. Albert Greenberg of Tampa and the late H. Woolf, who dug their first dirt pools by hand in the early 1930's, started an industry that today supplies the majority of all tropical fish sold. Their choice of location (in the vicinity of Tampa, Florida) has proven to be excellent. Today this area supports some 30 different fish farms. The water table is extremely high and even in the driest years fresh water remains within 5 feet of the surface. For the most part the temperature seldom falls to a chilling point. Vast underground water reserves are available, and by utilizing the pressure from deep wells (500 to 1,500 feet) a flow of warm water (74°F. constant the year round) can be fed into each pool. This not only warms the water in the winter and cools it in the summer, but also helps control the ever present dangers of fouling, stagnation and drought.

The sizes of individual dirt pools vary. The preference of the individual operator is the governing factor, but generally speaking a pool of 75 to 100 feet in length, 15 feet wide and 7 feet deep (at the deepest end) is most commonly used. The water level will remain constant, as a 3-inch overflow drain is provided for each pool. This carries the excess water off into drainage ditches.

Grading and sorting are two extremely important phases of the commercial hatchery business. Once the fishes are removed from the pools, the work has only begun.

An aerial view of a large but compactly arranged fish farm in Florida.

Small trucks with a relatively large payload are the most efficient means of transporting equipment and supplies around a fish farm.

A dirt pool such as the one described above can be dug in two and a half hours. A half-yard bucket dragline is used. The dirt removed is banked around the perimeter of the pool to give additional protection against flood and erosion. One end is always dug deeper than the other. This enables the water to collect at the deepest end, when a pool must be pumped dry, thus facilitating cleaning and poisoning.

As a general rule varieties are not mixed in the same pool. The reason for this is not necessarily because the fish will or can interbreed, but rather that the eventual culling operation makes it far too time-consuming to be practical.

The most important single factor for a successful operation is the quality of the original stocking. Quality of a livebearer is determined by two equally important factors:

    (a) color and body development

    (b) purity of strain.

These desirable traits are accomplished by careful selective breeding. This is a constant and most important part of the fish farmer's work. New strains are always in the process of development. In recent years the increased variety of livebearer strains has made a virtual riot of rich colors available to everyone at most reasonable prices.

It is a constant source of pleasure and wonder to realize that from the original dull greens and grays available from the wild platy fish selective breeding has produced 23 standard varieties. To further illustrate this tremendous variety, simply check any offering sheet from a Florida fish farmer and you will see that they all work with 5 basic species. These are Guppies, Mollies, Swordtails, Platies and Platy Variatus. The last list I checked (1961) indicated that from these 5 original species 67 different color varieties are offered.

The life span of the average pool is approximately one and a half years. At the end of that period the dirt pool must be completely reset. This means that the pool must be pumped dry. This is done with a portable 4-inch water pump run by a gasoline motor. As soon as the pool is dry the treatment starts. Hydrated lime is carefully thrown on the now exposed sides and bottom, one hundred and fifty pounds being the minimum amount used. This will sweeten the soil and also kill any remaining fish. The pool is then allowed to refill itself. This will usually take 48 hours. Another three or four days are allowed to pass, and then the pool is fertilized with cotton-seed meal, sheep manure, etc. This will start the food cycle (bacteria→protozoa→crustaceans→fish). A few days after the application of the fertilizer live *Daphnia* is added. At the end of three weeks the pool is ready to receive fish, and if all has been properly done the pool will be teeming with microscopic life. This will give the new stock a fast start. It will take a minimum of eight to twelve months before this pool is ready for harvest. During this time the pool must be kept clean of

Large pools must first be pumped partially dry before seining operations are begun.

This fish farmer is netting brine shrimp to feed to young fishes.

weeds; this is best done with arsenic compounds which must be carefully applied. Frogs, snakes, birds, water insects, crawfish, drought, flood, excessive heat, excessive cold, water fouling, and the introduction of wild fish by birds are just some of the problems that beset the fish farmer. It is not a business for faint hearts or weak backs.

Fish are removed from the pools by trapping. The bait used is a fish meal paste. Two types of traps are employed. The most popular trap is a large wire basket trap which is set in the afternoon and allowed to fill with fish until needed the next day. As these are made of $\frac{1}{4}$-inch hardware cloth, and cannot be overcrowded, there is no danger of the fish suffocating. Smaller plastic or glass "barrel traps" are used during the day. These must be carefully supervised. If too many fish are trapped too quickly they will suffocate. Work starts at the crack of dawn, as the most productive trapping can be done in the first two hours of daylight.

Two methods of grading are currently being employed. The older and more efficient method from a cost point of view is to have the fish graded on the spot in the field. There is no advantage to this other than speed and the subsequent savings in labor cost. The disadvantages are many. The people grading are not supervised and they always have the pressure of time on them, as they have other traps working which must be watched closely. As a result they must at times work faster than is possible to do a good job. In addition, the grading is done outdoors and it is inevitable that at times of extreme heat or cold the water used for the grading purposes will become over-heated or severely

A wire basket trap in operation; the fishes can swim in, but they cannot get out again.

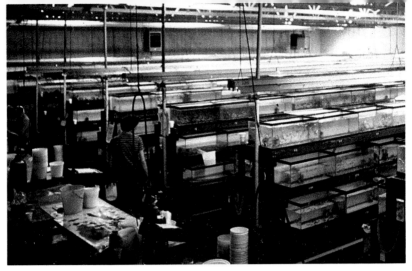
Constant surveillance is the keynote during acclimatization.

chilled. The other system, which is employed by all of the most progressive firms, is an indoor grading operation. The fish are removed from the pools and then immediately taken to a grading room. The fish are then carefully and accurately graded for size and color. Off-color fish are removed and destroyed so that when the fish are returned to the pool the strain will be strengthened by the removal of any poor quality fish.

Orders are assembled 48 hours before shipment. The fish are held in various chemical solutions which will condition them for the rough trip they must make to their ultimate destination. The very best drugs for livebearers are germicidal dyes such as acriflavine and methylene blue. These apparently prevent disease by sterilizing wounds and sores. Tetracycline, Terramycin, or sodium sulfathiozole are used in combination with one of these dyes to heal the wounds. Epsom salts stimulate the secretion of the fish's body slime, which further protects it from disease. When the fish are ready for shipment they are in top condition.

Livebearing fish are also produced in the Miami, Florida area in concrete pools of large size. As the cost of construction of these pools is so much greater than a comparably sized dirt pool all of the Miami farmers have small pools, and the quantity of fish produced is much lower. In recent years the Miami operations have more and more specialized in imported wild fish and the raising of egg-layers. A very great percentage of the livebearers sold from Miami are actually produced in the Tampa area and sent to Miami for conditioning, sizing, and eventual sale.

Some of the livebearing fish sold in England and Europe are produced in Singapore and Hong Kong. These fish are all small and cannot be compared to the American-produced fish in size, variety, or color.

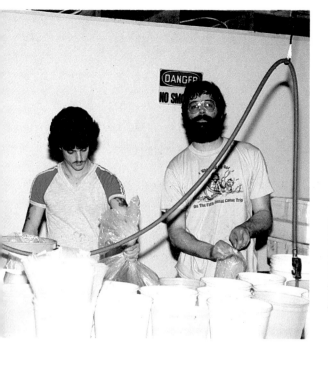

The bag containing the fish is given one last check before the inflating operation begins; even with the new and improved methods of transportation, it is still possible to crowd the fish.

The nozzle of the oxygen line is inserted into the neck of the plastic bag; if the opening is held too loosely, some of the oxygen will escape while the bag is being filled.

The Importance of Fast Air Transport

In recent years, the price of fishes, especially the rarer species, has come down considerably. Hobbyists, of course, are reluctant to look a gift horse in the mouth. They have given little thought to the reasons behind the lower prices; they are much more likely to have pocketed their savings and been grateful for the price reduction. But whether they've thought about it or not, there are some basic economic factors involved in their windfall. Increasing popularity of the hobby is one big reason. As more people make a demand for fish, dealers are able to rely more and more on a large volume of small-markup sales instead of a few high-markup sales. Individual unit prices therefore decline, to the benefit of hobbyists.

But there are other factors, too, one of the biggest being the availability of fast air freight to large commercial breeders and importers. Air freight is an asset to hatcheries because it is a time saver. When shipping tropicals, anything that saves time saves lives; the longer a fish is in transit, the greater are the chances that it will arrive dead or dying. Mortality of transported fishes is a very real expense. Whether this cost be absorbed by wholesaler or retailer matters little to the hobbyist; what does matter is that the cost of fishes killed or debilitated on the way to his favorite fish store is ultimately passed on, at least in part, to him. What hurts the dealer hurts the hobbyist; conversely, anything that helps the dealer also helps the hobbyist. Fast air freight applied to the tropical fish field has helped a lot, and not only in the area of price. Without air freight it would be next to impossible to bring in some of the weird beauties that are on the market today. Some of the most colorful fishes, especially marine fishes, would be completely unobtainable.

But although air transport has had a healthy effect on the hobby, there are still problems. Airlines are still hampered by the weather, more so than other transportation media. Also, the advantages of speed of transport must be paid for; air rates are high. Luckily, progressive shippers have been able to develop methods for safely shipping many fish in just a little water, thus cutting down on freight costs and allowing the advantages gained by rapid delivery to be passed along to the hobbyist.

One method used to reduce the weight of shipments is to pump pure oxygen into a large plastic shipping bag filled with water to only about one-seventh of its capacity. The fish have less room to swim, but they can be packed closely, because the water constantly absorbs fresh oxygen. This process can be made doubly effective by putting tranquilizers into the water. In this way the fish are less active and give off less carbon dioxide, the real killer when fishes are crowded.

C - 45.00

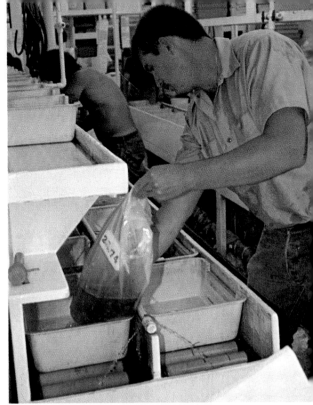

The bag has now been filled adequately; note that the straight outline of the sides of the bag indicate that the trapped gas is under considerable pressure.

Despite precautions, the fish are still headed for a little rough treatment in transit, and the bag must be sealed as thoroughly as possible. All loose ends are bound up.

The bag containing the fish is now placed into an insulated cardboard container; in colder weather, room must be left for additional insulation.

All the steps in preparation are completed, and the fish will soon be on their way to the airfield.

Even these new methods, however, cannot eliminate the painstaking work done by the commercial people to provide hobbyists with a large selection of healthy tropicals. The fish still have to be bred and raised to good size, collected, sorted, acclimated, and packed. So far, there have been few short-cuts in these systems. The most efficient transportation in the world can't help a breeder to raise nice Sailfin Mollies, nor can it give him a hand in sorting and checking his stock so that only the healthiest, most vigorous fishes are shipped. These things are still done mostly by hand. There's a lot of work involved, but it's worth it.

Tropical fish farms situated in warm areas can efficiently raise large quantities of livebearing species like these beautiful mollies in outdoor pools, but a constant check has to be kept on the quality of the fish in the pools in order to prevent deterioration of the stock's quality.

C - 48.00

ABRAMIS SP./*Bream*

Range: Europe and northern Asia.
Habits: Peaceful; a bottom-feeding species which will help clean up food which has been left uneaten by other fishes.
Water Conditions: Not critical.
Size: Up to 12 inches.
Food Requirements: Will thrive on almost any food. Of course, living foods are preferred.
Color Variations: A silvery fish, with no outstanding colors.

The Bream occurs in small schools in ponds and sluggish streams in European and northern Asiatic waters, where it is often caught by anglers. Sexes can only be distinguished in fairly large specimens, when the females become heavy with roe. This fish is not a very popular aquarium inhabitant, but young specimens may be kept with other cold-water species such as Goldfish. There are numerous species of this genus and all have very similar appearance and habits. They are members of the family *Cyprinidae*, the carplike fishes. Capturing young specimens for aquarium use should be a fairly simple matter. The best time to catch them is early summer, when the fry which have hatched in the spring have begun to grow. The best net is a seine, dragged along the bottom near the shore. Take only small specimens, which will most easily adapt themselves to aquarium life, and give them a large aquarium with clean water and good aeration. Avoid crowding; being a cold-water species, they have fairly high oxygen requirements, which they will not get if their quarters are overcrowded. Do not place their aquarium where the sunlight will raise the water temperature.

Photo by Dr. Herbert R. Axelrod.

ABRAMITES MICROCEPHALUS (Norman)/*Marbled Headstander*

Range: Lower Amazon and the Guianas.

Habits: A peaceful fish, suitable for the community aquarium. Has been accused of nibbling plants.

Water Conditions: Water should be soft and slightly acid. This species prefers water which has been well aged.

Size: 5 inches maximum; matures at 3 inches.

Food Requirements: Living foods which remain on the bottom, such as Enchytrae or *Tubifex* worms are preferable.

Color Variations: Body color is light brown, with a number of indistinct darker bars forming a marbled pattern.

This fish should be given a roomy, well-planted aquarium. They love to browse, searching for food on the bottom and nibbling algae growths. Avoid using tender plants such as Water Sprite or *Anacharis*, but decorate their aquarium with tough-stalked plants like *Sagittaria* or *Cryptocoryne*. Then they will confine their nibbling to cleaning algae off the leaves. Sex differences are slight: the female has a heavier body and a little less color. We have heard of only one account of their spawning, when they bred in typical Characin fashion among some bushy plants. All the eggs but one fungused, and this one hatched and was raised successfully. Once they have been acclimated to a tank and they find conditions to their liking, *Abramites microcephalus* is a fish which may easily outlive all the others in a community aquarium. When algae become scarce, an occasional meal of chopped spinach will be relished.

F-2.00

ACANTHODORAS SPINOSISSIMUS/*Spiny Catfish, Talking Catfish*

Range: Middle Amazon region.
Habits: Mostly nocturnal; will not molest any fish it cannot swallow.
Water Conditions: Not critical. Temperatures should range between 76° and 82°.
Size: Maximum 6 inches, matures at 4 inches.
Food Requirements: Prefers living foods, especially Daphnia, Tubifex or Enchytrae. Earthworms should be chopped if fed.
Color Variations: Body color light brown, with a dark brown marbled pattern over the body and fins.

As the popular names indicate, this is a spiny fish, capable of emitting a sound. This is a faint croak, which you would have to listen very attentively to hear. As with many of the Catfishes, they are mostly nocturnal by habit, shunning bright light. For this reason they should be provided with adequate hiding places, such as flat rocks under which they can dig. We can find no record of their spawning in captivity, but it is thought by some authorities that it is probably a nest-builder which exercises a certain amount of parental care. There are no known external sexual characteristics. Great care should be exercised in handling this fish; the first spine of the dorsal and pectoral fins is very stiff and sharp, and can inflict a painful wound. This is a fish which one could have in a large tank for months at a time without ever seeing it. Not only does it prefer to remain hidden below rocks, but it also has a habit of burying itself in the gravel, in which case it is very likely to uproot some plants. It first became available to aquarists when it was imported into Germany in 1921. It was not until some years later that it found its way into the United States.

Photo by Harald Schultz

*ACANTHODORAS U₁/*Chocolate Catfish*

Range: Middle Amazon Region; This specimen collected by the author in the Rio Urubu, Brazil.

Habits: Nocturnal; it digs into the soft mud during the daytime and is very difficult to catch.

Water Conditions: Not critical; in Brazil it lives in small, hot, dirty pools.

Size: Known from only one specimen which grew to 4 inches in length.

Food Requirements: Prefers worms, frozen brine shrimp and beef heart. Accepts the bulkier dry foods as a substitute.

Color Variations: Body chocolate brown, with creamy white stripe running laterally through the sides. Fins trimmed with white.

The Rio Urubu, near the small town of Itacoatiara, contains some beautiful fishes, from the famous Discus to the vicious Piranha. In some of the tiny intermittent feeder streams which carry water to the Roi Urubu during the rainy season are to be found some very interesting fishes. Nearly all of the fishes in these streams are Catfish since the Characins have long before died from lack of oxygen. By poking our nets into the mud and straining out whatever the mud contains, we sometimes come up with some interesting surprises. When Harald Schultz and I (HRA) caught this beautiful Chocolate Catfish (a name I gave it when I was talking about the fish to other aquarists), the same net also had a few snakes in it, too!

I don't know whether any other fishes like this one will ever be found, or whether a scientist will ever take the time to go to the United States National Museum in Washington and look at my collection long enough to classify this fish, but the fish is beautiful, and once the middle of the Amazon is opened up for professional fish collecting, this fish will have a future.

*The fish pictured has been identified as an adult *Platydoras costatus*.

F-4.00

*ACANTHODORAS U_2/*Spiny Chocolate Catfish*

Range: Rio Urubu, Brazil.
Habits: Nocturnal.
Water Conditions: Very tolerant of any type of water except cold and salt water.
Size: This excellent specimen grew to 2 inches in length.
Food Requirements: Prefers worms.
Color Variations: Body chocolate brown, with broad white stripe running the length of the sides, from tip of caudal to above eye. Fins edged in white.

As this is being written, it is fairly certain that this fish is not an *Acanthodoras*, but it looks so much like the fish on the facing page, *Acanthodoras U_1*, that the two fishes belong close to one another. Interestingly enough, both fishes were caught by the author on the same day in the same general area. This fish was caught in a trap at night. Nighttime is playtime for most Catfishes (except *Corydoras*) and even in Africa it is much easier to catch Catfishes at night than during the daytime.

This fish is called U_2 because it is "Unknown Number two" of this group. Actually a German scientist used this system first. "U" in German stands for *unbekannt*, which means "unknown." Thus the same letter makes it easily applicable herein.

It is unfortunate that the Rio Urubu has never been fished commercially by aquarium fish collectors. It is only overnight by boat from Manaus, certainly only one hour's flight by small plane, and there are many interesting fishes to be found there.

After catching this beauty, it was shipped to my laboratory where it grew to a maximum of two inches. After photographing it, it was preserved and donated to the collections of the United States National Museum, Smithsonian Institution, Washington, D.C. When it is properly identified, a revision will appear in this book.

*This fish has been identified as a juvenile *Platydoras costatus*.

ACANTHOPHTHALMUS KUHLII (Cuvier & Valenciennes)
Coolie Loach, Leopard Eel

Range: North-east Bengal, Assam, Malaya, Burma, Java, Sumatra, Borneo, Singapore and Malacca.

Habits: A peaceful little fish found on muddy bottoms in its native waters. Hides from bright light and becomes active at night.

Water Conditions: They prefer clean, clear water with a temperature of 76° to 82°. The use of coarse gravel should be avoided.

Size: 3½ inches; matures at 3 inches.

Food Requirements: A good scavenger, which can be counted on to pick up much of the food other fishes leave uneaten.

Color Variations: Body color yellowish, with wide dark brown bands on the sides. Green belly on ripe females.

The Coolie Loach has long been a favorite among aquarists. It has the ability to slither into almost inaccessible places and eat any food which would otherwise die there and foul the water. The trouble is that most aquarists think that it can subsist only on "leftovers." This is far from the truth, and enough living foods should be fed to insure a good supply for the "Coolies." These fish have a protective tough transparent skin over the eyes which enables them to dig into the sand without injuring themselves. If the sand is too coarse and has sharp edges, however, the nose and mouth can be injured, resulting in a wound which often becomes covered with fungus and may easily cause death if not caught early enough. The generic name *Acanthophthalmus* means *thorn-eye*, and the German aquarists call them *Dornaugen*. This is because of the tiny spine which projects above each eye.

F-6.00

ACANTHOPHTHALMUS MYERSI (Harry)/*Slimy myersi*

Range: Southeast Thailand.

Habits: A nocturnal swimmer; prefers hiding during the day and wholesalers use inverted, split coconut shells in their aquaria.

Water Conditions: Prefers soft, acid water with a pH of 6.2 and a temperature in the low 80's.

Size: Less than 3 inches.

Food Requirements: Worms, frozen brine shrimp and anything that will fall to the bottom and not require teeth to chew.

Color Variations: The specimen illustrated is an old specimen. The younger specimens have more black than yellow, just the opposite of the proportion shown here.

The family Cobitidae, the Loaches, contains such familiar genera as *Botia*, *Lepidocephalus*, *Noemacheilus* and *Acanthophthalmus*. All of these fishes have one thing in common: under their eyes they have a sharp spine which in a resting position is hidden from view, but when danger threatens, the spine sticks out and is sharp enough to cut the skin. In Thailand, the author (HRA) has found, on one occasion, a small dead snake that had obviously died from swallowing a Loach whose spines had punctured the throat of the snake. The Slimy Myersi is so-called because it seems to have a slimier skin than the other Loaches and is thinner. When a few hundred are kept together in a tank, they "ball up" and are very sensitive to light, preferring to remain hidden in the sand or in a dark corner. They are not to be recommended for the community aquarium, as you will never see them . . . except at night and then the slightest shadow will send them darting back into hiding. As only one importation prior to 1962 has been the sole exposure that the American public has had to this fish, not too much is known about its breeding habits, but it can be assumed to be a difficult fish to induce to spawn.

Photo by Dr. Herbert R. Axelrod.

ACANTHOPHTHALMUS SEMICINCTUS (Fraser-Brunner)
Half-Banded Loach

Range: Sunda Islands.

Habits: Peaceful, often remains hidden when the light is bright and comes out at night.

Water Conditions: Clean, clear water with a temperature of 76° to 82°. Do not give them a bottom with coarse gravel.

Size: A little over 3 inches.

Food Requirements: An excellent scavenger which will pick up uneaten food, but should get its share of live food, too.

Color Variations: Body yellowish, with a series of irregular brown bands reaching halfway down the body.

This species has often been confused with the so-called "Kuhli" or "Coolie" Loach, which it resembles very closely. Probably many hobbyists who think they have *Acanthophthalmus kuhli* actually have this species, and vice versa. In any case, both species are very attractive as well as useful. Their activities, which are largely nocturnal, include a very thorough cleaning of the bottom gravel and much food is eaten which would have been out of reach of the other fishes. Coming as they do from streams with muddy bottoms, their mouth is quite soft and coarse gravel will easily cause severe injury if the hungry fish pushes its mouth against it. For this reason the use of a finer gravel is recommended in a tank with these fish, which are very hardy otherwise and may live for years in captivity. It is positively amazing how a fish with such small, seemingly ineffective fins can move as swiftly as it does when frightened by just slithering through the water with a wriggling, snakelike motion. These fish make better scavengers than any of the other so-called "scavenger" species. They can get into places which are inaccessible to the heavier-bodied fishes. Importers handling this fish in quantity often suffer severe losses because they maintain the fish in cold water and treat them with ineffectual drugs. Only sulfa drugs can help these fish (use 1 teaspoonful per 5 gallons per day; it doesn't discolor the water).

Above: A very rare albino *Acanthophthalmus semicinctus* which appeared in a shipment from Singapore. Below: *A. shelfordi* from Borneo.

ACANTHOPSIS CHOIRORHYNCHUS (Bleeker)/*Long-Nosed Loach*

Range: Southeastern Asia, Sumatra, Borneo, Java; occurs in fresh water only.
Habits: Mostly nocturnal; in the daylight hours, it usually remains buried in the gravel with only its eyes showing.
Water Conditions: Neutral to slightly acid water, temperatures between 75° and 85°.
Size: Wild specimens attain a length of 7 inches; in captivity they remain smaller.
Food Requirements: Living foods only: tubifex worms, white worms, *Daphnia*, etc.
Color Variations: Basic color yellowish, with dark brown markings and a silvery belly. There is a row of dark spots on the sides.

Although this fish likes to dig in the sand, don't count on him to clean up and eat leftover foods. He may do this when very hungry, but his preference is worms, and they should be wriggling. This species is one for which you must search frequently, and then often without success. Most of the daylight hours are spent buried in the sand, right up to the eyes. For this reason you must provide a fine grade of gravel, or injuries may result when they dig in. Small fishes are perfectly safe with *Acanthopsis choirorhynchus*; they are seldom molested. One thing to be remembered if small specimens are purchased is that they will grow, and space will soon be a problem. So many people forget this, or have the attitude that they will cross the bridge when they come to it when buying the young of large fishes. It is better to be prepared before this happens, or to stick to fish species which stay small. Because of its retiring habits, this fish is not very popular, and breeders have not yet gotten them to spawn. Because they are nocturnal, their habits would have to be observed under very dim light, and a very strong possibility exists that they bury their eggs.

ACARONIA NASSA (Heckel) *Big-Eyed Cichlid*

Range: Northern Amazon region.
Habits: Nasty, greedy and pugnacious; cannot be trusted in the company of fishes smaller than itself.
Water Conditions: Not critical; temperature about 76°.
Size: Up to 8 inches.
Food Requirements: A heavy feeder; likes food in large chunks. Cut-up earthworms, pieces of raw fish or smaller whole fish are consumed eagerly.
Color Variations: Sides greenish to light brown, with a number of darker bars on the sides. Eyes and mouth unusually large.

This is one of those species which sometimes gets mixed into a shipment of other fishes when about an inch in length. At that size they are quite attractive with their big eyes and dark horizontal stripe which tilts upward somewhat like that of *Cichlasoma festivum,* and the dealer who gets them has little trouble selling them. His trouble comes a few months later when the customer brings back some big nasty Cichlids with the complaint that they ate everything in sight, including some valuable fish. The writer recalls getting two little ones when they came in a shipment of mixed Dwarf Cichlids. They were small, and their unfriendly attitude towards the others was soon noted and they were given a 20-gallon tank of their own. Here they were given large chunks of whatever food was available: pieces of shrimp cut to fit their large mouths, raw fish, fish which had become sick or crippled, and even dog food from cans! Everything went down their capacious gullets, and they got bigger and sassier until a friend expressed the desire to take them over, and they were gratefully given to him. They were about 5 inches long at the time, and maybe they are growing yet!

F-11.00

ACERINA CERNUA/*European Perch*

Range: Near the mouths of streams in Europe, sometimes in brackish water.
Habits: A predatory species which is best kept with its own kind.
Water Conditions: Not important, as long as the water is clean. Aeration is beneficial, and the tank should be well planted.
Size: Up to 6 inches.
Food Requirements: Live foods should consist of Daphnia, Tubifex worms and Enchytrae; for larger specimens chopped earthworms.
Color Variations: Body color dirty green, with a peppering of small black dots over the sides, dorsal fin and tail.

This is not a fish which can be kept in a community aquarium, especially with different fishes, but young specimens make fairly good aquarium fishes in a cold-water set-up. They are not infrequently kept in European aquaria, and mention is made of them in case some of them should ever find their way into shipments to the United States. The Kaulbarsch, as it is known to German aquarists, requires a good amount of space compared with tropical species. In their natural waters they prefer a weedy bottom, into which they lay long strings and bundles of eggs in the springtime. At this time the females are easily distinguished by their increased girth and the males by their heightened colors. Aeration is advisable at all times, to compensate for the otherwise lessened oxygen content in the aquarium. There is no parental care given to eggs and fry, however there is a good chance that the fry might be given the parental attention of being eaten up by the hungry parents, who are ever on the prowl looking for something edible. Therefore, if there is a spawning and it is desired to raise the fry, remove the parents when egg-laying is completed.

F-12.00

ACESTRORHYNCUS CACHORRO (Fowler) *Pike Characin, Cachorro*

Range: Upper Amazon, Peru.
Habits: Will eat or damage any other fish put with it.
Water Conditions: Requires much room and a good deal of heat, 80° to 82°.
Size: About 12 inches.
Food Requirements: Will only take living foods, preferably smaller fishes.
Color Variations: Upper half of body brown, silvery below. Bright golden stripe runs from the operculum to the caudal base. Middle caudal rays black.

One look at the torpedo-shaped body, the hungry eyes and Barracuda-like teeth of this fellow identifies it as a predatory species of the worst kind. Unlike the Pike, which lies quietly half-concealed or cruising along almost motionless like a twig in the water, *Acestrorhyncus cachorro* prefers to pursue its prey, and it is seldom that it cannot overtake it. It is the bane of fish collectors, who get a great many fish damaged or eaten whenever their catch includes one of these. What is more, they must be picked up with caution, or those needle-sharp teeth will tear into the fisherman's hand. Natives where this fish exists seek it for food, and its flesh is supposed to be very delicate in flavor. When captured the tiny scales are easily damaged, leaving the fish a prey to disease. Because of its large size and nasty disposition it is highly improbable that this rather colorful fish will ever be bred in captivity. Don't let the picture fool you! This picture was taken in Brazil immediately after the author (H.R.A.) caught it, and those little fish which were put in with it probably didn't last very long after he found them. It is not rare in its native waters, but seldom shipped, for obvious reasons.

F-13.00

Photo by Dr. Herbert R. Axelrod.

ACHIRUS ERRANS (Ribeiro)/*Brazilian Freshwater Sole*

Range: Originally described from The Amazon and the Rio Paraguay, this specimen was collected by the author in the Rio Araguaia, near Aruana, Brazil.

Habits: A slow, lazy swimmer, it waits on the bottom until food swims by and then it lunges savagely and its huge mouth opens to engulf whatever it attacks.

Water Conditions: They prefer a sandy bottom so they can lie partially imbedded in the sand camouflaged from view. They are not the scavengers they are supposed to be and they require warm, soft acid water. Prefer a temperature of 78°F.

Size: The largest size collected by the author was 4 inches.

Food Requirements: They prefer live, moving foods such as baby Guppies, but as they grow larger they take larger foods. They also take *Tubifex* worms.

Color Variations: These fish change color easily to blend in with their habitat.

Freshwater soles are not rare. Even the Atlantic Ocean Sole, *Achirus fasciatus*, comes into the freshwater rivers that empty into the ocean, but they never live long in an aquarium. No one has ever imported the true freshwater Brazilian Sole. This fish lives very well in the home aquarium and spends its entire life in freshwater. The author collected thousands of this species deep in the Brazilian jungle. Additional Brazilian Soles include *Achirusachirus* (Linnaeus), which ranges from Florida's Gulf of Mexico down to Argentina on the east and Peru on the West; *Achirus garmani* (Jordan); *Achirus jenynsi* (Guenther); *Achirus mentalis; Achirus microphthalmus;* and *Achirus punctifer.*

These fish are very interesting aquarium subjects, but they must be kept with fishes that are larger than themselves. In nature they only eat live food that swims by unaware of the danger lurking beneath them.

F-14.00

*AEQUIDENS AWANI (Haseman)/*Golden Cichlid*

Range: Rio Guaporé, Brazil.
Habits: Peaceful except when spawning. These fish are very much like the more familiar *Aequidens portalgrensis.*
Water Conditions: Not very sensitive to water changes as long as the temperature is between 68 and 88°F.
Size: To five inches.
Food Requirements: Will eat anything. They prefer worms and frozen brine shrimp.
Color Variations: The golden color is more intense in the wild specimens. The photographer, Harald Schultz, photographed these fish within hours after collecting them in Brazil.

This is one of the most beautiful of the "peaceful" cichlids. Its golden color becomes much more intense when the fish begins to spawn. Unfortunately, these fish, like the other golden species, lose most of their golden attractiveness in the next generation. Several times this species has spawned and each time the young looked like green *Aequidens portalegrensis* young, without a hint of the golden color of their parents. Perhaps there may be a closer relationship between these fish and *A. portalegrensis*, since they spawn alike. Unfortunately, the author has never attempted to cross the two species.

Like most cichlids, the Golden Cichlid likes warm water and an aquarium all to itself. Spawning is accomplished easily with a well suited pair. A 20-gallon aquarium should be set up with two inches of gravel on the bottom and a large flat rock upon which the pair will spawn.

*The fish pictured may be a local color variety of *Aequidens portalegrensis.*

Photo by H.J. Richter.

AEQUIDENS CURVICEPS (Ahl) (incorrectly **Acara thayeri**)
Flag Cichlid, Thayer's Cichlid

Range: Amazon River and its tributaries.

Habits: Peaceful except when spawning; does not dig and uproot plants as much as most Cichlids. Can be safely kept in community aquaria.

Water Conditions: Water should be soft and about neutral to slightly acid. Temperature about 76°; for breeding 83°.

Size: 3 inches, breeds at 2½ inches.

Food Requirements: Live foods such as Tubifex worms, Enchytrae, Daphnia, mosquito larvae, etc. If earthworms are fed, they should be chopped.

Color Variations: Back brownish green, sides silvery gray shading to blue posteriorly. Anal and caudal fins have bright blue dots.

This is probably the most peaceful member of the genus *Aequidens*, with the possible exception of *A. maronii*. Because of their comparatively smaller size, they can be bred in aquaria as small as 10 gallons, but of course a larger aquarium gives the fry a better start. The male, easily distinguished by his longer, more pointed dorsal and anal fins, will signify his intentions to spawn by taking possession of a particular spot and cleaning off a rock or section of the glass. He then half drives, half coaxes a female to the spot. Finally, after a few false starts she pastes row after row of eggs on the surface which was prepared, closely followed by the male who fertilizes them. They then guard the eggs and fan them with their fins, also frequently pick at them to remove any foreign matter. In 4 days the eggs hatch. After the fry are free-swimming they should be fed with infusoria and very fine dried food, later with newly hatched brine shrimp.

F-16.00

A male *Aequidens curviceps* guarding its nest of eggs which have been laid on the surface of a rock after the pair meticulously cleaned it.

F-17.00

AEQUIDENS HERCULES (Allen)/*Hercules Cichlid*

Range: Upper Amazon and Peru.
Habits: Very sensitive for a cichlid. Prefers hiding in dark corners.
Water Conditions: Prefers warm, soft slightly acid water.
Size: To four inches.
Food Requirements: Prefers small earthworms, bits of beef and frozen brine shrimp. Eats coarse grained dry foods, especially pelletized foods.
Color Variations: During spawning the males become very colorful.

Cichlids are, as a general rule, not the most popular fishes to keep in one's aquarium. When they want to spawn, they tear up all the plants and attack fishes that come near their nest. This species acts more like an African Cichlid than a South American Cichlid. It hides on the bottom and prefers dark corners to the open tank. It spawns very secretively, prefering an overturned flowerpot to an open stone. Every time this pair spawned, it ate its eggs, so too much information about their spawning isn't available. Perhaps the water wasn't exactly to their liking? At any rate, fishes of the genus *Aequidens* spawn very readily, so it shouldn't be anticipated that there will be any trouble with this species.

F-18.00

AEQUIDENS MARIAE (Eigenmann)/*Mary's Cichlid*

Range: Upper Amazon, Peru and Colombia.
Habits: Fairly peaceful with fishes its own size. A bit dangerous when spawning.
Water Conditions: Not too sensitive to water conditions. Does best in water from 76 to 88°F., with a pH of 6.8 and as soft as possible.
Size: To five inches.
Food Requirements: Prefers live foods such as *Tubifex* worms, earthworms and small fishes. Willingly accepts frozen brine shrimp, dried foods, especially those which are pelletized, and bits of beef.
Color Variations: Tank-raised specimens have less intense blues and greens.

This is a fish which can easily be imported in great quantity because it has such a large range in areas where a considerable amount of fish collecting goes on anyway. This fish is found in the same waters as the Neon Tetra! According to scientific reports, this species is found in Barrigoon, Curnaral, Cano, Caruiceria, Villavicencio, Bogota, Quebrada and Cramalote, Colombia ,and from Yarinacocha, Rio Morona, Iquitos and Yurimaguas, Peru. In Brazil it is found in the upper Amazon, the part they call Solimoes, which runs from near Manaus to Benjamin Constant. It is a very colorful Cichlid with interesting spawning habits if offered the proper environment. Set up a 15- or 20-gallon aquarium in which the water has been darkened with a little tea. Be careful that the pH doesn't go below 6.8, as this fish likes dark water. Use black gravel on the bottom to make the aquarium even darker and let the top grow thick with floating plants. This is the water in which the fish will become extremely colorful and active. By feeding the pair plenty of small earthworms and *Tubifex*, they can be brought to breeding condition. They breed like *Geophagus jurupari*.

AEQUIDENS MARONII (Steindachner)/*Keyhole Cichlid*

Range: Surinam, Demarara River, British Guiana.
Habits: Very peaceful; has been known to breed in community aquaria without molesting the other fishes. Seldom uproots plants.
Water Conditions: Clean water, neutral to slightly acid. Temperatures should be a bit higher than the others, about 83° to 85°.
Size: 3½ inches, begins to breed at 2½ inches.
Food Requirements: Live foods of all kinds, but not too large.
Color Variations: Basic color light brown, mottled with darker brown on the side. Dark vertical bar from forehead through the eye and keyhole-shaped marking.

This is a beautiful, highly desirable Cichlid; the only thing which can be said against it is that it is not very easy to spawn. Sexes are not easy to distinguish, as both develop long filaments on the dorsal and anal fins. However, when they are ready to spawn and the little tube begins to project from the vent, it will be noticed that the female's tube is heavier. A well-mated pair will spawn in the usual Cichlid manner: a smooth surface is cleaned off and the eggs are placed here and fertilized. Both fish usually take turns fanning and mouthing the eggs, which can number up to 300 but are usually less. Hatching takes place in 5 days, and the parents usually take excellent care of their offspring, but of course there is a possibility for exceptions. Because they are peaceful to the point of shyness, it is advisable to give this fish a well-planted aquarium; the possibility of retreat when any real or imagined danger threatens gives the fish a feeling of greater security. It will often be found in cases where a pair refuses to spawn that they have been given an aquarium which is not planted heavily enough.

F-20.00

AEQUIDENS PORTALEGRENSIS (Hensel)/*Port Acara, Black Acara*

Range: Santa Catarina, Rio Grande do Sul, Bolivia, Paraguay, Rio Uruguay.
Habits: Moderately peaceful, but should not be kept with smaller fishes. Will do some digging, and some plants may be uprooted.
Water Conditions: Not critical. Temperature 72° to 76°. Large aquaria are recommended, because spawns are often large.
Size: 5 inches, attains maturity at 3 inches.
Food Requirements: Has a robust appetite, and to the usual menu of live foods may be added such items as chopped beef heart, canned dog food, etc.
Color Variations: Body greenish brown; each scale has a dark border. Dorsal, anal and caudal fins have a reticulated pattern.

A popular Cichlid species, one of the easiest to breed. Because of their size and the fact that they generally produce many young, a large aquarium should be given them. This will obviate the necessity for transferring some of the young to other aquaria while they are still small to prevent crowding. Sexes are fairly easy to distinguish. Females are slightly smaller, and males have long, flowing dorsal and anal fins. This species is likely to do some digging, and therefore plants with a firm root-stock, such as the *Cryptocoryne* species or *Sagittaria* should be preferred. A rock with a flat surface should also be provided. When the parents are ready to spawn, and with a healthy pair this will be quite often, they will clean off this rock and deposit on it a great many eggs. Parental care is usually very tender, and a family of these fish is an intriguing thing to watch. Young hatch in four to five days, as is usual with Cichlids, after which time the parents dig a number of shallow depressions in the bottom gravel. The fry are moved from one to the other of these depressions, and any youngster with the temerity to try to swim away is promptly gobbled up by the parent and spat back into the protection of the depression.

F-21.00

As the female *A. portalegrensis* spawns, the male (right) hovers close by waiting for his turn to fertilize the eggs. Photo by Ruda Zukal.

A male *A. portalegrensis* in the act of fertilizing a newly laid clutch of eggs. Photo by Ruda Zukal.

Photo by Dr. Herbert R. Axelrod.

AEQUIDENS PULCHER (Gill) (formerly **A. latifrons**)/*Blue Acara*

Range: Panama, Colombia, Venezuela and Trinidad.

Habits: Is very apt to bully smaller fishes; should be kept only with their own kind or larger fishes.

Water Conditions: Not critical; water should be kept well filtered, because the fish are likely to stir up the bottom by digging.

Size: 6 inches; will begin to breed at 4 inches.

Food Requirements: All kinds of live foods, supplemented by chopped beef heart, earthworms, etc.

Color Variations: Body color bluish gray, covered with rows of light blue dots on body and fins. Males have elongated dorsal and anal fins.

The Blue Acara may be easily distinguished from the other Acara species by its unusually broad forehead. It is more apt to be troublesome to keep than the other species, but it has the fact to its credit that it is one of the easiest to breed, and also one of the least likely to eat its own eggs and fry. It is also probably the most robust of all the Acaras, and if given the proper attention will outlive many other aquarium fishes. Spawns like the others, but loves to dig, and can be expected to uproot many plants. When replacing plants, do not put them back where they came from, or they will be uprooted again. Sometimes this fish, instead of cleaning off a flat surface, will dig down until the slate bottom is reached, and will spawn on the surface thus afforded. Preliminaries are apt to be a bit more boisterous than with the others. A pair will sometimes seem to be getting ready to tear each other to pieces by locking their jaws together and kicking up a tremendous commotion all over the aquarium and then wind up by settling down to a very affectionate spawning. They are almost always model parents and will seldom eat their eggs or young.

Aequidens pulcher spawning.

AEQUIDENS TETRAMERUS (Heckel)/*Pishuna*

Range: Found throughout northern South America from British Guiana, throughout Brazil as far south as Rio de Janeiro.
Habits: A typical Cichlid with typical Cichlid behavior.
Water Conditions: Insensitive to minor water changes. Appreciates warm water but does well in water from 64-86°F., pH 6.0-7.4; water up to 10DH.
Size: 6 inches. Becomes mature at 4 inches.
Food Requirements: Eats all types of bulky foods, whether living or not. Prefers frozen brine shrimp and *Tubifex*.
Color Variations: Males are darker and more intensely colored during the breeding period.

So far has this fish ranged that it has been known under a number of different names from different places. Heckel first described this fish in 1840 as *Acara tetramerus* from the Rio Branco of Brazil. Eigenmann and Bray in 1894 used this species to establish the genus *Aequidens*. In 1891 Eigenmann and Eigenmann called this fish *Astronotus tetramerus* from the Amazon. Linnaeus called the fish *Labrus punctatus* in 1758, though there is a question about whether this was exactly the fish he meant or not. Castelnau called it *Chromys punctata* from Rio Tocantins in 1855. Even Heckel, its original describer, called it *Acara viridis* from Mato Grosso, *Acara diadema* from Venezuela, *Acara pallidus* from Rio Negro, and *Acara dimerus* from Cuiaba. Schomburgk in 1843 called the fish *Pomotis bono* "from all the rivers of Guiana." It has also been known as *Chromys uniocellata*, Rio Ucayali as described by Castelnau and as *Acara uniocellata* by Guenther, who copied it from Castelnau. This is one of those fish which is to be found throughout South American waters which are warm enough to suit it.

ALEPIDOMUS species/*Spotted Cuban Glassfish*

Range: Cuba.
Habits: A peaceful, quiet species which is very rare at the time of this writing due to the Communistic influence in Cuba and its effect upon the fish business.
Water Conditions: Unknown.
Size: Three inches.
Food Requirements: Prefers live food with dry food at rare intervals.
Color Variations: None known.

Not too much is known about this fish except that it is closely related to the Cuban Glassfish, *Alepidomus evermanni* which was imported into the United States by Albert Greenberg of Tampa, Florida.

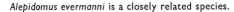

Alepidomus evermanni is a closely related species.

F-26.00

ALESTES CHAPERI (Sauvage)/*Chaper's Characin*

Range: West Africa, Upper Guinea, Gold Coast to the Niger River.
Habits: Peaceful if kept with fishes of its own size.
Water Conditions: Water should be soft and slightly acid.
Size: Attains a length of 3½ inches.
Food Requirements: Dried food is taken when hungry, but any kind of live food is
  preferable.

This is one of the African Characins which we do not see very often, but
due to increased facilities from that area we may see it a bit more frequently,
and also get better acquainted with it. Although it was first introduced into
Germany in 1911, nobody can yet tell with certainty which are males and
which are females without first dissecting them. How they breed has also
not been determined. Some illustrations picture this fish as bright green;
this is not so. The large scales are opalescent, and gleam with a light green
tint. The short stripe which begins at the caudal base and passes through
the middle caudal rays varies with age; in younger specimens there is a dark
diamond-shaped marking behind the gill-plate which then becomes a thin
stripe and widens into a heavier stripe about three-quarters down the body.
Dorsal fin and tail are brick-red. The upper part of the dorsal and the tips of
the caudal lobes are greenish. This is one of the fishes which give the collector
many a headache: they get a whole lot of them rounded up into a net, and
suddenly all of them jump out! Remember this, and keep your aquarium
covered.

Photo by Dr. Herbert R. Axelrod.

ALESTES LONGIPINNIS (Günther)/*Long-Finned African Tetra*

Range: Tropical West Africa, Sierra Leone to Belgian Congo.
Habits: Timid, an active swimmer which remains in the middle reaches of the aquarium.
Water Conditions: Water should be soft and slightly acid, preferably filtered through peat moss.
Size: To 5 inches.
Food Requirements: Larger sized live foods; can be accustomed to frozen foods or beef heart.
Color Variations: Back olive green; sides yellowish, with a black stripe running through the caudal peduncle and middle rays of the tail. Eye red.

Alestes longipinnis has the advantage over *A. nurse* in that it does not get anywhere near as big. As a matter of fact, only half the size is attained, a distinct point in its favor in that it is possible to keep them quite easily if a large tank is used. Be that as it may, this species has had no recorded spawnings either. As with *A. nurse*, sexes can be distinguished by the shape of the anal fin, rounded in the male and with a straight edge in the female. Besides, the male has a high, pointed dorsal fin while that of the female is considerably smaller and round. Both sexes have a horizontal stripe which begins in the middle of the body at a point above the after end of the anal fin and is carried by the middle rays through the fork of the tail. The eye is another attractive feature, a bright red. Like *A. nurse*, this is a timid fish which is likely to hide if kept with more boisterous fishes. There should be enough plants to allow them to take cover if necessary, and at the same time enough open space that they will not feel hemmed in. Avoid using a lot of rocks, and keep their water clean and well aerated. First introduced to the hobby about 1928.

ALESTES NURSE (Rüppel)/*Nurse Tetra*

Range: Widely distributed in tropical African water, Nile to Senegal.
Habits: Somewhat shy, very active. Prefer to swim in groups in the middle reaches of the aquarium.
Water Conditions: Water should be soft and slightly acid, preferably filtered through peat moss. Temperature 75 to 78°.
Size: To 10 inches. Usually offered for sale at 3 to 4 inches.
Food Requirements: Large live foods such as cut-up earthworm or fully grown brine shrimp. Can be accustomed to frozen foods.
Color Variations: Body light brown, yellowish towards the belly. Fins of immature specimens pinkish to light red.

It is extremely unlikely that an average hobbyist will ever raise these fish to their full size in a home aquarium. The colors are far from spectacular, although the young specimens usually sold have pink to reddish fins, a characteristic which is lost as the fish grows older. One thing which can be said for them is that they are active, graceful swimmers and are well suited to a large aquarium where a constant activity rather than brilliant colors is desired. Probably because of their large size and active nature, there have been no recorded spawnings in captivity, although their wide distribution in African waters indicates an active as well as prolific nature. Sexes can be easily distinguished even while they are young. The females have an anal fin which is straight at the edge, while the males have one with a rounded edge. These fish do not take very well to prepared foods. Best bet of course are the larger-sized live foods such as cut-up earthworms, but they can also be won over to lean raw chopped beef or chopped beef heart. They no doubt can also be taught to accept frozen mature brine shrimp. Swatted flies and small beetles are taken greedily.

*This fish is now known as *Brycinus nurse*.   F-29.00

ALESTOPETERSIUS CAUDALUS (Boulenger)
Yellow-Tailed African Characin

Range: Congo River and its tributaries.
Habits: Peaceful unless kept with smaller fishes which it could devour.
Water Conditions: Water should be soft and slightly acid, well aerated. Aquarium should be kept covered to prevent jumping. Temperature 78°.
Size: About 3 inches.
Food Requirements: Will take dried foods, but a preponderance of live foods should be given.
Color Variations: Males have lemon-yellow dorsal, anal and caudal fins. Dorsal is white edged and black tipped and caudal has a black streak.

Here we have another beautiful example of the kind of Characin which can be found in the region of the Congo River. Like its close relation the *Phenacogrammus interruptus* the males are very easy to distinguish from the females. One distinction is that the dorsal fin is considerably larger in the males and bright yellow, edged in white and tipped with black. Mature specimens have a frayed edge on this fin. The tail fin also has a distinct characteristic: the middle rays are black and form a point of their own. Females have only a slight tinge of yellow in the fins. There is no existing account that this fish has ever bred in captivity; being an active swimmer, there is a possibility that the comparatively tiny confines of even a large aquarium hinder it to such an extent that it will not try. However, a ripe, mature pair is very likely to attempt spawning even when circumstances do not permit them to do the same things which they do in their native waters. The aquarist who wants to be the first to spawn an unusual species must begin by carefully conditioning his fish with frequent feedings of the best foods available to him, and then making close observations.

F-30.00

Photo by R. Zukal.

AMBLYDORAS HANCOCKII (Cuvier & Valenciennes)
Hancock's Amblydoras

Range: Peruvian and Bolivian Amazon and tributaries, and the Guianas.

Habits: Mostly nocturnal; prefers a well-shaded tank. Will seldom uproot plants, and does not harm other fish they cannot swallow.

Water Conditions: Temperatures between 75° and 78°, water about neutral to slightly alkaline. A shady tank is best.

Size: To 6 inches.

Food Requirements: Small live foods are preferred, such as *Daphnia*, tubifex or white worms.

Color Variations: Sides light brown, with a mottled darker marking. A white stripe extends from the gill-plate to the caudal base.

This attractive Catfish is often confused with and sold as *Acanthodoras spinosissimus*. Although it is also spiny, *Amblydoras hancockii* is not in a class with its cousin. It is more peaceful and can be trusted in a community aquarium. When frightened it has the capability of burying itself in the sand, with only the large eyes looking out. It can do this so skilfully that the bottom is not roiled, and seldom is there ever a plant uprooted. Sexes may be distinguished quite easily: males have spotted bellies, and females do not. Secondarily, females have a narrower white band on the sides and the whiskers are not as distinctly ringed. Also, the pectoral and dorsal rays are more strongly hooked in the male than in the female. *Amblydoras hancockii* has not so far been bred in captivity, but in their native waters they have been observed to build nests from leaves, deposit their eggs in these and then guard eggs and young until the young are able to fend for themselves. A Dutch firm, Hanselmann, was the first to import this fish, in 1950. It was at about this time that the first ones found their way into the United States as well.

F-31.00

AMIA CALVA (Linnaeus)/*Bowfin, Mudfish, Dogfish*

Range: Found in the United States from Vermont to the Dakotas, from Florida to Texas.

Habits: A vicious, voracious fish, not to be kept with any fish smaller than itself.

Water Conditions: Capable of living in any water which is not poisoned, though it prefers warm water from 70 to 85°F.

Size: Males grow to 20 inches; females to 30 inches.

Food Requirements: This is a fish which will only eat live foods. Small earthworms are acceptable. Larger specimens can be taught to accept beefheart and other meat products.

Color Variations: A very variable fish.

Here is a truly interesting fish. The illustration shows a baby not more than two inches long. He has a lot of growing to do, and in two years he will be about 1½ feet long! The fish *Amia calva* is of great interest to zoologists because of its relation to many pre-historic forms. The adult coloration is blackish olive with green reticulations on the sides. The lower side of the head has dark spots. The male has a black ocellus (eye-spot) edged with orange at the upper base of the caudal fin. You can see the spot clearly in this young male. The fish is very common in Florida, especially in the lowland swamps and the larger, still pools. The young are very interesting and they poise like snakes above their prey and strike with a fast darting action. They are always moving. They live for hours out of water and the author has successfully shipped them by air for 30 hours packed only in damp moss.

The jaws are equipped with an outer series of conical teeth, behind which is a row of rasp-like teeth. They have small teeth on the vomer, palatines and pterygoids. This fish is best kept alone or with fishes as large or larger than itself. It makes a fine pet and learns to eat from your hand. Try keeping one in an unheated 50-gallon aquarium. They do very well if kept at room temperature and fed well.

F-32.00

Photo by H.J. Richter

ANABAS TESTUDINEUS (Bloch)/*Climbing Perch*

Range: India, Ceylon, Burma, Thailand, Cochin-China, Tongking, Southern China, Philippine Islands and Malaya.

Habits: Aggressive, should be kept by themselves. Large aquarium should be provided, and kept covered.

Water Conditions: Not critical; has a wide temperature tolerance, 65° to 85°.

Size: Up to 10 inches; becomes mature at 4 inches.

Food Requirements: Eats almost anything; in the absence of live foods, canned dog food with a high beef content is an acceptable substitute.

Color Variations: Dirty gray to greenish, with a dark spot at the caudal base and another just behind the gill plate.

The Climbing Perch, which incidentally is not a perch, has long been a great curiosity, and it used to be that a show which featured aquarium fishes counted on the antics of this fish to attract many people. A board was placed above an aquarium and one of these fish was netted out and placed on it. It would waddle the length of the board and plop back into the water, to the tireless amusement of the audience. In its native haunts the fish inhabits swampy places where when the water begins to dry out it must make its way from puddle to puddle across dry land until it finds another body of water. They are used as a food fish, and the natives pack them in baskets with a little wet grass, keeping them alive in this way. It seldom spawns in the aquarium; males may be distinguished by their darker colors. The floating eggs receive no attention whatsoever, and hatch in slightly less than two days. Spawns may be very large, and it may be necessary to distribute the fry among several aquaria to prevent crowding. Copious feeding should be provided as soon as the youngsters begin to swim, and the only problem thereafter will be what to do with them all.

Photo by Dr. Herbert R. Axelrod.

ANABLEPS ANABLEPS (Linnaeus)/*Four-eyes*

Range: Northern South America from the Guianas and Venezuela to the Amazon in Brazil.

Habits: Surface fish spending most of their time on the surface of the water with their bulging eyes exposed to the air. In nature they move quickly over the surface of the water.

Water Conditions: They prefer very hard, warm water. Their natural habitat is usually brackish water canals. They are not found in large rivers or fast moving streams.

Size: They grow to about one foot long.

Food Requirements: They prefer live food such as small fishes, worms and insects, but they can be tempted to take frozen brine shrimp and bits of beef heart on occasion.

Color Variations: Brownish to olive green, with dark stripe on sides.

Two South American species of *Anableps* are known. The one illustrated (two months old) is *A. anableps* and is distinguished primarily by the conspicuous violet stripes on its sides. The other species, *A. microlepis* has approximately the same range (Guianas and the Amazon) but is not found on the west coast of South America. The stripes on the sides of *A. microlepis* are not as distinct as on *A. anableps;* the scale count on *A. anableps* is 50-55 while *microlepis* has 81-90. The Four-eyes is a large fish and has eyes in elevated sockets which give it the ability to see in air as well as water. The pupil is divided by a horizontal cross-partition. This is a live-bearing species and gives birth to its young in small non-uniform batches. The young are about two inches long when born. The sexes are left- and right-handed, with a right-handed male mating with a left-handed female. Sexes are easy to ascertain as the male has a gonopodium-like adaptation on his anal fin which is a scaly tube. There is a great preponderance of females in this species. The author (HRA) once collected some 200 *Anableps anableps* in British Guiana by laying a net in water less than two inches deep. The fish were "herded" onto this shallow bed and the net swiftly lifted. Of the 200 fish collected, only three males were apparent. This is not a fish for the beginner, as feeding is a problem, the fish being unable to swim to depths to eat.

ANCISTRUS HOPLOGENYS (Guenther)/*Pearl Sucker*

Range: Widely dispersed over South America from British Guiana to the Rio Paraguay which separates Paraguay from Brazil.

Habits: A nocturnal fish which clings to the glass but prefers "nightwork."

Water Conditions: A very hardy species which does well in any type of water as long as it is not too salty. It can be safely maintained in water at a temperature of 66 to 86°.

Size: The usual size is under 5 inches.

Food Requirements: Eats every type of food usually offered aquarium fishes. Should be offered live foods on occasion.

Color Variations: The black body color varies from dark, slate gray in some species to an intense blue-black.

The family Loricariidae contains such familiar fishes as *Plecostomus*, *Xenocara*, *Farlowella* and *Loricaria*, as well as *Ancistrus*. *Ancistrus* is closely related to *Xenocara*.

This species is one of the most colorful in the genus and though it has a very wide range, it is found in each area in very limited numbers. This should be a very simple fish to spawn as it rarely gets larger than four or five inches. Males have more and longer tentacles than females (this photo shows a female). *A. lithurgicus*, the similar species, has thus far been found only in British Guiana and it is well differentiated by the more profuse tentacles, especially on the male. Specimens of *hoplogenys* have been found in Gluck Island, Packeoo Falls, Essequibo, and Rupununi Pan, British Guiana; not too much is known about the fish, as it is only rarely imported.

ANCISTRUS LINEOLATUS (Fowler)/*Bristle-Nose*

Range: Upper Amazon, Colombia.
Habits: Does not attack other fishes, but two males of the same species would be likely to fight. A nocturnal feeder.
Water Conditions: Clean, roomy tank in not too bright a location. As these come from far inland, no salt should be added to the water.
Size: About 6 inches.
Food Requirements: Should get some vegetable as well as animal nourishment. Tubifex worms, *Daphnia*, brine shrimp, and chopped spinach.
Color Variations: Body bluish, with dark mottlings. Fins brown, with irregular stripes and dots.

There are quite a few species of this freakish-appearing fish, but they come in so seldom that the name "Bristle-Nose" is applied to all of them. A look at these always reminds one of the picture of a dog which has just made the mistake of attempting to bite a porcupine. A number of bristles, some of them branched, cover the upper part of the head and mouth, standing out in all directions. The size and thickness of these odd growths varies at different times of the year, and it is thought that they attain their greatest vigor and luxuriance during breeding season. This fish prefers a heavily planted tank, for this gives him a chance to get out of the bright light. Chances are you will seldom see him, as he will come out into the light only when driven by hunger. This is one of those fishes who is so ugly that people are attracted to him by his sheer ugliness. As with other fishes which are equipped by Nature with "whiskers," these are sensitive tactile and olfactory accessory organs. They permit him to feel his way around in the darkness and smell whatever food particles there are to be found on the bottom.

Photo by Harald Schultz.

ANCISTRUS TEMMINCKI (Valenciennes)/*Temminck's Bristle-Nose*

Range: Upper Amazon, Peru and the Guianas.
Habits: Generally peaceful toward other fishes, but two individuals cannot always be trusted to get along peacefully.
Water Conditions: Clean, well-oxygenated water is essential. Once established in a tank, they should be moved as little as possible.
Size: About 6 inches.
Food Requirements: All small live foods are readily accepted, and an occasional meal of chopped spinach is beneficial.
Color Variations: Head dark brown, body bluish. Body and fins covered with light spots.

This species differs from the *Ancistrus lineolatus* in that the snout is not so broad and that the body has more spots on it. Although the bristles on the fish in the picture are rather small, don't let that fool you! At other times of the year, they can be so bristly that you may wonder how he gets any food through them. Like the other bristly-mouthed species, this one is also a night feeder. In order to insure that they get their fair share of the feedings, it is well to put in some food before turning out the light. Then the others would not gobble it up before the Bristle-Nose gets it. Care must be taken not to overfeed, though. So far nobody has bred them in the aquarium to the best of our knowledge, and nobody has yet found a way to tell the boys from the girls without cutting them up. Given time and a number of fish to work with, these mysteries may be cleared up, as have many others which formerly seemed impossible and today are everyday occurrences.

*ANOPTICHTHYS JORDANI (Hubbs & Innes)/*Blind Cave Characin*

Range: Cueva Chica, in San Luis Potosi, Mexico.

Habits: Peaceful, will not only leave other fishes alone, but will find much uneaten food.

Water Conditions: Temperatures may range from 68° to 90°. Slightly alkaline and hard water seems to be preferred.

Size: 3½ inches, will breed at 2½ inches.

Food Requirements: Will eat any fish foods, living or dried. If it is desired to breed them, feed live foods for a week before.

Color Variations: Pinkish body with colorless fins; males have slimmer bodies.

One of the most interesting examples of natural adaptation is the Blind Cave Characin, an evolutionary variety of *Astyanax mexicanus*. Here we have a fish which has lived for countless generations in total darkness; it no longer had any use for eyes, and so it lost them. To compensate for this it has a strange sense which prevents it from bumping into things and hurting itself. The sense of smell is also very keen, and it can find food every bit as well as sighted fishes. To spawn this fish, it is advisable to give them an aquarium of about 10 to 15 gallons capacity, with a double layer of pebbles or marbles on the bottom. Eggs are expelled in a more or less haphazard fashion, and if there is no means of keeping the parents away from them, they will be gobbled up almost as quickly as they are laid. Immediately after egg-laying has been completed and the breeders show no more interest in each other, they should be removed. Hatching takes place in three to four days, and on the sixth or seventh day the fry become free-swimming. Feedings of infusoria may be supplemented with very fine dried food, and growth is very rapid. In about a week newly-hatched brine shrimp may be substituted as a diet, followed by other larger foods.

* Now known as *Astyanax fasciatus mexicanus.*

F-38.00

ANOSTOMUS ANOSTOMUS (Linné)/*Striped Headstander*

Range: British Guiana; Amazon River above Manaos.
Habits: Mostly peaceful; prefers large aquaria which are well-planted. Likes to nibble algae.
Water Conditions: Fairly soft water is preferable, neutral to slightly acid. Temperature 76 to 78°.
Size: 7 inches; usually collected and sold at 3 to 4 inches.
Food Requirements: All living foods are preferred, but dried or frozen foods are also taken. Diet should be supplemented with green foods.
Color Variations: Brilliantly colored, with two golden stripes running horizontally on a dark brown background and a golden belly.

A small, pointed head with a mouth which points upward characterizes this handsome fish. As is usual with fishes which have this type of mouth, it is a partial vegetarian. Occasional feedings of boiled spinach (chopped and sold in little jars as baby food) are eagerly consumed and very beneficial. All efforts at breeding this fish have so far been unsuccessful. Some conditions cannot be duplicated in the aquarium; for instance, a fish may be able to spawn only at greater depths than any aquarium can offer, or require more swimming space than he can get in the largest aquaria. Again, there may be an item on its native diet which will bring the fish to spawning ripeness and which we cannot supply or duplicate. Even though the fish has been known to aquarists since 1924 and closely related genera like *Nannostomus* and *Nannobrycon* have spawned readily, we are still very much in the dark with this one. Once one of the "difficult" species is bred successfully in the aquarium, it is very likely that succeeding generations of the fish will be comparatively easy to propagate. This has been the case with the Angel Fish, and later the Neon Tetra.

F-39.00

ANOSTOMUS TAENIATA (Kner)/*Lisa*

Range: The Amazon from Brazil to the upper Amazon in Colombia and Peru.
Habits: Jumps at the slightest provocation. Its tiny mouth indicates it must have small particled food.
Water Conditions: Prefers warm, soft, slightly acid water. Temperature 76°.
Size: To 5 inches.
Food Requirements: Small particles of dry food and tiny worms are accepted. Frozen brine shrimp is a favorite food.
Color Variations: Some have a more or less intense golden pattern and darker background coloration.

This species has been known under nearly every genus in the family! Kner called it *Schizodon taeniatus* in 1859, representing its range as the Rio Guaporé, Barra do Rio Negro and Mato Grosso; Cope in 1878 called it *Laemolyta taeniata* and said it came from Pebas, Peru; Guenther, in 1864, called the fish *Anostomus taeniatus;* while Fowler in 1950 uses *Laemolyta* as the proper genus. Because of the mouth's being subcircular in cross-section and because its behavior in an aquarium is absolutely *Anostomus*-like (with upside down feeding, high jumping and sensitivity to shadows), the author decided to stick to the Guenther categorization.

The beauty of this fish in good condition is dazzling, as you can see from this Harald Schultz photo. Schultz took this photo in South America within hours after he collected it in the Rio Guaporé. The Brazilians call this fish "Lisa" which is the same girl's name in English. Rare importations of this fish and many unsuccessful attempts at spawning have left many frustrated lovers of this type of fish. All *Anostomus* are hardy and live a long time, much longer than most other Characins. Interestingly enough, no one has repeatedly spawned any of the fishes of the genera *Anostomus, Schizodon* or *Leporinus,* all fishes which are closely related.

F-40.00

ANOSTOMUS TRIMACULATUS (Kner)/*Three-Spotted Headstander*

Range: Amazon Basin and the Guianas.
Habits: Moderately peaceful; may be kept safely with fairly large fishes.
Water Conditions: Soft and slightly acid water, temperature 76° to 78°.
Size: 8 inches; specimens are usually sold at about 4 inch lengths.
Food Requirements: Live foods and dried foods, with the addition of occasional
    feedings of green foods such as chopped spinach.
Color Variations: Body silvery gray, scales have tiny black dots. Three prominent
    spots, one on the gill-plate, one in the middle and the other at the caudal base.

This fish is a bit large for the average aquarium, but is quite peaceful. It is
wise with this type of fish to provide an aquarium which is in a bright
location, to encourage a growth of algae, which will be nibbled. With a
vegetarian species like this one, it is also advisable to provide plants which
have strong stalks such as *Sagittaria, Cryptocoryne* and the like. These plants
will be well cleaned of algae but not chewed, as the tender leaves of Water
Sprite or some other soft-leaved plant would be. As with *Anostomus
anostomus*, we are still waiting to hear of this species being successfully
spawned. This species may prove to be even more difficult, as it becomes still
larger. Sexes are not distinguishable to our knowledge, and it is possible
that the females have roe which never actually ripen in the close confines of
captivity. This is a fish which if given conditions it likes may live to a ripe
old age in the aquarium. Young specimens, when they first arrive have a
rosy-pink tail fin which seems to fade when the fish becomes older. The
head-down swimming position which is typical of the species is also evident
here.

*APAREIODON PONGOENSIS (Allen)/*Pongo Pongo*

Range: Pongo de Menseriche, Peruvian Amazon.
Habits: See below.
Water Conditions: Soft acid water is preferred. Temperature ranging from 74 to 86°, is preferred.
Size: About 2 inches maximum.
Food Requirements: Prefers live foods but can readily take frozen brine shrimp and prepared, dry foods.
Color Variations: None.

One day while visiting the petshop of Earl Schneider (co-author with Whitney of *All About Tropical Fishes*), my attention was called to this fish because of its unbelievable swimming habits. The fish never stopped swimming at a very rapid rate in a rather tight circle in schools. Schneider had about twelve fish in the school and they swam very quickly in a circle about 4 inches in diameter, making a complete circle about twice every three seconds. They always swam about two inches off the gravel in the aquarium, which was about twelve inches deep. Their activity was anything but relaxing and reminded one immediately that this was probably an unnatural behavior, because the fish was imprisoned in such a small area. I took the fishes to my own aquarium and within a few minutes they had schooled again and started the same "ratrace" even though I placed them in a 50 gallon aquarium! This behavior didn't seem to disturb the other fishes, though; they all stayed away from the circling group. The only time they break schooling is when food is introduced into the aquarium. They swim very fast while feeding, but this is a usual Characid characteristic.

* Now called *Parodon pongoense*.

APELTES QUADRACUS (Mitchill)/*Stickleback*

Range: Brackish and salt water from Labrador to Virginia.

Habits: Cannot be kept with other species; very scrappy.

Water Conditions: Prefers water to which some salt has been added, about a table-spoonful per gallon. Aquarium should be unheated.

Size: 2 inches; breeds at a slightly smaller size.

Food Requirements: Live foods only; brine shrimp or Daphnia preferred.

Color Variations: At breeding time, males develop bright red bellies. Body is light green, mottled with darker green.

Were it not for their very interesting breeding habits, we would never get to hear of this little fellow as an aquarium inhabitant. The Stickleback is very common in brackish waters along the North Atlantic coast, where it is found in weedy locations in bays and estuaries, sometimes travelling upstream into fresh water. When the weather begins to get warm in the spring and early summer, the males develop their breeding colors and the females become heavy with roe. Males tear off bits of plants and build a nest among the weeds, cementing the stuff together with a sticky salivary secretion. The nest is a ball about the size of a walnut, with a tunnel through the middle. The female is coaxed into the nest, and her head and tail protrude from each end. The male joins her and a mighty quivering takes place which almost threatens to tear the nest apart. About a dozen eggs are expelled, after which the fish swim out and recuperate, then the process is repeated. When she has completed her duties, the female is driven off and should be removed to prevent bloodshed. The male is usually an excellent parent and the young are soon able to tear up newly hatched brine shrimp.

APHANIUS FASCIATUS (Valenciennes)/*Banded Minnow*

Range: Coastal waters of all the Mediterranean countries.

Habits: Will not annoy other fishes, but best kept with only their own kind.

Water Conditions: Slightly hard, alkaline water with a small addition of salt (1 teaspoonful per gallon.) Tank should be well planted.

Size: To 2¼ inches.

Food Requirements: Small live foods, also the addition of vegetable matter in the form of algae, spinach or lettuce leaves.

Color Variations: Back olive-green, sides bluish, belly white. Vertical rows of bluish bands adorn the sides. Females lighter.

Aphanius fasciatus is very similar in color to *Aphanius iberus*, with the exception that the light bars on the sides are fewer in number but a little more distinct. Its range is considerably greater, being found along the coast in all the Mediterranean countries, from strongly brackish to fresh waters. The *Aphanius* species are ready spawners, the male sometimes being so eager that the female is damaged if she cannot seek refuge from his amorous attentions. The eggs hatch in 10 to 14 days, and have been successfully mailed in insulated glass bottles or vials, sometimes even in damp cotton. This is an excellent way for hobbyists to "share the wealth" and make available at the low mailing costs fishes which are not otherwise available to others. It is of course important to have the eggs arrive at their destination before their incubation period is completed, so sending by regular mail instead of "air mail special delivery" is misplaced economy. Egg mailing has been made possible all over the world, thanks to the speed of modern plane service. Not only the eggs of this species but also those of any fish with a long incubational period can be mailed.

Photo by Dr. Herbert R. Axelrod.

APHANIUS IBERUS (Cuvier & Valenciennes)/*Spanish Minnow*

Range: Spain and Algeria.
Habits: Peaceful and very active. Best kept 2 females to 1 male.
Water Conditions: Neutral to slightly alkaline fresh water. Temperature 72 to 76°.
Size: To 2 inches.
Food Requirements: Should be given live foods whenever possible. Other foods are eaten unwillingly or ignored.
Color Variations: Body greenish blue, with about 15 light blue bars. Tail blue with light edge. Females have much less color and colorless fins.

The Spanish Minnow has the distinction of being one of the few aquarium fishes native to Spain. Feeding them is a bit of a problem, because they are not easily accustomed to prepared or frozen foods. It is best to have a ratio of 2 females to each male, as the males are exceptionally vigorous drivers. Eggs are laid near the surface in bushy plants, and are not eaten by the parents unless they are driven by hunger. Of course, their safety is assured if they are taken out. Hatching takes place in 6 to 8 days. Usually a fish which takes this length of time to hatch has the yolk-sac completely absorbed at the end of the incubation period, but this is not the case here. Do not attempt to feed them until they have become slender and are swimming freely. Growth is rapid, and it is best to keep the faster-growing ones separated so that they will not drive the smaller ones away from their share of the food. They are best kept with other active species of their own size; when kept with larger fishes they are likely to become shy and remain hidden. This species has been known to science since Cuvier and Valenciennes named them in 1846.

F-45.00

APHANIUS MENTO (Heckel)/*Persian Minnow*

Range: Iran, Syria, Asia Minor, in strongly brackish to fresh waters.

Habits: Will not annoy other fishes, but best kept with only their own kind with similar water requirements.

Water Conditions: Slightly hard, alkaline water with 1 teaspoonful of salt per gallon added.

Size: To 2 inches.

Food Requirements: Live foods with some vegetable matter added.

Color Variations: Back olive-green, sides bluish, belly white. Vertical rows of bluish spots adorn the sides. Females lighter with less spots.

The Persian Minnow often confused with the look-alike but morphologically different *A. sophiae,* from the same general region, is among the most handsome and the most popular of the little-known *Aphanius* group. Their range is much more limited than that of *Aphanius fasciatus,* but they are reputed to be quite numerous where they occur. The upper fish (the female) in the picture looks distinctly pinchbellied, but this may be a sign that she has recently gotten rid of her eggs rather than ill-health. The difference in coloration for the sexes is very much apparent here. Note how the male has brighter, more sparkling colors and most of all, more than double the amount of blue spots on the sides. Persian Minnows are easy to breed, but if possible two or more females should be used for one male. Otherwise he will drive her tirelessly until she no longer has any eggs left and then keep right on until her fins are in tatters. Eggs are large and easily seen. They can be picked out with tweezers by tearing away the bit of leaf on which they hang and then placing the eggs in a hatching-tank by themselves. They hatch in 10 to 14 days and the hardy fry are easily raised.

F-46.00

APHYOCHARAX ALBURNUS (Günther)/*Golden-Crowned Aphyocharax*

Range: Maranon River, also South Brazil in the Paraná region.

Habits: Peaceful and very active; should not be kept with timid species as their constant activity might prove annoying to them.

Water Conditions: Soft, slightly acid water in a well-planted tank. There should be plenty of swimming room and a cover. Temperature 75 to 80°.

Size: To 2¾ inches.

Food Requirements: Live or frozen foods preferred, but dry foods also accepted.

Color Variations: Bluish silvery body with a slightly more pronounced horizontal stripe. Top of head gold, caudal peduncle and lower caudal region red.

Its bluish silvery body is certainly not enough to give the Golden-Crowned Aphyocharax any amount of distinction. Many of the small fishes netted by a collector are dumped back unceremoniously because of their lack of color, but these are different: they wear a shiny gold crown. This is best accentuated by lighting their tank from the top and providing a dark background. There are some other fishes which have a similar sort of spot atop their heads. Being school-fishes, the sight of them from above against a dark bottom would probably fool a kingfisher or crane on the lookout for a meal into believing that these were not fish but just some little water insects swimming by, something he would scarcely deign to notice. So it would seem that a golden fleck on a fish's head would be a means of saving it from becoming a meal, but another thought keeps on intruding itself with insistence: wouldn't the fish be all but invisible from above *without* that golden spot? One thing which the picture misses almost completely is a bright red caudal peduncle and lower caudal area. A very similar fish, *Aphyocharax erythrurus*, occurs in parts of British Guiana.

F-47.00

*APHYOCHARAX AXELRODI (Travassos)
Calypso Tetra, The Red Pristella

Range: Trinidad.
Habits: Peaceful; likes to swim in schools.
Water Conditions: Soft, slightly acid water. Temperature 75 to 80°.
Size: To slightly over 1 inch.
Food Requirements: Takes all food eagerly, but should have an occasional meal of live or frozen food.
Color Variations: After half of body pink, tail bright red. Belly silvery. Dorsal fin has a dark streak. Females lighter in color.

Anyone who has had experience with the other *Aphyocharax* species finds it very difficult to recognize this as one of them. Probably the only reason it had missed being "found" in all the biological surveys of the fishes of Trinidad is its close resemblance to *Pristella riddlei*. When the author found these fish in a small pool at the edge of the Piarco Airport, the collecting party gasped at the sight of a hundred "drops of blood" in the net. No fish as red as this one had ever before been found in Trinidad, which has more fish collectors per square mile than any other country in the world! Unfortunately most of the fish lose this brilliant red coloration a few weeks after they have been collected, though for some strange reason a few individual fish still retain almost all of the brilliance they had in nature. It is only on a continual diet of live and frozen brine shrimp that the intense red coloration can be brought back. This is the only species in the genus *Aphyocharax* to be found on the island of Trinidad and it has thus far only been found in the one small pool on the banana plantation in which the author (HRA) discovered it in 1959. The fish breeds easily, scattering adhesive eggs into heavy bunches of plants.

* Now known as *Megalamphodus axelrodi*.

F-48.00

*APHYOCHARAX RUBRIPINNIS (Pappenheim)/*Bloodfin*

Range: Argentina, Rio Parana.

Habits: Active, peaceful species which likes to travel in schools and may be trusted in the community aquarium.

Water Conditions: Requires clean, well-aerated water which is neutral to slightly acid. Temperature should average about 75°.

Size: 2 inches, begins to breed when slightly smaller.

Food Requirements: Not fussy, as long as there is enough; has tremendous energy, and therefore requires frequent feedings.

Color Variations: Steel-blue body with bright red fins. Males have more slender bodies and deeper colors.

One of the old favorites, and rightfully so. A small school of these lovely fish disporting themselves in an aquarium is a pretty sight. Not very sensitive to lower temperatures, but when kept cool most of the color fades out. To breed this fish, prepare an aquarium of about 10 gallons capacity with a layer of marbles, about 4 deep, on the bottom. Pour in water from the tank in which they were kept, to which is added one-third fresh tap water of the same temperature until it comes about 6 inches above the marbles. Select the heaviest female and the most active male and place them in this aquarium. A vigorous driving soon takes place which is punctuated by frequent stops, usually over the same spot. The pair assumes a side-by-side position and with a great deal of quivering a few eggs are expelled and fertilized. These eggs are non-adhesive and sink to the bottom among the marbles. When the female has become depleted and the pair begins to hunt for eggs, they should be removed. The eggs are very small and hatch after only 30 hours. Infusoria and the finest-grained dried foods should be fed at first when the fry begin swimming, growth is rapid.

* Now known as *Aphyocharax anisitsi.*

F-49.00

Photo by Col. J. J. Scheel

APHYOSEMION ARNOLDI (Boulenger)/*Arnold's Lyretail*

Range: Niger River Delta, in ditches and swamps.
Habits: Should be kept by themselves in a well-planted aquarium.
Water Conditions: Soft, well-aged water which is acid, pH about 6.5.
Size: About 2 inches, begins breeding at 1½ inches.
Food Requirements: Living foods such as Daphnia, Tubifex worms and brine
    shrimp.
Color Variations: Males have a blue-green body, becoming indigo toward the tail.
    Deep red streaks on gill-plates and edgings on tail fin.

One of the most beautiful of a genus which is noted for its beauty. There
are some color variations which show up with this fish. In addition to the
above color description, is it well to add that the dorsal and anal fins are
also edged with red, and there are numerous red spots all over the body.
Females do not have the lyre-shaped tail fins, and are a comparatively dull
brown in color, with some red spots on the body and fins. This is not a fish
which is too easily kept. Well-aged water is almost a must, and a well-
established tank which is heavily planted is best. If there is no layer of mulm
on the bottom, provide a substitute by putting in a half-inch layer of well-
boiled peat moss from which the water has been poured off. Eggs are laid
in this bottom layer, and may be found by gently stirring and then picking
them up with a glass tube. They are then placed in a small jar and stored in a
dark location. In 30 days the eggs should begin to hatch. Unhatched eggs
in which the embryos have become fully developed may be placed in a dish
which contains water which has been deliberately fouled, from which the fry
must be removed immediately after they hatch.

F-50.00

APHYOSEMION AUSTRALE (Rachow)/Lyretail, *Lyretail Panchax*

Range: Southern Cameroon to Gaboon.
Habits: Peaceful; will not bother other fishes, but will do better if kept by themselves.
Water Conditions: Soft, well-aged acid water.
Size: 2 inches; will begin breeding at 1 inch.
Food Requirements: *Daphnia, Tubifex* worms, Enchytrae, brine shrimp, etc.
Color Variations: Chocolate brown body with carmine spots and streaks. Males have
large, beautiful finds edged with purple and tipped white.

Probably the most popular of the so-called "Panchax" species, which includes
genera like *Epiplatys, Aphyosemion, Aplocheilus, Pachypanchax* and *Aplocheilichthys.* Even while very young, males can be distinguished by their
beautiful lyre-shaped tail. Females are comparatively drab: brown, with
rounded fins and only a few red spots for color. A very easy breeder. Males
drive almost ceaselessly, and it is better to use several females for each male.
Floating plants may be used to receive the eggs, which hang from the leaves
by a sticky thread. Eggs are not eaten. There are several ways to hatch the
eggs. One of the easiest is to let them spawn for a week or so and then remove
either the plants or the fish. Another is to remove the eggs by feeling the
plants for hard little lumps, which look like glass beads. The eggs hatch in 10
to 15 days, depending upon temperature. Strangely, eggs kept at a lower
temperature (about 70°) will hatch more quickly than those kept warmer.
Youngsters are free-swimming at once, and may be fed with newly hatched
brine shrimp right away. As they grow up they must be sorted frequently
A golden or reddish-golden color variety of this fish, previously described as
a separate subspecies under the name *A. australe hjerreseni,* is available.

Male of orange aquarium variety first raised by Hjerresen in 1953.

Golden Lyretail . The streamers of the caudal fin were lost and have regenerated.

F-52.00

APHYOSEMION BIVITTATUM BIVITTATUM (Lönnberg)
Two-Striped Aphyosemion

Range: Cameroon and Niger Basins, in small streams and swampy areas.
Habits: Peaceful, but does better if kept with its own kind.
Water Conditions: Well-aged acid water, temperature about 76°.
Size: 2½ inches, breeds at 1½ inches.
Food Requirements: Live foods such as Daphnia, Tubifex worms, Enchytrae, brine shrimp, etc.
Color Variations: Body color reddish brown, almost white on the belly. Two dark horizontal stripes. Long red dorsal and lyre-shaped tail fins.

This beautiful *Aphyosemion* species likes a tank of its own which is not too brightly lighted and well planted. Once it has established itself, it will do quite well and give its owner much pleasure. It deposits its eggs on fine-leaved plants near the surface, but we have also observed that occasionally an egg is buried in the bottom sediment. For this reason, no matter how thoroughly the plants are gone over for eggs, an occasional youngster shows up, seemingly from nowhere. *Aphyosemion* eggs are quite firm, even hard to the touch, and may be handled with little danger of breaking them. However, if hatching time is close at hand, it has been known to happen that an occasional youngster pops out from its shell. There is some danger of the parents eating their young after they hatch; the trick is to keep them well-fed. The young also learn very early in life that it behooves them to stay away from anything larger than they are. Any fish which does not learn this early in life does not live very long. As with the others, hatching time is 10 to 15 days and the young grow well if started on newly hatched brine shrimp.

APHYOSEMION BIVITTATUM HOLLYI (Myers)
Holly's Aphyosemion, Blue Aphyosemion

Range: Equatorial West Africa.
Habits: Peaceful, but does better if kept with its own kind.
Water Conditions: Well-aged acid water, temperature about 76°.
Size: 2½ inches, breeds at 1½ inches.
Food Requirements: Live foods such as Daphnia, Tubifex worms, Enchytrae, brine shrimp, etc.
Color Variations: Body color blue, turning to green posteriorly. Irregular dark bars on upper half of body. Lower lip black.

Why this beautiful color variety is not bred more is a mystery. Besides the colors described above, there are numerous purple dots and irregular markings in the body and all the unpaired fins. The long filaments of the lyre-shaped tail are not as prominent as in *A. bivittatum bivittatum*, but in most specimens the colors are deeper and more distinct. These fish, as well as other *Aphyosemion* species which do not bury their eggs, may be spawned successfully in small aquaria, about one or two gallons. Using these reduces the area in which the eggs may be laid and makes them easier to find. Occurring as they do in small ditches and pools in their native haunts, they do not feel as cramped as a more active fish might. Do not let their leisurely movements fool you, however; they can move rapidly if the occasion demands, and are lively jumpers. Never come to the conclusion that because the water level is a bit low they cannot jump out of an uncovered aquarium. Many a good fish has been found on the floor dried up because someone thought they couldn't jump out. A sheet of glass is a small investment and will keep your valuable fish where they belong.

F-54.00

APHYOSEMION CALLIURUM AHLI (Myers)/*Ahl's Aphyosemion*

Range: Tropical West Africa.

Habits: Peaceful in the community aquarium. Males sometimes stage "battles" between themselves, but there is seldom any damage.

Water Conditions: Soft, slightly acid water. Water used for spawning should have a pH value of about 6.5. Temperature 74 to 78°.

Size: To 2½ inches.

Food Requirements: Any of the smaller living foods, especially daphnia. Frozen foods are taken unwillingly, and dried foods only when hungry.

Color Variations: Body yellowish to blue with bright red dots. Ventral, caudal, anal and dorsal fins with red inner edge and yellow outer edge. Pectorals blue.

Aphyosemion calliurum ahli is one of the most beautiful members of the genus *Aphyosemion*. The bright yellow outer edges of the fins make it a stand-out in any aquarium. There is a considerable variation in body colors: some strains have a blue body, and others a green or even yellowish tone. Selective breeding can establish any of these color strains, and many Killie breeders have their own favorite preferences. The fish breeds easily, like most of the egg-hanging *Aphyosemion* species, and two pairs placed in a breeding aquarium can produce about 40 eggs daily for quite a time. It has been found, however, that after two weeks of spawning the eggs prove to be infertile if the sexes are not separated and given at least a week's rest. The practice is a good one to follow with all the *Aphyosemion* species, not only this one. Incubation period is two weeks, give or take a couple of days. Most breeders have stopped using plants when spawning this group, and instead are using the "mops" made of nylon.

APHYOSEMION CALLIURUM CALLIURUM (Boulenger)
Blue Calliurum

Range: Liberia to Loanda.

Habits: Peaceful in mixed company, but they are happier with just their own kind.

Water Conditions: Soft, slightly acid water. For spawning, pH value should be about 6.5. Temperature 74 to 78°.

Size: To 2¼ inches.

Food Requirements: Live foods; frozen or dried foods are taken reluctantly.

Color Variations: Body bluish to light brown with red bright dots. Dorsal and anal fins edged with blue and covered with red streaks. Tail has blue edges.

There is no trouble at all in distinguishing between this variety and Ahl's Aphyosemion. There is a total absence of yellow in the fin edges of the male, the place of the yellow being taken by a light blue. Instead of a red area below this edge the red is scattered all over the anal and dorsal fins in streaks. The tail also has these streaks, but there is a red area below the blue edge. The females of both varieties look the same. Note how the female, the lower fish in the picture, has her red dots in nice, even rows while those of the male are scattered all over the body. It is a good policy for those who own both varieties to be careful to avoid mixing up the females. Results, if any, of a mating between a male of one variety and a female of another could result in a hybrid which is far inferior in color to either variety, as well as a fish which might easily be sterile. Spawning, of course, is the same as in the other egg-hanging species. Eggs are deposited singly near the water's surface in plants or any reasonable plant substitutes given them by their owner. Eggs hatch in 12 to 16 days and the fry begin eating at once. They are hardy and grow rapidly.

F-56.00

*APHYOSEMION COERULEUM (Boulenger)/*Blue Gularis*

Range: Niger Delta to Cameroon.
Habits: Should be kept by themselves; will swallow smaller fishes, and fight with larger ones.
Water Conditions: Well-aged acid water with little hardness. Add a tablespoonful of salt for each gallon of water.
Size: 5½ inches; will begin to breed at about 3 inches.
Food Requirements: Heavy eaters, which prefer large chunks. Chopped earthworms, fully grown male guppies and half grown females are considered delicacies.
Color Variations: Body color blue; dark bars toward the tail, which has three prongs, yellow above and orange below with a bright blue edge.

We would hear little about this fish were it not for its one saving grace, its beautiful coloration. Otherwise it is big, greedy for only live foods, which makes it difficult to feed, scrappy and difficult to breed. The one thing to their credit is that a male in full color is just about the most gorgeous thing

Young male

that the world of fresh-water fishes has to offer. Their breeding aquarium, which should be at least 15 gallons capacity, must be well shaded. The eggs are very sensitive to light. The bottom should be covered with a layer of fine sand, rather than coarse gravel. Sometimes eggs are laid near the surface in floating plants, but they are usually buried in the sand. Gentle stirring brings them to the surface where they may be picked up with an eyedropper. A brown glass jar is the best container for them at this stage. Infertile eggs turn white and should be removed immediately. Hatching time is 4 to 5 weeks at 75°.

*This fish was long known in the aquarium hobby as *Aphyosemion coeruleum*. Colonel Jorgen Scheel, author of *Rivulins of the Old World*, the monumental standard reference volume on killifishes of Asia and Africa, has indicated that *Aphyosemion sjoestedti* is the correct name for the fish known to hobbyists as the Blue Gularis and that the name *Aphyosemion coeruleum* is a synonym for *A. sjoestedti*. The Golden Pheasant, long recognized by hobbyists under the name *Aphyosemion sjoestedti*, is correctly named *Roloffia occidentalis*.

APHYOSEMION COGNATUM (Meinken)/*Red-Spotted Aphyosemion*

Range: Lower Congo River, in the vicinity of Leopoldville.
Habits: Peaceful, but best kept by themselves.
Water Conditions: Soft, acid, well-aged water.
Size: $2\frac{1}{2}$ inches, breeds at $1\frac{1}{2}$ inches.
Food Requirements: Live foods: Daphnia, Tubifex worms, Enchytrae, etc.
Color Variations: Reddish brown body with wine-red dots which also pepper the fins.

Although this species does not have some of the striking colors which characterize most of the others, it is a very beautiful and easily kept fish. Males have an oddly-shaped dorsal fin which has the longest rays toward the tail, making it look as if it had been stuck on backwards. Although this species will not take quite as much abuse as *A. australe* and some of the others, it is fairly hardy and easily bred. It is a comparatively new fish to the hobby, having first made its appearance in 1950 in Germany, where it was identified by the well-known expert Hermann Meinken. This is one of the top-spawning species. A small aquarium is provided which contains some floating fine-leaved plants or a substitute such as a bundle of nylon yarn which has been tied to a cork. The fish readily accept this substitute and spawn into it. After a few days this mop is removed and the strands separated. Eggs are seen stuck to the threads with a fine sticky string. They may be lifted off by this string with a pair of tweezers, to be placed in a jar where they will hatch in about 14 days. Young may be fed on newly hatched brine shrimp.

Photo by Col. J.J. Scheel

APHYOSEMION FILAMENTOSUM (Meinken)/*Lyretail from Togo*

Range: Tropical West Africa.

Habits: Peaceful in the community aquarium, but better kept with their own kind or similar species.

Water Conditions: Water should be soft and slightly acid, temperature about 76°. A well-planted or well-shaded aquarium is best.

Size: Males about 2¼ inches, females about 1¾ inches.

Food Requirements: Live foods essential; will eat frozen or dried foods only when very hungry.

Color Variations: Upper part of the body olive-green. Gill plates bright blue with carmine streaks. Dorsal fin large and rounded.

Do not judge *Aphyosemion filamentosum* by the illustration; this is a male that has just reached full size and is only beginning to get his adult finnage. This consists of two long white tips at the upper and lower points of the tail and a number of longer rays in the anal fin, which give the fin a fringed appearance. Therefore the name *filamentosum*, meaning filamentous. With most *Aphyosemion* species, the female is about the same size, but here the female is considerably smaller and has a far more modest coloration and finnage. Her tail is round, her anal fin is not fringed, and she has only a few red spots on her body. This is one of the top-spawning species, and the male is a very active driver. For this reason it is best if possible to give him two or three females, so that he can divide his attentions between them rather than run one ragged. Eggs are laid a few each day in the plant thickets near the surface, and hatching time may vary from two weeks to a month. The fry are small but grow well with proper feeding, and are full grown at 5 to 6 months of age. This species is related closely to *A. gardneri*, but has different colors.

F-60.00

APHYOSEMION GARDNERI (Boulenger)/*Steel-Blue Aphyosemion*

Range: Coasts of Nigeria and French Equatorial West Africa, where it occurs in small bodies of water.

Habits: Should be kept by themselves; males will fight and tear fins if two are kept together.

Water Conditions: Well-aged soft, acid water.

Size: 2½ inches. Will begin spawning at 1½ inches.

Food Requirements: Living foods such as Daphnia, Tubifex worms, Enchytrae, etc.

Color Variations: Males are a greenish blue which shades to a deep steel blue toward the tail. There are many purple dots and markings.

Although this species has been known since 1908, it has very seldom found its way into this country. The fact that they are not easy to breed is doubtless the reason. This is another of the bottom spawners; an aquarium for spawning them may be prepared by putting a layer of peat moss about ½ inch thick on the bottom of a 5-gallon aquarium. The peat moss must be well boiled to remove any excess acidity. Soft water is then poured in and when the peat moss settles, the pair of fish is introduced. Some cover such as floating plants and a few rocks may also be added, to provide an occasional refuge for the female when she is chased too hard. Spawning takes place in the loose peat moss, and close observation will show the preferred locations. The eggs are removed by gently stirring up the peat moss and siphoning them out with an eyedropper. Once the preferred spawning sites are established, much work can be avoided by placing a shallow glass dish filled with peat moss or silicate sand in these spots, then gently lifting out the dish to remove the eggs. Eggs are stored in darkened jars in soft water, to which has been added a little methylene blue. Eggs hatch in 6 weeks.

F-61.00

APHYOSEMION LABARREI (Poll)/*Labarre's Aphyosemion*

Range: Congo River and tributaries, near the mouth.
Habits: Peaceful, inclined to be shy. They jump, and their tanks should be kept covered.
Water Conditions: Neutral to slightly acid water. An addition of salt, one teaspoonful per gallon, may be beneficial. Temperature 74 to 78°.
Size: To 2 inches.
Food Requirements: Small live foods; frozen or dried foods accepted reluctantly.
Color Variations: Body blue with a horizontal stripe of deep red. Upper half has rows of small red dots, lower half irregular larger spots. Female almost colorless.

The slim outlines of *Aphyosemion labarrei* are no indication that the fish are in poor health. Neither are the partly folded fins of the male (upper fish). They're healthy enough; they just don't *look* it! This is one of the newer species, having first been identified by the great authority on African fishes, Dr. Max Poll, in 1951. Their range is very limited; Dr. Poll reports them from a small region near the mouth of the Congo River. This may mean that the fish comes from tidal waters and that the addition of a small amount of salt to their water might be beneficial. It is worth trying, in any case. Although we have not run across any accounts of their spawning, it is fairly certain that this is one of the egg-hanging *Aphyosemion* species. We seldom see this fish; probably most hobbyists are led astray by their seemingly unhealthy appearance and steer clear of them for this reason. It is to be hoped that this beautiful fish will find a more widespread popularity. Spawning them and distributing the eggs will surely be an effective means toward making them more popular, as it has been for so many other similar species which have an incubation period which is long enough to permit mailing of eggs.

*APHYOSEMION PETERSI (Sauvage)/*Yellow-Edged Aphyosemion*

Range: Gold Coast and French Equatorial Africa.
Habits: Peaceful; does better when kept by themselves, but may be kept in community aquaria.
Water Conditions: Well-aged water of about 8 degrees of hardness.
Size: Males 2½ inches, females 2 inches.
Food Requirements: Live foods such as Daphnia, Tubifex worms, Enchytrae, brine shrimp, etc.
Color Variations: Males olive-green to brown with dark narrow bands. Red dots on body and unpaired fins, yellow lower edge on anal and caudal.

This fish was first discovered in 1882, and came into prominence again in 1952 when some were brought in to be sold to aquarists in this country and Germany. It is a peaceful species, and the writer recalls keeping a number of them in a community aquarium for some time. They do not have the gaudy beauty found in many of the *Aphyosemion* species, but rather a quiet charm all their own. This is another top-spawning species; eggs are laid near the surface in bundles of floating plants or their substitutes. Here is another plant substitute which may be used, besides those already given: tie a bundle of Spanish moss which was previously well boiled to a cork, to keep it near the surface. If you do not care to pick out the eggs and want to save time, simply leave the bundle with the breeders for about 10 days, take it out, snip off the cork and tie it onto another bundle. Eggs hatch in 10 to 15 days like the others, and the youngsters are quite easy to raise. Another word of warning which would bear to be repeated is that this species is also a good jumper, so keep your aquarium covered
*This fish is now known as *Roloffia petersi.*

*APHYOSEMION SJOESTEDTI (Lönnberg)/*Golden Pheasant Gularis*

Range: Upper Guinea to the Cameroons.
Habits: Better kept by themselves; definitely not a fish for the community aquarium.
Water Conditions: Soft, acid water. Temperature 75 to 80°.
Size: To 3½ inches.
Food Requirements: Live foods of all kinds.
Color Variations: Throat and gill-covers indigo blue, the latter covered with red markings. Body light brown with a golden horizontal stripe. Female paler.

Here is a fish to try anyone's patience to the breaking point! The Golden Pheasant Gularis comes from a region in which the dry seasons are exceptionally long. This means that eggs are laid before the waters recede completely and then the eggs which have been buried in the mud go into a sort of resting period from which they are released when months later the rains begin to fall and the areas where the eggs were laid again begin to fill with water. Hatching follows very quickly and the fry grow at a furious rate until they become mature and lay their own eggs in the few months before the evaporating waters leave them stranded. Of all the so-called "annual" fishes this one has the longest incubational period: 3 to 6 months. In the aquarium a pair is allowed to spawn into a 1-inch layer of peat moss on the bottom for several weeks, until the female has become depleted. The peat moss with the eggs in it is then removed and placed in a covered container where it is kept damp, but not wet. Here is where the patience comes in: 3 months at least must go by, and then if the eggs do not hatch the peat moss is dried again and further attempts are made until success is achieved.

*This fish is now known as *Roloffia occidentalis.* See page F-58.00.

APISTOGRAMMA AGASSIZI (Steindachner)/*Agassiz's Dwarf Cichlid*

Range: Middle Amazon region.
Habits: Fairly peaceful except when spawning.
Water Conditions: Fairly soft, almost neutral water. Temperature about 78°.
Size: 3 inches; begins breeding at 2 inches.
Food Requirements: Live foods, Enchytrae and Tubifex worms preferred.
Color Variations: Body color variable, from light brown to bluish gray. Horizontal line from tip of snout to tip of the pointed tail.

This is one of the more spectacular of the Dwarf Cichlids because of its attractive colors. These seem to vary, depending upon the locality where the fish or its ancestors were caught. Here the fish adapts itself to its surroundings: specimens from a locality where the bottom is dark assumes a darker coloration, and vice versa. The blue variety is exceptionally beautiful. The dark horizontal line is bordered with bright blue, and the fins edged with orange. Females are much smaller and have a round tail. One of the big advantages with Dwarf Cichlids is that they do not require a large aquarium for breeding. Ten gallons is ample with this one. Some retreats should be provided, such as a flowerpot laid on its side and a few rocks. The pair should be carefully fed in advance and in the best of condition. They will soon inspect one particular spot and begin by cleaning it carefully. The female then lays row after row of eggs, which the male fertilizes. Then the female suddenly takes over. She drives away the male and guards the eggs, which hatch in 4 days. The male should be removed when he is done with spawning, to prevent bloodshed.

F-65.00

Photo by Dr. Herbert R. Axelrod.

APISTOGRAMMA AMBLOPLITOIDES (Fowler)
Peruvian Dwarf Cichlid

Range: Rio Ucayali, Peru.
Habits: Usually peaceful, but may get aggressive when spawning.
Water Conditions: Soft, slightly acid water. Temperature 75 to 80°.
Size: About 4 inches.
Food Requirements: Live or frozen foods.
Color Variations: Body brownish with a violet overcast. Series of vertical bars on sides. Fins bluish with patterns of dark streaks.

As we follow that most tremendous of all rivers, the Amazon, into Peru we note that it splits into three main streams, the Tigre, the Marañon and the Ucayali. From these streams come some of our most beautiful aquarium fishes, most of which are shipped by air from the attractive and fairly modern little city of Iquitos. From the Rio Ucayali comes this modest little *Apistogramma* species, which is shorter and blunter of body than most species of the genus. The vertical bars are not always in evidence and are sometimes replaced by a diagonal stripe, at which time the black spot in the upper center of the body becomes very prominent and the diagonal stripe passes through it from the gill-cover behind the eye to the base of the soft rays of the dorsal fin. Such a stripe is unusual, and the best example of another fish which has one is *Cichlasoma festivum*, the Flag Cichlid. The fins are mostly rounded and not at all like most of the *Apistogramma* species, and this fish could easily be mistaken for one of the *Aequidens* or *Cichlasoma* species. Because of its lack of bright colors, it is highly unlikely that this species will ever attain any amount of popularity.

F-66.00

APISTOGRAMMA CACATUOIDES (Hoedemann)
Cockatoo Dwarf Cichlid

Range: Dutch and British Guiana.
Habits: Peaceful, but better kept by themselves.
Water Conditions: Soft, slightly acid water. Temperature 75 to 80°.
Size: Slightly over 2 inches. Female about ½ inch smaller.
Food Requirements: Live or frozen foods.
Color Variations: Olive to greenish sides with a dark horizontal stripe. First elongated dorsal rays black. Female becomes yellow when spawning.

This Dwarf Cichlid was known to hobbyists for many years simply as "Apistogramma U2", a name which came to us from Germany. "U" in this case stood for *"unbekannt"*, or "unknown." What the "2" stood for and if there was ever a "U1" was never explained. The fish itself, on the other hand, became well-known even if its specific name was not yet given. It finally fell to Dr. Hoedemann to identify and name it. The Cockatoo Dwarf Cichlid is a perky little fellow whose aggressive manner is mostly bluff. Given a number of hiding-places, several pairs have been known to spawn at the same time and raise the young to the free-swimming stage. Once the female is guarding eggs she develops a bright yellow color and a mean disposition toward her mate. He becomes a very worried and harassed individual until removed to another tank, and if the female has to rush from her duties with the eggs to keep the male at a proper distance she is likely to get so excited that she will eat her eggs. Once the male is removed from the scene she usually proves to be a good mother, and it is an amusing sight to see her leading the fry like a mother hen with chicks.

APISTOGRAMMA CORUMBAE (Regan). Some works call this fish
Apistogramma commbrae/Corumba Dwarf Cichlid

Range: Upper Parana and Rio Meta region.
Habits: Peaceful except when spawning.
Water Conditions: Prefers older, well-established tanks which are well planted and
offer some hiding places. Temperature 76° to 78°.
Size: Males 2 inches, females 1½ inches.
Food Requirements: Diversified live foods when conditioning for spawning;
otherwise, some dried foods may also be given.
Color Variations: Yellowish brown body with a dark horizontal stripe and some
indistinct vertical bars. Females have lighter colors.

This fish could easily be confused with a member of a closely related genus,
Nannacara anomala, and we strongly suspect that it has happened often.
Body form is shorter and more blunt than the other *Apistogramma* species.
Because of this smaller size, it is possible to spawn them in a small aquarium.
When the *Apistogramma* species first became popular in this country, dealers
would demonstrate this fact by putting a pair in a 2-gallon aquarium and
letting them breed there. This procedure, while it is often effective, is not the
safest way. They spawn on a rock, in or on a flowerpot, or in a corner of the
aquarium. Immediately after spawning is completed, the otherwise docile
little female becomes a little tigress and will furiously drive away the male
every time he approaches the eggs. Using a smaller aquarium gives the male
less chance for escape, and there is an excellent chance that he will be killed.
On the other hand, a male which is ready to spawn might easily damage a
female which has not reached the point of ripeness where she is ready to
release eggs. A heavily planted aquarium of at least 5 gallons is recommended.

*APISTOGRAMMA KLAUSEWITZI (Meinken)
Klausewitz's Dwarf Cichlid

Range: Central Amazon region.
Habits: Peaceful, but better kept by themselves.
Water Conditions: Soft, slightly acid water. Temperature 75 to 80°.
Size: About 2 inches, female slightly smaller.
Food Requirements: Live and frozen foods.
Color Variations: Brownish olive body, with large black spot in the center, through which runs a horizontal stripe. Another stripe from center of body to tail.

One of the newest of the Dwarf Cichlids is *Apistogramma klausewitzi*, which was named in March, 1962 in honor of Dr. Wolfgang Klausewitz, the famous German ichthyologist. The head is very narrow when compared to the other *Apistogramma* species. The male is easily distinguished by his high, jagged dorsal fin, which increases in size as the fish gets older. There is also a considerable elongation of the first ray of the ventral fins which makes them almost long enough to reach to the base of the tail. Doubtless we will see more of these attractive little Cichlids when they become more available. Breeding should give no more difficulty than with the other species and there is no reason to believe that in this case things will be any different. This species was found by Harald Schultz, the famous ethnologist, while on an expedition in the Central Amazon region to study the little-known Indian tribes native to that area. Wherever he goes his fish-collecting equipment travels with him; the aquarium hobby is deeply indebted to this great man for his active interest in the many phases of natural science outside of his chosen profession.

*This fish is now known as *Apistogramma steindachneri*.   F-69.00

Photo by Dr. Herbert R. Axelrod.

*APISTOGRAMMA sp.

Range: Central Amazon region.
Habits: Generally peaceful in mixed company, but best kept in small aquaria in pairs.
Water Conditions: Not critical, but soft, slightly acid water is best. Temperature 75 to 80°.
Size: To 2½ inches, females about 2 inches.
Food Requirements: Live or frozen foods.
Color Variations: Body brownish to slightly yellow. Tail has bright yellow marks with black spots. Dorsal and anal fins elongated into streamers.

A taxonomic examination of this *Apistogramma* species might possibly reveal that this is merely a color variation of *Apistogramma cacatuoides*. The big difference seems to be in the caudal fin, which in the male specimen pictured here shows black-spotted yellow markings in the upper and lower rays. Attempts have been made to breed selectively with the goal of spreading these markings all over the tail. Progress has been made, but to the best of our knowledge it has not been done completely as yet. This species has the disdinction of laying eggs which are brick-red. Once the eggs have been laid and fertilized the male becomes very timid and allows the scrappy little female to chase him away, a thing which she would not dare to do under normal circumstances. This is a sure way to tell that there are eggs hidden somewhere, when the otherwise docile female becomes the "boss" of the family. Once the male is removed the female is able to give her undivided attention to the eggs and young, which hatch in 3 to 5 days. Once they can fend for themselves it is best to remove the female.
*The fish pictured may be *Apistogramma borelli*.

F-70.00

Photo by K. Pavsan.

APISTOGRAMMA ORTMANNI (Eigenmann)/*Ortmann's Dwarf Cichlid*

Range: British Guiana and the middle Amazon region.

Habits: Peaceful and may be kept in the community aquarium, but should be taken out when they show signs of wanting to spawn.

Water Conditions: Well-aged slightly acid water; temperature 76° to 78°.

Size: 3 inches for males; 2 inches for females. Will spawn when 2/3 grown.

Food Requirements: Diversified live foods, alternated with frozen or dried foods.

Color Variations: Body brownish to slate-gray. Female's fins become bright yellow when spawning.

A peculiarity of the *Apistogramma* species is the wide variability of form in the tail fins of the males. *A. agassizi* has a tail which comes to a single point; *A. corumbae's* is round and *A. ortmanni* has a square tail in which the top and bottom rays are slightly elongated in some specimens. This species does not have the brilliant colors of some of the other members of the genus, but it has the saving grace that it is easy to breed and the parents do not often eat their eggs nor young. As with the other members of the genus, the female becomes very "bossy" after the eggs are laid, and while the male might be damaged somewhat, he is usually just driven away and not hurt unless he gets really "nosey." To make life easier for the otherwise very busy female, it is also recommended that he be removed after the spawning is completed. Usually the first inkling that the parents have spawned is the bright yellow finnage of the female and the way she bustles back and forth to a particular spot where the eggs may be found on closer examination. Eggs hatch in 4 to 5 days and the fry are able to eat brine shrimp when they swim.

Photo by Dr. Herbert R. Axelrod.

APISTOGRAMMA PERTENSE (Hasemann)/*Amazon Dwarf Cichlid*

Range: Central Amazon region between Manaos and Santarem.
Habits: Peaceful in mixed company, but best kept by themselves.
Water Conditions: Soft, slightly acid water. Temperature 75 to 80°.
Size: Males to 2 inches, females somewhat smaller.
Food Requirements: Live or frozen foods.
Color Variations: Colors vary from brown to greenish. Horizontal stripe from eye to a large spot at the caudal base. Faint bars adorn the sides.

Although this not unattractive little Dwarf Cichlid does not have many of the frills of its cousins, it is nevertheless a desirable fish; for one thing these are probably the best parents of all the Dwarf Cichlids. They seldom eat their eggs, and do not seem to go in for all the hysterical histrionics the others resort to when they imagine their precious eggs are threatened. Even the female does not become quite the tigress that most females of the *Apistogramma* species develop into once there are eggs to be guarded. If the tank where they spawn is not too small she will sometimes tolerate the presence nearby of her mate, and pairs have been known to raise their young in perfect harmony. This is a risky proposition at best, however, and if the safety of the fry is to be assured it is much better to leave them with the mother or, better yet, to allow the eggs to hatch artificially with a gentle stream of air flowing past them. When hatching eggs artificially there must be no contact between the air bubbles and eggs.

Photo by H.J. Richter

*APISTOGRAMMA RAMIREZI (Myers & Harry)
Ram, Ramirez's Dwarf Cichlid, Butterfly Cichlid

Range: Rio Orinoco basin, Venezuela.

Habits: Timid, very peaceful. Should have their own well-planted, well-heated (80°) aquarium.

Water Conditions: Aged water, slightly acid. Tank should be placed so that some sunlight falls in every day for several hours. Temperature 80°-85°.

Size: Males 2 to 2¼ inches, females only slightly smaller.

Food Requirements: Live foods only, preferably Enchytrae or Tubifex worms. Dried foods are seldom touched.

This little beauty has been the alternate joy and despair of many an aquarist. They are very beautiful, and they are just as hard to breed as they are lovely. However, the job is not an impossible one. A pair which eats eggs and fry consistently should be separated from their eggs and artificial hatching resorted to if offspring are desired. German breeders use a system by which they raise many *A. ramirezi*. A number of small stones are provided, of which the parents choose one upon which to spawn. When spawning is over, the stone is lifted very carefully and placed into a jar which is hung under the outlet tube of an outside filter, that is to say, the tube which returns the clean water to the aquarium. The clean, flowing water running over the eggs keeps them free of sediment and provides the same action which the female gives when she fans them with her fins. Fry will hatch in 60 to 72 hours, and eggs which have turned white should be removed with an eyedropper. Fry will swim out with the overflowing water when they are able to swim, at which time feeding begins with infusoria, to be followed by newly hatched brine shrimp and finely chopped Tubifex worms.

*This fish is now known as *Microgeophagus ramirezi*.   F-73.00

APISTOGRAMMA REITZIGI (Ahl)/*Reitzig's Dwarf Cichlid*

Range: Central Rio Paraguay region.
Habits: Peaceful. Does better by itself, but may be kept in community aquaria.
Water Conditions: Clean, aged water neutral to slightly acid. Temperature 76° to 78°.
Size: Males 2 inches, females 1½ inches.
Food Requirements: Diversified live foods which are small enough for such a small fish. Dried foods may be fed occasionally.

This is probably the smallest known Cichlid. The outstanding characteristic of the males is the long, flowing dorsal and anal fin, both of which reach almost to the tip of the tail. This species has been known to use a broad plant leaf instead of a rock surface for spawning. One of the signs of approaching spawning has been described by some breeders: females will begin to herd a swarm of live Daphnia as they would a school of their young. Another is the heightened coloring, especially of the yellow in the belly region. Usually the female takes no part in the preparation of the spawning site, and shows no interest until the male finally coaxes her there. It is comical to see the male, after spawning is completed, attempt to help with the eggs. The female will have no part of it, however, and keeps driving him away with vim and vigor. He is finally forced to hide in a corner, and would be much better off if he were taken out of what was once, but is no longer, his happy home. The female of this species will seldom eat her eggs or offspring. Incidentally, the eggs of this species have a distinction of their own: they are brick red!

Apistogramma macmasteri is one of those species that has been circulating around for a while but only recently has been officially named.

Apistogramma trifasciatum is readily identified by the third stripe extending from the pectoral fin base to the origin of the anal fin.

Two unidentified Dwarf Cichlids of the genus *Apistogramma*, collected by Harald Schultz in Brazil. In every small pool in the Brazilian Amazon there are new species of tiny Cichlids.

APLOCHEILICHTHYS FLAVIPINNIS (Meinken)/ *Yellowfinned Lampeye*

Range: Lagos, Africa.
Habits: Peaceful, best kept in a group of at least a dozen. Because of their small size, they should be given their own quarters.
Water Conditions: Soft, slightly acid water is the best. Temperatures 74° to 78°.
Size: About 1¼ inches.
Food Requirements: Small live foods only are accepted.
Color Variations: Body yellowish with a greenish gleam. Dorsal and anal fins yellow with a blue edge, ventral fins orange.

These little beauties from Africa have the additional feature of being very easy to breed. If a number of them are put together, males and females pair off and in a short time a small cluster of eggs is seen hanging from the vent of some of the females, in a manner similar to that of *Oryzias javanicus*. The eggs are soon brushed off when the female swims through some plants, and in 12 to 18 days the very small fry hatch. Here the writer might be taken to task for the statement that they are very easy to breed. They are, but the tiny fry are a problem to feed. Only the smallest infusoria can be handled, and growth is extremely slow. Once they have been brought to a size where they can eat newly-hatched brine shrimp, then things become more normal and growth is speeded up greatly. All it takes is a lot of patience, which is eventually well rewarded. These fish have a short life span, usually not much over a year. Remember this if you wish to have them constantly in your aquaria, and always have some growing up. It should also be noted that these fish are active jumpers and their aquarium should be covered at all times.

F-78.00

APLOCHEILICHTHYS KATANGAE (Boulenger)/*Katanga Lampeye*

Range: Katanga, in the Congo region.
Habits: Peaceful; best kept in a group of at least a dozen. Should not be kept with large fish.
Water Conditions: Soft, slightly acid water. Temperatures 74° to 78°.
Size: About 1¾ inches.
Food Requirements: Small live foods exclusively.
Color Variations: Males have a yellow head and back. Body sides shimmer bluish. Dark line runs the length of body. Fins yellowish. Females less bright.

Small Cyprinodonts like the Katanga Lampeye are the perfect answer to the hobbyist who likes his fishes small and brightly colored and has enough patience to wait through the period when it seems the fry will never get any bigger. Like the others of the genus, this one also has a short life span, which should serve as a warning not to wait too long before letting them spawn. This is best done by giving them a bundle of *Nitella* or *Riccia*, where the eggs are found clinging singly or in small clusters. As with the *Aphyosemion* species which spawn near the surface, there are three choices of procedure if the eggs are to be allowed to hatch: Remove the eggs by tearing off a bit of the plant on which they hang and place them in a hatching tank; take out the parent fish and allow the eggs to remain where they are, or remove the entire plant bundle, eggs and all, and place it in a hatching tank. There is another method which was not mentioned because an occasional fish might be eaten: Don't disturb anything, and catch the fry when you see them swimming near the surface. Eggs are quite large and take about 3 weeks to hatch. Fry grow slowly at first, but make up for it later on.

F-79.00

APLOCHEILICHTHYS LOEMENSIS (Pellegrin)/*Loëmé Lampeye*

Range: Coastal streams of French Congo and Portuguese Congo.
Habits: Stays hidden unless kept in schools of 6 or more. Otherwise peaceful.
Water Conditions: Neutral to slightly alkaline water with a slight salt addition
(1 teaspoonful to the gallon). Temperature 75 to 80°.
Size: To 2 inches.
Food Requirements: Live foods of all kinds, preferably those which remain near
the surface.
Color Variations: Body olive to brownish with an irregular dark horizontal stripe.
Fins are colorless.

The Loëmé Lampeye is still a very rare thing among hobbyists. So rare is
it that it took a lot of searching to get any data on it. According to Dr. Max
Poll's notes published by the Museé du Congo Belge in 1952, this fish appears
in the coastal streams of French Congo and Portuguese Congo. This species
attains a length of 2 inches and is one of the larger members of the genus.
Like the others, *Aplocheilichthys loemensis* is a school fish and is not happy
when only one or two specimens are kept. In their natural waters they
appear in large schools and their large, almost luminous eyes give the appearance of tiny insects moving through the water. Doubtless this is an effective
sort of camouflage, and a guess would be that it protects them from fishing
birds and other predators. The fact that they appear in tidal waters may be
an indication that the presence of a little salt in the water would be helpful.
In some coastal waters the salinity is higher at some times of the year than
at others, and it is a distinct possibility that at such times or at other times
when it is at its lowest spawnings take place. If we knew what these conditions
were, they could be easily duplicated.

APLOCHEILICHTHYS MACROPHTHALMUS (Meinken)/*Lamp-Eyes*

Range: Nigeria, near the coast, where they occur in small freshwater streams, swimming against the current.
Habits: Peaceful, but should never be kept with large fishes, because of their small size.
Water Conditions: Water should be soft and about neutral. Temperature 76° to 78°.
Size: 1½ inches, spawns at about 1 inch.
Food Requirements: Small living foods, as well as dried foods.
Color Variations: Large, bright green eyes; green stripe horizontally. Males have red dots in the tail.

Here we have a fish whose name is longer than its body. For all its small size, it is very colorful. The best way to show them off is to keep them in a small school, a dozen or so. They stay in a group and their large, green, almost luminous eyes are best seen when the light comes down on them from above. Spawning them presents little difficulty. When the female is ready, and this can be seen by the eggs which are clearly visible through her body wall, she may be placed with a male which is lively and shows good color in a tank of about 5 gallons capacity. A bundle of *Nitella* or a few strands of *Myriophyllum* are placed with them. Temperature should be about 76°. After a great deal of driving the pair come together in a plant thicket and after a great deal of quivering, an egg is expelled. The egg is amazingly large when compared to the size of the female. Spawnings are small, and may last over a period of several days. Eggs hatch in 8 to 10 days, and the fry must be carefully fed on very fine dried food after a week on infusoria. Growth is extremely slow, and full size is not attained until after at least a year has passed.

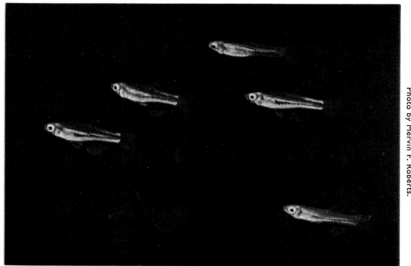

Photo by Mervin F. Roberts.

APLOCHEILICHTHYS MYERSI (Poll)/*Myers' Lampeye*

Range: Belgian Congo, in the Leopoldville region.
Habits: Peaceful, but because of their tiny size they cannot be put in community with any other fishes. Happiest in a school of 12 or more.
Water Conditions: Soft, slightly acid water. Temperatures 74° to 78°.
Size: 1 inch or slightly less.
Food Requirements: Small live foods exclusively.
Color Variations: Body olive-green which reflects a bright blue. Males have elongated dorsal fins, yellow at the base. Females have smaller, plain fins.

This is the smallest member of a genus which does not have any large ones. The Germans call it "Kolibrifisch," or "Hummingbird-fish." The name is an apt one, when one sees the brilliant colors and darting movements of this little beauty, as well as its small size. Rosario La Corte, a well-known breeder in Elizabeth, New Jersey, once showed the writer a tankful of these fish, of varying sizes. He explained that for a long time it was a mystery to him where the young fry were coming from in the bare tank which contained only an inside filter. The mystery was solved when it was discovered that a corner of the filter was loose and the fish were swimming in. An examination of the glass-wool revealed dozens of eggs. This method of spawning is not recommended, because of the possibility of the parent fish injuring themselves in the glass-wool. It is better to make use of the spawning methods given for *Aplocheilichthys katangae*. It is not essential to remove the parent fish. If well-fed, there is little cannibalism and many of the young ones can be raised right with the parents. Fry are hardy, but grow slowly at first. Once beyond this stage, growth is more rapid.

APLOCHEILICHTHYS PUMILUS (Boulenger)/*Tanganyika Lampeye*

Range: Lakes Edward, Kivu, Victoria and Tanganyika and their affluents.
Habits: Peaceful; prefer to be kept in a school instead of singly or in pairs.
Water Conditions: Water should exceed 10 degrees of hardness, alkalinity about 7.5 pH.
Size: About 1¾ inches.
Food Requirements: Living foods preferred, but it is possible that they may be trained to take frozen or prepared foods.
Color Variations: Light brown body and fins, with a blue horizontal stripe.

Contrary to the places where most *Aplocheilichthys* species are found, this one is native to the large lakes of Africa and the streams flowing into them. The waters in this area of the African Continent are mostly strongly alkaline, and in the aquarium we must attempt to duplicate these conditions. The water should not only be alkaline to begin with, but must also remain that way. This means frequent filter cleaning and if an undergravel filter is used the acid wastes of the fish must be removed and compensated for by frequent changes of part of the water. Even with the best of care these fishes have only a short life-span, and an individual that passes the ripe old age of one year is a regular Methuselah. There have been no accounts of the spawning of these fish, but a safe bet is that they spawn in a manner similar to that of *Aplocheilichthys flavipinnis*, the female expelling her eggs in a bunch which hangs from her vent, where they are immediately fertilized by the male and later brushed off when she swims through some plants. When we get more shipments of some of the beautiful fish species native to the Tanganyika region, we may get to see some more of these.

Photo by Dr. Herbert R. Axelrod.

APLOCHEILICHTHYS SCHOELLERI (Boulenger)/*Egyptian Lampeye*

Range: Egypt.
Habits: Peaceful; being a bit larger they may be kept with other peaceful species of approximately the same size. Happiest in a group of 12 or more.
Water Conditions: Soft, slightly acid water. Temperatures 74° to 78°.
Size: 2 inches.
Food Requirements: Small live foods exclusively.
Color Variations: Body bluish to greenish. Scales edged black. Dorsal and caudal fins light blue, sometimes edged red. Females grayish green.

This Egyptian member of the Lampeye group is seldom available to hobbyists. The Nile is not as productive of small, colorful fishes as for instance the Congo, and there is not as much profit for a collector to look for aquarium fishes here. Still, the Nile is a huge body of water and there may be many species which so far have gotten little attention from the natives because they are too small to eat, but which would elicit a joyful gasp from even a hardened aquarist. As has happened in many other parts of the world, transportation is always becoming faster and taking people to more and more previously unattainable places. These places are sometimes rich in fish life and provide the treasured "newcomers" to our hobby. There are few thrills which can compare to the finding of a "new" species, especially if it is one which is colorful and likely to cause a sensation in the aquarium world. Of course, investigation frequently proves that the species is merely a rediscovery of a fish which has been known to science for many years. However, collectors are forever on the lookout for something new, and a surprising number of new species have turned up in the last decade.

F-84.00

Photo by Edward C. Taylor

APLOCHEILUS BLOCKI (Arnold)
Dwarf Panchax, Green Panchax, Panchax from Madras

Range: Madras, India.
Habits: Peaceful, but should not be kept with large fishes.
Water Conditions: Well-aged water which is soft and slightly acid.
Size: Males 2 inches, females slightly smaller.
Food Requirements: Will eat dried foods, but this *must* be supplemented with live
foods.
Color Variations: Body green, with rows of light green to golden dots on the sides.
Females have lighter colors and fewer dots.

Aplocheilus blocki is the smallest of the genus. It was named after a Captain
Block of Hamburg, Germany, who brought in a great many Bettas around
1909 and included this fish in one of his importations. The fish has never
achieved a very great popularity, possibly because it does not possess the
flashing colors of some of the other members of this family. Nevertheless it
has a quiet beauty and does not grow so large that it endangers the smaller
members of a community aquarium. It prefers the upper reaches of the water.
Because of its small size, it can be spawned in a limited space. A 2-gallon
aquarium will accommodate a pair comfortably, and eggs will be found among
the surface plants with a fair amount of regularity. These will hatch in about
2 weeks, but the young will be found to be rather small. Infusoria must
therefore be fed at first, but they will soon be large enough for newly hatched
brine shrimp. From here on raising them is easy. Like the other members of
the group, this species is an accomplished jumper, and the aquarium in which
they are kept should be kept covered with a pane of glass.

Photo by Edward C. Taylor

APLOCHEILUS DAYI (Steindachner)/*Day's Panchax, Ceylon Panchax*

Range: Ceylon.
Habits: Will not annoy anything it cannot swallow. May be kept in company with larger fishes.
Water Conditions: Neutral to slightly acid. Temperature 76° to 78°.
Size: 3½ inches, females only a little smaller.
Food Requirements: Dried food will be taken, but live food should be supplemented at least occasionally.
Color Variations: Sides are green with rows of golden dots. Females have a row of half-bands on the lower half of the body.

Like the other *Aplocheilus* species, *Aplocheilus dayi* will spend most of their time in the upper regions of the aquarium. Here they lie, pike-like, waiting for whatever comes their way in the line of food. They also have the pike-like habit of drifting up to their prey very casually until it is just to one side of their head. A quick, almost imperceptible movement and presto! It's gone! Unlike the *A. blocki*, this fish needs a bit more room in which to spawn, but this is not to say a large tank. One of about 5 gallons capacity is enough for spawning purposes; keep it covered. Of course, they may be kept in larger quarters at other times. This fish is a top-spawner, and their eggs will be found at fairly regular intervals in the plants near the surface. There will never be a large spawning at any one time; with this family of fishes only a few eggs ripen each day, and these are the ones which will be laid. They will not be eaten, and may be allowed to accumulate for several days before gathering. Of course, this will result in hatchings which will be spread out over a length of time as well, and there will be a disparity in size when the fry grow up, so they must be sorted frequently.

APLOCHEILUS LINEATUS (Cuvier & Valenciennes)
Panchax Lineatus, Striped Panchax

Range: Malabar and Madras, India, and Ceylon.
Habits: Best kept by themselves; although usually peaceful except with small fishes, they sometimes harass other fishes.
Water Conditions: Neutral to slightly acid soft water. Temperature 76° to 80°.
Size: 4 inches; will begin to spawn at 2½ inches.
Food Requirements: Live foods such as Daphnia, Tubifex worms, Enchytrae, and grown-up brine shrimp. Dried foods may be fed occasionally.
Color Variations: Males have rows of golden and red dots on the sides. Females are olive green and have a number of vertical bars on the sides.

Aplocheilus lineatus are best kept in an aquarium of their own, where they will show off to excellent advantage. Fully grown specimens if kept in a community aquarium may swallow fishes as large as male Guppies or White Clouds; besides this they may take a violent dislike to another member of the aquarium and drive him around unmercifully. Its beauty, when fully grown, makes it worthy of its own aquarium. Several pairs may be kept in a 15-gallon aquarium. When spawning is desired, separate several females and feed them well until they become well-rounded. Then select the best male and put them together in an aquarium of about 5 gallons capacity, using two females to each male. Provide plenty of floating bushy plants; in a few days they will be festooned with eggs, which hang from them by a thread, like balls from a Christmas tree. Then return the breeders to their original aquarium. In 10 to 15 days the good-sized fry will be seen swimming around just below the surface, where they will feed greedily on newly-hatched brine shrimp, and grow rapidly.

APLOCHEILUS PANCHAX (Hamilton-Buchanan)
Panchax panchax, Blue Panchax

Range: India, Burma, Malay Peninsula, Thailand, Indo-Australian Archipelago.
Habits: Will not bother anything they cannot swallow, and may be kept in community aquaria which does not contain small fishes.
Water Conditions: Soft, slightly acid water, preferably well aged. Temperature 75° to 78°.
Size: 2½ to 3 inches, will begin spawning when 3/4 grown.
Food Requirements: Mostly living foods such as Daphnia, Enchytrae or Tubifex worms. Frozen or dried foods may be given occasionally.
Color Variations: Very variable; body usually light brown to light blue. Male's tail fin has a deep blue to black edge.

For a *Panchax*, this is one of the best-behaved members of the family. They are seldom quarrelsome, and as a rule they are easy to keep. Because they are not as flashy as some of the other members of the family, we do not see them as often as most of the others. Coming as they do from a very wide range, it is to be expected that this fish would show a variety of body colors. This it does to such an extent that it was once thought to be several species, and older literature list the same fish under a number of names. For a time it was also confused with *Aplocheilus dayi*, until it was established that *A. panchax* does not occur in Ceylon, although it covers most of the rest of the range for the genus. The Blue Panchax spawns like the other species, among floating plants or substitutes such as nylon mops, bundles of nylon fibers or Spanish moss. A temperature of about 78° works best for spawning. If eggs are removed for hatching, they may be handled with the fingers; if tweezers are used, do not grasp the eggs directly with the tweezer points. The concentrated pressure can easily damage the shells. Close the points behind the egg, and then lift them up. Eggs hatch in 12 to 15 days.

F-88.00

ARAPAIMA GIGAS (Cuvier)/*Arapaima, Pirarucu*

Range: Entire tropical South American region, usually in the deeper, larger streams.
Habits: Because of their size, any more than one to a large tank would be unthinkable.
Water Conditions: Water conditions are not particularly important with this species. Temperature 75 to 80°.
Size: To about 8 feet in the open. Captive specimens seldom over 2 feet.
Food Requirements: In captivity they will eat nothing but small living fishes.
Color Variations: Small specimens are almost totally lead-gray, with slight hints of red in the after section of the body.

The only reason this huge fish is included in a work of this kind is that small ones about 2 feet in length are occasionally exhibited in large aquaria. The author (WV) recalls seeing one on exhibition in the public aquarium of the Georgetown Museum in British Guiana, and another in a 50-gallon aquarium at a trade show in New York City. This one caused quite a stir when it jumped out of the tank and flopped about for quite a while before it was recaptured and dumped back into its tank, which was covered with a heavy glass pane weighed down with several rocks after this experience. This is the largest of the South American freshwater fishes and probably the most important food fish among the natives who live along the Amazon and its larger tributaries. They are skinned and the flesh is cut away from the bones, then dried in the hot sun. These dried slabs are then shipped to the towns, where they bring a good price. While in Leticia, Colombia I saw a cargo of dried Arapaima being unloaded and could not help but marvel at the size of the slabs of flesh which were piled there, and try to estimate the size of the fish they came from.

F-89.00

ARNOLDICHTHYS SPILOPTERUS (Boulenger)
Arnold's Characin, Red-Eyed Characin

Range: Tropical West Africa, especially the Lagos region and the Niger Delta.
Habits: A peaceful species, which is usually out in front.
Water Conditions: Soft, neutral to slightly acid water. Temperature 78° to 82°. Water should be clean and well aerated.
Size: Seldom exceeds 2½ inches.
Food Requirements: Has a good appetite, and will eat dried as well as live foods; some live foods should be provided, however.
Color Variations: Male has iridescent sides with a golden belly; females have silvery bellies. Both sexes have large black dorsal spot.

Arnold's Characin is one of the most common of the African Tetras. The large, iridescent scales are most attractive when seen with the light behind the viewer. There is a faint horizontal line which also reflects all the colors of the rainbow. Although it has been known to aquarists since 1907, it has never been reported as having been bred in captivity. A clue could be taken from its life habits: it is known to swim in large schools near the surface of open waters. Maybe this fish is one of those which prefer to spawn in more or less large numbers, and it would be necessary to keep a school of them together in a large aquarium before results could be looked for. Unfortunately, we are not likely to see a large number of these fish at any one time. They are lively swimmers, and any time the collectors get them into the seine, they have the exasperating habit of playfully leaping over the top of it. This species is also sensitive to water changes, and should not be moved from one tank to another any more than can be helped. Once they have become established in an aquarium and find conditions to their liking, there is a good chance that they will live a long time.

F-90.00

ASTRONOTUS OCELLATUS (Cuvier)
Oscar, Peacock Cichlid, Velvet Cichlid

Range: Eastern Venezuela, Guianas, Amazon Basin to Paraguay.
Habits: Only very small specimens may be kept with other fishes; when bigger, they will attack and swallow smaller fishes.
Water Conditions: Not critical. Temperature 72° to 82°. Breeds at 78°.
Size: 12 inches, spawns at half size.
Food Requirements: A very greedy eater which prefers its food in large chunks. Live fish, snails, dog food, raw beef heart, etc.
Color Variations: Dark brown with light brown to yellow mottled markings. Youngsters go thru various color changes. Red ocellated spot at tail base. Males have red markings on body.

Many breeders have a pair of Oscars which they use as a "garbage can." Any fish which are crippled, ill or dead are thrown to the Oscars, much as the Christian martyrs were thrown to the lions. They make short work of them, and are usually looking for more. A pair will generally get along quite well, but sometimes battles occur. A separation of several days by placing a pane of glass between them will sometimes calm them down. Usually they are excellent parents, guarding their eggs and fry, but as so often happens with Cichlids, eggs might be eaten. If this is done frequently, the parents or eggs should be removed, and the eggs hatched artificially by placing an air-stone near them, causing a gentle circulation. Spawns are generally large, and may number as high as 1,000 eggs. Young hatch in 3 to 4 days, and grow rapidly if fed generously. First food should be newly hatched brine shrimp, graduating to larger foods as the fish grow. Parents should have a large aquarium, and if there are any plants, they are likely to be uprooted. Provide some large smooth rocks and deep gravel; they like to dig.

Photo by Dr. Herbert R. Axelrod.

ASTYANAX BIMACULATUS (Linné)/*Two-Spotted Astyanax*

Range: Northeastern and Eastern South America south to the La Plata Basin.

Habits: Peaceful if kept with other fishes of about the same size.

Water Conditions: Water characteristics not important, if clean. Temperatures 70° to 75° are optimum.

Size: To 6 inches; in captivity usually half that size.

Food Requirements: Live or frozen foods preferred, but prepared foods also taken if hungry.

Color Variations: Body silvery to light gold. Oval black spot on the shoulder just behind the operculum, and another at the caudal base.

This is one of the fishes which is generally discarded by collectors because they have no bright colors and are generally too large to ship economically for the price they would bring. They are very hardy and once they have become accustomed to a large, well-planted tank will prove to be very attractive, especially if a number of them are kept together. They should not be kept with other species which are considerably smaller than themselves, or the usual condition of bullying will take place. Sexes are quite difficult to distinguish with any amount of certainty until the females develop eggs, at which time their rounder contours provide the only certain method of sexing. If it is desired to spawn them, a pair should be given their own tank of at least 15 gallons capacity. At a temperature of about 78°, active driving by the male takes place and soon a great number of eggs are dropped among the plants and haphazardly about the tank. Hatching takes place in 24 to 36 hours, and after 5 days the yolk-sac is absorbed and the fry become free-swimming. Raising them is easy; newly-hatched brine shrimp can be fed at once and growth is rapid.

*ASTYANAX MEXICANUS (Filippi)/*Mexican Tetra*

Range: Texas to Panama.
Habits: Will get along with other fishes of its size; very likely to eat plants.
Water Conditions: Not at all critical, but slightly alkaline water is best. Temperature
    70 to 75°.
Size: To 3½ inches.
Food Requirements: All foods accepted, but there should be some vegetable sub-
    stances included, such as lettuce or spinach leaves.
Color Variations: Body silvery with a light greenish stripe. Fins yellowish to reddish.

The only Characin which can be collected in United States waters is *Astyanax
mexicanus*. It is the northernmost representative of a widespread genus which
comprises about 75 species all the way down to Argentina. This species
occurs from Panama up to the Rio Grande, and can be found in Texas
streams which empty into this river. A very hardy fish, they require a generous
amount of space and are not averse to sunlight. An unfortunate habit of
nibbling at plants makes them unlikely ever to win a popularity contest
among aquarium hobbyists. This habit can be curbed somewhat by giving
them fresh lettuce leaves to nibble on. Spawning is very similar to that of
most Tetra species. The male drives the female through the plants and eggs
are scattered in all directions. The eggs are not very sticky, and many fall
to the bottom. Once the pair has finished, an egg-hunt is begun, and if they
are not removed most of the eggs will be eaten. Hatching takes place in 24
to 36 hours, but it is not until 5 days later that the fry absorb their yolk-sacs
and begin to swim freely. They are able to tear up newly-hatched brine
shrimp at once, and are easily raised.

*This fish is now known as *Astyanax fasciatus*.   F-93.00

*ASTYANAX MUTATOR (Eigenmann)
Mutator. British Guiana natives call it "Punkay"

Range: British Guiana.
Habits: Should not be kept with smaller fishes, whom it may attack.
Water Conditions: Soft, slightly acid water. Temperature 75 to 80°.
Size: About 2¼ inches.
Food Requirements: Will accept just about anything.
Color Variations: Silvery body with indistinct shoulder-spot and a dark oval spot
  at the caudal base. Fins slightly pink.

There are dozens of *Astyanax* species which occur all the way from the southern border of Texas all the way south into Argentina. Most of them are very similar in appearance, and in many cases it takes a real taxonomic examination to distinguish the species. Most are very drab fishes, and *Astyanax mutator* is hardly an exception. There is a very indistinct shoulder spot, a distinct spot at the caudal base, a silvery body and a little pink in the fins. An ichthyologist could cover the page with a minutely detailed account of head measurements, tooth counts and descriptions, scale and fin ray counts, body measurements, etc., etc., there is really very little of interest about *Astyanax mutator*. We seldom see this fish, for the simple reason that hobbyists don't want it. Many thousands of fishes like these are tossed back or even left on the shore by collectors who are searching for worthwhile, commercially valuable fishes and the collectors are not going to waste their time and money catching fishes nobody wants when they can move to another stream and get something desirable.

* This fish is probably a new species, presently unidentified.

F-94.00

BADIS BADIS (Hamilton-Buchanan)/*Badis, Dwarf Chameleon Fish*

Range: India.

Habits: Peaceful, but will hide a great deal when kept in a community aquarium.

Water Conditions: Not critical; a well planted aquarium should be provided, with several small flowerpots laid on their sides.

Size: Up to 3 inches, will begin breeding at 2 inches.

Food Requirements: Live foods only, in sizes tiny enough for their small mouths.

Color Variations: Very variable; yellow to blue with dark markings which come and go frequently. Males have concave bellies, females do not.

This interesting little Nandid has all the characteristics of the Dwarf Cichlids. It will find life a bit frightening in the community aquarium, unless it has an adequate number of places in which it can hide if danger threatens. When kept by themselves in a small aquarium, they breed readily. A rock or leaf surface, or the inside of a flowerpot if one has been provided, will be cleaned scrupulously by the male. The female is then coaxed to the spot and if she is ready to spawn, will hang 50 to 60 eggs on the surface. Sometimes a plant leaf or the corner of the aquarium is selected. Unlike the Dwarf Cichlids, the female does not take complete charge of the eggs and fry, but shares it with her mate. Eggs hatch in 2 to 3 days, and the fry are very small and helpless at first. Not until 2 weeks have passed do the youngsters become independent of their parents. Infusoria should be fed initially, and when they become large enough to handle newly hatched brine shrimp, growth becomes rapid. This has always been a favorite among European aquarists, and was first imported into Germany in 1904. Its only drawback is the fact that it insists on live food only.

Photo by Dr. Herbert R. Axelrod.

BADIS BADIS BURMANICUS (Ahl)/*Burmese Badis*

Range: Burma.

Habits: Peaceful, but will hide a great deal if kept in the community aquarium.

Water Conditions: Not critical; should have a well-planted aquarium with a number of hiding-places.

Size: About 2½ inches.

Food Requirements: Small live foods only.

Color Variations: Sides covered with rows of red dots, interspersed with blue in the upper half of the body. Large dark spot at caudal base.

Think this subspecies of *Badis badis* is a new one? Well, you're wrong by more than 40 years! The late Johann Paul Arnold, the well known authority on aquarium fishes, mentioned in his book *Fremdländische Süsswasserfische* that he first acquired and bred this fish in 1920, but that it did not find much favor in Germany and that they died out, not to reappear until 1934 when another shipment arrived from Rangoon. It was finally established as a subspecies in 1936 by Dr. Ernst Ahl. In body form it resembles *Badis badis*, but the colors differ considerably. The sides are covered with numerous rows of red dots, interspersed in the upper half with blue ones. At times there are 6 to 9 dark bars which extend halfway down the sides. Colors do not make such drastic and startling changes as with *Badis badis*, but spawning procedure is exactly the same for both. The female Burmese Badis carries the same colors as her mate, but they are not as bright. Like *Badis badis*, it is much better to keep a pair of these fish by themselves in a small aquarium, because they will hide almost constantly if put in the company of other fishes.

Photo by Dr. Herbert R. Axelrod

BALANTIOCHEILOS MELANOPTERUS (Bleeker)/*Bala Shark*

Range: Thailand, Sumatra and Borneo.
Habits: Active and peaceful. A skilled jumper which requires a covered tank.
Water Conditions: Neutral to slightly alkaline. Temperature 74 to 78°.
Size: To 14 inches. In the aquarium it seldom exceeds 5 inches.
Food Requirements: All sorts of live foods are preferred. Also fond of oatmeal
which has been previously boiled.
Color Variations: Body silvery to slightly golden, lighter below. Fins are yellow
with a deep black edge.

There have been frequent importations of the Bala Shark in the last few years, and although they have commanded a high price the demand is still greater than the supply. Do not let the popular name "Shark" fool you into thinking that this is a ferocious, predatory fish. The sole reason for the name is a superficial resemblance of the dorsal fin's shape to that of the oceanic marauder. This is a perfectly peaceful fish which minds its business at all times. It goes over the bottom frequently and thoroughly, picking up bits of food that were overlooked by the others. This is done without a great deal of stirring up of the gravel and sediment. Add to this useful trait the fact that it is attractively colored and easily fed, and you have the reasons for its popularity. Only one thing can be said in its disfavor: it may grow too large for the home aquarium. It is said to grow to 14 inches in Borneo and Sumatra, but specimens from Thailand attain only 8 inches. Of course, these sizes are greatly curbed in the aquarium, and it is seldom that we see one more than 5 inches long. Not yet bred in captivity. There is an account of one jumping 6 feet out of the water.

Photo by Dr. Herbert R. Axelrod.

BARBODES BINOTATUS/*Spotted Barb*

Range: Thailand, Malaya, parts of East Indies.

Habits: Will not molest species of its own size, but is best kept apart from smaller species to avoid nipping and bullying.

Water Conditions: Soft, slightly acid water. Should have large tank; settlings should be kept to the minimum. Temperature 74 to 78°.

Size: Up to 6½ inches, usually seen much smaller.

Food Requirements: Takes almost all live, frozen and dried foods.

Color Variations: Silver, overcast with blue. Dark area at bases of dorsal and caudal fins.

A rather plain fish, the Spotted Barb has never been popular. First of all, its lack of color would cause it to be passed over in favor of more showy specimens, but there is also another reason: it gets too big. On the other hand, some hobbyists prefer large, active fishes, especially if they are able to provide them with the big tanks they need. Big in appetite as well as size, *B. binotatus* needs lots of food, but if fed well enough they will respond and breed readily. Getting the fish to spawn is not difficult, considering its size, but a large tank is necessary, for the fish is very active during pre-spawning maneuvers. The Spotted Barb lays adhesive eggs into thickets of plants, and it does not at first try to eat them. If the eggs are not removed promptly enough, however, the fish, spurred on by a very hearty appetite, will seek out and devour them. Eggs hatch within 48 hours at a temperature of 78°; when free-swimming, the fry should immediately be fed plenty of newly hatched brine shrimp. Fry grow quickly, but they require a large tank for best growth. The Spotted Barb is often accused of being an uprooter of plants; where this tendency is noted, anchor firmly.

BARBODES CALLIPTERUS (Boulenger)/*Clipper Barb*

Range: Cameroon and Niger River, West Africa.
Habits: Usually peaceful, but some specimens are fin nippers.
Water Conditions: Soft, slightly acid water preferred. Temperature 70 to 85°.
Size: Up to 3 inches.
Food Requirements: Live foods are preferred, but dry foods and frozen foods are accepted if not fed exclusively.
Color Variations: Body is silvery, with pink-orange tint to tail. Black splotch at tip of dorsal fin in both male and female.

This Barb is not often seen today in the fish shops, and it has not really been missed much, although it was fairly popular many years ago. In comparison with some of the other Barbs, it has little to offer in the way of attraction, although Barb specialists would welcome the fish for at least one reason: it is tough to breed, and it therefore offers a challenge to their ingenuity. One difficulty in breeding the Clipper Barb is the fish's insistence on spawning under different conditions at different times. One time it may spawn in water which is pH 6.6 and DH 6, whereas at some other time of the year it will reject these conditions and force the breeder to work out alternative water compositions. Like many of its relatives, the Clipper Barb likes a well planted tank; some of the plants should be of the soft variety, which will enable the fish to add some vegetable matter to its diet. *Nitella* is good for this purpose, but *Nitella* is in many localities too expensive to be used as a diet supplement, so some other plant must be offered. If another plant is used, it should be a fine-leaved variety, because in this case the same plant can also serve as a spawning medium into which the fish may lay its eggs.

F-99.00

BARBODES CAMPTACANTHUS (Bleeker)/*African Red-Finned Barb*

Range: Tropical West Africa.
Habits: Peaceful when small, but inclined to aggressiveness when older.
Water Conditions: Soft, slightly acid water. Temperature 75 to 85°
Size: Up to 6 inches, usually seen much smaller.
Food Requirements: Accepts all foods.
Color Variations: Silvery, with horizontal bands and streaks. Male has reddish fins, while female's are yellowish.

Unlike some of its relatives within the genus *Barbodes*, *B. camptacanthus* needs to be kept warm, an ideal temperature for successful maintenance being 80. This is because it is a more strictly tropical species than some of the other *Barbodes*, many of which come from waters in which temperatures never get very high, usually keeping at the 60-70 level. Many hobbyists automatically assume that a fish which comes from Africa is bound to need very warm water, but this is definitely not the case. For example, many African fishes are found in swiftly moving mountain waters, waters which are necessarily cool. *Barbodes camptacanthus* is a pretty little Barb which presumably breeds in standard Barb fashion, although no definite accounts are available at this time. If a spawning attempt were to be made, there would be little difficulty in telling the sexes apart, as the male ventral and anal fins are considerably more red than those of the female, whose predominant finnage coloration is yellow. A few years ago this fish was being brought into the country in large numbers and was beginning to establish itself with aquarium hobbyists, but it seems that importations are no longer being made, and the fish is now very seldom seen.

F-100.00

BARBODES DORSIMACULATUS (Ahl)/*Blackline Barb*

Range: Sumatra.
Habits: Active and peaceful.
Water Conditions: Soft, slightly acid water. Temperature 70 to 85°.
Size: 1½ inches.
Food Requirements: Accepts all foods, small living crustaceans being preferred.
Color Variations: Silvery body, darker on the back; wedge-shaped black mark in dorsal fin. A thin black line runs from behind gills to base of tail.

Although the physical characteristic made mention of in this fish's specific name would ordinarily lead hobbyists to choose a name such as "Spotted Dorsal" for the popular name of this species, this is not the case, probably because there are many other Barbs that would qualify under the same name, thus adding to the confusion that already exists in both the popular and scientific terminology applied to these Cyprinid fishes. In any event, the thin black line along the side of the fish serves hobbyists as more of a distinguishing characteristic than the black marking in the dorsal. Aside from these markings, there is little to keep the species from being completely neglected as a plainly colored not-too-desirable aquarium inhabitant. About the best thing that can be said about the color pattern is that the fish would provide a nice contrast to more brightly colored fishes. To the best of our knowledge, this fish has not yet been bred in the home aquarium. This, plus its relative drabness, makes it a fish which is not seen too often. If the Blackline Barb had just a few added hints of color it could possibly become a favorite, because it does have two advantages: it is small and peaceful.

F-101.00

Photo by Helmut Pinter

BARBODES DUNCKERI (Ahl)/*Big-Spot Barb, Duncker's Barb*

Range: Malay Peninsula.
Habits: Can be nasty; has a tendency to eat plants.
Water Conditions: Neutral, slightly soft water. Temperature 70 to 85°.
Size: Up to 5 inches.
Food Requirements: Accepts all foods.
Color Variations: Generally plain light brown, with rosy hue to back and yellowish
tone to fins. Black splotches on sides, with largest just below dorsal.

The slight yellow and rose coloration of the Big-Spot Barb keeps it from being a completely drab species, but this slight attractiveness is not enough of an advantage to offset its two major drawbacks, which are its large size and its quarrelsome nature. Many of the large Barbs are inclined to be troublesome when they attain their full size and are kept with other, smaller, species, but *Barbodes dunckeri* can be mean even when it is still young, and even when it is kept with fishes of the same size or larger. As the fish gets older, the dark splotches along the sides of the fish begin to fade out, until only the largest marking, the one below the dorsal fin, remains distinct. The Big-Spot Barb spawns into bundles of fine-leaved plants; considering the mature size of the fish, it is best to use large tanks for both spawning and raising the young. A peculiarity of the spawning procedure is that the female of this species is often the aggressor at the beginning, with the male taking the initiative only after the chase has begun. To avoid trouble at this time, the sexes should be separated for an appropriate interval prior to the actual spawning. *B. dunckeri* eggs fungus easily.

F-102.00

Photo by G. J. M. Timmerman.

BARBODES EVERETTI (Boulenger)/*Clown Barb*

Range: Malaya, Sarawak, Borneo.
Habits: Requires a large tank; should not be kept with small fishes.
Water Conditions: Water should be fairly soft and neutral. Temperature about 76°.
Size: About 4 inches.
Food Requirements: Healthy eaters; will extend their appetites to plants in the aquarium.
Color Variations: Back reddish brown, shading to yellowish toward the belly. Two wedge-shaped markings and large round spots on the sides.

This is one of the most beautiful of the larger Barbs. The fins are deep brick red at times, and the dark markings are bluish. Often one sees these fish sold at a size of 1½ to 2 inches, and wonders how many of them will grow to their full size of 4 inches. *Barbodes everetti* is a very hardy fish whose only drawback is the same as that met with in many of the other large Barbs: they just *can't* be trusted not to nibble at the plants! In order to satisfy this hunger for vegetable matter, an occasional lettuce leaf or spinach leaf should be offered to distract them from the plants and also to add to their well-being. Strangely enough, the American breeders produce this fish by the thousands, but the German ichthyologist Hermann Meinken mentions in his work *Die Aquarienfische* that the German breeders have not yet succeeded in breeding them. He mentions the possibility that this fish might be the result of a natural hybridization between two other Barbs, but this seems a bit far fetched. Many American breeders spawn their Clown Barbs in refrigerator liners or very large tanks, and they do not have any more trouble with them than with any of the other large Barbs; like the others, the Clown Barb is prolific.

Photo by Dr. Herbert R. Axelrod.

BARBODES FASCIATUS (Bleeker)/*Striped Barb*

Range: Sumatra, Borneo.
Habits: Peaceful and active.
Water Conditions: Slightly acid water; hardness is not too important, unless at extremes.
Size: Up to 5 inches; rarely seen at this size.
Food Requirements: Accepts live and frozen foods and most dry foods.
Color Variations: Body is yellowish silver, transversed by bars; in females, the bars are less distinct. Fins are rust colored.

An odd thing about the Striped Barb is that the stripes which have given rise to its common name run lengthwise from near the gills to the tail, rather than vertically, as is common with many other Barbs. Unfortunately, this is not enough of a distinction to make the fish popular, and it is rarely seen in dealers' tanks. The Striped Barb is peaceful and suitable for large community tanks, particularly if fairly large fishes are kept with it, but it will do better if maintained with members of its own species. It is reported that the fish spawns like most of the other *Barbodes* species, that is, that it scatters its eggs into plant thickets; the eggs hatch within a day and a half when kept at the same temperature as used for spawning, which should be about 80°. Sex differences between adults of the species are indicated only by the fullness of the female and the comparative lack of clarity in her stripes. Also, some authorities maintain that the black edging at the frontal rays of the dorsal fin are shorter and less distinct in the female, but this cannot be relied upon as a definite indicator of sex.

BARBODES FASCIOLATUS (Günther)/*African Banded Barb*

Range: Angola, West Africa.
Habits: Active and fairly peaceful.
Water Conditions: Neutral to slightly acid water. Hardness not too important, as long as extremes are avoided. Temperature 70 to 85°.
Size: 2½ inches.
Food Requirements: Takes all foods, but live foods are accepted much more readily.
Color Variations: Over-all silver color, with bluish overtones. Small vertical black markings on sides; number of bars is variable.

This West African Barb is prettier than some of its Barb cousins from Africa, but it will certainly never rival the popular Asiatic Barbs in the favor of hobbyists. First of all, it has none of the brilliant coloring of such Asiatic species as the Tiger Barb; secondly, it is very seldom seen, because no commercial efforts have been made to breed this species, and also because it is very seldom imported. In order for a fish to begin to get popular, it must of course be put on the market in quantities sufficient to make hobbyists aware of its existence. This has never been done with *Barbodes fasciolatus*, and it seems unlikely that it ever will be done, because the few scattered importations made thus far have stirred up almost no interest in hobbyists. As of this writing, *Barbodes fasciolatus* has not been bred in the home aquarium, but there is little reason to suppose that its breeding habits would be different in any significant degree from those of its close relatives. The African Banded Barb is less of a plant eater than other African Barbs, but it is still not to be trusted with tender plant specimens. Nibbling on plants indicates that the fish is not getting enough plant matter in its diet.

F-105.00

BARBODES HEXAZONA (Boulenger)/*Belted Barb, Six-Banded Barb*

Range: Malay Peninsula, Sumatra.
Habits: Active, peaceful.
Water Conditions: Soft, slightly acid water. Temperature 74 to 80°.
Size: 2 to 2½ inches.
Food Requirements: Takes all foods.
Color Variations: Black bars on yellowish body, fins tinged with red.

A great deal of confusion has resulted from the close resemblance of many of the Barbs to one another. Such is the case with a number of fishes within the genus *Barbodes*. An illustration of the difficulty of categorizing these fishes correctly comes up when we make a comparison between two such fishes as *Barbodes hexazona* and *Barbodes pentazona*, the Six-Banded Barb and the Five-Banded Barb; both look very much alike, and both are almost identical in the matter of scale and fin counts, two of the most important considerations in cataloguing species within a given genus. About the only difference which makes itself immediately obvious is the black bar running through the eye. This bar is present on *Barbodes hexazona* but absent on *Barbodes pentazona*, so that *hexazona* would have six "zones" or banded areas, and *pentazona* would have only five, as indicated by the respective names. In markings and form *B. hexazona* resembles *Capoeta tetrazona*, the Tiger Barb, but the former is much less colorful and at its best is only a pale imitation of its more popular cousin. The Six-Banded Barb breeds in typical Barb fashion, scattering its eggs into plant thickets, but it does not spawn readily.

BARBODES HOLOTAENIA (Boulenger)/*Spot-Scale Barb*

Range: Tributaries of the Central Congo River.
Habits: Peaceful and active.
Water Conditions: Soft, slightly acid water. Temperature 70 to 85°.
Size: Up to 4¾ inches.
Food Requirements: Accepts all foods.
Color Variations: General coloring of grayish brown, shading to silver in belly region. Crescent-shaped marking on each scale.

This big Barb breeds readily, but the young are not easy to raise; they are quite small for a fish of this size. Although the Spot-Scale Barb has little to recommend it in the way of coloring, the crescent marking which appears in each scale gives the fish at least an interesting appearance, even if it is not of enough importance to create a real demand for the fish. One color note is introduced into the over-all drab pattern by the eyes, the upper portion of which is a light red. Oddly, this characteristic does not appear in all *Barbodes holotaenia;* some specimens have the half-red eyes, but others do not. When the fish was first imported it was believed that the presence or absence of red coloration to the rim of the eye was indicative of sex, but later developments showed that this was incorrect, for sometimes two fishes with colored eyes would spawn successfully, and at other times two fishes without any red color to their eyes would also spawn successfully. From this it was concluded that the coloring of the eye has nothing to do with sexual distinction, but is more probably due to a geographical variation in color. This fish is now very seldom seen.

BARBODES LATERISTRIGA (Cuvier and Valenciennes)
T-Barb, Spanner Barb

Range: Java, Borneo, Sumatra, Thailand, Malay Peninsula.
Habits: Peaceful at smaller sizes, but inclined to bully smaller fishes when it reaches full size.
Water Conditions: Soft, slightly acid water. Temperature 70 to 85°.
Size: Up to 8 inches, but usually seen much smaller.
Food Requirements: Takes all foods, particularly live foods.
Color Variations: General body color yellowish olive, with slight reddish tint to fins. Vertical band beginning below dorsal; horizontal stripe from base of tail almost to vertical band. Also has vertical band midway between eye and first vertical band. Black spot above anal fin.

One thing that can be said in favor of *Barbodes lateristriga* is that it moves more slowly than many of its relatives within the family Cyprinidae; unlike some of the other Barbs, the T-Barb is not given to the swift back and forth pacing that is so characteristic of the smaller Barbs. It can be assumed in general that the larger Barbs are less darting than their relatives, but this does not always hold true; for example, *B. fasciatus*, the Striped Barb, also reaches a good size, but it is a quick mover nevertheless. The T-Barb is no longer considered one of the really common aquarium fishes, but it still has a following with hobbyists who like to maintain at least one tank of large fishes; it is well suited to this use. As is to be expected with so large a fish, many eggs are laid. These eggs are scattered in and around plant thickets, and the parents, although not averse to eating their eggs, are not to be counted within the ranks of the really avid egg-eaters. The fry are large (or at least comparatively large by Barb standards), and the fry are therefore easier to raise than most other Barb fry; for best results, the fry should be kept at temperatures in the upper region of their range for the first few weeks.

BARBODES PENTAZONA (Weber and De Beaufort)
Banded Barb, Five-Banded Barb

Range: Malay Peninsula, Borneo.
Habits: Active and fairly peaceful.
Water Conditions: Soft, slightly acid water. Temperature 74 to 78°.
Size: 2 inches.
Food Requirements: Accepts all foods, especially small live foods.
Color Variations: Body yellowish, with bluish-black bars. In good condition, fish
   has reddish cast to body and red on fins.

This pretty fish, which is considered by some authorities to be identical with
or at the most a variety of *Barbodes hexazona*, is more colorful than its six-
banded relative. Aside from that, and from the fact that *B. pentazona* is
considered to be easier to coax into spawning, there is little difference between
the two. Neither of these two fishes has attained any great degree of popularity,
partly because they are imported so seldom and partly because they are unable
to compete with the colorful beauty of the Tiger Barb, which they resemble
in markings. Still and all, they are attractive, and in a sunny, well planted
tank they make a nice display. Oddly enough, *Barbodes pentazona* is as easy
to spawn as *Barbodes hexazona* is difficult. *B. pentazona* spawns in the
customary Barb manner, but the mating act is accompanied by more "dan-
cing" and less chasing from one end of the tank to the other than with its
relatives. Sexing adult specimens is not difficult, as the female is fuller in
form and is less colorful; in the female the pectoral fins are clear, but in the
male these fins have a pink flush, varying in intensity with the condition
of the fish. Newly emerged fry are small and require small foods.

F-109.00

BARBODES SCHWANENFELDI (Bleeker)/*Tinfoil Barb*

Range: Sumatra, Borneo, Malacca, Thailand.
Habits: Peaceful and very active; a very good jumper. A plant eater.
Water Conditions: Soft, slightly acid water; sediment should be kept to minimum.
  Temperature 74 to 78°.
Size: Up to 14 inches.
Food Requirements: Takes all foods, but should have plenty of vegetable matter in
  its diet.
Color Variations: Silver, with black ridge extending along back into dorsal fin; fins
  pink-orange, with colors becoming brighter depending on the fish's condition.

Usually offered for sale at a size of about two inches, this fish grows rapidly
and is soon too big for all but the largest tanks. As it grows older the body
continues to deepen, and what the hobbyist had originally bought as a small,
streamlined Barb is now a fat giant. Even at its full size, however, the Tinfoil
Barb does not lose all of its attractiveness, for the orange coloring of the fins
is heightened with age, which is the reverse of the usual procedure, as most
fishes lose their bright colors as they increase in age and size. This fish has
not been bred in the U.S. yet, but it is presumed that the general spawning
pattern of large Barbs would be adhered to. Sex differences have not been
noted, but the male is probably the more colorful of the pair, as is true with
other Cyprinids. The Tinfoil Barb, while not disdaining meaty foods, needs
a lot of vegetable matter. If this is not provided in regular feedings, the fish
will take out its hunger on the plants in the tank, beginning with the softest
and working its way up to the more tough-leaved varieties. For such a large
fish, *Barbodes schwanenfeldi* is well mannered and rarely picks on other species.

BARBODES UNITAENIATUS (Gunther)/*Red-Finned Barb*

Range: Southwest Africa, Angola.
Habits: Peaceful at all but largest sizes.
Water Conditions: Neutral, slightly soft water. Temperature 75 to 88°.
Size: About 3 inches.
Food Requirements: Accepts all foods.
Color Variations: Over-all body color is brownish yellow, interrupted on the sides by a black stripe with a silver edge. Fins reddish.

The popular name of this species might lead to the supposition that the fish has a very distinct and attractive color pattern to recommend it to hobbyists, but this is not so. The red coloration in the Red-Finned Barb is more of a subdued pink; indeed, if the fish is not kept in proper condition, this color fails to show at all. It certainly never approaches the brilliant red coloring so obvious on the fins of the Bloodfin, *Aphyocharax rubropinnis*. Still and all, it does have a slight rosy tint, and this is sufficient to make it desirable for some of the more enthusiastic Barb fanciers. Coming as it does from Africa, *Barbodes unitaeniatus* was never in good supply, and, since it didn't excite the hobby very much when it was offered for sale, it seems that it will be seen more and more infrequently as time goes on. Perhaps it will at some future date disappear from the aquarium scene altogether. If the Red-Finned Barb is to be maintained in a community aquarium, it should be kept with fishes which like warm water, because *B. unitaeniatus* has a decided preference for high temperatures, and it cannot exist comfortably in cool water. One advantage of the fish is that it attacks soft-leaved plants less frequently than other Barbs.

F-111.00

Photo by S. Kochetov

Initially identified as *B. chlorotaenia*, these fish are now considered to be specimens of *B. usumbarae*.

Although this fish, *Barbodes usumbarae*, is a very drab African species, it managed to become popular for a short while. The species has a very restricted range.

Photo by Dr. Herbert R. Axelrod.

The lack of body depth in this African Barb, *Barbodes viviparus*, makes it look more like a *Rasbora* species than a Barb. As indicated by the fish's specific name, this species was at one time thought to be a livebearer.

Barbodes anema is elongated in shape, much like *B. vivibarus*, but its dorsal fin is shaped differently. The fish pictured may be *Beirabarbus aurantiacus* of the Zambesi system.

BARILIUS CHRISTYI (Boulenger)/*Copper-Nose*

Range: Lower Congo River and its tributaries.
Habits: An active fish which can only be trusted with others which are as large or larger.
Water Conditions: Slightly acid, clean, well aerated water. Temperature 72° to 76°.
Size: Up to 6 inches.
Food Requirements: Has a healthy appetite, and will take dried as well as living foods. Is particularly fond of insects which have been thrown on the surface.
Color Variations: Greenish, with a copper-colored snout and a number of short, dark vertical bars on the sides.

Judging from the way it carries itself, *Barilius christyi* is a fish which comes from moving streams. Axelrod verified this on his 1957 African expedition. It should therefore be given a roomy aquarium with clean water and some aeration. Here it shows its attractive, metallic colors. If possible, it is best to keep it in a small school of about 6 or more. They are very active, and will almost surely jump out if their aquarium is left uncovered. Females can only be distinguished when fully grown. At this time they show a deeper belly while the males are more slender and also more highly colored. We have only one account of their spawning, and that a sketchy one; they spawn in the same manner as *Danio malabaricus*. A tank of at least 15 gallons is provided, and a layer of pebbles or glass marbles is placed on the bottom. A ripe pair, or better yet, several pairs are placed here. The water should not be more than 10 inches above the layer of pebbles or marbles. If all goes well, the fish will pursue each other in a very lively manner dropping eggs at intervals, these fall between the pebbles.

F-114.00

BATHETHIOPS FOWLERI (Poll)/*African Moonfish*

Range: Belgian Congo.

Habits: An active fish which gets along well with other community fishes.

Water Conditions: Prefers slightly acid, clean water with a pH of about 6.8 and a DH of 4.

Size: Under 2 inches.

Food Requirements: Eats all kinds of foods, but is especially fond of frozen brine shrimp. Live foods should be offered once a week.

Color Variations: The fins are redder on newly imported specimens, and unless they are fed brine shrimp they never get the red back. Sides are very blue on some specimens.

The famous African fish collector Pierre Brichard sent these specimens to Ross Socolof (who had a wholesale fish importing business in Brooklyn in 1957). Socolof offered them as "African Moonfish" because they were so round and shined so beautifully in reflected light, a characteristic of our moon. The fish sold well, but no one was ever able to breed them. As a matter of fact, African Tetras have been very difficult to breed as a rule, while South American Tetras are fairly easy to breed. As soon as Brichard heard that this fish sold so well, he immediately collected them by the thousands, only to have his whole collection aborted by the Congo war which followed their Independence Day! Brichard is collecting this species again, but in very limited numbers, and the interest in this species has quieted down. It is quite possible that very soon this fish will be imported in huge quantities and will once again take the place it deserves in every community aquarium.

A very dazzling sight is a school of about 50 of these fish in a 50-gallon aquarium which is lit by the Sylvania Gro-Lux fluorescent tube which makes the blues and reds in fishes so extravagantly rich.

Photo by H.J. Richter

BEDOTIA GEAYI (Pellegrin)/*Madagascar Rainbow*

Range: Madagascar.

Habits: Peaceful and active; never molest their tankmates.

Water Conditions: Somewhat alkaline water required, about pH 7.3 or 7.4. Temperature 76° to 78°.

Size: 2½ to 2¾ inches.

Food Requirements: Not a fussy eater; will eat dried foods readily, but should get live food at least occasionally.

Color Variations: Body greenish with a dark stripe running from the eye to the caudal base. Dorsal, anal and caudal have dark edges.

This fish usually makes an immediate hit with all who see it for the first time. While it is not as gorgeous as some of our outstanding beauties, it has a quiet charm and alert liveliness which make it desirable and we venture to predict that some day when it becomes more obtainable it will be one of the popular favorites. Some of the males which have been more blessed by Mother Nature have an added attraction: the ends of both caudal lobes are tipped with a bright red. This is also seen in some of the females to a lesser extent. The double dorsal fin identifies it as a member of the family of *Atherinidae*, to which belong the well-known Australian Rainbowfish and the Celebes Rainbowfish. These species have the characteristic that they prefer alkaline water, and *Bedotia geayi* are not at all happy when placed in the slightly acid water to which most egg-laying species are usually relegated. Given water which ranges from neutral to slightly alkaline, however, they soon feel very much at home. They spawn near the surface in closely-bunched plants, only a few brown eggs every day. Eggs and fry are not usually eaten, and the youngsters are easily raised on brine shrimp.

F-116.00

BELONESOX BELIZANUS (Kner)/*Pike Top Minnow, Pike Livebearer*

Range: Southern Mexico, Honduras to Costa Rica, Nicaragua and Guatemala.
Habits: Very vicious; cannot even be trusted with smaller members of their own family.
Water Conditions: Roomy tank which has been heavily planted is ideal. Water should have an addition of salt, 1 tablespoonful per gallon.
Size: Males 6 inches, females 8 inches.
Food Requirements: Will only take living foods of larger sizes. Small living fishes are ideal.
Color Variations: Sides are grayish to olive-green, with numerous tiny black dots on the sides.

If you like your fish nasty, this one is for you. This would be an ideal species for a guppy-breeder who has to keep weeding out the undesirable specimens to make way for the good ones, and therefore has a constant supply of unwanted fish. The Pike Livebearer is very similar in habits to his namesake the Pike: always hungry, ever ready to sneak up on some unsuspecting prey and gobble it up. One look at the pointed snout and sharp teeth will confirm this. The small, needle-pointed teeth are not designed for slashing and chewing, but are grasping teeth which enable it to hold its prey and prevent its escape. This it cannot do unless its captor opens his mouth, and *Belonesox* will do this only to get it further down his throat and swallow it. Females which are ready to deliver young, as their swollen belly would indicate, should be placed in their own well-planted quarters at a temperature of about 85°. The youngsters are quite touchy at first, and must also be protected from their greedy mother. Daphnia is a good food for them to start out with, followed by fully grown brine shrimp or baby guppies. Keeping this fish fed is the greatest problem.

BELONTIA SIGNATA (Günther)/*Comb-Tail*

Range: Ceylon.
Habits: Vicious toward smaller fishes; should be kept only with those which are able to take care of themselves.
Water Conditions: Large tank is required. Water not critical. Temperature should be at least 76°.
Size: 5 inches.
Food Requirements: Very greedy; will take coarse dried foods, but prefer chunks such as pieces of earthworms, or lean raw beef.
Color Variations: Sides are a reddish brown, lighter in the belly region, outer edge of the tail is fringed.

This species is very similar to the Paradise Fish, *Macropodus opercularis*, not only in appearance but in habits. As in the other Anabantids, the male may be distinguished by his longer, more pointed fins and slightly brighter colors. Like the Paradise Fish to which it is related, they are very heavy eaters, and it may be a bit difficult to keep a tank in which a number of them are quartered spotlessly clean. In the winter months when live foods are not so easy to come by, other foods may be substituted such as pieces of shrimp, chunks of clam or crab meat, or pieces of lean beef. This fish builds a bubble-nest in which a great number of eggs are placed. Sometimes a pair will share parental duties in guarding the eggs and fry, but more often one or the other will be constantly driven away. If this happens, take out the fish which is being chased. When they become free-swimming, the youngsters have no further need of parental attention. There is always the chance that the appetite of the parents might overcome their affection, and they should also be removed. This is not a fish for the community aquarium.

F-118.00

Photo by Dr. Herbert R. Axelrod.

BETTA BELLICA (Sauvage)/*Slender Betta*

Range: Perak, in Malaya.

Habits: Not a good fish for the community tank. Although there is not the aggressiveness between males as with *B. splendens*, they are best kept alone.

Water Conditions: Not critical, but a high temperature (76° to 85°) must be maintained.

Size: About 4 inches.

Food Requirements: Should get living foods, with occasional supplements of dried foods.

Color Variations: Sides reddish-brown, with a large green spot on the gill-cover and several rows of green dots on the sides.

Looking at this species and comparing it with a wild specimen of *Betta splendens*, one cannot help but wonder what the result would have been if the breeders had bestowed as much care and time on *B. bellica* as they did on *B. splendens*. Perhaps the result would have been even more beautiful than the gorgeous *B. splendens* one sees today. But *B. bellica* is more beautiful than the wild *B. splendens*. Would aquarium-bred specimens have yielded the wide variety of colors and huge fins that *B. splendens* has? All these are interesting speculations to which, if we ever know the answer, we will not know it for a long time to come. This attractive fish is longer and more slender in the body than *B. splendens*, and the males can be distinguished by their longer ventral fins. Unfortunately they have proven to be not quite as active as their illustrious cousins, and they seem to spend most of their time moping about near the bottom. They spawn by building bubble-nests.

Photo by E. Roloff.

BETTA BREDERI (Myers)/*Breder's Betta*

Range: Java and Sumatra.
Habits: Although they are not vicious, it is best to keep this species by themselves.
Water Conditions: Not critical, as long as the tank is clean. Temperature about 78°.
Size: To 3¼ inches.
Food Requirements: Live foods exclusively.
Color Variations: Yellowish brown with lighter-colored vertical bands. Scales on the sides of the males have a bluish shimmer.

While it is not as glamorous as its illustrious cousin *B. splendens*, *B. brederi* has some interesting spawning habits which make it more or less unique. This species is not a bubble-nest builder like most of the other Labyrinth Fishes, but a mouthbreeder. After the nuptial embrace, the male catches the large eggs in his folded anal fin and fertilizes them. Then the female picks them up from there in her mouth and offers them to her mate by spitting them toward him. Sometimes he refuses one or two and she has to pick them up again and spit them at him once more. This little game goes on until all of the eggs are safely lodged in the brood-pouch of the male, which extends from his mouth to his throat. The eggs hatch in about 40 hours, but the fry continue to be carried about until they are capable of swimming and hunting for their own food. Raising them is not difficult, and their aquarium should be kept covered for two reasons: first, to prevent them from gulping chilled air and second, to prevent a scum from forming on the surface which would interfere with the youngsters coming up to breathe the atmospheric air.

F-120.00

BETTA SPLENDENS (Regan)/*Betta, Siamese Fighting Fish*

Range: Thailand, Malaya, Cochin China.
Habits: Usually peaceful with other fishes of its own size, but two males in the same aquarium will fight until one retreats.
Water Conditions: Not critical; breathing atmospheric air as they do, they can be kept in very small containers. Temperature should not go below 78°.
Size: 2 to 2½ inches.
Food Requirements: Will take dried foods, but should get an occasional meal of live foods.
Color Variations: Many colors have been developed: red, green, blue and combinations of these colors.

Next to the ubiquitous Guppy and Goldfish, this is probably the most popular of all aquarium fishes. Their brilliant colors are a monument to the fish-breeder's art, and has been developed by selective breeding from a rather nondescript greenish, short-finned fish which is still bred in Siam today for fish-fighting. Fish-fighting is as much of a sport in Siam as cock-fighting is in many other parts of the world. The procedure is simple: two males are placed in a small aquarium and wagers are made and taken as to the outcome. The fish tear away at each other furiously until one or the other is over-come by exhaustion or weakness. The vanquished is then fished out by its owner, who either disposes of it or nurses it back to health, and the winner's owner collects his money. The *Betta splendens* is easily bred.

Bettas are available in a multitude of colors ranging from brown and black to orchid, red, and blue.

BIOTOECUS OPERCULARIS (Steindachner)/*Green Dwarf Cichlid*

Range: The Amazon River System of Brazil.

Habits: Typically nocturnal; hugs the bottom of the aquarium and hides amongst plants and any other nook it can find.

Water Conditions: Not very sensitive to water conditions as long as the temperature is between 70 and 85° and not too acid or alkaline. Tolerates a pH of 6.0 to 8.0.

Size: Under 4 inches.

Food Requirements: Prefers worms to anything else, but eagerly takes frozen brine shrimp and beef heart. Also likes the pelletized foods.

Color Variations: A very variable fish which blends in with its background very easily. The males have a purple caste on their belly and their body is transparent green.

This fish was first discovered in 1891 in Lake Saraca and the Amazon River by Vila Bela. At that time it was placed in a separate genus, *Saraca*, named after the lake in which the fish was found. It is the only species from Brazil in this genus. Pellegrin placed the fish in the genus *Biotoecus* in 1903, along with the authors of this genus, Eigenmann and Kennedy, because it was discovered that *Saraca* was a genus of butterflies established by Walker in 1865. The fish has appeared often in scientific literature because it is a "misfit" and lies so closely related to such genera as *Batrachops, Apistogramma, Chaetobranchopsis, Cichla* and *Aequidens*.

The fish spawns rather easily if properly fed on live foods such as small garden worms, *Tubifex* worms and frozen brine shrimp. The pair seeks seclusion, sometimes even going into a darkened flowerpot, where about 60 eggs are laid in a small circle. They exercise extreme parental care and zealously guard their young until a week after they are free swimming. It is advisable to remove the parents as soon as the young are free swimming and able to take freshly hatched brine shrimp.

BOTIA BEAUFORTI (Smith)/*Beaufort's Loach*

Range: Thailand.
Habits: Generally peaceful toward other fishes; mostly nocturnal. Will remain mostly in the darker portions of the aquarium.
Water Conditions: Soft, slightly acid water, well-aerated. Tank should have a number of hiding-places and be dimly lighted.
Size: To 8 inches.
Food Requirements: Live foods, especially *Tubifex* or white worms preferred; frozen and prepared foods also eaten, and food left by other fishes.
Color Variations: Grayish-green body with 4 rows of dots on the sides, each dot surrounded by a lighter area. Dorsal and anal fins orange.

Don't try to keep *Botia beauforti* unless you have a large tank. The 8-inch size given is a maximum, but 6-inch specimens are not at all unusual. One of the distinguishing marks of this species is the lack of taper in the body toward the caudal base, which is almost as wide at this point as it is at the middle of the body under the dorsal fin. The snout is not as underslung as in most of the other species, sticking almost straight out. This species has a double spine under the eye. *B. beauforti* should not be kept singly, but rather in a group. If kept singly, they may develop a nasty attitude toward their tankmates; on the other hand, if kept in a group a sort of "pecking order" is established among themselves, and they should be provided with a number of hiding-places for the protection of the weaker ones. After a while each fish will select a spot for himself and spend most of his time there, defending it against all intruders. In their home waters they swim in schools in streams with their heads to the current, feeding on whatever comes rolling down to them; because they come from flowing waters, their tank should be clean and well-aerated.

BOTIA HORAE (Smith)/*Hora's Loach*

Range: Thailand.

Habits: Peaceful, mostly nocturnal. Will remain mostly in the darker portions of the aquarium.

Water Conditions: Soft, slightly acid water, well-aerated. Tank should have a number of hiding-places and not be brightly lighted.

Size: To 4 inches, usually smaller.

Food Requirements: Live foods, especially *Tubifex* or white worms preferred; frozen and prepared foods also eaten, and food left by other fishes.

Color Variations: Greenish yellow sides. Black stripe extends from top of snout along the top of the back, ending in a bar at the caudal base.

The *Botia* species all have a protective device which is shared by few other fresh-water fishes, but is not at all uncommon among the marine groups. There is an erectible spine, sometimes two, under each eye. This inflicts a painful but non-poisonous sting when the fish is handled. This has proven to be the downfall of many a bird or larger fish which caught a *Botia* and did not spit it out quickly enough, to have it lodge in its throat and choke on it. This is no satisfaction at all to the *Botia*, which cannot usually dislodge itself either and dies in the process. *B. horae* is not only an attractive fish with its green body and black stripe along the back, but also remains within the 4-inch range and does not outgrow its welcome in a medium-sized tank. Although they adapt well to a life in captivity and live to a good age, there are no records of their ever having spawned in captivity. It is even questionable which are the males and which the females, and they do not seem to attain a sexual maturity in the aquarium. Usually some factor is missing which would be undesirable in a home aquarium, such as a mud bottom.

BOTIA HYMENOPHYSA (Bleeker)/*Banded Loach*

Range: Malaya, Thailand, Singapore, Java, Sumatra and Borneo.
Habits: Occurs in flowing streams of fresh water. Mostly nocturnal; shuns light and stays in the darker portions of the aquarium.
Water Conditions: Should be given clean, well-oxygenated water; temperatures between 75° and 80°.
Size: In captivity about 6 inches. Wild specimens are said to attain 12 inches.
Food Requirements: Will take any living foods, including small fishes. Will also rummage around the bottom for uneaten leftovers.
Color Variations: Sides are a light brown, with reddish overtones and 13 to 15 dark, narrow vertical bands.

This attractive Loach is a useful addition to an aquarium of larger fishes, but should not be trusted with smaller ones which could be swallowed. It is nocturnal in habits to a great extent, and should be provided with a number of retreats such as rock caves. Care must be taken to place the rocks for these caves on a firm foundation, or they will be undermined and fall on the fish which is doing the digging. This Loach is found in flowing streams, so it is best provided with clean, well-filtered and well-aerated water. For some unexplained reason, they will sometimes dash madly from one end of the aquarium to the other, stirring up the bottom sediment and anything else which is loose. Perhaps this is sheer playfulness. Sex differences have never been fully determined, and if they have ever spawned in captivity it has never been observed nor reported. They take well to captivity otherwise, and specimens have been observed to grow to a ripe age in the confines of an aquarium. The probable reason why spawning activity has never been observed may be that the nocturnal nature of this Loach would confine its activity in this direction to the hours when there is little light.

BOTIA LOHACHATA (Chaudhuri)/*Pakistani Loach*

Range: India and Pakistan.

Habits: A typical Loach with bottom-dwelling habits.

Water Conditions: Prefers very soft, slightly acid water with high temperatures in the 80's.

Size: Seldom larger than 4 inches in length.

Food Requirements: This species often starves in an aquarium for they must have worms in their diet, preferably *Tubifex* worms.

Color Variations: This is a very variable species. The Indian variety is less colorful than the Pakistan variety.

The Pakistani Loach is famous only because it is one of the very few fishes from Pakistan which have made aquarium history. The Pakistani people are very active in the aquarium field and their new aquarium in Karachi must be applauded as a major contribution to "living museums of the world." This Loach has never been exported from Pakistan in commercial quantities only because there are so few exporters in the small country. But shipments arrive regularly from India, especially Bombay, where they are collected in large quantities. The Indian variety is probably a subspecies, if not a separate species, as it is very much lighter in color and is much smaller, but there is so much variability from population to population that it is impossible to determine the differences between the two varieties with a statistical analysis of the validity of certain meristic differences.

With such colorful competitors as *Botia macracantha* it is doubtful that this species will ever have major economic value as an aquarium fish, for it spends too much of its time hiding.

BOTIA LUCAS-BAHI (Fowler)/*Barred Loach*

Range: Thailand.
Habits: Peaceful toward other fishes if kept in a group; mostly nocturnal.
Water Conditions: Soft, slightly acid water, well-aerated. Tank should have a
number of hiding-places and be dimly lighted. Temperature 73° to 76°.
Size: To 3 inches.
Food Requirements: Live foods, especially *Tubifex* and white worms preferred;
frozen and prepared foods also eaten, as well as food left by other fishes.
Color Variations: Sides grayish-green with 10 to 15 vertical bars extending from the
back halfway down the sides. Dorsal fin partly or totally black.

Botia lucas-bahi has such a similarity to *Botia hymenophysa* that there is a
strong suspicion among taxonomists that one may be merely a sub-species
of the other. The main difference seems to be that *B. lucas-bahi* has a dorsal
fin which is either wholly or partly black, or at the very least edged with black.
This species is also found in flowing streams, and for this reason their water
should be clean and well-aerated, and high temperatures should be avoided.
Like the other *Botia* species, *B. lucas-bahi* has not been bred in the aquarium.
Sexual maturity seems to come only after several years of good feeding and
good living conditions, and only then can the females be distinguished from
the males by their more rounded bellies. The writer has no doubt that before
long someone, perhaps someone who has never bred fish before, will come
up with a breeding of one of the *Botia* species. In Thailand they simply
throw a dozen or so into a pool and let Nature take its course. In the aquarium
it is not as easy to duplicate natural conditions, but a close enough approxi-
mation has been achieved to breed many fishes which have for many years
been considered impossible.

Photo by Dr. Herbert R. Axelrod

BOTIA MACRACANTHA (Bleeker)/*Clown Loach*

Range: Sumatra, Borneo and the Sunda Islands.
Habits: Peaceful, not quite as nocturnal as some of the other species.
Water Conditions: Clean, well-aerated water. Temperatures should not exceed 76°.
Size 12 inches maximum, but most specimens do not exceed 4 inches.
Food Requirements: They like to grub for leftover morsels at the bottom, but should also get some living foods.
Color Variations: Yellowish red body with three black vertical bands. Fins are bright red.

The Clown Loach is the most popular and colorful member of the genus. It does not appear to be quite as sensitive to light as the others, and therefore has the added attraction of being more apt to stay in sight. However there should also be places provided where they can get into a shady spot to rest their eyes. This is a very active species, and often swims up and down the glass sides of the aquarium for no apparent reason. To the best of our knowledge there have been no successful spawnings observed in the aquarium, probably due to the fact that conditions which are present in their natural environments are missing in the aquarium. For instance, the fish may spawn in soft mud, which would never be permitted by an aquarist who wants to see his fish and plants. Some day some fortunate aquarist will be successful, and a very desirable aquarium fish will become more available at a lower price. At the present time it is also not known what the external sex differences are, and it is impossible to tell the males from the females without killing them. Some day we may also hear from some observant Asiatic naturalist who studies the life habits of this fish in its native environment.

Photo by Dr. Herbert R. Axelrod.

BOTIA SIDTHIMUNKI (Klausewitz)/*Dwarf Loach*

Range: Thailand.
Habits: Peaceful, playful, seem to be less nocturnal than the other species.
Water Conditions: Soft, alkaline water, well-aerated. Temperature 73° to 76°.
Size: 1½ inches.
Food Requirements: Small live foods preferred, other foods accepted.
Color Variations: Back golden brown, sides silvery to light yellow. A number of dark spots along the sides connect with saddle-shaped marks above.

This lively little fellow is sure to find favor with any hobbyist who sees it. Although it is a *Botia*, it has none of the faults found among other members of the genus. They aren't always hiding, and do not seem to have the dislike for the lighter spots that the others have. *B. sidthimunki* is the smallest known member of a group which with some species gets rather big. The writer had some which were not yet full-grown when he got them. They were about 1 inch in length. One day there was only one where there were formerly three. After a thorough search it was found that the other two had squeezed into the intake tube of the outside filter, where they were found happily grubbing around in the glass-wool. It was some time before they became too large to squeeze through the narrow openings, and they frequently had to be netted out of the filter. This species is a recent introduction, named by Dr. Wolfgang Klausewitz in 1959. It is doubtless the most active and playful of the *Botia*.

Photo by H.J. Richter

BRACHYDANIO ALBOLINEATUS (Blyth)
Pearl Danio (golden variety known as Gold Danio)

Range: Moulmein Region of India, Burma, Thailand, Malacca and Sumatra.

Habits: Very active swimmer, likes sunny tanks with clean, well-aerated water. Likes to swim in schools with others of its own kind.

Water Conditions: pH and hardness not critical. Aquaria need not be large, but should provide a good amount of open space for swimming.

Size: 2½ inches.

Food Requirements: A good eater like most active fishes. Will thrive on dry as well as living foods, but some living foods should be included occasionally.

Color Variations: Mother-of-pearl body color, with an indistinct reddish stripe beginning at the center of the body and ending at the caudal base.

This little fish has all the attributes of a good aquarium inhabitant. It is above all peaceful; it does not outgrow a small aquarium; it eats all foods, and besides is one of the most easily-bred egg-layers. A small school of these fish with the sun playing on them in a well-planted aquarium is a very pretty sight. This is the only fish which the writer has had spawn for him in the dark of a paper pint container on the way home from the store. The approved way of spawning them is to place them in a long aquarium with about 4 inches of half fresh and half aged aquarium water. The bottom should be covered with several layers of large pebbles or glass marbles. The pair (some breeders use two males to one female) should be healthy and in good condition, which the female shows by her increased girth. They begin driving almost at once, and dropping eggs which are non-adhesive and fall among the pebbles or marbles. Temperature should be 74° to 76°. When the female has become depleted, the fish are netted out. Fry hatch in 36 to 48 hours, and are easily raised on very fine food to a point where newly hatched brine shrimp may be taken, after which growth is quite rapid.

F-131.00

BRACHYDANIO KERRI (Smith)/*Kerr's Danio*

Range: Koh Yao Yai and Koh Yao Noi Islands, Thailand.
Habits: Peaceful, active, best kept in a group.
Water Conditions: Not critical; water should be clean and well-aerated.
Size: 1½ inches.
Food Requirements: Small live foods preferred, frozen and prepared foods also taken willingly.
Color Variations: Body deep blue with a golden line from the gill-cover to the caudal base. Another irregular gold line below. Fins yellow.

This is one of the lesser-known species of a popular genus. Why it has not "caught on" is one of those mysteries. It is every bit as peaceful, active and hardy as the Zebra or Pearl Danio, and its colors are certainly far from unattractive. It is every bit as easy to breed as the others, and raising the young presents no problems, either. Maybe some day some breeder will make a great "discovery" and suddenly everybody will wonder why they have been passing them up all these years. Like the other Danios, the best way to keep them is in a school of about a dozen, with enough swimming space to suit their active nature. They will not interfere with any other fishes in the tank with them, unless their tankmates are fishes which are made nervous by their constant activity. This species has been known to science since 1931, and was first introduced to hobbyists in Germany in 1956. Strangely enough, this species is not very popular among European hobbyists either. The European hobbyist seems to prefer species which present a little difficulty, and as a rule avoids the livebearers and "easy" egglayers.

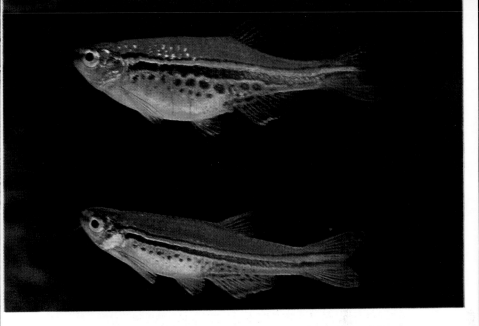

BRACHYDANIO NIGROFASCIATUS (Day)/*Spotted Danio*

Range: Upper Burma to Rangoon and the Moulmein region.

Habits: Active swimmer, does not require a large aquarium, but some open space should be provided.

Water Conditions: Clean, well-aerated water, pH and hardness not critical. Temperatures should be between 72° and 77°.

Size: Slightly under 2 inches.

Food Requirements: Dried and frozen foods as well as living foods are eagerly eaten, but should not be too coarse.

Color Variations: Body color brown on the back to yellowish on the belly. Bluish stripe from the side, with spots underneath and on the anal fin.

Like the other Brachydanio species, *B. nigrofasciatus* is an active, peaceful and hardy fish. This fish was once known as *Brachydanio analipunctatus*, and got its present name in 1932. Being a smaller and not quite as strikingly colored fish, we do not see it as often as *B. rerio* or *B. albolineatus*, but it is every bit as satisfactory in the aquarium. Rather than keep it in pairs, it is better to put about 6 to 12 together, as they like to congregate in schools. Both sexes are very similar in coloration, but the females may be distinguished by their fuller, heavier bodies. Like the other *Brachydanio* species, this one lays non-adhesive eggs, which should be allowed to fall between layers of pebbles or glass marbles, to prevent their being eaten by the parents. This is one of the few egg-laying genera in which the various species can be hybridized, and interesting results can be produced, but unfortunately the offspring are usually sterile. This has its advantages, too. If the offspring were fertile, we would soon be unable to get pure strains of these attractive fishes, as has happened with some of our livebearing fishes.

F-133.00

BRACHYDANIO RERIO (Hamilton-Buchanan)
Zebra, Zebra Danio, Striped Danio

Range: Coromandel Coast of India, from Calcutta to Masulipatam.
Habits: Peaceful, active, likes to travel in schools.
Water Conditions: pH and hardness not critical. Prefers clean, well aerated water, being native to flowing streams.
Size: About 2 inches.
Food Requirements: A heavy eater, like all active fishes. All foods are accepted, but some live foods should be included.
Color Variations: Body color silvery to yellowish, with wide blue stripes horizontally. These stripes are repeated in all unpaired fins except the dorsal.

This is probably the most popular among the egglaying fishes, and for good reasons. The Zebra Danio is hardy, always active, and will never attack any of its tankmates. Besides, it is easily bred, easily fed, and will withstand much abuse without serious consequences, making it just about the perfect aquarium fish. Many advanced breeders, the writer included, remember it as the first egglayer they ever spawned, and in almost all cases many of the fry were raised successfully. There are many methods of breeding the Zebra Danio which, like the other *Brachydanio* species, lays a non-adhesive egg. All of these methods have the same purpose, to keep the parents from eating their spawn. Of course, the layer of pebbles or marbles technique described for the other *Brachydanio* species is still the most popular, because it gives the breeders the most swimming area. Another is a bag of nylon mesh wide enough to let through the eggs but not the breeders, which is suspended in the breeding aquarium. Still another is a bed of glass rods spaced slightly apart and placed so that they lie about an inch above the bottom. Fry hatch in 36 hours, and are easily raised.

F-134.00

BRACHYGOBIUS AGGREGATUS (Herre)/*Philippine Bumblebee*

Range: Philippine Islands.

Habits: A typical Goby that spends most of its time "hopping" from one spot to another, often attaching itself to the glass with modified ventral fins.

Water Conditions: Hard, alkaline water is preferred, with very high temperatures in the 80's being necessary.

Size: Under 2 inches.

Food Requirements: Live food is a necessity; small worms are best.

Color Variations: The intensity of the yellow is very variable and many specimens are found without any trace of yellow whatsoever.

As is mentioned under *B. xanthozona*, considerable confusion exists between which species is which. For a much higher authority than Prof. Sterba's book (published in Eastern Germany), we refer to the Axelrod-Schultz *Handbook of Tropical Aquarium Fishes*, from which we quote the following:

"*Brachygobius xanthozonus* (Bleeker) with 8 dark cross bars or black girdles and 50 scale rows along the side, has been badly confused with *B. doriae*, which has only 3 black bars or girdles and 27 to 30 scales. The color variety show above with narrow black bars between the main broad black bars has been illustrated in aquarium books as *B. doriae*, with the true *doriae* being called *xanthozonus*. The species illustrated on this page is *B. aggregatus* Herre (*Philippine Journal of Science*, 72 (4):361, pl. 4, 1940, type locality, Philippines). Counts: Dorsal VI-I, 6; anal 1,6; scales 22 to 26."

The photograph above is the same which appears in Axelrod-Schultz and shows how variably this species may be mottled. Undoubtedly there are additional species to be found in areas lying between the Philippines, Borneo and Singapore, from which we know the three species listed here.

BRACHYGOBIUS DORIAE (Günther)/*Doria's Bumblebeefish*

Range: Borneo and the Malayan Archipelago.
Habits: Should be kept by themselves in a small aquarium. Hiding-places should be provided.
Water Conditions: Water should have an addition of one heaping teaspoonful of table salt per gallon. Temperature 75° to 78°.
Size: Up to 1 inch.
Food Requirements: Small live foods exclusively.
Color Variations: Body color dirty yellow, covered with irregular blotches of dark brown.

These interesting little fish come from partly brackish waters, and for this reason their water should have an addition of table salt, one heaping teaspoonful per gallon. Like most of the Goby group, the ventral fins are joined and form an efficient sucking disc, by means of which they can attach themselves to stones or any other flat surface. Because of this they do not have to battle against any current which comes along. When the pull is too strong to swim against with its little fins, the fish merely attaches itself to a stone or any other firm object that happens to be handy until things quiet down. *Brachygobius doriae* spawns in a very similar manner to many of the Cichlids. The male cleans off a patch in a secluded spot, such as the inside of a flowerpot. The eggs are laid here and then the male guards them. Hatching time varies greatly from one egg to the other, but at the end of 5 days the fry should all be out. Two days later they are free-swimming. All this time the male is guarding them fiercely, but there is no point in leaving him there when the young are able to take care of themselves, and they could be eaten.

BRACHYGOBIUS XANTHOZONA (Bleeker)/*Bumblebeefish*

Range: Sumatra, Borneo and Java.
Habits: Should be kept in a small aquarium by themselves. Hiding-places should be provided.
Water Conditions: Water should have an addition of one heaping teaspoonful of table salt per gallon. Temperature 75 to 78°.
Size: To 1¾ inches, usually smaller.
Food Requirements: Small live foods exclusively.
Color Variations: Body color yellow with 4 wide dark vertical bands. Both dorsal fins and anal fin are black.

Nobody who has ever watched a bumblebee buzzing from flower to flower on its wings which are so tiny in proportion to its body can ever dispute that it has its underwater replica in this little fish with its short, round black-and-yellow body and undersized fins. *Brachygobius xanthozona* has been the source of some scientific argument lately. There were some who said that the name is incorrect and the right name is *B. nunus*, and others who claimed that the correct name should be *B. aggregatus.* In his very comprehensive work "Süsswasserfische aus Aller Welt" Professor Günther Sterba lists the three species and describes the very slight differences which exist between them. These might be described as color varieties of the same fish, but the fact remains that there are *other* differences which cannot be shrugged off, such as the count of the second dorsal and anal fin-rays. In *B. xanthozonus* both of these fins show I/8-9. In *B. nunus* the count is I/7, and in *B. aggregatus* it is I/6. In other words, if your fish has one stiff ray and six soft rays in the second dorsal and anal fins, it must be *B. aggregatus*, etc.

Photo by K. Paysan

BROCHIS COERULEUS (Cope)/*Short-Bodied Catfish*

Range: Upper Amazon, also in the Ambiyacu River, a tributary in Peru.

Habits: Peaceful, feeds on the bottom, where it is useful in picking up uneaten foods left by other fishes. Seldom uproots plants.

Water Conditions: Not critical; sensitive to only one thing: there must be *no* salt in the water. Temperatures should range between 76° and 80°.

Size: About 2½ inches.

Food Requirements: Eats any kind of prepared foods, but should get an occasional feeding of tubifex worms, of which it is very fond.

Color Variations: Lighter part of body gold, sides greenish gold, underparts light yellow.

Being a comparative newcomer, we do not have a very satisfactory amount of information on this Catfish. At first sight, this fish looks like a stubby *Corydoras aeneus*, but there are enough important anatomical differences to put it into another genus. The body is much higher and more compressed; the adipose fin is considerably larger and has one ray which is spiny and gives the fin a pointed appearance; the armor-plates on the head also extend into the snout. There are no known external sex differences, with the possible exception that the armor-plates in female specimens may not meet as closely as in the males, which would probably be more noticeable in females with eggs. Although quite a few are being imported at the present time, so far we have seen no accounts of their being bred. Our guess would be that they spawn like the *Corydoras* species, but like so many guesses it may be wide of the mark. It is an attractive, interesting, peaceful fish and like the *Corydoras* species, it would find a ready market among hobbyists. Like many other difficult spawners, a few generations of tank-bred specimens would produce fish which would be accustomed to life in the aquarium and spawn readily.

F-138.00

BUNOCEPHALUS CORACOIDEUS (Cope)/*Two-colored Banjo Catfish*

Range: Throughout Brazil and as far east as Ecuador and south to Uruguay.
Habits: A bottom dwelling Catfish that is nocturnal in habit and ugly in appearance.
Water Conditions: Tolerant of any water with a pH from 5.0 to 8.0 and a temperature between 60 and 85°F.
Size: About 6 inches.
Food Requirements: A true scavenger which ingests everything to be found at the bottom of the aquarium whether or not it is digestible.
Color Variations: It is generally a dark gray with no obvious "two color." This misnomer came from a translation of its previous scientific name, "*B. bicolor*", which has been invalidated.

Some fish are famous for their beauty . . . some for their ugliness . . . and the Banjo Catfish happens to be the latter case. This fish is so unfishlike that it is hard to tell where its eyes are, or, where its mouth opens. Its lack of beauty is more than balanced by its interesting reproductive habits and the ease with which it spawns in home aquaria. Sex is easily distinguished because females are much fatter and fuller than males. After selecting an active pair, place them in an aquarium all by themselves and feed them heavily on *Tubifex* or small earthworms. Spawning usually is easier in the spring and if you have the pair well conditioned after a month on live foods, you can induce spawning by changing 50% of their water with *fresh* tap water of the same temperature. In 48 hours the pair will spawn. Sometimes they spawn under a fallen leaf but other times they spawn on a large rock and incubate their eggs like a chicken . . . by sitting on them!

For the amateur, it is impossible to distinguish between most of the *Bunocephalus* species, so this one will serve as a model for the entire genus.

BUTIS BUTIS (Hamilton Buchanan)/*Crazy Fish, Ca Bong*

Range: Throughout the Asian area bounded by China, Indochina, Indonesia and the Philippines.

Habits: A typical Goby which clings upside down to plants and rocks and swims upside down as well.

Water Conditions: Not very particular about water conditions, but since it is found in some brackish water areas, it is assumed that it has a tolerance for hard water.

Size: About 4 inches.

Food Requirements: Prefers live foods, but is an active scavenger and cleans rocks and plants of algal growths incessantly.

Color Variations: Very variable in color. The color plate, a drawing from Chevey's book, shows a good average coloration.

The author (HRA) entered the aquarium depot of Lee Chin Eng in Djakarta, Indonesia in 1959 and was greeted with the exclamation: "Dr. Axelrod! I've discovered a new fish!" The author quickly investigated the fish and remarked, "I doubt that it's new, but it sure is acting crazy." That night Lee wrote a letter to a German importer and said he had "Axelrod's new Crazy Fish." The name stuck in Europe and in the United States, and the Crazy Fish is becoming a very popular scavenger. The Crazy Fish, even with its big mouth, doesn't seem to be too dangerous to smaller fishes, but this may have been because he was so well fed. The ones kept by the author worked 24 hours a day working over every rock and plant leaf sucking in whatever there is to suck in from such surfaces. Their bellies were always full and the fish were always healthy. Newborn fishes didn't disappear into their stomachs as far as the author could determine. In 1822 Hamilton-Buchanan described the fish from India as *Cheilodipterus butis*. In 1837 Cuvier and Valenciennes renamed it *Eleotris humeralis*, thinking it a different species. Cantor in his *Catalogue of Malayan Fishes* (1849) united the two species under the name *Eleotris butis*. Bleeker in 1849 called it *Eleotris prismatica* and again, in 1852, *Eleotris melanopterus*. Finally in 1861 Bleeker discovered that all of these were the same fish, and he renamed them *Butis butis*.

CAECOBARBUS GEERTSI (Boulenger)/*Blind African Barb*

Range: Found only in a cave at Thysville, Lower Congo (Belgian Congo).

Habits: An ever-moving blind species that locates its food with its long tactile barbels, which act as feelers. Smaller fishes are not safe with this species.

Water Conditions: They are not particular in choice of water as long as it gets no colder than 70°F. and no hotter than 85°F.

Size: To about 3 inches.

Food Requirements: Readily accepts all types of foods, both live and prepared. Especially fond of frozen brine shrimp and beefheart.

Color Variations: A pale, relatively colorless pink species.

While the author (HRA) was on an expedition in Africa, he and Pierre Brichard went to the fishery officer to get permission to collect a few specimens of the blind fish from the cave at Thysville. The officer was furious that we should have asked, for these are a "natural resource" of the area and could not be collected under any circumstance. We soon discovered that with a small bribe we were able to collect as many as we wanted. The cave at Thysville is a beautiful natural cave and is kept as a national park of sorts. How many people visit it is quite another story.

About 500 specimens have thus far been exported from the Congo, most of them finding their way to large public aquaria which were able to pay the high price for them (they sold for about $25 each). To date no one has been able to breed them, but then again no one with any real talent has tried. Since the Blind Cave Tetra, *Anoptichthys jordani*, was so relatively easy to breed, there is reason to believe that this species should be simple also.

CALAMOICHTHYS CALABARICUS (Smith)/*Snake Fish*

Range: Niger Delta, Calabar, Cameroon.
Habits: Largely nocturnal, spends most of its time on the bottom. Best kept only with its own kind.
Water Conditions: Not critical; is not dependent upon the oxygen content of the water for breathing.
Size: Up to 15 inches; tank-raised specimens do not attain this size.
Food Requirements: All living foods which are not too large to be swallowed are accepted, also strips of lean beef, beef-heart, or earthworms.
Color Variations: Back olive to brown, shading to yellow on the belly. Fins colorless except pectorals which have orange base and a black spot.

This interesting fish sometimes is included in African shipments. It looks more like a snake, an illusion which is further enhanced by its motions. In its habitat it occurs in pools which sometimes dry out in the dry season. Like the Lungfish, it is capable of burying itself in the mud and leaving only a tiny hole for breathing. The dorsal fin of this fish is interesting: it is broken up into a series of small finlets, like those found on the Mackerel family in ocean waters. The air-bladder is paired, with one much larger than the other. This acts as an accessory breathing organ. This fish, like some of the others, is also said to be occasionally found at night out of the water, traveling through the wet grass from one pool to another. It propels itself not only in a snakelike manner, but also with the help of its long, powerful pectoral fins. Has never been spawned in captivity, but observers say there may be a possibility of internal fertilization, because the anal fin becomes pointed at times, possibly becoming an intromittent organ. To strengthen this belief, developing eggs have been found in females at certain stages of the season. It builds a grass nest in the water.

CALLICHTHYS CALLICHTHYS (Linnaeus)/*Armored Catfish*

Range: Eastern Venezuela, Trinidad to Buenos Aires.
Habits: Quite active for a Catfish; in its native waters it prefers quiet water and a muddy bottom.
Water Conditions: Not critical. Temperatures should not exceed 75°. Well-rooted plants should be used, lest they be uprooted.
Size: 7 inches; tank-raised specimens do not usually exceed 5 inches.
Food Requirements: A very greedy eater. Prefers living foods, up to and including small fish.
Color Variations: Body color olive-green to gray. Pectoral fins edged with orange.

This Catfish is not uncommonly imported, and a certain number of them are usually available to aquarists. The armor-plates on the sides form a herringbone pattern, and there are even plates protecting the head. This fish has a huge appetite, and should not be trusted with small fishes, or his appetite will extend to them. If kept in a large aquarium which is to their liking, they often live to a ripe old age. If it is desired to spawn this fish, a very large aquarium is required. In the summer months, a pool might be given them, although we have not heard of this procedure being used. Sex differences are very slight, but the females have slightly duller colors and a deeper, more rounded body. The male is said to build a bubble nest, in which he keeps and guards a huge number of eggs. The meager reports of spawnings do not state how long the eggs take to hatch, and one report ends with the eggs being eaten. Successful aquarists who have gotten beyond this stage tell us that the fry grow very quickly, and that they attain the size of one inch in a matter of three weeks.

CAPOETA ARULIUS (Jerdon)/*Longfin Barb*

Range: India, Travancore, Canvery.
Habits: Peaceful, especially when kept with Barbs of an equal size. Very lively.
Water Conditions: Soft, slightly acid water; tank should be placed so as to receive occasional sunshine. Temperature 74 to 78°.
Size: Up to 4¾ inches.
Food Requirements: Live foods of all types, plus frozen foods. Frozen foods of small size, such as frozen *Daphnia*, should not be fed often. Accepts dry foods.
Color Variations: Top of body reddish, shading to silvery green in belly area. Anal and caudal fins tinged with red.

Here is one of the frequent Barb importations which comes into the country, enjoys favor for a while, and is then more or less forgotten in favor of more colorful or interesting fishes. The Longfin Barb's main claim to beauty lies in the attenuated middle rays of the male's dorsal fin, although under proper lighting the fish takes on a decidedly pleasing metallic overcast. In the tanks of dealers they do not show up well, particularly if they are offered for sale while still young, before the male has gained his distinctive feature. The Longfin Barb is peaceful; about the only time the fish evidences animosity to others is during spawning time, when one male may threaten his brothers to keep them away from the females. Spawning takes place in thick bundles of floating plants, after much energetic driving by the male. The eggs, which are adhesive and stick to the plants, are eaten eagerly by the parents.

F-144.00

CAPOETA CHOLA (Hamilton-Buchanan)/*Swamp Barb*

Range: Burma, Eastern India.
Habits: Peaceful and active; when confined to small tanks, becomes less active.
Water Conditions: Soft, slightly acid water. Temperature 70-80°.
Size: Up to 5 inches.
Food Requirements: Accepts all live and frozen foods, and most dry foods.
Color Variations: Body silvery, with greenish highlights. Large black spot at base of caudal fin; lower portion of dorsal also black, especially in males. Red spot on gill covers.

The Swamp Barb is so named because in its home waters in Asia it is encountered most often in low-lying, swampy areas, with much small vegetation. It is frequently found in land given over to rice culture, and this would almost lead one to the conclusion that the fish likes, or is at least able to stand for long periods, dirty water. This is definitely not so! Like most of its relatives, the Swamp Barb, despite its name, feels best in large, clean, well filtered tanks; when not provided with surroundings of its preference, *Capoeta chola* soon declines and loses whatever faint traces of color it possessed when kept in water more to its liking. The colors spoken of here are definite, even though they are not pronounced enough to make the fish desirable for its looks alone. When the Swamp Barb is in good condition, the red coloration of the operculum is very evident, and it makes a nice contrast to the circular black blotch at the peduncle. Out of condition, however, this red color is subdued, in some cases vanishing almost completely. The Swamp Barb is not difficult to breed, as it quite readily scatters its eggs among thick bunches of plants, but the fry need lots of room for proper growth.

CAPOETA HULSTAERTI (Poll)/*Butterfly Barb*

Range: Central Congo region near Coquinatville.
Habits: Peaceful, almost shy; should be kept only in company with very small fishes or their own kind.
Water Conditions: Soft, clean, neutral to slightly acid water, temperature about 78°. Should be moved from tank to tank as little as possible.
Size: 1 inch, mostly a little smaller.
Food Requirements: Small live foods preferred, but some fine-grained prepared foods are accepted.
Color Variations: Body color brownish gold, with a black crescent behind the gill-plates. Large black spot in center of body. Males have black mark on dorsal fin.

The Butterfly Barb is a fairly recent introduction to aquarists. Original shipments were only males, which are easily distinguished by the yellow dorsal, anal and ventral fins. These are bright yellow, with black tips. Females have very little color at all in these fins. It was amusing at first when the males came in by the hundreds that everybody had a different way to find the "females" by looking for some tiny difference. As the specimens at hand died and were dissected, the truth finally dawned and African shippers began to collect females as well as males and ship them out. Nevertheless, although the fish has been with us for several years now, it is still seldom bred. The few successful breeders tell us that it breeds like the other Barbs by depositing its eggs in bushy plants. The fry are tiny, and spawnings are small. Raising them is quite a task. Perhaps some day a breeder will discover the magic formula, and will be able to turn them out in quantity. No doubt the tank-raised generations will be a little more adaptable to a life in captivity, and it might easily be that some day we will see a good supply of this lovely fish. They are very delicate.

F-146.00

CAPOETA MELANAMPYX/*Ember Barb*

Range: India.
Habits: Peaceful and active; a good jumper.
Water Conditions: Soft, slightly acid water. Temperature 74 to 78°.
Size: 3 inches.
Food Requirements: Takes both live and prepared foods.
Color Variations: Yellowish brown, with black spot near tail and below dorsal and
black band behind the eye. Male (at spawning) purple-red, with dark fins.

This new import is one of the most colorful Barbs to be brought to the attention of hobbyists in a long time. The male, when in condition, takes on a beautiful red color, accentuated by the dusky black of the fins. Luckily, the red coloring is kept throughout the year, even outside spawning time, but it is most bright during the spawning period. The female, normally plain in color, also takes on a red hue at this time, but she is never as intensely colored as the male. The Ember Barb spawns in the usual Barb manner, but the males are very hard drivers, and harm might come to the females if sufficient hiding space is not provided. Dense masses of floating plants provide good hiding places, but even caves can be used to provide refuge. Eggs hatch in two days at a temperature of 75°, which is the correct spawning temperature. Fry are ready for newly hatched brine shrimp as soon as they have absorbed their yolk-sacs; they grow quickly, but only if given enough room. Crowding will stunt young of this species very much, as will poor feeding within the first few weeks. This hardy and peaceful new Barb should soon become a lasting favorite if imported in quantity.

F-147.00

CAPOETA OLIGOLEPIS (Bleeker)/*Checker Barb*

Range: Sumatra.
Habits: Peaceful and active.
Water Conditions: Soft, slightly acid water is desirable, but small variations in water composition are easily withstood. Temperature 74 to 78°.
Size: About 2 inches.
Food Requirements: Takes all foods.
Color Variations: Yellowish brown above, lighter below. Male's fins reddish, edged with black. Dorsal fin of female has smaller black edging. Under proper lighting, an iridescent purple spot shows at base of caudal fin. Two rows of black dots along body.

Definitely one of the most desirable of all the Barbs, the Checker Barb has much to recommend it. It is small, hardy, peaceful, easy to breed, and active; also, although by no means brilliant, it is an attractive fish. In prime condition, the male of the species takes on a pleasing red-orange hue to his fins, and the coloring of the upper portion of his body becomes darker, providing a handsome contrast. When in good condition, it is very easy to tell the sexes apart, but even when the male has not assumed his courting dress there is little difficulty, for the female is fuller and the black edging of her dorsal fin is less pronounced. For so small a species, the scales are quite large and distinct, which adds to the attractiveness of the fish. The Checker Barb spawns in typical Barb fashion, but the newly hatched young, which emerge from the eggs in about 2½ days, are very small and require very tiny first foods. Once past the first six days, newly hatched brine shrimp are accepted and the young need no special precautions after that time. Because of their size, they do not need large tanks, but to show them to best advantage they should be given a long tank and kept in schools.

CAPOETA PUCKELLI (Boulenger)/*Two-Spot African Barb*

Range: Congo River near Leopoldville.
Habits: Peaceful, may be combined with other peaceful species.
Water Conditions: Soft, slightly acid water. Temperature 74 to 78°.
Size: Females 2½ inches, males 2 inches.
Food Requirements: Prepared and frozen foods taken just as eagerly as live foods.
Color Variations: Body color silvery, with a small black spot at the dorsal base and another one at the caudal base.

This small African Barb has masqueraded under several names. The first ones we saw were called "Barbus bimaculatus," which makes a certain amount of sense, as "bimaculatus" means "two-spotted." Then a Dutch magazine, "Het Aquarium," showed the same fish, and the author of the article told how he had purchased them as "Barbus bifasciatus," which would make no sense, as "bifasciatus" would mean "with two bars." Then the article went on to identify them as *Barbus pobeguini*. Another work shows *B. pobeguini* as a fish with a large dark mark fairly high in the dorsal fin, but this fish has a small mark right at the base, which led to further doubts. When we sent some preserved specimens to Dr. Leonard P. Schultz at the Smithsonian Institution in Washington, D.C. he identified them as *Capoeta puckelli*, which name we are accepting here. Most of the African Barbs do not breed readily in captivity, but these are exceptions. Sexes are easily distinguished in mature specimens by the disparity in length and girth between males and females, and a pair given a clean tank with a partial change of water will spawn readily in the manner of the other Barbs.

Photo by G. J. M. Timmerman.

CAPOETA PARTIPENTAZONA (Fowler)/*Banded Barb*

Range: Malay Peninsula.
Habits: Active, a fast swimmer inclined to nip fins of slower fishes.
Water Conditions: Soft, slightly acid water; tank should be well planted and receive good light. Temperature 72-82°.
Size: Two inches.
Food Requirements: Accepts all foods, especially small live foods.
Color Variations: Yellowish body, with five vertical bands, one band running through dorsal fin onto top portion of back. Fins reddish.

Here is another Barb of the "Banded Barb" grouping, similar to *Capoeta tetrazona*, *Barbodes hexazona*, and *Barbodes pentazona*. These Barbs are much alike in coloring and general markings, but, since *Capoeta tetrazona*, the Tiger Barb, is so much more crisply marked, the others have lost favor during the years and are seldom seen any more. Indeed, it appears that they will rarely ever be brought back into the country in large numbers, because the Tiger Barb is now so cheap and plentiful that the others would be hard put to give it a battle in the popularity race. *Capoeta partipentazona* has one advantage over the Tiger Barb, however: although it is a nippy fish, it seldom carries its harassment of a victim to the same extreme as the Tiger Barb, contenting itself with occasional passes at the object of its misplaced attentions, whereas the Tiger Barb will often hound its victim so persistently that the fish jumps clear out of the tank to avoid pursuit, even if it is a fish ordinarily thought of as being a non-jumper. Oddly enough, *Capoeta partipentazona* and *Capoeta tetrazona* usually get along well together when kept in the same tank, members of both species forming little schools of their own.

F-150.00

Photo by G. J. M. Timmerman.

CAPOETA SEMIFASCIOLATUS (Günther)/*Half-Striped Barb*

Range: Southern China.
Habits: Peaceful.
Water Conditions: Soft, slightly acid water; tank should be densely planted. Temperature 70 to 80°.
Size: 2½ inches.
Food Requirements: Takes live, frozen and dry foods.
Color Variations: Greenish-brown, fins flushed with orange; bars on sides, not extending all the way down.

Much controversy has arisen over this fish and one which is supposed by some to be a golden variety of it. The latter fish, the golden one, is often identified as *Barbus schuberti*, although this name has no real basis, but is a trade name. Other authorities maintain that the golden variety is in reality another Barb traveling under the specific name *sachsi*, basing their belief on the fact that there are important differences between the fish. In any event, the golden variety is certainly more colorful than the Half-Striped Barb, and this has accounted for the almost complete replacement of *C. semifasciolatus* in the affections of aquarists. The golden variety has the further distinction of being the more easily bred of the two, and they are usually in good supply at low prices. There is no significant difference between the spawning habits of the two, both breeding in the normal Barb fashion, but *sachsi* needs less coaxing. The Half-Striped Barb derives its name from a peculiarity of the barred pattern on the sides of the fish; unlike many of the other vertically banded Barbs, the stripes on *C. semifasciolatus* are less wide and do not traverse the whole depth of the fish.

CAPOETA TETRAZONA (Bleeker)/*Tiger Barb, Sumatra Barb*

Range: Sumatra, Borneo.
Habits: A very active fish and a fast swimmer; inclined to nip the fins of slower species.
Water Conditions: Soft, slightly acid water. Temperature 70 to 85°.
Size: Up to 3 inches.
Food Requirements: Takes both live and prepared foods. Should also have vegetable matter included in dirt.
Colour Variations: Sides yellow, interrupted by four wide black stripes. Bottom portion of dorsal fin black. Upper portion of dorsal trimmed in red; upper and lower lobes of tail and ventral fins red; snout red. An albino variation is also available.

The Tiger Barb has much to recommend it. It is flashily colorful, hardy, easy to breed, and usually in good supply. Also, it is cheaper now than it ever was, possibly because it is being bred on such a large scale both in this country and the Far East, especially Hong Kong. About the only drawback the fish has is that it is inclined to nip its tankmates; long-finned fishes are usually the victims in these cases, but the Tiger Barb is not particular in its choice, and other fishes are also pursued. Oddly enough, some schools of Tiger Barbs are kept in a community tank without ever doing any damage; in this regard, one or two *tetrazona* are likely to do more fin nipping than six or seven, presumably because the Barbs in the larger group are so busy chasing each other that they don't have time to bother other species. For spawning *C. tetrazona*, which spawns in typical Barb fashion, use water which is softer than the water in which they are customarily maintained. For example, if their regular tank water is 8 DH, they will spawn more readily in water of 6 DH. The fry are small at first but grow rapidly, especially if given plenty of room; if kept in small tanks, they will not attain their full size.

Photo by H. Hansen, Aquarium Berlin

CAPOETA TITTEYA (Deraniyagala)/*Cherry Barb*

Range: Ceylon.
Habits: Peaceful; a good community fish.
Water Conditions: Soft, slightly acid water; well planted tank. Temperature 72-82°.
Size: 2 inches.
Food Requirements: Accepts both live and prepared foods; particularly likes small living crustaceans.
Color Variations: Coloring depends on mood and condition of the fish; deep cherry red or plain light brown, with shades between. Male always more intensely colored than female. Dark line crosses body horizontally.

Of the five or six Barbs that have gained lasting popularity in this country, the Cherry Barb ranks right near the top. Small, peaceful, and undemanding, it has been around for a long time and will stay around for many years to come. For the beginning Barb enthusiast, perhaps no other Barb, with the possible exception of the Checker Barb, has so much to recommend it. In coloring, prior to spawning, it is particularly attractive, with the body suffused with a rich reddish-brown sheen. During the actual spawning act this color is intensified to an oxblood hue, and although the deepness of the color at this time is not of long duration (it loses much of its dark, rich quality after spawning) the fish is still nicely colored if maintained under proper conditions. Inducing the species to spawn is not difficult if they have been well treated during their period of acclimatization; eggs are scattered into plant thickets, where they are eagerly sought out and eaten by the parents, who should be removed as soon as possible. The fry, which are very small, emerge from the eggs within 1½ days at a temperature of 78°, and when they become free-swimming they need the very small of live foods.

Photo by Gunter Schmida

CARASSIOPS COMPRESSUS (Krefft)/*Australian Sleeper Goby*

Range: Coastal regions of eastern Australia.

Habits: Should be kept with fishes of its own size or larger, or some aggressiveness will be shown.

Water Conditions: Not critical. Water should have a slight salt content. Temperature 74° to 77°, no lower.

Size: About 6 inches maximum, seldom exceeds 4 inches in captivity.

Food Requirements: Should get mostly living foods; will eat dried foods only when forced by hunger.

Color Variations: Reddish brown body, with many black dots. The after dorsal fin and anal fin have dark edges with white dots.

Australia has few fishes to offer from its fresh waters which are really bright in color, but many of them are worth keeping for their interesting habits. *Carassiops compressus* is not a highly active species, but it is capable of changing its colors to a deep dusky hue at the slightest provocation. At such times one would scarcely recognize them as the same species. The entire body becomes very dark, and the eyes take on a green or sometimes deep blue color. Like so many Australian fishes, this one has a distinct space between the spiny and soft rays of the dorsal fin, forming two separate dorsal fins. This fish has never to our knowledge been bred in captivity. Occurring along the coastal regions as they do, their water may require a certain amount of salinity before eggs and sperm ripen. This of course is only a theory which has not as yet been proven (or disproven).

F-154.00

Photo by Gunter Schmida

CARASSIOPS GALII *Pink Sleeper from Australia*

Range: The coastal waters of Australia.
Habits: A fin nipper which should only be kept with fishes its own size.
Water Conditions: Prefers slightly alkaline, hard water. Brackish water is tolerated.
Size: It is rarely found to exceed 4 inches.
Food Requirements: Prefers live foods, but takes pelletized foods and frozen foods readily.
Color Variations: Some specimens have red, brown and blue edges on their fins.

One of the close relatives of *Carassiops compressus* is the Pink Sleeper which has been found to be more plentiful and more salable than *compressus*. At best neither of the two species are "best sellers" and the question of which is more desirable is academic. When kept in a school of about a dozen fish in a 20-gallon aquarium with hard water, the fish become very active and colorful, but they seem to be extremely short-lived. The longest that one has stayed alive on record is less than a year; perhaps this is due to the manhandling the fish gets before it is shipped, as none have been tank-raised to the best knowledge that we have available.

Aquarists in Australia receive the fish very well and claim it to be an excellent community fish, but our experience here is that the fish is nasty and nips the fins of larger fish while swallowing fishes up to half its own size! It is not recommended for the community aquarium regardless of what our friends from "down under" say.

Photo by Dr. Herbert R. Axelrod.

CARASSIUS AURATUS AURATUS (Linné)/*Goldfish*

Range: Originally from China, now introduced into temperate waters the world over.
Habits: Peaceful; large-finned specimens should not be kept with other fishes which might nip the fins.
Water Conditions: Water characteristics not critical, but should be clean and well-aerated. Best temperatures 50 to 70°.
Size: Sizes vary with breeds. Average size in the aquarium 3 to 4 inches.
Food Requirements: Prepared and frozen foods taken just as eagerly as live foods.
Color Variations: Has been bred into various colors and color combinations of red, black, white, yellow, etc.

The hobby of fish-keeping owes its popularity more than anything else to the Goldfish. They are mentioned as early as 970 A.D. by the Chinese and in the Sixteenth Century their care and breeding, which was at first a plaything of the nobility, became commonplace and a number of fancy breeds were developed. Because of their innate love for beauty and living things, the Chinese and Japanese have remained the world leaders in the development and production of the many fancy breeds of Goldfish available today. We see such freakish fishes as the Lionhead, Pompom, Telescope, Celestial, Eggfish and many others too numerous for this small space. There are fish with short single fins, and others with long flowing fins. Some breeds have double fins; some have large, sail-like dorsal fins and others have no dorsal fin at all. Some are pure white, others are midnight black. Still others vary from light yellow to deep red, and some are peppered with red, white, black, yellow and even blue. Goldfish have a wide temperature tolerance, and fish which have been kept outdoors can live under a layer of ice for quite a time. They are also kept successfully in the tropics.

F-156.00

A beautiful white fantail with red cap.

Red and white lionhead goldfish.

F-157.00

A new variety of goldfish is this Chocolate Goldfish above.

Shubunkin Goldfish.

Lionhead-type Goldfish. Above, with dorsal fin, Oranda. Below, without dorsal fin, Lionhead.

F-159.00

CARNEGIELLA MARTHAE (Myers)/*Black-Winged Hatchetfish*

Range: Venezuela, Peru, the Brazilian Amazon, Rio Negro and the Orinoco.
Habits: Active jumpers, have to be kept in a covered tank, preferably a long one. Peaceful; may be kept with other non-aggressive species.
Water Conditions: Soft, slightly acid water. Temperature 76 to 80°.
Size: 1⅜ inches, usually a bit smaller.
Food Requirements: Floating prepared foods eaten when very hungry, but best are live foods like mosquito larvae or wingless fruit-flies.
Color Variations: Silvery body, black horizontal line edged with gold on top. Pectoral fins have a black area inside.

The Black-Winged Hatchetfish is the smallest known member of the genus *Carnegiella*. The name *marthae* was given to this species in 1927 by Dr. George S. Myers because they were favorites of his wife Martha. They are easily distinguished from the other Hatchetfishes not only by a black edge on the keel of the belly back to the caudal base, but also by a black area inside the long pectoral fins. These pectoral fins are called "wings" because their length and size gives them that appearance, but they are not wings in the sense that the fish can fly with them, any more than the well-known marine Flying-Fish fly with theirs. These pectoral fins are actuated by the most powerful muscles the fish has, and give it enough impetus to leave the water and glide for a considerable distance along its surface. Insects which congregate in this area are efficiently snapped up on these "flights" and this fact gives us a clue as to why the Hatchetfishes are not the easiest fishes to keep and feed, and why they seldom spawn in captivity. This is where the ingenuity of their owner comes into the picture, figuring out how to feed them live insects without having them escape into the room.

F-160.00

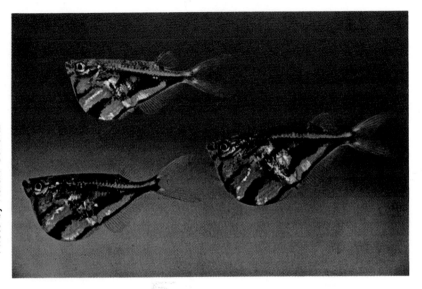

*CARNEGIELLA STRIGATA (Günther)/*Marbled Hatchetfish*

Range: British Guiana, middle and upper Amazon region, especially in jungle streams.
Habits: Occurs in schools near the surface. In the aquarium they are peaceful, but are likely to jump if a cover is not provided.
Water Conditions: Soft, slightly acid water. Temperature about 78°.
Size: About 1¾ inches.
Food Requirements: Will readily accept dried foods which float on the surface, but anything which falls to the bottom cannot be picked up.
Color Variations: Body mother-of-pearl, iridescent, with three dark, wavy lines extending from a horizontal line on the back to the belly.

This is one of the most attractive of the Hatchet Fishes, first introduced to aquarists in 1912. Most works say that it has never been bred, but the fact is that it has happened, but only rarely. The sexes can be distinguished by looking at the fish from above; the females are slightly wider in the body. The rare descriptions of the spawning say that tiny eggs are laid in plant clusters at the surface, and to the best of our recollection very few if any of the fry were hatched and raised. One of the obvious assumptions as to why the fish will not spawn readily is that there is some food, possibly winged, which the fish will devour in their natural habitat, which the aquarist cannot duplicate. Probably the best food would be mosquito larvae, because these spend a great deal of time at the surface, and being an insect, would be the food most relished by a fish which gets its food at the surface. Another insect food which has been developed of late is the *Drosophila*, or wingless fruit fly. It is easily cultured and will not make a nuisance of itself by flying around the rooms after they hatch. This is the easiest to keep of all the Hatchet Fishes.

* Now known as *Carnegiella strigata fasciata.*

F-161.00

*CARNEGIELLA VESCA (Fraser-Brunner)/*Marble Hatchetfish*

Range: British Guiana.

Habits: Found in shaded pools where it leaps from the water for insects flying very close to the surface of the water.

Water Conditions: Very sensitive to temperature and water changes. Prefers very soft, slightly acid water.

Size: Under 3 inches.

Food Requirements: This species must have small live food. Dropping wingless *Drosophila* flies onto the surface of the water is an ideal way to feed this species. They also take small amounts of floating foods containing dried brine shrimp.

Color Variations: This species is probably a subspecies of *Carnegiella strigata*.

When Fraser-Brunner described this fish, he separated it from *Carnegiella strigata* because of certain minor meristic and color characteristics and the fact that this species is to be found in British Guiana while *C. strigata* is an Amazonian species. Since that time the author has found intermediate forms in the Rio Urubu, Brazil and adjacent waters and is of the opinion that *C. vesca* is not a valid species. It is included here only because it is slightly different in its aquarium requirements. The genus *Carnegiella* contains the smallest species of the subfamily *Gasteropelecinae* according to George Myers. Myers' very capable student, Stanley Howard Weitzman, made a thorough study of the fish under discussion (*Stanford Ichthyological Bulletin*, Vol. 4, No. 4, August 23, 1954) and he proved that *Carnegiella vesca* does "flap" its pectoral fins. He also recorded a buzzing sound which he believes comes from this flapping motion. It is generally accepted that the Hatchet-fishes of the subfamily Gasteropelecinae are the only true "flying fish" which moves its pectoral fins to aid in its flight. The other so-called flying fishes, such as the marine Exocoetidae and the freshwater African *Pantodon*, do not

* Now known as *Carnegiella strigata strigata.*

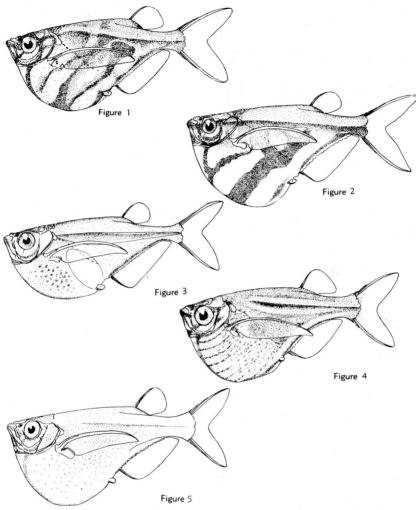

Figure 1

Figure 2

Figure 3

Figure 4

Figure 5

The illustrations above are taken from Agustin Fernandez-Yepez' article "A Revision of the South American Characid fishes of the Genus *Carnegiella*" which appeared as a *Stanford Ichthyological Bulletin* edition, Volume 3, No. 4, August 21, 1950. They can be used as a key to the species of Hatchetfishes which have appeared on the aquarium over the past 30 years. Figure 1: *Carnegiella fasciata* (Garman). Figure 2: *Carnegiella strigata* (Guenther). Figure 3: *Carnegiella myersi* (Fernandez-Yepez). Figure 4: *Carnegiella marthae* (Myers). Figure 5: *Carnegiella schereri* (Fernandez-Yepez).

voluntarily move their pectorals in flight, but probably use them for stabilization while in "flight." It is the author's (HRA) opinion that thoracic lines are not stable characteristics, and the author has collected populations in which these lines varied greatly.

CATOPRION MENTO (Cuvier)/*Wimple Piranha*

Range: Lower Amazon, Bolivia, Guianas.
Habits: Peaceful, but will attack small fishes.
Water Conditions: Soft, slightly acid water in a well-planted tank.
Size: About 4 inches.
Food Requirements: Larger live foods are best. Otherwise, frozen foods or bits of fish, shrimp, clams or oysters.
Color Variations: Silvery body; orange to red spot on the operculum. Black spot on the side just behind operculum; anal red, caudal black.

Catoprion mento has all the ferocious appearance of a true Piranha as well as an attractive set of colors of its own, which makes it an interesting aquarium fish capable of being kept in a community tank without danger to its tank-mates, unless they are small. They resemble a Piranha so convincingly that even the natives who collect them are sometimes fooled. The writer recalls netting Pencilfishes and other small Characins with a few native helpers in a small stream in British Guiana. One of the natives yelled "Perai" when the net came up and a Wimple Piranha flopped about in it. They warned me not to touch it or I might lose a finger, and did not calm down until I picked it up, pried its mouth open and told them "Look, no teeth!" Strangely enough, a little while later we fished a different spot in the same stream and came up with some *real* Piranhas, and then it was my turn to warn the natives to be careful, because these fellows *had* teeth. Although the Wimple Piranha cannot compete with the real Piranha in dental equipment, they *do* have small teeth which they will not hesitate to use on something as small as, say, a Guppy or Neon Tetra.

CHALCEUS MACROLEPIDOTUS (Cuvier)/*Pink-Tailed Chalceus*

Range: The Guianas.
Habits: Peaceful if kept in a school with no small fishes in the same tank.
Water Conditions: Not critical; best temperature about 76°. Once they have become established, they should be moved as little as possible.
Size: To 10 inches.
Food Requirements: Generous feedings are necessary, using earthworms, *Tubifex* worms or chopped beef heart.
Color Variations: Bluish sides; fins are brown to reddish, tail pink to bright red.

This is another fish which is often offered by dealers while it is still very young, and grows and grows until it has become too big for all available tanks. If given an aquarium of at least 50 gallons capacity which is well planted and aerated, a group of about a half-dozen *Chalceus macrolepidotus* makes a very attractive picture. They are active and always on the move, and their big scales have a highly metallic gleam. When in particularly good condition, the fins as well as the tail become bright red. They are excellent jumpers, and when being seined in their native Guiana waters most of them will leap nimbly over the net rather than let themselves be caught. A glass cover on their aquarium is therefore essential if one does not want to find them on the floor some morning. When in British Guiana, the author noticed that the Indians were always quick to pounce upon these fish when their large size made it advisable to discard them. They considered them a delicacy which they seldom got otherwise, because their slender shape and active habits made it difficult to shoot them with a bow and arrow, the Indians' accepted method of catching fish.

CHANDA BACULIS (Hamilton)/*Pla Kameo* or *Burmese Glassfish*

Range: Burma, India and Thailand in the Sikuk River, in the headwaters of the Menam Chao Phya, in the lower Menam Nan and in the Bung Borapet.

Habits: A dainty, but beautiful small fish that requires copious amounts of live food such as microworms and *Daphnia*.

Water Conditions: Strictly a freshwater species which prefers the higher temperatures in the lower 80's.

Size: The smallest of the large genus *Chanda*. Rarely larger than 2 inches.

Food Requirements: Prefers live foods, but accepts frozen brine shrimp and some dry foods in pellet form.

Color Variations: This photo is of the Burmese race. The Siamese race has, according to Smith, "an intensely black edge on the spinous dorsal fin and the glistening golden spot on the occiput."

The genus *Chanda* (incorrectly referred to as *Ambassis, Hamiltonia, Bogoda* and *Pseudambassis*) is not the small genus that aquarists think it is. In Thailand alone there are nine species (*kopsii* which is also found in the East Indies, Philippines and Malaya; *commersonii* from Australia, Africa, India, East Indies and the Philippines and which grows to about 4 inches; *thomasi* from India and Malaya and which grows to about 7 inches; *wolfii* from Borneo and Sumatra which grows to about $7\frac{1}{2}$ inches; *siamensis* which is the same size as *baculis*; *ranga* from India, Bengal and Burma; *gymnocephala* which is found in East Africa, Australia, India, Malaya, East Indies, Philippines and China and grows to about 3 inches; and *buruensis* which grows to about $2\frac{3}{4}$ inches and ranges from Sumatra to the Philippines, down to the Australian Archipelago) and they range in habitat from pure fresh water, to brackish and pure marine water. As a general rule they like hard water, but the freshwater species, such as *baculis*, require soft water and high temperatures.

CHANDA BURUENSIS (Bleeker)/*Siamese Glassfish*

Range: Thailand, Malaya, Sumatra, Celebes, and the Philippines.
Habits: Best kept by themselves. Even then, two males in the same tank might pick on each other.
Water Conditions: Native to brackish waters, which must be duplicated in the aquarium by adding 2 tablespoons of table salt to each gallon.
Size: To 2¾ inches. Aquarium-raised specimens usually under 2 inches.
Food Requirements: Small living foods such as newly-hatched brine shrimp and small worms. Dry foods taken only when starving.
Color Variations: Body glassily transparent. Black stripe on second dorsal and anal fins and black edge on upper part of first dorsal fin.

Because of its lack of bright colors we do not often see this Glassfish among importations. *Chanda buruensis* is longer in the body than its better-known cousin *Chanda ranga*. The males do not sport a blue edge on the second dorsal and anal fins, but there is a good deal of black in these fins, and in the first dorsal as well. Males are likely to have little disagreements, and for this reason a tank which affords some opportunity for concealment is recommended, where the defeated ones can escape the bullying of their victors. Like *Chanda ranga*, *Chanda buruensis* will not accept any but living foods. They spawn readily, but the resulting fry are very small and getting them to a size where they can handle larger foods is a real problem. A good Rotifer culture would be the answer, but these are not always very easy to come by. Once they are large enough to take newly-hatched brine shrimp, the battle can be considered won. This fish is doomed to an "ugly duckling" status wherever it is kept. It is nowheres near as pretty as *Chanda ranga*, and besides is not as easy to collect. It was first introduced to aquarium hobbyists in 1953, but has not yet attained great popularity.

Photo by R. Zukal

CHANDA RANGA (Hamilton-Buchanan)/*Glass Fish, Glass Perch*

Range: Northern India, Bengal to Burma.

Habits: Very numerous in rice paddies and other shallow bodies of water in their habitat; peaceful in the aquarium.

Water Conditions: Requires somewhat hard water with a light salt content. Once established in an aquarium, they should be moved as little as possible.

Size: 2 inches; in nature they become slightly larger.

Food Requirements: Some prepared foods are unwillingly accepted, but the bulk of foods given should be alive.

Color Variations: Body light amber with a glassy transparency. In the males, the soft dorsal fin and the anal fin have a bright blue edge.

Here we have one of the old favorites, known to the aquatic world since 1905. As for the scientific world, Hamilton-Buchanan first identified and described it in 1822. It is interesting to note that this little fish is so numerous in India that farmers often use it for fertilizer. In the aquarium it is not so prolific; at first it was considered one of the difficult ones, but the truth is that the fish breeds quite readily, but the fry are so small that they usually die of starvation before they become large enough to eat foods like newly hatched brine shrimp. An annoying trait the fry also have is that they do not hunt for food, but will snap at it when it swims near them. Males are distinguished by the bright blue edge on the soft dorsal and anal fins, of which there is only a trace on the females. A 5-gallon aquarium is of sufficient size for spawning, and eggs are deposited in a clump of floating plants like *Riccia* or *Nitella*. The aquarium should be placed in a sunny location, and the fish disturbed as little as possible. Best temperature is about 76°. Eggs hatch in one day, and when they begin to swim, fry should be provided with the smallest infusoria.

Photo by Gene Wolfsheimer.

CHANNALLABES APUS (Günther)/*Eel Catfish*

Range: Congo and Angola regions.
Habits: Mostly nocturnal. Young specimens will not bother the other fishes, but it is best to keep larger ones by themselves.
Water Conditions: Not critical; temperatures 70 to 75°.
Size: Up to 12 inches.
Food Requirements: Greedy eaters which will consume great amounts of Tubifex worms. Other foods may be substituted, such as beef heart or pieces of fish.
Color Variations: Dark brown throughout. Sex differences unknown.

Channallabes apus resembles nothing as much as a young Eel with whiskers. The body is compressed laterally and the dorsal, caudal and anal fins form an unbroken line from the back to the anus. The ventral fins are missing completely. The head is very small and at first sight one might be led to believe that a large brown worm had somehow gotten into the aquarium. They are very hardy and long-lived, and because of an accessory breathing organ are not dependent upon the oxygen in their aquarium water. They are greedy eaters and their diet of Tubifex and white worms may be augmented by pieces of beef heart, raw shrimp or fish cut into small pieces. They get to be about a foot long and have never to our knowledge been spawned in captivity. There is little likelihood that anyone will ever try it, either; such a venture would undoubtedly be a scientific achievement, but commercially the result would merely be a lot of wormlike Catfish which nobody would want. This odd Catfish has been known to science for a long time. It was named by Günther in 1873. Aquarium hobbyists saw the first importation of this species when they were brought into Germany in 1956.

CHARACIDIUM FASCIATUM (Reinhardt)/*Banded Characidium*

Range: South America, Orinoco region in the north to La Plata region in the south.

Habits: Comes from streams where there is some current, therefore requires fresh, clean water in an uncrowded aquarium.

Water Conditions: Clean, well-oxygenated water, about neutral. Temperatures should not exceed 75°.

Size: $2\frac{1}{2}$ inches.

Food Requirements: Not a fussy eater, but prefers living foods.

Color Variations: Body yellowish-brown, lighter toward the belly. Dark horizontal stripe, and 10 dark bars.

Because of its lack of bright colors and rather retiring habits, this fish does not very often find itself in the tanks of aquarists. It stays mostly in the lower reaches of the aquarium, and often digs into the gravel for bits of food. Males are recognizable by their larger fins, which are yellowish in color. Spawning is accomplished in the lower parts of the tank, and as many as 150 eggs may result. The very tiny eggs hatch in 30 to 40 hours, and the fry begin to swim in 3 days. Remaining near the bottom as they do, they often remain undetected until they have grown considerably. Fine infusorian food is of course indicated for a short time, until they have grown a bit and their small mouths can handle such morsels as newly hatched brine shrimp. Because they can pick food from the bottom, some of the infusoria substitutes could probably be used with success, but of course living infusoria is preferable. Once they begin to put on size, growth is rapid and in four weeks they may be as long as $\frac{3}{4}$ inch. There is a record of their introduction as early as 1913, but it is believed that this species was known to aquarists even earlier.

CHARAX GIBBOSUS (Linnaeus)/*Glass Headstander*

Range: Guianas, lower and middle Amazon region and Rio Paraguay.
Habits: Perfectly peaceful and harmless.
Water Conditions: Not critical, temperature should average about 76°.
Size: 6 inches; aquarium specimens are usually much smaller.
Food Requirements: Prefers live foods, but dried foods may be fed when others are not available.
Color Variations: Mostly transparent, with an indistinct shoulder-spot. Scales in the upper half of body show an iridescent sparkle.

Here we have a fish which looks fierce, but actually is a "shrinking violet." As the name describes, it has a *gibbous* or *humpbacked* appearance. The head is small in contrast to the body, and the mouth large. A strange characteristic is that the head is at an angle to the body, and when the fish swims in its characteristically downward tilted position, the head is practically straight. Because of its lack of colors, this is a fish which is not often imported, and still more seldom bred. Males are slightly smaller than their mates, and have a more slender build. Because of their size, a large aquarium is required if spawning is desired. Some bundles of bushy plants are provided, and the fish soon lose much of their accustomed sluggishness when courtship begins. Eggs are released among the plants, and the spawning is apt to be quite large. Incubation period is 30 hours, and the resulting fry are very small. The first days are critical, and an abundance of infusoria are essential. Once they begin growing and larger foods can be provided, they will be found to be very hardy. This fish was first introduced into Germany about 1910.

F-171.00

CHEIRODON AXELRODI (Schultz)/*Cardinal Tetra*

Range: Upper Rio Negro and tributaries.
Habits: Perfectly peaceful and active. Likes to swim in schools, and therefore it is best to keep at least 6 of them together.
Water Conditions: Water should be soft, clean and on the acid side, about 6.5 or lower, in order to show the fish in its brightest colors.
Size: 2 inches.
Food Requirements: All foods, either live or prepared, should be given with their small size in mind. Not a fussy eater.
Color Variations: Back is brown on top. Horizontal stripe a brilliant blue-green. Lower part of body bright red, belly white.

This living jewel is without a doubt the most gorgeous of all aquarium fishes. It was also the cause of a great controversy where the name was concerned. In an issue of "Tropical Fish Hobbyist" which was published on February 20, 1956 the fish was described by Dr. Leonard P. Schultz and assigned the name *Cheirodon axelrodi*. The "Stanford Ichthyological Bulletin" published on February 21, 1956 ran a description of the new species by Myers and Weitzman, and named it *Hyphessobrycon cardinalis*. For a long time many publications, especially the German ones, called it by the latter name. Finally in November, 1957 the International Commission of Zoological Nomenclature met and voted to give the name *Cheirodon axelrodi* priority. Coming as it does from waters which have a rich content in humic acid and very little mineral content, this little fish is not one of the easy ones when it comes to getting them to spawn. It has been done, however, and can probably be repeated a little more easily when several generations of tank-bred specimens have been produced which have accustomed themselves to our harder water. Meanwhile, we must depend upon imported specimens for our supply.

F-172.00

CHILODUS PUNCTATUS (Müller & Troschel)
Spotted Headstander

Range: Northeastern South America between the Amazon and the Orinoco.

Habits: Very peaceful; pays no attention to the other fishes. Rather shy, and should be moved as little as possible.

Water Conditions: Slightly acid to neutral water, very soft. Temperature should range between 75° and 80°.

Size: About 3½ inches.

Food Requirements: Diet should be largely vegetarian; lettuce or spinach leaves are nibbled frequently. Some dried food and live food also.

Color Variations: Body color silvery gray; large scales have dark areas which form rows of dots. Caudal and dorsal fins have pink flush.

This peaceful fish forms an interesting addition to any community aquarium. It swims in a normally head-down position, and is very fond of nibbling algae from rocks and plants. As additional vegetable nourishment, lettuce leaves and spinach leaves are enjoyed. Females are about ½ inch longer than the males, and the body is considerably heavier. A large aquarium is preferred, with much clear space for swimming. The fact that the fish has not spawned in captivity until now is probably due to the fact that aquarists have been feeding them as they have their other fishes. An account of their breeding tells how there was always a lettuce leaf in the aquarium for them to nibble on. During spawning a remarkable change in coloration takes place. The horizontal line disappears and a large round dark shoulder-spot which is visible at no other time shows up. Eggs which are non-adhesive are released near the surface and sink unmolested to the bottom. After 4 days they hatch. The fry are difficult to see, and are able to eat newly hatched brine shrimp at once. Growth is rapid, according to the German aquarist who had the successful spawning.

Photo by Edward C. Taylor

*CHRIOPEOPS GOODEI (Jordan)/*Florida Bluefin*

Range: Southern Florida.

Habits: An active species which will sometimes pursue other fishes, but seldom attack them.

Water Conditions: Should be kept in roomy aquaria, well planted and cool, 60° to 65°.

Size: 1¾ to 2 inches.

Food Requirements: Small-sized live foods only. Dried foods are accepted only if the fish are starving.

Color Variations: Black horizontal stripe, body yellowish brown above and lighter below. Males have black-edged blue dorsal and anal fins.

This is a common little fish in Florida, but in spite of this we seldom see it offered by dealers. Probably the reason they do not like to handle them is that many people who buy them try to crowd them into a tank with tropical species, a thing which this fish does not like at all. They should not be crowded, and they cannot stand the 76° to 80° temperatures we give to most of our tropical species. Given a roomy tank which is well planted and temperatures which range from 60° to 65°, the males will put on a nice display and spawnings will be observed among the fine-leaved plants. Only 3 to 5 eggs will be expelled by one female per day, but this is kept up for about 5 weeks. The eggs hatch in about 14 days at 65°. Higher temperatures result in many infertile eggs. When they hatch, they can be brought to the surface by placing a light over the darkened tank. They are then lifted out with a spoon and transferred to a rearing tank with similar water. After a week of infusoria feeding they are able to take newly-hatched brine shrimp.

*Now known as *Lucania goodei*.

CICHLA OCELLARIS (Bloch & Schneider)/*Eyespot Cichlid, Lukanani*

Range: Widely distributed throughout tropical South America, except in the La Plata System.

Habits: A predatory fish which cannot be kept with smaller species; it will even attack others of its own size.

Water Conditions: Large, well-aerated aquarium is an absolute necessity. Temperature about 76°.

Size: To 24 inches.

Food Requirements: Will eat only living foods like large earthworms, smaller fish, dragonfly and other large larvae, tadpoles, etc.

Color Variations: Silvery body with several dark bars, ocellated spot in the tail, lower fins and lower half of tail dark red.

This fish holds as important a spot among South American game fishes as our North American Largemouth Bass does in this country. They seize a plug or spoon with the same ferocity and give the angler every bit as much of a battle as their North American cousins. Tell any angler in British Guiana that you know where the Lukanani are biting, and he will invariably drop everything and get out his fishing tackle. Besides being a gamester, the Lukanani is also a delight to eat. Small specimens sometimes find their way into dealers' tanks, but they are usually a disappointment unless their purchaser likes his fish big and rough. Feeding them is also a never-ending problem and, although our records say they will eat only living foods, they could probably be trained to accept chunks of beef-heart, as can many fishes of a similar nature. There are no external marks of sex distinction, and it is doubtful if there was ever a pair brought to maturity in the aquarium. To our knowledge, there are no written accounts of their ever having spawned in captivity, and an aquarium suited to a job of this sort would have to be a large one indeed.

F-175.00

CICHLASOMA AUREUM (Günther)/*Golden Cichlid*

Range: Guatemala and southern Mexico.
Habits: Like the large Cichlids, they should not be trusted with smaller tankmates
which they might bully. They are also apt to dig.
Water Conditions: Not critical.
Size: Wild specimens attain a length of 6 inches; tank-raised specimens considerably
smaller.
Food Requirements: Any of the live foods, including some of the smaller water-
beetles. Some vegetable matter, such as lettuce or spinach leaves, are also taken.
Color Variations: Yellowish olive-green, with a number of indistinct dark bars, and
a large dark spot toward the after half of the upper part of body.

This is one of the larger, lesser-known of the Cichlid family. There have
been some discrepancies in the descriptions of the habits of this fish; some
say they are perfectly peaceful, and will not dig holes in the bottom, and others
insist that they will bully smaller fishes and will uproot any plants when
placed in the community aquarium. They should have a tank of their own at
least when they are ready to spawn, as many a Cichlid which is very peaceful
ordinarily becomes a "bad actor" at this time. Another important characteristic of this fish is that they require a certain amount of vegetable matter
in their diet. This is a warning to the aquarist that any soft-leaved plants,
such as Water-Sprite (*Ceratopteris*) should be avoided as plants in an aquarium
in which this fish is kept, and the tough-leaved ones such as *Sagittaria* or
the *Cryptocoryne* species should be given preference. Spawning is done in
typical Cichlid fashion, with the male and female dividing the parental duties
between them. Fry are easily raised. People who have raised them say that
the parents should not be disturbed in any way while eggs are present, or
they will be eaten.

F-176.00

CICHLASOMA BIMACULATUM (Linné)/*Two-Spot Cichlid*

Range: Northern South America, except in the Magdalena River.
Habits: Typical Cichlid, but not as nasty as some. Should not be kept with smaller fishes.
Water Conditions: Not critical; slightly alkaline is best, not too hard. Temperatures 74 to 78°.
Size: To 8 inches. In the aquarium it seldom attains 6 inches.
Food Requirements: Live or frozen foods, or substitutes like beef heart, pieces of raw clam, mussel, shrimp, etc.
Color Variations: Grayish-brown sides with a silvery belly. Large black spot in the center of the body and another at the caudal base.

The Two-Spot Cichlid has a very wide distribution, occurring in most of the streams in northern South America. They frequently show up in streams where one would not expect to find any but the dwarf species of Cichlids. The author once found a pair tending their young in a tiny stream in British Guiana, where the water was nowhere more than a foot deep. This is not one of the brilliantly-colored Cichlids, and there might be a certain amount of variability in coloration depending on age and where the fish came from, as is the case with most species which have a wide distribution. As the fish gets older most of the colors fade to a silvery gray, and the two spots on the sides which are scarcely noticeable become very prominent. Once a pair have become accustomed to each other they get along well, and usually make excellent parents. Of course, the best way to assure good breeding pairs is to raise about a half-dozen young ones together and then allow them to make their own selections. This assures pairs which are equally ready for spawning, and cuts chances for misfortune down to a minimum. One of the old favorites among Cichlids, it was introduced to hobbyists in 1912.

* CICHLASOMA BIOCELLATUM (Regan)/*Jack Dempsey*

Range: Rio Negro and Amazon Basin; also reported in Costa Rica.
Habits: Very aggressive, and loves to dig and uproot plants. Should be kept only with large fish which can take care of themselves.
Water Conditions: Not critical; temperature should average about 76°, slightly higher when it is desired to spawn them.
Size: 8 inches for males. Females slightly smaller.
Food Requirements: Has a healthy appetite; chopped-up earthworms are a delicacy, and chopped beef-heart small enough to be swallowed easily.
Color Variations: Mature males are deep brown to black, with a black round spot at the center of the body and another at the tail base.

Were it not for their beauty we would seldom see these fish. Besides the background colors mentioned above, the males are peppered with light blue spots all over the body and fins. Females show only a few of these spots, and have shorter fins. Another point of beauty on the male is the bright red edge on the dorsal and anal fins. A pronounced roughneck, it is almost sure to harass smaller fishes put in with it, so make sure if it is going into a community tank that its tankmates are of a comparative size. For all its other bad habits, the Jack Dempsey is a very gentle parent and breeding a pair is not usually fraught with a great deal of difficulty. Both parents take excellent care of eggs and fry, and the youngsters are quite pretty when they are about an inch long. At this time the large spot on the sides is very prominent, and ringed with blue or greenish yellow. It is possible with a healthy, vigorous pair, to raise as many as 1000 youngsters in a single season.

C. biocellatum is no longer a valid name for the fish pictured; the fish is now known as *C. octofasciatum.*

F-178.00

CICHLASOMA CORYPHAENOIDES (Heckel)/*Chocolate Cichlid*

Range: Widely in the Amazon region, but not plentiful.

Habits: Not peaceful; even when kept with their own kind, the bigger ones are very apt to pick on the smaller.

Water Conditions: Not critical, but temperature requirements are a bit high. 80° is best, and never let the water go below 70°.

Size: Males up to 10 inches, females slightly smaller.

Food Requirements: Greedy eaters, preferring large chunks. Earthworms, pieces of beef heart or canned dog food are best.

Color Variations: Chocolate brown body, which color may vary in shade. Dark spot in center of the body, and W-shaped marking just behind eye.

One of the harder-to-keep large Cichlids, this one is seldom imported. They are big, ferocious and a bit touchy where temperature is concerned. The hobbyist who likes their coloration, which is admittedly attractive, soon tires of their greed and inability to get along with any tankmate which can't lick them, of which there are mighty few. Because they are not ready sellers, most breeders have preferred not to try propagating them, even if they had the proper amount of space required. Add to this the fact that the fish does not occur in great numbers in any part of the Amazon where collecting is done, and you have the reason why we seldom see the fish. They were first introduced into Germany in 1911 by the old firm of Siggelkow, in Hamburg. Occasionally an exporter will include a few young specimens with his shipments. These eventually grow to a huge size, and in some cases their owner actually gets to like them. For all their bad habits, they have never been reported to uproot plants, although they do some digging. Perhaps some day this fish, like the Oscar Cichlid, will come into his own and also enjoy a certain amount of popularity.

Photo by Aaron Norman

CICHLASOMA FACETUM (Jenyns)/*Chanchito*

Range: Southern Brazil (Rio Grande do Sul, Rio Parana and tributaries).
Habits: Likely to be quarrelsome, and uproot plants. Should not be kept with smaller fishes.
Water Conditions: Not critical; temperatures should be between 75° and 80°.
Size: In their habitat, up to 12 inches. In the aquarium, about 8 inches.
Food Requirements: Greedy eaters; larger specimens may be fed canned dog or cat foods in addition to insects, garden worms, water beetles, tadpoles and pieces of fish or lean beef. Will only eat dried foods if very hungry.
Color Variations: Body color greenish, with a number of darker bands. Fins are dark at the base, becoming reddish and with a dark red edge.

If you like your fish rough and tough, this one is for you. The Chanchito has the distinction of being the first Cichlid to be bred in captivity, and we suspect that the reputation which many Cichlids have gotten, whether it be for being quarrelsome or for digging plants and raising the devil in general, may be traced back to the behavior of the Chanchito. Whatever their bad habits may be, they are usually good parents. They lay their eggs on a flat stone, flowerpot or one of the glass sides of the aquarium and then both parents take meticulous care of their spawn, mouthing them often to make sure that no dirt settles on them. In 3 to 4 days the young hatch and are immediately transferred to holes which the parents have been digging previously. The yolk sacs are absorbed in about another week, and the youngsters then begin to swim out of the holes, to be herded back by the watchful parents. Feeding is best begun with newly hatched brine shrimp, and they soon outgrow this. This is followed with daphnia, then larger foods like tubifex worms and Enchytrae. The young are very attractive in color, but soon become ruffians like their parents.

F-180.00

Photo by Ruda Zukal

CICHLASOMA FESTIVUM (Heckel)/*Flag Cichlid*

Range: Widely spread all over the central Amazon region.

Habits: Fairly peaceful for a Cichlid; small specimens make good community tank fish, but when they grow larger should have their own tank.

Water Conditions: Conditions are not as important as the fact that the water should be clean and have an exceptionally high oxygen content. For this reason they should be given plenty of room.

Size: Up to 6 inches.

Food Requirements: Varied diet of living foods; will eat dried foods unwillingly.

Color Variations: Body color yellowish to greenish gray. With a dark line extending obliquely from the mouth to the after end of the dorsal fin.

No danger of confusion here with any of the other Cichlid species. The line which runs upward diagonally from the mouth to the tip of the dorsal fin identifies it without question. Differentiating between the sexes is another story; males are a bit larger, with longer fins, but a not fully developed male and a fully developed one could easily be mistaken for a pair, and the only way to be really sure is by comparing the genital papillae, or breeding tubes, when they are ready to spawn. The female's tube is much thicker than the male's. This fish is found in a very large area in the central Amazon region, and fish collectors often find them a nuisance when netting other species. There would be many more shipped, but their heavy oxygen requirements do not permit them to be crowded in shipping containers for any length of time. A rather shy fish; they should be given a well-planted aquarium which permits them to hide when danger threatens. They are often found in the company of the popular Angelfish, and get along well with them in the aquarium. First imported into Germany in 1908, and first bred in 1911.

CICHLASOMA MEEKI (Brind)/*Firemouth*

Range: Northern Yucatan.

Habits: Peaceful for a Cichlid; will get along with most fishes which do not harass it.

Water Conditions: Not critical; requires large tank with some open space and rocks for shelter.

Size: 5 inches; females about 4 inches.

Food Requirements: Predominantly living foods, such as daphnia, tubifex worms, grown brine shrimp, etc.

Color Variations: Body bluish gray, darker on the back and a number of vertical bars and a horizontal stripe. Fins reddish.

One of the most beautiful and popular Cichlids. Pairs usually get along fairly well together, but when spawning the male may forget his manners if the female is not ready for him, and may kill her if she is not removed until her eggs are developed. At this time the male shows his colors at their best. There is a bright red area which extends over his belly and his chin, even to his mouth. The female's colors are much more subdued, and her fins are shorter. They are usually good parents, and the young are easily raised. There was another species which was identified as *Cichlasoma meeki* by Hildebrand in 1925, and later was established as another species, *Cichlasoma guiza* Hildebrand, in 1934. This species was first introduced in 1937, at which time its beauty created quite a commotion among aquarists in this country and in Europe. This fish is recommended only if the hobbyist has a large aquarium which presents a good number of hiding-places. There have been a number of reports where this fish has spawned in a community aquarium and raised its young without injuring any other fishes kept with it.

F-182.00

CICHLASOMA NIGROFASCIATUM (Guenther)/*Convict Cichlid*

Range: Guatamala, El Salvador, Costa Rica and Panama. A related species is found in the upper Amazon near the Colombian-Peruvian border.

Habits: A typical cichlid not to be trusted with smaller fishes.

Water Conditions: Not particular about water. Moderately hard water suits it fine with temperatures between 68 and 80°F.

Size: To 6 inches; breeds at 3 inches.

Food Requirements: Eats everything but does exceptionally well on frozen brine shrimp and frozen beef heart. The young thrive on microworms from their free-swimming stage on.

Color Variations: This is a very variable species. Some races show a yellow back and purple sides; others are plain silver with the characteristic stripes. As the fish ages and stripes diminish in number.

This is a typical Cichlid which exhibits extremes of color variations between the six-inch adults form and the young which have as many as ten dark vertical bands covering the body. As the fish gets older the stripes disappear until some specimens raised in the author's tanks have lost almost all of their stripes. The fish are very simple to breed if they are given the barest of essentials. Set up a 15- or 20-gallon aquarium. The bottom should be sand to a depth of about 2 inches. The pair will select a spawning site on a rock or inverted flowerpot and spawn as soon as they have been prepared for the reproductive act with copious feedings of frozen brine shrimp, beef heart and *Tubifex* worms. They exercise extreme parental care of the spawn and will probably dig holes in the sand after the young are free swimming in which to herd the young. The fry do very well on microworms until they are old enough for larger forms of live foods.

If their aquarium has plants in it, they will usually be ruthlessly uprooted and chewed to bits before the breeders feel secure enough to breed.

F-183.00

Photo by Aaron Norman

CICHLASOMA SEVERUM (Heckel)/*Convict Fish*

Range: Northern South America to the Amazon River, except in the Magdalena River.

Habits: Typical of the large Cichlids, it will become quarrelsome when breeding time rolls around. Requires a large aquarium, and will uproot plants and dig many holes in the gravel.

Water Conditions: Not critical; clean, slightly alkaline water seems to be best.

Size: Up to 8 inches.

Food Requirements: Small specimens may be fed with all the various live foods; when they become large, chopped garden worms should be given on occasion.

Color Variations: Young specimens show a number of dark vertical bars, which later fade with the exception of one which connects the last rays of the dorsal and anal fins. Sides are spotted red, especially in the males.

Like *Astronotus ocellatus*, young specimens of this fish do not greatly resemble their parents, and often create a problem when they grow up. Young fish are usually peaceful and their owner gets the mistaken impression that this attitude will continue. As they get bigger, they will "pair off" in the usual Cichlid fashion and proceed to prepare a site for spawning. Every other fish which dares to come near is driven away fiercely, and bloody fights may ensue. If given their own tank, spawning proceeds normally as a rule, and eggs and fry are seldom eaten. There is also an albino variety of this fish available today, with a light golden body and pink eyes. We have not heard whether or not this variety is more peaceful than the normal variety, but in all probability it is not. The young normally colored *Cichlasoma severum* have a high, compressed body on which the vertical bars are very prominent, giving them their popular name "Convict Fish." At this size they are often confused with young Discus Fish, *Symphysodon discus*, and have been sold as such.

F-184.00

CLARIAS BATRACHUS (Linnaeus)/*Pla Duk Dam* or the *Albino Clarias*

Range: India, Ceylon, Burma, Malaya, East Indies, Philippines, Indo-China and Thailand.

Habits: An amazing fish which jumps out of aquaria and walks for long distances without dying.

Water Conditions: Hardy and tolerant to any water which is not too salty nor too cold. Can tolerate temperatures from 50 to 90°F.

Size: Grows to at least 18 inches long in nature.

Food Requirements: Eats anything usually offered to aquarium fishes.

Color Variations: There are two natural varieties; a normally colored gray form and an albino form which is freely found in nature.

The catfish of the genus *Clarias* are an extremely interesting group of fishes, for they have a huge accessory breathing organ in the branchial cavity which enables them to utilize atmospheric oxygen in the same way that higher animals do. As a result, their gills have atrophied to the point where they are practically useless and it has been demonstrated that if they are maintained in an aquarium with a floating glass cover, where they are unable to gather atmospheric air to breathe, they die of suffocation. As if this were not enough, they are one of the very few species which exist in nature in an albino form. Somphongs Lekaree, the famous Bangkok fish exporter, has a race of them growing in a pool in his backyard. Smith reports adult albino forms having been found in other areas. The aquarium market is always able to supply limited quantities of wild albino forms. Catfish seem to be the only fishes which exist in an albino form in nature. The albino forms of other fishes are probably destroyed because of their lack of protective coloration. The author (HRA) did find an albino *Acanthophthalmus*, however. Smith reports the following incident:

"*On August 13, 1926, a friend brought the writer a fish that in the late afternoon of the previous day was picked up on a metaled driveway in his yard in Bangkok. The fish had left a small canal 15 meters away and was proceeding toward another canal 35 meters away. It was placed in a flat jar of water in the writer's office. It left the jar during the night (apparently by jumping), dropped from a table to the floor, passed through a short corridor, traversed a large exhibit room, went the entire length of a long hallway, and was found in a lively condition just inside the front door at 11 p.m. It was released the next morning, having earned its freedom.*"

COBITIS TAENIA (Linnaeus)/*Weatherfish, Spined Loach*

Range: Extremely wide, covering parts of both Europe and Asia.

Habits: Peaceful and inclined towards shyness.

Water Conditions: Water conditions for this species are not of special importance, as long as extremes of pH and DH variations are avoided. Can take temperatures lower than 60°, but a range in the low 70's is best.

Size: Up to 4 inches.

Food Requirements: Takes all foods, but particularly likes living foods which congregate near the bottom, such as worms.

Color Variations: Over-all coloration is yellowish-brown, with rows of markings on the sides.

The range of this fish is so wide that many authorities, no doubt working at least in part on the theory that no single animal should be allowed to cover so much territory, have broken the species up into at least seven sub-species, according to geographical origin. No matter where it comes from, this little Loach is a peaceful addition to the community tank, where it is most often kept as a scavenger under the mistaken notion that the fish lives by choice on left-over food particles. This same fate overtakes many of the hapless Catfish within the genus *Corydoras;* looked upon as garbage disposal units, the fish, whether Loach or Catfish, gradually wastes away. This is unfortunate, for although *Cobitis taenia* can be by no means considered as a really strikingly pretty fish, it is interesting and worthy of better treatment. One point to note about the many members of the family Cobitidae, to which all of the aquarium Loaches remain, is that these fishes are regarded to have the capacity to forecast weather conditions. Changes in barometric pressure are evidenced by increased or decreased activity of the fish, giving rise to the popular name of many Loach species: Weatherfish.

COLISA CHUNA/*Honey Dwarf Gourami*

Range: India.
Habits: Peaceful and shy.
Water Conditions: Soft, slightly acid water desirable.
Size: 2½ inches.
Food Requirements: Will accept some dry foods, but prefers small living foods,
especially crustaceans.
Color Variations: Tan body with yellowish cast; dorsal fin of male shades from plain
light brown to gold. Dark stripe on sides.

This peaceful little Anabantid, very similar in size and configuration to the
popular Dwarf Gourami, is a recent introduction to the aquarium scene,
although the fish was catalogued and described before the turn of the century.
Apparently it was not received with enough enthusiasm to merit its importation on a large scale, for it has made but a very limited appearance in the
tanks of dealers throughout the country. Although the Honey Dwarf is a
pleasing fish of warm but not startling coloring, it is no rival to its relative
Colisa lalia, the male of which species is a truly beautiful fish. *Colisa chuna*
is a bubblenest builder which spawns like the Dwarf Gourami, but *chuna*
uses less vegetable matter in the construction of its nest. Also, the male
Honey Dwarf Gourami is inclined to be more tolerant of the hesitancy of
the female to spawn, whereas the male *Colisa lalia* will damage the female if
she is not provided with enough refuge. Like the Dwarf Gourami, *Colisa
chuna* does best at a temperature between 75 and 82°

COLISA FASCIATA (Bloch & Schneider)/*Giant Gourami*

Range: India: Coromandel Coast, Northwest and North Provinces, Assam.
Habits: Peaceful, a good community fish.
Water Conditions: Not critical; they like warm water, about 78° to 80°.
Size: Males about 4¾ inches, females a little smaller.
Food Requirements: They eat anything, and have tremendous appetites.
Color Variations: Body color light brown, which shimmers blue in certain lights. A
series of bands on the sides alternate bluish green and orange.

This attractive fish looks somewhat like a larger edition of the popular Dwarf
Gourami. Because it is considerably larger, some people tend to shy away
from it, fearing that it might be aggressive. This is not so; it is even a bit shy,
and tends to be scary if placed in a tank where it cannot hide when real or
imaginary danger threatens it. Breeding is very easily accomplished, and a
well-mated pair may easily make a nuisance of themselves by breeding too
often. Like the other *Colisa* species, they prefer to anchor their bubble-nest
to a floating plant, and a few should be provided. When they are ready to
spawn, the water should be reduced to only 3½ to 4 inches deep. After a
number of false tries, the pair will eventually produce as many as 800 eggs,
which hatch in about 24 hours. The fry become free-swimming in two more
days, at which time the male may be removed; the female should be removed
when she is finished laying eggs. The fry should be fed liberally with fine
dried food, and it is an advantage to add aeration at this time. Sorting the
fry after they begin growing will prevent cannibalism.

COLISA LABIOSA (Day)/*Thick-Lipped Gourami*

Range: India, Upper and Lower Burma.
Habits: Peaceful, rather shy. A good fish for the community aquarium.
Water Conditions: Requires warmth, about 78° temperature. Otherwise not critical as to water conditions, if extremes are avoided.
Size: 4 inches, usually somewhat smaller.
Food Requirements: Live foods preferred, but in the absence of these, prepared foods are acceptable.
Color Variations: Bluish horizontal stripe, not always present. 8 to 10 dark vertical bands, on a blue background. Ventral fins red.

The Thick-Lipped Gourami, while not as popular or quite as colorful as the Dwarf Gourami, is also worthy of a place in the community aquarium. Like the other members of the *Colisa* genus, this fish is a bit on the shy side, and should have an aquarium which is rich in plant life and permits the fish to duck out of sight if he feels circumstances warrant it. *C. labiosa* is one of the easiest of the Gourami group to breed. The males seem to get a kick out of making bubble-nests, and are less likely to get rough when a female is not ready for spawning. Care must be taken not to combine this or for that matter any other thread-finned fish with a greedy species such as some of the Barbs, or in a very short time the long, thin ventral fins will be reduced to stumps. In time the fins grow back, but the new fin is often a bit crooked at the point where growth began. As with so many other species, *C. labiosa* was first made available to aquarists in 1911 by a Berlin firm which imported them from Rangoon. In 1926 the fish were again imported from Bassein. The name "Thick-Lipped" is not entirely exact. The lips are quite thick, but a thin black line above them makes them look thicker.

COLISA LALIA (Hamilton-Buchanan)/*Dwarf Gourami*

Range: India, Bengal and Assam.
Habits: Very peaceful; likely to be shy and retiring if kept with fish which annoy it.
Water Conditions: Water should be neutral to slightly acid; enjoys a tank which gets a good amount of sunlight.
Size: Largest males never exceed 2½ inches, females 2 inches.
Food Requirements: Not a fussy eater. Dried foods accepted, but should be alternated with live foods.
Color Variations: Males have alternating blue and red diagonal stripes on the body and unpaired fins. Females have lighter bodies and fins.

The Dwarf Gourami is one of the beloved hardy perennials of the aquarium fish world. Even in its native India it is extensively kept in aquaria, which is an unusual thing because with aquarium fishes there is usually no respect for a native fish. At least this seems to be the case in this country, where there are some native fishes which are valued in other countries as aquarium specimens, but scarcely ever seen here. The Dwarf Gourami is unusual among the bubble-nest builders in that it includes bits of plants, twigs and other debris in its nest. The result is a firm bundle which holds together for a long time after the fry have hatched. The eggs are tiny, and if not provided with fine infusoria at first the fry are likely to starve. Once past the critical stage, however, when they are large enough to handle newly hatched brine shrimp, they prove hardy and growth is rapid. The famous naturalist Francis Day described them as early as 1869 as "the most beautiful amongst the numerous species of freshwater fishes I have ever seen," and sent four dozen to the London Zoo. The shipment was unsuccessful, however.

COLOSSOMA species

Range: Branches of the Amazon.

Habits: Not to be trusted with small fishes.

Water Conditions: Soft, slightly acid water is indicated, but is probably of no great importance. Temperature 70-80°.

Size: Up to 8 inches.

Food Requirements: Very reluctant to accept dry foods, but will take live and frozen foods.

Color Variations: Generally plain silver body, with black specklings and red in the fins.

All of the *Colossomas* are big, ungainly fishes, with few attributes that would suit them to the home aquarium. First of all, they are big and must consequently be maintained in big tanks; also, they are closely related to the Piranhas and share, at least to a small degree, the nasty temperaments of their more notorious cousins. Of course, these very qualities are what makes the Piranha species attractive to some hobbyists, and it sometimes happens that a *Colossoma* will be billed in a dealer's display tank as a "Man-eating Fish" to attract attention. The *Colossoma* species, especially the older fish, are popular in public aquariums, where size of a fish is no objection and where there is a complete supply of the proper dietary items.

COPEINA ARNOLDI (Regan)/*Splash Tetra, Jumping Characin*

Range: Amazon River, in the region of Rio Para.
Habits: Very peaceful, but should be kept always in a covered aquarium, because of its jumping habits.
Water Conditions: Neutral to slightly acid, temperature between 75° and 78°.
Size: 3 inches; females about 2½ inches.
Food Requirements: Live foods preferred, but will take dry food when hungry.
Color Variations: Brownish sides, becoming yellowish in the belly region. Males have larger fins, and the black marking in the dorsal more pronounced.

We have many odd ways of reproduction in aquarium fishes, but this species probably has the oddest. In nature, a pair will seek out an overhanging leaf and together leap out of the water and cling to this leaf long enough to paste several eggs there. They then drop back, to repeat the process again and again until there are more than 100 eggs in a closely-packed mass on the underside of the leaf. The eggs do not hatch until 3 days later, during which time the male remains under the leaf and every 15 minutes or so splashes water on them with his tail to keep them from drying out. The reason for this behavior is not definite, but a study of the ecology of this fish would probably disclose that there are some egg-eating parasites or maybe snails present in these waters, which would wipe out any unprotected eggs in the water but could not catch the tiny fry once they begin swimming. In the aquarium, these fish will breed if the tank is half-full of water and a piece of slate is leaned against the inside edge so that half is out of water. Once the fry hatch and fall into the water, the parents should be removed to prevent them from eating their fry.

COPEINA CALLOLEPIS (Regan)/*Spotted Copeina*

Range: Amazon Basin.
Habits: Peaceful; a good community fish. Should be kept in covered tank.
Water Conditions: Soft, slightly acid water. Temperature 72 to 82°F.
Size: Up to 3 inches.
Food Requirements: Not too particular, but not all dry foods are accepted.
Color Variations: Over-all body color brownish-purple, fins shading to red. Definite red spot in base of dorsal fin of male.

There is a simple beauty to this fish. Not flashy in color, *Copeina callolepis* is possessed of a subdued warm coloring that is highlighted by occasional bright spots of red and lavender. The most striking of these spots lies immediately between the gill covers and the pectoral fins; under correct lighting, this spot shows up like a brilliant jewel. Also, the fish has a gliding swimming motion which lends additional grace to its appearance. All in all, *Copeina callolepis* gives the impression of refined elegance, especially if it is kept with fishes more stubby in body form, for then the streamlined charm of the Spotted Copeina is most pronounced. Distinguishing the sexes is easy with mature specimens, because the male's dorsal fin is very definitely longer and more tapered; also, he is more elongated in shape. Although *Copeina callolepis* closely resembles *Copeina arnoldi*, its breeding pattern is quite different. Instead of jumping from the water to lay its eggs, the Spotted Copeina deposits its eggs on submerged plants, usually broad-leaved plants, such as broad-leaf Amazon Sword Plants. At a temperature of 78° the eggs hatch in about a day, and the fry require small foods.

Photo by Harald Schultz.

COPEINA EIGENMANNI (Regan)/*Eigenmann's Copeina*

Range: Middle Amazon region (?).
Habits: Peaceful, prefers to swim in the upper reaches of the tank. A skillful jumper; tank must be kept covered.
Water Conditions: Soft, slightly acid water. Temperature about 78°.
Size: To 2½ inches.
Food Requirements: They accept dry food, but prefer live foods which remain near the top.
Color Variations: Back brown, dark horizontal line edged with gold. Male's dorsal fin red with black spot; all other fins yellow.

The *Copeina* group is a bit of a paradox. *Copeina arnoldi* has the unusual, almost freakish method of spawning where the pair jumps out of the water and fastens their eggs to the underside of an overhanging leaf or rock, then splashing water up against the eggs until they hatch. *Copeina guttata* spawns like the Sunfishes, making a depression in the bottom gravel and depositing the eggs there until they hatch and guarding the young afterward. *Copeina callolepis* usually spawns on a submerged leaf. Now we have a *new* one, *Copeina eigenmanni*. To the best of the author's recollection, they were made available to hobbyists on only one occasion, when a shipment of them came in about 1957. If any of these were spawned, we have never heard of it or seen any of the tank-raised progeny. Until the collectors find some more and send them up, we will have to content ourselves with just the memory, and keep wondering how *these* fellows spawn! One thing we do know: these fish can jump through the smallest openings and their tank should be covered at all times, or they are very likely to be found on the floor some morning when we go to feed them.

Photo by Dr. Herbert R. Axelrod.

COPEINA GUTTATA (Steindachner)/*Red-Spotted Copeina*

Range: Central Amazon region.

Habits: Peaceful; good community tank fish if not kept with others much smaller than themselves.

Water Conditions: Not critical; a wide range of temperatures is tolerated, with optimum temperatures around 75°.

Size: Wild specimens attain a size of about 4 inches, in captivity 6 inches.

Food Requirements: Heavy eaters which will take prepared foods, but they should also be given live foods whenever possible.

Color Variations: Bluish sides, fins in the female yellow, reddish in the male. Males also have rows of red dots on the sides.

It is highly unusual for a fish which is kept in captivity to grow as large as it would in its natural waters. But every rule has its exceptions, and with this fish it is a rare one indeed: *Copeina guttata* become larger in captivity than it does in the wild. There may be several reasons for this, but in all probability the answer is in the food supply. In their natural waters *Copeina guttata* occur in large schools and there is a very good chance that they might not get enough food to satisfy their robust appetites. The same has been observed with trout and other fishes which occur in habitats where there was a food shortage. The fish matured but remained much smaller. *Copeina guttata* has another claim to being unusual. It is a true Characin, but does not spawn in a manner which is usual for Characins, and would be more likely to be found among the Cichlids. The male scoops out a depression in the gravel in an open spot, and a large number of eggs is deposited into this depression. Here they are guarded and fanned by the male. Fry hatch after 30 to 50 hours and are easily raised. *Copeinas* are jumpers, so be sure to keep their tank covered at all times.

F-195.00

Photo by Dr. Herbert R. Axelrod.

COPELLA VILMAE/*Rainbow Copella*

Range: Discovered by Harald Schultz in the Brazilian Amazon.

Habits: A very typical member of the *Copeïna-Copella* group. Keep in covered tank as this species may jump.

Water Conditions: Prefers warm, slightly acid, soft water.

Size: To about 2½ inches.

Food Requirements: Eats any small particled food, especially dried pelletized foods. Also requires some live foods or frozen brine shrimp in order that the male will keep his beautiful colors.

Color Variations: Not all males are as colorful as the photo shows. They tend to lose their redness and the two blue-green spots if they are not properly fed and cared for.

When Harald Schultz, the expedition leader for *Tropical Fish Hobbyist* magazine, discovered this fish in Brazil he immediately wrote the author: "I've found the most beautiful *Copeina* in the world! It has a blood red belly and two beautiful metallic blue spots. I am sending you the fish soon so you will believe that the pictures I am enclosing are really of living fishes that I didn't paint myself. I have always been looking for a fish as beautiful as the Cardinal Tetra (*Cheirodon axelrodi*) to have named in honor of my wife Vilma, and I think this is it!!"

CORYDORAS ACUTUS (Cope)/*Blacktop Catfish*

Range: Upper Amazon.
Habits: Peaceful.
Water Conditions: Soft, slightly acid water desirable. Temperature 73 to 80°F.
Size: 2½ inches.
Food Requirements: Accepts all foods.
Color Variations: Brownish-gray body, with metallic glistening area at gill covers. Large irregular black spot at top of dorsal.

Although this little Catfish is rarely seen, it makes a good aquarium subject, as it is peaceful and hardy. Specimens of this fish are usually found among importations of more popular Corydoras species. In dealers' tanks they are almost always mixed in with other *Corydoras*, as there have been no direct attempts at importing this fish as a separate species, for it is little known and has no following among the aquarium public in general. For the casual tropical fish store browser, *Corydoras acutus* has no special charm, and when purchased it is usually the last, or one of the last, specimens to be chosen from the general "scavenger" tank. *Corydoras* specialists, however, are always on the lookout for Catfish which differ in some respects from the most common members of the genus, and for them *Corydoras acutus* presents at least one interesting point: the angle of indentation between the upper and lower caudal lobes is wider than with most other *Corydoras* species, and the separation is less sharp, thus giving *Corydoras acutus* a more fan-like tail than its relatives. Little is known of the breeding habits of the Blacktop Catfish, but the fish in all probability spawns like *Corydoras aeneus*.

F-197.00

CORYDORAS AENEUS (Gill)/*Aeneus Catfish*

Range: Widely distributed over South America from Trinidad to the La Plata.
Habits: Very peaceful; constantly going over the bottom for scraps of leftover food. Useful in keeping the tank clean.
Water Conditions: Neutral to slightly alkaline; water should have no salt added to it. These fish come from absolutely fresh water.
Size: 2¾ inches, usually a bit smaller.
Food Requirements: All dried foods are accepted, but to keep them in really good shape an occasional feeding of tubifex worms should be given.
Color Variations: Greenish brown on the sides, darker above and a dirty yellow underneath. There is a darker zone on the sides.

This is probably the most well-known among the popular Armored Catfishes, and its popularity is well deserved. They are comical fellows, their alert eyes always looking around while grubbing around the bottom in search of food. Probably their eyes are not as useful in finding food as their barbels, which are their accessory taste organs and permit them to find food where many other fishes cannot, even in the dark. This fish has little to fear from any enemies; it has sharply-spiked anal and dorsal fins which would make a larger fish feel as though he was biting into a pincushion. His armor plates, which he wears on his body in place of scales, give a hard, bony surface to a smaller fish which would feel inclined to nibble on him. With such protection, who needs teeth ? The natives have an odd way of catching these fish. They choose a small pond where the ripples tell them that there are Catfish there surfacing for air. Then they build a dam where the water enters and let the pond run dry. This leaves the Catfish flopping around in the mud, where the collectors can walk out and pick them up. Needless to say, they are careful not to step on them with their bare feet!

*CORYDORAS AGASSIZI (Steindachner)/*Agassiz's Catfish*

Range: West Brazil; Amazon region, Nauta, Ambyacu River, Maranon, Rio Jurua.
Habits: Peaceful; useful in that it feeds off the bottom and gets much food left by other fishes.
Water Conditions: Neutral to slightly alkaline; water should have no salt content.
Size: 2½ inches.
Food Requirements: Will do a good clean-up job, but if really good fish are desired, should get frequent live food feedings.
Color Variations: Back brown, sides silvery to yellow, with darker markings. Anal and caudal fins have rows of spots.

This attractive little Catfish has a shorter, thicker body than most of the other species, almost like *Brochis coeruleus.* Although it has been known to science as far back as 1912, aquarists did not see them until a single specimen was brought into Germany in 1936. This is one species which cannot be sexed by color alone, as indeed very few of them can. We cannot go by fin shapes either, although usually the dorsal fin of the males is more pointed. The best way to arrive at a fairly accurate conclusion is to look at them from above. The females are a little bigger and their body shape is heavier. So far there have been no accounts of their spawning in captivity, possibly because there have been not very many fish available. It is interestingly marked: the upper half of the sides is marked with wavy lines, and the head is covered with tiny spots. There are vertical rows of dots in the anal and caudal fins. The caudal fin is a bit bigger and more deeply notched than most of the other *Corydoras* species. With all their rooting in the bottom, the *Corydoras* will seldom uproot a plant. They always seem to know when to stop.

*This fish is now known as *C. ambiacus.*

Photo by Dr. Herbert R. Axelrod.

CORYDORAS ARCUATUS (Elwin)/*Skunk Catfish, Tabatinga Catfish*

Range: Amazon region, above the city of Tefe.

Habits: Peaceful; being a bottom feeder makes it especially valuable for finding and eating leftover food.

Water Conditions: Neutral to slightly alkaline water; it is important to leave out any salt. Temperature about 76°.

Size: About 1¾ inches.

Food Requirements: Besides food left by other fishes, an occasional feeding of live foods should be given.

Color Variations: Body light gray, with a dark stripe running from the mouth all along the back and ending in the lower part of the tail.

According to existing literature, this attractive Catfish has not yet been bred in captivity. Probably the most important reason why the *Corydoras* species are so seldom bred is because most hobbyists consider them as strictly scavengers, and will put one into each tank to eat any food left by the other fishes in that tank. If two are used, no attention is paid to whether they are a pair or not. We would doubtless hear of many spawnings if pairs were given their own tanks and well fed with living foods. Sexing is not the near impossibility it was once considered. Looking at a group of mature fish from above, it will be seen that some of them are wider in the body than the others; these are the females. These Catfish do not eat their eggs; all that is required is that there are no other fish in the tank to eat eggs or fry. In Germany this species is known as "Stromlinien-Panzerwels," or "Streamlined Armored Catfish." Many thousands of them have been imported since 1938, when they were first introduced to the aquarium hobby. It would be interesting to see a batch of youngsters; probably the stripe down the back does not appear right away, but develops later.

F-200.00

CORYDORAS BARBATUS (Quoy and Gaimard)/*Banded Corydoras*

Range: Brazil (Southeast).
Habits: Peaceful.
Water Conditions: Soft, slightly acid water desirable; temperature 72 to 82°F.
Size: Up to 5 inches.
Food Requirements: Takes all foods.
Color Variations: Light brown body covered by large black markings. Belly color pink.

While *Corydoras barbatus*, because of its size, is not considered to be one of the better Catfishes for the community tank, the fish is occasionally brought into the country and put on the market. Usually only young specimens are sold, and many purchasers are amazed to find that their Catfish, which they originally supposed would grow no larger than the popular *C. aeneus*, is soon outgrowing its tank. For hobbyists with big tanks this is no problem, but for the hobbyist who buys a couple of *Corydoras* just to fit into the general framework of a small community tank, *Corydoras barbatus* is best left alone. To the best of our knowledge this fish, like so many of the other *Corydoras* species, has not been bred, but it is reasonable to believe that the Banded Corydoras follows the general spawning pattern of the genus.

Photo by Dr. Herbert R. Axelrod.

CORYDORAS CAUDIMACULATUS (Rössel)/*Tail-Spot Corydoras*

Range: Rio Guaporé, Brazil.
Habits: Peaceful; will not disturb fish or plants.
Water Conditions: Slightly alkaline water is best. Avoid sharp edges on rocks or gravel, as the mouth is easily damaged.
Size: About 2 inches.
Food Requirements: All food which falls to the bottom is eaten, but there should be some live as well as prepared foods.
Color Variations: Sides, head and fins peppered with small dots; large black spot at caudal base.

While this book was still under preparation, our good friend Harald Schultz sent us some specimens of newly discovered fishes, of which this was one. Tropicarium, in Frankfurt, Germany also received some and Herr Fritz Rössel, of the Natur-Museum und Forschungs-Institut Senckenberg lost no time in identifying it as a new species. The short body might almost lead one into believing that this is a species of *Brochis*, but the profile of the head is rounded like the other members of the *Corydoras* group. The German breeders have already been successful in breeding this fish, and there are no deviations from the usual *Corydoras* breeding procedure. There are some excellent spawning photos, to which space has been allotted in this work. It is to be hoped that spawnings will be frequent and successful enough to ensure a good supply of this attractive fish, which bids fair to become one of the favorites. One unusual thing about this species is that even the adipose fin carries a number of dots. In most spotted *Corydoras* species, the adipose fin is scarcely large enough for this, but in one picture we are able to count 10 dots appearing there. This gives an idea of how small the dots are.

F-202.00

CORYDORAS COCHUI (Myers and Weitzman)/*Cochu's Catfish*

Range: Central Brazil.
Habits: Peaceful.
Water Conditions: Neutral water, medium soft, Temperature 72-85°F.
Size: About 1½ inches.
Food Requirements: Accepts all regular aquarium foods, provided they are small enough to be swallowed.
Color Variations: Whitish gray belly, upper body grayish brown with irregular dark markings. Fins, even pectorals, marked with black.

Corydoras cochui ranks with *Corydoras hastatus* as among the smallest *Corydoras* known to aquarists. It is a pretty little Catfish, more elongated in body form than its relatives, and it is interesting and peaceful, although it does have a tendency to be shy. Unlike *Corydoras hastatus*, it remains true to normal Catfish behavior by spending the great bulk of its time at the bottom of the aquarium rooting in the gravel for food. Because of its size, it makes less commotion while going about its business, and this is valuable in tanks containing fishes which do not relish having their prancings interrupted by a heavy-bodied 2½-inch Catfish whizzing by at breakneck speed as it shoots to the surface of the water for an occasional gulp of air. For hobbyists who are in the habit of regarding the various *Corydoras* strictly as scavengers, however, the size of Cochu's Catfish is not an advantage, but a disadvantage, for it stands to reason that a small *Corydoras* is going to eat less than a medium-size or large *Corydoras*; in addition, *C. cochui* is a little more finicky in its eating habits. This fish was named after Fred Cochu of Paramount Aquarium.

Photo by Harald Schultz.

CORYDORAS ELEGANS (Steindachner)/*Elegant Corydoras*

Range: Amazon Basin (Upper).
Habits: Peaceful.
Water Conditions: Slightly acid to slightly alkaline medium-soft water. Temperature 73 to 83°F.
Size: 2 inches.
Food Requirements: Accepts all foods, but is particularly fond of small worms.
Color Variations: Dark gray body with black stripes, one broad and one narrow.

The "Elegant" in this fish's popular name is derived from its specific scientific name, not from any special coloring or markings that would entitle it to such a fancy name. It is certainly a lot plainer than many of the other *Corydoras* species, some of which have been extracted from the "scavenger" category and are now being kept for their good looks alone. However, it is a good community Catfish, and its desirability is enhanced by the fact that it is small, seldom reaching over two inches in length. Breeding has not been observed, although attempts have been made to spawn this fish. The fish pictured are still fairly young; as they mature, they will develop heavier bodies, with more dorsal "hump". The irregular outline of the dorsal fin of the fish at left is the result of damage suffered during transportation; it is not to be relied on as a sexual characteristic.

CORYDORAS GRISEUS (Holly)/*Gray Catfish*

Range: Brazilian Amazon region, in small tributary streams.
Habits: Peaceful. Will not bother other fish, even very small ones.
Water Conditions: Slightly alkaline water is best, with no salt content. Temperature about 76°.
Size: About 2 inches.
Food Requirements: Although dried foods are picked up eagerly from the bottom, live foods should also be fed regularly.
Color Variations: Body gray, fins transparent, face sooty black.

It is possible that this rare little Catfish has often been passed up by collectors who considered them a little plain for the average hobbyist's tastes. However, their greatest charm lies in their simplicity of color. It seems that there are never enough aquarists who are interested in the *Corydoras* species to propagate them in quantity, and about nine-tenths of the ones available today are wild imported stock. Catching these seems like simplicity itself: schools numbering in the hundreds can be seen browsing over a flat sandy bottom. A long seine is spread out and held in place, and then the fish are driven into this with another seine which is pulled along the bottom. A goodly amount of them are seen swimming ahead of the seine, and a large haul is anticipated. Then when the stationary net is approached and the fish see that they are about to be trapped, suddenly they seem to vanish into thin air (or should it be thin water?). They quickly bury themselves in the sand and let the net pass over them, coming up again and swimming away when the danger has passed. *Corydoras griseus* was first exhibited in Munich in 1938, and there have been few importations since.

CORYDORAS HASTATUS (Eigenmann and Eigenmann)
Corydoras, Pygmy Corydoras

Range: Amazon Basin, Mato Grosso, Paraguay
Habits: Very peaceful and inoffensive.
Water Conditions: pH and hardness values not of great importance, as long as extremes are avoided. Temperature 70 to 85°F.
Size: 1½ inches.
Food Requirements: Accepts all regular foods.
Color Variations: Over-all body coloring plain gray with green cast; two dark stripes along sides, one at middle of body and the other at lower part of body, between ventral and anal fin. Large spot at tail.

Here is a little Catfish which represents a departure from normal *Corydoras* body shape and behavior. First of all, it is a good bit smaller and more streamlined than other *Corydoras*, the difference in body shape being so marked as to lead to this fish's being placed by some authorities into a separate genus, *Microdoras*. Whatever its scientific standing, the Dwarf Corydoras is an interesting addition to a community tank. Contrary to the actions of its relatives, *Corydoras hastatus* swims mainly in the middle reaches of the water; it spends little time on the bottom, or at least much less than the other Corydoras. Generally considered as one of the easiest Catfishes to spawn and raise, the Dwarf Catfish goes through the rather frenzied mating procedure of the other Catfishes, but the fish is much more likely to choose plants for the site of egg deposit; the fry are large for so small a fish. One disadvantage in keeping the Dwarf Catfish in a community tank is that other fishes pick at it much more frequently than they do the larger *Corydoras* species. This is odd, because *C. hastatus* possesses comparatively as much armor as other members of the genus.

F-206.00

CORYDORAS JULII (Steindachner)/*Leopard Catfish*

Range: Small tributaries of the lower Amazon.
Habits: Very peaceful and active. Constantly poking on the bottom for bits of food which were overlooked by the others.
Water Conditions: Not critical; best water is slightly alkaline and not very hard.
Size: To 2½ inches.
Food Requirements: All sorts of foods are taken, but enough should be fed so that the Catfish will get his share.
Color Variations: Body silvery gray and covered with black spots. These spots give way to wavy lines about the head and gill-plates.

One of the most popular and attractive members of the *Corydoras* family is *Corydoras julii*. Fortunately the supply is usually good. It is a strange thing about the *Corydoras* Catfishes: practically all of the fish we see for sale have been caught wild in South America and imported into this country. The *Corydoras* species are not as difficult to spawn as many other species which our hatcheries produce, but nobody wants to spawn *Corydoras*. Like the Neon Tetra, it is cheaper to import them than it would be to raise them. If we were ever cut off commercially from South America (Heaven forbid!) our breeders would soon bend their efforts to producing *Corydoras*, and as a result the collectors would lose a good-sized chunk of business when things were straightened out again. The *Corydoras* species are not at all an easy proposition to catch, either. They occur in good enough quantities in most of the streams, and can be seen by the thousands poking around for edibles in the sand. When they are trapped so that it seems that they have no place to swim but into the net, they quickly bury themselves in the sand and the net passes harmlessly over them. It has to be seen to be believed!

F-207.00

Photo by Dr. Herbert R. Axelrod.

CORYDORAS METAE/*Masked Corydoras, Bandit Catfish*

Range: British Guiana.
Habits: Peaceful and active.
Water Conditions: Medium soft water, pH slightly acid to slightly alkaline. Temperature 73 to 85°F.
Size: 2¼ inches.
Food Requirements: Accepts all foods, particularly *Tubifex* worms.
Color Variations: Reddish-tan body with broad dark stripes, one through the eye and one running backward along the back from the frontal portion of the dorsal to the caudal peduncle.

This pretty Catfish looks a lot like *C. arcuatus* and *C. myersi,* and the three are often confused by hobbyists. Unfortunately, while *C. metae* must be given the nod over the other two in good looks, it is seen less frequently and is therefore less often available to the hobbyist who would like to own some relatively pretty Catfish. *Corydoras metae* will take place in a mass spawning activity in which the males and females gather around a central location and begin the ritual of laying, fertilizing and depositing the eggs. As with *Corydoras paleatus,* the females are more aggressive than the males in initiating the reproductive maneuvers; at the end of the courting actions, the males lie passively on their sides and allow the female to make contact between her mouth and the male's genital pore. Then the female swims to the place to deposit the eggs, usually a spot on the glass sides of the aquarium, cleans the spot with her mouth and in so doing deposits some of the sperm which she has taken from the male. With *C. metae* the eggs are deposited singly, and they soon become very tough and tightly bound to the surface on which they're laid. The fry, which hatch in about five days, are large.

CORYDORAS MICROPS (Eigenmann and Kennedy)
Light-Spot Catfish

Range: Rio Sao Francisco, Sao Paulo, Paraguay, Rio de La Plata.
Habits: Peaceful.
Water Conditions: Neutral water, medium soft. Temperature 68 to 75°F.
Size: 2½ inches.
Food Requirements: Takes all foods.
Color Variations: Many light blotches scattered over a dark background; belly area white, shading to pink.

One of the more distinctively marked *Corydoras, C. microps* is no longer available in good quantity today, although it was at one time imported for a short while. Perhaps the reason that it was seen for so short a time is due to the fact that this Catfish, coming as it does from a spot far removed from the equatorial regions where other South American species originate, is not suited to a really "tropical" tank with temperatures in the high seventies and low eighties. Under such conditions *Corydoras microps* is uncomfortable and becomes subject to diseases which would not plague it if it were kept in cooler water. *Corydoras microps* has never been bred in the home aquarium, but there is good reason to believe that it spawns in the same manner as its cousins within the genus *Corydoras*.

F-209.00

Photo by Dr. Herbert R. Axelrod.

CORYDORAS MYERSI (H. Ribeiro)/*Myers' Catfish*

Range: Small tributaries of the Amazon above the mouth of the Rio Negro.
Habits: Very peaceful and active, harmless to all but the smallest fry.
Water Conditions: Neutral to slightly alkaline, temperature about 76°.
Size: To 2½ inches, usually a little smaller.
Food Requirements: All sorts of food are taken, but enough should be fed if other fishes are present to give the Catfishes their fair share.
Color Variations: Body reddish to yellowish brown. Dark horizontal line begins at dorsal fin and extends to the caudal base.

Corydoras myersi is frequently sold in this country as *Corydoras rabauti*, but *C. rabauti* is a much smaller species from a different habitat. Probably aquarium hobbyists have never seen the real *C. rabauti* as yet. *C. myersi* is one of the few *Corydoras* species which the author has been privileged to observe in the act of spawning. There is a great deal of hustle and bustle, which ends with one of the males lying on his side on the bottom. The female swims up to him and nuzzles him in the region of the vent, at the same time releasing 2 or 3 eggs in a pocket formed by her ventral fins. She then swims up to a spot on the glass side which was previously cleaned off, and rubs her mouth against this spot. Then she pushes her belly against the same spot and the sticky eggs are pasted against the glass. A very interesting color change comes over the young: until they are about ½ inch long they are real beauties. The front half of the body, including the head, is green and the after half is red! Unfortunately these colors are not permanent and a remarkable thing happens: the green becomes darker and forms the stripe, while the red fades and covers the rest of the body.

F-210.00

CORYDORAS NATTERERI (Steindachner)/*Blue Catfish*

Range: Brazil, Rio de Janeiro to Sao Paulo.
Habits: Peaceful.
Water Conditions: Neutral, medium soft water. Temperature 72 to 82°F.
Size: Up to 3 inches.
Food Requirements: Accepts all regular foods.
Color Variations: Over-all light brown with greenish cast; when spawning, the fish becomes a pleasant light blue-green, which color is more pronounced in the male. Wide dark stripe on sides.

In the photo above, the Blue Corydoras is pictured at just the proper moment to bring out the colors which have set this Catfish apart from all others; while other Corydoras can very definitely be attractive, their attractiveness is usually achieved through markings, such as stripes and spots, rather than through general body color. Although *Corydoras nattereri* does possess a stripe, this is not its distinctive feature, because stripes are not rare on the Catfish, but color is. Unfortunately, the color of the fish is not always at its brightest, and it takes a while for this Catfish to show up at its best. Rarely will *Corydoras nattereri* live up to its potential in the tanks of dealers, who have neither the time nor the space to give the fish the conditions it needs. In the tanks of a hobbyist who is willing to provide this little Catfish with more than the bare essentials, however, it soon rewards its owner by assuming the coloration that sets it apart from all other *Corydoras* species. Unfortunately, *Corydoras nattereri* is no longer in good supply.

CORYDORAS PALEATUS (Jenyns)/*Peppered Corydoras*

Range: Southern Brazil and parts of northern Argentina.
Habits: Peaceful.
Water Conditions: Neutral, medium soft water. Temperature 70 to 80°F.
Size: Up to 3 inches.
Food Requirements: Accepts all regular aquarium foods; especially likes worms.
Color Variations: Original type was a dark gray fish, with mottled patches of black on the body and spots on fins. An albino variety now exists.

Pictured above are two of the albino variety of *Corydoras paleatus*, a strain which is very far removed in color pattern from its forebears. The original *Corydoras paleatus* was a comparatively dark species with many dark blotches, irregularly joined, on its sides. This original variety was one of the first of the *Corydoras* species to become popular in this country, but it has fallen by the wayside and is no longer as popular as it once was. However, the fish has maintained at least a small degree of its past popularity in Germany, where the albino form was developed. One of the first of the *Corydoras* species to be bred (and one of the easiest), *C. paleatus* follows the pattern whereby the male, after an attentive courtship of the female, lies on his back or side and allows the female to lie across him, her mouth in contact with his underside. She then swims away from him and attaches her eggs, which have been expelled during the "contact" position, to a spot which she has cleaned with her mouth. This spot may be a leaf, a rock, or a part of the aquarium glass. The first eggs are usually deposited singly, but as the process is repeated more eggs are deposited at each trip.

C. melanistius melanistius.

CORYDORAS PUNCTATUS PUNCTATUS (Bloch)/*Spotted Catfish*

Range: Guianas to the Amazon.
Habits: Peaceful; useful for picking up food missed by others.
Water Conditions: Neutral to slightly alkaline water. Temperature 74 to 78°.
Size: To 2¼ inches.
Food Requirements: Willingly eats any kind of foods, but should get live or frozen foods several times a week.
Color Variations: Body grayish with a little bronze near the gill-plates. Rows of spots on sides and in tail, with a large spot in the dorsal region.

There is a great similarity in markings between *Corydoras punctatus punctatus* and *C. melanistius melanistius*. This species, it seems, has slightly larger dots on the sides. The author saw a great many of these attractive little Catfish in the British Guiana streams and no doubt there are many local varieties, each one marked a little differently. Any ichthyologist who undertakes to classify and identify all of the *Corydoras* species once and for all has a lifetime of work ahead of him, and when he is finished there will be just as many questionable species which have been found and put on the market meanwhile that his successor will have as much or more work with which to carry on.

F-213.00

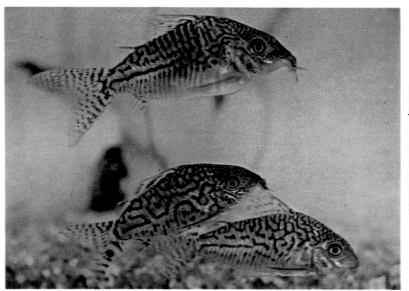

Photo by Dr. Herbert R. Axelrod.

CORYDORAS RETICULATUS (Fraser-Brunner)/*Network Catfish*

Range: Amazon Basin.

Habits: Peaceful.

Water Conditions: Neutral to slightly alkaline, medium-soft to slightly hard water. Temperature 72 to 83°F.

Size: About 2 inches.

Food Requirements: Takes all common aquarium foods; but not so fond of worms as other *Corydoras*.

Color Variations: Olive gray body, lighter towards the belly; body covered with a network of lines which are especially close together in the area of the head. Black spot on dorsal of young specimens.

Although this Catfish is very rarely seen, it would make a nice addition to a collection of *Corydoras*, for it is an attractive fish. The vermiform markings covering the body and head give a striking appearance to the fish; luckily, these markings are not subject to appearance or disappearance depending on the mood or physical condition of the fish. The markings are always there in fairly distinct form, although it is possible that they can become less clear when the fish is kept under extremely poor conditions. *Corydoras reticulatus* does, however, have one prominent marking which is not present at all times, although, again, this is not subject to mood or to physical condition. Rather, it is dependent on age; the spot is present in the dorsal fin of young specimens but absent in the dorsal fin of older fish. Older fish, instead of having the spot, have a pattern of small dark dashes similar to the markings in the tail, but less dense.

F-214.00

CORYDORAS TREITLII (Steindachner)/*Long-Nose Corydoras*

Range: Eastern Brazil.
Habits: Peaceful.
Water Conditions: Neutral water desirable, but pH may vary slightly above or below this value; soft water not necessary, but advisable. Temperature 72 to 82°F.
Size: Up to 3 inches.
Food Requirements: Takes all regular aquarium foods.
Color Variations: Gray-green body with black blotches and short bars. Lighter in belly area.

Although this fish has been known to ichthyologists since 1906, when it was classified by Steindachner, it has never appeared in quantity on the American market, or at least not under its correct name. However, it was seen in Germany in the early 1930's but it did not attract much attention there, even though German hobbyists worked with it for a while in an effort to breed it. It defied these efforts and soon dropped out of circulation, but not before it had stirred up a little controversy regarding its correct taxonomic stature. This was mainly because of the peculiarly shaped head which was different from the head shape of *Corydoras* species known to hobbyists at that time, being much more elongated. Because of a similarity in coloring, it was also supposed for a short time to be a variety of *Corydoras elegans*, but this point was later resolved. As *Corydoras treitlii* has no pronounced advantages over the more common *Corydoras* species, it is unlikely that the fish will ever again make an appearance, except when it is sent to this country in shipments of "mixed" Catfish.

Photo by Dr. Herbert R. Axelrod.

CORYDORAS UNDULATUS (Regan)/*Wavy Catfish*

Range: Eastern South America, La Plata region.

Habits: Does not grub into the bottom like most other species. Should therefore be fed live foods, especially tubifex worms.

Water Conditions: Temperature 73° to 76°. Tank should be clean, with no sediment on the bottom.

Size: Females 2 inches, males slightly smaller.

Food Requirements: This fish is not a scavenger, and should be given generous quantities of live foods.

Color Variations: Body yellowish olive, becoming yellow toward the belly. Sides covered with black dots in a wavy pattern. Males smaller and more slender.

There are many species of *Corydoras*, and it seems that there are always more coming in. Because of the mistaken idea by many hobbyists that they are strictly scavengers which will live happily on the leavings of other fishes, they are too often kept one to a tank where they lead a miserable half-starved existence. The *Corydoras* have vigorous appetites, and in order to get them to breed they should be fed generously with living foods. Under these conditions they can be gotten to breed quite frequently. *Corydoras undulatus* has not been introduced in any numbers until quite recently, although it was first imported into Germany in 1909. So far there have been no accounts of their having been bred in captivity, but there is no doubt that their breeding procedure is no different from that of other members of the genus. Males are easily distinguished from the females: they are considerably smaller and much more slender. This species is very active and once they have become accustomed to a tank will live for a long time.

A pair of *Corydoras aeneus* photographed during courtship prior to spawning.
Photos by Ruda Zukal.

Continued on next page.

Group spawning is not rare among the *Corydoras* Catfish. Notice the single egg held between the pelvic fins of this *Corydoras aeneus*. Photo by Ruda Zukal.

Immediately after fertilization, the eggs are attached to leaves or stems of plants. Photo by Ruda Zukal.

Though Axelrod discovered scores of catfishes, this species was not discovered by him. It was brought into the U.S.A. by K. Swegles and Axelrod found it in the shipment. The fish eventually was named *Corydoras axelrodi* and comes from Colombia.

In the absence of plants, the eggs may be attached to any other object or surface on hand, such as the filter box or glass wall of the tank. Photo by Giancarlo Padovani.

Several *Corydoras* eggs photographed through the glass wall of a tank. Photo by Giancarlo Padovani.

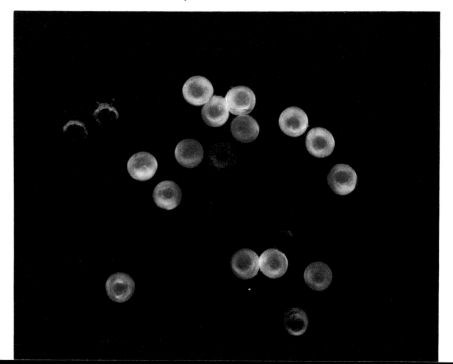

This *Corydoras* species, as yet unidentified, is called *Corydoras* U-2.

Corydoras species.

Corydoras haraldschultzi, from Brazil.

Corydoras bondi.

The extended upper lobe of the tail fin is characteristic of several *Corydoras* species and is not diagnostic. This fish is *Corydoras melini*.

It was indeed unfortunate that the author (HRA) only found one of these fish in the Rio Araguaia in Brazil since it seems to be a "fat cat." This specimen was described as a new species and named *Corydoras pauciradiatus* by Drs. Weitzman and Nijssen.

This *Corydoras* was captured in the Araguaia River in Brazil.

Corydoras sterbai, from Brazil.

CORYNOPOMA RIISEI (Gill)/*Swordtailed Characin*

Range: Trinidad, Colombia and Venezuela.
Habits: Peaceful, hardy; a good community fish.
Water Conditions: Not critical; temperatures between 72° and 82°. A sunny, well-planted tank and clear water show it at its best.
Size: Males 2¾ inches, females 2 inches.
Food Requirements: Will take prepared foods. Best foods are daphnia, tubifex worms and especially white worms, of which they are very fond.
Color Variations: Silvery, with a dark horizontal stripe which becomes more pronounced toward the caudal base.

Exactly what goes on when this interesting fish breeds has long been a mystery to scientists and aquarists alike. What first strikes the eye is the magnificent finnage of the males and also a peculiar paddle-like extension of the gill-plates, which reaches more than halfway down the sides of the males. What the exact function of these extensions is has been argued back and forth for many years. They are kept folded back except during courtship, when the male swims toward the female with these paddles extended at right angles. Strangely enough, there seems to be some sort of internal fertilization, because females which have been separated from their mates for some time have surprised their owners by laying eggs which hatched! Whether the male conveys his sperm with the oar-like appendages, or whether the female gets the sperm into her body in another way has not yet been explained in a satisfactory manner. Some even claim that the female takes in the sperm through her mouth, but then it would have to travel through her stomach. A sac containing living sperm has been found among the eggs of females which were cut open. How did it get there?

F-225.00

Photo by Harald Schultz

CREATOCHANES CAUDOMACULATUS (Günther)/*Tail-Spot Tetra*

Range: Guianas and the central Amazon region.
Habits: Active and quarrelsome; should be kept only with their own kind.
Water Conditions: Soft, slightly acid water. Temperature 75 to 78°.
Size: To 5 inches.
Food Requirements: All kinds of live foods, live baby fishes preferred.
Color Variations: Body silvery-gray to brownish. A silvery stripe runs the length of the body. Upper caudal lobe has a large white spot.

There are certain fish species which a collector almost always ignores, for fear that he will be "stuck" with them and not be able to dispose of them even at a low price. The *Creatochanes* species are a perfect example. The collector will go out and try to load up with the desirable species, discarding those which lack color or have some other undesirable traits such as being nasty toward other fishes, eating plants, growing too big, etc. But sometimes things do not go too well and at the end of a hard day's work there are still many unfilled cans. The answer of course is to load up with some of the fish he has been discarding rather than return with a light load. *Creatochanes caudomaculatus* is not such a "bad actor", but it is not advisable to try keeping them with other species. Even among themselves there are sometimes some pretty vigorous scraps. Otherwise it is not an unattractive fish, and a tankful swimming back and forth might even evoke an occasional second look. They should have a large tank with generous planting at the sides and back, and plenty of swimming space in the center. Once they have established themselves, they usually prove to be very hardy.

Photo by K. Paysan.

CRENICARA MACULATA (Steindachner)/*Checkerboard Cichlid*

Range: Central Amazon region.
Habits: Fairly peaceful, but should have their own tank.
Water Conditions: Soft, neutral to slightly acid water, temperature about 78°.
Size: Males, to 4 inches; females, to 2 inches.
Food Requirements: Varied live foods.
Color Variations: Body yellowish with two rows of alternate square spots on the sides. Male's ventral fins have blue and orange streaks.

Many hobbyists who have seen the Checkerboard Cichlid were not unduly impressed at first. This is because the fish is seldom seen under the best conditions. Put a lot of half-grown fish in a bare tank, and they hardly ever rate a second look. But put a fully-grown pair which is ready to spawn in a well-planted tank which is to their liking, and you have a male which will outshine most of the Cichlid family. The Checkerboard Cichlid is a fish which, it seems, nobody can produce in quantity. A pair will produce a beautiful spawning and the next time under identical conditions everything will go wrong. Possibly with this fish the time of sexual ripeness varies between spawnings, and a pair which achieves this state once may not come due again at the same time. Keeping several pairs and observing them closely would probably do the trick, but good pairs are quite expensive and not easily come by. This is a member of the Cichlid family which is just about too big to be considered a Dwarf Cichlid, and still too small to be called a regular-sized one. Although it has been known to science since 1875, aquarium hobbyists did not see it until 1938.

F-227.00

CRENICICHLA DORSOCELLATA (Hasemann)/*Eye-Spot Pike Cichlid*

Range: Amazon River and its tributaries near Santarem and Manaus.

Habits: Slightly more peaceful than the other *Crenicichla* species, but cannot be trusted with other fishes.

Water Conditions: Should be provided with a number of hiding-places as retreats for any which are attacked. Temperature 75° to 78°.

Size: Up to 8 inches in their native waters.

Food Requirements: Generous feedings of live foods are necessary. They take dried foods only when very hungry.

Color Variations: Back bluish-green, with seven dark bands on the sides. Black ocellated spot in the middle of the dorsal fin.

Many beautiful fishes are shunned by hobbyists because of their vicious, predatory habits. This is often the case with the *Crenicichla* species. Without a doubt they are handsome fishes, but to keep them in company with other fishes would be placing the lives or at least the fins of their tankmates in jeopardy. There is a *Crenicichla* species, *Crenicichla alta,* which is known as "Sunfish" in British Guiana. This fish has a gorgeous array of colors, but it is the most hated predator of all the fishes in that country. Fish farms which store fishes for shipment abroad will sometimes get a tiny "Sunfish" into one of their pools and not have any inkling that it is there until the ragged fins and dead bodies of the other fishes are noticed. The culprit must then be netted out and removed before the pool can yield any more saleable fishes again. *Crenicichla dorsocellata,* although it is a fairly nasty customer, is not quite so ferocious as its cousins, but should never be kept in a community tank with smaller fishes. Although this species was first brought into Germany in 1913 as *Crenicichla notophthalmus,* there have been only a few importations since.

CRENICICHLA GEAYI (Pellegrin)/*Half-Banded Pike Cichlid*

Range: Central Amazon region.
Habits: Predatory and vicious. Can only be trusted with fishes with similar habits in large aquaria.
Water Conditions: Not critical; temperatures 73 to 76°F.
Size: To 8 inches; imported specimens usually much smaller.
Food Requirements: Large living foods, preferably live smaller fishes.
Color Variations: Body greenish. Dark horizontal line from snout to center rays of tail. A number of bars extend across the back to the center line.

The Half-Banded Pike Cichlid is another of the "rough customers" among the Cichlid group. This one does not even have the distinction of having any gay colors to ornament it, but it is a good illustration of how a fish's colors and markings can be an asset to its habits when it is on the lookout for a meal, which is almost constantly during the daylight hours. Picture this fish almost motionless in a clump of aquatic plants. The resemblance to a slime-covered twig with shadows of plant leaves on it would be close enough to deceive any smaller fish and lull it into a very false sense of security. When the prey gets close enough, a rush of that torpedo-shaped body, followed by a gulp of that big mouth, reduces the small fish population by one and the Pike Cichlid is already thinking about how good the next victim will taste. As is the case with most predators, at spawning time they usually become the best of parents. In the aquarium a well-mated pair can usually be counted upon to give a good exhibition of Cichlid parental care. It goes without saying that this fish is definitely not a candidate for any community aquarium, even when young.

Photo by Uwe Werner

CRENICICHLA LEPIDOTA (Heckel)/*Pike Cichlid*

Range: From the Amazon down to northern Argentina.
Habits: A predator which cannot be trusted with other fishes, especially those of a size it can swallow.
Water Conditions: Not critical; temperature 73 to 76°. Tank should be well planted and afford a number of hiding-places.
Size: To 8 inches.
Food Requirements: Large living foods, preferably smaller fishes.
Color Variations: Grayish-green back, mother-of-pearl sides, belly brown, gray or white. Light golden or white spots all over sides and fins.

The *Crenicichla* species have very little to recommend them. True, they are not unattractive to the eye, but in mixed company they are real terrors. They select a spot among the plants where they are likely to be unobserved, and when a smaller fish swims by they dart out, pike-like, and swallow it. In order to keep them in the best of shape, their owner should have a constant supply of larger-sized live foods like dragonfly larvae and water-beetle larvae, or best of all some "expendable" smaller fishes like Guppies which are either deformed or do not make the grade as fancy stock with the Guppy breeders. As is usually the case with the "nasty" Cichlids, a well-mated pair almost always proves to be good parents. Spawning takes place in a depression in the gravel, and a great number of small white eggs results. When the fry hatch, the male takes charge of the brood, but the female need not be removed. She soon realizes that she must keep her distance, and does so. While guarding eggs and fry, they should be fed heavily to lessen the temptation to eat their own eggs and fry. This species develops beautiful colors in the breeding season.

Members of the genus *Crenicichla* are known for their ferocity and predatory habits, but in many cases these are ignored in favor of their attractive color patterns. Notice the attractive head and tail pattern and red dorsal fin of this *Crenicichla strigata* photographed in a dealer's display tank. Photo by Aaron Norman.

Slightly more colorful than most of the *Crenicichla* species is *Crenicichla wallacei*, which comes from many parts of British Guiana. This specimen came from the Rio Araguaia in Brazil.

Photo by Harald Schultz.

Photo by Dr. Herbert R. Axelrod.

CRENUCHUS SPILURUS (Günther)/*Sailfin Tetra*

Range: British Guiana and central Amazon region.
Habits: Probably a predator; do not keep them with any smaller fish.
Water Conditions: Soft, definitely acid water is required. Temperature 75 to 78°F, never lower.
Size: To 2½ inches.
Food Requirements: All sorts of live foods, preferably the larger ones like cut-up earthworms and young livebearers.
Color Variations: Body reddish brown, belly yellowish. Large black spot on caudal peduncle. Male has large dorsal and anal fins with reticulated markings.

We hear some conflicting things about this very beautiful Tetra. One authority says they are peaceful, but the consensus seems to be that they are predatory and may not be trusted in mixed company. Judging by the size of the mouth, we are inclined to side with the latter school of thought. There are also two camps on the question of spawning habits. All authorities agree that the fry have never been raised, but some say that they spawn Characin-fashion among plant leaves while others have them laying their eggs on rocks and large-leaved plants. According to one source, the eggs are bright red and are guarded Cichlid-fashion by the male. Some day someone will come along and say in no uncertain terms that he has observed a successful spawning of the fish and earn the gratitude of the aquarium world by giving an accurate, authoritative account of the entire procedure. Although at this time the fish has been known to aquarists for 50 years, we have not seen anything but contradictory reports. One thing is fairly certain, that the fish is quite sensitive and does not adapt readily to captivity, but once it has adapted some aquarists are able to keep them for several years.

F-232.00

CTENOBRYCON SPILURUS (Cuvier & Valenciennes)/*Silver Tetra*

Range: Northern South America from Surinam to Venezuela.
Habits: Peaceful with fishes of its own size or larger, but likely to pick on smaller ones.
Water Conditions: They prefer clean water, and their tank should be large. Temperatures may range from 68° to 76°.
Size: About 3 inches.
Food Requirements: Greedy eaters, they may extend their appetites to some of the plants. Will also take all kinds of dried foods.
Color Variations: Silvery, with an indistinct horizontal stripe of lighter color, and a black shoulder spot and another at the caudal base.

Many people buy this fish at a stage where they are half-grown, because of their lively habits and·pretty silvery coloring. After they have had them for some months, they find that the fish has grown to a size much larger than they have bargained for. In a large aquarium and with no smaller fish to pick on, the Silver Tetra will live for a long time and always be out in front where they can be readily seen at all times. Breeding them does not present much difficulty; given enough room and a partial change of water, driving is apt to be vigorous, and some plants uprooted. A large female may produce as many as 2000 eggs. Mating is accomplished by the pair swimming with tilted bodies in tight circles. As with most of the Tetra family, the parents must be removed as soon as they have finished spawning, or they will find most of the eggs and eat them. Fry emerge after 50 to 70 hours, and become free-swimming after the third or fourth day. Once they have put on a little growth they are easily raised, and what to do with them all may easily become a problem. This fish was first described in 1912 from a few single specimens which found their way into shipments.

CTENOPOMA ANSORGEI (Boulenger)/*Ornate Ctenopoma*

Range: Tropical West Africa, Chiloango.
Habits: Peaceful when given plenty of space and kept with fishes of the same size or larger.
Water Conditions: Not critical, but the water must be kept warm, 78 to 84°.
Size: To 2¾ inches.
Food Requirements: Large live foods, preferably small living fish. Cut-up earthworms or pieces of beef-heart are also taken greedily.
Color Variations: Body brownish, with 6 or 7 bluish to greenish bars on the sides, extending into the dorsal and anal fins.

Africa has few labyrinth fishes to offer, and the members of the genus *Ctenopoma* are almost the only ones. Most of them make good aquarium citizens, but they must be kept with fishes of their own size or larger. They will not usually harm a fish they cannot swallow, but can handle a sizeable mouthful, having a large mouth. *Ctenopoma ansorgei* is easily the most attractive member of the family, with its alternating reddish and bluish bars which not only cross the body but also extend into the dorsal and anal fins. The *Ctenopoma* species are quite hardy and might even be classified as "tough," but *C. ansorgei* is a bit of an exception in that it is somewhat sensitive to lowered temperatures. This species has been spawned in captivity. The male, distinguished by its brighter colors, is said to build a firm bubblenest. The young are easy to raise. This fish is a greedy eater and very fond of the larger live foods, especially small fish. Their tank should be a roomy, well-planted one. It is interesting to watch a *Ctenopoma* stalk its prey. It glides rather than swims, its large eyes never losing sight. An unbelievably quick lunge, and the little fish is gone!

Photo by Dr. Herbert R. Axelrod.

CTENOPOMA CONGICUM (Boulenger)/*Congo Ctenopoma*

Range: Lower Congo River, Chiloango, Ubangi.
Habits: Fairly peaceful with larger fishes. Likes a large, well-planted tank.
Water Conditions: Not critical, but temperatures should be kept high, about 78°.
Size: To 3¼ inches.
Food Requirements: Large live foods, small living fish preferred. They can be trained to accept pieces of fish, shrimp, etc.
Color Variations: Body brownish with a dark mottled pattern. Caudal base has a dark ocellated spot.

This is one of the less attractive members of the family, which has only an indistinct mottled pattern on the sides. The only distinct mark is a bright "eye-spot" at the base of the tail. It has been proven with some of the marine Butterfly Fishes that this "eye" at the other end of the body serves to confuse an enemy or a prospective meal. Whether this is also true with this species has never been observed, but it has been found that these eye-spots usually serve such a purpose. For instance, there is a moth with a large eye-spot on each under-wing which uses these spots to frighten away birds by imitating the eyes of an owl. *Ctenopoma congicum* is said to be quite easy to spawn, although the feat is seldom attempted because of the small demand for this fish. The male chooses a dark corner of the tank, often a spot under a floating leaf. Here he builds a bubblenest. When this is completed he concentrates on getting the female to cooperate by getting under the nest. He wraps his body around her like a *Betta* and everything proceeds accordingly. Eggs hatch in 24 to 30 hours and the fry become free-swimming in 2 to 3 days. They are very easy to raise.

F-235.00

Photo by Kremser

CTENOPOMA FASCIOLATUM (Boulenger)/*Banded Ctenopoma*

Range: Tropical West Africa, especially the Congo region.
Habits: Peaceful, but cannot be trusted with fishes which are small enough to swallow.
Water Conditions: Not at all critical, but should not be kept at temperatures less than 78°.
Size: About 3 inches.
Food Requirements: This fish prefers food in chunks. Pieces of lean beef or fish, cut-up earthworms or small balls of tubifex worms are best.
Color Variations: Olive-green on the back, shading to a yellowish white underneath. Females do not show as bright coloration as the males.

The African Labyrinth fishes can best be compared to the East Indian Gourami species. They are a very durable lot, and will withstand a great deal of abuse. The author once emptied an aquarium for cleaning, and forgot to fish out one of these. There was scarcely any water left in the tank, only a few puddles where the rocks had rested in the gravel. Hearing a splash about three days later, I was astonished to find this fish in about a quarter-inch of water. Naturally he was immediately put into another tank, as good as new. He lived for a long time thereafter. This fish is rarely bred, and for this reason we seldom see them in dealers' establishments. Their requirements are very modest: enough food and a good amount of heat, never below 76°. Their mouths are rather large, and a small fish might be considered a tidbit if left with them.

CTENOPOMA KINGSLEYI (Günther)/*Kingsley's Ctenopoma*

Range: Widely scattered from Senegambia to the Congo region.
Habits: Very predatory and nasty; should not be kept with other fishes.
Water Conditions: Not critical, but temperature should be high, about 78°.
Size: To 8 inches.
Food Requirements: Will eat just about everything, but prefers living fish.
Color Variations: Body slate-gray to brownish, with an indistinct eye-spot near the tail.

Ctenopoma kingsleyi is the largest known species of the *Ctenopomas*. It is also the least desirable species to keep. It gets big, up to 8 inches, and quite nasty. This species could be easily confused with *C. congicum*. There is also an eye-spot of sorts on the caudal base, but no pattern on the sides. This unusual group of fishes evidently occurs in places where the water sometimes partly dries out. They are able to cover considerable distances over land and through wet grass, thanks to their air-breathing ability. When the pool in which they are living dries out, they hop out and flop along until they locate another pool. They do not have the panicky terror which most fish have when out of water and seldom get stranded, but usually manage to find a pool before they dry out. Because of their lack of colors, large size and predatory habits this fish is seldom exported from Africa, and we scarcely ever see them. Sex differences are unknown, and they have never bred in captivity. This species has been known to science since 1896, when Günther identified them. They were first introduced to the fish hobbyists in 1933. Understandably, they have not become popular.

CTENOPOMA OXYRHYNCHUS (Boulenger)/*Mottled Ctenopoma*

Range: Tributaries of the lower Congo River.
Habits: Peaceful with fishes of the same size or larger.
Water Conditions: Not critical, but temperatures should be kept high, 79 to 84°.
Size: To 4 inches.
Food Requirements: Larger live foods preferred, especially living fishes.
Color Variations: Basic color brown, with dark mottled markings. Dark line runs
diagonally from the mouth through the eye to the first dorsal rays.

Ctenopoma oxyrhynchus is one of the beauties of the group. Its marbled sides
and varying shades and the fact that it does not grow as big as most of its
cousins makes it the most desirable member of a not very desirable genus.
According to Ladiges, the younger specimens have a coloration very similar
to the South American Leaf Fish, and stalk their prey in the same manner.
As they grow older the permanent markings appear. The females are distinguished by their more rounded fins. This species does not build a bubblenest
like the others, nor is one needed. The eggs have an oil content which
makes them lighter than water and causes them to float at the surface.
During this time the tank should be tightly covered. Like the other *Ctenopoma*
species, this one also requires warm water. Breeding temperatures should be
82 to 84°, and an uncovered tank where the fish are kept at high temperatures
and the fish are gulping atmospheric air at room temperatures would obviously lead to trouble, unless the room is heated to tank temperatures. Eggs
hatch in 24 to 32 hours and the fry become free-swimming in 2 to 3 days.
Having a large mouth, they are easily fed and grow rapidly.

F-238.00

Photo by H.J. Richter.

*CTENOPS PUMILUS (Arnold)/*Pygmy Gourami*

Range: Cochin China, possibly Thailand, Malaya and Sumatra.

Habits: Peaceful, but because it is shy it is best to keep them only with their own kind. Will not harm plants.

Water Conditions: A large aquarium is not required, but it should be well planted and well heated. 80° is good, and for spawning 85°.

Size: Males about 1¼ inches, females slightly smaller.

Food Requirements: Will take prepared as well as the smaller live foods.

Color Variations: Both sexes are darker above than below, and have a longitudinal stripe which consists of a row of lighter and darker spots.

Colisa lalia, referred to as the "Dwarf Gourami," is generally considered to be the smallest of the Labyrinth Fishes, and it was until this little beauty moved into the picture, so now we have a fish which we have to call the "Pygmy Gourami." A tankful of these with the sun shining on them makes a lovely picture, with their deep blue eyes and purplish spots sprinkled all over the body and fins. Sexes are not always easy to distinguish, but the males usually have a bit of an edging on their dorsal and anal fins, and these fins are a bit larger and come to more of a point. These fish love a warm temperature, and are apt to be "touchy" to keep if it is not given to them. Spawning them is very much dependent upon the compatibility of the pair. We have seen the rankest amateurs get spawning after spawning, and some of the so-called "experts" unable to get them to breed for them at all. There is a small bubble-nest, usually hidden under a floating broad leaf, into which about 50 eggs are laid. They hatch in about 30 hours, and the male takes care of the brood, for which reason the female should be removed after she has finished. The fry are not difficult to raise.

*Ctenops pumilus is now known as *Trichopsis pumilus.*

F-239.00

*CTENOPS SCHALLERI (Ladiges)/*Three-Striped Croaking Gourami*

Range: Thailand.
Habits: Peaceful; emits a faint croaking sound, especially during spawning activity.
Water Conditions: Soft, slightly acid water. Temperature 73 to 77°F.
Size: About 2½ inches.
Food Requirements: Live or frozen foods of all kinds. No dry foods are mentioned in the account, but they would probably be accepted as well.
Color Variations: Body brownish with 3 horizontal dark stripes and many light-blue flecks. Fins are edged with red.

Most of us have at some time or other become acquainted with the original Croaking Gourami, *Ctenops vittatus*, which has been kept by aquarium hobbyists for many years. This new species was sent to E. Roloff, the well-known German authority, from Bangkok, Thailand to Karlsruhe, Germany. Herr Roloff was quick to recognize it as a new species. The fish were collected by Dieter Schaller about 135 miles northeast of Bangkok, where he found them in ponds and small pools in clear, lightly brown-tinted water with a fairly heavy plant growth. Roloff placed a pair in a small tank which was planted with a single *Cryptocoryne* plant. The male built a small bubblenest under one of the leaves. They embraced in typical Labyrinth Fish fashion, and after each frequent embrace 3 to 6 eggs were produced. The male guarded the eggs, which hatched on the third day. He was a good father and guarded the more than 200 fry very closely. They became free-swimming on the 7th day and were easily raised.

Ctenops schalleri is now known as *Trichopsis schalleri*.

F-240.00

Photo by H.J. Richter.

*CTENOPS VITTATUS (Cuvier & Valenciennes)/*Croaking Gourami*

Range: Cochin China, Thailand, Malaya, Sumatra, Java and Borneo.
Habits: Peaceful and shy; should be kept by themselves because of their high temperature requirements.
Water Conditions: A well-covered, well-heated aquarium is necessary, or this fish may prove to be sensitive. 82° to 85° should be maintained.
Size: Males, a little over 2½ inches, females slightly smaller.
Food Requirements: Will take dried foods if hungry, but prefers live foods, especially white worms.
Color Variations: Sides are striped and bluish in color, fins spotted. Males have longer filaments on the dorsal, anal and caudal fins.

The most attractive feature of this otherwise rather plain fish is its beautiful deep-blue eyes. Another unusual thing about it is that it is able to make tiny croaking noises, usually while spawning. One must listen quite attentively to hear them, but they are distinct. The species is by no means a newcomer, having been known to hobbyists in Germany since before the turn of the century. The old-time hobbyists who had to heat their aquaria with gas or alcohol flames had trouble keeping this fish alive, but nowadays when it is a simple matter to boost the temperature with a thermostatically controlled electric heater and hold it in the lower 80's, it is not difficult to keep such fishes. If given a sunny aquarium which is shallow and well-covered, pairs will begin to spawn in the Spring months. A few broad-leaved plants should be there with the leaves floating, for the preferred spot will be under these leaves. Fry hatch in 24 to 35 hours and are tiny at first. Changes in temperature must be avoided at this time, and an infusoria culture is a necessity for food. Once they have been brought to a size where they can take newly-hatched brine shrimp, they will do well.

Ctenops vittatus is now known as *Trichopsis vittatus.*

F-241.00

CUBANICHTHYS CUBENSIS (Eigenmann)/*Cuban Minnow*

Range: Western Cuba.
Habits: Will do well in an uncrowded and well-planted aquarium; although it some-
times occurs in brackish waters, an addition of salt is unnecessary.
Water Conditions: Should be kept in a sunny location; water temperatures 75° to 78°.
Size: About 1½ inches, usually smaller.
Food Requirements: This species will seldom eat dried foods unless very hungry.
All sorts of living foods are taken.
Color Variations: Ground color yellowish to reddish, with a series of blue stripes.
Males have a blue edge on the dorsal and anal fins.

The scientific name of this attractive little fish means "Cuban fish from
Cuba." How this was arrived at Heaven only knows. At least it leaves no
doubt as to the fish's range. This little fellow makes no bones about it: he
just doesn't care for dried foods, however rich they are supposed to be in
mineral, vitamin and wonder-drug content. Unless he is very hungry, no
attention will be paid to these tidbits. Even frozen foods do not elicit much
interest; the food has to be alive and moving. This fish shares a peculiar
breeding habit with a few of the other Cyprinodonts. Instead of a few single
eggs being expelled at a time and hung on plants, the female expels the eggs
in a bunch, and they hang like a tiny bunch of grapes on a string from her
vent. This string is quite durable, and she may swim around with it for hours
before it is torn off, leaving the eggs hanging on a plant leaf or anything she
might brush against. The fry hatch after 10 to 12 days, and are very small at
first. The water should be kept warm, about 78°, and for the first week
infusoria must be fed. One they have grown to where they can take brine
shrimp, the rest is fairly easy.

F-242.00

CURIMATA Species

Range: Northern Brazil.
Habits: Peaceful; may be a plant nipper.
Water Conditions: Soft, slightly acid water. Temperature 73 to 78°F.
Size: About 3 inches.
Food Requirements: The ones we have had ate all kinds of foods.
Color Variations: Silvery body; dorsal fin tip is black, as are the tips of the caudal lobes.

There are many, many *Curimata* species listed in scientific literature. Although its body form establishes firmly that this is a *Curimata*, the black tip of the dorsal fin and the tips of the caudal lobes cannot be applied to any of the species we have seen described. Either it is a new species or there is one long dead tucked away in a jar of formalin on the shelf of a museum somewhere, and a scientific paper to describe it in the museum's library. Most of the *Curimata* species are disregarded or discarded by the collectors, who net them quite frequently but have no use for such colorless and probably uninteresting fishes which find no market among hobbyists who want colorful specimens or those which have interesting habits to make them desirable. One of the most tedious jobs a collector has to do is to spread his nets and drag them in to shallow water; usually the catch is a good one, but it must then be sorted. First of all, the fish which are too big are taken out and thrown up on the bank. Fresh fish are always a desirable delicacy to the natives, who quickly snap them up. Then the "good" fishes are sorted out. Damaged or colorless specimens are discarded.

CYNOLEBIAS ADLOFFI (Ahl)/*Banded Cynolebias*

Range: Southeastern Brazil

Habits: Should be kept by themselves. Males become scrappy.

Water Conditions: Tank should have a layer of about an inch of peat moss on the bottom. Temperature 72 to 76°F.

Size: Males to 2 inches, females a little smaller.

Food Requirements: Live foods of all kinds which are small enough for easy swallowing.

Color Variations: Body of males yellowish brown with a series of dark narrow bands on the sides. Fins light blue. Females almost colorless.

No problem distinguishing between males and females in Banded Cynolebias, or for that matter any other *Cynolebias* species. The female has almost no color, and the male seems to have enough for both. Besides, note carefully the great difference in the dorsal and anal fins of the two sexes; one would swear that they were two different species! Although they are extremely interesting fishes and beautiful as well, we do not see them offered very frequently for sale. Dealers are reluctant to stock them. Their short life span necessitates making a quick sale, and customers who expect to have their fish for a long time often complain bitterly when their fish dies a perfectly natural death after two or three months. If one can get a few half-grown specimens, it is an amazing thing to see how quickly they grow and blossom into full adulthood. Spawning them is an easy matter. A layer of peat moss on the bottom and a healthy pair is all that is needed. After the female has become considerably thinner the peat moss is netted out and stored in a slightly moist state for 3 to 5 weeks. Eggs hatch in a few hours when the peat moss is put back in the water.

CYNOLEBIAS BELLOTTI (Steindachner)/*Argentine Pearl Fish*

Range: La Plata region.

Habits: Should have a good-sized aquarium to themselves.

Water Conditions: Not critical; tank should stand in a sunny spot, and a wide variety of temperatures is tolerated, but 72° to 75° is best.

Size: 2¾ inches, females a little smaller.

Food Requirements: A heavy eater; should be generously fed with live foods whenever possible, but will also accept dried foods occasionally.

Color Variations: Males in good condition are a gorgeous deep blue with white dots all over the body. Females are mottled brown.

This is one of the amazing group known as "annual" fishes. They occur in water-holes which evaporate in the course of the dry season, eventually to dry out altogether. Naturally all fish life and most of the plant life dies, but the fish have already laid their eggs in the mud on the bottom. When the rains begin, the eggs hatch and the little fish appear in swarms, eating greedily and growing at an amazing rate until they attain maturity in a few months and lay their eggs in the mud, completing this unique life-cycle. This life-cycle is difficult but not impossible to reproduce in the aquarium. A pair will spawn readily, using a layer of peat-moss as a substitute for the mud bottom. Then the eggs are taken out with the peat-moss, which is allowed to dry out, but not completely, for about a week. The eggs are then replaced in the aquarium, and then hatch, sometimes taking as long as two to three months. The fry grow with amazing rapidity, and become mature in six to seven weeks. This fish is seldom seen on sale, and those few which are usually offered are old and far beyond their prime. A healthy pair is well worth keeping, for they are beautiful as well as interesting.

F-245.00

Photo by G. J. M. Timmerman.

CYNOLEBIAS NIGRIPINNIS (Regan)/*Black-Finned Pearl Fish*

Range: Parana River region in Argentina, above Rosario.
Habits: Peaceful toward other fishes, but does best when kept with only their own kind.
Water Conditions: Soft, slightly acid water. Temperature 72 to 76°F.
Size: To 1¾ inches, females slightly smaller.
Food Requirements: Small live foods are best. Frozen foods are accepted, but only as a second choice.
Color Variations: Male's body and fins velvety black, covered with small greenish to blue dots. Females light brown with darker spots and mottlings.

"Like stars in a summer night," is the very appropriate way one writer describes the color pattern of this beautiful fish. The entire body and fins are a velvety black, sprinkled with small light green to light blue dots. The contrast between the colors becomes very much greater while the fish are spawning, at which time the males may be classed among the most beautiful aquarium fishes. As with the other *Cynolebias* species, the females are so different that it is difficult to recognize them as belonging to the same species as their gorgeous mates. The fins as well as the body are much smaller. She does not share the black color at all; her body color is a light tan to brown, mottled and spotted with a slightly darker color. Males are eager breeders, and they are constantly seeking out the females and trying to coax them to the bottom, which should have a layer of peat moss. They assume a side-by-side position, then almost stand on their heads and push into the peat moss to deposit their eggs. The peat moss is then removed and stored in a slightly damp condition for 3 to 6 weeks. Water is then added and the young hatch in short order.

CYNOLEBIAS WHITEI (Myers)/*White's Cynolebias*

Range: Savannah ponds of the Mato Grosso Region, Brazil.
Habits: Peaceful toward other fishes, but best if kept to themselves.
Water Conditions: Soft, slightly acid water. Temperature 72 to 76°F .
Size: To 3 inches, females slightly smaller.
Food Requirements: Live or frozen foods. Dried foods accepted only when very hungry.
Color Variations: Body brownish with bluish dots, fins reddish with blue dots. Females have a black spot on the side and another at tail base.

Here we have a *Cynolebias* species which does not resemble the other members of the group in body form. This is not short and chunky but longer, with flowing, pointed dorsal and anal fins, more like a *Pterolebias* species. The fish was named by Dr. George S. Myers for General Thomas D. White, who discovered it in Southeastern Brazil, in the Mato Grosso region. Like the other annual fishes, it occurs in ponds that disappear in the dry months, to fill up again when the rainy season gets under way. Naturally such a fish has a very short life span and most dealers shy away from them, but a fish with so much beauty generally finds takers in short order, and if the fish is still fairly young when he gets it, it will not be old when he sells it. The usual method of spawning is the same as for the other *Cynolebias* species, with peat moss as the spawning medium, but it has been found by Rosario S. LaCorte and other breeders who have spawned this fish that it will also accept fine-grained sand for the purpose. This is much easier to work with than peat moss; the sand is placed in a shallow dish on the bottom and removed when there are eggs. Procedure from here is the same as for the others of the species.

Photo by Dr. Herbert R. Axelrod.

CYNOPOECILUS LADIGESI (Myers)/*Ladiges' Gaucho*

Range: Northwest of Rio de Janeiro in pools which dry out seasonally.
Habits: Must be kept by themselves.
Water Conditions: Soft, slightly acid water. Temperature 75 to 79°.
Size: To 1½ inches.
Food Requirements: Small live foods.
Color Variations: Body green with bright red bars which extend into the vertical fins. Eyes are a beautiful green. Females plain greenish-brown.

The *Cynolebias* and *Cynopoecilus* species, like their African counterparts, occur in small pools which dry out periodically each year. *Cynopoecilus ladigesi*, which was first known as *Cynolebias splendens*, is a very vigorous spawner, and if possible a number of females should be used for each male. A small tank is all that is needed, with a 1-inch layer of peat-moss on the bottom. Eggs are deposited in the peat-moss. After this has gone on for about a week, the parents are removed and placed in another similar tank, and most of the water is drained off from the first tank. It is then placed in a shaded location where the temperatures run from 68 to 75° for a period of 15 to 20 days. The contents are then poured into a fine-meshed net and gently squeezed out. Then the peat-moss is loosened again and placed in a jar. This is covered lightly, and if the surface becomes dry a few drops of water are sprinkled on it. In three weeks the peatmoss with the eggs is placed in a tank of soft, slightly acid water, where the eggs hatch very quickly, most of them within a few hours. Dust-fine dried food is taken immediately, and the fry put on growth very rapidly.

Photo by H.J. Richter

CYNOPOECILUS MELANOTAENIA (Regan)/*Fighting Gaucho*

Range: Southeastern Brazil.

Habits: Do not put two males in the same tank, or they will fight until one or both are badly mutilated or dead.

Water Conditions: Occurs in ditches and water holes, some of which dry out in the hot season; can adapt to almost any water.

Size: Males about 2 inches, females slightly smaller.

Food Requirements: Should be given live food of all kinds. Dried foods are accepted, but not willingly.

Color Variations: Males have a wide dark horizontal stripe, and the sides are covered with rows of green dots. Females are smaller-finned.

Like the *Cynolebias* species, the *Cynopoecilus melanotaenia* is a fish which is short-lived, and therefore not often found in the tanks of dealers, who prefer fishes which they can keep over a period of time if they cannot sell them quickly. These fish occur in a variety of conditions, which leads one to wondering just exactly what their breeding habits are. One authority says that they lay their eggs in mud like the *Cynolebias* species, and that the eggs undergo a drying-out process. Then there is another authority who says that they spawn like the *Aphyosemion*, *Aplocheilus* and *Rivulus* species, laying their eggs in bushy plants near the surface. Possibly both are right, and the fish adapts its breeding habits to its surroundings. This of course is pure conjecture, and would take much work to establish conclusively. The author once watched an *Aphyosemion bivittatum* pair spawn on the bottom of the aquarium, burying the eggs in the sand. This is a fish which is supposed to spawn into bushy plants near the surface exclusively; what made them do it? There were plenty of bushy plants near the surface where they could have spawned to their hearts' content! When Axelrod collected several hundred near Porto Alegre and put them into a plastic bag, he found hundreds of eggs in the bag 3 days later, even though the fish were in the dark!

CYPRINODON NEVADENSIS (Eigenmann & Eigenmann)
Desert Minnow

Range: Nevada.
Habits: Usually peaceful, but best kept by themselves because of their high temperature requirements.
Water Conditions: Water should be somewhat alkaline and warm, about 85°.
Size: Up to 2½ inches.
Food Requirements: Live foods preferred, but they can probably be trained to accept frozen foods.
Color Variations: Body greenish yellow with dark brown bars. Females paler and with a spot in the dorsal fin.

Cyprinodon nevadensis is a highly interesting fish to a student of paleontology as well as ichthyology. We know that there is a *Cyprinodon variegatus* native to the coastal fresh and brackish waters of Maine all the way down to Texas. So what is another fish of the same genus doing all the way out in Nevada? The two fishes are very similar in form as well as in color. The answer is fairly obvious: in prehistoric times, the ocean covered much of California and parts of Nevada. The fossils found in these areas bear this out. But few of the creatures which lived in the salt and brackish waters in those dim days were able to survive when the waters receded, and the bodies of water which were left gradually became fresh. Only highly adaptable fish like the Desert Minnow were able to make the change, which of course was very gradual and lasted over many thousands of years. To the best of our knowledge the Desert Minnow has not been spawned in captivity. If it is, and this should not be difficult, it would be interesting to determine if what has been the result of thousands of years of evolution can be overcome in a few generations by acclimating the fish back to salt water.

F-250.00

*CYPRINUS CARPIO (Linné)/*Carp*

Range: Originally from the temperate waters of Asia, now widespread.
Habits: Young specimens are peaceful, but constantly stir up the bottom in search of food.
Water Conditions: Will adapt to any water; best is slightly alkaline. Temperature 65 to 70°; can be kept much colder in pools.
Size: In natural waters they sometimes exceed a yard in length.
Food Requirements: Will eat anything edible.
Color Variations: Entire body and fins olive green to reddish, with some dark brown markings on sides.

Doubtless the most useful freshwater food fish in the world is the Carp. It has been introduced into many ponds and streams in temperate waters, where it adapts quickly, often living a good many years and, if food is sufficient, growing to a large size. Sport fishermen consider the Carp a troublesome nuisance. They do not like to catch them, and a hungry Carp will eat thousands of fish eggs of more desirable species daily. A new sport has been developed by archers with a view to reducing the numbers of Carp: fishshooting. In tropical countries this art is taught to little toddlers as soon as they have the strength to pull a bow-string. Here one sees very little hookand-line fishing. Small to medium-sized fish are shot with bow and arrow, and larger ones are speared. The Carp is much more respected in Europe and the Asiatic countries, probably because there are hardly any sport fishermen and not as many food fishes as we have in our fresh waters. Only young specimens can be kept in the home aquarium; these are useful in that they keep the bottom free of all left-over food; trouble is that they stir things up very vigorously.

* The koi shown here are probably derived from *Cyprinus carpio.*

F-251.00

Photo by H.J. Richter

DANIO DEVARIO (Hamilton-Buchanan)/*Bengal Danio*

Range: Northwest India, Orissa, Bengal and Assam.

Habits: Peaceful, very active. Should not be combined with nervous, slower-moving fishes.

Water Conditions: Not critical; water should be near neutral, clean and not too hard.

Size: To 4 inches.

Food Requirements: A hearty eater; will take dried as well as live or frozen foods.

Color Variations: Body greenish, back bluish. Several vertical yellow bars, and three blue stripes, interspersed with yellow.

Danio devario is a slightly smaller fish than *Danio malabaricus*, the well-known Giant Danio. It would probably be every bit as popular, but its colors are not nearly as brilliant. Like the Giant Danio it is a very active species and could easily cause a tankmate with more sluggish habits to become very nervous. It is always a good policy when mixing fishes in a so-called "community aquarium" to pay attention not only to whether the fishes will hurt each other or not but also to choose fishes with almost equal dispositions. There is no place, for instance, for a nervous, timid fish in the same tank as such ever-active fellows like the Danios. It would not be able to stand the constant hustle and bustle, and would not get anywhere near its share of the food. For this reason there are very few "community tanks" where all the fishes are well matched and happy. The Bengal Danio comes to our shores very seldom, and because it looks like a poorly-colored Giant Danio chances are that it will never become a really popular fish. Breeding habits for *Danio devario* and *Danio malabaricus* are exactly the same. Both are sturdy, hardy fishes and live in the aquarium for a long time.

DANIO MALABARICUS (Jerdon)/*Giant Danio*

Range: Quite common on the west coast of India and Ceylon.

Habits: Peaceful in the community aquarium. Will not bother anything it cannot swallow.

Water Conditions: Prefers clean, sunny water, pH and hardness not important. Temperatures 75° to 78°.

Size: Wild specimens are said to attain 6 inches; in the aquarium they seldom exceed 4 inches.

Food Requirements: Will consume dried as well as live foods; like any active fish, it should be generously fed.

Color Variations: Body light blue, with 4 or 5 steel-blue stripes, yellow between. Fins are reddish. Males are more slender and brighter colored.

This is one of the old favorites among aquarium hobbyists. It has good reason to be popular: it is peaceful, active, easy to breed, and colorful. It is at home in any aquarium, as long as it is not too small for its size and active habits. Unless it is abused pretty badly, it is seldom attacked by disease. Unlike the *Brachydanio* species, the Giant Danio lays adhesive eggs in the manner of the Barb species. A thicket of bushy plants is placed at one end of a large aquarium (about 20 gallons or more). If possible, the aquarium should stand in a sunny spot. The water should be fresh and clear, and the bottom may be covered with glass marbles or pebbles, because the fish sometimes will spawn in the open areas and the eggs could be eaten. Driving is very active, and hundreds of eggs often result. When finished, the parent fish should be removed. Fry hatch in 1 to 2 days, but some will take a little longer. For the next 3 to 5 days, until the yolk-sac is absorbed, the youngsters will be seen hanging from the glass sides and plants. Then when they begin swimming, food must be provided. Infusoria is not necessary; fine dried food is also eagerly accepted.

F-253.00

DATNIOIDES MICROLEPIS (Bleeker)/*Siamese Tiger Fish*

Range: Thailand, Sumatra and Borneo.
Habits: Peaceful; will not harm any fish it cannot swallow.
Water Conditions: Neutral to slightly acid. Temperature 74 to 78°.
Size: To 15 inches in its natural waters, much smaller in the aquarium.
Food Requirements: Larger live foods or chunks of shrimp or raw lean beef.
Color Variations: Body yellow to cream or pinkish, with black vertical bars.

A recent introduction to the world of aquarium hobbyists is the Siamese Tiger Fish. It is a handsome fellow, and the black and yellow bands of the body form a pleasant contrast to the green of a well-planted tank. It is a large fish with a big mouth, and although peaceful enough toward others of an equal size, it cannot be combined with tankmates which could be swallowed. In its native Thailand it is said to attain a 15-inch length, but in the aquarium it could not be expected to attain half that size. We have had reports that when the fish is displeased with its surroundings it not only sulks but loses its yellow coloring and becomes almost entirely black. Feeding is not much of a problem. Smith, in his book *The Freshwater Fishes of Siam, or Thailand*, mentions keeping them in an aquarium where they thrived on shrimp and raw meat. They have not yet been bred in captivity, and it still remains to be seen if they attain maturity at the smaller sizes attained in the aquarium. In Thailand this fish is highly respected as food, so highly that the fishermen keep them for themselves and market the rest of the catch.

DATNIOIDES QUADRIFASCIATUS (Sevastianov)
Four-Barred Tiger Fish

Range: Thailand, India, Burma, Australia.
Habits: Peaceful; will not molest other fishes, but will swallow those which are small enough to be eaten.
Water Conditions: Neutral to slightly acid. Temperature 74 to 78°F.
Size: To 15 inches in their natural waters.
Food Requirements: Larger live foods, chunks of shrimp or raw fish.
Color Variations: Yellowish to coppery in color with 8 to 10 dark brown bars, some of which unite as the fish grows older.

Our picture shows a young specimen of *Datnioides quadrifasciatus*, the Four-Barred Tiger Fish. When it has grown a little more, the fish will look more like our picture of *Datnioides microlepis*. One of the ways of telling them apart is that *D. microlepis* has much smaller scales: 105 in the lateral line, while *D. quadrifasciatus* has only 70. One must not take the name *quadrifasciatus* too literally ("four bars"). We turn again to H. M. Smith as our authority with the statement that there may be as many as 8 to 10 vertical bars, some of which become confluent with age. On the other hand, the bars of *D. microlepis* remain distinct at all ages. Neither of these species has been propagated in the aquarium, but with the increasing popularity and the ever-increasing influx of these species, we have every reason to believe that in the not-too-far-distant future there will be accounts of how they breed. Do not keep either of the Tiger Fish species with small fishes. They mind their business at all times and are not quarrelsome, but anything that can be engulfed in that big mouth and swallowed is considered food.

DERMOGENYS PUSILLUS (Bleeker)/*Malayan Halfbeak*

Range: Singapore, Sumatra, Borneo, and Thailand.
Habits: Should be kept by themselves. If more than one male is put into a tank, they will fight continually.
Water Conditions: Water should have an addition of 1 tablespoonful of salt to every gallon of water. Temperature 75 to 78°.
Size: Males to 2 inches, females to 2¾ inches.
Food Requirements: Living foods like Daphnia or mosquito larvae.
Color Variations: Back brown, sides greenish. Males have a red spot on the dorsal fin.

Every once in a while an East Indian shipment contains a number of Half-beaks, which should be enough to ensure a constant supply of these interesting livebearers. This is not so; fact is, this livebearer is a very difficult proposition to breed, and even to keep. They occur in brackish as well as fresh water, and the addition of some salt to their water is beneficial. Probably there is some item of food in their native waters which we cannot or do not give them, and as a result they are short-lived in the aquarium. Males often indulge in battles which result in injury to the beak, the result of which usually is death. Females will give birth once or twice to a dozen young or so, and then most subsequent births are premature, or are born dead for some other reason. Another possibility which comes to mind is that there might be some tiny trace element which is native to their home waters, but which is absent in the aquarium. Perhaps some day we will have the answer, or someone will take extra pains with them and produce a healthy strain which will be hardy and fertile. Even if it does happen, the bellicose nature of the males will always be a drawback to their popularity.

DISTICHODUS AFFINIS (Günther)/*Silver Distichodus*

Range: Lower Congo region.
Habits: Peaceful; can be trusted with other fishes, but requires a large aquarium.
Water Conditions: Soft, slightly acid water, temperatures 75 to 80°.
Size: To 5 inches.
Food Requirements: Large amounts of live or frozen foods, with an addition of vegetable matter like lettuce or spinach leaves.
Color Variations: Sides silvery with a greenish-blue back. First dorsal rays black. Other fins bright red.

The *Distichodus* genus is easily distinguished from most of the other African Characins. The head is small in comparison to the rest of the body, and most of the tail is covered with tiny scales. *Distichodus affinis* goes the rest of them one better: the anal fin is also covered with scales. The shape of the tail lobes is unique as well. Both the upper and lower lobes are round, and a deep cleft separates them. This is one of the smaller species, and one of the least colorful. There is one thing which is a big drawback where the *Distichodus* are concerned: they cannot be trusted in a planted tank, as they have strong vegetarian tendencies. This must also be remembered when they are in an unplanted tank, and their feedings should be augmented with an occasional lettuce leaf or spinach leaf. This interesting group has never been spawned in captivity, and it is doubtful if this feat will ever be accomplished unless an exceptionally large tank or pool is used for the purpose. It must also be remembered that *Distichodus* are shy fishes, and although the tank cannot be planted it is also possible to arrange rocks, roots, etc., in such a manner that hiding-places are provided.

Photo by Jim Greenwald

DISTICHODUS FASCIOLATUS (Boulenger)/*Shark-Tailed Distichodus*

Range: Congo Region.
Habits: Peaceful with other fishes, but requires a large aquarium.
Water Conditions: Soft, slightly acid water. Temperature 75 to 80°.
Size: Up to 12 inches.
Food Requirements: Large amounts of live or frozen foods, with the addition of vegetable matter such as lettuce or spinach leaves.
Color Variations: Sides brownish to silvery, with narrow vertical bands. Young specimens have spotted caudal base.

In contrast to the oddly-shaped, deep-bodied members of the group, the Shark-Tailed Distichodus has a body which is a little longer and slimmer than the others. The caudal fin is unusual: the upper lobe is long and pointed, while the lower is much rounder and shorter. The picture is of a young pair, and the fins have been somewhat damaged. As can be seen, the colors are drab and there is little likelihood that they will ever set the aquarium world on fire with their beauty. Besides, it has the *Distichodus* habit of plant-eating which might be tolerated in a more highly-colored species, but not in an Ugly Duckling like this one. Besides its vegetarian tendencies, this species has the added disadvantage to home aquarists that it gets altogether too large for the average aquarium. The caudal base of young specimens is covered with dark spots, a characteristic which disappears when the fish gets older. Like so many of the larger species, we still cannot be sure how the *Distichodus* group breeds. Perhaps some day someone with a very large aquarium and a great deal of patience will find out and give the world a report of his findings.

F-258.00

DISTICHODUS SEXFASCIATUS (Boulenger)/*Six-Barred Distichodus*

Range: Lower Congo region.
Habits: Peaceful toward other fishes, but will nibble plants.
Water Conditions: Neutral to slightly acid, temperatures 75 to 80°.
Size: To 10 inches.
Food Requirements: Large amounts of live or frozen foods; supplemented with green foods like lettuce or spinach leaves.
Color Variations: Body pinkish to white with six dark bands. Fins are brilliant deep red.

The Six-Barred Distichodus is a large, handsome fish which is better adapted to a large tank in a public aquarium then in the comparatively cramped quarters a hobbyist can offer. It is fairly well distributed throughout the Congo region, but does not occur in the upper reaches. There is a similar species which grows bigger and has an almost identical coloring and markings, *Distichodus lusosso*. The most outstanding difference between the two is that *D. lusosso* has a head that is ridiculously small and pointed for the big, wide body while that of *D. sexfasciatus* is shorter and in better proportion. As with the other *Distichodus* species, this one should also get a generous proportion of green foods in its diet, and will supplement these with any plants it may find. Some hobbyists who wish to have a planted tank and also keep a plant-eater like this one set up a background of plants and then insert a glass pane in the back. This robs the tank of some of its area, but is a good way to keep the fish and plants separated. If the fish are fed a good amount of green foods, they will not feel frustrated if they cannot get at the growing plants.

DORMITATOR LATIFRONS (Richardson)/*Western Sleeper*

Range: Pacific coast from California south through Mexico and Central America.

Habits: Should not be kept with small species. A greedy eater which may attack other fishes when hungry.

Water Conditions: Fairly hard water (about 15 DH) with some salt added, about a teaspoonful per gallon. Tank should be well planted.

Size: To 10 inches in natural waters; mature at 4 inches.

Food Requirements: Eats just about anything; the important thing is to provide enough for its ravenous appetite.

Color Variations: Body brownish with a greenish shimmer. Scales each carry a dark spot. Underside yellow to reddish.

Dormitator latifrons occurs on the West Coast of the United States down through Mexico and Central America. It is distinguished from its East Coast counterpart, *Dormitator maculatus*, by having a very wide head. Both are very sluggish, sometimes showing scarcely any movement and lying in a clump of plants for hours at a time. One would think that a fish which burns up such little energy would not require much in the way of food but the Sleepers are uncommonly greedy eaters, able to put away their own weight in food daily. This species is covered with reddish-brown dots, one appearing on each scale. These dots are continued on the fins. When acquiring a fish with a wide range like this one, it is a mistake to assume that its tolerances of temperature are as wide too. It must be remembered that specimens from the northernmost limits are accustomed to lower temperatures than the same species caught in the southernmost limits of the range. This is not a migratory fish, and the ones from cool waters have spent countless generations in these waters. It helps greatly if you know where your fish were collected and govern yourself accordingly.

Photo by Dr. Herbert R. Axelrod.

DORMITATOR MACULATUS (Bloch)/*Spotted Sleeper*

Range: Atlantic coastal waters from the Carolinas to Brazil.
Habits: Inactive and predatory; should not be kept with small fishes.
Water Conditions: Water should have a salt content, about a teaspoonful to the gallon. Temperatures should range from 70 to 75°.
Size: To 10 inches.
Food Requirements: Eats anything and everything. Bits of raw fish are especially relished.
Color Variations: Sides brown to greenish, with many irregular dots. Dorsal, anal and caudal fins have rows of small dots.

The Spotted Sleeper is not strictly a tropical species, although its range extends down into Brazil. The northernmost extreme of its habitat is the Carolinas. This is one of the highly adaptable fishes which is found in salt water, as well as brackish and fresh waters. In the aquarium it displays a constantly vigorous appetite which belies its sluggish nature. It is an omnivorous eater, and smaller fishes of a size to be swallowed are considered special tidbits. This species has been spawned in captivity. They spawn very much like many of the Cichlid family. Both fish clean off a rock, and a large number of eggs are deposited by the female and fertilized by the male. The tiny fry hatch in a day at 75°, and when the fry begin to swim it is best to remove the parents. Infusoria should be fed at first, followed by newly hatched brine shrimp and later by larger foods. Not a very satisfactory aquarium fish, the Spotted Sleeper is as inactive as its name indicates and spends most of its time in hiding. This species has been known to science for a long time; it was given its scientific name in 1785, and was first introduced to hobbyists in 1901.

Photo by Dr. Herbert R. Axelrod.

EIGENMANNIA VIRESCENS (Valenciennes)
Green Knife Fish

Range: Widely distributed all over northern South America.

Habits: Mostly nocturnal; very greedy eaters which are best kept by themselves.

Water Conditions: Water should be well aged and clean. Temperatures 76 to 80°. This fish is very sensitive to fresh water.

Size: To 18 inches.

Food Requirements: Almost any food is taken greedily; preferred of course are the larger live foods, but they also eat chunks of beef-heart and oatmeal.

Color Variations: Greenish sides with a number of dark bars which fade as the fish grows older.

The Knife Fishes are a very interesting group because of their unusual shape and manner of swimming. Most of them are nocturnal by nature and are happiest when in a well-shaded tank. Their swimming motions are most interesting, and it is difficult to understand how a fish which is equipped with only pectoral fins and an anal fin can swim so rapidly and maneuver so well. Propulsion is accomplished by a rippling motion of the anal fin. If the fish is swimming forward and wishes to reverse direction, he simply reverses the rippling motion and swims backward just as easily. The Green Knife Fish grows to a large size, about 18 inches, which puts him in a class where he is adaptable only for large show aquaria when fully grown. Young specimens do not tarry long in growing up, either. They have an immense appetite which never seems to be satisfied, and growth is quite rapid. Of course, the full 18-inch size is seldom attained in captivity and specimens kept in the aquarium are frequently stunted to about half that size. This is one of the species where a hobbyist might buy a 3-inch fish and get a surprise some months later at how big the little fellow has gotten.

EIRMOTUS OCTOZONA (Schultz)/*False Barb*

Range: Bung Borapet, Thailand.
Habits: Peaceful and inoffensive toward other fishes and plants.
Water Conditions: Soft, slightly acid water is best. Temperature 74 to 80°F.
Size: To about 2½ inches.
Food Requirements: Not choosy; will eat dried as well as live or frozen foods readily.
Color Variations: Body transparently greenish with eight dark bars and a few dark spots irregularly placed between. Fins light pink.

When this handsome little fish was sent to our office in 1957, we were quite sure that this was a Barb species of some kind, but search as we might through our literature we could not find one where the description exactly fitted the fish. The big surprise came when Dr. Leonard P. Schultz, Curator of Fishes in the National Museum in Washington, D.C., made a complete taxonomic examination of the specimens we sent him and informed Dr. Axelrod that this was not only a new species but a new genus. It differs from the known genera which we call the "Barb" group by having several lines of sensory papillae on the head, and lacking a complete lateral line. Because it looks and acts like a Barb but is not a Barb, we are giving it the popular name "False Barb." This is a highly desirable aquarium fish which will doubtless become an overnight favorite if it is ever imported in numbers and bred. Breeding should offer no difficulties, but this is a rash statement, because some day there may be some available and the writer (WV) could be faced with a challenge like: "All right, wise guy, you said it was easy; go ahead and spawn them if you're so smart!"

F-263.00

ELASSOMA EVERGLADEI (Jordan)
Dwarf Sunfish

Range: North Carolina to Florida.

Habits: Very timid with other fishes; should be kept by themselves in a small aquarium.

Water Conditions: Slightly alkaline water. Room temperatures, about 65 to 70° are perfect.

Size: About 1¼ inches, females a little smaller.

Food Requirements: Small live foods are best, like sifted *Daphnia*, newly hatched brine shrimp, etc.

Color Variations: At spawning time males are velvety black with many shimmering green scales. Females are more grayish and have smaller fins.

Why is it that the aquarium hobbyist places such a high value on fishes which come from another part of the world and ignores the beautiful and interesting species which he can find in his own country? Our native American fishes, by and large, are not the most colorful and practical aquarium fishes in the world, but there are some which certainly deserve a little more attention. The Dwarf Sunfish is one of these. Coming from the Everglades in Florida, they can withstand a variety of temperatures. Because of their tiny size, a pair can be kept quite comfortably in a 1 or 2 gallon aquarium. Eggs are usually placed on a plant leaf and hatch in 2 to 3 days. Spawnings vary from 30 to 60 eggs. Parents guard the eggs and young, which are easily fed in their first days on dust-fine food. This fish has an odd manner of propelling itself along the bottom at times: the long ventral fins are alternately swished back and forth along the bottom, giving the fish the appearance of "walking." The Dwarf Sunfish can be highly recommended for an outdoor pool during the warm months. A single pair will often produce hundreds of young in a summer with hardly any attention.

ELASSOMA ZONATUM (Jordan)/*Banded Dwarf Sunfish*

Range: USA, southern Illinois to Alabama and west to Texas.
Habits: Peaceful, but because of their size, timidity and requirements should be kept in a small tank by themselves.
Water Conditions: Soft, slightly acid water. Temperatures need not be regulated; room temperatures suffice.
Size: To 1½ inches.
Food Requirements: Small live foods of all kinds.
Color Variations: Grayish green sides with tiny black dots all over; large black spot in the center, and 11 or 12 dark bands. Tail streaked with black.

Elassoma zonatum, although it occurs over a very wide range in our own USA, is seldom collected and can be counted among our "rare" aquarium fishes. The range is somewhat vaguely defined as southern Illinois to Arkansas, and west to Texas. They are most easily observed in a small aquarium, and are not particularly sensitive to low as well as high temperatures. Males are quite frisky at spawning time and are an interesting sight to watch. Eggs are usually laid on a plant leaf, but they may also be found on a rock or the glass aquarium sides. Hatching takes place in 2 to 3 days and the parents pay no further attention to the fry, except for the questionable one of occasionally eating one or more. Oddly enough, the young spend most of their time near the surface of the water. Here they may be fed finely powdered dry food until they have become large enough to handle the smallest live foods. The Dwarf Sunfishes are intriguing and interesting fishes which require only a small space and no extra heat, and their only disadvantage is their insistence on being fed nothing but living foods. It remains to be found out if they will accept frozen foods, which they probably will.

F-265.00

Photo by Edward C. Taylor

ENNEACANTHUS GLORIOSUS (Holbrook)
Diamond Sunfish

Range: Eastern United States from New York to Florida.
Habits: Peaceful when kept with fishes of its size.
Water Conditions: Slightly alkaline water which is kept unheated at room temperatures.
Size: To 3 inches.
Food Requirements: Variety of live or frozen foods. Dried foods are accepted unwillingly.
Color Variations: Olive to brown sides, generously sprinkled with sparkling blue dots. Female has smaller fins and less dots.

Enneacanthus gloriosus is doubtless one of the most beautiful of our American Sunfishes, as well as one of the most peaceful. Occurring as it does in the eastern coastal states of the United States, it should be rated as a cold-water species and should not be kept in a heated aquarium, unless there is danger of the water freezing. They may be kept in company with other cold-water species. One way the cold-water species differ from our tropical aquarium fishes is that spawning usually takes place at a very definite time of the year, and egg ripeness cannot be induced at any time by heavy feeding, higher temperatures, adding fresh water or all the other tricks we use with the tropical species. With this particular species there are usually two periods of ripeness, one in the spring and the other in late summer. As is often the case, we must turn to the European authorities for information on how to spawn an American fish in the aquarium. According to Rachow, spawning takes place among fine-leaved plants and at this time the male may treat the female with excessive roughness. The female should be taken out when finished. Fry hatch in 3 days and are very easy to raise.

F-266.00

EPALZEORHYNCHUS KALLOPTERUS (Bleeker)/*Flying Fox*

Range: Sumatra and Borneo.

Habits: Peaceful, even toward the smallest fishes.

Water Conditions: Not critical. An active fish, therefore aquarium should be of a good size. Sunny location best, as it provides algae.

Size: Said to attain 5½ inches, but specimens in captivity do not usually exceed 4 inches.

Food Requirements: Omnivorous; should have some vegetable substances in its diet, such as is provided by algae.

Color Variations: Back olive-green, golden horizontal stripe, belly white. Fins brownish red at base, with a black marking above.

Most of our so-called "scavenger" fishes are only tolerated because of their useful habits. They keep a tank bottom clear of uneaten food, and many of them also clear the rocks and plants as well as the glass sides of an aquarium of algae. Here we have a fish which does all these things, and is beautiful and active as well. Unfortunately we only see them once in a while, for the very good reason that so far there has been nobody who has had the good fortune to get them to spawn for him. As with some of the other "difficult" fishes, the wild specimens may exceed the measurements given, and never attain these measurements in captivity. As well as not attaining full size, it is also possible that they never attain a proper maturity. Much research is possible in this direction, and it also may be that some of the clever Chinese fish breeders around Hong Kong, who are able to give the fish almost natural conditions the year round in their outdoor pools, will come up with an answer. Even if we do not find out what the answer is, we will then get specimens which are more accustomed to a life in captivity, and which in time will also spawn for us.

EPALZEORHYNCHUS SIAMENSIS (Smith)/*Siamese Flying Fox*

Range: Thailand.
Habits: Peaceful, can be kept with any other fishes.
Water Conditions: Neutral to slightly alkaline water. Temperature 74 to 80°F.
Size: To 5½ inches.
Food Requirements: Omnivorous; diet should be supplemented with vegetable substances.
Color Variations: Sides green with blue or purple flecks, belly white, black stripe from head to middle rays of the tail.

This is a rare fish not only in the aquarium, but also in its home waters. The fishermen in the region of Thailand from where it comes call it *"pla lab mue nang"* or "lady's fingernail fish" and say it is good to eat. Where the resemblance lies between the fish and a lady's fingernail is not made clear; perhaps the scales look like a Siamese lady's fingernail, or it may be that the gill-covers have this appearance. We can do nothing but wonder. In the aquarium the Siamese Flying Fox does not have the beautiful fins sported by its close relation *E. kallopterus*, but its body colors almost make up for it. Back and sides are green with flecks of light blue or purple, top of the head is bright green and there is a black horizontal stripe running from the head through the middle rays of the tail. Underneath the fish is white and the dorsal, caudal and pectoral fins are pale green. It is a fairly active fish which does a great deal of poking about for algae and bits of left-over food. This of course is usually insufficient and there should be enough food for the fish to get its fair share. The tank should get a good amount of sunlight to promote a sufficient growth of algae.

F-268.00

EPICYRTUS SP./*Transparent Tetra*

Range: British Guiana.
Habits: Peaceful toward other fishes and plants.
Water Conditions: Soft, slightly acid water. Temperature 72 to 78°F.
Size: About 1¾ inches.
Food Requirements: Not known, but will probably eat just about everything.
Color Variations: Body greenish and very transparent; scales have an opalescent sparkle and each has a tiny black dot. Large black spot at tail base.

When I (WV) saw this picture it took me back to the savannah country around Lethem, British Guiana. Louis Chung, the well-known collector, had one in a one-pint rum flask we had picked up. This tiny improvised aquarium served to show him how a fish would stand up under the *worst* conditions a fish could get. Our little *Epicyrtus* was as good after three days as the day he went in, and had passed the test. Later that week we caught some of them in the Tabatinga River and I could admire the fish in its real colors. The tiny scales had an opalescent sparkle and the body was even more transparent than the picture shows. Kept with other fishes it proved to be peaceful, and it looked as if the aquarium hobby would be enriched by one more fish species. Since that time, however, I have not seen them again. Perhaps this fish disappeared from the Tabatinga; at the time it was the height of the dry season and the river was little more than a creek. The probability is that the dealers turned thumbs down on them, not considering them colorful enough. Personally I liked the fish very much and would like to see them again.

Photo by Col. J. J. Scheel.

EPIPLATYS CHAPERI (Sauvage)

Range: West Africa
Habits: Peaceful; will not bother anything it cannot swallow.
Water Conditions: Prefers soft, acid water and a certain amount of sunlight.
Size: Males slightly under 2 inches, females a little smaller.
Food Requirements: Will eat dried foods when hungry, but prefers live foods of all kinds.

Recent taxonomical work has shown that the fish long known to hobbyists as *Epiplatys chaperi* in actuality is *Epiplatys dageti; Epiplatys chaperi* is a distinct but little-seen species.

It is also a ready breeder. A pair can be put into a small aquarium with a few floating plants. Only a few eggs will be laid each day, and they can be picked out with the fingers. They are quite hard, and do not break readily. These are then placed separately in small containers, where they will hatch in about 14 days. The young fry are free-swimming at once, and food must be provided. The best way to feed them is with small amounts of newly-hatched live brine shrimp. The fry spend almost all of their time at the surface, so it is advisable to place a light above the surface, to bring up the brine shrimp nauplii where the fry can get at them.

EPIPLATYS FASCIOLATUS (Günther)/ *Striped Panchax*

Range: Sierra Leone, Liberia to Nigeria.

Habits: Not safe with smaller fishes. Should be kept in a covered tank to prevent them from jumping.

Water Conditions: About neutral and not very hard (10 to 15 DH) with 2 teaspoonsful of salt added for every gallon.

Size: To 3¼ inches.

Food Requirements: Prefers the larger sizes of live foods, but can be trained to take frozen foods.

Color Variations: Males have a brownish body with a blue shimmer. Scales each have a red dot. Six narrow dark bands. Tail green with reddish-brown edge.

There is a great deal of resemblance between this species and the preceding one, but a closer inspection shows a much more elegant finnage on the male, the lower fish in the picture. One can also see the light tip of the elongated ventral fin below the blur caused by the waving pectoral fin. Something which is only faintly seen is the pattern of red dots, each scale carrying one. Fishes of the *Epiplatys* genus are easily spawned as a rule, laying their eggs in the plants near the upper reaches of the aquarium. The eggs in the female ripen only a few at a time, and for this reason spawning is extended over a prolonged period. As a result the young hatch a few at a time as well. With such assorted sizes growing up together it would naturally follow that once the biggest of the lot got big enough to swallow the smallest he would do so, and for this reason the hobbyist who wants to raise the most fish possible has to have a number of well-planted tanks ready rather than just one and periodically grade his youngsters as to size. *Epiplatys* eggs are somewhat light-sensitive, and the incubating eggs will fungus readily if they are not shaded.

Photo by Col. J. J. Scheel.

EPIPLATYS GRAHAMI (Boulenger)
Graham's Panchax

Range: Southern Nigeria.
Habits: Lively and peaceful with others of about its own size.
Water Conditions: Soft, slightly acid water is best. Temperatures 75 to 79°.
Size: To 2¼ inches; females slightly smaller.
Food Requirements: Live foods in variety; dried foods only in an emergency.
Color Variations: Body yellowish with a number of slanting dark bars on the sides.
Lower jaw has a bright red bar. Females darker.

This species can easily be confused with several others which are very similar
in appearance, *E. macrostigma* and *E. sheljuzhkoi*. The only distinguishing
mark is a bright red band in the lower jaw. Although it is an active fish, it
is not as productive as most of the other *Epiplatys* species. It should be kept
in a well-planted and not too brightly lighted aquarium, to approximate the
conditions in the weedy, well-shaded jungle streams where they are found.
As they are skillful jumpers, their aquarium should be kept covered at all
times. You will find that if a pair or more are kept in their own tank, a few
youngsters will be found every once in a while swimming at the surface; they
can be lifted out with a spoon to a tank of their own where they are not in
constant danger of being swallowed. Of course, if more young are desired the
eggs must be hunted out and hatched in a tank of their own. Hatching time
is 10 to 14 days, and the young are able to swim and eat at once. Raising them
is no problem, as they have sharp eyes and are skilled at hunting their food.
They should be sorted frequently to prevent the larger ones from swallowing
the smaller ones.

F-272.00

EPIPLATYS LONGIVENTRALIS (Boulenger)/*Banded Panchax*

Range: Tropical West Africa, principally South Nigeria.
Habits: Peaceful toward any fish it cannot swallow.
Water Conditions: Soft, slightly acid water. Temperature 75 to 80°.
Size: To 2¼ inches.
Food Requirements: Live foods preferred, dried foods only when nothing else is available.
Color Variations: Body light brown with dark bars slanting back. Anal and caudal fins have black edges, caudal with a bright yellow border inside.

The Banded Panchax is one of the lesser-known species of the genus *Epiplatys*, and because of its quarrelsome nature and larger size is not favored quite as much as the smaller species. Nevertheless it is attractively colored and the few which occasionally put in an appearance do not go begging for takers very long. This is definitely not a fish which could be combined with smaller specimens in a community aquarium. Those which it could swallow would be stalked and engulfed, and the others which would be a little too large for these attentions would be bullied. It is also a mistake to keep two large males together. Even if there are enough females to keep them both busy, there would be a constant struggle for supremacy. A healthy pair will spawn readily, hanging their eggs in fine-leaved plants near the surface. The so-called "spawning mops" of nylon yarn are also accepted in lieu of plants. Eggs hatch in 12 to 14 days and during the incubation period should not be exposed to bright light. While they are growing, fry should be sorted frequently to keep the same sizes together, otherwise there will be many losses among the smaller ones from being eaten by the larger ones.

EPIPLATYS SEXFASCIATUS (Gill)/*Six-Banded Panchax*

Range: West coast of Africa from southern Liberia to the mouth of the Congo River.
Habits: Fairly peaceful with fish of their own size.
Water Conditions: A well-established, well-planted tank which is not too small is preferred. Water should be soft and slightly acid.
Size: Large specimens attain a length of 4 inches; average is smaller.
Food Requirements: Any kind of living food is preferred. Frozen or dried foods are usually passed up.
Color Variations: Back greenish olive, darker on the sides. Six dark bands extend from the middle to the lower part of the body.

This attractive little fish is not quite as brightly colored as the others in the "Panchax" group, and is therefore not seen as often in dealers' tanks. In a community aquarium they are inclined toward shyness, and often keep themselves hidden. One thing they seem to like is a light which comes down on them from above, and some broad-leaved plants. The males take up a position under the leaves, and when a female or another male swims by, scoot out with flashing colors. It is advisable once they are established in an aquarium which is to their liking, to move them as little as possible. This is of course good advice with any fish, but some adapt to varying conditions more easily than others and the Six-Banded Panchax is not one of these. When spawning this fish, it is best to use a ratio of two or even three females to one male. If only one female is used and the male still wants to spawn after she is depleted of her eggs, she is likely to be beaten up pretty badly. Eggs are deposited singly on plants near the surface, and may be removed to small containers, where they will hatch in 10 to 14 days. Fry are easily raised.

*EPIPLATYS SHELJUZHKOI** (Poll)/*Sheljuzhko's Panchax*

Range: West Africa, in the region of Abidajean.
Habits: Peaceful toward any fish they cannot swallow.
Water Conditions: Soft, slightly acid water. Temperature 72 to 80°.
Size: To 2½ inches.
Food Requirements: Live foods of all kinds. Can be trained to eat frozen foods.
Color Variations: Males have a brownish body with rows of red spots on the sides.
Females have less color and fewer spots.

Epiplatys sheljuzhkoi has been confused with a great many other *Epiplatys* species which it resembles very closely, and the mistakes are quite understandable. The distinguishing characteristic here, we are told, is that the horizontal rows of red dots are nice and regular in the lower half of the body as well as the upper. An attractive as well as very hardy species, which spawns readily in the manner of the other *Epiplatys* species. One of the great advantages of working with the Killifishes in general is that their long incubational period, about 2 weeks, makes it possible for hobbyists to exchange eggs by air mail all over the world. The eggs can be placed in a vial which contains water, or even in a damp nylon mop where the fish laid them. The mop is slipped into a plastic bag which is then sealed and put into an envelope. It is surprising how much abuse and crushing the eggs can stand, and there is seldom any damage. In this way there have been many exchanges made among fish hobbyists the world over and the hobby has benefited greatly *Epiplatys sheljuzhkoi* is now considered to be a subspecies of *Epiplatys chaperi.*

F-275.00

ESOMUS DANRICA (Hamilton-Buchanan)/*Flying Barb*

Range: Singapore and parts of India; numerous in ditches of rice-paddies.
Habits: Peaceful; spends most of its time at or near the surface. Not a fussy eater; eats dried as well as live foods.
Water Conditions: Not critical, as long as the water is clean. Some sunlight should fall into the tank.
Size: Said to attain 5 inches in native waters; in the aquarium about 2½ inches.
Food Requirements: Should have food that floats or stays near the top. *Daphnia* will gather under a light, and mosquito larvae come up for air.
Color Variations: Back silvery gray; dark horizontal line. Belly almost white. Sides have a violet sheen.

A covered tank is a necessity with these fish; their large pectoral fins have enough drive to send them on a good-sized leap out of the water, and they will soon learn to restrain themselves if they bang their heads a few times on the cover-glass. The *Esomus* species have a distinguishing characteristic: a pair of long "whiskers" flows from the corners of the upper lip underneath the body. These barbels are almost half the entire length of the body. This is another fish which is likely to "go begging" because many hobbyists pass it by, due to a lack of bright colors. However, there is a vast difference between the bare tanks in a dealer's establishment and a well-planted, well-lighted tank, and once established in one of these, our fish takes on a different appearance. A small school of Flying Barbs is attractive in a tank where most of the other fishes are found in the middle and lower reaches, and provide some action in the upper reaches. Males are smaller and slimmer than the females. Very prolific spawners, usually in floating plants in the corners. The parents must be removed immediately after spawning, and the tiny fry hatch in less than a day.

F-276.00

ESOMUS MALAYENSIS (Mandée)/*Malayan Flying Barb*

Range: Malayan Peninsula and South Vietnam.
Habits: Peaceful and very active, preferring to swim in schools near the surface.
Water Conditions: Not critical, but the water should be clean and well aerated. Temperature 72 to 75°.
Size: To 3 inches.
Food Requirements: Good eaters; accept dried as well as live or frozen foods.
Color Variations: Sides bluish, with a silvery white belly. Large black spot with golden border at the caudal base.

The Malayan Flying Barb is distinguished from the others by having an indistinct horizontal stripe and at the base of the tail a black spot approximately the diameter of the iris of the eye. Around this is a ring of gold. Nature provides many fishes with "eye-spots" on the body, and it is easily understood how a larger fish looking for a meal and swimming into a school of these fish could be greatly confused by seeing so many real and false eyes staring at him and shift his area of operations elsewhere. An eye-spot is also a protection to a fish swimming by itself. A predatory fish on the lookout for a meal might mistake the spot for the real eye and snap at a point behind it where the body should be, to his disappointment. The Malayan Flying Barb should be provided with a tank which affords a good deal of swimming space, and the tank must be kept covered to prevent the fish from jumping out. If spawning is desired, the bottom should be thickly planted and the water clean and well aerated. A pair will usually spawn in or near the corners, and about 500 eggs from a well-rounded female is not at all an unusual achievement.

F-277.00

ETROPLUS MACULATUS (Bloch)/*Orange Chromide*

Range: India and Ceylon.
Habits: Fairly peaceful with fishes of its own size, but cannot be trusted completely.
Water Conditions: Water should be fresh and clean, with a little salt added, about a teaspoonful to each gallon.
Size: About 3 inches.
Food Requirements: Should be provided with living or frozen foods; dried food taken only when very hungry.
Color Variations: Sides lemon yellow to orange, with a round black ocellated spot in the upper center of the body. Fins sooty black.

Asia provides us with a great many of our finest tropical aquarium fishes of many kinds, but is extremely stingy with the aquarist when it comes to Cichlid species, most of which come from South America and Africa. Here is one exception which has become very popular in the half-century it has been known to the aquarist. Colors are a happy combination of yellow and black, which always gives a good contrast against the green of the plants. A healthy pair in a well-planted aquarium is particularly beautiful when an additional contrast of black gravel is provided. In form these fish greatly resemble the Sunfishes of North America, and their breeding habits are very similar. Sometimes a rock or wide plant leaf is selected, but this fish prefers to find an open space and dig an excavation there until it reaches the slate aquarium bottom, which it will then clean meticulously. The female usually provides little help, leaving this job to the male. Eggs are attached to this surface, then carefully tended by both parents. Young hatch in 4 to 6 days, and about a week later begin to swim. Newly-hatched brine shrimp may then be fed.

F-278.00

ETROPLUS SURATENSIS (Bloch)/*Banded Chromide*

Range: India and Ceylon, in the mouths of streams and bays.

Habits: Somewhat quarrelsome; should be trusted only with fishes of its own size or bigger.

Water Conditions: Requires a generous addition of salt to the water, a tablespoonful to the gallon, or 10% sea water added.

Size: Wild specimens may measure up to 16 inches, but we seldom see them more than 3 inches in length.

Food Requirements: Should be generously fed with a variety of live foods, or frozen full-grown brine shrimp.

Color Variations: Body grayish green to brownish green, peppered with small silvery dots. At times, dark bands appear.

This fish is better known to the natives of India as an article of food than as a candidate for the average aquarium. They are usually found in the brackish river mouths, and sometimes ascend the rivers into fresh water, like the Scats which come from the same area. They seem to prefer these brackish waters to marine environments, and are seldom found in salt water. Occasionally some small specimens come in with shipments as a rarity, but their "chip-on-the-shoulder" attitude with their tankmates, along with their inability to do well in fresh water, will always keep them from becoming favorites among aquarium hobbyists. An interesting thing to note is that this fish was first identified as "*Chaetodon suratensis*" by Bloch in 1790, which put it in the same family as the marine Butterfly Fishes. Then Cuvier and Valenciennes named it "*Etroplus meleagris*" 40 years later, and Günther combined the generic name given by Cuvier and Valenciennes with the specific name given by Bloch, and in 1862 the fish's present name became official. This fish has never spawned in a small aquarium, probably never attaining maturity in the aquarium.

EXODON PARADOXUS (Müller & Troschel)/*Bucktoothed Tetra*

Range: British Guiana and Brazil.

Habits: Small specimens are mostly peaceful toward other fishes, and bigger ones are likely to fight among themselves.

Water Conditions: Should have a large, sunny tank with plenty of vegetation. Rather high temperatures are required, not under 78°.

Size: Attains a size of about 6 inches, but specimens in the aquarium seldom exceed 4 inches.

Food Requirements: Should get mostly live foods, but will also take frozen foods and pieces of fish, shrimp, etc.

Color Variations: Lemon yellow body with large black spot in the upper middle of the body. Fins are reddish.

This is a prolific fish in its native waters; wherever it occurs, there are huge schools of them. The natives have an amusing use for them: when they have any dirty dishes to clean, they merely set them in the river and let the "Miguelinhos", as they are called locally, pick them clean. The always-hungry hordes soon find the easy pickings, and nibble every bit of food off of the dishes. The native women have a warm affection for this little fish, and come to look upon them almost as pets. South American aquarists tell us that a number of these little beauties can be raised together, and never cause any trouble. The sad truth is that if a number of grown specimens are put in the same tank, they soon injure each other in many cases. However, there have been a few accounts of them spawning in the aquarium. According to these accounts, they spawned in the usual Tetra fashion, that is to say, they scattered eggs in bushy plants. The eggs hatched and the fry were of good size and easy to raise. This fish will live to a good age if conditions suit it; all it asks is live food, and a sunny, well-planted tank in a sunny location.

F-280.00

Photo by Dr. Herbert R. Axelrod.

FUNDULUS CHRYSOTUS (Holbrook)
Golden Ear

Range: Eastern coast of the United States from South Carolina to Florida.
Habits: Peaceful if kept with fishes of its size.
Water Conditions: Although it sometimes comes from brackish waters, it will tolerate fresh water as well. Temperatures 73 to 78°.
Size: To 3 inches.
Food Requirements: Has an excellent appetite and will eat dried as well as live or frozen foods.
Color Variations: Sides greenish with rows of red dots. Females have less color and fewer dots. Bright golden spot on each gill-cover.

As with most of our American fishes which are suitable for the aquarium, the Golden Ear finds little respect in its own country. In this case its unpopularity is largely undeserved. It is not uncomfortable at temperatures which we reserve for our tropical species and it is a willing spawner. Even when it is kept in a community tank it is not unusual to find a few youngsters from time to time which have escaped the depredations of the bigger fishes. At spawning time it is not advisable to keep too many males together, or there may be fights. It is also a good idea (in the interest of the females) to use two or three females for each male when spawning this fish, because the males are hard drivers. Eggs are laid in bushy plants at the rate of a few each day. They hatch in 8 to 15 days, and if they are not removed daily the parents will eat every egg they find. There is also a problem which is common with the Panchax group while the young are growing up. There is a great variety of sizes, and eventually the danger results that the smaller ones might be eaten by the larger ones. Raising them is very simple if they are fed frequently.

F-281.00

FUNDULUS NOTTI (Agassiz)
Star-Head Top Minnow, Masked Minnow

Range: Mississippi and Louisiana north to Ohio and Illinois.

Habits: Best kept only with their own kind, as they are likely to attack other species kept with them.

Water Conditions: A good-sized tank should be provided, with thick vegetation and good aeration.

Size: 2½ inches.

Food Requirements: Live foods are preferred, and dried foods taken only as a last resort.

Color Variations: Olive to brown body; male has a series of vertical bars on the sides, and the female rows of horizontal dots.

It is a strange and almost inexplicable thing that among aquarium hobbyists a fish seldom has any value or interest unless it comes from some far-off place. There are many species which come from our own native waters and make excellent aquarium fishes, but because they are readily available most hobbyists all but ignore them and if we want to know anything about their life habits we must often turn to European works; in many cases the fish is highly valued among European aquarists and much has been written about them. *Fundulus notti notti* is one of these "neglected" fishes which we see respectfully mentioned in European literature, and which we seldom even see for sale in this country, where they are available in great numbers in such states as Mississippi and Louisiana. As with most of the *Fundulus* species, the sexes are easily distinguished by the brighter colors and larger fins of the males.

A male *Fundulus notti notti;* juvenile fish are shown in the color photograph opposite.

Living habits are similar in their natural waters: large schools swim mostly just below the surface of the water, in contradiction to their name *Fundulus,* which means "bottom." Most males of the *Fundulus* species are vigorous drivers at breeding time, and it is best to provide each one with several females in order to prevent them from getting hurt. Eggs are deposited on bushy plants, and are usually left alone by the parents. It is best to leave the parents in the breeding tank for a week to 10 days, as there are only a few eggs deposited each day. Hatching takes place in 12 to 14 days. The young are free-swimming at once.

Photo by Dr. Herbert R. Axelrod.

FUNDULUS HETEROCLITUS (Linné)/*Zebra Killie*

Range: Atlantic Coast from Canada to Mexico.
Habits: Fairly peaceful, but may pick on smaller fishes.
Water Conditions: Water should be alkaline and hard (about 20 DH), with some salt added (at least a teaspoonful to every gallon).
Size: To 4½ inches.
Food Requirements: All kinds of live foods, also dried foods which have a vegetable content, such as the so-called "Molly foods."
Color Variations: Sides greenish brown, with a number of narrow blue bars. Females have less color and bars are only faint or absent.

You will probably notice that the colors described above do not account for the reddish fins in the picture and that the bars in the female (below) are almost as prominent as in the male. The fish in the picture are a color variety of *Fundulus heteroclitus*. The author (WV) has seen them with yellow fins, but never with red ones like these. The Zebra Killie is probably the most common small fish along the Atlantic Coast, ranging from Canada down to Mexico. It prefers the brackish waters of the bays and river mouths but is frequently found in fresh water; it was always my opinion that they returned to brackish water to spawn until I found them in all sizes, from half-inch babies to 4-inch monsters, in a completely landlocked fresh-water pond. During the summer months most of the establishments that sell live bait along the New Jersey coast have a supply of live "Killies" at all times. In the aquarium they are peaceful if not very colorful citizens which thrive very well once they have become established. Tanks are best left unheated. Males are vigorous drivers and eggs are laid in plant thickets near the bottom. Incubation period is 6 to 12 days.

F-284.00

FUNDULUS NOTATUS (Rafinesque)/*Black-Striped Killifish*

Range: Texas, Louisiana and Mississippi north to Wisconsin.
Habits: Fairly peaceful unless kept with fishes it can swallow.
Water Conditions: Should be kept in unheated aquaria at room temperatures. Plant growth should be ample, and tank should be roomy.
Size: About 3¼ inches; fish from the northern part of the range are smaller.
Food Requirements: Should get live foods only; they take dried foods only when very hungry.
Color Variations: Light to medium brown, with darker spots on the back and a black horizontal stripe from the snout to the caudal base.

Fundulus notatus is another species which is seldom kept by American hobbyists even though it occurs over a wide range which includes our Central Southern States and extends as far north as Wisconsin. Strangely enough, many of the *Fundulus* species have an odd characteristic which is shared by the *Epiplatys* species of Africa: there is a shiny spot on top of the head. The purpose of this spot has been the source of much conjecture among scientists, and most of them agree that these spots reflecting up from a school of fish swimming near the surface would look like a swarm of insects and would attract real insects to a spot just above the water's surface, where the hungry fish could snap at them. *Fundulus notatus* is distinguished by a black stripe which is indistinct in young specimens, becoming distinctly defined with age. The stripe is especially distinct with mature males. It must be remembered when keeping this and other *Fundulus* species that they are native to much cooler waters than the tropical species, and should be kept in an unheated aquarium at room temperatures. Eggs are laid in bushy plants and hatch in about 10 to 14 days.

Photo by Dr. Karl Knaack.

GAMBUSIA AFFINIS AFFINIS (Baird & Girard)
Mosquito Fish

Range: Southern United States from eastern Texas to Alabama.
Habits: Aggressive and pugnacious; not for the community aquarium.
Water Conditions: Will tolerate a wide variety of water conditions, with temperatures ranging from almost freezing to about 85°.
Size: Males to 1¼ inches, females to 2¼ inches.
Food Requirements: Wide variety of foods is eaten greedily, especially live foods.
Color Variations: Sides gray with a bluish shimmer, back brown. Some specimens have a number of black blotches on the sides.

Although it is not a desirable aquarium fish, *Gambusia affinis affinis* is without a doubt the most useful member of the fish world which we will ever see. It has been introduced into many bodies of water all over the warm parts of the world, there to thrive and multiply and, most important of all, to satisfy its greedy appetite with the hordes of mosquitoes which would otherwise go unchecked to plague the human population and cause many outbreaks of malaria. *Gambusia affinis affinis* is a livebearer which is particularly well adapted for the job. It can make itself at home in fairly dirty waters and is as much at ease in tropic temperatures as it is in the sometimes near-freezing waters of its native climes. Its appetite is enormous; a healthy fish can consume its own weight in mosquito larvae every day. It is prolific and the young grow very rapidly. But put this fish in an aquarium and we quickly become aware of its true nature. It is very aggressive toward its tankmates, frequently tearing their fins to shreds. It is strange that one of man's most useful fishes should be given a generic name derived from the Spanish slang word *gambusino*, which means "worthless."

F-286.00

Photo by G. J. M. Timmerman.

GAMBUSIA AFFINIS HOLBROOKI (Girard)/*Holbrook's Gambusia*

Range: Southern New Jersey to Florida.
Habits: A bit scrappy for the community aquarium; best kept in a tank by themselves.
Water Conditions: Not at all important, as long as the water is clean and well aerated. Unheated aquaria kept at room temperature are best.
Size: Males to $1\frac{1}{4}$ inches, females to $2\frac{1}{2}$ inches.
Food Requirements: A greedy eater which will accept practically anything in the way of fish food.
Color Variations: Males have many black patches covering the body, sometimes almost solid black. Females have smaller black patches.

Holbrook's Gambusia is a subspecies of *Gambusia affinis* in which the males have a great many black speckles and sometimes, as in this case, are almost completely black. The female also frequently carries black markings, unlike the plain one shown here. A fish as black as the male in our picture seldom occurs in natural waters. Many are born this way, but a fish which is black among light-colored brethren has the proverbial two strikes against him. His color makes him conspicuous, too conspicuous for his own good. A fish owes his life to being inconspicuous, and one that cannot blend in with his background has to be exceptionally alert and agile at all times to avoid becoming an item on a bigger fish's menu. In the aquarium it is a different story; if one desires a black strain in a fish which has an inclination toward melanism, one merely picks out the blackest ones and breeds selectively until the desired amount of blackness is reached. With this subspecies the goal of getting a pure black strain has been almost attained with the males, but so far the blackest females still show a lot of patches of the original color.

GARRA TAENIATA (Smith)/*Siamese Stone-Lapping Fish*

Range: Thailand.
Habits: Peaceful toward even the smallest fishes.
Water Conditions: Slightly alkaline water with a good amount of sunlight. Tank should be well-planted and afford some hiding-places.
Size: To 6 inches. Becomes mature at half that size.
Food Requirements: Accepts all foods, but should be allowed to browse occasionally in an aquarium which has a growth of algae.
Color Variations: Back reddish brown, belly silvery; deep black horizontal line from gill-covers to caudal base. All fins reddish.

It used to be a problem what to do to get rid of algae in the aquarium, but now with the many algae-eating fishes which have become available the situation reverses itself. Some of these species, which include *Epalzeorhynchus*, *Gyrinocheilus* and others, do their clean-up jobs so well that the hobbyist often wonders if they are getting *enough* algae. *Garra taeniata* is well-known to the natives of Thailand, who call it *pla lia hin*, or "Stone-Lapping Fish." Its actions may well be described as stone-lapping, and the probability is that it comes from briskly-flowing streams where it would have to use its mouth not only for removing algae from rocks or other firmly-anchored objects but also to hang on when the current would make it a hard job to use its fins for swimming against it. Like *Epalzeorhynchus kallopterus* this is a very handsome fish and it is to be hoped that in the near future there will either be more importations or that some breeder with a "wet thumb" will supply them in quantity. Keep this fish in a covered aquarium, as it is a skillful jumper which can find its way through small openings such as those allowed for heaters, etc.

An unidentified species of *Garra,* possibly also *Garra taeniata.*

GASTEROPELECUS STERNICLA (Linnaeus)/*Silver Hatchetfish*

Range: Restricted to the Peruvian Amazon, Guianas and the Orinoco Basin in Venezuela.

Habits: A top feeder which spends most of its time waiting quietly for a passing insect.

Water Conditions: Prefers warm, soft water with a pH of about 6.4.

Size: About 2 inches maximum.

Food Requirements: Floating foods, Wingless *Drosophila* flies and floating bits of frozen brine shrimp.

Color Variations: Nearly identical in color to *Gasteropelecus levis.*

There is only one big difference between this fish and G. *levis* that is meaningful as far as aquarists are concerned. G. *sternicla* is usually the larger of the two species and it is much hardier. Aquarists are unable to differentiate between the two species just by looking at them. Those fishes which come from the lower Amazon basin, usually being exported from Belem, are G. *levis.* The fish from the Guianas, Venezuela and from the Peruvian-Colombian Amazon, are G. *sternicla.* Of course there are certain morphological differences, too. G. *levis* does not, according to Weitzman, have maxillary teeth. G. *sternicla* has 2 to 4 maxillary teeth. A third valid species, G. *maculatus*, has a relatively deeper body and is found in the northern parts of South America between Panama and the Maracaibo Basin in Venezuela. Weitzman says that *sternicla* usually has a lighter color pattern than *levis* but this is probably due to whether the fish came from the black waters of the Amazon or the muddy brown waters. Black water fishes are usually more silver; brown water fishes are darker. Fishes from practically sterile black waters (such as the Rio Negro) are very difficult to maintain for long in an aquarium. There has never been any successful incidence of spawning occurrence with this genus.

GASTEROSTEUS ACULEATUS (Linné)
Three-Spined Stickleback

Range: Most of Europe, North America, Algeria, northern Asia.

Habits: Inclined to be pugnacious toward other fishes, and therefore should have their own tank.

Water Conditions: Water should be slightly alkaline with a salt content of about a teaspoonful of salt per gallon. Temperature 60 to 65°.

Size: Up to 4 inches.

Food Requirements: Living foods only, such as *Daphnia, Tubifex* worms and white worms.

Color Variations: Sides greenish to brownish, sometimes with darker marbled markings. At spawning time the males have bright orange to red bellies.

The Three-Spined Stickleback is one of the most widely distributed freshwater fishes in the temperate zone. Not only does it occur in completely fresh water, but it is also especially numerous in brackish water bays and estuaries. It is an interesting fish for a cold-water aquarium, especially in the early and middle spring months. At this time the males put on their brilliant colors and go into their interesting courting activities. They become distinctly unfriendly toward other males who intrude into their territories and drive the females very actively. The correct ratio during breeding is two or three females to every male. A number of rooted grasslike plants like *Vallisneria* are a help to the male, who anchors his nest among the leaves. This nest is built in the shape of a ball with a hole through the middle. As a building material bits of plants, etc., are used. These are held together by a sticky secretion from the male's kidneys. After she has laid her eggs the female is driven out of the nest and frequently one or two more add their eggs as well. The eggs hatch in 10 to 14 days, and the fry are carefully guarded by the male.

F-291.00

Photo by H.J. Richter

GEOPHAGUS BRASILIENSIS (Quoy & Gaimard)
Brazilian High-Hat, Pearl Cichlid

Range: Eastern coastal regions of South America from Bahia to the La Plata.

Habits: Fairly peaceful for a Cichlid. Larger specimens should be kept only with their own kind, or with other Cichlids their own size.

Water Conditions: Not critical, temperature should be about 78°. A pair should have a well-planted tank of about 20 gallons or more to spawn in.

Size: In their native waters, about 12 inches. About half that in captivity.

Food Requirements: Live foods preferably. Can be accustomed to pieces of fish or shrimp, etc.

Color Variations: Body color grayish green, covered with pearly dots. Large fish develop a large spot on the sides.

This is a popular food fish in the parts of Brazil where it occurs. The picture shows a young immature specimen. Colors vary greatly as the fish grows up, and a peppering of mother-of-pearl spots becomes more and more prominent. There is also a large black spot on the sides, which is very variable in intensity. Until the fish become large, the only sure way to tell sex is by comparing the breeding tubes when the fish are ready for spawning. That of the male is slender and pointed, and the female's blunt. Older males develop a fatty accumulation which gives them a considerable lump atop their foreheads. This becomes largest when the fish are ready to spawn. A usually preferred spawning site is a cleft between two rocks, which could be substituted by an empty flowerpot standing upright. Eggs and young are seldom eaten and the young, which hatch in 4 to 5 days, are carefully tended by the parents who keep moving them from place to place in holes dug for them. When they have begun to swim, it is best to separate them from their parents who might at any time forget their affection for their babies and let their hunger pangs carry them away.

Photo by H. Hansen, Aquarium Berlin

GEOPHAGUS JURUPARI (Heckel)/*Eartheater, Demon Fish*

Range: Northeastern South America to the Guianas.

Habits: Generally peaceful; fond of digging in the sand searching for edible bits, but seldom uproots plants if they are well-rooted.

Water Conditions: Temperature should be kept high, about 80°. Water should be neutral to slightly acid.

Size: Up to 9 inches in the wild state, but not over 6 inches in captivity.

Food Requirements: Will eat dried foods, but should be given an occasional feeding with live foods. White worms and tubifex preferred.

Color Variations: Sex differences very slight; males have slightly more pointed anal and ventral fins. Body covered with blue dots, streaks on head.

The large, flat, pointed head of this Cichlid, with its big eyes, are what usually attract the hobbyist to this fish. Like the *Corydoras* Catfishes, it is constantly digging for food particles in the bottom. Their real claim to being something unusual is their manner of breeding. They will lay their eggs in typical Cichlid fashion, then guard and fan them for a day or so. The eggs are then picked up by the male, or female, or both, and incubated in the mouth. After they hatch, the babies will seek refuge in the parent's mouth until their size no longer permits them to be accommodated. Breedings of this beautiful fish are rarely reported, and we are dependent mostly on importations for the stock which is offered for sale. Although the males may be recognized by their more pointed anal and ventral fins, this difference is not highly pronounced, and the only sure way to sex them is to look for the breeding tubes when the fish are ready for spawning. The male's will be slender, and the female's much heavier. A well-mated pair will generally spawn with regularity once they have become accustomed to their surroundings. A tank of at least 20 gallons is recommended.

Photo by Dr. Herbert R. Axelrod.

*GEOPHAGUS THAYERI (Steindachner)

Range: Throughout central Brazil and all the Amazonian tributaries.
Habits: A large, beautiful fish which is rarely imported but which exists in quantity in nature. It should have a large aquarium.
Water Conditions: Not sensitive to water conditions, but is in best color when it is kept in soft, slightly acid water at a temperature of about 76°F.
Size: To about 6 inches.
Food Requirements: As with most Cichlids, they prefer large, bulky live foods such as small garden worms, but they eagerly take pelletized fish foods and frozen foods.
Color Variations: A similar fish exists with a narrow dark bar through the eye and a black spot on the anterior dorsal spines. This fish is *Acarichthys heckeli* (Mueller & Troschel).

While fishing in the Rio Urubu about 20 miles north of Itacoatiara, in 1959, the author (HRA) collected this very specimen. In a few hours it was in a photo tank and had its beautiful form recorded for history! This was one of the few fishes, from the thousands the author collected, that really impressed him. After spending several hours looking for a likely female of the species, the author gave up in vain. In the next river, he caught hundreds of them and shipped them back to the United States alive. They were not the "smash hit" he thought they would be and that was the end of what could have been a very interesting addition to the aquarium field. No one was able to breed them even though some of the finest fish breeders in Florida tried it.

They probably breed as a mouthbreeder, but there is no direct evidence to support this supposition. No young were ever collected, so it is quite possible that the young look nondescript. Females are much less colorful than males.

*This fish is now known as *Acarichthys heckelii*.
F-294.00

GIRARDINUS METALLICUS (Poey)

Range: Cuba.
Habits: A livebearing fish which greedily gobbles its young if they are not protected with a heavy planting of fine-leaved plants.
Water Conditions: Does best in hard water with a slightly alkaline pH of 7.4.
Size: Females reach 3 inches; males about 2 inches.
Food Requirements: They eat everything, but they should have some frozen brine shrimp or live foods in their diets from time to time.
Color Variations: The blue-metallic sheen on the male is very temporary and only fish in perfect condition have any color at all.

In every stream in Cuba which is fed with cool, fresh water from the mountains, you can find a small pool which doesn't have too much current. These pools will usually be heavily stocked with *Girardinus*. But who cares! The fish are silvery gray to olive green at their best. Plain Guppies are much more colorful and more interesting and they cost about $\frac{1}{5}$ of the cost of these rare fish because nobody is breeding the latter. Even though livebearers are supposedly easy to breed, there are many which refuse the best and most skillful breeders' hands and they cannot be economically reproduced.

A very heavily planted aquarium with hard water is necessary to have these fish at their best. The German aquarists feed them mosquito larvae, probably their natural food, and enjoy much success with them, but only the very serious aquarist would consider having them at all, as they are as colorless as any fish can be.

The males have the typical double-pointed gonopodium which is not quite as long proportionally as the gonopodium of the Yellow Belly (*Glaridichthys falcatus*). Females are much larger, sometimes being twice as large as their males. The female will drop about 20-30 fry per month on a very predictable schedule if conditions are uniform.

GLARIDICHTHYS FALCATUS (Eigenmann)/*Yellow Belly*

Range: Cuba.

Habits: A livebearing, surface-feeding small fish which has never achieved the popularity it deserves.

Water Conditions: Prefers hard, alkaline water with a pH of 7.5.

Size: Males attain 2 inches; females 3 inches.

Food Requirements: Prefer live foods, but eagerly taken.

Color Variations: The extremely large females of this species have a light golden hue with a much yellow belly.

In the same ditches which were discussed under *Girardinus metallicus*, these fish are also to be found. They are much more colorful than the *Girardinus* and look almost like a golden female Guppy. They do not, however, cross with a Guppy and this has been verified by the author (HRA) who tried placing female *Glaridichthys* with male *Lebistes* and vice versa. Though some of the male *Lebistes* made "passes" at some of the females, the author was unable to ascertain any sperm transfer after pipetting the female's oviduct for sperm packets for which the male Guppy is so famous. Perhaps the male Guppy didn't release sperm packets at all; or, more logically, because of the morphological difference between the fishes, the sperm packets could not find their way into the reproductive tract of the female *Glaridichthys*. Male *Glaridichthys* with female *Lebistes* were unamorous and none of the premarital play which might be necessary to stimulate the female Guppy was observed, and consequently no offspring from either cross was found. Some petshops offer these fishes as "Mosquito Fish" . . . and they truly are . . . but *Gambusia* and *Heterandria* seem to have claimed that name.

GNATHONEMUS MACROLEPIDOTUS (Peters)/*Scaly Mormyrid*

Range: Southeastern Africa.

Habits: Nocturnal; remains hidden during daylight hours and comes out to feed at night. Peaceful.

Water Conditions: A well-planted tank with shady spots and a number of hiding-places is a necessity.

Size: To 10 inches.

Food Requirements: Mouth is tiny, and only the smallest of live foods can be taken. Also nibbles at dead plants.

Color Variations: Olive-gray to brownish, lighter toward the belly.

The African Mormyrids, of which this is one, are not very satisfactory aquarium fishes. True, they are very odd in appearance and are peaceful by nature. But put one of them in a well-planted tank and you'll only get an occasional glimpse of him! They are shy and retiring in bright light, which is consistent with their nocturnal nature. If there are places to hide, your Mormyrid will find them and his dark colors will blend into the shadows until he is all but invisible. There he will stay until darkness approaches, which is the signal for him to come out and begin to hunt for worms or whatever else he can find on the bottom. The mouth opening is very small, and only the smallest live foods can be swallowed. Tubifex worms are especially relished. There are no known outward sex differences and this odd fish has never been spawned to our knowledge. An aquarium in which Mormyrids are kept should be provided with a good number of shady spots and retreats among the rocks in which these fish may hide during bright daylight. If Mormyrids are kept in company with other fishes, it is best to put in a feeding toward dusk to ensure their getting their share of food.

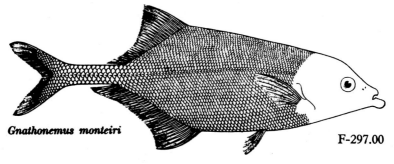

Gnathonemus monteiri

F-297.00

GNATHONEMUS TAMANDUA (Poll)/*The Worm-jawed Mormyrid*

Range: Congo River in the vicinity of the Stanley Pool, Leopoldville, Congo.
Habits: Inhabits quiet pools which have bottoms covered with fallen logs and trees. This is a very sensitive fish which prefers privacy, quiet and darkness.
Water Conditions: Prefers warm water at a temperature of about 80°F. with a pH of 7.2 and as soft as possible.
Size: Known from only a few dozen imported specimens which were under 8 inches.
Food Requirements: A true bottom-feeding scavenger which eats worms, pelletized dry foods and frozen brine shrimp.
Color Variations: The color pattern of this fish is basically constant with many minor variations from individual to individual.

Go to any small lake or pool in Africa and find yourself a pile of logs, rocks, mudholes or fallen branches and you are almost certain to find one of the Mormyrids. There are at least one hundred different members of this very interesting family. All have highly specialized mouths and most have dorsal and anal fins which are set back on the lower third of the body. Most have a thin caudal peduncle and have the general body shape of a submarine. They are very delicate fish and do best in an aquarium which has been set up and designed especially for them. Their aquarium requires a minimum of light and a maximum of privacy. Their diet should be substantially augmented with *Tubifex* worms and frozen brine shrimp. Feeding is one of the major problems in keeping this fish. In the 1950's and early 1960's, Pierre Brichard, working out of Leopoldville, Belgian Congo, shipped thousands of this species along with other mormyrids to Europe and the United States. Most of them arrived dead. The author (HRA) visited Brichard and fished with him. Brichard is a master fish collector but a terrible aquarist. He couldn't keep the fishes alive after he caught them since he didn't have the proper foods. Imagine feeding these fish ground coconuts?? Dry food doesn't serve these fish too well and the only way the world had a fair chance of seeing these fish was if Brichard and the other African collectors shipped them within a few days of their having been collected.

*GOBIOCHROMIS TINANTI (Boulenger)/*Dwarf African Cichlid*

Range: Central Africa, especially the Congo.

Habits: A bottom dweller that spends most of its time in hiding.

Water Conditions: Prefers water that is warm (80°F.) and neutral. The closer to 7.0 and a hardness of 3 degrees, the better.

Size: A maximum size of 6 inches is rare.

Food Requirements: Will only eat live foods, though some pelletized dried foods and frozen brine shrimp serve well.

Color Variations: This is primarily a colorless group of fishes.

The Dwarf Cichlids from Africa have been noticeably lacking in their number. In South America there are hundreds, if not thousands of species of Cichlids to be found, from the very tiny to the huge *Cichla ocellaris*. In Africa, aside from the *Tilapia*, there are a great variety of Cichlids, but only a few from each genus (see the TFH booklet entitled AFRICAN CICHLIDS, which lists a hundred species and illustrates many in full color).

The only claim to fame that this fish has is that it is one of the first of the fishes which were supposedly to have come from Lake Tanganyika which was so easy to breed and had such interesting breeding habits. Interesting, perhaps, for the beginning aquarists, but not so for the advanced aquarist.

To breed *Gobiochromis* set up a 10- or 15-gallon aquarium in which you have about 4 inches of gravel and a few flowerpots lying over on their sides. Chances are that the pair will select one of the flowerpots and spawn inside it. Some may even spawn on the inside top of the flowerpot, but you never can be certain of exactly where they will take a fancy to spawn.

*This fish is now known as *Leptotilapia tinanti*.

F-299.00

GOBIUS SADANUNDIO (Hamilton)/*The Knight Goby*

Range: Indonesia, Burma, Indochina, India and the Philippines.
Habits: A bottom dwelling fish which requires live food or it begins eating fishes half its own size. Will take frozen brine shrimp as a substitute.
Water Conditions: Originally from brackish water areas, this fish is not at home in soft water conditions. Add salt to the water, at least one tablespoon for 2 gallons.
Size: Up to about $3\frac{1}{2}$ inches.
Food Requirements: Must have copious feedings of live foods, preferably worms. Frozen brine shrimp is eagerly taken once the fish has become accustomed to it.
Color Variations: Not a very colorful fish; the black markings are extremely variable.

Many writers place this fish in the genus *Stigmatogobius* and were it very significant, the authors would have delved more deeply into the proper taxonomic position of this fish. But to the aquarium trade, the name *Gobius sadanundio* is very meaningful and the same fish under another name would not sell at all. No one knows for sure why this fish has become so popular that it should be flown all the way from the Middle East to the United States. No one knows why it sells so well and for so much money. There are many more beautiful Gobys, such as the Bumblebee Goby, but this seems to be a perennial favorite. They are hard to keep in good health without proper feedings of worms and they require at least 10% of their water to be sea water or a fair substitute thereof. When all is said and done they will probably jump out of the tank and dry out on your living room rug, but people still buy them. Perhaps you can find a reason for this fish being a member of your community tank, where, if you don't feed him, he'll start chewing on fishes about half his own size.

F-300.00

GYMNOCORYMBUS TERNETZI (Boulenger)/*Black Tetra*

Range: Paraguay and Rio Guaporé Basins in Southern Brazil, Argentina and Bolivia.
Habits: A fast moving fish which is responsible for some fin nipping but it cannot do real damage to fishes larger than itself.
Water Conditions: This is not a warm water fish as so many people think. It does best in temperatures in the upper 60's and very low 70's.
Size: In Nature specimens as large as 3 inches are found; tank raised specimens rarely grow larger than 1½ inches.
Food Requirements: This fish requires live food to be at its best, but it can live for years with nothing but pelletized dry food and a bit of frozen brine shrimp now and then.
Color Variations: The blacker the specimen the better the fish. The colder the water the blacker the fish. Washed out Black Tetras are probably another species.

This is one of the most popular aquarium fishes and they all came from a few pairs which were imported into the United States in the 1930's from Paraguay and Argentina by Guenther Schott who operated, at that time, the Columbia Aquarium (now defunct). Schott brought in hundreds of thousands of *Corydoras paleatus* from Argentina and once in a while he brought in other fishes of interest. So simple was this fish to breed that every successful breeder had thousands of them. Mr. Victor Scafuro, probably the world's first tropical fish salesman, tells of the time they sold for as high as $10 per pair and that was in the 1930's. Lately their price has been under $1 and they are still very popular, probably because they are so hardy. In the usual aquarium situation, these are the last fish to die.

GYMNOCORYMBUS THAYERI (Eigenmann)/*Black Tetra*

Range: Upper Amazon, Bolivia and Colombia in warmer waters.

Habits: A fast swimming fish which should be well fed at all times if kept in a community aquarium.

Water Conditions: Prefers warmer, softer and more acid waters than its much blacker cousin, *G. ternetzi.*

Size: Not larger than 2 inches.

Food Requirements: Prefers copious feedings of live foods, but does equally well if fed frozen brine shrimp and a varied diet of prepared foods. Some live food should be offered weekly.

Color Variations: A lighter fish than *G. ternetzi.*

Undoubtedly many of the Black Tetras swimming around in aquariums now under the name of *Gymnocorymbus ternetzi* are *G. thayeri*. This fish is much smaller than its cousin, reaching a two inch maximum in nature. This photo shows a fish collected and photographed by Harald Schultz on his 1962 TFH Expedition to Rio Guaporé. This is really an intermediate area for this fish and may represent a new subspecies. Then, too, *ternetzi* is more relatively deep-bodied, the depth going 1.6 into body length while *thayeri* has a length which is twice its depth; thus, this is the real test. Of course, the fish becomes more rounded as it grows older and only fully grown fishes can pass this "test."

Spawning of this species is very simple and it is merely a matter of separating the sexes and finding enough live foods to bring them into the peak of condition. Any live foods can do it, though *Daphnia* and *Tubifex* worms seem to be best. Dry food is eagerly taken but the fish must have some live food if it is to breed successfully.

F-302.00

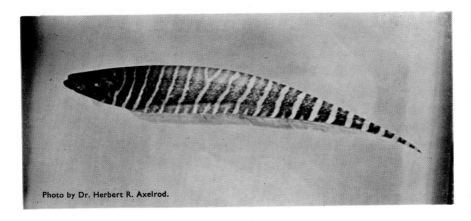

GYMNOTUS CARAPO (Linné)/*Banded Knife Fish*

Range: Guatemala south to the La Plata.
Habits: Mostly nocturnal; a predatory species best kept by itself.
Water Conditions: Not critical; temperatures 76° to 78°.
Size: Is said to attain 23 inches. Imported specimens seldom over 6 inches.
Food Requirements: Pieces of beef-heart, fish or shrimp; prefers small fish above all.
Color Variations: Sides yellowish to reddish, darker toward the back. A series of slanting lighter bars on the sides.

The Knife Fishes are extremely interesting oddities in the aquarium. There is no dorsal fin nor caudal fin; where a fish would normally have a tail, the body simply comes to a point. There are pectoral fins, but they contribute little to the fish's locomotion and simply serve to steer it. It propels itself by means of a rippling motion of the long anal fin. This rippling motion can be reversed instantaneously and the fish can swim backward with the same ease as forward. *Gymnotus carapo* is not adapted for keeping in a community aquarium. Its favorite food is smaller fishes, on which it generally feeds while the tank is in almost complete darkness. These fish do not congregate in schools when in their natural waters; the author saw them caught in British Guiana, and at no time were there more than three or four among a netful of other fishes. There are no known external sex differences, and the species has never been bred in captivity. Once they have become accustomed to their tank, this fish may attain a surprising age, 10 years or more. They were first introduced to aquarists through an importation into Berlin in the year 1910.

GYRINOCHEILUS AYMONIERI (Tirant)
Chinese Algae-Eater

Range: Widely distributed throughout Thailand.
Habits: Small specimens usually peaceful.
Water Conditions: Clean, well-aerated, slightly alkaline water. To promote algal growth, a generous amount of sunlight should enter the tank.
Size: Seldom exceeds 5 inches in the aquarium.
Food Requirements: Vegetarian; grazes on algae much of the time. Will also take dried foods or a piece of crushed lettuce or spinach leaf.
Color Variations: Sides brown, belly light. Dark horizontal line extends from snout to caudal base. A number of indistinct darker bars on the sides.

Whoever got the wild notion of calling this fish the "Chinese Algae-Eater" was far off base. Thailand, its home, is a long ways from China. *Gyrinocheilus aymonieri*, although it has been known to science since 1883, was not imported alive until 1955. In its native waters it attains a length of about 10 inches, but in the aquarium a length of more than half that is unusual. Like many of our Sucker Catfishes, *Gyrinocheilus aymonieri* has an underslung mouth which forms a sucking disc. With this it is able to anchor itself to a rock or some other stationary object in swiftly moving water. There is an unusual thing in connection with this: in addition to the slit behind the gills where the water is exhaled there is another slit which admits fresh water for breathing. The observed respiratory rate is 230 to 240 per minute. This interesting fish is of strictly vegetarian habits, and will do an excellent job of cleaning up algae in a surprisingly short time. If no algae are available, a crushed lettuce or spinach leaf will do nicely. So far nothing is known of their reproductive habits. Rostral tubercles are developed by both sexes at a length of about 4 inches.

HAPLOCHROMIS BURTONI (Günther)/*Burton's Nigerian Mouthbreeder*

Range: Probably Nigeria.
Habits: Usually too aggressive to be kept with smaller fishes. Should have a tank of their own.
Water Conditions: Neutral to slightly acid; Temperature 76 to 78°.
Size: About 4 inches; females slightly smaller.
Food Requirements: A greedy eater; some vegetable substances should be given besides the usual live or frozen foods.
Color Variations: Body steel blue with lighter markings; dorsal and caudal fins blue with red spots, anal has a row of large orange spots.

The two species *Haplochromis burtoni* and *Haplochromis wingati* are so similar that no doubt both have been offered as "Nigerian Mouthbreeders." A comparison of this species and *H. wingati* will show the similarity, and the difference may be seen by comparing the anal fins. That of *H. wingati* has small orange spots, while this one has spots which are considerably more pronounced. A German scientist, Dr. Wolfgang Wickler, has made a very interesting observation about the function of these spots. The female turns around and picks up the eggs almost as soon as she lays them. When she has a mouthful of eggs the male spreads his orange-spotted anal fin on the bottom in front of her. The spots resemble more eggs and she pecks busily at his fin, trying to pick up the spots. As she does this he releases his sperm, which mixes thoroughly with the eggs in her mouth. The question still remains to be answered whether *H. wingati* has smaller eggs which are matched by the smaller spots, and does Mother Nature use the same trickery? The writer has had *H. wingati* spawn for him on frequent occasions, but never made close enough observations to give a definite answer.

Photo by H.J. Richter

⋆ **HAPLOCHROMIS MULTICOLOR** (Hilgendorf)
Dwarf Egyptian Mouthbreeder

Range: All over eastern Africa south to the lower Nile.
Habits: Fairly safe in the community aquarium.
Water Conditions: Not critical, temperatures between 75 and 80°.
Size: Males to 3 inches, females slightly smaller.
Food Requirements: Live and frozen foods preferred; dry foods are taken, but the fish do not do as well.
Color Variations: Most of the color is in the fins: anal fin of the male is tipped with red, and the other unpaired fins have rows of pretty dots.

One of the most unusual and intriguing methods of reproduction is that of the mouthbreeding Cichlid species. *Haplochromis multicolor* is the smallest of the group and also the most usually available, and it is with this species that the hobbyist usually makes his first acquaintance. The actual egg-laying is frequently missed, and their owner is unaware that there was a spawning ⋆This fish is now known as *Hemihaplochromis multicolor*.

F-306.00

A pair of Egyptian mouthbreeders.

This female Egyptian Mouthbreeder   exhibits the typically distended jaw and mouth area and sunken belly of the female Egyptian Mouthbreeder that has been orally incubating eggs for a protracted period.

F-307.00

Fry are visible to the rear of this female Egyptian Mouthbrooder.

until he observes the bulging throat of one of the females. Here is what happens: the male digs a shallow hole, usually in an out-of-the-way corner. This done, he coaxes and almost forces the female to join him in the hole, and eventually 30 to 80 eggs are laid. The female then picks up the eggs in her mouth, which is made more capacious by the presence of a sac in the throat region. Here the eggs remain for 10 days until they begin to hatch, constantly provided with circulating water by the breathing motion of the mother, and constantly moved around by a sort of chewing motion. When the fry hatch, they are faithfully guarded by the mother; if danger threatens, she opens her big mouth and lets the little ones swim inside, where they are packed in like sardines in a can.

This attractive little fish, usually in good supply and available at very reasonable prices, is a very good species for hobbyists who want to breed and raise Cichlids. They lack the size of the mouthbreeding *Tilapia* species and the nasty temperament of some of the mouthbreeding Lake Malawi cichlids and are therefore more easily accommodated by hobbyists who can't provide large tanks or separate quarters for quarrelsome species. The ease of breeding and raising at least a few of the fry to adult size makes them an excellent choice for examination of the spawning habits of mouthbreeding species.

Photo by Dr. Herbert R. Axelrod.

HAPLOCHROMIS WINGATI (Cadenat)
Nigerian Mouthbreeder

Range: Kano, Nigeria.
Habits: Usually too aggressive to be kept with any of the smaller fishes; should have a tank of its own.
Water Conditions: Not critical; best conditions seem to be water of a slightly acid character. Temperature 76 to 78°.
Size: Males about 4 inches, females slightly smaller.
Food Requirements: Besides the usual carnivorous diet given to Cichlids, there should also be some vegetable food offered, such as lettuce leaf.
Color Variations: Males have a steel-blue body with dark vertical markings; anal fin has a row of brilliant orange spots. Females are duller.

The author has good reason to remember the day when this gorgeous Mouthbreeder probably made its first entrance into the country. There was an African shipment and its recipient was leaving on a business trip; the author and another hobbyist were asked to divide the shipment and take care of it. We got the entire thing split up between us and there finally remained three small immature nondescript silvery fish which were obviously a Cichlid species of some kind. Because we feared that they might be a large *Tilapia* species, neither of us wanted these fish particularly. Finally the author consented to take them along with him; they grew rapidly and in no time at all turned out to be the most beautiful fish in the entire lot! *Haplochromis wingati* is apt to be very aggressive at times, but its beautiful colors richly warrant giving it a tank of its own. Spawnings are frequent and conform to the pattern of the Dwarf Egyptian Mouthbreeder. A fully-grown male of this species seen with the sunlight coming from behind the viewer is a gorgeous sight, rivalling in color many of the most beautiful African Cichlids. Some vegetable matter should be included with their food.

A pair of Kissing Gouramis in the act of kissing. So far as is known, there is no sexual explanation for this act as even young, sexually immature fish will indulge in it from time to time.

HELOSTOMA RUDOLFI (Machan)/*Kissing Gourami*

Range: Sumatra, Borneo, Java, Malaya and Thailand.
Habits: Likes plenty of space and a sunny tank. All but the largest individuals get along with other fishes very well.
Water Conditions: Not critical. Likes a warm tank, 78° to 85°.
Size: Reaches a length of 10 inches, but usually smaller.
Food Requirements: A greedy eater; loves to graze on algae on plants and glass sides, but this is only an appetizer; should be generously fed with live or frozen foods several times daily.
Color Variations: Entire body pink to yellowish.

People never seem to tire of the spectacle of a pair of these fish going through their "kissing" antics. It is very comical to watch two of them face each other, then pucker their thick, rubbery lips and press them against each other's, being very careful to make them meet squarely. Whether this is just a game with them is a question which has been argued pro and con, but it seems that as they seem to perform this strange (for a fish!) ritual less and less as they get older. For many years this fish was known as *Helostoma temminckii*, but the fact is that we seldom ever see the real *H. temminckii*, which is greenish in color and has a dark stripe in the dorsal and anal fins. *H. rudolfi* was thought to be an albinistic form, but was later established as a distinct species. *H. rudolfi* has become so popular that most aquarists have never seen the real *H. temminckii*. Both have similar breeding habits: the male builds a sloppy bubble-nest, which soon falls apart. It is not needed in any case; the eggs float, and may number up to a thousand or more. The fry hatch in 48 hours and also float until they have absorbed their yolk-sac.

Photo by Dr. Herbert R. Axelrod.

HELOSTOMA TEMMINCKII (Cuvier and Valenciennes)/*Green Kisser*

Range: Thailand, Indonesia, Sumatra, Borneo, Java, Malay Peninsula and Cambodia.

Habits: Prefer a large aquarium. Plants are not necessary though they do enjoy "chomping" on them to remove whatever has fallen onto them or grown over them. They are a very easily overcrowded fish and unless they are given plenty of room their growth is stunted and they develop a "hollow belly" and die.

Water Conditions: The water conditions are not critical, but they do much better in slightly hard water with a pH of 7.0 and a temperature in the 80's.

Size: Up to one foot long.

Food Requirements: A greedy eater which never tires looking for food. The·r major diet should consist of frozen brine shrimp and worms now and then. They seem to get along very well on salmon eggs (the dried prepared form available as a fish food) and shredded shrimp, though this usually fouls the water.

Color Variations: This is the wild, green form. It is doubtful whether *H. rudolfi*, the pink Kissing Gourami ever existed in Nature. The author (HRA) never heard of a pink variety having been found in Java as the literature claims. This is still doubtful, and it is possible that the pink variety was developed as a sport from some tank-raised stock, while this present variety is the true species. But, unfortunately, it's always easier to prove that a certain fish does exist in an area than to prove that it does not, and as time goes on it will be even more difficult as cities and modern technology push back the frontier, killing fishes and birds with it.

The species illustrated is what the trade calls the Green Kisser. It is far from the fish which Dr. Hugh M. Smith describes from Thailand as "Fish as long as 10 to 12 cm (4 to 5 inches) from Bung Borapet proved very attractive in small balanced aquaria in Bangkok. The general bright silvery skin is relieved by vertical black bars on the head, black longitudinal stripes on the body following rows of scales, a black vertical band at the base of the caudal fin, and black spinous dorsal and anal fins." About all this species illustrated has is the "black vertical band at the base of the caudal fin." The author has seen hundreds of the above species . . . is there still another ?

F-312.00

HEMIANCISTRUS NICEFORDI (Fowler)/*Clown Sucker Catfish*

Range: Upper Amazon and Colombia.
Habits: A typical Sucker Catfish of the "Plecostomus" type. It likes to loaf about the bottom or attach itself to the glass front on the aquarium.
Water Conditions: Not sensitive to water conditions as long as the water is warm (over 76°F.) and not too hard or alkaline. Tolerates a pH of 6.0 to 7.0 and water less than 15 DH.
Size: Up to 10 inches, though only a few dozen specimens have been collected.
Food Requirements: As a scavenger, it doesn't require too much in the way of live foods, but it does like plenty of frozen brine shrimp and pellet type dry foods.
Color Variations: The spots are lighter or darker on various individuals to be found.

What a beautiful fish this is! When Fowler first described it in 1943 in the Proceedings of the Academy of Natural Sciences of Philadelphia, from a specimen collected in the city of Florencia on the Rio Orteguasa, Colombia he couldn't believe that such a fish existed. How often had he heard tales of a "Brick Red Plecostomus"? But this was a scientific report by a famous ichthyologist. Then, nearly 20 years later, Harald Schultz, on a TFH expedition (TFH are the initials for "Tropical Fish Hobbyist Magazine"), found the fish again and photographed it for the files and records of TFH. Here it is. It has never been brought alive into the United States and it is doubtful that any living specimens ever found their way into any aquarium prior to 1962. New methods of collecting and storing fishes found way out in the wilderness will help bring some of these rare beauties into the home and then this fish, along with other rarities, will be more plentiful in your petshop.

HEMIANCISTRUS VITTATUS (Steindachner)/*Striped Sucker*

Range: The Amazon and the Rio Paraguay.

Habits: A typical bottom feeder which spends most of its time loafing about the bottom of the aquarium, chomping on plant leaves trying to get every bit of algae growth from it. Shy and spends much time hiding.

Water Conditions: Prefers water a bit on the cool side in the neighborhood of 70°F.

Size: Up to 9 inches long, but known from only a few specimens.

Food Requirements: Does very well on frozen brine shrimp and pellet foods. Should be offered some *Tubifex* worms now and then.

Color Varieties: As the fish gets older the black bands get heavier and more definite in their color pattern.

In 1882 Steindachner described this fish as *Chaetostomus vittatus* in a Viennese scientific journal. He listed the exact location of the type as coming from the Amazon, with other specimens coming from the Tajapuru, Rio Xingu no Porto do Moz and the Rio Madeira. Throughout its history since that time it has had various names. Eigenmann and Eigenmann in 1889 called it *Hemiancistrus vittatus*; Regan, in 1904, put it into the genus *Ancistrus*; Ribeiro and Gosline, individually, called it *Peckoltia vittata*. The authors feel that this designation is as correct as possible.

It is one of the more attractive Catfishes, but there doesn't seem to be enough of them in any one place to warrant an all-out collecting trip for them. They will probably continually come into this country a few at a time, but as soon as helicopters are available in quantity to help fish collecting, this is one of those fish which will most benefit.

HEMIBRYCON TRIDENS (Eigenmann)/*Jumping Anchovy*

Range: Upper Amazon and Peru.

Habits: A school fish which jumps from the water to catch flying insects. Very peaceful but requires a large tank with a great deal of swimming space.

Water Conditions: Prefers moving water, or water that is heavily agitated. Temperature should be 78°F. and the softer the better. A pH of 6.6 is best.

Size: Up to 5 inches.

Food Requirements: Prefers live food such as the wingless *Drosophila* flies which can be sprinkled onto the surface of the tank, but they do well on dried foods and frozen brine shrimp.

Color Variations: Some specimens have more or less red in the tail.

Imagine a beautiful babbling brook just near a small waterfall on the outskirts of Manaos, Brazil. It is a hot day and you have just finished your day's collecting work and have taken a shower under the waterfall. You sit down to rest, light your pipe and watch the fish springing from the water after flying insects. Suddenly you realize that you are there to catch fish, not smoke pipes, and you net some of these beautiful flashes of silver. Impatiently you put them into the photo tank where you can better observe them and figure out what kind of fish they are. That's how this photo found its way to the top of this page! Dramatic? No! But that's about the most exciting thing I can write about them, for they died immediately after I (HRA) removed them from the photo tank and they only lived in large tanks without overcrowding and only with heavy aeration. This importation of this species is very unlikely unless the new "sleeping" drugs help them.

HEMICHROMIS BIMACULATUS (Gill)
Jewel Cichlid

Range: Widely distributed throughout tropical Africa.
Habits: Besides being very pugnacious, it has the nasty habit of digging up plants.
Water Conditions: Not critical; temperatures should be quite high, about 80°.
Size: To about 6 inches, usually smaller.
Food Requirements: Live foods preferred, frozen foods accepted.
Color Variations: Sides greenish yellow with two large dark spots. At breeding time body turns bright red with many blue dots.

It is strange that such a nasty, pugnacious Cichlid species as the Jewel Cichlid is one of the most docile and devoted of parents. If it were not for their mean disposition, this beauty would certainly be one of the most popular of the Cichlid group. The body colors of both sexes undergo quite a change when the time for breeding comes. The sides, which normally are a yellowish green, take on an intense red hue, sprinkled with gleaming blue dots, which no doubt gives rise to the popular name. Once they begin spawning their owner may soon be faced with a problem; namely, what to do with all the young Jewel Cichlids which everybody seems to admire but nobody wants. Once a pair has mated, there is seldom any trouble with them afterwards, but selecting a well-mated pair sometimes presents a problem. If you get a male that is ready to spawn and a female that is not, very often the result is a dead or mangled female. Always make sure that when a pair is introduced into a tank there is plenty of refuge such as rocks and plant thickets. A flowerpot placed in a dark corner will usually be the preferred site for spawning, which takes place in the usual Cichlid manner.

HEMICHROMIS FASCIATUS (Peters)/*Five-Spotted Hemichromis*

Range: West Africa, widely distributed from Senegambia to the Congo.
Habits: Very quarrelsome towards other fishes. Should be kept by themselves.
Water Conditions: Occurs in both fresh and brackish waters. In the aquarium they adapt to any water condition.
Size: Fully grown, about 12 inches.
Food Requirements: Will consume any unwanted fish, or will settle for chunks of fish or beef heart.
Color Variations: Sides yellowish in younger specimens, becoming bronze colored as the fish matures. Five large spots on the sides.

Some hobbyists like nasty fishes, and choose a fish like this with the full knowledge of what they are getting; others buy a fish without realizing how big it will get, and buy them more or less blindly. A fish like this will prove a disappointment to those people, and they soon realize that the bigger they get, the nastier. Many breeders keep a few of these as a sort of "garbage can with fins" which will eat any and every unwanted fish. The five large spots on the sides often turn into bands, and when they decide to go about spawning, a startling transformation in color takes place: the entire body becomes suffused with blood-red, the bands become deep black and the dorsal fin develops stripes of red, yellow and white. Sexes are difficult to distinguish; males have slightly more pointed dorsal and anal fins. As with many other Cichlids, at breeding time the spawning tubes show a distinct difference when extended. The female's is wide and blunt, and the male's is pointed. Like most vicious Cichlids, these make very devoted parents. A great many eggs are usually laid on a rock, and carefully guarded. The parents stay with the young until they are ready to spawn again. Axelrod discovered they love to sleep in old auto tires in the Congo River.

HEMIGRAMMUS ARMSTRONGI (Schultz & Axelrod)
Gold Tetra

Range: British Guiana.
Habits: Peaceful; prefers to be kept in a school.
Water Conditions: Not critical, but water should be somewheres near neutral.
Size: About 1¾ inches.
Food Requirements: Live foods preferred, but frozen and prepared foods are also readily accepted.
Color Variations: Body gleaming gold, with a small black spot on the caudal base. Above and below this spot there are tiny red areas.

The Gold Tetra is a fish which looks as if it were sprayed with gold paint all over the body. A large, well-planted tank with a school of these very attractive fish constantly and playfully on the move needs little else to recommend it. When the author visited British Guiana, he was told that this fish was very common in the drainage ditches around the sugar fields and rice paddies just outside of Georgetown. There is a peculiar thing about this little beauty: they do not lose their color in captivity, and they breed readily. But the offspring do not have the golden color! In their native waters, they are always golden. This will be an interesting subject for experimentation, and, when the answer is found, another step ahead will be taken in man's knowledge of fishes and what the causative factors are concerning their coloration. It may put us one step further along the road to knowing how to restore the lovely colors with which many fishes are so generously endowed in their native waters, and which fade when the fish is transferred to the aquarium. Although the ones bred in captivity have no gold color, they tend to get more red in the fins.

F-318.00

HEMIGRAMMUS CAUDOVITTATUS (Ahl)/*Buenos Aires Tetra*

Range: Region around Buenos Aires.

Habits: Fairly peaceful with fishes about its size; should not be kept with thread-finned fishes, whose fins it nips.

Water Conditions: Neutral to slightly acid. Can withstand temperatures around 70° for a time. Should be kept about 76° normally.

Size: About 4 inches.

Food Requirements: Seems to like dried foods as well as live foods; has a good appetite and should be fed generously.

Color Variations: Sides metallic silver with a lighter lateral line. Diamond-shaped black spot at caudal base. Fins are reddish.

This is one of the most easily-kept of the Tetra family. Being a rather large species, one of the requirements is a tank which will give them a generous amount of swimming-room. Another requirement is a generous amount of food. Lacking this, they are likely to take a few mouthfuls out of the plants. Another habit which is not exactly to their credit is their habit of attacking an Angelfish or Gourami and trimming its fins down to stubs. This is not viciousness on their part, just hunger. When properly and generously fed, they will not resort to these antics. Coming as they do from semi-tropical Buenos Aires, aquarium temperatures need not be very high. They will be quite comfortable in the low 70's, and around 76° they will usually exhibit a willingness to spawn. A bunch of bushy plants should be placed at one end of the tank, and about one-fourth of the water drained off and replaced with fresh water. The pair is best separated for a day or two and well fed. When placed in the breeding tank they will soon begin to drive and scatter a large number of eggs all over. These hatch in about 72 hours, and the fry are easily raised.

HEMIGRAMMUS GRACILIS (Reinhardt)/*Glowlight Tetra*

Range: The Guianas and adjacent regions of the Amazon.
Habits: One of the most peaceful of all Tetras.
Water Conditions: Should have a clean aquarium at all times, with slightly acid, soft water.
Size: About 2 inches maximum, usually a bit smaller.
Food Requirements: Will eat dry food, but this should often be augmented with live and frozen foods.
Color Variations: Body greenish and very transparent, with a brilliant, glowing red or purple line running from the upper edge of the eye to the caudal base.

The early and middle 1930's brought fish hobbyists two of the most beautiful aquarium fishes. One was the Neon Tetra, and the other was the Glowlight Tetra. To show off the Glowlight Tetra to its best advantage, some pains must be taken to provide it with its proper setting. The bottom should be covered with black gravel, and nicely planted. A moderate light should come from above. All that needs to be done then is to place our little jewels in their setting and wait a few hours for them to get used to their surroundings. A dozen or more swimming about in a school will make the most hardened fish fancier sit up and take notice. From the time of its introduction there has been a great amount of confusion as to the proper name for this fish. For a time it was long known incorrectly as *Hemigrammus erythryzonus,* a name which rightfully belongs to another fish which is not nearly as beautiful. In 1955 Dr. Leonard P. Schultz set things straight, but to this day many books still refer to it by a number of incorrect names. Breeding should not be attempted with fish which are less than 15 months old. The young are very small and should be fed on infusoria for at least one week.

F-320.00

HEMIGRAMMUS HYANUARY (Eigenmann)/*January Tetra*

Range: Amazon tributaries near Leticia, Colombia.

Habits: Very peaceful; prefers to be in a school with others of its own kind.

Water Conditions: Not critical; best is water which is neutral to slightly acid in character.

Size: About 1½ inches.

Food Requirements: Live or frozen foods are of course preferred, but dried foods are also accepted eagerly.

Color Variations: Body greenish to olive above, belly white. Golden line runs from gill-plate to caudal base, and a black spot covers lower half of caudal rays.

The January Tetra is a fish which is not regularly imported into this country, and most of the specimens we get to see have become inadvertently mixed in with shipments of such gaudy fishes as Neon Tetras or Cardinal Tetras. These are often collected when very small, and weeding out all the unwanted specimens from a shipment of less than half-grown fish is almost an impossibility. Overlooking its lack of colors, the January Tetra is an attractive fellow with peaceful habits who will never harm your other fishes or plants. Their small claim to colors lies in a horizontal golden stripe and a good-sized squarish black spot in the lower half of the middle caudal rays. Males have a black adipose fin, as can be seen in the lower two fish shown in the picture. The fact that they are hardy is fairly obvious to anyone who has ever kept them. We have had some in our office tanks for almost two years, where they have been thriving even without special treatment. Probably the reader is wondering why this fish is called the January Tetra. The original specimens were collected in a place called Lake January by the great ichthyologist Eigenmann in 1918.

F-321.00

HEMIGRAMMUS OCELLIFER (Steindachner)/*Head and Tail Light*

Range: Widely distributed throughout the Amazon region, especially in the southern part.

Habits: Mostly peaceful, if kept with fish their own size.

Water Conditions: Not critical, but warm temperatures are preferred. A temperature of 78° to 80° should be maintained.

Size: About 1½ inches.

Food Requirements: Will get along very well on dry foods when live foods are lacking.

Color Variations: Body silvery greenish. First dorsal, anal and caudal rays white at the tips. Upper half of eye and upper half of caudal base golden.

This popular Tetra has become a favorite among hobbyists since the first ones were introduced into the United States in the early 1930's. It has much in its favor: it is peaceful, does not get too large, will not chew plants, and will gratefully accept almost anything in the way of food which is offered. Add to these qualities the fact that it is attractive and easily bred, and there is no mystery as to the reason for its popularity. This fish should not be kept singly or in pairs. A small school of at least six in a roomy aquarium which is lighted from above will show up best; here we are able to see the gleaming spot of gold in the upper half of the eye and at the base of the tail flashing as the fish move always busily about in the open portions of the aquarium. Males are distinguished by their longer, more slender bodies and also a thin streak which runs horizontally across the anal fin. A breeding tank of about 8 gallons should be provided, with a layer of glass marbles on the bottom. Water temperature about 78°, pH about 6.5 and hardness about 5 degrees. Given these conditions, the fish will spawn readily and often.

HEMIGRAMMUS PULCHER (Ladiges)/*Garnet Tetra*

Range: Peruvian Amazon, Loreto region.
Habits: Peaceful; will not bother plants or other fish.
Water Conditions: Prefers a roomy, well-planted tank. Most important requirement
  is warmth, 78° to 80°.
Size: About 1¾ inches.
Food Requirements: Will not refuse dried foods, but should be given frequent
  changes to live or frozen foods.
Color Variations: Greenish body, with a small shoulder-spot and indistinct hori-
  zontal line. Upper half of caudal base deep red, with black area below.

Because it resembled the *Rasbora heteromorpha* in body form and had a
large black spot in the after end of the body, this fish was known for a time as
the "poor man's Rasbora." As so often happens with some names, the
situation has become reversed and the Rasbora has dropped considerably in
price since the days when the Garnet Tetra first made its appearance in 1938,
and at the present time there are not very many Garnet Tetras on hand.
Therefore one will usually find that the Garnet Tetra commands a higher
price. Notwithstanding, it is a very attractive little fish and a small group of
them will make a beautiful appearance in any tank. One of the few things
which can be said against them is that they are slightly sensitive to disease
if their aquarium is allowed to drop in temperature. Given a good thermostatic heater which will keep the water at a constant 78° to 80°, they will put
on their most glowing colors. Males and females are equally beautiful, and
the females are distinguished by their stockier build and slightly deeper
bellies. Not a ready spawner, but patience and good feeding will sometimes
be rewarded.

F-323.00

HEMIGRAMMUS RHODOSTOMUS (Ahl)/*Rummy-Nose Tetra*

Range: Lower Amazon region, around Aripiranga and Para.
Habits: Peaceful; is most at home with lively fishes of about its own size.
Water Conditions: Best kept in a well-planted, well-established, well-heated tank. Temperature about 80°.
Size: 1¾ to 2 inches.
Food Requirements: Will get along fairly well on dried food, but should get an occasional meal of live or frozen food.
Color Variations: Body silvery, almost transparent. Nose bright red; tail has large black spot above and below.

To be a good aquarium citizen, a fish should be small, peaceful, nicely colored and not shy. Our friend here is all of these things. When kept in an aquarium which is well established and well planted, a small school of these fish flit around always active and alert, their noses glowing. Take the same group of fish and place them in a bare tank where the temperature is about 76° or lower, and the water is not to their liking; immediately the fish become almost unrecognizable. The nose fades to the palest of pinks, and the black markings on the tail are so indistinct that they can scarcely be seen. This fish has been the despair of many dealers. When they display them in a community aquarium, everybody wants them, and when they fish them out of their stock tanks, the customers quickly decide that they don't want them after all. Often no amount of explaining will convince the customer that once they have spent a few days in an aquarium at home they will be very bit as pretty as the ones in his community aquarium. This fish is one of the more difficult ones to breed, and once accomplished the tiny young are very difficult to raise.

HEMIGRAMMUS ULREYI (Boulenger)/*Tetra ulreyi*

Range: The upper reaches of the Paraguay, where it enters Brazil.

Habits: Peaceful; will not harm plants or other fish.

Water Conditions: Most important thing is temperature, which should be kept from 78° to 80°.

Size: Males about 1½ inches, females about 1¾ inches.

Food Requirements: Will eat dried foods, but should be varied with live or frozen foods.

Color Variations: Body silvery with some transparency. Dark, wedge-shaped line on side gives way to an indistinct horizontal line.

For many years, this fish has gone unrecognized and another one has masqueraded under its name. Finally, the distinction has been made and the other fish which has gone under the name of "*Hemigrammus ulreyi*" for many years has been classified as *Hyphessobrycon heterorhabdus*. Because it was considerably less attractive, *Hemigrammus ulreyi* was not collected. At first the bigger, fatter, less colorful females were not thought to be the same species and were thrown back, with the result that breeders tore their hair out looking for infinitesmal differences and selecting what they thought were pairs and getting no results because they were actually working with two males! As may be seen in the accompanying picture, the fish shown here is a female. The males are considerably smaller and more slender. Another way of sexing them is by a look at the silvery sac which contains the organs, easily discernible by placing a light behind them. The female sac is blunt, and the male's is pointed. Most of the Tetra species can be sexed in this manner, and it is much more reliable than going by outward appearances. According to even the latest works, this species has not yet been bred.

Photo by Dr. Herbert R. Axelrod.

HEMIGRAMMUS UNILINEATUS (Gill)/*Featherfin Tetra*

Range: Trinidad and northern South America from Venezuela to Brazil.
Habits: Peaceful; a heavy eater which should have plenty of swimming room.
Water Conditions: Should have a sunny aquarium with fairly high temperatures, 78° to 80°.
Size: Attains a length of 2 inches; most specimens smaller.
Food Requirements: Like all active fish, a heavy eater. If possible, should be fed several times daily. Will take dried foods, but live foods should also be fed.
Color Variations: Body silvery with a gold horizontal stripe. First rays of the dorsal and anal fins white, with a black streak behind. Brazilian variety has red fins.

This is not one of our most colorful of the Tetras, but the fish enjoys a great popularity nevertheless, because of its ceaseless activity. Besides always being on the go, it is always out where it can be easily seen. One of our old favorites, this fish has been known to aquarium hobbyists since 1910, when it was first imported from Para in Brazil. Since then shipments have also been made from Venezuela and Trinidad, proof of the fish's wide range. Like most of the Tetras, it is best to keep a small school of them. A sunny aquarium with clear water and a temperature of about 78° will have them chasing around all day. Given a tank to themselves a pair, or better yet two males and one female will soon begin driving about madly and depositing eggs all over the bushy plants. When the female begins to hide from the males and egg-hunts are begun and the parents should be immediately removed or there will soon be very few eggs left. A successful spawning may number as many as 500 eggs which hatch in about 60 hours. After 2 to 4 days the fry become free-swimming at which time they may be fed very fine dried food or infusoria. Growth is very rapid under good conditions. The Brazilian variety males have an anal hook.

F-326.00

Two pairs of the Beldt Strain of Featherfins, *Hemigrammus unilineatus.*

*HEMIODUS QUADRIMACULATUS VORDERWINKLERI
(Pellegrin)/*Barred Hemiodus*

Range: British Guiana.
Habits: Peaceful and active; prefers to be kept in groups. A jumper; tank must be kept covered.
Water Conditions: Neutral to slightly alkaline, with good planting and a sunny location.
Size: To almost 5 inches.
Food Requirements: Should be given a good percentage of vegetable foods in addition to the usual live or frozen foods.
Color Variations: Body brownish with a violet shimmer. Three black bands cross the body; caudal peduncle black. Caudal lobes have black edges.

It is the dream of everyone who works with fishes or for that matter any living things, some day to get lasting recognition by having his name appear in a scientific name given to a new species, and the writer feels that having even a subspecies named in his honor is a great distinction accorded to only a few fortunate people. These names stand for hundreds of years, and it is extremely unlikely that the present system of nomenclature will ever be revised. As for the fish, it looks very much like the original *H. quadrimaculatus* described by Eigenmann in his book "The Freshwater Fishes of British Guiana," and at the time of writing we have not yet seen Dr. Gery's paper which makes this subspecies official. Probably there is some slight variation in color; the black area in the subspecies covers the entire caudal peduncle and in the original it covers only the lower half. The black bands seem wider, too. This fish is a very agile jumper and a covered tank is a real necessity. It does well in captivity, and a group in a well-planted tank is a pretty sight with the sun shining on them.

* *Hemiodopsis quadrimaculatus* is probably the correct designation.

F-328.00

*HEMIODUS SEMITAENIATUS (Kner)/*Half-Lined Hemiodus*

Range: The Guianas, middle and lower Amazon and Matto Grosso.
Habits: Very active, should be kept in a covered aquarium to prevent their jumping out. Usually peaceful toward other fishes.
Water Conditions: Water should be clean and clear, other conditions not important, except temperature which should not drop below 76°.
Size: Is said to attain 8 inches; most specimens seen are about half that.
Food Requirements: Will accept dried foods, but is very fond of vegetable matter in its diet, and for this reason is likely to nibble plants.
Color Variations: Body color silvery, back bluish and belly white. Black spot in center of body ends in a horizontal line which passes through lower lobe of tail.

One look at the slender, graceful lines of this fish will tell us that it is a fast, active swimmer. Its large tail will propel it through the water at a rapid enough rate to enable it to leap clear of the surface, and therefore a covered aquarium is a necessity or some day it will be found on the floor. Here is one fish which was often damaged by banging its nose against the hard sides of the old-fashioned shipping cans. The modern methods of shipping largely eliminate this by giving the fish the resilient surface of a plastic bag to bang his nose on, making it almost impossible for the fish to injure itself. In the aquarium, this fish will often live to a ripe age once it has adapted itself to the water, which it does very readily. Their one drawback is that they require a certain amount of vegetable matter in their diet, which they will take by nibbling plants. This, of course, can be eliminated by not planting the aquarium into which they are placed, and feeding them an occasional spinach leaf or lettuce leaf. They will sometimes disturb the quieter fishes with their great activity, but do not harm them otherwise. There are no records of their ever breeding in captivity.

* Now placed in the genus *Hemiodopsis.*

F-329.00

*HERICHTHYS CYANOGUTTATUS (Baird & Girard)
Texas Cichlid

Range: Southern Texas and northern Mexico.

Habits: All the bad Cichlid habits: digs a great deal and uproots plants; usually quarrelsome if kept with other fishes.

Water Conditions: Not critical; not sensitive to temperature drops. Best breeding temperature about 75°.

Size: In native waters up to 12 inches. In captivity seldom exceeds 6 inches.

Food Requirements: Larger specimens require chunks of food, such as cut-up earthworms or pieces of beef-heart or other lean meat.

Color Variations: Body bluish gray, with a number of dark bands in the rear half. Many bluish or greenish spots all over the body.

Most of the larger Cichlids have very little in the way of good qualities, and this one is no exception. One unusual thing which can be said of it is that it is the only Cichlid which is native to the United States waters. It is the northernmost American Cichlid, found as far up as the Rio Grande and some of its tributaries in southern Texas. It is a prolific fish, and very likely to be found in profusion wherever it occurs. There are probably several local names for this fish, but *Texas Cichlid* is the most easily recognized by aquarium hobbyists. Anyone who intended to keep them should provide them with a Texas-size aquarium, 40 gallons or better. Once they have made themselves at home here, a pair may some day begin digging holes all over the place. Once the surroundings are bare enough for their satisfaction, they usually select a flat stone and begin to clean it carefully and meticulously. Then the female, after acting coy for a while, will allow herself to be coaxed to the stone and will deposit 500 eggs or more on it, closely followed by the male who sprays them with his sperm. The fry hatch in 5 to 7 days

*The name of this species has been changed to *Cichlasoma cyanoguttatum*.

HOLOBRYCON PESU (Mueller & Troschel)/*Mourning Tetra*

Range: Amazon River system and the Guianas.

Habits: A beautiful school fish which can grace every large community aquarium with its fast moving, darting action and its voracious appetite.

Water Conditions: Not very sensitive to the water in which it is kept as long as the temperature ranges between 75 and 85°F. It tolerates salt, but does better in soft, acid water with a pH of 6.6.

Size: Under 4 inches.

Food Requirements: Though it does better on a weekly ration of live foods, it has been kept for a year without anything but frozen brine shrimp and dry food.

Color Variations: As the fish gets older, the black edge on the tail gradually fades and the intense black on the adipose gradually covers the whole adipose.

There are some fishes which never become popular because they are so easy to get and so hardy that they are inexpensive. If this fish came from the Congo or from Australia it would be a very popular fish because its sides are gleaming silver with a reddish blue cast and its adipose fin is stark black, contrasting beautifully with its black-edged tail. This black "outergarb" is what suggested the name "Mourning Tetra" to the author (HRA). Perhaps with a popular name, the fish might achieve the popularity it deserves. A 50-gallon aquarium filled with about 60 of these fish, three inches long and with the Gro-lux lighting to catch the highlight of the red in the eye and to deepen the reddish blue cast, is a breathtaking sight, especially if the tank has a black background. This is one fish you will see more of as time goes by.

HOPLOSTERNUM LITTORALE (Hancock)/*Cascudo, Hoplo*

Range: Brazil, Peru, Bolivia, Paraguay, Argentina, Trinidad, Guianas and Venezuela.
Habits: A bottom swimming fish which comes to the surface for air every few minutes. It is as peaceful as any fish this size.
Water Conditions: It prefers soft, acid water, but is found in all kinds of water. Temperatures of the water are not important as in nature it is found in water which varies in temperature from freezing to 90°F.
Size: To 8 inches.
Food Requirements: Since the fish is so easy to spawn, it must be fed properly to insure spawning success. It will eat any food that other fishes can eat. Frozen brine shrimp and *Tubifex* worms bring it into condition fastest.
Color Variations: A variety with isolated black spots is another species.

When this fish first came to be known to aquarists, and that was very early, since the fish has been known scientifically since 1828, when it was described from the Demerara River in British Guiana, it had a strange fascination because of its unusual breeding habits. The fish would select a spawning site which was usually on a floating leaf or at best a floating log. They would spawn under the leaf and the leaf would float away, the eggs taking as long as two weeks to hatch if they happened to be floating into colder waters. In an aquarium a simple method is to float a soup plate upside down. The pair should be isolated in a bare 20-gallon aquarium and fed heavily. They spawn within a few days if the pair is ready and the female plump. They lay a few hundred eggs and the eggs adhere to the dish. The dish can be removed and the youngsters hatched in the same manner as Angelfish eggs, that is, with the plate tilted against the sides of the tank and with the airstone playing a stream of bubbles against it. A few drops of 5% methylene blue added to the water will keep down the fungus infection. The young are remarkably free swimming immediately after they detach from the glass. They don't take on their Catfish shape for a few weeks, but they do take newly hatched brine shrimp and do best on microworms which they scavenge from the bottom with voracious appetites.

F-332.00

HOPLOSTERNUM THORACATUM (Valenciennes)/*Port Hoplo, Atipa*

Range: Found throughout South America except Uruguay.
Habits: A bottom feeder with the same characteristics as *H. littorale*.
Water Conditions: Same as *H. littorale*.
Size: Up to 6 inches.
Food Requirements: Same as *H. littorale*.
Color Variations: There is extensive variation in the length and thickness of the barbels and the location and intensity of the spots on the body.

There are usually three species of *Hoplosternum* recognized from South America: *littorale*, *shirui* (named for the Brazilian name of the fish given it by the Indians) and *thoracatum*. Some authors claim that there are several subspecies of *H. thoracatum* based upon slight meristic characteristics and the fact that they occur so widely ranged. The present authors take the opinion that they are all one species. They all freely interbreed and the individual differences which have been noted as subspecific characteristics are merely within the tolerances of individual variation within a single spawning family. The third species, *H. shirui* Fowler, was described by Fowler in 1939 from the Rio Ucayali, Contamana, Peru. The fish has no significant differences from the ordinary *littorale* which is so familiar to everyone, and Dr. Gosline even included it as a minor race of *littorale*. For aquaristic purposes there are only two species and they are illustrated here. Both spawn in approximately the same manner, though *littorale* is much easier to induce to spawn than *thoracatum*.

HORADANDIYA ATUKORALI (Brittan)/*Midget Minnow*

Range: Ceylon.

Habits: Peaceful and active; timid in the presence of larger fishes.

Water Conditions: Can take both soft, acid water and hard, alkaline water, as long as extremes are avoided. Temperature 72 to 83°.

Size: 1¼ inches.

Food Requirements: Accepts all foods that are small enough to be swallowed.

Color Variations: Over-all body color plain olive brown, with stripe running along the sides from opercle to base of tail. All fins clear.

A little fish whose size would lead one to the belief that the species is delicate, *Horadandiya atukorali* is really pretty tough and is able to live under conditions that would soon kill off other species. Originally thought to be a *Rasbora* species, this hardy Cyprinid was first brought into the United States by Captain Henri Carpender, a sea captain who was able to purchase or trade for new fishes during his many voyages around the world. The Midget Minnow spawns by laying adhesive eggs in plant thickets; the eggs, as is to be expected from the size of the parents, are very small. The newly hatched fry are also very small, and they therefore require feedings of infusoria, as they are unable to swallow brine shrimp nauplii during the first days of their life. *Horadandiya atukorali* eggs have a fairly short incubation period (about a day and a half to two days); perhaps it is fair that the fish should be able to begin its free-swimming life comparatively quickly, because it doesn't get a chance to enjoy life very long. They are considered past their prime at an age of one year, and they don't linger too long once they reach this point.

F-334.00

HYPHESSOBRYCON BIFASCIATUS (Ellis)/*Yellow Tetra*

Range: Southeastern Brazil, near the coast.
Habits: Very peaceful; will not attack other fishes or plants.
Water Conditions: Neutral to slightly acid; temperature 72 to 76°.
Size: Up to 2 inches.
Food Requirements: All foods gratefully eaten, prepared as well as live or frozen.
Color Variations: Body lightly yellow, with two dark streaks on the shoulder. Streaks are darker in young fish, and the fins red.

This looks like a larger, yellow version of the Flame Tetra. We do not often see it because there is little collecting done in the regions to which they are native, and besides no collector will ever get rich collecting this species. They are not particularly colorful and the demand for them would be very light. They are extremely hardy in the aquarium and stand up very well even when slightly abused. Young specimens of the Yellow Tetra are considerably prettier than the fully grown ones. Their fins when half-grown are an attractive red and make a nice contrast to the yellow color of the body as well as the two black streaks. As the fish grows older the red leaves the fins completely and the yellow color as well as the black streaks become washed out. This is an easy species to breed. Spawning takes place among bushy plants, and the parents must be removed as soon as the spawning is completed. Eggs hatch the day after they are laid, after which the tiny young can be seen hanging from the glass sides and the plants. Once the yolk-sac is absorbed and they begin to swim, feeding may be begun with very fine foods, to be followed in a few days with newly-hatched brine shrimp.

Photo by S. Frank

HYPHESSOBRYCON CALLISTUS BENTOSI (Durbin)
Bentosi Tetra

Range: Lower Amazon region.

Habits: Peaceful; prefers to be kept in a school of fish its own size or better yet, its own species.

Water Conditions: Soft, slightly acid water preferred, temperature 75 to 78°.

Size: About 1½ inches.

Food Requirements: Prepared foods readily accepted, but live or frozen foods preferred.

Color Variations: Sides reddish, black spot in dorsal. Spot on side which is very plain in some others of the group is only faintly indicated.

There has long been a question as to whether the group to which this fish belongs is composed of a number of distinct species, or if the group is all of the same species with a number of subspecies. In 1954 Hoedeman suggested that six fishes which were until then considered to belong to separate species were actually what is referred to as "the *callistus* group," consisting of six subspecies. There were *Hyphessobrycon callistus bentosi, H. c. callistus, H. c. minor, H. c. serpae, H. c. copelandi* and *H. c. rosaceus.* All the members of this group, and especially *Hyphessobrycon callistus bentosi,* have a beautiful red coloration in their natural waters, much of which leaves them when placed into the confines of an aquarium. It stands to reason that a small fish like this would sense very little feeling of being shut in when placed in a rather large aquarium, so the answer must lie in one of two other factors: water conditions and feeding. Since giving them a wide variety of water conditions has produced no effect, it is safe to assume that our fish are missing something in their diet which would bring back the red color. We still have much to learn about the nutritional requirements of fishes.

Photo by S. Frank.

HYPHESSOBRYCON CALLISTUS CALLISTUS (Boulenger)
Callistus Tetra

Range: Rio Paraguay.

Habits: Peaceful, active. Should have a well-planted tank and be kept in a school of not less than six individuals.

Water Conditions: Fish will show their best colors if the water is slightly acid and very soft. Temperature best around 76°.

Size: About 1½ inches.

Food Requirements: Prepared foods accepted, but to keep them in the best of condition they should get live or frozen foods frequently.

Color Variations: Body red with a black vertical wedge-shaped shoulder spot. Dorsal almost completely black; anal with a black edge.

Hyphessobrycon callistus callistus is probably one of the most misnamed of all aquarium fishes. This is one of the cases where for years a fish is known by a certain accepted name, in this case *Hyphessobrycon serpae*, as was this one. Then later on, after taxonomic investigation, the apple-cart is upset by the announcement that this is not *H. serpae*, but *H. callistus*, and another announcement that the species *bentosi*, *serpae*, *callistus*, *copelandi*, *minor* and *rosaceus* are merely subspecies of *Hyphessobrycon callistus*. Meantime, *Hyphessobrycon callistus serpae*, the real one, has put in an appearance. *H. c. callistus* can be distinguished by the fact that the dorsal fin is almost completely black and that there is a distinct shoulder marking. In *H. c. serpae* black covers only about half the dorsal fin area, with a light area on the upper tip and the rear and bottom edges. The shoulder spot in this species is only faintly indicated. To make matters still more confusing, it is highly probable that breeders have made a complete and utter hodgepodge of things by attempting to get a brighter red in the body by crossing the subspecies.

F-337.00

Photo by S. Frank.

HYPHESSOBRYCON (CALLISTUS) ROSACEUS (Durbin)
Rosy Tetra

Range: Essequibo River, British Guiana.
Habits: Peaceful, should be kept in groups of at least six.
Water Conditions: Soft, slightly acid water is best. Temperature 75 to 80°.
Size: To 2 inches.
Food Requirements: Prepared foods accepted, but live and frozen foods preferred.
Color Variations: Back light brown, sides silvery, belly white. After half of body
has a bright rosy flush. Males have long, black-tipped dorsals, other fins red.

The Rosy Tetra is the largest member of the so-called *"callistus* group." A
handsome fish such as this deserves a few extra pains to bring out its best
colors. To do this, rule number one is to give it a dark background. If your
tank has its back to a wall and gets its light from the front, that is good. If
the front light is sunlight, that is even better. As for the background, paint
the back glass with dark green paint, either the ordinary type or the crackle
finish paint sold for the purpose by most petshops. When this is done, cut
down the glare still further by using black gravel instead of the natural
color. Planting of course should be concentrated in back and on the sides,
with an open area in front center. This done, and of course the other fixtures
attached, the stage is set for the star attraction, a group of Rosy Tetras. Try
this some time; it's well worth the trouble if you have the available space,
and an aquarium like this is the best possible argument against the variegated
clutter of the usual "community" aquarium. A tank with only one species of
fish in it provides something which you will never find with a mixed population: harmony!

Photo by Harald Schultz.

HYPHESSOBRYCON EOS (Durbin)/*Dawn Tetra*

Range: British Guiana.
Habits: Very peaceful; should be kept in a school of not less than six.
Water Conditions: Slightly acid and soft water, temperature 75 to 78°.
Size: To 1¾ inches.
Food Requirements: Prepared foods accepted, but live or frozen foods are preferred.
Color Variations: Coppery to gold body, with a prominent black spot on the caudal base. Fins have a rosy tinge.

Every once in a while the fish world is offered some fish or others which are called "Dawn Tetras," but the real *Hyphessobrycon eos* is one which is seldom seen and about which little is known, in spite of the fact that Durbin named the fish in 1909 and hobbyists saw the first specimens in 1933. Probably the only reason there is so little known about their spawning is not that they are particularly difficult, but that there have been so few specimens to work with. Although it is not one of the "flashy" individuals, it can be readily seen that the Dawn Tetra is far from unattractive, and in a well-planted aquarium it has a quiet beauty all its own. Like the other members of the genus, this beauty becomes most evident when a number of them are kept in a school. This is one of the fishes for which the author kept his eyes peeled while in British Guiana, but none of the waters we fished yielded any of them, nor were any of them among the large variety of fishes which Louis Chung was holding for shipment. We did, however, see a number of *Hyphessobrycon* species which were merely a silvery gray with a black spot on the caudal base. Could we have thrown some back by mistake?

F-339.00

Photo by R. Zukal.

HYPHESSOBRYCON FLAMMEUS (Myers)
Flame Tetra, Red Tetra, Tetra from Rio

Range: Region near Rio de Janeiro.
Habits: Peaceful; best kept with other small fishes and in a school of at least six.
Water Conditions: Not critical; water is best if slightly acid and soft, but this is not absolutely essential.
Size: To 1¼ inches.
Food Requirements: Prepared foods accepted, but live or frozen foods are preferred.
Color Variations: Sides coppery, becoming red in after portion. Two black streaks adorn the sides. Fins bright red, anal of the male edged with black.

The aquarium hobbyist who wishes to try his hand at spawning one of this group is strongly recommended to try the Flame Tetra. Not only is the task an easy one which is usually successful, but the rewards enjoyed later on are well worth the effort. A good-sized, well-planted aquarium which contains a good number of healthy, colorful youngsters is a sight at which even a hard-boiled old-timer will gaze repeatedly. There is nothing shy and retiring about a Flame Tetra; they enjoy being out in the open and disporting themselves, looking for all the world like a flock of tiny red-winged butterflies. Sexing is not much of a problem: besides being less full-bodied and having brighter colors, the males have a slightly wider black margin on the anal fin, which has a straighter edge than that of the females. Spawning occurs among fine-leaved plants, and their owner is sometimes amazed at the amount of eggs which can be released by such a small female. Hatching occurs in two to three days, and once the fry begin to swim they must be fed with very fine-grained prepared foods or infusoria. Growth proceeds rapidly; with good attention, the fry are raised to maturity in about six months.

F-340.00

Photo by R. Zukal

HYPHESSOBRYCON GRIEMI (Hoedeman)/*Griem's Tetra*

Range: Brazil, in the vicinity of Goyaz.
Habits: Perfectly peaceful; like the other small members of the family, they also prefer to be kept in groups of at least six.
Water Conditions: Soft, slightly acid water is best but not necessarily essential. Temperature 75 to 78°.
Size: About 1¼ inches.
Food Requirements: Prepared foods are accepted, but live or frozen foods are preferable.
Color Variations: Sides brownish to greenish, with two vertical streaks of black. Anal and caudal fins show a pink tinge.

Griem's Tetra is one of the more recent introductions, and a beautiful one it is. It was introduced in 1956 and named by Hoedeman in 1957. In size and shape it resembles *Hyphessobrycon flammeus*, and the same two streaks appear on the sides. The picture only hints at the slightly greenish color of the sides, which becomes lighter around the second streak of black. The deep pink of the caudal and anal fins is only slightly indicated in most available specimens, but with good care and feeding it becomes increasingly evident. This color is also often lost when the fish is frightened by being placed in a too-bare aquarium, or in an aquarium where it is being constantly pursued by larger fishes. Probably the reason why we do not see this fish more frequently is because in a bare dealer's tank they appear washed-out and their beauty is unappreciated. They certainly deserve a place in a collection of such small Tetras as *H. flammeus, H. innesi, Cheirodon axelrodi, Pristella riddlei* and the like. Breeding *H. griemi* is not quite the easy matter that it is with *H. flammeus*, but it is far from difficult. Procedure is similar in both cases, but results are not as frequently successful.

Photo by Dr. E. Schmidt.

HYPHESSOBRYCON HARALDSCHULTZI (Travassos)
Harald Schultz's Tetra

Range: Ilha do Bananal, Goiaz, Brazil.
Habits: Peaceful; should be kept with a number of their own kind.
Water Conditions: Soft, slightly acid water. Temperature 75 to 78°.
Size: Just under 1 inch.
Food Requirements: Will take prepared foods, but live or frozen foods are better suited.
Color Variations: Body color rosy pink, belly white. Fins reddish except dorsal, which has a black spot in a white area. Small black shoulder spot.

Here we have another example of what happens all too frequently with so many of our aquarium fishes. When Harald Schultz found this little fish in the Ilha do Bananal in Goiaz, Brazil, he made a rough sketch of it in its life colors and sent it along to us. This sketch showed the color of the body and all fins, with the exception of the dorsal, to be a brilliant red. When a shipment of the living fish came and we got them into an aquarium, we wondered if they could possibly be the same ones. These had only a slight rosy flush, somewhat less than that of the Rosy Tetra. This we attributed to the rigors of their long journey, but their colors never brightened again. Nevertheless, even with its paler-than-original colors the fish is very attractive and peaceful as well. The taxonomic description by Dr. Haraldo Travassos appeared in the February, 1960 issue of *Tropical Fish Hobbyist*, and he here mentions that *H. haraldschultzi* is closely related to *H. callistus*, but distinguished from this species by the black spots in the dorsal fin and also by differences in dentition. Coloration and dentition differences also distinguish it from other members of the group.

F-342.00

HYPHESSOBRYCON HERBERTAXELRODI (Gery)
Black Neon Tetra

Range: Rio Taquary, Brazil.
Habits: Peaceful toward other fishes; prefer to be kept in a group of at least six.
Water Conditions: Soft, slightly acid water preferred but not essential.
Size: About 1¼ inches.
Food Requirements: Hearty eaters; prepared foods as well as live or frozen foods are eaten with equal gusto.
Color Variations: Back brownish, lower half of sides deep black. Between these areas runs a bright white line. Fins have little or no color.

The so-called "Black Neon" has caused quite a furore in German aquatic circles. In the author's opinion this is indeed a handsome fish, but not handsome enough to cause such excitement. Like the Neon Tetra, the contrasts are very striking, even if in this case the colors are only black and white. In a well-planted aquarium, a number of them swimming around makes a pleasing sight with the broad, velvet-black area on the lower half of the sides and the startling, enamel-white stripe above it. When the light comes from above, this white stripe takes on a gleaming light-blue color which we cannot see in the picture. Another color which is only faintly indicated is the red in the upper half of the eye. Discovery of this species can be attributed to the sharp eyes of Mr. Karl-Heinz Stegeman, who spotted them in a shipment of fishes coming from the Rio Taquary in the State of Mato Grosso, Brazil. This was in the early part of 1960, and the taxonomic identification by Dr. J. Gery was published in the May, 1961 issue of *Tropical Fish Hobbyist*. Although no doubt this fish has been bred by hobbyists, we have only heard of it being bred by commercial breeders.

Photo by Harald Schultz.

From the savannah of northeastern Brazil comes the pretty little *Hyphessobrycon stege-manni* which was discovered by Harald Schultz and named for Schultz' good friend Karl Stegemann. Mr. Stegemann left Germany and moved to Sao Paulo, Brazil where he opened an aquarium shop. These two photos show the young fish (above) as compared to the older fish.

Photo by Dr. E. Schmidt.

F-344.00

Photo by S. Frank

HYPHESSOBRYCON HETERORHABDUS (Ulrey)
Flag Tetra, False Ulreyi

Range: Lower Amazon region (Rio Tocantins, Rio Para); Rio Caete; Rio Negro.
Habits: Peaceful and very active.
Water Conditions: A little sensitive if not given soft, slightly acid water. Temperature
  should be kept around 78°.
Size: About 2 inches.
Food Requirements: Will take dried food readily, but should also get frequent
  feedings of live or frozen foods.
Color Variations: Back olive-green, sides silvery. A three-colored stripe runs along
  the sides, colored red, gold and black.

This very attractive Tetra masqueraded under a false name for many years.
When it was first introduced into Germany in 1910, it was mistaken for
Hemigrammus ulreyi. Call it what you may, it is a pretty little fish, and an
asset to any aquarium. Trouble is, we seldom get to see any numbers of these
fish. Breeders have not yet been successful in producing good numbers of
tank-raised specimens, and we are still dependent upon imported specimens
for our aquaria. They usually take very well to captivity, and the females
seem to fill up with eggs, but the usual result is either nothing at all or only a
few youngsters. A study of the ecological conditions in their home waters is
indicated, to find out if there are any special water conditions which induce
spawning in this fish, though they are always found in the same waters as
Cheirodon axelrodi, another hard fish to breed. Sexes may be distinguished by
the difference in shape between the body cavities. The female's is blunt and
rounded, and the male's is more pointed. Probably in time there will be
successful spawnings, using the methods which have already been found
successful in spawning the other difficult *Hyphessobrycon* species: soft, acid,
bacteria-free water and the other requisites.

F-345.00

Photo by R. Zukal.

* HYPHESSOBRYCON INNESI (Myers)/*Neon Tetra*

Range: Peruvian Amazon, Yarapa River.

Habits: Very peaceful, should be kept only with small fishes or in a tank of their own.

Water Conditions: Soft, clear, slightly acid water is preferred, and brings out their best colors. Best temperature about 76°.

Size: Maximum 1½ inches; most specimens seen are about 1 inch or less.

Food Requirements: Medium or finely ground dried foods, with occasional feedings of small live foods.

Color Variations: Back is dark, with a brilliant green to blue stripe from the eye to the adipose fin base. Bright red from the belly to caudal base.

The Neon Tetra is undoubtedly the most popular among the egg-laying fresh water fishes in aquaria today. Probably its only drawback is its small size, which would make it a meal for larger fishes if put into an aquarium with them. Like the other small Tetra species, their brilliance is made even more effective if they are kept in a school of a dozen or more. For contrast, their aquarium should be given a dark bottom. Black gravel is best. The Neon Tetra has an interesting history. It was discovered by natives who showed it to A. Rabaut while he was on a collecting expedition searching for butterflies. Realizing the importance of what he had, he brought back some with him to France. The first ones to reach America were shipped from Germany on the ill-fated dirigible " Hindenburg " which was to crash a short time later. Breeding this beautiful fish is not an impossibility, but most attempts result in failure. The most important ingredient is soft, acid water and a compatible pair. The eggs are very sensitive to light, and usually only a fraction of them hatch no matter what precautions are taken.

* The Neon Tetra is now scientifically known as *Paracheirodon innesi.*

F-346.00

HYPHESSOBRYCON ORNATUS (Ahl) ×
HYPHESSOBRYCON ROSACEUS (Durbin)
Hybrid of Rosy and Ornate Tetra

Range: *H. ornatus* comes from the Guianas, and *H. rosaceus* from British Guiana.
Habits: Peaceful; will not harm other fish or plants.
Water Conditions: Soft, slightly acid water is preferable. Temperature 75 to 80°.
Size: 1½ inches.
Food Requirements: Prepared foods accepted, but live or frozen foods preferred.
Color Variations: Body olive greenish to brownish. Ventral, anal and caudal fins are
  flushed with red. Upper part of dorsal fin black.

Most aquarium hobbyists are prone to think of hybridizations as being
feasible only with the livebearing species. The fact is that interspecific
hybridizations, that is, crosses between fishes of the same genus but different
species, are frequently possible. The result in many cases is a fish which is
undeniably attractive but not quite as attractive as either parent. Another
result is that if the young of this hybridization, assuming that the hybrids are
fertile, are bred back to a pure-bred adult of one of the original species, we
get a fish which is not exactly one or the other and besides is seldom good
breeding stock. Note the female of this hybridization, the lower fish. Even
though this is only the second generation of this cross, she already shows a
secondary male characteristic, the high, flaglike dorsal fin. The females of
neither *H. ornatus* nor *H. rosaceus* have such high dorsal fins.

F-347.00

HYPHESSOBRYCON PERUVIANUS (Ladiges)/*Loreto Tetra*

Range: Upper Amazon region.
Habits: Peaceful, a bit shy; should not be kept with large or aggressive fishes.
Water Conditions: Soft, slightly acid water is best, but not absolutely essential.
Size: 2 inches, most specimens smaller.
Food Requirements: Live foods preferred, but frozen or prepared foods accepted without any trouble.
Color Variations: Back light brown to olive, deep black stripe below. Dorsal fin reddish and the caudal fin deep red.

No matter how much care is taken when writing a book on aquarium fishes to make the thing absolutely flawless, this is an absolute impossibility. The author goes over his references carefully and uses a scientific name which has been unquestioned for a score or more of years, to find that by the time the book is completed and printed this name has become invalidated and is supplanted by another. We have been calling this fish *Hyphessobrycon metae* for many years, having been assured that this is the correct and proper name. Now Dr. Gery tells us, in our own magazine no less (May '61), that *Hyphessobrycon metae* is a different fish altogether, and that aquarium hobbyists in all probability have never yet seen it. Call it what you will, this fish is as peaceful as they come and several of them kept by the author have proven to be very hardy. As this fish comes from the same districts as the Neon Tetra, breeding may prove to be difficult. To the best of our knowledge it has yet to be done. At the time the author visited Señor Rafael Wanderraga's "fish farm" on the Loreto Baja in Colombia, there were none of these fish to be found among all the thousands there.

HYPHESSOBRYCON PULCHRIPINNIS (Ahl)/*Lemon Tetra*

Range: Brazil, in the vicinity of Pará.
Habits: Peaceful; happier in a group of at least six.
Water Conditions: Soft, acid water is desirable but not essential. Temperature 75 to 80°.
Size: To 2 inches.
Food Requirements: Live foods preferred, but frozen and prepared foods accepted.
Color Variations: Back brownish to greenish, sides very transparent. First rays of ventral and anal fins brilliant yellow with black behind them.

It is a fairly safe assumption that the two fish shown here are not a pair, but two males. The females have a fuller, deeper body and a narrower black edge on the anal fin, if indeed any edge exists at all. As can be readily seen, this is not a highly colorful fish, but the small streaks of brightest lemon yellow and bright red upper part of the eye make it an excellent "contrast fish," especially when combined with other Tetras which have a great deal of red in them. Spawning these little beauties is not always simple. Females frequently have a bit of trouble expelling eggs, and it may sometimes be necessary to combine a male with several females before a successful spawning is achieved. Eggs are laid in fine-leaved plants in the usual *Hyphessobrycon* manner. Once the fry have hatched they sometimes prove to be a bit "touchy" at first, and the mortality rate is likely to be high. Once through these trying stages, however, they are fairly easy to raise. The fish is sometimes called *Hemigrammus erythrophthalmus*, a name which is not valid scientifically, although *erythrophthalmus*, which means "red eye," certainly describes the fish aptly.

F-349.00

*HYPHESSOBRYCON RUBROSTIGMA (Hoedeman)
Tetra Perez, Bleeding Heart Tetra

Range: Colombia.
Habits: Peaceful if kept with fishes of its own size.
Water Conditions: Slightly acid, soft water. Temperature 74 to 78°.
Size: To 3 inches.
Food Requirements: Live or frozen foods preferred; prepared foods taken if hungry.
Color Variations: Sides light brown with a bluish shimmer. Anal fin white at the base with a thin black edge. Dorsal pink with large black spot.

For some months after its introduction this very attractive fish was known to the hobby only as "Tetra Perez." At that time a large number of immature fish were found by a collector and shipped from Colombia. It is amusing to see how some of our present-day authorities took these immature specimens and jumped to conclusions. Professor Sterba in his book *Süsswasserfische aus Aller Welt* gives their maximum size as 3.5 centimeters, which is less than $1\frac{1}{2}$ inches, and illustrates his account of the fish with a sketch of obviously half-grown specimens, which purports to show them in their natural size. To everyone's surprise, these little fellows which arrived in 1956 grew and grew until they became larger by far than the Rosy Tetra. Most of the color is concentrated in the bright pink of the dorsal fin with its large black area in the middle, and in the startling blood-red spot just above the belly region. This is not a fish for the small aquarium; it is an active species which requires a good deal of "elbow-room" and should get it. Given this, a well-conditioned pair will spawn readily and in a manner similar to that of the other *Hyphesso-brycon* species.

* Also known as *Hyphessobrycon erythrostigma.*

F-350.00

HYPHESSOBRYCON SCHOLZEI (Ahl)/*Black-Lined Tetra*

Range: Vicinity of Pará, Brazil.
Habits: Peaceful; will not harm other fish or plants.
Water Conditions: Soft and slightly acid water preferable but not essential. Temperature 74 to 78°.
Size: To 2 inches.
Food Requirements: Prepared foods accepted readily, but should be supplemented with frozen and live foods.
Color Variations: Sides silvery with a bluish sheen; black line from gillplate to caudal base, where it ends in a black spot. Fins slightly pinkish.

The Black-Lined Tetra is not one of the flashy individuals which takes the aquarium world by storm, but it has a quiet charm which has kept it in the tanks of aquarium hobbyists with a fair amount of consistency ever since its introduction in 1936. The reason most probably is that it has just about all the desirable traits except color. And if one sees this fish in the proper light, there is some color which is quite evident. When in a position where sunlight bounces off its scales, these show an opalescent gleam, and the black stripe has a bluish, almost luminous glow at its upper edge. Besides, all the unpaired fins have a slight pink tinge when the fish is in good condition. All these things are lost when they are put in a tank where there are not enough plants and the lighting is not proper, and the Black-Lined Tetra becomes just a silvery fish with a black stripe. This is one of the easiest members of the genus to breed. They spawn like many other *Hyphessobrycon* species, hanging their eggs among fine-leaved plants. A tankful of quarter-grown youngsters makes a surprisingly attractive and lively picture, and they are easily raised.

HYPHESSOBRYCON SERPAE (Durbin)/*Tetra Serpae*

Range: Amazon River, Madeira and Guaporé regions and upper Paraguay.
Habits: Mostly peaceful, but will sometimes take a dislike to a fish and nip fins.
Water Conditions: Soft, slightly acid water. Temperature should not drop below 76°
at any time.
Size: Up to 1½ inches, usually smaller.
Food Requirements: Does very well on dried foods, but of course should get
occasional feedings with live or frozen foods.
Color Variations: Body silvery to golden, back olive-green, belly silvery. Tail red.
Dorsal fin black, red at base and white tipped.

It is a pity that we cannot give this beautiful Tetra an absolutely clean
record of behavior. With other fishes of the same approximate size it is
usually a model citizen, but put it with something smaller, like a Neon Tetra,
and it will often pursue them and tear at them unmercifully. Eventually
there will be a number of sub-species grouped under this general species, and
some authorities are calling this fish *Hyphessobrycon serpae serpae*. Others
will be *Hyphessobrycon serpae minor, Hyphessobrycon serpae callistus*. In some
works there is even reference to *Hyphessobrycon serpae rosaceus*, which we
have referred to here under its original name *Hyphessobrycon rosaceus*. With
so many changes and differences of opinion, it is difficult to figure out who
will come out on top and which name will finally be the official one. To get
back to this little Tetra, it is a very durable fish and once accustomed to its
surroundings it will usually live a long time. It is easily spawned, and the fry
are not difficult to raise by the usual methods. It is a very rare fish and many
different species are sold under the name of *Serpae*.

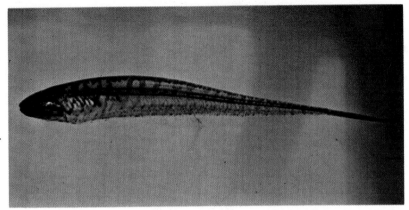

HYPOPOMUS ARTEDI (Kaup)/*Spotted Knife Fish*

Range: French Guiana.
Habits: Peaceful toward other fishes which are not small enough to be swallowed. Likely to be belligerent toward their own kind.
Water Conditions: Not critical, but the fish is sensitive to fresh water. Tank should be well planted and offer a number of places to hide.
Size: To 17 inches.
Food Requirements: Prefers larger-sized live foods or chopped lean beef.
Color Variations: Yellowish to brownish with darker spots.

Tell a non-hobbyist that there is a fish which has no dorsal fin, no tail fin and no ventral fins, and also has its anus just below its head, and he will doubt your sanity! Then tell him that this fish swims by rippling its anal fin and can swim as easily backward as forward by reversing this rippling motion, and your friend will begin to make excuses to get away as quickly as possible, before you get violent. Better have one of these fish around to show him before you tell him these things. There are Knife-Fishes fairly well distributed in tropical Asia, Africa and South America. They are seldom caught in large numbers, and putting together two males often results in a pitched battle in which the defeated fish is likely to be killed if he is not rescued. In spite of this seeming bloodthirstiness, *Hypopomus artedi* is rather shy in its behavior toward other fishes, provided of course that they are not small enough to become an item on his menu. This shyness unfortunately manifests itself by the fish's almost constant hiding among the plants and rocks. There are no known external sex differences, and to the best of our knowledge there have been no accounts of their breeding.

HYPOSTOMUS PLECOSTOMUS (Linnaeus)
Sucker Catfish, Plecostomus

Range: La Plata region, Rio Grande do Sul, Trinidad.

Habits: Peaceful toward other unrelated fishes, sometimes very scrappy among themselves.

Water Conditions: Slightly hard, alkaline water preferred, temperature 75 to 80°.

Size: To 2 feet in natural waters; most captive specimens get no longer than 12 inches.

Food Requirements: Live worms or frozen foods eaten greedily, also cut-up pieces of earthworms.

Color Variations: Grayish to dark brown with irregular dark markings. Fins sometimes show rows of dark spots.

Not all of our aquarium fishes are beautiful; a few are so ugly that their unbelievable ugliness makes them interesting, and the Plecostomus is one of these. The eyes, for example, do not look like anything that any living creature could see through but rather like a pair of lumps with a lighter-colored circle inside and a dot in the middle. There seems to be no transparency to them. The mouth is a round, underslung affair with which the fish can attach itself to a flat surface and rasp off the algae, of which it is very fond. This makes it a very useful citizen in a tank which is plagued by algal growths. The Plecostomus is a fish which is most active at night, and during the day generally remains hidden by the hour in the shade of some rock. Do not let this preference for a shady spot dissuade you into putting this fish into a tank where there is little sunlight, because our friend will always find a spot to his liking during the daylight hours and at night come out and graze on the algae which is prone to proliferate in a tank which is sunny and has fairly alkaline water. Perhaps it has been bred, but if so the feat is a rare one.

HYPSELEOTRIS CYPRINOIDES (Cuvier & Valenciennes)
Chameleon Goby

Range: Australia, also reported from Sumatra.
Habits: Peaceful; all foods readily accepted.
Water Conditions: Slightly alkaline, fairly hard water preferred. Temperature 73 to 78°.
Size: About 2½ inches.
Food Requirements: Will eat anything, but may also include plants in its menu. Should get live foods occasionally.
Color Variations: Usually a muddy brown with a darker horizontal stripe. Male's fins have a blue edge, dorsal fin has blue dots.

Australia is the home of this seldom-imported fish, and it is also reported from Sumatra. It is a regular chameleon in the way it can undergo color changes with startling speed. Its usual color is a rather muddy brown with a darker horizontal stripe, but in no time at all it can assume dark colors, as in the picture. Along with the darker colors the fish frequently develops a pair of startlingly light blue eyes. Most of the Goby group are lazy and not good swimmers. Some have very inadequate swim-bladders and merely hop about on the bottom from one place to another. Not so with this one; they swim normally and prefer the middle reaches of the aquarium. They are very hardy and the author has kept some for a number of years without any special attention. Males can be distinguished by a blue edge on the fins and a number of large blue dots in the dorsal fin. The female's fins are transparent and the blue edge is missing. The few works which describe the fish mention the fact that it has been spawned in captivity, but no further details are given. This is a peaceful species which will not bother its tankmates.

Photo by H.J. Richter

JORDANELLA FLORIDAE (Goode & Bean)/*American Flagfish*

Range: Florida, especially in the southern portion.

Habits: Males are apt to be very quarrelsome, especially at spawning time; it is best to give pairs their own aquarium.

Water Conditions: Prefers a sunny aquarium, with slightly alkaline water. Temperature should be around 70°, slightly higher for spawning.

Size: About 2 inches.

Food Requirements: Will eat dried as well as live foods, but should get a good deal of vegetable matter in its diet.

Color Variations: Basic color olive-green. Males have red stripes in body and fins. Females have a checkered pattern of spots.

A fish, like a prophet, is often without honor in its own country. The European hobbyists value this Cyprinodont highly, but in American aquaria it is quite rare. This also holds true for a great number of other beautiful native American fishes. Of course, temperatures which we give to our tropical species are a bit too high for these beauties, but even a small aquarium at room temperatures suits them fine. Its breeding habits are unusual for a Cyprinodont. Eggs are often hung among surface plants in the usual Cyprinodont manner, but sometimes we also find them near the bottom or on the

Jordanella floridae male

bottom, guarded by the male. It is not usually necessary to remove the female; she is rarely molested. Spawning may last over a period of a week. The male takes care of the young Cichlid-fashion after they hatch. Incubation lasts 5 to 6 days. After the young have put on some growth, they should be given their own aquarium, preferably a sunny one which has taken on some algae growth. Given these conditions, the young will flourish and in about 3 months will be ready to raise families of their own. This species was first introduced to hobbyists when shipped to Berlin in 1914.

Photo by H. Hansen, Aquarium Berlin

JULIDOCHROMIS ORNATUS (Boulenger)/*Julie*

Range: Lake Tanganyika, Africa.

Habits: Because of their special water requirements, they should be kept by themselves. If more than one male is kept, each should have his own spot.

Water Conditions: Very hard and alkaline water, made by treating it with sodium bicarbonate and calcium. Temperature 75 to 80°.

Size: About 3 inches.

Food Requirements: Very finicky eaters which seem to prefer *Tubifex* worms and glass larvae.

Color Variations: Lemon yellow with three dark brown horizontal stripes in the upper half of the body. Large dark spot at the caudal base.

Lake Tanganyika is a place which has a very interesting geological history. Far back in prehistoric times there was a terrible drought throughout most of Africa which killed off most of the life in this huge area. Only a very few deep lakes had any water at all left in them, and among these was Lake Tanganyika. Life continued to flourish here while it was staging a slow comeback in other bodies of water, and therefore the fauna of this huge lake predates by far that of the bodies of water which were again formed after the drought. Scientists have identified more than 200 species of Cichlids in this lake *alone*, most of which are peculiar to Lake Tanganyika and occur nowhere else on earth. Among these are such beauties as *Julidochromis ornatus*. Because there is a great deal of limestone in the Tanganyika region, the waters of the lake are highly alkaline and very hard. This eliminates them as candidates for the community aquarium, because most fishes would not be able to stand for any length of time the type of water which the Julies need to thrive. A few rare instances have been observed where the fish were coaxed into spawning, and we hope to hear more.

Photo by Dr. Herbert R. Axelrod.

KRYPTOPTERUS BICIRRHIS (Cuvier & Valenciennes)/*Glass Catfish*

Range: India and the Great Sunda Islands.
Habits: Peaceful, should not be kept singly. They should also not be kept with very active fishes.
Water Conditions: Water should be slightly alkaline and have a hardness which does not surpass 10 DH.
Size: To 4 inches.
Food Requirements: Should be given living foods such as *Tubifex* worms, white worms, *Daphnia*, etc.
Color Variations: Body yellowish and very transparent; upper side of head almost black. Violet spot above the pectoral fins.

The Glass Catfish is one of the most transparent of all aquarium fishes. As with most of the other transparent species, the body organs are enclosed in a silvery sac, which shows how compressed and far in front these organs are in some fishes. As they are not nocturnal in their habits, they do not need a darkened aquarium. They are also happier when kept in a group, and should not be combined with other fishes which are highly active. Their tank should be well planted, and they seem to enjoy getting under a broad leaf and remaining there with their fins undulating. They are not a bottom-grubbing species, and food which reaches the bottom is seldom retrieved by them. Note how the two long barbels, or "whiskers," stand straight out rather than point downward, as do those in the bottom-feeding Catfish. This is because they are tactile rather than olfactory organs. Although they have been frequently available since their introduction in 1934, we have seen no records which described their ever having been bred in captivity. Seen in a light which is reflected by their tiny scales, they show colors which are beautifully opalescent.

Photo by Dr. Herbert R. Axelrod.

LABEO BICOLOR (Smith)/*Red-Tailed Shark*

Range: Thailand.
Habits: Apt to be a bit scrappy among themselves, but peaceful toward other fishes.
Water Conditions: Slightly alkaline water of about 10 DH. Temperature 75 to 78°.
Size: To 4¾ inches.
Food Requirements: All kinds of live foods, besides some vegetable matter in addition, like lettuce or spinach leaves.
Color Variations: Deep brown to black body color, ending in a red caudal base and tail.

The person who first referred to this group of fishes as "Sharks" certainly had a healthy imagination. True, the *Labeo* species have a rather high dorsal fin, but its shape does not even faintly resemble the sickle-shaped dorsal fin of the real Shark which is seen so frequently in our offshore marine waters. There is no other resemblance either between the shy, mild-mannered Red-Tailed Shark and its vicious, ever-hungry namesake. The only time the Red-Tailed Shark gives any inkling of a "chip on its shoulder" is when one male intrudes into another's territory. With most fishes which stake out a claim this is the signal for a fierce battle, and there is a great deal of bustle and bluster with the Red-Tailed Sharks as well. The only thing is that, lacking the dental equipment and sharp fin rays, the Red-Tailed Shark is at a real disadvantage and his ferocity is mostly bluff. Lately there have been shipments of many small specimens, and it is suspected that the Thailand breeders propagate them in their pools. Females are recognizable by their heavier bodies and we have seen accounts which stated that they had been bred, but no details were given.

Labeo erythrurus, the Red-Fin Shark, behaves much like *Labeo bicolor*. Spawning accounts for this fish mention that the male has a black band at the rear edge of the anal fin. From the heavy belly and the lack of a black edge to the anal fin, it is assumed that the fish illustrated is a female.

Labeo variegatus is a fairly large fish that behaves like both *L. bicolor* and *L. erythrurus*, but it is seen less frequently.

F-361.00

LAMPRICHTHYS TANGANICUS (Boulenger 1898)

Range: Lake Tanganyika, Africa.
Habits: Peaceful, quite shy; should be kept in a well-planted, covered tank.
Water Conditions: Slightly alkaline, temperature about 76°.
Size: Males about 4 inches, females slightly smaller.
Food Requirements: Living foods, such as daphnia, tubifex worms, and adult brine shrimp.
Color Variations: Body brownish, with a light blue horizontal stripe. Sides are covered with rows of small, light blue dots. Females duller.

Lake Tanganyika is a place where the ichthyologist has long had a field day with many species which were known from no other place. There is also much to interest the aquarist, among them some gorgeous specimens like this fish. Seeing a pair swimming around with the sun shining on them is a sight guaranteed to make any aquarist gasp. The rows of tiny dots gleam brightly with an incandescent blue. The picture gives a good idea, but the fish must be seen in the proper light to be appreciated. They are peaceful, even timid. Other fishes kept with them which are large enough not to be swallowed are left alone. Being an active fish, a large tank is preferable and should be covered to prevent their loss by jumping. So far, very few of these lovely fish have found their way to our shores, so there is still much left to be found out about them. If they are ever spawned, and they probably will be, we will have another fish which will find its way into the hearts as well as the aquaria of hobbyists all over the world. Until then, there will be many transportation problems which will make the price of the few fish available very high.

LAMPROLOGUS COMPRESSICEPS (Boulenger)/*Compressed Cichlid*

Range: Lake Tanganyika, Africa.
Habits: Peaceful toward other fishes, but cannot be trusted with those it could swallow.
Water Conditions: Alkaline water, about pH 8.0. Temperature 76 to 80°.
Size: 4 to 4½ inches.
Food Requirements: Large living foods, such as grown brine shrimp, small fishes or cut-up earthworms.
Color Variations: Deep brown to black body color, with a series of lighter vertical bars. Fins are covered with rows of small dots.

There are many Cichlid species in Lake Tanganyika which the hobbyist has not yet seen, and doubtless many which are still unknown to science. The fascinating thing about the fish life in this huge lake is that for the most part it is a world unto itself and for the greatest part the fish species native here can be found in no other place on earth. *Lamprologus compressiceps* looks just like what its specific name indicates, "with a compressed body." Its body is so compressed that if it remained motionless among some plants and were seen head-on, it would look like one of the stems. The large mouth usually is an indication of a vicious fish, but this one will not bother anything it cannot swallow. The method by which the natives catch them is interesting. In order to bring them up alive, they must dive to a depth of more than 60 feet and feel among the rock clefts for the fish. These must be handled with caution, because being pricked by one of the sharp spines causes a very unpleasant itching. Is it any wonder that the few specimens which have become available so far are expensive? We have seen no accounts of their spawning activities as yet.

F-363.00

LAMPROLOGUS LELEUPI (Poll)/*Lemon Cichlid*

Range: Lake Tanganyika, Africa.
Habits: Inoffensive; can be kept with other fishes which can tolerate their water conditions.
Water Conditions: Alkaline water, about pH 8.0. Tank should be well planted, and other hiding-places provided as well.
Size: To 4 inches.
Food Requirements: Prefers living foods on the small side, such as *Daphnia* and other crustacea.
Color Variations: Body is lemon yellow with the exception of the eyes, which are brilliant blue.

The Lemon Cichlid is a fish which, once it has adapted itself to life in the aquarium, should prove to be one of the most popular of the smaller Cichlids. The blue eyes and yellow body coloration make a delightful contrast against a dark background in the aquarium. In an article by Dr. Werner Ladiges which was published in a German magazine, the first spawning was described. The males are distinguished by a larger head and more robust body. A pair was selected and given a tank of their own, which besides plants contained a flowerpot from which the bottom was knocked out. They spawned Cichlid-fashion in this flowerpot, and the eggs hatched in three days. The parents were left with the eggs and the female assumed all of the parental responsibility. Of the approximately 150 eggs which were laid, almost all hatched and the fry were raised without difficulty. It was noted that in the imported specimens there was a predominance of males over females, which possibly might be a local condition in the waters where they were caught. It is sincerely hoped that things quiet down in Africa in the not-too-far-distant future and permit collectors to fish unmolested in the waters of the lake once more.

Photo by Dr. Herbert R. Axelrod.

LAUBUCA DADIBURJORI (Menon)/*Dadio*

Range: Vicinity of Bombay, India.
Habits: Active fish which if possible should be kept in a small group. Jumpers; keep their tank covered.
Water Conditions: Soft to medium-hard water, temperature 72 to 77°.
Size: 1¼ inches.
Food Requirements: Accepts dried foods as enthusiastically as live or frozen foods.
Color Variations: Body is olive-yellow in color. Dark blue horizontal line, edged with gold above. Fins except pectorals are reddish.

The Dadio is never likely to win any prizes for its coloration alone, but it has everything else to recommend it. It is active, gregarious, and will accept anything in the food line which comes its way. It is not particularly sensitive to water conditions and seems to breed readily. The specific name honors its discoverer, Shri Sam J. Dadyburjor of Bombay, India. In June, 1960 we received a few specimens and sent them to Herr E. Roloff in Karlsruhe, Germany. He gave them a long tank of their own, such as is used for spawning the *Danio* species. In one corner he placed a nylon "mop," which is merely a tassel of nylon yarn attached to a cork to make it float. The tank was otherwise bare and the fish had no choice but to spawn into the nylon threads. Herr Roloff thinks, however, that they normally attach their eggs to the underside of a broad plant leaf. There were less than 100 eggs laid, and the parents were removed immediately afterward. Hatching began on the next day, but the fry did not begin to swim until the sixth day later. They were fed infusoria at first, then brine shrimp, which they accepted eagerly. In three months they were mature.

Photo by Dr. Herbert R. Axelrod.

LAUBUCA LAUBUCA (Hamilton-Buchanan)/*Indian Hatchetfish*

Range: India, Burma, Sumatra and Malaya.

Habits: Peaceful, prefers the upper reaches of the aquarium. Active swimmers, they are also skilled jumpers. Keep their aquarium covered.

Water Conditions: Neutral to slightly acid, soft water for spawning. Otherwise, water conditions are unimportant. Temperature 75 to 80°.

Size: Up to 2½ inches.

Food Requirements: Will eat any food. Being a top feeder, they prefer a food which does not sink rapidly.

Color Variations: Body green to bluish with a violet sheen toward the tail. Dark horizontal stripe with gold edge, ending in an ocellated spot.

The Indian Hatchetfish does not have the deep, keeled body which is characteristic of the South American Hatchetfishes. Also it is not a Characin, as they are, but a member of the Cyprinid family. Some works refer to it as *Chela laubuca*, but the generic name *Laubuca* is by far the most commonly used. Here we have a fish which is attractively colored, easily fed, not difficult to spawn and easy to keep; still, hobbyists never seem to get excited about them. This is a paradox which exists with some species. Sometimes, suddenly, a fish "catches on," and people who have known and avoided a particular species for years suddenly fall all over each other to get them. The spawning act of *Laubuca laubuca* is interesting. An aquarium with a large water surface is best. There need be no precautions against the eating of the eggs by the parents; if well fed they show little inclination to do so. Males are distinguished by their thinner bodies and brighter colors, and little attention is paid to the females until about dusk. After an active pursuit the male embraces the female from the left with his fins, and a large number of eggs result. They hatch in about 24 hours at a temperature of 78°.

F-366.00

*LEBISTES RETICULATUS (Peters)/*Guppy*

Range: Trinidad, Venezuela, Barbados and parts of northern Brazil and the Guianas.
Habits: Peaceful, very active and prolific.
Water Conditions: Soft, slightly alkaline water is best. Clean, well-filtered water is important for healthy conditions. Temperature 74 to 78°.
Size: Males to about 1½ inches, usually less; females to about 2¼ inches.
Food Requirements: Good eaters; should be fed a variety of foods, either live, frozen or prepared. Frequent small feedings are preferable.
Color Variations: Wild males have gray bodies with black and vari-colored markings. Fancy specimens are bred in all imaginable colors and fin shapes.

So popular is the little Guppy that many hobbyists have given up all their other fishes to devote their activities and tank space to these beauties. There are several international societies devoted to the breeding and study of Guppies alone, and no other fish has ever captured the imaginations of so many followers. Wild specimens are not particularly pretty: short fins, a gray body and some black markings with a few spots of red, yellow or green would describe the males, and a plain gray body the females. From these the breeders have developed many strains in a rainbow of colors and with long, flowing fins in a variety of shapes. Many countries in the tropics have taken advantage of the prolific nature and wide adaptability of the wild fish and have introduced them in mosquito-infested areas, where they could be counted upon to do an excellent job of eating the mosquito larvae almost as quickly as they hatched.
*Now alternatively known as *Poecilia reticulata.*

F-367.00

Guppies have been selectively bred to an extent where there are virtually hundreds of different color variations and fin forms. Seen in this photo are some of the red veiltail strain.

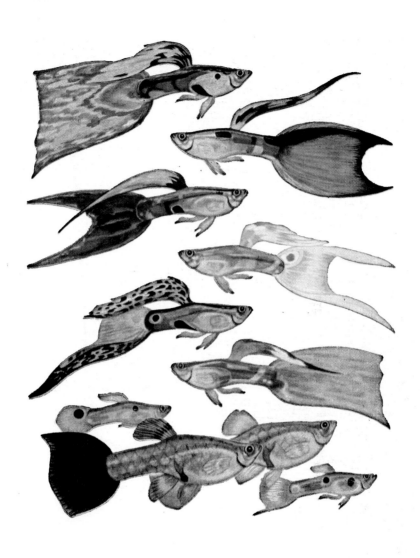

(From **All About Guppies**, by Dr. Leon F. Whitney and Paul Hahnel.)

Sometimes guppies are bred so that all of the fins (including the gonopodium) become elongated as in this one.

A deltatail female guppy.

A double swordtail male. Single swordtails normally have the lower portion of the tail developed into the sword.

A female guppy dropping live young. One baby can be seen above the female's head, another is about to be born head first.

Photo by Edward C. Taylor

LEIOCASSIS SIAMENSIS (Regan)/*Barred Siamese Catfish*

Range: Thailand.
Habits: Peaceful toward fishes it cannot swallow; mostly nocturnal in its habits.
Water Conditions: Soft, slightly acid water which has been aged for at least a week. Temperature 72 to 77°.
Size: To 6¼ inches.
Food Requirements: All sorts of live or frozen foods.
Color Variations: Body color brown to bluish, with four light vertical bars. Fins brown.

This is a comparatively new species of Catfish which was first offered to hobbyists in 1953. Today, we do not see them offered for sale very frequently, but fish shows seldom fail to attract quite a number of entries. This is a clear indication that the fish has a long life-span. There is a considerable variation in the body colors. Most specimens have an attractive coffee-brown color, but others are a bluish black or a grayish blue. These are probably local color variations, because the colors change very little with the moods of the fish. Being a nocturnal species, hiding-places will be sought out and used during the bright daylight hours. They prefer the larger sizes of living foods, and a special delicacy is a medium-sized earthworm cut up into several pieces. There are no visible sex differences and thus far there have been no accounts of their reproductive habits. A characteristic of this group is the large-sized adipose fin, which is also seen in the *Synodontis* species from Africa. The large mouth indicates that it could swallow smaller fish in the same aquarium, so do not keep your fancy Guppies or Neon Tetras in its company or they might disappear.

Photo by Dr. Herbert R. Axelrod.

LEPOMIS GIBBOSUS (Linné)/*Sunfish, Pumpkinseed*

Range: Maine to Florida west to the Mississippi.

Habits: Should be kept by themselves or with others of the same genus.

Water Conditions: Tank should be roomy and the water clean. Room temperatures suffice without any additional heat.

Size: Seldom larger than 6 inches.

Food Requirements: Hearty eaters which require frequent feeding with large live foods such as chopped earthworms, or frozen foods like beef-heart.

Color Variations: Sides bluish, belly yellowish in the females and bright orange in the males. Dark vertical bars on the sides, and red spots.

Our native Sunfishes have little to recommend them as aquarium fishes, except that they are colorful and interesting. Keeping them with tropical species is out of the question, because the temperature requirements are too far apart. Besides, a Sunfish could not be trusted with any but the toughest Cichlids and other "rough customers" among the tropicals. On the credit side of the ledger, Sunfishes are easily acclimated to a clean, good-sized tank and are quite colorful. The best ones to get for aquarium keeping are caught in the early summer months and are one to two inches long. At this size they accept captivity well if they are uncrowded, and are not likely to be as belligerent toward each other as larger ones would be. As is the case with so many of our native fishes, they are quite popular in Europe as cold-water aquarium fishes, and much space is devoted in foreign literature to their spawning habits. The male fans out a depression in an open space and then lures the female into it. Eggs are laid here and guarded by the male, who drives away the female after she has finished. Eggs hatch in 2 to 3 days, and the fry are easily raised.

F-373.00

LEPOMIS MEGALOTIS (Rafinesque)/*Longeared Sunfish*

Range: Eastern United States, Canada to Mexican border.
Habits: Best kept by themselves.
Water Conditions: Not critical, but water should be clean and well-aerated.
Size: Wild specimens 8 inches, in the aquarium seldom over 5 inches.
Food Requirements: Hearty eaters whose live food diet can be supplemented with chopped beef-heart, liver, etc.
Color Variations: Greenish sides, belly yellowish. Lips blue, sometimes green. Fins greenish.

The Longeared Sunfish occurs in practically the same habitat as the Common Sunfish. Its chief mark of distinction is an elongated extension of the black tab at the point of the opercle or gill-plate. In colorful males this "ear" is edged blue, sometimes yellow or red. They are often regarded as a "panfish" and are accepted as food by game-fishermen when the larger ones they are seeking prove scarce or elusive. Their flesh makes excellent eating, but they are very bony. In the aquarium, it will be found that medium-sized specimens which have recently reached maturity are the most brightly colored and that these colors tend to "wash out" as the fish grow larger. It will be found that the Longeared Sunfish prefers a little more sunlight than the others, and their tank should be in a position where it gets a few hours of direct sunlight daily. During the winter months these fish should get a "rest period" of lowered temperatures, about 40° to 45°. This is essential to their well-being, and if they do not get this period the number and quality of the eggs laid the following spring may easily be a disappointment. Spawning is the same as described for the Common Sunfish.

F-374.00

LEPORINUS FASCIATUS (Bloch)/*Banded Leporinus*

Range: Widely distributed in South America from the Guianas to the La Plata.
Habits: Active and peaceful toward other fishes, but inclined to be destructive to plants. Keep their tank covered; they jump.
Water Conditions: Neutral to slightly alkaline water. Being active, they require a good-sized tank. Temperature 73 to 78°.
Size: In their home waters to 13 inches. In captivity, seldom over 6 inches.
Food Requirements: Omnivorous, with a preference for vegetable matter. Crushed lettuce leaves or spinach leaves should be frequently provided.
Color Variations: Body light to golden yellow with about 10 black vertical bands.

The Banded Leporinus is doubtless the most popular and brightly-colored fish of this group. The alternating black and yellow bands stand out very effectively against a green plant background. Young specimens have only a few black bands, and as the fish grows older these bands split and form two separate ones. In their native waters they swim in a head-down position and constantly graze on the algae which covers the plant surfaces. In the aquarium they will do the same and when all the algae has been cleared away they will switch their attentions to the soft shoots and plant leaves. A good substitute is to give them a frequent supply of crushed lettuce leaf, but of course there is always the danger that they will pass up the lettuce and re-direct their attentions to the aquatic plants again. Another ruse, which many aquarists will frown upon, is to use the new plastic plants. They resemble the real article and provide shelter for the fishes, but once they get a few trial nips they are left strictly alone. The Banded Leporinus attains the respectable size of 13 inches in its native waters, and the Indians have a high regard for them as food.

Photo by Dr. Herbert R. Axelrod.

LEPORINUS FREDERICI (Bloch)/*Frederici*

Range: The Guianas to the Amazon River.
Habits: Peaceful toward other fishes. A jumper; tank must be kept covered.
Water Conditions: Neutral to slightly alkaline. Temperature 75 to 80°.
Size: In nature, up to 16 inches. In captivity, seldom over 6 inches.
Food Requirements: Live or frozen foods, with frequent feedings of vegetable substances such as crushed lettuce leaves or chopped spinach.
Color Variations: Body grayish-green to light gold at the caudal base. A number of black spots from the center of the body to the tail.

Leporinus frederici is a sort of "poor relation" when seen with its more colorful cousins. Its colors are modest, almost drab; still, it moves with an attractive, easy grace which probably accounts for its limited popularity. Most of the *Leporinus* species are prized for food in their native countries, and collectors who net them must make it very plain to their native workers that they may keep fish above a certain size and that the smaller ones go into the cans. This is a difficult fish to catch in their native waters, and many of them go sailing high over the top of the net in magnificent leaps when they feel confined. The native boys who handle the nets must duck with lightning-like reflexes when a fish comes flying at them, or they could easily get a black eye. This jumping ability is shown to a lesser degree in the confines of an aquarium, and a cover must be kept on at all times. Kept in large public aquaria, the fish can attain a size up to 16 inches, as it does when wild. Usually they are sold at a size of 3 to 4 inches and do not grow larger than about twice this size, even in a large home aquarium. We have never heard of them being bred in captivity.

LEPORINUS MACULATUS (Mueller & Troschel)
Spotted Leporinus

Range: Upper and lower Amazon, Peru, Espirito Santo, Rio de Janeiro, Sao Paulo, Rio Paraguay, Guiana.

Habits: Peaceful, active. Should have a covered tank, as it is likely to jump.

Water Conditions: Neutral to slightly acid. Temperature about 76°. Water should be well aged.

Size: 3½ to 4 inches.

Food Requirements: A good eater; will eat dried as well as all kinds of live foods.

Color Variations: Light brown body color, with rows of large black oval to round spots on the sides.

A fish does not have to be brightly colored to be popular, and this one is an example of a fish which is surely destined to be popular if it ever becomes readily available. This may soon be the case. Herbert R. Axelrod saw this fish being spawned by the thousands on his recent world tour, by Chinese breeders in Hong Kong. This means that we should soon see small specimens of this attractive fish, at a price well within reach of the average aquarist. What is more, the tank-raised specimens should be much easier to spawn than their wild ancestors, having been in aquaria all of their lives and accustomed to the comparatively cramped quarters allotted to them. It was at one time considered impossible to spawn the Angelfish in the aquarium, but after the first ones were successfully raised it became easier with each successive generation, and now some of the rankest beginners have raised them. The Spotted Leporinus is said to spawn much like the Barbs, scattering eggs all over the aquarium and then eating them if not taken out. This should be one fish which would be easy to raise, judging by the appetite the grown ones have. Like the other Leporinus species, a little green food should be given.

LEPORINUS MELANOPLEURA (Günther)/*Spot-Tailed Leporinus*

Range: West Brazil, between the Amazon River and Rio de Janeiro.
Habits: Peaceful toward other fishes; a jumper which must be protected by keeping its tank covered.
Water Conditions: Neutral to slightly alkaline. Temperature 75 to 80°.
Size: To 8 inches; usually sold at 3 to 4 inches.
Food Requirements: All live foods and frozen foods. Prepared foods also accepted, and an addition of vegetable matter is very beneficial.
Color Variations: Body light brownish, belly yellowish. Dark brown to green horizontal stripe; tail base reddish with tiny brown dots.

Leporinus melanopleura is distinguished by having a body which is not quite as elongated as that of the other *Leporinus* species. Another distinguishing trait is a number of tiny brown dots on the caudal base. Whether or not it is a sexual characteristic is questionable, but some specimens have a dark edge on the dorsal and caudal fins. These are presumed by some to be the males, and the plainer colored ones the females. This species does not attain the size of most of the other *Leporinus* species, but with a maximum size of 8 inches it is by no means a small fish. The first ones to be sold to hobbyists reached the market as early as 1926, but to date there have been no accounts of any spawnings. One of the theories as to why some aquarium fishes have eluded all efforts to spawn them is that the larger species which have been stunted for some time in an aquarium which does not allow them full development never attain sexual maturity.

LEPTOLUCANIA OMMATA (Jordan)/*Swamp Killie*

Range: Southern Georgia to Florida, in swamps.
Habits: Peaceful, but should not be kept with larger fishes.
Water Conditions: Neutral to slightly acid water. Tank should be well planted. Temperature 70 to 75°.
Size: To about 1½ inches.
Food Requirements: Small living foods preferred, but dried foods accepted when hungry.
Color Variations: Males yellowish to light brown. Vertical dark bars cross after half of body. Ocellated spot at tail. Females have another above anal fin.

The body shape of this little Minnow bears a great resemblance to a related genus of Cyprinodonts native to parts of Africa, the *Aplocheilichthys* species. The Swamp Killie is not a particularly beautifully colored fish, but makes up for this by being peaceful and hardy. Females are slightly larger than their mates and are easily distinguished by the fact that they have one more spot. The males have an ocellated spot at the caudal base; this spot is not as distinct in the females. An extra spot just above the anal fin occurs in females only. With good feeding and a constant temperature of 75°, a pair will soon spawn among fine-leaved plants. The eggs are very small and hatch in about 10 days. At first they should be fed infusoria, and once they have graduated to larger live foods such as baby brine shrimp, growth is very rapid. It is interesting to speculate as to why an "eye-spot" occurs in some fishes. Probably the reason is that a predatory fish which sees the eye-spot going by in the dim waters would be fooled into thinking that this was the real eye and snap at where the body should be, getting a mouthful of water instead of a mouthful of fish.

Photo by J. Elias

*LIMIA NIGROFASCIATA (Regan)/*Humpbacked Limia*

Range: Haiti and Dominican Republic.
Habits: Peaceful toward other fishes, but is very much apt to eat its own young.
Water Conditions: Slightly alkaline water and temperatures not lower than 78° are required.
Size: Males up to 2 inches, females slightly larger.
Food Requirements: Not critical; will take dried foods as well as live or frozen foods.
Color Variations: Olive green back and sides, belly region lighter. A number of dark, uneven dark bars adorn the sides. Gonopodium black.

If it were not for the fact that this livebearer requires rather high temperatures as compared with the others, the Humpbacked Limia would probably be one of the popular favorites. True, the colors of almost all the *Limia* species are not the brightest, but this one has an attractive caudal and dorsal fin, which it spreads like a fan whenever a female comes into view. One of the most interesting features of this fish is the transformation of shape in the males as they get older. The back and lower posterior region accumulate fatty tissue, and they have a deformed appearance which makes them look like a fish with a spinal curvature, in spite of the fact that the spine remains perfectly normal. An unusual bit of coloration which also appears in the males is the relatively long, black gonopodium. Rather than the normal 4 weeks of "gestation" the females may take as long as 6 weeks before they release their young. Broods are small in number, but make up for it by their size. They are hearty eaters and grow rapidly. Young males look perfectly normal until after maturity is passed, when they assume their odd shape.
*Now alternatively known as *Poecilia nigrofasciata*.

*LIMIA ORNATA (Regan)/*Ornate Limia*

Range: Haiti.

Habits: Peaceful toward all but newly-born young, including their own.

Water Conditions: Not critical, but tank should be in a sunny location and not drop below 78°.

Size: Males a little under 1½ inches, females just under 2½ inches.

Food Requirements: Besides live, frozen and dried foods, they should get some vegetable nourishment.

Color Variations: Dark olive green, shading to yellowish in the belly. Dorsal, anal and caudal fins peppered with spots.

Just why this *Limia* species should be called "*ornata*" is not exactly clear. Even the few who like them would hesitate to say that they are particularly ornate. Of course, they do have a slight claim to colors; they are attractively spotted, reminding one somewhat of the *Phalloceros caudomaculatus reticulatus*. Another feature they have in common with this livebearer is that the female is considerably bigger than the male. As with the other *Limia* species, these must also be kept in a warm tank, about 80°. This species is also shy unless a heavily-planted tank is given to them. Youngsters should be netted out when they are first discovered, or they are very likely to be eaten in short order. This fish was first introduced to hobbyists in 1912, when it was brought into Hamburg, Germany. At that time aquarium heating was not the simple thing it is nowadays with thermostatically controlled heating, and not much luck was had with them. Because of their lack of bright colors and the slightly higher temperatures they require, plus the fact that many of the livebearers are losing the popularity they once had.

*Now alternatively known as *Poecilia ornata*.

Photo by G. J. M. Timmerman.

LIMIA VITTATA (Guichenot)/*Banded Limia*

Range: Cuba.

Habits: Peaceful; likes to nibble algae, but will seldom damage plants.

Water Conditions: Slightly alkaline water with about 1 teaspoonful of salt per gallon added. Recommended temperature 78°, with a sunny aquarium.

Size: Males about 2½ inches, females about 4 inches.

Food Requirements: Not critical; will take dried foods as well as live and frozen foods, but should also get some vegetable nourishment.

Color Variations: Greenish to yellowish body, with a horizontal stripe. Some males have a series of dark vertical bands and yellow dorsal and caudal fins.

A sunny tank with high temperature are the prime requirements for this *Limia* species. The fact that a tank of this sort will produce some algae is grist for their mill, because this species loves to graze on algae. As a rule they confine their appetites to this, and do not as a rule nip at the plants in the aquarium. As a precaution it is well, however, to avoid using the softer-bodied plants like Water Sprite. In the absence of algae a leaf of spinach or lettuce will give the necessary vegetable nutrition. This fish is inclined to be a bit shy in a sparsely-planted aquarium, and will not be at ease unless the planting is heavy. This will also afford protection to the young fry when they are born, and give them a place to hide from their ever-hungry parents. As with the other *Limia* species, broods are not very large numerically, but make up for their small number by being unusually big when they are born, which makes them very easy to raise. An important point is to give the youngsters a sunny aquarium, where they can pick at algae to their hearts' content.

*Now alternatively known as *Poecilia vittata*.

F-382.00

LORICARIA PARVA (Boulenger)/*Whiptailed Catfish*

Range: Paraguay and the La Plata region.

Habits: Occurs in fast-flowing streams, therefore requires well-aerated water. Peaceful toward other fishes.

Water Conditions: Temperatures should be kept in the lower 70's, and there should be plenty of room, as well as a growth of algae.

Size: Up to $4\frac{1}{2}$ inches.

Food Requirements: Food should be small, and tubifex worms are taken greedily, but most important is some vegetable matter, like lettuce leaves.

Color Variations: Body color brown to greenish, lighter underneath. 6 to 8 dark bands. Fins almost colorless.

The Whiptailed Catfish is very much likely to be overlooked in the average aquarium. Its colors blend with most gravel bottoms, and the fish spends a great deal of time on the bottom motionless with fins folded. Its form is interesting, reminding one of some of the armor-plated fossil fishes to be seen pictured now and then. Up to a short time ago, it was considered impossible to breed this fish, but the job has since proven to be far from impossible. Thanks to the skill of some German breeders, we know that they required a large quantity of vegetable matter in their diet to get them into condition. After that came the hard job: raising the young. They breed in dark places like the inside of flowerpots or tubes about $1\frac{1}{2}$ inches in diameter. The male guards the eggs until they hatch and then pays them no further heed. The young must have a continuous supply of algae, or they will suffer a deficiency disease which will render them sterile if it does not kill them.

MACROGNATHUS ACULEATUS (Bloch)/*Spiny Eel*

Range: India, Burma, Thailand.
Habits: Fairly peaceful with fishes its own size or not too much smaller, but it has been known to attack tiny species and half-grown individuals of larger species.
Water Conditions: Soft, slightly acid water best. Temperature 75 to 85°.
Size: Up to 10 inches.
Food Requirements: Usually reluctant to accept dry foods, although will sometimes pick these up from the bottom. *Tubifex* worms are eagerly accepted.

Spiny Eels in general appeal to hobbyists because of their interesting habits and odd shape, although it is true that some of them are also considered as attractive, as their various bars and spots form pleasing patterns. The fish are definitely eel-like in shape, but they are no longer considered to be true eels, even though authoritative ichthyologists of the last century classified them as such. The most interesting habit of Spiny Eels (both *Macrognathus* and *Mastocembelus* species are known by this popular name) is their ability to dig into and remain buried in the aquarium gravel, where they sometimes remain for long periods of time with just the head sticking out, or even completely buried. Another characteristic, but one of more annoyance and less pleasure for their owner, is their propensity to escape from whatever tank they are kept in. This is accomplished more by a "climbing" maneuver than by jumping, and the method serves the Spiny Eels well, because they are often able to leave a tank from which even the best jumping or leaping species are unable to escape. For this reason it is best to cover their tank especially well, for they can "climb" through the smallest openings.

F-384.00

This beautiful Paradise Fish represents a cross between *Macropodus opercularis* and *Macropodus concolor*, the resulting hybrid more closely resembling the latter than the former. Note the handsome development of the upper and lower caudal threads, and the fine extension of the anal filament. Hybrids between species of other genera of fishes are not rare, but the offspring are very seldom an improvement on either parent. Usually, even when combining two pretty fishes, the resulting hybrid young are pale by comparison with the parents, and they have the additional disadvantage of being sterile and frail. This hybrid, however, proved to be equally as hardy as its rugged parents.

MACROPODUS OPERCULARIS (Linneus)/*Paradise Fish*

Range: China, Formosa, Hainan south to Cochin China.
Habits: Very quarrelsome, even toward their own kind.
Water Conditions: Very adaptable to any water conditions. An unheated aquarium suffices, and for breeding 70 to 75° is high enough.
Size: About 3 inches.
Food Requirements: A greedy eater; should be fed often and generously. All kinds of foods are accepted.
Color Variations: Body attractively banded with alternating deep blue and red bands. Fins blue with lighter stripes, tail red with green bands.

The Paradise Fish is the granddaddy of all tropical aquarium fishes. Actually it can only be called a semi-tropical species, and they have been known to survive freezing temperatures when kept in outdoor pools. A pair of Paradise Fish in top condition is a breathtaking sight, and it is a pity that such a gorgeous creature should have so much against it as an aquarium fish. They cannot be kept in community with other fishes, especially smaller ones. In any case the temperatures which would be comfortable for most tropicals would be too high for the Paradise Fish. Anyone who has despaired of ever being able to breed any aquarium fishes could get a pair of these and be almost sure of success. The males build bubble-nests very frequently, and a female which is not yet ready for egg-laying should be kept away until she is, or the nasty-tempered male may mutilate or even kill her. A great number of eggs which float are laid, to be gathered by the male and placed in the nest. The male's ferocity becomes most apparent when spawning is over and he guards the nest, and the female should be removed. Young hatch in 30 to 50 hours and are very easy to raise.

MALAPTERURUS ELECTRICUS (Gmelin)/*Electric Catfish*

Range: Tropical Africa, except for some lake and river systems.
Habits: Decidedly predatory, not safe with other species.
Water Conditions: Neutral water in the medium soft range is best. Temperature 73 to 83°F.
Size: Over two feet in nature, but rarely seen at this size when offered for sale.
Food Requirements: Wants small live fishes, which are usually swallowed whole. Will also eat plants.
Color Variations: Pinkish-gray body covered with irregular black spots; crescent-shaped black marking in tail, with two vertical bars at extreme rear of body. Area between bars is creamy white.

Usually kept for its attraction as a novelty, the Electric Catfish is a real show specimen, for it is both interesting and, in a subdued way, attractive. The most interesting point about *Malapterurus* is, of course, the fish's capacity for discharging an electric current. This current is much weaker than that generated by the South American Electric Eel, *Electrophorus electricus,* but much stronger than that of the African Elephant-Noses of the family Mormyridae. Much speculation has gone into the question of discovering the exact use to which the Electric Catfish puts its odd talent, with some authorities claiming that the Catfish uses its electricity as a weapon of offense by which *Malapterurus* stuns its prey, and others claiming that it is used chiefly as a type of sonar, for the Electric Catfish has very small and poorly developed eyes. Perhaps the former conclusion is closer to the truth, because *Malapterurus* is a very clumsy swimmer and definitely needs help in catching its victims. For this reason the Electric Catfish is often unable to catch its food, even with the help of its electric organs, if it is maintained in a very large tank. Reports state that this fish is a mouthbreeder.

Photo by Aaron Norman

*MASTACEMBELUS SP.

Spotted Fire Eel

Range: Java, Borneo, and Sumatra.
Habits: Mostly nocturnal and a bit shy at first. Hiding-places should be provided.
Water Conditions: Not important as long as the water is clean. Temperature 75 to 78°.
Size: To 18 inches.
Food Requirements: Very fond of worms and other live foods such as *Daphnia* and brine shrimp.

A real oddity which sometimes reaches our shores is the Spotted Fire Eel. Its unusual body shape and hooked, trunklike snout make it a stand-out in any collection. Like so many species that can undulate the dorsal as well as the anal fin, it can swim backward as well as forward, and is a mighty tricky proposition to get into a net. It is largely nocturnal in its habits and unfortunately does not come out often, except when it is hungry and smells food. It is most at ease when a number of hiding-places such as rocks or plant thickets are provided. Often, too, it burrows into the gravel with only its eyes and snout protruding. Once it has gotten accustomed to its surroundings, it makes more and more frequent appearances and gets to know and trust its owner. We have seen no accounts of this species spawning in captivity, but a related species, *Mastacembelus pancalus,* is known to scatter its eggs all over the bottom. After they hatch, the fry hide in the bottom sediment.

*Probably *M. erythrotaenia.*

Photo by S. Frank

MEGALAMPHODUS MEGALOPTERUS (Eigenmann)
Black Phantom Tetra

Range: Brazil.
Habits: Peaceful and active.
Water Conditions: Soft, acid water is best, especially for breeding.
Size: 1½ inches.
Food Requirements: Accepts live, frozen and dried foods; diet should contain a good percentage of live foods.
Color Variations: Over-all body color dusky black, except for silvery stomach area. Black more intense in males; females have red adipose and ventral fins.

The Black Phantom Tetra is a very pretty fish whose colors can best be described as a combination of the markings of the Black Tetra and Serpae Tetra. Additionally, it is a small fish and, unlike some of its Tetra relatives, a peaceful one. The Black Phantom Tetra can be sexed easily when mature, so there is no problem in picking pairs for breeding purposes. The male has a much larger dorsal fin, although this difference is not as noticeable as with some of the other easily-sexed Characins, such as *Hyphessobrycon rubrostigma*, the Bleeding Heart Tetra. But just to make sure that there is no confusion, the fish makes it a little easier for prospective breeders, by adding another sure sign of sex, this one holding good even before the fish have reached maturity: the ventral and adipose fins are blood red on the females and black on the males. *Megalamphodus megalopterus* spawns in thick bundles of plants (nylon spawning mops may also be used), and for a small fish it is quite prolific, sometimes scattering up to 400 eggs at one spawning. The eggs hatch in a little over a day at a temperature of 78°, but they are quite susceptible to fungus, especially if put into a tank with too much light.

Photo by H.J. Richter

MEGALAMPHODUS SWEGLESI (Gery)/*Swegles' Tetra*

Range: Amazon region near Leticia, Colombia.
Habits: Peaceful; like the other Tetras, they prefer to be in schools.
Water Conditions: Soft, slightly acid water is preferred. Temperature 75 to 78°.
Size: About 1¼ inches.
Food Requirements: Easily fed. Prefers live foods, but frozen and prepared foods are also accepted.
Color Variations: Body reddish brown with a large lateral spot of black. Male's dorsal fin is higher and pointed, and female's smaller and round.

Megalamphodus sweglesi is an almost brand-new species which was named by Dr. J. Gery in the May, 1961 issue of "Tropical Fish Hobbyist Magazine." The specific name honors Mr. Kyle Swegles of the Rainbow Aquarium in Chicago, who found them near Leticia, in Colombia,in 1960. The fish closely resembles the *Hyphessobrycon* genus, and it is not evident that this is a member of a different group altogether until a painstaking taxonomic examination is made by an ichthyologist. The region from which this fish comes is an interesting one. Leticia lies at a point on the Amazon where several other rivers meet it, and the small feeder streams are especially rich in fish life. The exotic bird and plant life where the jungle comes to the water's edge put the viewer in another world, one which changes at every turn of the stream. It is here that the Peruvian Amazon begins, and we enter into the region from which comes the Neon Tetra. Swegles' Tetra is probably being bred in Germany at this time. The first ones to reach this country were passed on to our German friends, and it is certain that they have been making every effort to add one more colorful Tetra species to the ones we have.

Photo by Dr. Gerald R. Allen

*MELANOTAENIA SPLENDIDA
Pink-Tailed Australian Rainbow

Range: Queensland, Northern Australia.
Habits: Peaceful; a good community fish.
Water Conditions: Soft, slightly acid water preferred. Temperature 75 to 78°.
Size: To 5 inches.
Food Requirements: Not a choosy eater. Will take prepared as well as live or frozen foods.
Color Variations: Sides bluish with a violet tinge. Several red zigzag horizontal lines. Dorsal and anal fins with orange spots, tail pink.

A look at the deep body and disproportionately small head of *Melanotaenia splendida* reminds one of the odd *Distichodus* species which are native to Africa. Unlike the *Distichodus* species, however, they are not plant-eaters and do not attain the immense proportions reached by the queer-looking Africans. Once the breeders have put out good numbers of these fish, it may do to the Dwarf Australian Rainbow what that fish did to *Melanotaenia nigrans*. This was a gorgeous, peaceful fish and its only fault was that it would outgrow all but the largest tanks. With the introduction of the Dwarf Australian Rainbow there was a fish with a striking set of colors of its own, and almost at once the larger species all but disappeared. Now that there is a *third* Australian Rainbow, one cannot help but wonder if it will get the center of the stage and supplant the other two. The newcomer certainly fills the bill where colors are concerned, with its beautiful orange-speckled and black-edged dorsal and anal fins and pink tail.

* The current generic name of this species is *Nematocentrus*.

F-391.00

MELANOTAENIA MACCULOCHI (Ogilby)/*Dwarf Australian Rainbow*

Range: Northern Australia in the region of Cairns.

Habits: Peaceful; prefers being kept in small groups.

Water Conditions: Slightly alkaline water to which a little salt (about a teaspoonful per gallon) has been added is best. Temperature 74 to 78°.

Size: Up to 2¾ inches.

Food Requirements: Not a choosy eater; prepared foods accepted as readily as live or frozen foods.

Color Variations: Sides grayish silver, back brown, belly yellowish green. Seven reddish horizontal lines on sides. Fins red with a yellow edge.

At the time of writing, the Dwarf Australian Rainbow is the most popular of the aquarium fishes from that country. Whether or not the Pink-Tailed Australian Rainbow will supplant it in popularity remains to be seen. Fish hobbyists are apt to be a fickle lot and tire easily of a species to shift their attentions to another fish which often turns out to be less desirable. In any case, the Dwarf Australian Rainbow comes very close to being an ideal aquarium fish. It is peaceful, hardy and easily fed. It spawns readily and seldom eats its eggs except when very hungry. It does not uproot plants, nor does it nibble on them. Add to these traits a set of very attractive colors and you obviously have a fish which is fairly hard to improve upon. The male has something special to offer in the way of colors which we have never seen photographed: when pursuing a female during spawning time the colors not only become intensified but a wide lemon-yellow stripe appears on the sides, to disappear as quickly as it came. Eggs are laid in bushy plants; young hatch in 7 to 10 days and are very easily raised.

MELANOTAENIA NIGRANS (Richardson)/*Australian Rainbow*

Range: Northern Australia as far south as Sydney.
Habits: Peaceful; prefers to be kept in small groups. Very hardy.
Water Conditions: Neutral to slightly alkaline water to which a small amount of salt has been added. Temperature 65 to 75°.
Size: To 4 inches.
Food Requirements: Easily fed; accepts prepared foods as readily as live or frozen foods.
Color Variations: Back yellowish to greenish, belly white. Scales on sides have dark edges, giving a reticulated effect. Dark horizontal stripes.

This is the original Australian Rainbow, which has been known to the hobby since about 1927. By old standards it was quite large for the average tank, but the use of larger tanks has become more commonplace since those days, as well as accessory equipment such as aeration, filtration, etc. Some day someone will get a pair of these fish, which we see so rarely these days, spawn them and get the ball rolling by giving the young ones to some of his friends. It will be only a question of time when a demand is created for this peaceful, attractive fish and it comes into its own again. Breeding Rainbows is not at all difficult. A well-conditioned pair is placed into a tank of at least 15 gallons capacity which has been planted with *Myriophyllum, Cabomba* or some other fine-leaved plant. It is not necessary to watch the fish and remove them the minute they have finished spawning. They seldom touch their eggs. When a good amount of eggs can be seen hanging by little strings from the plants and the fish have lost interest in each other the parents can be removed. Incubation period is 7 to 10 days. The fry are hardy.

Photo by H.J. Richter

MESOGONISTIUS CHAETODON (Baird)/*Blackbanded Sunfish*

Range: New Jersey south to northern Florida.

Habits: Usually peaceful, but should not be trusted with smaller fishes. Also shy, and gets very nervous when with very active fishes.

Water Conditions: Water should be kept alkaline, and a part of it frequently changed. Temperature should be kept around 70°.

Size: 3 inches.

Food Requirements: Live foods only; it might be possible to induce them to eat frozen foods, but they will seldom take dried foods.

Color Variations: Body silvery to light yellow, with a number of dark bars running vertically. First ventral fin rays are orange.

Here is a fish which our readers along most of the states along the Atlantic Seaboard can catch for themselves, game laws permitting. The Blackbanded Sunfish is found in ponds and cypress swamps along the Atlantic Coast from New Jersey down to northern Florida. The best time to hunt them is in the early Summer, when the young ones have left the nest and are found along the shore in shallow water. These youngsters are best able to make the change to aquarium life, and there are fewer losses. There may be a great temptation to catch some adult specimens, but if you do this be prepared to lose some of your catch, as they do not acclimate themselves as easily to the aquarium. When transporting them do not crowd the containers; remember, a few live and healthy fish are better than a lot of dead ones! This fish is a great favorite with European hobbyists. The males build a nest by digging out a depression in the gravel. The females are then lured to this nest, and a great many eggs are expelled. These eggs are sticky and adhere to the gravel. Females are driven away, and should be removed. Males guard the eggs and later the young, but should be removed when the young leave the nest.

F-394.00

METYNNIS MACULATUS (Kner)/*Spotted Metynnis*

Range: Guianas down to the Rio Paraguay.
Habits: Peaceful toward other fishes of comparable size. Are happiest when kept in groups.
Water Conditions: Soft, slightly alkaline water is best suited. Tank should be roomy and afford some shelters. Temperature 72 to 76°.
Size: To 7 inches. Usually collected and sold at about 2 inches.
Food Requirements: Special attention must be given to their vegetable diet requirements by giving them lettuce and spinach leaves plus live foods.
Color Variations: Sides yellowish to brownish with many good-sized dark spots. All fins except pectorals have a dark edge.

The *Metynnis* species are related to the vicious Piranhas which are known and feared throughout most of tropical South America. Although there is a superficial similarity in body form, to an ichthyologist there is an immense difference in skull structure and in the digestive organs. The Piranhas are of course strictly carnivores, while the *Metynnis* species are almost as strictly vegetarians. Thus the hobbyist who keeps them in a community aquarium and feeds them as he does his other fishes is making the mistake of depriving them of their most important diet ingredient, vegetable substances. If their tank is planted the *Metynnis* will make up for this lack by chewing up the plants until they are all gone. This places a considerable strain on the ingenuity of the hobbyist: how to achieve an attractive background for his fish without using plants. This can be done surprisingly well by using rocks, driftwood and decorative roots. Males of this species are distinguished by the shape of the anal fin, which is considerably indented, while that of the female is straight or slightly rounded. There are no accounts on hand of this species ever being spawned.

F-395.00

Photo by Gunter Senff.

*METYNNIS SCHREITMUELLERI (E. Ahl)/*Schreitmueller's Metynnis*

Range: Amazon region, widely distributed.
Habits: Peaceful, fond of swimming in schools.
Water Conditions: Must be kept in a large aquarium. Hardness should be 10 to 15 DH, slightly acid, pH 6.8. Temperature 75 to 80°.
Size: Up to 6 inches.
Food Requirements: Will take and should get live or frozen foods, but most important item is vegetable nourishment, such as lettuce leaves, etc.
Color Variations: Sides silvery with a bluish sheen. Back olive green. Front part of anal fin brick red.

Schreitmueller's Metynnis is one of the old favorites among the genus. Whether any of them found their way to these shores is dubious, but German works refer to them as early as 1913. Here again we have a fish which will make a meal of any plants it finds in the aquarium. It might seem that decorating with the artificial plants one sees sold nowadays could cause a great deal of frustration to a fish which sees something which looks good to eat but isn't, but the fact is that a fish depends more on its sense of smell when it comes to locating its food than on its sight, which with many fishes is far from good. One must remember too that water is not by a long shot as transparent as other media, and a fish with poor eyesight is not as badly off as one which has been deprived of its sense of smell and taste. To get back to the subject, *Metynnis schreitmuelleri* has been spawned on occasion. A pair will swim through a plant thicket and cuddle against each other Tetra-fashion, releasing as many as 2000 eggs. These hatch in 70 hours at about 82° and the fry do not begin to swim freely until about a week later. They are easily raised on brine shrimp and finely chopped spinach.

* Now known as *Metynnis hypsauchen*.

A heavily parasitized *Metynnis*. Ectoparasites seldom kill the host unless they occur in such great numbers as to interfere with the normal functions of the fish.

Photo by Dr. Herbert R. Axelrod.

Photo by Dr. Herbert R. Axelrod.

MICRALESTES ACUTIDENS (Peters)/*Sharp-toothed Tetra*

Range: Nile River, Congo River, Lake Chad, Omo River, Zambesi River and Limpopo River.
Habits: Peaceful and active fish which requires adequate swimming room.
Water Conditions: Soft, slightly acid water which is clean and well aerated is best. Prefers warmth, about 78°, but a drop to 73° or so is tolerated.
Size: 2½ inches maximum.
Food Requirements: Not critical; may be maintained on dried foods with only occasional feedings of live foods.
Color Variations: Body silvery with a bluish sheen underneath. Horizontal stripe from gill-plates to caudal base. Dorsal tips have black marking.

What the Sharp-toothed Tetra lacks in bright colors it makes up for in activity and good behavior; it minds its own business and bustles around without bothering the others. Don't let the name "Sharp-toothed" scare you. These teeth do no damage to other fishes or plants. Because the collectors have so many highly colored and therefore better-selling species to offer, we do not often get to see these lesser-colored fish and to the best of our knowledge they have not yet been spawned in captivity. Again we have the possibility that the breeders have not tried very hard to propagate a fish which might be a "hard seller." The fish themselves might be quite willing to co-operate. Males are usually not difficult to distinguish by their slender form and more pointed and elongated dorsal fin. With their constant hustle and bustle a tankful of half-grown Sharp-toothed Tetras should present a pretty sight. This fish has a very wide range, and we have seen them in shipments from the Congo River, then had the same fish turn up in a shipment from the Zambesi River. The author (H.R.A.) collected this species in the Belgian Congo—perhaps the specimens then collected were the first to appear alive outside the Congo ?

F-398.00

MICROBRYCON (BOEHLKEA) FREDCOCHUI
Cochu's Blue Tetra

Range: Peruvian Amazon region, near Leticia, Colombia.

Habits: Peaceful but very sensitive; best kept with other fishes with similar characteristics.

Water Conditions: Soft, slightly acid water is highly important with this species. The addition of acid peat moss in the filter is beneficial.

Size: Up to 2¼ inches.

Food Requirements: Live or frozen foods; dried foods only when there is nothing else at hand.

Color Variations: Sides bluish violet, with a silvery bluish horizontal line. Dorsal and anal fins light orange; all fins have light tips.

Like many of the Tetras from the Upper Amazon region, Cochu's Blue Tetra is not seen at its best unless it has water which is to its liking. At this point of the huge river the water has very little mineral content, and there is an influx from other streams where the humic acid content is high, plus a great deal of rain water at certain times of the year, so we must approach these conditions by using water which is soft and has a certain amount of acidity. The most beautiful specimens of this fish ever seen by the author were in a large aquarium in the lobby of a hotel in Iquitos, Peru. Here they were kept in the company of several types of Pencilfishes as well as a good number of Neon Tetras. It was a surprise to see the Peruvians keeping their own native fishes, rather than some expensive (for them!) Barbs or Gouramis. Wherever one goes the fishes from far-off lands, whether they are beautiful or not, are the ones which are considered worth keeping. It could be that the Peruvians are aware that they have some of the most colorful fishes in the world. Dr. Gery studied this fish and named it *Boehlkea fredcochui*. We retain *Microbrycon* only because the fish is so popular and known under that name.

F-399.00

MICROGLANIS POECILUS *Dwarf Marbled Catfish*

Range: Brazil.

Habits: Peaceful, nocturnal. Tank in which they are kept should have a number of retreats where the fish can hide when the light is bright.

Water Conditions: Soft, slightly alkaline water is best. Temperature 75 to 78°.

Size: To 2¾ inches.

Food Requirements: Live foods preferred, especially worms. Frozen foods are second choice, then dry foods.

Color Variations: Body yellowish with marbled markings of dark brown. Caudal, anal and ventral fins clear with rows of dark spots.

The Catfishes are a tremendous group. They include fishes which are down-right ugly, some which are not quite as ugly but are kept for strictly utilitarian reasons and others which are quite pretty. Some have no objection to a brightly lighted tank, but others will come out into the light only when there is food available and they are hungry enough to subjugate their fear and hatred of the light to come out of hiding and quickly gobble up as much food as they can get into their mouths and then rush back again. *Microglanis poecilus* belongs to a minority group by being very pretty to look at and never getting to a size where the owner wonders whether to purchase a larger tank or cook it for dinner. At the present time they are so scarce as to be practically non-existent, but about a decade or so ago most well-stocked dealers had some. This is a fish which has varying colors, and if kept in an aquarium with a dark bottom is likely to remain dark, with less contrast between the light and dark areas. There are no external sex differences and no records of anyone having ever spawned them, although they have been known to science since 1880 and hobbyists since 1926.

*MICROPOECILIA BRANNERI (Eigenmann)/*Branner's Livebearer*

Range: Amazon Basin.
Habits: A fin-nipper.
Water Conditions: Alkaline, medium-hard water best. Temperature 70 to 80°F.
Size: 1½ inches; females up to 1¾ inches.
Food Requirements: Takes all foods.
Color Variations: Plain gray-brown fish with black vertical bars in body and large oval spot near tail.

One of the first of the livebearers to be brought into the country, this nasty little fish had a very fleeting popularity, because it had no real advantages other than its availability, and it was soon overshadowed by the introduction of other livebearers, most of them more colorful and peaceful. It is almost never seen these days, because the establishment of the large Florida fish hatcheries has assured a continual supply of colorful and popular livebearing species, and there is no longer any need to import colorless species from South America. The male of the species is smaller than the female and is distinguishable from her by the presence of a gonopodium and the fancier dorsal fin. In general, the fish look like small Guppies, but with different markings. *Micropoecilia branneri* is not nearly as prolific as the Guppy, however, and breeding the species is complicated by the fact that the parent fishes are very eager eaters of their own young, even more so than most other livebearers. Young are dropped over a protracted period, usually one or at most two at a time, and the total number born to any one female is always small. Although fully grown fish are hardy, the young do not do well, even with the best of care.

* Now known as *Poecilia branneri*.

Photo by Dr. Herbert R. Axelrod.

*MICROPOECILIA MELANOZONUS (Eigenmann)/*Blue Guppy*

Range: British Guiana.
Habits: Inclined to be nasty; a fin-nipper.
Water Conditions: Slightly alkaline, medium-hard water.
Size: 1½ to 2 inches.
Food Requirements: Accepts all regular aquarium foods.
Color Variations: Extremely variegated, although blue is the predominant color
of the male; female plain grayish brown.

Looking at the picture above, the viewer would almost certainly be tempted
to identify the fish as poor specimens of Guppies, perhaps some of the original
stock brought into the country. The fish pictured, however, are currently
placed in a different genus from the Guppies, although with such a marked
similarity it is entirely possible that they may be combined in the genus
Lebistes. This is a very ticklish question, though, because ichthyologists
base their decisions on much more fundamental considerations than outward
appearances. In the case of the livebearing fishes, for instance, the gonopodium of the male is of basic importance in classification; where the structure
of the gonopodium varies greatly from fish to fish, a separation is made, no
matter how much the species might resemble one another in size, general
body shape, and markings. However, these *Micropoecilia* have been successfully crossed with *Lebistes reticulatus* by Dr. Herbert R. Axelrod, and this
opens the door to putting the fish into the same genus.

F-402.00   * Now known as *Poecilia parae.*

Photo by Harald Schultz

*MIMAGONIATES BARBERI (Regan)/*Barber's Tetra*

Range: Southern Brazil, Paraguay and northeastern Argentina.
Habits: Peaceful and very active; prefers to swim in schools. Does not harm plants.
Water Conditions: Soft acid water which is clean and well aerated. Temperature about 76°. Tank should be in a sunny location. Prefers tannic acid stained water (brown water).
Size: 1¾ inches.
Food Requirements: Should be generously fed with live foods.
Color Variations: Body color brown, with a dark blue horizontal stripe. Anal fin edged with dark blue, dorsal edged with white and blue underneath.

Mimagoniates barberi looks more like a member of the *Danio* genus than one of the Characins. They are always alert, and forever on the move, traveling in schools whenever a number of them are put into the same aquarium. They love sunlight, and are especially happy and active when the sun shines into their tank. In their native habitat they inhabit small, fast-flowing, cool streams where the water is rich in oxygen, and for this reason they should have adequate aeration in their tank. Males of this fish have an odd characteristic: the horizontal stripe extends into the lower rays of the tail. Where the dark rays occur the tail is not evenly notched, but the dark rays come out and give an almost square appearance to the lower caudal lobe. This characteristic is only slight in the females, which gives a sure method for choosing pairs. They have been spawned on a few occasions, but reports do not tell much beyond the fact that they spawned in a similar manner to the other small Characins, that the eggs hatched in one day and that the fry were very hard to raise. Many imported specimens which are seemingly healthy seem to waste away for some mysterious reason in the aquarium. The author (H.R.A.) collected and shipped thousands from Santos, Brazil to Florida.

* Now known as *Coleurichthys tenuis.*

Photo by Dr. Herbert R. Axelrod.

*MIMAGONIATES INEQUALIS (Eigenmann)/*Croaking Tetra*

Range: Southeastern Brazil, Rio Grande do Sul.
Habits: Peaceful and active. Does not disturb plants.
Water Conditions: Should be kept in a roomy aquarium at a temperature slightly
lower than most tropical species, 70 to 74°.
Size: Males about 2¼ inches, females about 1¾ inches.
Food Requirements: Not a fussy eater; besides live foods, will also eat dried foods.
Color Variations: Body brownish above, silvery white below. Front and upper edge
of eye bright red. Dorsal and anal edged yellow, with black below.

For many years this fish was classified as *Glandulocauda inequalis*, and it
remained for Dr. Leonard P. Schultz of the United States National Museum
to combine the two genera in a paper published in "Tropical Fish Hobbyist,"
October, 1959. As the name implies, this fish has the power to make tiny
croaking noises. These are made by getting a gulp of air at the surface, then
swimming below and releasing it. This is likened to the chirp of an insect by
some. Something which has not yet been fully explained goes on when this
fish breeds. There is an active driving beforehand, but then the female leaves
the male and lays the eggs without any further contact with the male. The
usual explanation for this is that some sort of an internal fertilization takes
place, and this has been backed by some authorities who have cut open females
and removed eggs and a sac which was found to contain sperm. They were
able to fertilize the eggs with this sperm, but one thing still remains to be
fully explained: How did the sperm-sac get there? A similar problem exists
with a few other fishes, such as *Corynopoma riisei* and *Pseudocorynopoma
doriae.*

* The fishes shown are *Glandulocauda inequalis* (left, top)
and *Coelurichthys microlepis.*

MISGURNUS ANGUILLICAUDATUS (Cantor)/*Weatherfish*

Range: Japan and northern China.
Habits: Peaceful with other species.
Water Conditions: Water conditions not too important, as long as extremes are avoided.
Size: Up to 8 inches.
Food Requirements: Takes all regular aquarium foods, but living worms are preferred.
Color Variations: Over-all brownish body with dark mottlings.

Like the other Cobitid fishes, most *Misgurnus* species are often thought to be Eels, because of their elongated cylindrical shape. The name "Weatherfish" is derived from the fact that the fishes are known to be sensitive to changes in barometric pressure, and their changes in motion during periods in which the barometric pressure changes sharply have given the fish the reputation for being able to forecast the weather accurately. Changes in activity accompanying a drop in pressure, signifying a storm, are especially noteworthy. In the home aquarium the fish are interesting for their habit of diving head-first under the gravel, sometimes keeping the whole body completely out of sight, other times keeping the head or part of the head above the level of the sand. This makes it difficult to tell at a glance exactly how many *Misgurnus* are in a tank (if the tank contains a bottom in which the fish can hide), and it is always a surprise for a viewer to find four or five healthy, active fish in a tank which to all intents and purposes contained nothing just a few minutes before. If this species is to be kept it is best to pick one or two small fish, as large ones stir up the gravel too much.

MOENKHAUSIA DICHROURA (Kner)/*Spot-Tailed Moenkhausia*

Range: Paraguay.
Habits: Peaceful and active; tank should be covered, as this fish can jump.
Water Conditions: Soft, acid water preferred. Temperature 68 to 75°.
Size: To 3 inches.
Food Requirements: A good eater which is not fussy as to food. Should get some live or frozen foods, however.
Color Variations: Back is light brown, sides silvery with a shiny horizontal stripe. Tail yellow with two black areas and white tips.

This is a good fish to show someone who considers himself an authority on aquarium fishes and ask him to identify. Nine times out of ten he will give it a careless glance and say it is *Rasbora trilineata*, a fish from the East Indies which is very familiar to hobbyists and has an almost identical pattern in the tail. Then it will be your turn to ask him if he ever saw a *Rasbora* with an adipose fin, which is sure to cause the "expert" to look again, this time more carefully. The author was almost fooled the same way, but first asked where the fish came from. The dealer, who had a tankful and did not know what they were either, admitted that they came from South America and gave me a pair to get identified for him. They are pictured here and lasted in my tanks for several years with no special attention. They did not indulge in the usual *Moenkhausia* habit of nipping plants, nor did they ever bother any of their tankmates. Eventually they jumped out through an opening left a little too wide. Only once since then have I ever seen them for sale. They certainly deserve a better distribution, but are probably neglected because of their resemblance to a better-known species.

F-406.00

Photo by G. J. M. Timmerman.

MOENKHAUSIA OLIGOLEPIS (Günther)/*Glass Tetra*

Range: British Guiana and the upper Amazon region.
Habits: Quite peaceful, but must not be kept with smaller fishes.
Water Conditions: Soft, slightly acid water and a large tank are required.
Size: 4½ inches, usually smaller.
Food Requirements: Must be fed generously with mostly live or frozen foods. If
hungry they may nip plants.
Color Variations: Body silvery to gray. Upper half of eye bright red. Large black
area at caudal base. Fins have a pink tint.

Most people who buy this fish get young ones without realizing how they
grow and grow until they find themselves with bigger fish than they had
bargained for. *Moenkhausia oligolepis* is a hardy fish, and asks little more
than a large aquarium and plenty of food. Lately there has been an albino
form on the market, which has a white body, pink fins and red eyes. Whether
these albinos attain the size of their normal brethren we cannot say for sure,
but we have had small ones and found them to be every bit as hardy as the
others. The Glass Tetra has been accused of being a plant eater, and rightly
so. However, an examination of the intestines discloses the fact that they are
short, which is not at all typical of a fish which normally lives on a vegetable
diet. We may therefore assume that the Glass Tetra is normally carnivorous,
and eats plants only when hunger drives it to eat anything edible. We must
therefore take this fish's appetite into consideration and feed it as we would
any active, large, carnivorous fish. If this is done we can keep them in a well-
planted aquarium without any fear of the plants being damaged.

F-407.00

Photo by Dr. Herbert R. Axelrod.

MOENKHAUSIA PITTIERI (Eigenmann)/*Diamond Tetra*

Range: Environs of Lake Valencia, Venezuela.
Habits: Peaceful and very active.
Water Conditions: Large, well-planted tanks are best. Temperature 75 to 80°.
Size: To 2½ inches.
Food Requirements: A good eater which will take practically any kind of food, but should have a supplement of vegetable matter, like lettuce leaves.
Color Variations: Body color yellowish, darker above. Upper half of body gleams golden, and the lower part iridescent. Unpaired fins milky violet.

The Diamond Tetra is without a doubt the beauty of the *Moenkhausia* group. It has an opalescent sparkle to its scales which is not found in many other aquarium fishes, and it grows to only about half the size attained by the Glass Tetra. This is not to say that the Diamond Tetra requires only about half the space allotted to its larger cousin; it is happiest when it has ample "fin-room." Although they are not entirely innocent of the crime, the Diamond Tetras do not have the immense appetite for plants which is characteristic of *Moenkhausia oligolepis*, and if properly fed a well-planted tank is not in very great danger from their depredations. This is an extremely hardy and long-lived fish, and once established in a tank which suits them they will live for a long time. They are also easier to spawn, but are by no means an "easy" species. Eggs are laid among bushy plants in a manner similar to the large Tetras. The young hatch in 48 to 60 hours and after the yolk-sac is absorbed are very easy to raise.

MOGURNDA MOGURNDA MOGURNDA (Richardson)
Purple-Striped Gudgeon

Range: Central and northern coastal Australia.
Habits: Should be kept with its own kind or larger fishes which can take care of themselves, or it may bully its tankmates.
Water Conditions: Alkaline water with a slight addition of salt is best. Temperature 72 to 78°.
Size: 4 inches.
Food Requirements: Should get a preponderance of live or frozen foods.
Color Variations: Colors vary with individuals. Gill-plates have purple stripes; body and fins have spots and stripes of varying colors.

We do not see many really good aquarium fishes from Australia. Most of them come from the coastal regions and require partly brackish water. With very few exceptions Australian fishes are not very active and do not have very bright colors. The Purple-Striped Gudgeon is an exception where color is concerned, but is a fish which cannot always be trusted to leave its tankmates alone. Many a nipped fin can be traced to them. Old-time aquarists often counsel: "Beware of a fish with a large mouth." This does not necessarily mean that all large-mouthed fishes are nasty. The all-time "nasty prize" goes to the African *Phago* species, which will pursue and pick at a fish until its fins are gone, and then proceed to pick at its scales and skin until it is dead. And they have small mouths! To return to the Purple-Striped Gudgeon, they spawn quite willingly on rocks and the glass sides of the aquarium. The male takes charge of the eggs and keeps fanning them thoroughly for about a week, at which time they begin to hatch. It is best to remove him at this time and leave the fry to fend for themselves. Thanks to their large mouths, they have no trouble with brine shrimp babies and grow quickly.

Photo by Dr. Herbert R. Axelrod.

*MOLLIENESIA LATIPINNA (Le Sueur)/*Sailfin Molly*

Range: Southeastern coastal United States south to Yucatan.

Habits: Peaceful toward other fishes, but best kept by themselves in a large, well-planted aquarium.

Water Conditions: Slightly alkaline water with a light addition of salt, a teaspoonful to the gallon. Temperature 78 to 84°.

Size: Males, to 4 inches; females, to 5 inches.

Food Requirements: A hearty eater which should be fed frequently with a preponderance of foods which have a vegetable content.

Color Variations: Body greenish, back light brown. Dorsal fin of the male is very high and broad with rows of red, brown and green dots.

One of the most abused of all aquarium fishes is the Sailfin Molly. Very seldom does one see them kept with a perfect understanding of their requirements and habits, and consequently the specimens one sees are of a very poor quality. In the first place, the fish in its natural waters usually seeks a place where the water is shallow and becomes quite warm during the day. For this reason fish kept in captivity should be kept at higher temperatures than one generally gives to tropical species. Pursuing the topic still further, the warmer water holds less oxygen than the cooler water and in order to give them the oxygen they require, Mollies should have a large, uncrowded tank. A study of their internal organs as well as observation of their habits tells us that they are largely vegetarians, and their food should contain a good percentage of vegetable matter. Coming as they do from mostly brackish water, the addition of salt to their aquarium water is important. Females about to have young should not be moved if possible, and breeding traps should not be used. Given a well-planted aquarium of her own, a Molly will seldom eat her young.

*Now alternatively known as *Poecilia latipinna*.

F-410.00

Above and below: These two photos show the great difference in color pattern between Mollies of the same species. Both photos show *Mollienesia latipinna*, but each particular strain represents a divergence from the color pattern of the original wild fish.

Lyre Tail Black Mollies.

Photo by Dr. Herbert R. Axelrod.

*MOLLIENESIA SPHENOPS (Cuvier & Valenciennes)/*Sphenops*

Range: Mexico and Central America, also parts of northern South America.

Habits: Individual specimens show marked differences in behavior; some are completely peaceful, and others are nasty.

Water Conditions: Hard, alkaline water best; tank should have plenty of plants and be well lighted.

Size: Up to 4 inches; usually seen about half this size.

Food Requirements: Doesn't like dry food unless it contains a high percentage of vegetable matter. Small crustaceans form a good meaty portion of the diet.

Color Variations: Many intermediate color varieties, most commonly gray or black body with orange markings.

It is unfortunate that so many beginning hobbyists pick Mollies as the fish with which to begin their aquaristic activities. The various Mollies are really not a beginner's fish, because they are rather touchy about how they are handled, and they soon die, or at least give evidence of extreme discomfort, when kept by the person who is still learning the rudiments of good aquarium technique. Still, many people are attracted to the Mollies in general, and it is lucky that the genus contains at least one species that is not so tender as its relatives. The Sphenops Molly is such a fish, for, although it is not as tough as some other livebearers, like the Platies and Guppies, it is generally more robust than *Mollienesia latipinna* and *velifera*. First of all, it requires less space for proper growth, but it has other advantages besides this. It is easier to feed, as it accepts dry and frozen foods more readily, and it is easier to keep with other species, because it is not so dependent on the special water conditions needed for the other Mollies. A pretty fish, *Mollienesia sphenops* is usually seen as one of three varieties: plain black, mottled black with orange tail, or gray-green with orange tail. The male fish has the orange tail.

*Now alternatively known as *Poecilia mexicana*.

Photo by A. van den Nieuwenhuizen.

*MOLLIENESIA VELIFERA (Regan)/*Sail-Fin Molly*

Range: Yucatan.
Habits: Individuals vary; some are peaceful and some, especially large males, are bullies.
Water Conditions: Hard, alkaline water with salt added is best.
Size: Up to 5 inches.
Food Requirements: Needs plenty of vegetable matter, especially algae, in diet, but also takes meat foods.
Color Variations: Steely-blue body covered with many iridescent green and blue dots; dorsal fin trimmed in orange. Orange throat area on both sexes. Three dark blotches below beginning of dorsal fin of male.

The difference between *Mollienesia velifera* and *Mollienesia latipinna*, simply put, is that *velifera* is a bigger fish with a bigger dorsal fin. In other visible particulars the two are very similar, and the similarity is compounded by the fact that many of the *velifera* found on the market today are smaller than their forebears, thus bringing the fish into even greater physical alignment. They are also quite alike in their food preferences and water requirements, and they are both unsuited to the beginning hobbyist, even though they are often chosen as "starter" fish by the uninformed. *Mollienesia velifera* is not often seen today, mostly because *latipinna* can be found wild in the southern states along the Gulf Coast, where it is sometimes caught and shipped as a pool-raised fish. When in good condition, *Mollienesia velifera* is tough to beat for looks, for it is truly a beautiful fish, especially with the majestic dorsal fin at full spread. But they are not too often seen at their best; many times they can be viewed in a dealer's tanks with clamped fins, shimmying, instead of swimming, their way around the tank. When Mollies in general and *M. velifera* in particular are unhappy, they let you know quickly.

*Now alternatively known as *Poecilia velifera*.

MONOCIRRHUS POLYACANTHUS (Heckel)/*Leaf Fish*

Range: Tropical South America; Amazon, Rio Negro, British Guiana.

Habits: Occurs in sluggish streams, where it feeds on smaller fishes and aquatic insects. Peaceful in the aquarium toward anything it cannot swallow.

Water Conditions: Soft, slightly acid water, temperature about 78°.

Size: Up to 4 inches.

Food Requirements: Small ones may be fed with the usual live foods. Larger ones must get living smaller fishes.

Color Variations: Light brown, mottled with darker markings. Darker lateral line from eye to caudal base, with two other lines emanating from eye.

Unless he knows what to look for, a collector would probably pass by dozens of these before he realized that they were fish, so perfect is their camouflage. Not only does their color make them look like a dead leaf in the water, but they also have the faculty for swimming like one. They can turn on their side and drift along almost imperceptibly by paddling with their almost transparent pectoral fins. Not only does this throw their enemies off guard, but it also permits them to get close to their unsuspecting prey. They work their head toward a selected morsel, then suddenly open a surprisingly large mouth. The prey is sucked along with the inrushing water, and the Leaf Fish has had his meal. In the aquarium these conditions must be duplicated, and the Leaf Fish will consider it beneath its dignity to forage for food, and prefers to stalk it. A supply of small, expendable fishes must therefore always be on hand. Some hobbyists who were possessed of infinite patience and had a great deal of time at their disposal found that it was sometimes possible to tame Leaf Fish and get them to swallow a strip of cut fish by dangling it in front of them. They breed easily and lay sticky eggs under a leaf.

MONODACTYLUS ARGENTEUS (Linné)/*Mono*

Range: Malayan and African coastal waters.
Habits: Shy, often gets panicky when frightened. Best kept in a small group in a roomy tank.
Water Conditions: Slightly alkaline water with about a teaspoonful of salt to each gallon is acceptable.
Size: Wild specimens attain 9 inches. Seldom exceed half that in captivity.
Food Requirements: All sorts of live foods.
Color Variations: Body silvery, with a golden sheen above. Two black vertical bars, one through the eye and the other through the pectoral base.

The Mono is an example of a fish which is native to brackish and even completely marine water, but it frequently ascends rivers for a time, a habit which gives it a tolerance for fresh water. It must be remembered that they must have some salt in their water if they are to be kept successfully in the aquarium. Monos are never at their best unless kept in a marine aquarium, where their colors deepen, they eat ravenously and grow rapidly. These beautiful fish have never been spawned in captivity, probably because they confine these activities to salt or brackish waters. Many fishes like this never attain sexual maturity in captivity under any conditions, even in a marine aquarium. We still have a great deal to learn about the spawning rhythms of many of our aquarium fishes, and what triggers them. This is what adds zest to the aquarium hobby and makes it possible for an informed amateur to lend a hand to the ichthyological experts by making his findings known. The Mono is a good fish to keep with others which have the same requirements as to a slight salinity in the water, such as fishes of the genus *Mollienesia*.

F-416.00

Photo by Dr. Herbert R. Axelrod.

MONODACTYLUS SEBAE (Cuvier & Valenciennes)/*Fingerfish*

Range: Tropical West African coast.
Habits: Shy; should be kept in a very large, well-planted tank.
Water Conditions: Alkaline water with some salt added, about a teaspoonful for each gallon. Temperature 76 to 80°.
Size: Wild fully-grown specimens up to 8 inches.
Food Requirements: All sorts of live foods.
Color Variations: Body silvery, brownish above. Four dark bars cross the body. These bars fade with age.

The Fingerfish is rarely collected and shipped to dealers, and if a few occasional ones survive the rigors of travel from Africa and get established in an aquarium, they may soon outgrow all but the largest tanks. The overall length of grown specimens is given as 8 inches, and the body is one-third higher than it is long, resulting in a fish which is almost 11 inches high! A fairly active fish with these dimensions, it may be readily imagined, would require lots of "fin-room." This rare beauty is a showpiece for public aquaria, which would be best equipped to handle them. The body shape is somewhat reminiscent of that of the Angelfish but the dorsal and anal fins are much simpler, while the ventral fins are so small as to be mere vestiges. There is a dark bar which passes through the eye, a faint one which passes through the pectoral fin base, another which extends from the tip of the dorsal fin to the tip of the anal fin and still another at the caudal base. With advancing age these markings become more indistinct, presently almost disappearing.

MORMYROPS ENGYSTOMA (Boulenger)

Range: Lower Congo River.

Habits: Should not be kept with smaller fishes which it could swallow. Usually peaceful with the larger fishes.

Water Conditions: Neutral to slightly acid water. Temperature 75 to 80°F. Tank should be well planted and partly shaded.

Size: To 14 inches.

Food Requirements: Tubifex or small earthworms are the preferred foods, and crushed snails are also enjoyed.

Color Variations: Color of body almost uniformly gray with an indistinct horizontal darker line. Small heart-shaped area of black in the tail.

Some of the oddest and most interesting fishes in the world occur in Africa, in the Nile and Congo Rivers. These are the Mormyrids, a group of fishes which will never be distinguished for any bright colors but which nevertheless have the strangest imaginable body shapes. Look at the body proportions in this picture of *Mormyrops engystoma*, for instance: the head is all out of proportion to the rest of the body, the dorsal fin is far back near the tail and the tail itself is so small that it looks as if it would do for a fish one-third its size. Scientists are particularly interested in the Mormyrid group. They have come to the amazing conclusion that the brain of these fishes, when weighed and compared to the weight of the rest of the body, is larger in proportion than that of a human being. Most of the Mormyrids are night feeders and are endowed with a keen sense of smell. The majority of them have tiny mouths with which they sift out worms, crustaceans and molluscs from the bottom mud. Most of them get too big for the home aquarium and reach us when very young. However, they grow slowly and take quite a while to outgrow their quarters.

MORULIUS CHRYSOPHEKADION (Bleeker)/*Black Shark*

Range: Thailand.
Habits: Peaceful toward other fishes, but likely to be scrappy among themselves.
Water Conditions: Water should be slightly alkaline, about 10 DH. Temperature 75 to 80°.
Size: To 24 inches.
Food Requirements: Will take practically any food, but exceptionally fond of algae and other vegetable matter.
Color Variations: Body black. Scales on sides each have a yellowish spot. Fins black.

Be sure you have a large tank if you intend keeping Black Sharks! In nature they attain a length of about two feet, and although they do not get to be this big in captivity, specimens a foot long are not unusual. Needless to say, the ones offered for sale are only three to four inches long. This is a fish with an excellent appetite; it spends most of its waking hours in search of food. Vegetable matter is preferred, and they can always be counted on to do an excellent job of cleaning up an algae-infested aquarium. Lacking this, a leaf of lettuce or spinach is also appreciated. Probably because ordinary-sized aquaria inhibit their growth, chances are that very few Black Sharks attain sexual maturity and both males and females look so much alike that they would have to be dissected to distinguish them. They are easily kept, and once established in an aquarium and left alone they can be counted on to live for many years. The usual practice is to keep one to a tank, because two or more kept together will frequently indulge in disputes. This fish has been known to science for a long time. Bleeker named them in 1849, and hobbyists made their acquaintance in 1932.

MYLOSSOMA DURIVENTRIS (Cuvier)/*Hard-Bellied Characin*

Range: Southern Amazon region, Paraguay, Paraná, La Plata.
Habits: Peaceful toward other fishes, but larger specimens are likely to damage plants.
Water Conditions: Soft, slightly acid water in a well-planted tank. Temperature 75 to 82°F.
Size: To 9 inches in their natural waters. Imported specimens much smaller.
Food Requirements: All kinds of live and frozen foods, supplemented with some vegetable substances like chopped spinach, etc.
Color Variations: Silvery with dark anal and dorsal fins. Tail almost transparent. A number of vertical bars appear on the sides.

For many years this species was imported and sold as *Mylossoma aureum*, but it was found that these fish were merely young specimens of *Mylossoma duriventris*, and the real *Mylossoma aureum* had not yet been imported. What probably contributed to the confusion was that, as is the case with many other fishes, there are several color changes as they grow up. Thus a dealer can easily be fooled into believing he has two different species when actually he merely has two sizes of the same species. *Mylossoma duriventris* gets to be 9 inches long in its native waters but it is rarely that we ever see them even approach this size in captivity. Like the *Metynnis* species, the larger ones (3 inches up) are likely to destroy plants, about the only thing that can be said against them. There are no recognizable sexual differences given in the reference works; probably if they ever show up we would see them only in grown specimens. A great many small specimens come in regularly from South America and hobbyists usually find them available in sizes from 1 to 2 inches. They should be kept in groups rather than singly or in pairs.

NANNACARA ANOMALA (Regan)/*Golden Dwarf Acara*

Range: British Guiana.
Habits: Peaceful and shy except when guarding young.
Water Conditions: Neutral to slightly alkaline. Temperature 74 to 78°.
Size: Males to 3 inches, females to 2 inches.
Food Requirements: Prefers live foods but can be trained to take ground beef heart, etc.
Color Variations: Forehead and back brown, sides gold to metallic green. Sides have two dark horizontal stripes. Male's dorsal fin edged with red.

Nannacara anomala is the perfect answer for the hobbyist who wants to observe the family life of Cichlids and does not have the large tank which would be required to spawn one of the larger kinds. A five-gallon tank is ample for the purpose, and it does not take long to get a pair ready. A week's feeding with a variety of live foods is generally all that is needed to get a healthy female almost bursting with eggs and an equally healthy male to put on his brightest colors. A flowerpot laid on its side is often a preferred spot, but the male may pick out a rock or clean off the glass in a corner of the tank. Fifty or seventy-five eggs is an average spawning and it may happen that the pair will share the duties of caring for the eggs and young. It may also happen, and usually does, that the little female will begin to harass her bigger mate and force him into hiding. If the male is left in, he may be badly injured or even killed, so he should be taken out. Eggs hatch in 2 to 3 days and the youngsters become free-swimming in 5 more days. Feeding may then be begun with newly-hatched brine shrimp, and growth is very rapid from here on.

NANNACARA TAENIA

Range: British Guiana.
Habits: Peaceful except when spawning. Will not disturb plants.
Water Conditions: Neutral to slightly alkaline, temperature about 76°.
Size: Large males attain a length of about 3 inches, females about 2 inches.
Food Requirements: Live or frozen foods. Eats dried foods when very hungry.
Color Variations: Olive green to golden body; all scales have a brown edge. Dorsal
has a red and black edge. Females have dark stripes.

This is not the most colorful of the Dwarf Cichlids, but it is one of the most
easily kept, and one most likely to raise a family. When this species was first
introduced in the early 1930's the dealers demonstrated how easy it was by
putting a pair in a small aquarium and letting them spawn there, which they
usually did. Considering how the Cichlids insist on privacy and lack of disturbance when they are guarding eggs, this speaks well for this species.
As with the other Dwarf Cichlids, the male is the Big Boss until the eggs are
laid and fertilized. Then the female takes complete charge, and woe betide the
male when he makes the mistake of coming anywhere near the eggs! The
little female harasses him until he is forced to cower in a corner. It is best
therefore to remove him before he gets hurt, and allow the female to have
her way. She usually makes a good mother, and the youngsters grow quickly.
Her coloration undergoes a change at this time: usually there are only two or
three horizontal stripes visible. When spawning or guarding eggs and young,
a number of vertical bars emerge, giving her a checkerboard pattern.

NANNAETHIOPS TRITAENIATUS (Boulenger)
Three-Lined African Tetra

Range: Upper Congo region.
Habits: Peaceful and shy.
Water Conditions: Not very critical, but the best is slightly acid and soft water. Temperature 74 to 80°.
Size: To 1½ inches.
Food Requirements: Live and frozen foods greatly preferred, but when not available dry foods can be given for a time.
Color Variations: Back brown, sides silvery with three dark horizontal stripes. Fins are reddish.

The African continent is notoriously stingy toward the aquarium hobbyist when it comes to producing Tetras. Most of the Characins from Africa have some drawback: either they become too big for the average home aquarium, or they gobble up the plants, or they cannot get along with other fishes, or they cannot be induced to spawn, etc., etc. The *Nannaethiops* species are a notable exception. *Nannaethiops tritaeniatus* is a small, peaceful fish which will not bother plants and can easily be gotten to spawn. They should be placed in a fairly large aquarium which gets a good amount of sunlight and is not very heavily planted. Best temperatures range from 74 to 79°. The reason for the fairly large aquarium is that sometimes spawns are surprisingly large. Eggs are scattered among plants and sometimes all over the bottom. At 77° the fry hatch in 26 to 32 hours, and in 5 days they become free-swimming. This is a fish which seldom shows its best colors unless conditions are ideal, and in the picture they definitely are not at their best. The lower half of the body should show a pink flush. Males are distinguished by their reddish fins and slightly higher dorsal fins.

Photo by K. Paysan

NANNAETHIOPS UNITAENIATUS (Günther)/*African Tetra*

Range: Equatorial Africa.
Habits: Peaceful; a good community fish which does not bother plants.
Water Conditions: Soft and slightly acid, Requires some warmth, about 76 to 78°. Some sunlight is beneficial.
Size: Males 2¼ to 2½ inches, females slightly larger.
Food Requirements: Live food preferred, but will take dry foods otherwise.
Color Variations: Dark brown to greenish, yellowish to silvery underneath. A dark horizontal stripe extends from the tip of the snout to the fork of the tail.

When this fish became known as the "African Tetra" there were not very many Tetra species available from the Dark Continent. Nowadays the popular name could cause confusion, because there are many. In fact, this fish is seldom seen at the present time, where once it was in fairly good supply. A hardy species, which may live for years once it has become accustomed to its surroundings. This is also one of the easier Tetra species to spawn, and may prove to be quite prolific. Females may be distinguished by the deeper body and larger size, while the males have a more pronounced horizontal stripe and a wider dark marking in the first dorsal rays. Eggs are scattered all over the plants and bottom. They hatch in 40 to 50 hours, and the tiny young begin to swim in about 5 days. An infusoria culture is a necessity for the first few days, and once they have survived this stage and are able to handle newly hatched brine shrimp the battle is won and the fish grow well from there on. This fish was first imported into Hamburg, Germany in the summer of 1931 by an aquarium society there, and the three males and four females spawned

NANNOCHROMIS DIMIDIATUS (Boulenger)/*Dimidiatus*

Range: Belgian Congo.
Habits: Usually very peaceful in the community aquarium.
Water Conditions: Soft, slightly acid water. Temperature 75 to 80°F.
Size: Males 3½ inches, females 2½ inches.
Food Requirements: All sorts of live foods, preferably those which sink to the bottom. Frozen foods also accepted.
Color Variations: Body dusky with a purplish sheen. Horizontal line with row of dark spots above. After part of dorsal fin and top of caudal fin bright red.

The genera *Nannochromis* and *Pelmatochromis* are very closely related, and a quick glance at *Nannochromis dimidiatus* might give rise to the suspicion that it is a *Pelmatochromis* species, the two being almost exactly alike in body form. However, there is a touch of greenish blue in the female's throat which reminds one of *Nannochromis nudiceps*. Give the pair a place where they can hide and it is fairly dark. A flowerpot with a notch out of the side such as is recommended for *Pelmatochromis kribensis* is just about perfect.

NANOCHROMIS NUDICEPS (Boulenger)/*Congo Dwarf Cichlid*

Range: Congo River region.
Habits: Apt to be a bit quarrelsome at times; best kept by themselves.
Water Conditions: Soft, slightly acid water is best. Temperature 75 to 80°.
Size: Up to 3 inches for males; females about an inch smaller.
Food Requirements: Live foods of all kinds; at times when none is available, frozen
foods may be provided temporarily.
Color Variations: Sides of body blue, belly bright green. Dorsal fin is orange with a
black tip and white edge. Upper half of tail striped.

There are only a few fishes from Africa which could be properly referred to
as Dwarf Cichlids, and the *Nannochromis* species are among these. As with
so many Cichlids, peace is never assured unless one male is kept to a tank,
unless the tank is a large one which will provide territories for all the males.
For the first few hours after being placed in an aquarium, each male will
search busily for a sheltered spot where he can spend his time and keep a
constant lookout for intruders. When an invasion occurs an otherwise peaceful
male will become a raging tyrant until the other beats a retreat. For this reason
provision for a number of places where an attacked fish can hide is highly
important where any Dwarf Cichlids are concerned, especially *Nannochromis
nudiceps*. Females are a docile lot, and submit meekly to the advances of the
males when they are ready to spawn. When the male has finished his duties
of fertilizing the eggs, the erstwhile meek little female turns into a tigress and
gives the male a severe drubbing every time he gets anywhere near the eggs.
For his safety he should be removed at this time and put into another tank
while the female guards the eggs and fry.

NANNOPERCA VITTATA (Castelnau)/*Australian Pygmy Perch*

Range: Western Australia in the vicinity of Perth.
Habits: Peaceful; will not harm other fishes or plants.
Water Conditions: Water should be clean and have an addition of a teaspoonful of salt to each gallon of water. Temperature 60 to 75°.
Size: To 3 inches.
Food Requirements: Live or frozen foods; they can be taught to take dried foods, but do not like them.
Color Variations: Dark brown sides with mottled markings. At breeding time, sides become black with an orange horizontal stripe and orange belly.

Most of Australia is a little too far south of the Equator to be considered a really tropical country. Only the fishes from the northern end of that continent live under actually tropical conditions, and for that reason we have only a limited number of tropical aquarium fishes from that huge country. Most of these fishes, like the native fishes of our own temperate clime, tend to be colorful only when the spawning season arrives, which is the case with *Nannoperca vittata*. Most of the year they are just a muddy brown, with the horizontal stripes barely distinguishable. In Australia the breeding season occurs between the months of July and January, at which time the fish take on brilliantly intense colors. There is a black area on the back which gives way to an orange stripe from the forehead to the caudal base. Below this is a black stripe from the mouth through the eye to the caudal base, and below this an orange area which covers the entire belly region. Eggs are laid in plants near the bottom, 8 to 10 being laid each day until a total of about 60 is attained. They hatch in 62 to 74 hours; according to the reports, the fry are hardy and grow slowly.

Photo by H.J. Richter.

NANNOSTOMUS ANOMALUS (Steindachner)/*Anomalous Pencilfish*

Range: British Guiana, Rio Negro and the central Amazon region.
Habits: Completely peaceful toward other fishes and plants.
Water Conditions: Soft, slightly acid water which is not too fresh. Temperature 74 to 80°F.
Size: To 2 inches.
Food Requirements: Small live foods greatly preferred, but frozen and dried foods accepted.
Color Variations: Yellowish brown sides with a black stripe. A gold stripe appears above this. Anal and lower caudal red; ventrals tipped white.

Some works are beginning to consider the species *Nannostomus anomalus* and *N. aripirangensis* both as subspecies of *N. beckfordi*. This practice has not and may not ever become widespread, and for this reason we are staying with the old nomenclature. To our mind *N. anomalus* is one of the prettiest of the Pencilfishes, as well as the easiest to spawn. The Pencilfishes are slightly more demanding as to the composition of their water than many of the other Characins. It is best to get them accustomed to one type of water and then give them this type at all times. To spawn them, assign a small tank (5 to 10 gallons) to a healthy pair and fill it with soft, aged, slightly acid water. Plant with *Myriophyllum* or some other bushy plant. A small amount of acid peat moss in the filter or hung in a small cloth bag near the bubbles of an airstone will stimulate the fish and they will show their best colors. Temperature should be raised to 80° and the male will soon begin to pursue the female, trying to get her to come to a stop among the plants and let him get beside her. Eggs hatch in about a day and the fry require infusoria for a week after they become free-swimming.

F-428.00

Photo by Dr. Herbert R. Axelrod.

NANNOSTOMUS ARIPIRANGENSIS (Meinken)/*Aripiranga Pencilfish*

Range: Region around Aripiranga, lower Amazon River.

Habits: Completely peaceful toward other fishes and plants.

Water Conditions: Soft, slightly acid water which has been aged for at least a week. Temperature 74 to 80°F.

Size: About 1¾ inches.

Food Requirements: Because of the small mouth, small live foods are best. Will also accept frozen and dried foods.

Color Variations: Brown body with a black stripe, edged with gold. Ventral fins blood-red with a light blue edge. Females have less color.

The Aripiranga Pencilfish is so closely related to *Nannostomus anomalus* that it is possible to produce hybrids by crossing the two species. These hybrids are not usually sterile, and as a result the present-day *N. aripirangensis* have been crossed at some time in a previous generation; unless we are sure that our fish are a direct importation from the Aripiranga region we cannot be sure that we have the real thing. Some unusual experiments have been made in animal behavior by hybridizing two closely-related fish species of which each has a different method of spawning. The result was a hybrid which was utterly confused when spawning was attempted, giving the animal behaviorists ample opportunity to make many exhaustive observations and put out reams of scientific papers. Not so with our *N. aripirangensis—N. anomalus* hybrids; both species have exactly similar spawning habits and the result is a healthy, more robust fish which seems to excel its forebears in color as well: the body has a great deal more red color such as is found in the male at spawning time. The entire caudal base assumes a bright gleaming red.

F-429.00

NANNOSTOMUS BECKFORDI (Steindachner)/*Beckford's Pencilfish*

Range: British Guiana, Paraná, Rio Negro, middle and lower Amazon.
Habits: Peaceful toward other fishes and plants. Should be kept in a group of their own kind or other related species.
Water Conditions: Prefers soft, slightly acid water but is not intolerant to other types. Temperature 75 to 80°.
Size: To 2 inches.
Food Requirements: Prefers the smaller living foods, but can be accustomed to taking frozen or dried foods when the others are not available.
Color Variations: Body brown above, with a wide black stripe running from the mouth to caudal base. Fins red at base in males, almost colorless in females.

Beckford's Pencilfish is fairly well distributed through most of the small streams of British Guiana, along with most of the other Pencilfish species. This species is fairly easy to breed, but the young in the first stages are difficult to feed because of their tiny mouths. For this reason most of the Pencilfishes sold today are still imported. In their native waters there are large schools to be found in the backwater streams, and collecting them is a very simple matter. As with most wild-caught fishes the colors are unbelievably brilliant and lovely, and it is hard to believe that the comparatively pale fishes one brings home and puts into the aquarium are the same ones. Rarely do the original colors ever return to their former beauty, but a pair which is spawning in the sunlight comes pretty close. Most of the Pencilfishes have an odd characteristic. At night, the body markings change greatly. This species loses its horizontal stripe and replaces it with three large spots; if one lights up a dark tank and then tries to identify some Pencilfishes, it is strongly advisable to wait awhile before doing so, and wait for their real colors to come back.

NANNOSTOMUS MARGINATUS (Eigenmann)/*Dwarf Pencil Fish*

Range: British Guiana.
Habits: Very peaceful; an excellent community fish.
Water Conditions: Neutral to slightly acid; requires heat, about 78°.
Size: Maximum about 1¼ inches.
Food Requirements: Prefers small live foods, but will take dry food if necessary.
Color Variations: Back chocolate brown, sides and belly silvery white. Three horizontal dark stripes, with gold between. Red spot on dorsal and ventrals.

The Pencil Fish group is very popular, and this is probably the most popular member of the group. Its small size makes it a candidate for a community tank containing only small, peaceful fishes. Many people make the error of mixing fishes of all sizes, as long as they do not harm each other. This is a mistake, because in many cases a fish like, for instance, this one, is constantly frightened by larger fishes swimming near it, and as a result spends much of its time hiding. Sexes are not easy to distinguish, except for the female's slightly heavier body, and a little more red in the dorsal and anal fins of the male. Breeding them is made difficult because of the fact that the parent fish are very quick to eat their own eggs. These eggs have very little adhesive power and most of them fall to the bottom. A bed of glass rods which lets the eggs through and holds back the parents is used with success here. The young are very small when they hatch, and have small mouths, which makes them difficult to feed. Even when fed with small infusoria, many of the fry are still likely to starve.

F-431.00

NANNOSTOMUS TRIFASCIATUS (Steindachner)
Three-Lined Pencilfish

Range: British Guiana, middle Amazon region, Rio Negro.

Habits: Peaceful toward other fishes and plants; should not be kept with very active fishes.

Water Conditions: Soft, slightly acid water which has been run through peat moss. Temperature 76 to 80°.

Size: To 2½ inches.

Food Requirements: Smaller-sized live foods are best, with frozen or dried foods given only when living foods are not available.

Color Variations: Three black stripes at side of the body, with red markings on anal, ventral, dorsal and caudal fins.

Most hobbyists who keep the Pencilfishes consider *Nannostomus trifasciatus* the beauty of the group, and are usually unanimous in expressing the opinion that this species is the most difficult to spawn. Strangely enough, in its habitat in British Guiana this was the most common species everywhere we fished. The usual catch was about as many *Nannostomus trifasciatus* as all the rest of the *Nannostomus* species put together. Our best catch was made in a little stream which meandered across a savannah in the vicinity of Lethem, near the Brazilian border. The banks were lined with palm trees and there was grass growing knee-deep right up to the water. The bottom was only slightly muddy and the water was stained brownish by decaying vegetable matter. The stream was no more than hip-deep in most places, but the variety of Characins caught there was no less than amazing. We even caught some Piranhas in this little stream, which was seldom more than 100 feet wide, scarcely enough to call it a creek. *Nannostomus trifasciatus* is one of the larger members of the Pencilfish group, attaining a length of 2½ inches. It is happiest in a sunny tank, with a number of its own kind.

NEMATOBRYCON AMPHILOXUS (Eigenmann)/*Rainbow Tetra*

Range: Calima region, Colombia.
Habits: Peaceful, inclined to be a bit shy.
Water Conditions: Soft, slightly acid water is best. Temperature 75 to 80°.
Size: About 2 inches.
Food Requirements: Live foods are best, but fish can be trained to accept frozen and dried foods.
Color Variations: Body golden to brownish, with a dark stripe running from the center of the body to the tail. Bright blue spots are above this line.

This hobby of ours sees many fish species which are hailed as "new" introductions, which indeed they are, but only as far as the hobby is concerned. Actually this gorgeous fish was first found and identified by Eigenmann more than fifty years ago. It is a constant source of amazement to modern-day fish collectors to find that after much traveling by plane, Jeep and other comparatively modern modes of transportation they find what looks like a new fish species and upon further investigation it turns out that Carl H. Eigenmann had been there and found the species near the turn of the century. How he got to these out-of-the-way places is the most amazing part of the whole thing. The Rainbow Tetra was re-discovered by William Kyburz in the Calima Region of Colombia while looking for a more convenient place to collect the Emperor Tetra, *Nematobrycon palmeri*. Unfortunately the Rainbow Tetra is never found in any large amounts, and unless it proves to be a ready breeder it may seldom be available to hobbyists. At the present time there are plenty of Emperor Tetras available, so chances are that when they get some specimens to work with, breeders will also produce numbers of these.

Another view of the gorgeous Rainbow Tetra, *Nematobrycon amphiloxus.*

NEMATOBRYCON PALMERI (Eigenmann)/*Emperor Tetra*

Range: San Juan Basin, Pacific slope of Colombia.

Habits: Peaceful, inclined to be a bit shy. Inclined to remain singly or in pairs rather than forming a school

Water Conditions: Clean, soft, slightly acid water is best. Temperature 72 to 78°.

Size: To 1¾ inches.

Food Requirements: Excellent appetite; will accept dried or frozen foods, but of course live foods are preferred.

Color Variations: Back dark brown, shading to a wide blue area. Below this is a wide black area. Belly golden. Dorsal, caudal and anal fins edged with black.

The *Nematobrycon* species were discovered in 1911 by the indefatigable Carl Eigenmann. In his huge work *The American Characidae* (Vol. 43), published in 1927, he cites another reference to the two species in 1922, and then they appear to have been forgotten until 1960, when a number of these beautiful fish arrived in this country. The Emperor Tetra comes from a very inaccessible region in Colombia, the San Juan Basin on the Pacific slope. Fortunately, breeders both in Europe and in the United States found that this fish was far from difficult to breed, and a permanent supply seems to be assured. They spawn like most Tetras, laying their eggs in bushy plants. Some breeders prefer to use spawning mops or bundles of fine nylon filaments, both of which are readily accepted and more practical to use than the usual bundles of *Myriophyllum* or other bushy plants. The fry are hardy and easy to raise once they have grown to a size where they can handle newly hatched brine shrimp. Males are distinguishable at an early age by their brighter colors and three-pronged tails.

F-435.00

Photo by H.J. Richter

NEOLEBIAS ANSORGEI (Boulenger)/*Ansorge's Neolebias*

Range: Central Africa, Chiloango region.
Habits: Peaceful, very shy in a community tank. Should be kept by themselves.
Water Conditions: Sensitive to hard, alkaline water. Water must be well-aged and should never undergo great changes. Temperature 75 to 82°.
Size: To 1½ inches.
Food Requirements: Small-sized live foods only.
Color Variations: Sides golden with a wide green stripe. Anal and ventral fins red, anal fin edged with black. Black bar at caudal base.

Anyone who sees the picture of this fish and then sees it for the first time in a dealer's bare tank is apt to be highly disappointed and accuse the photographer of taking liberties with the colors. Truth of the matter is that here we have a fish which pales very quickly when things around him are not to his entire satisfaction. Even when in color, there are two distinct color varieties, one golden in body and the other green. Both have a large amount of green in the wide horizontal stripe, but in one the rest of the body is greenish to violet, while in the other those portions are golden. One would never suspect that this is one of the Tetra family from its body shape. It has the short, heavy body that one generally associates with the Barbs, an illusion which is heightened by the fact that there is no adipose fin. The unique square dorsal fin looks like nothing one would find on a Tetra, either. The fish is sensitive to water changes and hard water. They breed readily, but the fry are difficult to raise. Eggs are laid in plant thickets and hatch in 20 to 24 hours. The tiny fry have small mouths and must be given very fine infusoria at first.

F-436.00

NEOLEBIAS LANDGRAFI (E. Ahl)/*Blue-Banded Neolebias*

Range: The Cameroons.
Habits: Peaceful, very shy in a community tank. Should be kept by themselves.
Water Conditions: Sensitive to hard, alkaline water or water which is too fresh. Temperature 75 to 82°.
Size: To 1½ inches.
Food Requirements: Small-sized live foods only.
Color Variations: Back reddish brown; wide blue stripe on the sides. Belly pinkish. Male's anal and ventral fins deep pink.

Neolebias landgrafi is almost a duplicate of *Neolebias ansorgei* in body form, and the colors are not greatly different. Where *N. ansorgei* has a wide green band, this band is light blue in *N. landgrafi*. Although the picture does not show it very plainly, there is a rosy pink flush on the underparts and the back is often a dark reddish. Like the other species, this one is also sensitive to hard, fresh water and if kept in a community tank there is a distinct possibility that one will scarcely ever see them. Given a well-planted tank of their own and generous feeding with live foods as well as soft, slightly acid, well-aged water with a temperature of about 80°, chances are very good that spawning will take place without too much delay. The male lures the female into the plant thickets with fluttering motions, and in a trembling side-by-side position 5 to 10 eggs are released at a time, with an occasional total of 300 finally being attained. If the tiny fry can get an adequate amount of very small infusoria for the first days, they soon put on enough growth to manage larger foods and put on quick growth. They mature in 6 to 7 months.

NOEMACHEILUS BOTIA (Hamilton-Buchanan)/*Mottled Loach*

Range: Upper India.

Habits: Peaceful toward other fishes and will not harm plants. Are useful in cleaning up unwanted algae and food left by other fishes.

Water Conditions: Water should be slightly alkaline but not very hard. Temperature 75 to 80°.

Size: To 4½ inches.

Food Requirements: Not at all fussy about foods. Should have some soft algae to pick at in addition to their regular diet.

Color Variations: Back greenish, belly pink. Sides have irregular spots and other markings, dorsal and caudal fins have rows of spots.

Most Loaches are not as attractively colored and marked as this one, which comes from India. The greenish, black-spotted sides contrast nicely with the pink belly region. The markings and square tail remind one of the European Loach *Cobitis taenia*, but *Noemacheilus botia* shows less tendency to hide from the bright light than its European cousin. Appetites are similar. There is a constant search for algae on rocks and plant surfaces, and a special delight is taken in uprooting tubifex worms from the bottom gravel. This is a very easy fish to keep, which will happily adjust to varying tank conditions and accept practically anything in the way of food. The stock of imported fish to date has been rather meager, and we have not heard of any spawnings. Even the better-known Loaches have in most cases steadfastly resisted most efforts to spawn them. Perhaps they insist on a layer of mud on the bottom, which would not be practical in a home aquarium. Much remains to be found out, and perhaps some day a thing which is considered an impossibility now will be a commonplace achievement tomorrow. This fish has been known to science since 1822.

F-438.00

NOEMACHEILUS FASCIATUS (Cuvier & Valenciennes)/*Barred Loach*

Range: Great Sunda Island.
Habits: Best given a tank of their own. Chooses and defends its own territories.
Water Conditions: Soft, slightly acid water. Temperature 75 to 80°F.
Size: To 3½ inches.
Food Requirements: Likes worms and other live foods, but not a fussy eater.
Color Variations: Body brown, belly white. Numerous yellow narrow bands on the
  sides. Fins tinted light yellow.

Although it has an elongated body and markings like our old friend *Acanthophthalmus kuhli*, the Kuhli Loach, plus a set of barbels, the similarity between the two fishes ends right there. *Noemacheilus fasciatus* does not have the snaky, eel-like motions of the Kuhli Loach, and has a more usefullooking and nicer-shaped set of fins. It carries itself more like a fish than like a large worm or small snake. The natives to the countries where the Loaches come from are fond of eating small fishes and have an interesting method of catching them. They divert a small stream by damming it and leading it away from its original bed. When the water has run off, they turn over rocks and dig into the gravel bed, capturing a great many Loaches of all sorts in the process. We have also heard of the South American collectors doing the same thing when collecting the *Corydoras* Catfishes. *Noemacheilus fasciatus* should have a number of hiding-places in their tank. Each fish carefully selects and takes possession of one of these nooks and defends it fiercely when another fish attempts to invade it. Although they have no teeth to speak of, they know every threatening gesture in the book and use them.

Photo by Dr. Herbert R. Axelrod.

NOEMACHEILUS KUIPERI (De Beaufort)/*Fighting Loach*

Range: Billiton Island.

Habits: Best kept by themselves in pairs, or several pairs in a large tank with a number of hiding places.

Water Conditions: Not critical, but the water should be clean. Temperature 75 to 80°.

Size: To 3 inches.

Food Requirements: Any kind of food accepted, but there should be live foods given at times.

Color Variations: Back brown, with about a dozen vertical yellow bars. Belly silvery to yellowish.

The Loach family is for the most part a peaceful one. There are a few members, notably the Clown Loach, which will take over a special spot and defend it from intruders, but such action is mostly bluff and seldom results in serious injuries. Our Fighting Loach goes one step further and not only defends its own territory but sometimes goes out looking for trouble. Females, which with most species are the docile ones, are just as pugnacious as the males where the Fighting Loach is concerned. Here is one Loach where the males are easy to distinguish: in the male the upper lobe of the tail is considerably longer, looking like a rooster's. Both sexes attain a length of 3 inches. Fighting consists mostly of maneuvers in which one attempts to grasp the other's pectoral fin. Although they have no teeth in their jaws, they can manage to tear away pieces of the fin membrane. As with most Loaches, there have been no reported spawnings. This is not to say that they cannot be spawned, because importations have not been received in any numbers. The pair photographed here came to us from Germany, where a few were received around 1960.

F-440.00

NOTHOBRANCHIUS GUENTHERI (Pfeffer)/*Guenther's Nothobranch*

Range: East Africa.
Habits: Somewhat pugnacious; should be kept in pairs in their own tank.
Water Conditions: Water should be soft and slightly acid. Temperature 75 to 80°.
Size: To 2½ inches.
Food Requirements: Live foods only.
Color Variations: Males have greenish-brown back and yellowish to bluish sides.
Tail is brilliant red. Females are brownish, with plain fins.

The adaptability of animal life to its surroundings is very graphically illustrated by the *Nothobranchius* group from East Africa. These fishes make
their home in shallow pools which are well filled in the rainy months and then
become gradually smaller and shallower as the dry season progresses, finally
to dry out altogether. In order to survive through this dry season a fish must
either be equipped to breathe atmospheric air and go into a period of estiva-
tion through the dry, hot months, or it must die and be survived by eggs
which can live through the dry season. The former is done by several of the
Lungfishes, and the latter is accomplished by several "annual" fishes, of
which this is one. The eggs hatch months later when the rains begin, almost

A pair of breeding *Nothobranchius guentheri*. The male is easily distinguished by its more colorful pattern than the pale colored female. Photo by Ruda Zukal.

The female is seen here, half-buried in the sand, as the male holds her down. A few eggs are laid which are fertilized immediately. Photo by Ruda Zukal.

NOTHOBRANCHIUS MELANOSPILUS (Meinken)/*Beira Nothobranch*

Range: Portuguese East Africa, in the vicinity of Beira.
Habits: Should be kept in their own tank.
Water Conditions: Soft, slightly acid water with a layer of peat-moss on the bottom.
Size: Males to 2 inches, females slightly smaller.
Food Requirements: Live foods only, and there should be an almost constant supply.
Color Variations: Males have bluish sides with red edges on the scales. Fins are deep red, anal and dorsal with a blue edge. Females have tiny red dots.

Nothobranchius melanospilus was found near Beira in Portuguese East Africa by E. Roloff. The specific name is a bit puzzling, because *melanospilus* means "black-spotted." One would expect to see a fish with black spots all over, but the spots are only on the head and gill-covers of the male. The female, the upper fish in the picture, is a very drab proposition by comparison. A hobbyist who keeps several species of *Nothobranchius* has to be very careful to keep the females either in labeled tanks or with their own males, because there is so little difference that things could be hopelessly confused and the result could be either sterile eggs or a lot of unidentifiable hybrids. This species is almost always ready to spawn if kept in good condition, almost too ready. If there is only one female available, a male will soon have her quite battered and she should be given a few days of rest. Like the other *Nothobranchius* species, eggs are buried in a layer of peat-moss on the bottom where they may be removed, peat-moss and all, when there is a let-up in the spawning. This is kept in a slightly moist stage for 3 to 4 weeks and the eggs hatch when they are put in water again.

Photo by Dr. Walter Foersch.

NOTHOBRANCHIUS PALMQUISTI (?)/*Palmquist's Nothobranch*

Range: East Africa.
Habits: Somewhat pugnacious; should be kept in their own tank.
Water Conditions: Water should be soft and slightly acid. Temperature 75 to 80°.
Size: To 2½ inches.
Food Requirements: Live foods only.
Color Variations: Males have greenish-brown back and distinctly yellowish sides.
Tail is brilliant red. Females are brownish, with plain fins.

Here is a *Nothobranchius* species which can be easily confused with *N. guentheri*. The difference lies in the basic body color, which in *N. guentheri* is blue and in *N. palmquisti* is yellow. In all probability this will eventually be recognized as a color variety of *N. guentheri*, but as far as we know the necessary research such as scale counts, fin-ray counts, anatomical measurements, etc., have not as yet been made, and until this is done we cannot be sure. An interesting sidelight on this and the other *Nothobranchius* species is that the eggs and a kit, known as "Fish-In-A-Flash," are now being sold. The kit includes brine shrimp eggs and a plastic container where the shrimp may be hatched for food. The fish eggs are placed in another, larger container. As they have already undergone their drying period the eggs hatch within a few minutes after they are placed in water. Because one never knows which species of *Nothobranchius* has been packed in the kit or even if it is a *Nothobranchius*, *Cynolebias* or *Pterolebias* species he has, it is a lot of fun for the experienced aquarist to hatch the eggs and raise the fry; in fact, even the most inexperienced beginner can do it.

F-444.00

Photo by Kremser.

NOTHOBRANCHIUS RACHOVII (Ahl)
Rachow's Nothobranch

Range: East Africa, in the vicinity of Beira.
Habits: Quarrelsome toward other fishes; should be given their own tank.
Water Conditions: Water should be soft and slightly acid. Temperature 75 to 80°.
Size: To 2 inches.
Food Requirements: Living foods only.
Color Variations: Sides brilliant turquoise blue with many red spots and streaks.
   Dorsal and anal fins bright blue streaked with red.

Any hobbyist who sees a beautiful male *Nothobranchius rachovii* in his full colors will never deny that this is one of the most beautiful freshwater fishes in the whole world. Like the other *Nothobranchius* species they have a few traits which keep them from being perfect. For one thing, they insist on live foods, and will seldom eat anything which is not moving. Males will frequently stage seemingly vicious battles which usually turn out to be harmless, but when kept with other fishes they are likely to become nasty. A jewel such as this deserves its own setting, and it is best to give them a tank with only their own kind. Like the other *Nothobranchius* species, their life-span is comparatively short and once they have attained maturity spawnings are frequent and feedings must be generous.

NOTROPIS HYPSELOPTERUS (Günther)/*Georgia Dace*

Range: Southeastern United States from Georgia to Florida.
Habits: Peaceful, active fish which will not molest its tankmates.
Water Conditions: Clean, soft, slightly acid water and a good-sized, well-planted tank are preferred.
Size: 3 inches.
Food Requirements: Will take dried as well as live or frozen foods.
Color Variations: Body color brownish with a black horizontal line. Males have dorsal fin and anal reddish at the base, shading to yellow.

Notropis hypselopterus is one of our most beautiful native fishes; it occurs in good numbers in Georgia's Okefenokee Swamp region. In spite of its obvious good looks, the usual antipathy toward any fish which does not come from some far-away place exists, and dealers will seldom stock them. The author once saw a tankful of beautiful specimens in a dealer's store, all males. When asked if there were any females available, the dealer said that the collectors had thrown away all of the females and kept only the more brightly-colored males, thinking that the females were something else. Coming as they do from our warmer states, this fish can be kept with tropical species. It is an active but peaceful fish which is usually swimming where it can be seen. For their complete well-being, they should get a period of two to three months each year in an unheated aquarium at room temperatures. At the end of this period their temperature can again be increased gradually. If this rest period is not provided the fish become sensitive to diseases. As is so often the case with native fishes, there is no account of their having been bred in the aquarium as yet.

F-446.00

NOTROPIS LUTRENSIS (Baird & Girard)/*Red Horse Minnow*

Range: Illinois, South Dakota, Wyoming to Nebraska, Kansas, Missouri, Arkansas, Texas and tributaries of the Rio Grande.

Habits: Peaceful; will not molest its tankmates at any time.

Water Conditions: Water must be clean and well-aerated, and fish should never be crowded. Temperatures may go as high as 80°, but nearer 70° is better.

Size: 3 inches.

Food Requirements: Prepared foods as well as live foods are eaten, but there should be a preponderance of live or frozen foods.

Color Variations: Males steel-blue with sides orange-red to crimson. Fins are red. Females lighter in color with plain fins.

Here is a fish which deserves a great deal of popularity, but seldom gets it. It occurs over a wide area, and the best ones for the aquarium come from the southern end of its range. The picture shows the fish in their normal coloration, which becomes much more brilliant when spawning condition is attained. Then the blues become deeper and the fins become *really* red. These fish prefer flowing streams and in order to make them feel at home, their tank should be well-aerated and briskly filtered. Mr. Jeff W. Moore, Curator of the Dallas (Texas) Aquarium is a great admirer of this fish, and there is an interesting article about it in the July, 1959 issue of *Tropical Fish Hobbyist*. He tells how a trio kept in a community aquarium which also contained tropical species spawned for him, right in the center of the tank. The male fanned away the fine gravel in a small area and then spawned for more than an hour, first with one female and then with the other. Since there were other fishes in the tank the eggs were eaten and since the fish is plentiful in the Dallas area, no further attempts were made to isolate and spawn them again.

Photo by Dr. Herbert R. Axelrod.

OMPOK BIMACULATUS (Bloch)/*One-Spot Glass Catfish*

Range: Ceylon, Indo-China, Thailand, Burma, Java and Sumatra.
Habits: Only small specimens are adaptable to aquaria, and they should not be kept singly. Single fish are short-lived.
Water Conditions: Very adaptable to practically any clean water. Temperature 74 to 82°.
Size: To 18 inches in native waters, about half that in the aquarium.
Food Requirements: Live or frozen foods preferred.
Color Variations: Body glassily transparent, with a well-defined dark spot on the shoulder and a faint lateral line.

Ompok bimaculatus is found throughout a rather wide range which includes Ceylon, Indo-China, Thailand, Burma, Java and Sumatra. It is a very popular fish wherever it occurs, not as an aquarium fish but as an item on the menu. Being fairly common, it is easy to get under ordinary circumstances. The natives often have pools which they plant with these fish, feeding them all sorts of table refuse and eventually reaping a rich harvest. The generic name *Ompok* was originally given to this fish by Lacepède in 1803, and he did a very questionable job on it which caused much confusion later. In his drawing he left out the tiny dorsal fin, and he also failed to mention it in his description. More than 30 years later Valenciennes dug out Lacepède's specimen and discovered that the little fin, which consists of 4 or 5 rays, was there all the time. Small specimens are frequently sent to our shores, but they soon outgrow their quarters. In the open, the fish may get to be 18 inches long, but in captivity a fish half that size is quite unusual. Unlike many Catfishes, this one is active and does not mind the daylight.

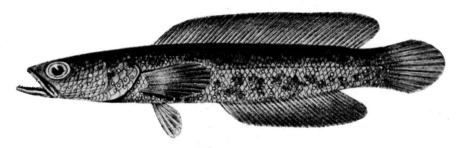

Ophiocephalus cyanospilus.

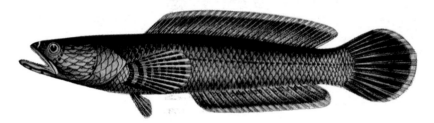

Ophiocephalus gachua.

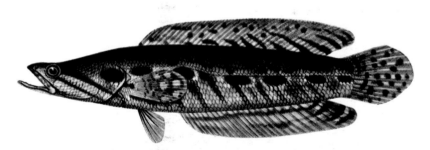

Ophiocephalus lucius.

The genus *Ophiocephalus* is a relatively large genus, closely allied to the genus *Channa*, containing elongated, primitive fishes possessing auxiliary breathing organs. They are large, mean fishes, and not suitable to home aquariums, except where kept alone as oddities or display specimens. The genus ranges over tropical Asia and Africa. To the best of our knowledge none of the various *Ophiocephalus* species has been bred in this country, but another Snakehead, *Channa asiatica*, has.

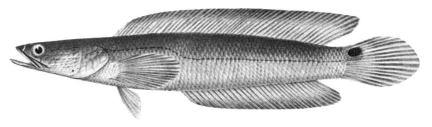

Ophiocephalus maruloides.

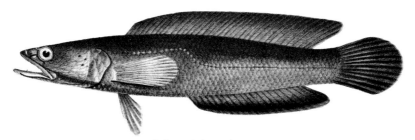

Ophiocephalus melanosoma.

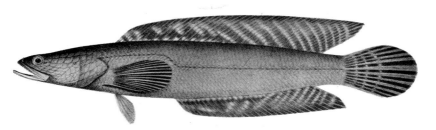

Ophiocephalus melanopterus.

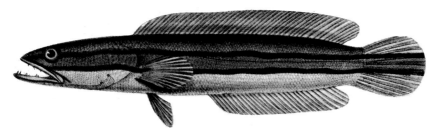

Ophiocephalus micropeltes.

F-450.00

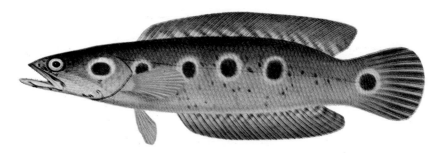

Ophiocephalus pleurophthalmus.

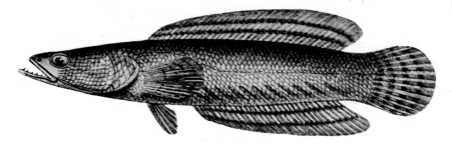

Ophiocephalus polylepis.

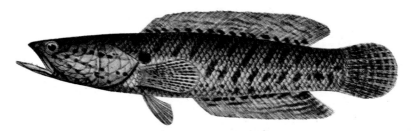

Ophiocephalus punctatus.

Ophiocephalus striatus.

Photo by Aaron Norman

ORYZIAS JAVANICUS (Bleeker)/*Javanese Rice Fish*

Range: Java and Malaya.

Habits: Peaceful toward other fishes, and will not harm plants.

Water Conditions: Water should be neutral to slightly alkaline, with a little salt added. Keep at high temperatures, 80 to 85°.

Size: Males to 1¼ inches, females to 1½ inches.

Food Requirements: Live foods greatly preferred; other foods are not picked up once they fall to the bottom.

Color Variations: Body light grayish-blue, fins yellowish. Eyes are a beautiful blue, and the anal fin has a blue edge.

The Javanese Rice Fish is not the most colorful of aquarium fishes, but it is an interesting one nevertheless. The glassily transparent body plainly shows the skeletal structure of the fish, and with the light shining on it from behind the viewer, the large anal fin shows a beautiful blue edge. Most interesting, however, is their manner of spawning. The male drives the female actively until they come to a quivering halt among the plants. Here the eggs are expelled and fertilized. Nothing unusual so far, but here is where the oddity comes in: instead of staying among the plants, the eggs hang in a bunch attached by a tough string to the female's vent, and are sometimes carried about in this manner for hours. Finally the string snags against something solid, usually a plant leaf or twig, and the eggs come to rest. Hatching takes place in 10 to 12 days, and the tiny youngsters must be provided with infusoria at first until they begin to grow. As soon as they reach a point where they can consume newly-hatched brine shrimp growth progresses more rapidly. Aquarium-raised specimens for some reason seem to lack something they get in their natural waters and do not get as large as their parents.

ORYZIAS LATIPES (Schlegel)/*Medaka*

Range: Japan and nearby islands.

Habits: Active and peaceful, although a male will occasionally rough up a female. A very good community fish.

Water Conditions: Slightly soft, acid water desirable, but not too important. Temperature 50 to 85°F.

Size: Females about 1¾ inches, males slightly smaller.

Food Requirements: Takes all foods.

Color Variations: There are two varieties, one golden and one (the original) plain grayish-green. The latter is now rarely seen.

The three primary requisites of a good aquarium fish are that the fish be hardy, easy to feed, and interesting. The Medaka possesses all three characteristics to a remarkable degree. It is very definitely one of the toughest of all aquarium fishes, outranking even the Guppy and White Cloud in its ability to withstand adverse conditions, particularly where water temperature is concerned. And it is easy to feed, accepting dry food day in and day out without declining, although of course it will not be at its best under such a feeding schedule. The Medaka is interesting in both its attractiveness and breeding habits, too. Certainly not a flashy fish, it is still quietly pretty, with its golden body (the old wild strain is no longer seen) set off by iridescent blue-green flecks and the beautiful, large almost-luminescent eye. The breeding habits of the fish offer a remarkable opportunity to view the life cycle from egg to free-swimming fry, for the eggs can be observed in bunches on the female, and they can later be observed in detail while they are attached to plants prior to hatching. In a heavily planted tank, the parents will leave the young alone. If highly inbred, the strain soon becomes hump-backed.

F-453.00

Photo by Dr. Herbert R. Axelrod

OSPHRONEMUS GORAMY (Lacepède)/*Gourami*

Range: Great Sunda Islands, introduced in other places as a food fish.
Habits: Peaceful; because of their size they should be kept only with large fishes.
Water Conditions: Not critical as long as the water is clean. Temperature 74 to 82°.
Size: Up to 2 feet in natural waters, about half that in the aquarium.
Food Requirements: Should get large amounts of shrimp, clams, mussels, etc., to which is also added vegetable matter such as boiled oatmeal.
Color Variations: Mature specimens are brownish to reddish on the sides, belly yellowish. Fins gray to reddish. Black spots sprinkle the body.

The Gourami is usually sold in sizes of 2 to 3 inches, at which size they are attractively banded and nicely shaped. The surprise comes when they grow and grow and grow. If allowed plenty of room and full scope is given to their huge appetite, the result is a large, heavy-bodied fish with thick, rubbery lips and a stupid expression. In their native range they are highly regarded as food fish, and the natives consider them quite a delicacy. According to existing literature on the subject, they build a bubble-nest and the male stands guard over the eggs and young. Sexes can be distinguished in mature specimens by a roundness in the dorsal and anal fins of the females. In males these fins are pointed. Mature fish a foot or more in length are said to be excellent show objects for large public aquariums. Their food should contain a good amount of vegetable matter, such as boiled oatmeal and the like. According to Rachow, old specimens become completely black in color. This fish has been known to science since 1802, and has been known to the aquarium hobby for a long time as well, having first made its appearance somewhere around the year 1895.

F-454.00

OSTEOCHILUS HASSELTI (Cuvier & Valenciennes)/*Hard-Lipped Barb*

Range: Thailand, Greater and Lesser Sunda Islands, Java, Borneo and Sumatra.
Habits: Peaceful if kept with fishes of its own size.
Water Conditions: Neutral to slightly acid water. Tank should be well planted and of a good size. Temperature 75 to 80°.
Size: Grows to a little over a foot in length in nature, about half that in the aquarium.
Food Requirements: Live foods with an addition of vegetable substance such as lettuce leaves.
Color Variations: Sides silvery to yellowish with 6 to 8 rows of dark dots running horizontally. Dorsal and caudal yellowish, other fins red, except pectorals.

Osteochilus hasselti is a well-known food fish in Thailand as well as Java, Borneo and Sumatra. It is a large, handsome, well-formed fish which unusually enough has two pairs of barbels on the upper lip and none on the lower. The mouth is well-adapted for algae-nibbling and tearing at other soft plants. The upper and lower lips are lined with papillae, and there is a bony structure behind the lower lip. In Central and Southeastern Thailand it is called *pla soi khao* because of a fancied resemblance to a dove which is called *nok khao*. This dove has small black and white spots on each side of the neck. The fish gets large in its home waters, having been reported a little over 12 inches, but this is rarely the case. Most mature specimens are 6 to 8 inches in length. The large dorsal fin is reddish, the pectoral fins are white to greenish and the caudal, anal and ventral fins are red. It has been known to science since 1842 and was introduced to hobbyists in 1931. Mature females can be distinguished by their greater girth, and if there have been any attempts to breed them there have been no reports that they have been successful.

Photo by Dr. Herbert R. Axelrod.

OSTEOCHILUS VITTATUS (Cuvier & Valenciennes)
Black-Banded Osteochilus

Range: Thailand, Java, Borneo, Sumatra and the Malay States.
Habits: Peaceful if kept with fishes of its own size.
Water Conditions: Neutral to slightly acid water. Tank should be well planted and of a good size. Temperature 75 to 80°.
Size: To 9 inches in their natural waters, about half that in the aquarium.
Food Requirements: Live foods with added algae or lettuce leaves.
Color Variations: Silvery sides with plain fins. A broad black lateral stripe extends from the eye to the middle caudal rays. Back is sometimes purplish.

In spite of the fact that it is as abundant in its home waters as *Osteochilus hasselti* and of a smaller, more practical size for the aquarium hobbyist, *Osteochilus vittatus* is seen even less among imported Thailand fishes than its better-known cousin. It is distinguished very easily by its broad black band which extends from the eye through the fork of the tail. In some highly-colored specimens the area above this stripe is purplish to purplish-black, making the lateral stripe difficult to distinguish. The body of *Osteochilus vittatus* is also distinguished by being more slender, and the dorsal fin is not the magnificent sail-like thing it is with *Osteochilus hasselti*. Seen from underneath, the mouth shows a horseshoe-shaped upper lip which is rough and horny, with a small underjaw which fits inside. The two pairs of barbels on the upper lip which help identify *Osteochilus hasselti* are also present here, and a large pore or warty growth appears on the middle of the snout. Sexual differences are not externally apparent, and we have yet to hear that this attractive fish has been bred in the aquarium. Introduced in 1954, there have been very few subsequent importations.

F-456.00

OSTEOGLOSSUM BICIRRHOSUM (Vandelli)/*Arowana*

Range: Guianas and most parts of the Amazon.

Habits: Only small ones may be kept together; big ones are best kept alone.

Water Conditions: Not critical, but water should be clean. Should be moved as little as possible. Temperatures 76° to 78°.

Size: To about 18 inches, possibly larger.

Food Requirements: Greatly prefers fish which can be swallowed whole, but can be trained to take pieces of raw fish, shrimp, etc., from the fingers.

Color Variations: Greenish body with large, iridescent scales. The two stiff "whiskers" are usually blue.

The Arowana gives its viewer a look into an ancient prehistoric world, the Jurassic Age. Fishes from this period are mostly known from fossil remains, and the Arowana is one of the few remaining living examples of this group. They make very interesting aquarium fishes, but only the largest aquarium will hold a full-grown specimen. Their swimming movements are very lithe and fluid, reminding one of those of a snake. The scales are very large and opalescent, reflecting many colors when the light hits them. The large, "landing-barge" mouth betrays the predatory nature and healthy appetite. Anyone who decides to keep one of these beauties should have a number of expendable small fishes on hand at all times for food. We have heard of their being trained to accept strips of raw fish from the fingers, which solves the feeding problem when there are no live fish on hand. Once an Arowana adapts itself to a tank and if given the proper attention, it will usually live to a ripe old age and make an interesting conversation piece. They become very tame and we have had reports that they frequently come up to their owners to be "petted."

F-457.00

OTOCINCLUS AFFINIS (Steindachner)/*Midget Sucker Catfish*

Range: Southeastern Brazil.
Habits: Peaceful.
Water Conditions: Soft, slightly acid water is best, with dense plant growth and good light. Temperature 70 to 85°F.
Size: 2 inches.
Food Requirements: Main staple is algae which is scraped off leaves, rocks, and glass sides of the aquarium, but will accept other foods.
Color Variations: Gray-brown, with wide dark band running laterally from eye to peduncle. Dark blotch at base of tail.

This is a good algae-eater for the small tank, or even for the large tank, if enough of them are used. *Otocinclus affinis* busies itself by going around the aquarium using its sucker-like mouth to rasp algae off wherever it may have formed in the aquarium. The fish is particularly useful, because of its size, in removing algae from places which are beneath the notice of larger sucker species, like the Plecostomus. But there is a strange thing about this little Catfish: there seems to be no middle ground in its adaptability to a given set of tank conditions; the Midget Sucker Catfish will do either very well or very poorly, with no in-between state. Unfortunately, it works out often that the fish does poorly, rather than well. This is in many cases directly attributable to a lack of sufficient algal growths (or a lack of the right kind of algae) in the tank to support the fish. Where not enough algae or only the wrong kinds of algae are available, *Otocinclus affinis* will linger for a while but eventually die off. Although the species is bred only infrequently, the feat is not impossible if the species is given good care. Eggs are placed *Corydoras*-fashion against the glass sides of the tank; the small eggs hatch in two days at 80°.

F-458.00

OTOCINCLUS ARNOLDI (Regan)/*Arnold's Sucker Catfish*

Range: La Plata Region.

Habits: Peaceful, will not harm other fishes or plants. Cleans algae from plants and rocks.

Water Conditions: Slightly alkaline water and a sunny tank are best. Temperaure 73 to 78°.

Size: To 2¼ inches.

Food Requirements: *Tubifex* worms are eagerly eaten. The grazing on algae that they do takes care of their vegetable requirements.

Color Variations: Body brown with darker blotches and a dark horizontal stripe. Dorsal fin and caudal fin streaked with dark spots.

Arnold's Sucker Catfish is one of the most useful of all aquarium fishes. The larger Sucker Catfishes often outgrow their quarters and can stir up quite a mess when they are rooting in the bottom. Many species also stake out territories and defend them, getting pretty nasty doing so. This is not the case with the little *Otocinclus*, which minds its business of grazing on patches of algae and is never a source of annoyance to other fishes. Its small size permits it to get into a lot of nooks and crannies which are not available to its larger cousins and dig out morsels in the form of uneaten food, etc. With the *Otocinclus* we need never worry about shallow-rooted plants being dug out, either. Their only interest lies in what is to be found on the surface of the bottom, and the closest they will come to rooting is when a *Tubifex* worm is found and dragged out. Spawning is very similar to that of the *Corydoras* species. Eggs are fastened to rocks, plant stems and leaves, glass sides or any available solid surface. After 2 or 3 days they hatch and begin their never-ending search for food, which may be offered in the form of very fine dried foods.

Photo by Harald Schultz.

OTOCINCLUS VITTATUS (Regan)/*Sucker Catfish*

Range: Rio Paraguay system.
Habits: Peaceful.
Water Conditions: Soft, slightly acid water. Temperature 70 to 83°F.
Size: About 2 inches.
Food Requirements: Prefers algae above all other foods, but some meaty items are taken.
Color Variations: Plain brown, with dark stripe on sides and black spots near caudal fin.

Otocinclus vittatus, like its relatives *O. affinis* and *O. arnoldi*, is considered by aquarists as a miniature version of the larger Sucker Catfish. It does an efficient job of eradicating algae, but the fish, being small, has a limited capacity and cannot be relied on to tackle too big a job. One *Otocinclus* in a small tank will suffice, but in a larger tank the hobbyist must be prepared to use more *Otocinclus* or replace them with larger Sucker Catfish. This, of course, is based on the assumption that the hobbyist is keeping the little Sucker Cats primarily for their value as algae-eaters, although some hobbyists prefer to keep them for their interesting habits alone, taking care of the job of algae eradication through their own efforts. Perhaps this is as it should be; with a little work and attention to detail on the part of the hobbyist, a tank can remain relatively free of algae, and in such cases there is no need to introduce fishes into an aquarium for the specific purpose of cleaning up a tank. *Otocinclus vittatus* has not been spawned in this country, but in all probability it follows the pattern of *O. affinis* and *O. arnoldi*, which have.

OXYGASTER ANOMALURA (van Hasselt)/*Knife Barb*

Range: Thailand, Java, Borneo, Sumatra, Malaya.
Habits: Peaceful and active; a jumper.
Water Conditions: Soft, slightly acid water best. Temperature 70 to 85°F.
Size: Up to 5 inches.
Food Requirements: Will accept live, dry and frozen foods. Despite its size, this fish prefers small foods.
Color Variations: A comparatively colorless, semi-transparent fish.

The Knife Barb, so named for its keeled, or "sharp" belly, is a harmless Cyprinid which is best suited to larger tanks, because it gets big and because it does best in a tank in which it has plenty of room to swim freely. Rarely imported, *Oxygaster anomalura* is not in great demand; it is not a pretty fish, nor is it especially interesting, so no one seems to miss it, although it was offered some years ago on the aquarium market. All of the *Oxygaster* species are restless, nervous fish. They swim back and forth from one side of the aquarium to the other almost continually, like the *Danios*, *Brachydanios*, and some *Puntius* species. However, *Oxygaster anomalura* keeps more to the upper reaches of the water than to lower and middle reaches; its mouth is definitely adapted to feeding at the surface. The Knife Barb has not been bred in this country, but a spawning report on *Oxygaster atpar* states that the mating pair go through vigorous circular motions before the eggs are laid. The eggs are small and non-adhesive, and they hatch in about a day at a temperature of 79°. The fry remain near the surface, where they can easily be fed on dust-fine dry foods.

OXYGASTER OXYGASTROIDES (Bleeker)/*Glass Barb*

Range: Thailand and the Great Sunda Islands.
Habits: Harmless to other fishes and plants. Likes to swim in schools.
Water Conditions: Soft, slightly acid water. Temperature 75 to 80°.
Size: To 8 inches in native waters; in the aquarium about 5 inches.
Food Requirements: Prefers live foods which remain near the surface, like mosquito larvae. Can be accustomed to dry foods.
Color Variations: Sides silvery to glassy transparent. Dark horizontal stripe through center of body, and a narrow one above the anal fin.

The Glass Barb loses most of its claim to the popular name as it becomes bigger. The two fish shown here are too small to even sex properly. In their natural water this species attains 8 inches in length, but in the aquarium a fish half that size is considered large. Small fish like those in the picture have a very glassy transparency, much of which is lost later. The dark spots in the caudal lobes also tend to disappear in time and our friends become very plain, greenish-silvery fish with a dark stripe running from behind the gill-plate to the caudal base and another much narrower stripe from behind the belly to the bottom of the caudal base. The upturned mouth indicates that it gets most of its food at or near the surface. Another thing to notice is the size of the pectoral fins, one of which can be seen on the lower fish. This is the mark of the jumper, a fish which can easily "take off" from the surface and land on your living-room rug. Never keep them in an uncovered aquarium. This is a very common fish in quiet waters of Thailand, but because of its lack of colors the collectors prefer to ship more colorful species which bring a bigger price.

F-462.00

PACHYPANCHAX PLAYFAIRII (Günther)/*Playfair's Panchax*

Range: East Africa, Seychelles, Madagascar.
Habits: Apt to be a bit "bossy" with smaller fishes. Should be kept in a sunny, well-planted aquarium.
Water Conditions: Neutral to slightly alkaline water. Temperature 73 to 78°.
Size: About 3 inches.
Food Requirements: Live foods of all kinds. Will take dried foods if hungry.
Color Variations: Males are brown on the back, shading to greenish yellow on the sides with rows of red dots. Females have lighter colors.

Here is a fish you can recommend unhesitatingly to anyone who wants to begin with an "easy" egglaying species. Playfair's Panchax will withstand just about any abuse you can hand out and keep on spawning merrily. This is a species which will lay a small amount of eggs daily over a period of time. Males are active drivers and many breeders keep several females extra so that the male can divide his attentions. Eggs are hung in bushy plant leaves near the surface, where they can be seen hanging by fine threads. The shells are hard and they can be picked carefully out with the fingers and placed in a separate tank for hatching. This takes place in 10 to 14 days and the youngsters can swallow newly-hatched brine shrimp at once. Growth is rapid and the young must be sorted frequently because of the disparity in size between the younger and the older ones. Once they have reached a size where they can no longer swallow each other all is well. *Pachypanchax playfairii* has an unusual trait which is worth mentioning: the scales, especially along the back, stand out instead of lying close to the body. This is natural, and must not be diagnosed as a disease symptom.

F-463.00

PANAQUE species/*Sucker Catfish*

Range: British Guiana, Brazil.
Habits: Peaceful.
Water Conditions: Soft, slightly acid water best. Tank should be well planted and well lighted.
Size: Up to 1 foot.
Food Requirements: Main item in diet should be algae, but other foods, including worms, are taken.
Color Variations: Very variable; basic body color is generally brown or gray, with dark speckling and dark bands. Bands are sometimes white.

The *Panaque* genus is another genus representing the many South American Catfishes of the family Loricariidae. For the layman it is difficult to distinguish *Panaque* species from many of the other Sucker Catfish close relatives within the family, such as the various *Ancistrus, Hemiancistrus, Hypostomus, Stoniella,* and *Plecostomus*. Generally, almost all Sucker Catfish imported from South America, with the exception of the *Otocinclus* and *Loricaria* species, have been lumped together as *Plecostomus* species. Rarely do hobbyists pay any attention to specific differences among them, for there is little interest in breeding the Sucker Catfish, although some hobbyists have tried. The *Panaque* species pictured above was brought into this country by Paramount Aquarium in 1961. The fish was caught in British Guiana, but *Panaque* species are also found in other South American localities. The species illustrated has an extension on the lower lobe of the caudal fin, a characteristic shared with other Sucker Cats. The "whiskers" at the side of the head are also quite prominent.

PANTODON BUCHHOLZI (Peters)/*Butterfly Fish*

Range: Tropical West Africa.
Habits: Harmless to other fishes, but better kept by themselves to prevent damage to their filamentous ventral fin extensions.
Water Conditions: Soft, slightly acid water is preferable. Tank should not be too heavily planted and have a large surface; it must be covered.
Size: To 4 inches.
Food Requirements: Prefers live insects, but can be trained to take bits of shrimp, etc., from a pair of tweezers.

One title the Butterfly Fish can certainly lay claim to is that it is unique. *Pantodon buchholzi* is the only species in the genus, and the genus *Pantodon* is the only one in the family Pantodontidae. Its appearance is also unique. The upturned mouth tells us that it is a surface feeder, and the size of the mouth is an indication that not only mosquitoes and flies but also larger beetles and the like can be handled with ease. The large pectoral fins which when outspread resemble a butterfly's wings can be used for gliding over short distances in much the same manner as the oceanic Flying Fishes. The Butterfly Fish inhabits weedy, slow-flowing pools where it lies almost motionless near the surface and waits for its prey to pass by. When an insect comes within range the fish explodes into instant action.

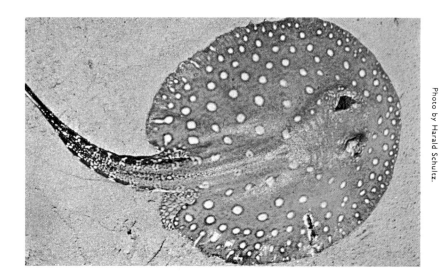

*PARATRYGON LATICEPS (Garman)/*Freshwater Stingray*

Range: Amazon Basin.
Habits: Spends all of its time on the bottom, sometimes almost covered. Small specimens are bottom feeders, and will seldom attack other fishes.
Water Conditions: Slightly alkaline water, fine gravel on the bottom. Temperature 75 to 80°.
Size: Up to 4 feet across.
Food Requirements: Worms, bits of shrimp, clam, etc.
Color Variations: Back brown to light brown with round cream-coloured spots. Belly white.

What is the most feared fish in South American waters ? Before you jump to wrong conclusions and say that is the Piranha, let me hasten to tell you that it is the Stingray. There are many times more instances of natives being injured painfully by its whipping tail than there are cases of Piranha bites. A Stingray will lie on the bottom in the sand and change its colors to blend exactly with its surroundings. Here it is the master of any situation. Other fishes cannot (and will not) attack it and its only danger is that of being trampled upon. This is where its very effective weapon comes into play. The "stinger" does not make much of a wound going in, but it has many barbs on its surface which rip the flesh when it is withdrawn. There is no injection of poison as with a snake, but the slimy coating causes an agonizingly painful swelling.
*Now called *Potamotrygon laticeps*.

PARAUCHENOGLANIS MACROSTOMA (Pellegrin)
African Spotted Catfish

Range: Tropical West Africa.
Habits: Peaceful, usually remains hidden in daylight and comes out at night.
Water Conditions: Soft, neutral to slightly acid water. Temperature 76 to 80°.
Size: To 9½ inches in natural waters, much smaller in the aquarium.
Food Requirements: All sorts of live or frozen foods.
Color Variations: Body brown, dark on the back and lighter below. Rows of dark
brown spots, large on the body and smaller on the head.

The African Spotted Catfish pictured here are small babies, as indicated by
the size of the sprig of *Elodea* just behind them. Fully grown they are recorded
to attain a size of 9½ inches, and at this size would be adaptable only to very
large aquaria. They are very attractive, but when placed in a large well-planted
aquarium even a diligent search often fails to find them. Add to this the fact
that they confine most of their activity to the night hours and it is easily understood why they haven't exactly caused a furore in aquarium circles. Like so
many of the other African Catfishes, this species has not been spawned in
captivity. Probably there have never been enough of them on hand to make
any real attempts in this direction, but it is a fairly safe bet that even if a few
big shipments came in the story would still be the same. There have been no
observed sex differences, and it is suspected with many of our "impossible"
species that they never attain sexual ripeness in the confines of an aquarium.
One of the reasons for this may be that there are certain food substances which
are common in their native waters but which we cannot provide.

PEDALIBRYCON FELIPPONEI (Fowler)/*Uruguay Characin*

Range: Uruguay.
Habits: Will not attack larger fishes, but will nip fins of smaller fishes. Also eats plants.
Water Conditions: Soft, acid water best.
Size: About 4½ inches.
Food Requirements: Takes all foods.
Color Variations: Silvery-gray, with round black spot at caudal base.

Pedalibrycon felipponei has one advantage: it can take colder water than most other South American Characins. Outside of that, the fish has little to recommend it; on the contrary, in fact, the Uruguay Characin has a few points in its disfavor. One of these is that the fish is a nipper, of both other fishes and plants. As such, it is not a sought-after species, and it is no longer seen in hobbyists' tanks. In the early days of the hobby, fishes such as this one had a chance to gain a little attention, simply because they had little competition. In these days of great variety of fishes offered for sale to hobbyists, a fish must have an attraction of some sort in order to be worth anything to a hobbyist; it is no longer possible for a dealer to be able to sell a fish just because it is a fish, which was true in the very beginning of the hobby when aquarists were anxious to lay their hands on any fish that came along, so long as it was the least bit different. The very short vogue enjoyed by *Pedalibrycon felipponei* didn't allow enough time for the few people who owned the fish to get well acquainted with it, so there are no evidences to show that it has ever been bred here.

F-468.00

Photo by R. Zukal.

PELMATOCHROMIS ANSORGII
Five-Spot African Cichlid

Range: Liberia to Nigeria, in fresh and brackish waters.
Habits: Peaceful for a Cichlid; does some digging, but usually around rocks. Plants
are seldom uprooted.
Water Conditions: Slightly alkaline, with an addition of about a teaspoonful of salt
per gallon of water. Tank should be well planted.
Size: Males to about 4 inches; females a little smaller.
Food Requirements: Live foods preferred, but they will also take frozen foods.
Color Variations: Sides are greenish-yellow with five spots which are sometimes
connected into a horizontal line. Belly of the female pink, male red.

The Five-Spot African Cichlid occurs in coastal waters of tropical West
Africa, where it is found in brackish as well as fresh waters. With such a fish
it is always a good idea to add some salt to the aquarium water, about a teaspoonful per gallon. This is just enough to make the water a tiny bit brackish,
but not brackish enough to do any harm to fresh-water plants. An unusual
marking of the females of this species is that when sexually mature they have
a gleaming white spot on the sides near the anal opening. They can be distinguished from the males in other ways besides: they are a little smaller in
size and the fins are smaller and more rounded. A well-mated pair will usually
get along well and spawn regularly, preferring the privacy of an overturned
flowerpot with a notch broken out of the rim to allow the pair to get in.

F-469.00

*PELMATOCHROMIS KRIBENSIS (Boulenger)/*Kribensis*

Range: Tropical West Africa, especially the Niger Delta.
Habits: Peaceful. Does some digging, but mostly under rocks. Plants are seldom up-
rooted.
Water Conditions: Soft, slightly acid water. Temperature 76 to 80 .
Size: Males, up to 3½ inches; females, to 2½ inches.
Food Requirements: Live and frozen foods.
Color Variations: Too many to describe in this small space. See illustration. Female
takes on a coppery flush when spawning.

The Kribensis was an immediate hit when it was first introduced in the early
1950's. One look at the picture of this gorgeous fish is enough to make it
obvious why. It is not large enough to really put it in a class with the big
Cichlids, and at the same time rather large to be called a Dwarf Cichlid. Its

P. kribensis female

behavior in mixed company is very mild, but for its most appealing feature, just look at the colors! It is best when first attempting to spawn a pair to keep them in separate tanks until the female becomes heavy with eggs. The ideal spawning site is the same as described for *P. ansorgii* , a flowerpot with a notch knocked out of the rim, set upside down on the bottom. There will be a great deal of activity by the male carrying out huge mouthfuls of gravel from inside the flowerpot when suddenly one day both will disappear, to come out very rarely. Then a very comical situation develops. The little female will forcibly eject the male every time he tries to go in. Put him in another tank, or he may get hurt. The female takes complete charge of the eggs and young, but should be removed when the youngsters become free-swimming.

The male is more slender, bigger, and has a broader forehead than the female. On the edge of his dorsal fin there is a silvery, gold-gleaming stripe which ends in the point. In the upper part of the tail fin there are 1-5 round dark spots which are edged in light yellow. The fins are violet in color.

The female has a large wine-red patch on the sides of her body, is more deeply colored, and has red ventral fins. Younger specimens do not show this full coloration.

*The name of this fish is now *Pelvicachromis pulcher*.

Photo by H. Hansen, Aquarium Berlin.

*PELMATOCHROMIS TAENIATUS (Boulenger)
Striped African Dwarf Cichlid

Range: Lower Niger River, West Africa.

Habits: Generally peaceful, even timid except when breeding.

Water Conditions: Soft, slightly acid water is best, temperature 76° to 78°. Tank should be well-planted and provide hiding-places.

Size: Male 3½ inches, female slightly smaller.

Food Requirements: Live foods preferred, but finely chopped beef-heart is also accepted and even relished.

Color Variations: Males have black spot on the gill-cover. Sides have two dark stripes. Upper third of tail orange with dark spots. Females plainer.

Pelmatochromis taeniatus is only slightly different from its much better-known cousin, *Pelmatochromis kribensis*. Both come from West Africa, and the few specimens which are imported now and then are frequently sold as *Pelmatochromis kribensis*. The two species look very much different in the color plates, but that of *P. kribensis* was made with the fish in breeding colors, while that of *P. taeniatus* depicts their normal colors. Both are beautiful and highly desirable species, and their habits are identical. When the female becomes heavy with eggs and the male begins to search for a spawning site, it has been found that the best one is a flowerpot with a notch about one inch in diameter cut or broken out of the edge. This is partly filled with gravel and set upright in a dark corner, covered with a piece of slate. The male will soon be swimming in through the notch and returning with mouthfuls of gravel. Then one day it will be noticed that the female has taken possession and will not let him enter. A careful lift of the slate will reveal that she is guarding eggs. In about ten days the young are swimming.

*Now called *Pelvicachromis taeniatus*.

PERIOPHTHALMUS BARBARUS (Linné)/*Mudskipper*

Range: East Africa, Madagascar, Sunda Islands and Australia.
Habits: Cannot be combined with any other class of fishes. Shy at first, but later can be tamed effectively.
Water Conditions: Water must have salt, 2 teaspoonsful to the gallon, added. There should be an area where the fish can climb out.
Size: To 6 inches.
Food Requirements: Worms and other living insects. Can be trained to take bits of shrimp from the fingers.
Color Variations: Variable; usually bluish-gray to brown above, lighter below.

The Mudskipper looks as though it were a fish which began developing into a frog and changed its mind when the metamorphosis was half completed. Its head with the eyes set into lumps on top certainly has a froglike appearance. The powerful pectoral fins are set in muscular elongations which appear like short forelegs and permit them to move over land with amazing nimbleness. They are in fact clumsy swimmers and can move more swiftly over land than they can swim in the water. Their habitat is usually a stretch of muddy tide-flats which become uncovered when the tide moves out. There is almost always a tangle of mangrove roots, and the Mudskippers are very adept at climbing onto these to get a wider range of vision. In the aquarium Mudskippers are not the easiest fishes in the world to keep. Their tank should be shallow and have a large surface. Their water, what there is of it, should have about two teaspoonsful of salt added to it per gallon. The sand should be sloped to come out of the water, and a few flat rocks may be placed at the water's edge. It is important that the air be warm and moist, so the tank must be kept tightly covered.

Photo by Paysan.

PHAGO MACULATUS (Ahl)/*African Pike Characin*

Range: West Africa, in the Niger River.
Habits: A decidedly nasty fish which will kill for the sheer pleasure of killing.
Water Conditions: Neutral, medium-soft water best.
Size: Up to 8 inches, but usually seen much smaller.
Food Requirements: Wants plenty of meaty foods, preferably live fishes, although it will also accept dead ones.
Color Variations: Over-all body color is olive to brown, with belly lighter. Spots along sides.

This mean fish is no longer available, because of the political disruptions in Africa which have put a crimp in collecting expeditions, but you can bet that *Phago* is not missed, except by a few hobbyists who are willing to put up with its vicious nature for the sake of owning an oddity. In effect, the African Pike Characin is the piscatorial counterpart of the weasel, for *Phago*, like the weasel, kills more than it needs to satisfy its hunger. It almost seems that the fish takes a pleasure in killing, and *Phago* even goes the weasel one better by torturing its victims before dispatching them.   The *Phago* illustrated is young; you can imagine what a full-grown specimen is capable of. Some authorities place this fish in a family distinct from the family Characidae, in the family Citharinidae.

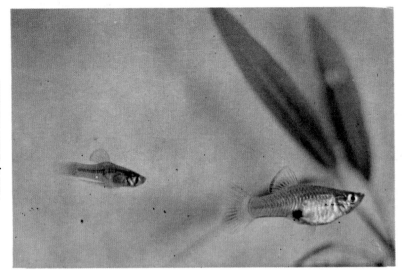

PHALLICHTHYS AMATES (Miller)/*Merry Widow*

Range: Atlantic coastal regions of Guatemala.
Habits: Peaceful toward other fishes, but very fond of eating its own young.
Water Conditions: Slightly alkaline water is best. Temperature 72 to 75°.
Size: Males, to 1¼ inches; females, to 2 inches.
Food Requirements: Should have some algae on which to nibble, as well as prepared, frozen and live foods.
Color Variations: Body greenish yellow with a bluish shimmer. Fins yellow. Males have a series of faint bars which are missing in the females.

The Merry Widow was a very popular livebearer several decades ago, but since then there have been many other more colorful fishes to attract the attention of the hobby, and it is rarely seen except in the collections of those who specialize in keeping the lesser-known livebearing fishes. An unsual feature of the male of this species is an exceptionally long gonopodium. There has long been a controversy on the copulative actions of livebearing fishes among experts. Some claim that the female is fertilized internally by an actual insertion into her body of the male's gonopodium. Others say that no insertion is made, but that the male simply touches the female's vent and releases the sperm there, where it is drawn into her body. Still others say that the copulative act is a more or less hit-or-miss affair and that the gonopodium is used merely to aim the sperm in the female's direction. If this is so, why are the livebearers equipped with so many different lengths and shapes of gonopodiums? There is still much to be done until science gets a satisfactory and conclusive answer; high-speed photography and other experiments should give results before too long.

Photo by H. Hansen, Aquarium Berlin.

PHALLOCEROS CAUDOMACULATUS RETICULATUS (Köhler)/
Caudo

Range: From Rio de Janeiro to Paraguay and Uruguay.

Habits: Peaceful at all times; not greatly inclined to eat their young if well fed.

Water Conditions: Slightly alkaline water, well-filtered and clean. Tank should stand in a sunny location.

Size: Males, up to 1 inch; females, to $2\frac{1}{4}$ inches.

Food Requirements: Small sizes of live and prepared foods, supplemented with algae which is nibbled from plants and glass sides.

Color Variations: Yellowish to golden with black spattered markings.

This is the little fish with the big name. The original "Caudo" is a nondescript little fish which has never found any favor, but this one with the yellowish background and black peppered markings is at least popular enough to be seen occasionally. There is also a golden variety with black markings, but this is a real rarity. In this species we have a real disparity in size between the sexes, the female being about twice the size of the male. His one-inch size makes him an unlikely candidate for the community aquarium, unless his companions are all small fishes like himself who would not swallow or bully him. Females are not very productive, and it must be expected that a percentage of the young will revert to the original coloring. The fry are a little delicate at first, but once they begin growing the battle is over. The author has always considered the Caudo as a nice little fish which deserved a more respected place in the live-bearing group, but in these days of fancy Guppies and a multitude of brilliantly colored breeds of other live bearers to be had these days, this not unattractive little fellow has fallen into a more or less "ugly duckling" role which he does not deserve.

Photo by Dr. Herbert R. Axelrod.

PHENACOGRAMMUS INTERRUPTUS (Boulenger)/*Congo Tetra*

Range: Congo Region.
Habits: Peaceful toward fishes of comparable size. A school fish, which prefers to swim in groups.
Water Conditions: Soft, slightly acid water which has been treated with the addition of an acid peat moss. Temperature about 76°.
Size: Males, to 3¼ inches; females to 2½ inches.
Food Requirements: Larger-sized live and frozen foods, supplemented by coarse prepared foods.
Color Variations: Large opalescent scales, fins grayish violet with white edges. Indistinct yellowish horizontal stripe.

Many authorities either have been slow or have refused to accept the present name *Phenacogrammus*, and still refer to the generic name as *Micralestes*. This good-sized Characin from the Congo River is a shining example of the refractive powers which are possible in a fish's scales. When bathed in sunlight, which their scales reflect, each scale becomes a prism which repeats all the colors of the rainbow. Another interesting thing about this fish is its ability to grow a number of feathery-looking appendages from the fork of its tail. They are quite prominent in the males and much less so in the females. Frequently they are bitten off by other fishes, but grow in again before long. Spawning the Congo Tetra takes a large tank and is not an easy task. According to Meder, who first spawned them in Germany, the temperature should be 75 to 77°, and the eggs are laid among plants near the bottom. When they are finished the parents should be removed. Hatching takes place in 6 days, and in 24 to 36 hours they are free-swimming. Being quite large, newly-hatched brine shrimp may be fed at once and growth progresses at a rapid rate.

Photo by R. Zukal

PIMELODUS CLARIAS (Bloch)/*Spotted Pimelodus*

Range: Central America south to central South America.
Habits: Peaceful with fishes too large to swallow, nocturnal.
Water Conditions: Any clean water suits this hardy fish. Temperature 68 to 78°.
Size: To 12 inches. Only young specimens suitable for the average tank.
Food Requirements: Larger live foods like cut-up earthworms preferred, but other foods like chunks of lean beef are also relished.
Color Variations: Grayish blue body with large irregular bluish-black spots. Fins have smaller spots.

This handsome Catfish looks very much like some of the *Synodontis* species from Africa. Because of the large size it attains (about 12 inches) it is not highly suitable for the average home aquarium when it reaches maturity. It has a very wide distribution, all the way from Central America all over the West Indies and down to central South America. Unfortunately it becomes most active at night and prefers to remain hidden in the daytime. As with most nocturnal fishes, they are seen most frequently in a well-planted tank which does not receive a great deal of sunlight. In such a tank they feel secure and make themselves quite at home. This is not an algae-eating fish. Generous feedings of such foods as cut-up earthworms or other carnivore fodder should be provided. Chopped beef heart or other beef is excellent, but care must be taken that the fish receive enough during the dark hours and at the same time that there is nothing left to foul the tank in the morning. This amount can be established by a little close observation in the beginning. *Pimelodus clarias* has been known to science for a long time, first having been named by Bloch in 1795.

PLECOSTOMUS BOLIVIANUS (Pearson)/*Bolivian Sucker Catfish*

Range: Bolivia, in the Amazon tributaries.
Habits: Seldom bothers other fishes.
Water Conditions: Neutral to slightly alkaline. Temperature 75 to 80°.
Size: To 6 inches.
Food Requirements: All live and frozen foods eagerly accepted, especially worms. Requires algae or a vegetable substitute like lettuce leaves.
Color Variations: Body dark green, fins light green with dark round spots.

The Bolivian Sucker Catfish will surely gladden the hearts of many aquarium hobbyists if it ever becomes generally available. Most of the Sucker Catfishes are characterized by their extreme ugliness, but it is completely forgotten when this fellow begins waving his banners, in this case a huge sail-like dorsal fin and a deep anal fin, both with large round black dots in neat rows. The tail also carries some rows of black dots, but they are not as round or spaced in as orderly a fashion. Strangely enough, only a few of these dots overflow onto the body, in the belly region. The body is well protected by rows of sharp spines on the sides and the stiff, sturdy first ray of the pectoral fins is similarly armed, making this fish not only a dangerous one to handle but also a difficult one to remove from the meshes of a net. All of the *Plecostomus* and many similar species are very difficult to capture in their native waters because they invariably seek out streams where there is a great deal of brushwood in the water where they can hide. Seining is an impossibility and the fish cannot be driven out into clear spots. They merely dodge from one hiding-place to another.

Photo by Dr. Herbert R. Axelrod.

POECILISTES PLEUROSPILUS (Günther)/*Porthole Livebearer*

Range: Atlantic and Pacific watersheds of Mexico and Guatemala.
Habits: Peaceful toward other fishes and does not harm plants. Seldom even harm their own fry.
Water Conditions: Neutral to slightly alkaline; avoid chilling and keep the temperature 75 to 80°.
Size: Males to 1¼ inches, females to 2 inches.
Food Requirements: Not fussy eaters; will consume all foods they can swallow, but of course should get some occasional live foods.
Color Variations: Males have brown sides with a greenish shimmer. On a lighter horizontal stripe there is a row of dark spots. Females lighter in color.

The aquarium hobbyist of today is very different in his attitude toward the livebearing species from his fellow-hobbyist of a few decades ago. A few colorful species have been developed into unbelievably colorful strains, and many of the comparatively drab ones have all but fallen by the wayside.

Breeders who could be producing these lesser-known fishes are so busy supplying the demand for Platies, Swordtails and Mollies for which there is a ready market that they do not take up their time and space with slow-selling species. Twenty years ago this little livebearer was in fairly good supply, as were many others which the younger hobbyists of today have never seen and in all probability will never see. *Poecilistes pleurospilus* is a model citizen in the community aquarium. They do not uproot or bite chunks out of plants and if fed properly will seldom attack their young. A very desirable fish, the Porthole Livebearer would be an asset to any livebearer collection. Unfortunately, because so few people have any desire to keep a fish which has no bright colors, we will only see the few which now and then find their way into shipments from their native countries.

F-480.00

POECILOCHARAX WEITZMANI Meinken • *Black Darter Tetra*

Range: The Upper Amazon (Solimoes) as well as the upper Rio Negro-Orinoco in heavily vegetated, slow-moving streams.

Habits: It stays on the bottom of the aquarium, barely rising even when it is hungry. It preys on slowly falling food particles whether they are live or not. They are extremely difficult to keep without live foods. The males are territorial even when not spawning.

Water Conditions: Warm, slightly acid water.

Size: 4 cm.

Food Requirements: Living foods that fall to the bottom, such as daphnia, tubifex worms, live brine shrimp, etc.

Only recently has this spectacular tetra been imported in any numbers, but it is still a very rare item in the pet trade. The slow movements and gigantic, fluttery fins reminded Dr. Axelrod, one of the few scientists to collect this fish, of the tropical American morpho butterflies and resulted in the common name "Black Morpho Tetra" being jokingly suggested for the species. The species has not been studied in detail in its natural habitat in the soft, acid, black water creeks of the Upper Amazon and Rio Negro, but what is known of its behavior in the aquarium indicates that it is somewhat territorial, otherwise peaceful, and rather lethargic. It also has gained a reputation for not feeding well even when provided with live foods.

The Black Darter Tetra has seldom or never been spawned in the aquarium, although there are rumors that it has bred in a few tanks in eastern Europe or Germany. Its close relative, the Sailfin Tetra, *Crenuchus spilurus,* is reputed to spawn somewhat like a nesting cichlid, even when guarding the nest, so we would not even venture to guess how the Black Morpho spawns.

F-481.00

Photo by Hans J. Richter.

*POECILOBRYCON EQUES (Steindachner)/*Pencilfish*

Range: Central Amazon region, possibly Rio Negro.
Habits: Peaceful; swims with the head tilted upward. Prefers to swim in schools.
Water Conditions: Soft, neutral to slightly acid water. Temperature 76 to 80°.
Size: To 2 inches.
Food Requirements: Most foods are taken from or near the surface. Mosquito
    larvae are particularly relished by mature fish.
Color Variations: Sides deep brown with five horizontal stripes, the heaviest of
    which runs into the lower caudal lobe.

At the time of writing there is a great deal of controversy about the proper
naming of the genera to which the various Pencilfishes belong, and which
species belongs to which genus. Every authority has his own ideas on the
subject and expresses them in his works. This fish, which was known for
many years as *Poecilobrycon eques*, has been referred to as *Nannobrycon* and
Nannostomus as well, depending upon whose works you are reading.

                               * Now known as *Nannobrycon eques.*

Photo by Hans J. Richter.

*POECILOBRYCON ESPEI (Meinken)/Barred Pencilfish

Range: British Guiana.
Habits: Peaceful and active. A skilled jumper whose tank should never be left uncovered.
Water Conditions: Soft water, neutral to slightly acid. Temperature 76 to 80°.
Size: To 1¾ inches.
Food Requirements: Not choosy as to foods, but very partial to live *Daphnia*.
Color Variations: Back olive brown, shading to silver toward the belly. Five tilted bars on lower half of body. Fins colorless.

This is the most recently introduced and most distinctively marked of all the Pencilfishes. The five black bars in the lower half of the body make it unmistakable even from 20 feet away. The fish was found in British Guiana by our good friend Louis Chung in 1956, and large numbers of them found their way to American and European dealers. The author helped collect many species of Pencilfishes in the Rupununi District savannahs with Mr. Chung, but this was not one of them. Of course this is no help in pinpointing their habitat, but at least we know two things: they *do* come from British Guiana, and they do *not* come from the savannah waters in the southwestern part of that fascinating country. The Barred Pencilfish has the distinction of swimming in an almost horizontal position, unlike most of the other *Poecilobrycon* species which tilt themselves upward. They are active and like to swim in small groups. A look at the picture shows a similarity of finnage, but the deeper body and more irregular markings of the upper specimen make it easily recognizable as the female. They are said to spawn in bushy plants like most of the other Pencilfishes.

* Now known as *Nannostomus espei*.

F-483.00

*POECILOBRYCON UNIFASCIATUS (Steindachner)
One-Lined Pencilfish

Range: Middle and lower Amazon tributaries, Rio Negro.
Habits: Peaceful and somewhat timid; prefer to be kept in a small group.
Water Conditions: Soft, slightly acid water. Temperature 74 to 78°.
Size: To 2½ inches.
Food Requirements: Live and prepared foods of small size, preferably food which will remain at or near the surface.
Color Variations: Back brown to gold; belly white. Wide black stripe from snout to lower caudal lobe, where there is a small red area.

The One-Lined Pencilfish has been known to science since being named by Steindachner in 1876, yet we see them so seldom that many works do not even list them. Their habitat is evidently confined to Brazilian waters, because Eigenmann does not mention them as appearing in British Guiana streams in his huge book on the fish life indigenous there.

* Now known as *Nannostomus unifasciatus.*

F-484.00

POLYCENTROPSIS ABBREVIATA (Boulenger)/*African Leaf Fish*

Range: Tropical West Africa, Lagos, Nigeria, Ogowe.

Habits: Greedy eaters which can swallow a fish almost as large as themselves. Not to be kept in a community tank.

Water Conditions: Soft, acid water is best. Temperature 78 to 82°.

Size: To 3¼ inches.

Food Requirements: Earthworms and smaller unwanted living fishes preferred, but can be trained to take chunks of beef heart.

Color Variations: Dark brown mottling on a lighter background. Black line from tip of snout to eye, another across the opreculum toward the belly.

The African Leaf Fish, unlike its South American counterpart, does not go around imitating a dead leaf all day, but the markings are similar and permit it to blend unnoticed into the background. Another point of similarity is the huge mouth, which can engulf a good-sized fish with no trouble at all. The tail is so transparent that it looks as if it had been chopped off; this and the huge head and mouth give the appearance of a fish which has been cut in half and allowed to swim around. The African Leaf Fish has a surprising manner of spawning: it builds a bubble-nest of large proportions, preferably under a floating leaf. The parents then circle underneath the bubbles in an upside-down position, releasing and fertilizing the eggs. For her safety the female should be removed when this is finished. The male guards the eggs and fry when they hatch after 48 hours. After they become free-swimming the male's job may be considered at an end and it is best to remove him. Thanks to their huge mouths the fry can consume good-sized foods and grow quickly. They should be sorted according to size frequently, or the smaller ones will be swallowed.

POLYCENTRUS SCHOMBURGKI (Müller & Troschel)
Schomburgk's Leaf Fish

Range: Northeastern South America and Trinidad.

Habits: Aggressive and capable of swallowing fish almost as large as themselves. Should not be kept in a community tank.

Water Conditions: Neutral to slightly acid and soft.

Size: To 4 inches.

Food Requirements: Smaller fish and pieces of earthworm preferred, but can be trained to take pieces of beef heart or other lean meat, shrimp or fish.

Color Variations: Male spotted with blue and green at spawning time. Dorsal, anal and caudal fins are black at this time. Females much paler.

The fact that there are members of the Nandid family found in South America, Africa and Southern Asia is a clear indication to some scientists that these continents were once connected. It is difficult to conceive that the thousands of miles of ocean between Brazil and Africa were once land, but when one considers the similarity between fishes like the *Polycentrus* in South America and *Polycentropsis* in Africa the whole thing becomes plausible. Schomburgk's Leaf Fish often finds its way up among other fishes shipped from South America. In behavior it is very similar to that of many of the Cichlids. A hiding-place is selected among the rocks and the eggs are deposited there. Hatching takes place in only 48 hours and the male, who takes full charge, fans and guards the fry. As soon as they are able to fend for themselves, the parents should be taken out. Nothing is gained by leaving them together, and the danger is eliminated that the youngsters will be mistaken for something good to eat. They grow well, but care must be taken to keep them sorted as to size, or otherwise the bigger ones will find that one of their brethren makes a tasty morsel.

Photo by Hans J. Richter.

POTAMORRHAPHIS GUIANENSIS (Schomburgk)
Freshwater Needlefish

Range: Guianas.
Habits: Must be kept away from other fishes. Likely to become very nasty.
Water Conditions: Soft, slightly alkaline water. Temperature 74 to 78°.
Size: Said to attain a length of 32 inches in native waters.
Food Requirements: Must be fed small living fishes.
Color Variations: Grayish green above, yellowish below. Black irregular stripe
extends from the snout to the caudal base.

At first sight one might be tempted to identify this slender, longbilled fish
as one of the Pipefishes, but a close look at its mouth tells us that this is not so.
The Pipefishes have a tubular, sucking-type mouth, but this fellow has a
mouth that opens wide and is armed with a series of needle-sharp teeth.
These jaws snap shut easily on its prey while moving, and once impaled on
those teeth no amount of squirming will loosen it. The jaws will open
occasionally until they have worked the prey into a position where it can be
swallowed. These fish, like their salt-water relatives the Bony Gars, spend a
great deal of time near the surface where they can take a lightning-like stab
with wide-open mouth at any fish unfortunate enough to approach them.
Sometimes they conceal themselves very effectively among plant leaves where
they wait patiently like a Pike for their prey to swim by. Keeping *Potamorr-
haphis guianensis* in the aquarium requires that they have a tank of their own.
Feeding them is likely to be the biggest problem: the prey must move or they
will not touch it. For this purpose there must be a constant supply of Guppies
or other living fishes on hand.

F-487.00

Photo by Aaron Norman

PRIONOBRAMA FILIGERA (Cope)/*Glass Bloodfin*

Range: Tributaries of Rio Madeira.
Habits: Peaceful, very active fish which prefer to be in group...
Water Conditions: Soft, slightly acid water is best. Temperature 74 to 78°. Tank
   should afford a good amount of swimming room.
Size: To 2½ inches.
Food Requirements: Prepared foods accepted, but live foods should be given at
   least several times a week.
Color Variations: Body transparent with a light blue tint, dark blue shoulder-spot.
   Anal and caudal fins red at the base, anal with a white edge.

It is frequently the misfortune of a fish that it is overshadowed by another
better-known species which it resembles. In this case we have a fish which
resembles the popular Bloodfin, *Aphyocharax rubripinnis*, to which it is closely
related. However, the Glass Bloodfin has a transparent quality which is not
found on the other. Both have a bluish gleam to the body, but the Glass
Bloodfin has a more distinctive finnage. The anal fin of the male is sickle-
shaped and white on the front edge. This white edge is usually extended to a
definite point. Unlike the common Bloodfin there is not much red in the anal
fin, but a definite amount in the tail. The Glass Bloodfin is an active, attractive
fish in its own right, and when kept in a group provides constant motion and
activity. They are skilled jumpers and the tank in which they are kept should
be kept covered at all times. They spawn in a helter-skelter fashion, the males
pursuing the females like Danios and scattering eggs all over the tank, where
most of them fall to the bottom. As soon as the driving is finished the breeders
should be removed, or the eggs will be eaten. Fry hatch in a day at 80° and
grow rapidly.

F-488.00

*PRISTELLA RIDDLEI (Meek)/*Pristella*

Range: Northern South America.
Habits: Peaceful and active; swims in schools.
Water Conditions: Soft, slightly acid water. Temperature 75 to 80°.
Size: To 1¼ inches.
Food Requirements: Not at all choosy; live foods should be offered as often as available.
Color Variations: Sides silvery to yellowish; dorsal and anal fins have large black spot on a white background. Tail reddish to bright red.

This perky little Tetra has long been a prime favorite among hobbyists, and for excellent reasons. It is active, always out where it can be seen, and harmless toward other fishes and plants; to top it off, it is a real beauty. In the past few years there has been an albino variety offered by the trade. These are pink-eyed and rather washed-out in appearance, and to the author's mind do not begin to compare with the original. For instance, I do not consider a red spot on a pink background to be as effective as a black spot on a white background. Still, there are many who deem this a lovely fish and a great improvement over the original. Breeding the Pristella is not a difficult task, but care must be taken to select a good pair. Picking a ripe female is ridiculously easy: the eggs can be seen plainly through her transparent sides with the aid of a light from behind the fish. The body cavity of the male comes to a point and we can only estimate by their interest in the females whether or not they are ready. It may be necessary to try several males before a proper one is found. Eggs hatch in a day and the fry are hardy and easily raised.

* Now known as *Pristella maxillaris.*

F-489.00

Photo by Dr. Herbert R. Axelrod.

*PRISTELLA RIDDLEI (Meek), albino variety/*Albino Pristella*

Range: Northern South America.
Habits: Peaceful and active.
Water Conditions: Soft, slightly acid water. Temperature 75 to 80°F.
Size: To 1¾ inches.
Food Requirements: Not choosy, but should get live foods as frequently as available.
Color Variations: Sides pinkish white; where the original fish has black markings, these are pink. Eyes are red.

For those who might be interested in seeing what the Albino Pristellas look like, we show a picture here. Albinism, the dictionary tells us, is a congenital deficiency of pigmentation. This happens quite frequently with captive specimens of fishes, and most hobbyists are fairly well acquainted with albinos of certain species, this one included. These are almost without exception tank-bred specimens, because in its native waters an albino in a school of its normal-colored brethren is a fish which stands out as an easy target for its enemies and is among the first to be singled out for extermination. In the aquarium some fishes which are albinos command a good price, and some are attractive in a sort of washed-out way. It must be remembered when keeping any of the albino varieties that the eyes are also without pigmentation and the light rays which strike them are practically unfiltered, causing what seems like normal light to be an almost unbearable glare. Therefore it is actually an act of kindness if we give them some shady spots where they can retreat when this glare gets to be too much for them.

* Now known as *Pristella maxillaris,* albino variety.

*PROCHILODUS INSIGNIS (Schomburgk)/*Flag-Tailed Prochilodus*

Range: British Guiana and the central Amazon region.
Habits: Peaceful, but its vegetarian habits may lead it to nip plants. A skilled jumper; tank must be kept covered.
Water Conditions: Soft, slightly alkaline water. Temperature 74 to 78°.
Size: To 14 inches. Imported specimens seldom exceed 5 inches.
Food Requirements: Mostly vegetable foods should be offered, such as lettuce leaf, spinach or boiled oatmeal. Live foods also accepted.
Color Variations: Body golden, dorsal, ventral and pectoral fins reddish. Anal and caudal fins yellow with black stripes.

This is one of the fishes which we seldom see except as babies. Larger ones would be highly expensive to ship, and the market for them would not be active. In their native Guiana they attain a size of 14 inches, at which size the natives catch them for food. Netting them is difficult; they leap nimbly over the net, often even over the collector's head, as soon as they feel the confines of the seine. A young specimen in full color is certainly a thing of beauty with its reddish fins and large striped tail. As the fish gets older the colors fade and finally it is scarcely recognizable as the same species. As is the case with many of these large fishes, no external sex differences have yet been observed. Perhaps some day a public aquarium will come up with a report of a spawning in one of their large tanks. We have learned about the spawning habits of many hundreds of fishes, but can do no more than speculate about the habits of so many more! *Prochilodus insignis* was known to science as far back as 1841 and was first offered to aquarium hobbyists in Germany around 1910. If it likes its conditions, it lives for a long time in captivity.

* Now known as *Semaprochilodus theraponura.*

*PROCHILODUS TAENIURUS (Valenciennes)/*Silver Prochilodus*

Range: Amazon Basin; no exact location given.
Habits: Peaceful, but very likely to nibble at plants. Tanks should be kept covered at all times, as they jump.
Water Conditions: Soft, slightly alkaline water. Temperature 74 to 78°. These are active swimmers, and they like a roomy tank.
Size: To 12 inches.
Food Requirements: Mostly vegetable foods should be offered, such as lettuce or spinach leaves; boiled oatmeal also accepted, besides live foods.
Color Variations: Body silvery with rows of black dashes. Dorsal, anal and caudal fins with black stripes. Ventral fins bright red.

Not as often imported as *Prochilodus insignis* but even more beautiful is *Prochilodus taeniurus*. The body, which in *P. insignis* is a slightly golden color and without markings, is silvery white and is covered with horizontal rows of black dashes. In the middle from a point below the dorsal fin to the caudal base is a thin black line which looks as if the pigment in a row of dashes flowed together. The same characteristic stripes seen in *P. insignis* adorn the caudal and anal fins of *P. taeniurus*, but the intervening areas are white. Note also the difference in the dorsal fins: that of *P. taeniurus* is striped black and white like the tail, while in *P. insignis* is unmarked and reddish. The outstanding feature of *P. taeniurus*, however, is the brilliant red of the ventral fins, the only splash of bright color in the whole fish. The thick, rough lips proclaim both species as algae-nibblers, and vegetable matter is an important item in their menu. Lacking this, the fish will become listless, sluggish and prone to disease. A large, well-lighted tank is a necessity with this fish, and another is a tight-fitting cover.

* Now known as *Semaprochilodus taeniurus.*

F-492.00

PSEUDOCORYNOPOMA DORIAE (Perugia)/*Dragonfin Tetra*

Range: Southern Brazil and the La Plata region.
Habits: Will not annoy other fishes or chew plants.
Water Conditions: Soft, slightly acid water. Temperature 70 to 76°F.
Size: To 3 inches.
Food Requirements: Will take any foods, but live foods of course preferred.
Color Variations: Body silvery, fins gray. All fins have a black tip. Males have a
dorsal and anal fin which have fringed tips.

There are never more than a very few Dragonfin Tetras available at any time.
It is not the easiest fish in the world to keep and breed, and does not ship
very well. In its native waters it sometimes has to withstand some very cool
temperatures, at times as low as 60°. This of course is not a recommendation
to keep it as cool as that, but it is a warning that high temperatures should be
avoided. Another thing the fish is sensitive to is drastic changes in water. But,
kept in a tank to which it has become accustomed, it may become a hardy
and undemanding fish which can live for many years. There is still a bit of
mystery attached to the spawning of this fish. The male expels his sperm in a
little packet which eventually finds its way into the female's body. When she
expels her eggs the packet releases some sperm cells and the eggs are fertilized.
Thus it is believed that a female is capable of laying fertile eggs for the rest of
her life without even the presence of a male. The big question is, how does
the female get the sperm packet into her reproductive tract originally? Some
day the animal behaviorists will tell us, but they have not done so yet.

PSEUDOPIMELODUS TRANSMONTANUS (Regan)
Peruvian Mottled Catfish

Range: Peruvian Amazon, near Iquitos.

Habits: Peaceful, but should not be trusted with fish which are small enough for it to swallow.

Water Conditions: Soft, slightly acid water. Temperature 75 to 80°F.

Size: To 5 inches, possibly bigger.

Food Requirements: Will eat almost any kind of food, but should get some live food, especially worms, when available.

Color Variations: Body dark blue, almost purple, covered with tiny white spots. Two very irregular pink bars on the sides, and transparent area in the tail.

Most Catfishes are not exactly God's noblest creatures where color is concerned, but this one is something pretty special. That it has nice colors is fairly obvious, and we are told that they are peaceful as well. Just the same, it is best to avoid tempting fate too much by remembering that the big mouth is capable of swallowing quite a morsel and might not hesitate to gulp down a smaller fish. Most of the *Pseudopimelodus* species come from waters near the Amazon River basin but this one comes from a point far upstream, the streams near Iquitos, Peru, where the Neon Tetras and many other beautiful fishes come from. The Indians in this picturesque country have found it profitable to collect fishes and bring them to the shippers who export them from this thriving little city. The aquarium hobby has even taken a foothold here and the author (WV) was agreeably surprised when he saw a large, beautifully set-up aquarium in a hotel lobby. It was crowded with many Pencilfishes and there were also a great many Blue Tetras (*Microbrycon cochui*). This must be a great source of satisfaction to Mr. Fred Cochu on his frequent flights there.

F-494.00

PSEUDOTROPHEUS LIVINGSTONII (Boulenger)

Range: Lake Malawi, Africa.

Habits: Quarrelsome; many rock caves or holes should be provided if kept with other cichlids.

Water Conditions: Alkaline and very hard. Optimum temperatures are about 75 to 80° F.

Size: Two forms are known (perhaps distinct species), one reaching a size of about 3½ inches and the other closer to 5 or 6 inches.

Food Requirements: Not fussy. Will take almost any food.

Color Variations: Not one of the species known to have color morphs. The pattern and color depicted here is the only one currently known.

Pseudotropheus livingstonii is one of the more interesting of the Lake Malawi cichlids. Although it is currently classified in the genus *Pseudotropheus*, whose members are all mbunas, it does not live among the rocks like the rest of them. It instead lives in the empty shells of a snail, *Lanistes*. Most of the individuals I have seen were kept in aquaria supplied with rocks and they seemed to do very well. It might be interesting to place some empty shells in the same aquarium and see if they would take up residence in them.

Spawning is similar to that of the other species of *Pseudotropheus*. The female incubates the eggs in her mouth. She should be removed from the community tank when holding eggs and isolated until the fry are well able to care for themselves. There are generally few eggs, about 20 or so, but the parental care ensures that most of them will have an excellent chance for survival.

The sexes are generally similar in appearance and no indication of how to sex them (aside from examination of the genital papillae) has been recorded. There are bluish individuals and yellowish individuals, the bluish ones possibly males, but this distinction may not hold up.

Most *P. livingstonii* are collected by trawling in relatively shallow water, somewhere between 30 and 50 feet deep. The empty *Lanistes* shells collected in this way are shaken to see if the small fish will fall out.

Pseudotropheus livingstonii. The blue color probably indicates that this fish is a male. Photo courtesy African Fish Imports.

PSEUDOTROPHEUS MICROSTOMA Trewavas

Range: Lake Malawi, Africa.

Habits: Quarrelsome. A large number of rock caves and holes should be provided.

Water Conditions: Alkaline and very hard. Optimum temperatures between 75 and 80° F.

Size: Reaches a length of about 5 to 6 inches.

Food Requirements: Omnivorous and will take almost any prepared food offered.

Color Variations: Few if any variations from the basic color and pattern are known.

Pseudotropheus microstoma may be known under several names or combinations of names due to its close affinities to *Pseudotropheus tropheops*. It has been called a form or morph of *P. tropheops*, a subspecies of *tropheops* (*P. tropheops microstoma*) or simply a species by itself (*P. microstoma*). Current opinion is that it is a full species, and it is treated as such here.

The female *Pseudotropheus microstoma* is less colorful than the male. Photo by Dr. Robert J. Goldstein.

Although very similar in appearance to many of the other mbunas, the fewer dark stripes crossing the body and the blunt head generally serve to distinguish this species from the others.

Its habits are similar to the well-known *P. zebra*. It is a mouth-brooder, with the female incubating the eggs in her mouth. Few eggs are deposited per spawning, usually about 20 to 30, although some may have more.

This species is not known to have different color morphs as in *P. zebra* or *P. tropheops*, but since it is recognizable mostly by its color pattern other morphs might be simply regarded as *P. tropheops* varieties. The males and females are distinguishable by color, the females being more drably colored compared with the bluish males which exhibit very dark bars.

In its natural rocky habitat, the male *P. microstoma* in full color stands out quite noticeably from the background. Notice that there are only four black bars crossing the body. Photo by Dr. Herbert R. Axelrod.

One of the more common morphs of *P. tropheops* and the one which may be considered typical of the species. Photo by Dr. Herbert R. Axelrod.

F-494.180

Photo by Dr. David Terver.

PSEUDOTROPHEUS TROPHEOPS Regan

Range: Lake Malawi.

Habits: One of the more peaceful of the mbuna but still retains the quarrelsome habits of these cichlids.

Water Conditions: As with most species of *Pseudotropheus*, this one can stand a wide variety of water conditions but does best (and will probably only breed) in hard alkaline water.

Size: About 3 to 4 inches.

Food Requirements: Omnivorous. Does well on a variety of foods including flake food.

Color Variations: A complex species with many color morphs.

Pseudotropheus tropheops is second only to *P. zebra* in the number of color morphs that have been reported. As collectors move to new areas of the lake, new morphs will undoubtedly be found.

This is another of the mbuna or rock-dwelling cichlids and in its natural habitat it lives among the rocks in relatively shallow water. The aquarium should be amply supplied with rocks. Plants and gravel are not necessary.

F-494.181

One of the more popular morphs is the Golden Tropheops which retains a bright yellow color throughout life. Photo by Dr. Herbert R. Axelrod.

P. tropheops typically feeds on the *aufwuchs* present on the surface of the rocks in the lake. This is impossible to duplicate in an aquarium, and substitute foods must be offered. This species is not particular about the type of food as long as it arrives in good quantity. Frozen brine shrimp, flake food, or any combination of prepared foods will be taken with relish. It is surprising that it does so well with a high protein diet since its natural food is primarily vegetable matter. This has been explained by some as being due to the high level of competition in the lake which forces the fish to rely on the *aufwuchs* as food. If they were able to get it, they would prefer a more balanced or higher protein diet. It has been reported that many of the lake cichlids grow larger in an aquarium than in their natural habitat. This could be due to a better diet than they are able to obtain in the wild.

Spawning is similar to that in most other mbunas. The actual spawning takes place among the rocks, apparently safely away from the other cichlids in the tank, and is not commonly observed. Many aquarists know that spawning has occurred only by the appearance of the female. Once spawning has occurred and she has a batch of eggs in her mouth, the lowered gular area is quite obvious. She is generally removed to more isolated quarters where hatching occurs some weeks later. The female is usually a good parent and the fry may be left in with her for the early stages of development and while the female regains her strength. It is not advisable to place the female back in the community or spawning tank too soon. In her weakened condition she might not be able to cope with the advances of the males in the tank and might eventually be killed by them. The fry are relatively easy to raise.

When adding mbunas to your tank it is advisable to move the rocks about before their introduction. *P. tropheops* is territorial (like the other mbunas) and will chase any newcomer from any cover or food until it is killed. By moving the rocks the territories are broken up and new ones must be established. Introducing new fishes at this time gives them an equal try at the territories.

Some paler colored varieties still retain the dark bands in the dorsal, anal and pelvic fins. Photo by Karl Knaack.

Above and below: *Pseudotropheus tropheops* males, the upper one in full breeding or dominant color, the lower one in a subdued or fright pattern where the bars become more visible. Photos by Warren E. Burgess.

The commonly occurring blackish 'tropheops' which is not usually imported because of its drab coloration. Photo by Dr. Herbert R. Axelrod.

A typical female *P. tropheops* color pattern. Females of this species are generally less colorful than the males. Photo by Warren E. Burgess

A distended gular region in a female generally means that the female is brooding eggs. Sometimes it is only a false alarm, however. Photo by Dr. Herbert R. Axelrod.

One of the yellow morphs of *P. tropheops* which has become quite pale over the sandy bottom. Photo by Dr. Herbert R. Axelrod.

This slender bodied *P. tropheops* has a parasite on the caudal fin (dark spot).
Many of the Lake Malawi cichlids become parasitized in this manner. Photo by
Dr. Herbert R. Axelrod.

A female *P. tropheops* possibly of the same variety as the male above. Photo by
Warren E. Burgess.

Species of the genus *Pseudotropheus* are algal scrapers. This head shot of a white morph *P. tropheops* shows the numerous orange or reddish colored bicuspid teeth which it uses for this job. Photo by Dr. Herbert R. Axelrod.

New morphs are constantly being discovered and imported. This orange-blotch female *P. tropheops* is one of the most recent introductions to the hobby. Photo by Dr. Herbert R. Axelrod.

An unusual color morph of *P. tropheops*. It may be one of the various forms or subspecies of 'tropheops' but it is difficult to determine without a number of specimens. Photo by Dr. Robert J. Goldstein.

F-494.189

The head of a male *Pseudotropheus zebra*. This species also has an outer row of many bicuspid teeth for algae scraping. Photo by Dr. Herbert R. Axelrod.

PSEUDOTROPHEUS ZEBRA varieties

With additional collecting around Lake Malawi new varieties of cichlids are constantly being found. *Pseudotropheus zebra* is one species in which the color forms or morphs are becoming better known. Unlike the angelfish (*Pterophyllum*) varieties, those of *P. zebra* occur naturally in Lake Malawi. They vary from the basic blue with black stripes (BB) to shades of red, white, mottled, blue, etc. With the ease of breeding this species it will be interesting to see if some of the crosses in colors will produce entirely new color varieties from those found naturally in the lake.

One of the rarest of the morphs of *P. zebra* is a mottled form generally called the marmalade cat. This morph is similar to the orange-blotched (OB) female which is so common but has a bluish tinge to the whitish portions of the pattern. Naturally, being so rare it commands a rather high price at this time and is constantly sought after by aquarists. So far no reports of marmalade cats being found among the progeny of domestically raised fish have been forthcoming.

P. zebra has many color morphs. This one has been called the Red Zebra. Photo by Dr. Herbert R. Axelrod.

One of the popular blue morphs of *P. zebra* generally called the Cobalt Blue Zebra. Photo by Dr. Herbert R. Axelrod.

This green colored Zebra may be included in the morph called the Cobalt Blue.
The Cobalts vary in color from all shades of blue to this greenish-blue color.
Photo by Gerhard Marcuse.

Above and below: In it's natural habitat *P. zebra* is always among rocks. The dominant male (below) exhibits greater contrast between the black body bars and the background color than does the non-dominant male. Photos by Dr. Herbert R. Axelrod.

Above and below: Female *P. zebra* often show a blotched pattern as seen below. Rarely, males are found with a similar pattern but with a bluish overcast (above) and are called Marmalade Cats. They command a high price. Photos courtesy African Fish Imports.

F-494.215

The dark blotches may be relatively heavy over the fish as in this one or only scattered. Photo by Dr. Robert J. Goldstein.

The background color of this female is similar to that of the above fish but the black blotches are almost non-existent. Photo by Dr. Herbert R. Axelrod.

An albino strain of *P. zebra* has been developed. The similarly colored White Zebras do not have the pink eyes that mark the albino. Photo by Ken Miner.

A typical scene among the rocks of Lake Malawi. Several species of mbuna are present including *Melanochromis auratus* and a dominant male *P. zebra*. Photo by Dr. Herbert R. Axelrod.

The striped pattern is common in the mbuna Cichlids. In any underwater scene several fishes will exhibit this pattern. Photo by Dr. Herbert R. Axelrod.

The *aufwuchs* is scraped from the rocks by the specially adapted teeth. Here the angle of attack is shown by some fishes. Photo by Dr. Herbert R. Axelrod.

It is rare to find an mbuna this far from the rock habitat. This *P. zebra* must be heading directly for the rocky cover. Photo by Dr. Herbert R. Axelrod.

The white morph of *P. zebra* is very attractive and is a favorite among aquarists. This one is a male. Photo by Dr. Herbert R. Axelrod.

The white and pale yellow morphs of *P. zebra*. The front fish is a male, the one behind is a female. Photo by Dr. Herbert R. Axelrod.

A relatively new morph, the Peppered Zebra, probably is derived from some of the blotched forms. Photo courtesy African Fish Imports.

A similarly patterned *P. zebra* but with larger blotches and a yellow background color. Photo by Dr. Herbert R. Axelrod.

The Cobalt Blue Zebra is quite common and many hundreds are shipped out
from Lake Malawi. Photo by Dr. Herbert R. Axelrod.

The individual here is of a type of morph which is found at Maleri Island in Lake
Malawi. Photo by Dr. Herbert R. Axelrod.

The tangerine morph shown here is sometimes confused with the red morph. When they are side by side, however, the difference in color is quite noticeable. Photo by Gerhard Marcuse.

A close view of a young *P. zebra*. At this age they are well able to care for themselves. Photo by Hans J. Richter.

The bright orange egg spots in the anal fin stand out against the dark background of the rocks. Photo by Dr. Herbert R. Axelrod.

A group of young *P. zebra*. This species is quite easy to spawn and raise. Photo by Hans J. Richter.

One of the darker varieties of *P. zebra*. With so many colorful morphs in this species the darker, unspectacular ones are passed by. Photo by Dr. Herbert R. Axelrod.

This female was found to be ripe with eggs. Photo by Dr. Herbert R. Axelrod.

PSEUDOXIPHOPHORUS BIMACULATUS (Heckel)/*False Swordtail*

Range: Mexico, Guatemala, Honduras and possibly Nicaragua.
Habits: Apt to be quarrelsome in a community aquarium. Should have a tank of their own.
Water Conditions: Not critical; should be kept warm, 76 to 82°F.
Size: Males to 1½ inches, females to 3½ inches.
Food Requirements: Greedy and will eat anything edible, but should get live foods at times.
Color Variations: Body greenish gray, middle scales with a dark edge. Large black spot at caudal peduncle.

The False Swordtail bears only a remote resemblance to the real article, *Xiphophorus helleri*. There is not even a small sword, and the gonopodium of the Swordtail is much smaller in proportion to its body size than that of *Pseudoxiphophorus bimaculatus*. This is a very hardy and productive fish, and females have been known to deliver as many as 150 young in a litter. This fish has a wide habitat range and there have been several subspecies described: there is a so-called "northern form" *P. b. jonesi* from the Orizaba Mountains of Vera Cruz. The coastal regions of the Gulf of Mexico yields three more, *P. b. bimaculatus* from the lowlands of Vera Cruz, *P. b. taeniatus* from Tabasco and *P. b. peninsulae* from Campeche and Yucatan. The subspecies *P. b. taeniatus* is known as the "southern form" and comes from the streams flowing into the Atlantic in Oaxaca and Guatemala, possibly also Nicaragua. In the aquarium they are not the most peaceful of fishes; the larger females especially are inclined to be quarrelsome. The young are interesting in form: the anal fin, especially in the males, is exceptionally deep and looks like a keel.

Photo by H. Abel.

PTEROLEBIAS PERUENSIS (Myers)/*Peruvian Longfin*

Range: Upper Amazon region.
Habits: Usually peaceful, but should be kept by themselves.
Water Conditions: Soft, considerably acid water. For spawning, a layer about 1 inch deep of peat moss should be provided on the bottom.
Size: About 3 inches for males, females about 2 inches.
Food Requirements: Live foods of all kinds.
Color Variations: Body light brown with a series of vertical bars. Dorsal and anal fins have rows of bluish spots. Tail spotted, tips black.

At the little city of Leticia, Colombia, the author was privileged to travel a short distance up the Amazon River to a point where Peru could be seen across the immense river. Here we went up a small tributary stream to the fish collector's trading post. Most of the smaller, brightly-colored fishes in the area were to be found in the storage troughs, and the author recalls being asked for a scientific identification of two species. One was *Colomesus psittacus*, and the other was called "Africano" by the natives. This turned out to be our friend *Pterolebias peruensis*. It would have been highly interesting to see where the Indians were catching these fish, but time did not permit. This is one of the "annual" fishes, which lays its eggs in the mud on the bottom of small bodies of water that dry out in the dry season. The fry hatch when the rains begin and the dried-out ponds fill up once more. In the aquarium they spawn in a layer of peat-moss on the bottom.

*PTEROPHYLLUM ALTUM (Pellegrin)/*Long-Finned Angelfish*

Range: Orinoco River.

Habits: Peaceful and slow-moving; should not be kept with active fishes.

Water Conditions: Soft, slightly acid water; because of their height, tank should be large or at least high. Temperature 75 to 80°.

Size: Length of body about 4 inches; height about 5½ inches.

Food Requirements: Live foods preferably; will take frozen foods in time, also bits of beef heart.

Color Variations: Silvery body with dark brown vertical bars which vary in number. Upper part of body covered with small brown dots.

This is no doubt the stateliest of the three Angelfishes. They are a bit difficult to ship because of the great height of the dorsal and anal fins. For this reason we seldom get to see specimens. Collectors would be unable to distinguish between half-grown *P. scalare* or *P. eimekei* and *P. altum*, and the only ones that come in are a few large specimens. The fish shown in this picture was one of three collected by Kyle Swegles, of the Rainbow Aquarium in Chicago, who was kind enough to let us have this one for photographing. Unfortunately *P. altum* has not yet been spawned in captivity. This is a good fish to keep in a very large or at least a very high aquarium. It is not as active as the other two species, and does not display the lively, snoopy curiosity that the others do. They move deliberately and haughtily from place to place with an air of regal aloofness and dignity. When the inevitable comes to pass and this fish decides to breed, it will be interesting to see what the breeders will be able to achieve by selective breeding. No doubt their aim will be to get those very long fins still longer. Whether this will be a desirable fish or just a freak remains to be seen.

* In 1975, the author (HRA) discovered the missing link between *Ptero-phyllum altum* and *Pterophyllum scalare* (see TFH magazine, February, 1976, p. 93, *The Rio Negro Angelfishes* by Warren Burgess). This resulted in the merging of *altum* with *scalare*. Thus, there are only two valid species in *Pterophyllum*, namely, *dumerilii* and *scalare*.

PTEROPHYLLUM SCALARE (Lichtenstein)/Angelfish, Scalare,
P. eimekei

Range: The Amazon basin, the Rupununi and Essequibo Rivers of Guyana, with specimens also found in French and Dutch Guiana.
Water Conditions: Clean, neutral water. Temperature 74°.
Size: 5 inches in length; 6 inches in depth.
Food Requirements: Freeze-dried or live foods.
Color Variations: This species is found in "Ghost" form without bars, in solid black, in "lace" form with some black markings, and with long fins. These are all mutant forms which have been fixed by inbreeding.

Lichtenstein first described this fish in 1823 as *Zeus scalaris* from Brazil. The name was subsequently changed to *Platax scalaris* in 1831 by Cuvier and Valenciennes and finally to *Pterophyllum scalaris* by Heckel in 1840. Günther changed the *scalaris* to *scalare* in 1862, and so it has been ever since. *P. scalare* is the Angelfish every aquarist is familiar with. Since 1928 when Ahl described *P. eimekei* from the mouth of the Rio Negro in Brazil, there has been considerable confusion as to which species was which. Dr. L. P. Schultz has carefully studied collected specimens of both species and found that the counts for the syntype of *P. eimekei* coincide with the median counts of *scalare* and thus concludes that *eimekei* is a synonym of *scalare*. The important lesson to be learned here is that tank-raised fishes do not have the same meristic characteristics as wild specimens and cannot normally be valuable in the description of a species.

The *scalare* is easy to breed and millions of tank-raised specimens are sold every year all over the world. Many color and finnage varieties have been developed.

F-499.00

A magnificent Veil Angelfish.

The beautiful All-Black Angelfish, developed by the Ludwigs of Detroit, Michigan.

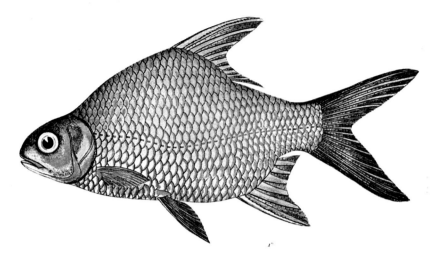

PUNTIOPLITES PROCTOZYSRON (Bleeker)/ *Yellow-Cheeked Barb*

Range: Thailand, Cochin China and Cambodia.
Habits: Peaceful if kept with large fishes.
Water Conditions: Not critical, but soft, slightly acid water is best.
Size: To 8 inches, seldom above 6 inches.
Food Requirements: Larger frozen foods or live foods.
Color Variations: Silvery sides with a pearly tinge; yellow spot on the gill-plates.

The Yellow-Cheeked Barb is in a genus all by itself, the genus *Puntioplites*. It is unlikely that we will ever see this one in numbers, as its only claim to any color is a touch of yellow on each gill-plate. Of course, its scales are nice and pearly, but there are other Barbs which have pearly scales and a lot more color than this one. This is a well-known food fish in Thailand, and if you want to add a few words of Siamese to your vocabulary, the Thai call it *pla kamang*. The dorsal fin does not take on the length and shape shown in the picture until the fish has attained maturity; *Barbodes schwanenfeldi* has a dorsal fin which greatly resembles this one. What takes this fish into a genus of its own is the saw-toothed edge on the first ray of the anal fin, and for this reason H. M. Smith created the genus *Puntioplites* in 1929. The usual length of adult specimens from Thailand is 5 to 6 inches, but specimens up to 8 inches are on record. It is highly doubtful if this fish will become popular but public tastes are unpredictable and the most unlikely-looking fish sometimes becomes a red-hot favorite overnight.

Photo by H.J. Richter.

PUNTIUS CONCHONIUS (Hamilton-Buchanan)/*Rosy Barb*

Range: India.
Habits: Very active; continually swims from one end of the tank to the other. Generally well behaved.
Water Conditions: Water can vary a little way from neutral in either direction. Likes a well planted tank, but must have swimming room. Temperature 72 to 76°.
Size: Up to almost half a foot, but usually seen much smaller, about half this size.
Food Requirements: Takes all foods.
Color Variations: In spawning condition, a beautiful purplish red suffuses body of males. Out of spawning condition, or under adverse conditions, a plain silvery fish. Black spot at peduncle.

The Rosy Barb's popularity has endured the test of time, and it seems destined to be with us always. When in breeding color, the males takes on a gleaming purplish red flush, and the black in his fins becomes accentuated. The female, which when not in breeding condition looks like a plain silvery fish, also improves in coloration when in spawning condition, but she never rivals the male in brilliance. They spawn by scattering eggs into bunches of plants, like so many of its relatives. Properly conditioned, the species is eager to spawn and requires no special preparations, except that for best results they require big tanks for both spawning and rearing the fry. A very prolific fish, the Rosy Barb is usually in good supply at low prices. Rosy Barbs are very active swimmers and very heavy eaters, often rooting around in the gravel much like Goldfish. They should be kept in long, low tanks, preferably by themselves; kept in a school, the males will swim around each other with fins fully spread and colors at their gleaming best in an effort to outshine their brothers. Although the Rosy Barb is considered as a peaceful fish, it occasionally nips slower species.

F-503.00

PUNTIUS FILAMENTOSUS (Cuvier and Valenciennes)/
Black-Spot Barb

Range: Ceylon, India, Burma.
Habits: Peaceful with fishes its own size; a good jumper.
Water Conditions: Slightly acid to neutral, not too hard. Temperature 74 to 78°.
Size: Up to five inches.
Food Requirements: Takes all foods.
Color Variations: Body color golden above to silver on lower sides and belly area. Large black spot at beginning of caudal peduncle. Fins red.

This fish deserves the title "Longfin Barb" almost as much *Capoeta arulius,* another Barb in which the adult males show extended dorsal rays. Colors in these two fishes are also somewhat similar, but *arulius* lacks the prominent dark blotch which shows so strongly on *P. filamentosus.* For breeding, a large tank should be used. The longer the tank, the better the results. Spawning pairs of this species will chase back and forth over the length of the tank a few times before settling down to the actual spawning act; the eggs are laid in bunches of plants, which should cover at least one-fourth of the bottom area of the tank. Once driving by the males has been begun, the fish should not be interrupted, as this often results in a complete cessation of breeding activity for a period of weeks. Eggs hatch in about two days, and the newly emerged fry are soon able to take newly hatched brine shrimp, which should be fed in large quantities because the young, like their parents, have hearty appetites. *P. filamentosus* has often been confused with *P. mahecola,* which it resembles in its young stages. Like many of the other Barbs, *P. filamentosus* appreciates some vegetable matter in its diet.

F-504.00

Above: A young male *Puntius filamentosus*. Below: A pair of *P. filamentosus* spawning. Note the male wrapping his body about the top of the female using her dorsal fin as a pivot. Photos by Hans Joachim Richter.

PUNTIUS GELIUS (Hamilton-Buchanan) *Dwarf Barb*

Range: Central India, Bengal and Assam.

Habits: One of the most peaceful of all the Barb species. In their native land they occupy quiet waters, usually in small schools near the shore.

Water Conditions: Not critical, but avoid too high temperatures. 72 to 75° is ample, also for breeding.

Size: Females $1\frac{1}{2}$ to $1\frac{3}{4}$ inches, males $1\frac{1}{4}$ to $1\frac{1}{2}$ inches.

Food Requirements: Good eaters, but food should be small because of the small mouths.

Color Variations: Back olive-green, belly silvery. Golden stripe runs the length of the body. A number of dark patches on the body.

Its small size and lack of brilliant colors keep this little fellow from being one of the most popular of the Barb species, but it has some qualities which should make it deserving of a greater popularity. One is a lack of sensitivity to lower temperatures, and another is that it does not present as many problems when being bred than most of the other Barbs. The spawning act usually takes place in the morning, with the female beginning by chasing and annoying the male until he turns the tables on her and drives her vigorously all over the tank. Unlike most of the other Barbs, these do not usually strew their eggs among the bushy plants, and prefer to stick them on the underside of broad-leaved plants, which should be provided instead of the usual *Nitella* or *Myriophyllum*. The parents do not indulge in the usual "egg-hunt" after breeding is completed, but leaving them in the breeding tank serves no further purpose. Fry hatch in about 24 hours, and may be seen hanging from the plants or glass sides for a time, after which they seem to disappear from sight. At this time they require a finely-ground food which should be first stirred into a small jar of water to make it sink.

F-506.00

PUNTIUS LINEATUS (Duncker)/*Striped Barb*

Range: Singapore and Malayan Peninsula.
Habits: Peaceful and active, harmless to plants.
Water Conditions: Soft, slightly acid water. Temperature 75 to 80°F.
Size: Up to 4 inches, usually smaller.
Food Requirements: All sorts of food accepted, but occasional meals of live foods are necessary for the best condition.
Color Variations: Body olive-green with four horizontal lines on the sides. Dorsal and anal fin show a pink flush at times.

It is a pity that this very attractive Barb is seldom available, and then only in limited numbers. It is a perfect aquarium fish with a pretty color pattern and an alert, perky carriage. It is usually out in front where it can be seen and admired, and its not-too-large size makes it practical to keep a number of them in an average-sized aquarium. It does not take bites out of your best plants as some Barbs do. The fact that it is one of the most difficult Barbs to breed successfully makes it a challenge to the experienced aquarist. The author (WV) knows a very successful hobbyist who has bred most of the difficult fishes but is still trying to get a good spawning out of his Striped Barbs. The females do not seem to fill up with eggs as they should, and when one of the rare spawnings takes place only a few hatch. Once we get a few generations which have spent their entire lives in the aquarium the story will be different. A school of half-grown Striped Barbs and another of Tiger Barbs in a large, well-planted aquarium should make a breathtaking exhibit at a fish show, sure to put the exhibitor in the running for a trophy.

Photo by Hans J. Richter.

PUNTIUS NIGROFASCIATUS (Günther)/*Black Ruby Barb*

Range: Ceylon.
Habits: Active swimmer, inclined to nip fins.
Water Conditions: Soft, slightly acid water. Temperature 75 to 82°.
Size: 2½ inches.
Food Requirements: Accepts all foods; small living foods preferred.
Color Variations: Male (in color) purplish red, with broad black bars and purple-black fins. Female lacks male's red color and black fins.

When in color, the male of the Black Ruby Barb is a beautiful fish in which the bright red of the front part of the body is set off against the deep black of the rear portion and the fins. Out of color, it is of no distinction, being a plain grayish-yellow banded Barb. Sexes are not difficult to distinguish, because the black bars on the male and the black in his fins is always more crisp and distinct than in the female, even when he is not showing his best colors. The Black Ruby Barb spawns in typical *Puntius* fashion, but the fish requires a larger tank than its size would indicate. The fry hatch more quickly if the temperature of the water is kept a degree or two below that used for spawning.

F-508.00

PUNTIUS SACHSI (Ahl)/*Golden Barb*

Range: Malay Peninsula.
Habits: Peaceful and active.
Water Conditions: Soft, slightly acid water. Temperature 70-82°.
Size: 2½ inches.
Food Requirements: Accepts both live and dry foods.
Color Variations: Golden, fins shading to red; indistinct horizontal bar on male.

The Golden Barb is a pretty and inoffensive fish which has achieved a good deal of popularity because it is easy to keep, cheap, peaceful, and easy to breed. Besides these good points, the fish also offers a very pleasing combination of colors in which the golden yellow of the body is set off nicely by the reddish fins and black markings. It is hard to see why this fish has been confused with *Puntius semifasciolatus*, the Half-Striped Barb, even though color patterns are not too important in identifying fishes. The Golden Barb is an easy breeders, and a prolific one, although not as prolific as its larger relatives. For spawning, fine-leaved bunch plants or their artificial substitutes, such as nylon mops, are required. The parent fish chase wildly back and forth over the length of the tank until the female is ready to enter the spawning area. Once there, the male and female quiver side by side, and the female releases the eggs, which are immediately fertilized by the male. During the first entrances into the plants, there may be no eggs expelled, but there are only a few such dry runs before the female is able to produce eggs. Eggs hatch in 24 hours at a temperature of 80°.

A pair of albino Barbs. Except for the lack of body and eye pigments, all other characters correspond with normally pigmented golden Barbs. Photo by Dr.
Dr. Herbert R. Axelrod

Unless kept under the proper aquarium conditions, the beautiful coloration of Barbs, especially the reddish tinge on the fins shown here, can easily fade.

PUNTIUS SOMPHONGSI (Benl & Klausewitz)/*Somphongs' Barb*

Range: Thailand.
Habits: Peaceful and active, but sometimes nips plant leaves.
Water Conditions: Soft, slightly acid water. Temperature 76 to 80°F.
Size: 4 inches.
Food Requirements: Has a good appetite and is not a fussy eater. Will accept dried as well as live or frozen foods.
Color Variations: Body silvery with an indistinct green stripe. Dorsal and caudal fins have an orange area with black tips.

If there is ever to be a good supply of this handsome Barb available to hobbyists, it looks as if they will have to be bred somewhere, unless a better source of supply is found in Thailand. Somphongs Lek-Aree, who is probably the best-known and most active collector in Thailand, declares that it is the rarest of all rare Thailand fishes, and that in all of his collecting expeditions he has found only six. Two died on the return trip and another died in his aquarium. The other three were sent as a Christmas present to Dr. Gerhard Benl in Munich, Germany. He and Dr. Wolfgang Klausewitz promptly named the new Barb in the collector's honor. Perhaps a pleasant surprise awaits the hobby and the fish actually *will* be spawned easily. Sometimes these so-called "rarities" are scarce in their home waters not because they are not prolific but because they have a great many natural enemies. Do not take the size given as the absolute maximum (4 inches). The ones mentioned may or may not still have a little growing to do. When putting this fish in a planted aquarium, make sure that there are no soft-leaved, delicate plants growing there. They have been found to nibble them.

PUNTIUS STIGMA (Cuvier & Valenciennes)/*Two-Spot Barb*

Range: Common throughout most of India.
Habits: Peaceful and active if kept with large fishes.
Water Conditions: Not critical, but soft, slightly acid water is best.
Size: To 8 inches.
Food Requirements: Heavy eater which will consume any kind of food.
Color Variations: Silvery sides with a black spot at the caudal base and another at
the dorsal base. Faint red line shows at spawning time.

Chances are that you will never see the Two-Spot Barb, because it is one of those fishes which is common enough in its home country of India but remains unpopular for two reasons: first of all it gets too big; secondly, its size might be overlooked if it had a set of attractive colors but the only bit of color is a faint streak of red on the side from the head to a black spot at the caudal base. There is another spot at the base of the dorsal fin which is not always evident. As a matter of fact, only the black spot at the caudal base remains at all times and the other markings may put in an appearance only when the fish is spawning. The Two-Spot Barb has been known to science since Cuvier & Valenciennes named it in 1843, and hobbyists first saw it in 1927. The fish did not cause any great commotion then and there have not been many imported since. Spawning is similar to the other Barbs but would probably require a large aquarium. Females are distinguished solely by their heavier bodies when the eggs ripen, plus the fact that the red stripe never shows on them. It might be well to watch these fish closely when putting them in a planted aquarium to see if they nibble on the plants.

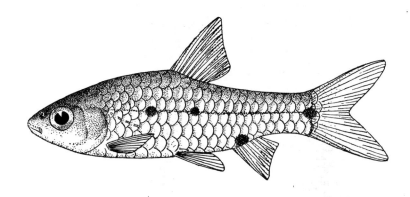

PUNTIUS STIGMATOPYGUS/*Mid-Spot Barb*

Range: Africa, in White Nile.
Habits: Peaceful and active.
Water Conditions: Neutral, medium-soft water; tank should be well planted, as
the fish is shy. Temperature 73 to 83°F.
Size: About 1½ inches.
Food Requirements: Will accept frozen and dry foods, but more readily accepts
small living crustaceans.
Color Variations: Over-all body color silvery, shading to gold, with four spots on
body, three arranged in a row along middle of body.

This tiny Barb from Africa was greeted with much enthusiasm when it
made its first appearance in the United States, because it was small, seldom
exceeding 1½ inches in length, even in mature specimens. When first imported, some hobbyists considered it as a juvenile form of a larger species,
as they preferred to believe that the fish was bound to grow a lot bigger than
it was. But they waited in vain, for this Barb stayed small, although specimens
kept in large tanks outgrew their brothers and sisters slightly. No great
effort was made to breed the few imported fish that had come in, and the
species died off. To this date, it has not been replaced, mostly because the
interest that was at one time shown in the African Barbs has largely died out,
and in the few scattered appearances that they make these days they are not
highly regarded. Perhaps at some future date an effort will again be made to
popularize these fishes, as was done in the middle and late 1950's.

Photo by G. J. M. Timmerman.

PUNTIUS STOLICZKAI (Day) *Stoliczka's Barb*

Range: Eastern Burma, near Rangoon.
Habits: Active and peaceful in the community aquarium. Should not be given small quarters for this reason.
Water Conditions: Like other Barbs, not critical. Temperatures 75 to 78°.
Size: A little over 2 inches.
Food Requirements: Frozen or live foods preferred, but dried foods accepted.
Color Variations: Back green, sides silvery, small dark streak behind the gill-plate and a large dark, gold-bordered spot near the tail base.

Stoliczka's Barb is often mistaken for the Two-Spot Barb, *Puntius ticto*. The markings on the body and fins are very similar, but Stoliczka's Barb is slightly higher in the body. It is also distinguishable by the bright golden zone around the dark spot near the caudal base. This and the bright rosy hue of the fins make it a very attractive fish. Their colors are best observed if a number of males are kept together. Some very vigorous but harmless battles take place, where there are seldom any torn fins. Each male tries to make the other retreat, and a great deal of butting and tail-slapping goes on. Although they are fond of searching among the bottom sediment for stray bits of food, they never stir it up or uproot any plants. For spawning, a tank of at least 15 gallons should be richly planted, or a great many eggs will be eaten. The eggs do not have any great adhesive power, and a great many fall to the bottom instead of adhering to the plants. Fry hatch in 30 to 36 hours and begin swimming two days later. Finely powdered dry food is fed after being stirred into a small amount of water to keep it from floating. This is best followed in 10 days with brine shrimp.

PUNTIUS TICTO (Hamilton-Buchanan)/*Tic-Tac-Toe Barb*

Range: Ceylon.
Habits: Peaceful; inclined to be timid when small, aggressive as it gets older and larger.
Water Conditions: Slightly soft and acid water recommended; not delicate. Temperature 75-80°.
Size: Up to 4 inches.
Food Requirements: Prefers live foods, but accepts dry and frozen foods.
Color Variations: Silvery, with two black spots on sides; dorsal fin of male trimmed with red, while female's has slight red tint.

As already mentioned under *Puntius stoliczkai*, *Puntius ticto* is considered by some authorities to be identical with Stoliczka's Barb, or at most a sub-species. Here they shall be considered as two separate species, because hobbyists have long treated them separately and distinguish one from the other by general body outline and color differences. *P. ticto* is a more stream-lined fish than *P. stoliczkai*, the male *P. ticto* being especially less deep in body contour. The Tic-Tac-Toe Barb is not continuously available, because importations of this fish are sporadic and because it is not being bred in quantity on a permanent basis by any of the large commercial breeders in this country, in contrast to such established Barb favorites as the Tiger Barb and Rosy Barb. The species scatters its adhesive eggs into bundles of plants placed about the spawning tank; like the other Barbs, it will eat its own eggs, but in this regard it is not so great an offender as some of the others. Also, the eggs seem to be more resistant to fungus attacks, even when not treated with standard fungus preventives, such as methylene blue. *Puntius ticto* grows quickly at first, later slowing down a bit; it reaches full size only in large tanks.

Photo by Dr. Herbert R. Axelrod.

PUNTIUS VITTATUS (Day)/*Banded Barb*

Range: Found mostly in rice-paddies throughout India.
Habits: Peaceful and active; prefers to move in schools.
Water Conditions: Not at all critical. Will adapt to almost any kind of water. Fairly soft water with a temperature of about 76° is best.
Size: 2 to 2½ inches.
Food Requirements: Will eat dried as well as live foods; easily kept.
Color Variations: Back yellowish to olive green. Sides brownish, belly silvery.

Why this one is called Banded Barb is a bit of a mystery. The only band this Barb has runs through the dorsal fin. Although this fish is very abundant in its native waters, its lack of bright colors keeps it among the seldom-seen species. It is, however, one of the most easily-kept fishes of the genus. It will accept just about anything in the way of food, and if there is a drop in temperature, these will be among the last to suffer from it. It is easy to distinguish a ripe pair, even if the colors of both sexes are almost alike. The female's body is much deeper, and she is usually somewhat bigger than her mate. *Puntius vittatus* seem to be happier when they are swimming in a school, and in their native waters they are seldom found singly, but usually in large schools. This fish has been compared to *P. conchonius* in ease of keeping. They seldom get sick, and make little demands of their owner. They spawn readily, scattering their eggs among plant thickets. Fry hatch in about 36 hours and become free-swimming a day or two later. This species has been known to aquarists since 1904, when they were first brought into Germany.

PUNTIUS WÖHLERTI (Trewavas)/*Sickle Barb*

Range: Mozambique, East Africa.
Habits: Peaceful and timid, inclined to hide.
Water Conditions: Soft, slightly acid water; temperature 72-82°.
Size: 1¼ inches.
Food Requirements: Prefers small live foods, but will accept dry and frozen foods.
Color Variations: Body light brown, shading to yellow in belly area. Red-violet stripe from behind gills to tail. Lower part of base of tail black.

Here's a little Barb that you won't see very often, for it is seldom imported. This is unfortunate, because it has some good points that would soon make it popular if it were ever brought into the country and sold in quantity. Apart from its diminutive size, which is enough of an advantage when the fish is compared to some of its close relatives, *Puntius wohlerti* also has another trait working in its favor: with mature specimens, there is no danger of confusing male and female, because there is a very definite physical characteristic which enables the hobbyist to tell the sexes apart. This is unusual in a Barb, because with most Barbs the aquarist must rely on such changeable evidences as comparative color brilliance, fullness of the body, etc. Although in most cases these are very valuable guides, they are not completely reliable unless the fish are in good enough condition to bring out the differences. Not so with the Sickle Barb! The anal fin of the male of this species (the upper fish in the illustration) is shaped much differently from that of the female, as the illustration brings out. The Sickle Barb breeds in normal Barb fashion, but they do not spawn readily.

PYGOCENTRUS CALMONI (Steindachner)/*Dusky Piranha*

Range: Guianas to the lower Amazon River.
Habits: Cannot be kept with other fishes, even its own kind. Fierce and predatory.
Water Conditions: Soft and slightly acid. Temperature 76 to 80°.
Size: To about 12 inches.
Food Requirements: Smaller living fishes preferred, or chunks of raw table fish or raw shrimp.
Color Variations: Body dusky gray with a golden area on the gill-plates. Anal fin reddish, dorsal almost black. Black area in fore part of tail.

The group of fishes known as Piranhas or Pirayas, the fishes about which so many blood-curdling tales are spun, includes several genera: *Serrasalmus*, *Rooseveltiella* and *Pygocentrus* are the nasty, razor-toothed ones that can inflict a severe wound if carelessly handled. According to the wild tales, the Piranhas travel in huge schools and are always ready to pounce upon anything that resembles food. The natives in most places where these fishes occur have no trepidations whatever when it comes to entering the water, but they would never think of cleaning a chicken at the water's edge and dipping in their bloody hands to wash them. These fish seem to have a powerful instinct to turn upon and destroy anything that has been injured, even one of their own number. Saying that Piranhas are harmless is like quoting the old fisherman's proverb: "Ninety-nine out of a hundred Sharks are perfectly harmless and will never bother anyone, but look out for that hundredth one!" *Pygocentrus calmoni* is kept like the other Piranha species, by itself, one to a tank. Never place the tank where children can reach it and put their hands in the water.

Photo by Dr. Herbert R. Axelrod.

Above and below: *Pyrrhulina brevis*, a South American Characin species in which the female is much larger than the male. This species lays its eggs on broad-leaved plants, where they are guarded by the male. The fry are very small and require very tiny food at first. Adults are good jumpers.

Photo by Dr. Herbert R. Axelrod.

F-519.00

PYRRHULINA RACHOVIANA (Myers) *Rachow's Pyrrhulina*

Range: Argentina, in the vicinity of Rosario.
Habits: A very active swimmer, which in spite of its small size should not be kept in too small a tank.
Water Conditions: Soft and slightly acid water, temperature about 75°.
Size: Up to 2 inches.
Food Requirements: Will eat dried foods, but should also get a variety of live or frozen foods.
Color Variations: Sides and back brown, becoming almost white in the belly region. Black spot in the dorsal fin of both sexes.

In the Characin family, it is unusual to find some members which exercise a certain amount of parental care. This is one of them. Males may be easily distinguished by their more slender bodies and brighter colors, also by a stripe which begins at the tip of the snout and continues about halfway down the body. This narrow stripe is only faintly indicated in the females. A tank in which these fish are kept should be provided with some broad-leaved plants, such as the *Cryptocoryne* species. Prior to spawning, a male will pick a leaf free of algae. If none of the leaves are to his liking, he may change his mind and dig a small depression in the gravel on the bottom. After a lot of vigorous driving, the female is lured to the clean leaf or other spawning site, and a surprising number of eggs, sometimes as high as 200, are deposited and fertilized. Then, instead of turning around and making a meal of them, the male drives away the female and guards the eggs as a Cichlid would, fanning them constantly with his fins. After about 20 hours, the eggs become loosened and fall from the leaf to the bottom. About 10 hours later the fry hatch.

F-520.00

PYRRHULINA VITTATA (Regan)/*Banded Pyrrhulina*

Range: Amazon in the Santarem region, Rio Tapajoz.
Habits: Very peaceful in the community tank.
Water Conditions: Soft, slightly acid water. Temperature 75 to 80°.
Size: To 2¾ inches.
Food Requirements: Small live foods preferred, but will also take frozen and
   prepared foods.
Color Variations: Body light tan with three large black spots. Line from mouth to
   behind operculum. Dorsal and anal fins of male edged blue.

The Banded Pyrrhulina is an attractive and peaceful little fellow which can
always be counted upon to "dress up" a community tank and never upset
the equilibrium there. This species is easily distinguished from the others
by the short, rather chunky body and the distinct narrow black line which
extends from the lower jaw through the eye to a point slightly behind the gill-
plates. The three markings on the sides could be described as large spots
rather than bands, but there is a golden band at the base of the tail. Males are
distinguished by a longer dorsal fin and a blue glint in this and the caudal fin.
The upper fish in the illustration shows this very plainly. This species is said
to be a ready spawner, but sometimes a bit of patience and a number of fish
is required for results. A pair will choose a broad submerged leaf and clean it
thoroughly, then lay eggs on the clean surface. The male guards and fans
them, and the fry hatch in 24 to 28 hours. Once they are swimming there is
no point in keeping the parents with them any longer. The youngsters should
get infusoria for at least a week, after which fine dried foods and then newly
hatched brine shrimp are fed.

Pyrrhulina spilota Weitzman, is one of the approximately 25 known species of *Pyrrhulina*. They are a pretty, hardy species which adapt readily to aquarium conditions. They eat all kinds of foods, preferring live or freeze-dried foods. Though this species hasn't been spawned as yet, the other known species show a typical cichlid breeding behavior even though they are Characins. The male guards the eggs!

QUINTANA ATRIZONA (Hubbs) *Black-Barred Livebearer*

Range: Cuba.
Habits: Because of their size, they should be kept only with small fishes. Otherwise they may tend to be shy.
Water Conditions: Not critical; prefers a sunny tank which is well heated, 76 to 78°.
Size: Males about ¾ of an inch, females about 1½ inches.
Food Requirements: Not choosy, but the food particles should be small in size.
Color Variations: Sides of a glassy transparency, with 3 to 6 dark vertical bars.

Although not very brightly colored, these little livebearers are very interesting. The gonopodium of mature males is very long, and reaches almost to the caudal base when folded back. At the tip is a distinct hook, similar to the one found on the *Gambusia* species. This fish is a comparatively recent introduction, the first ones being introduced in 1932. These first ones were said to have come from the vicinity of Havana, Cuba and also from Baracoa, in the eastern end of the island. Now there seems to be some doubt as to whether they come from Cuba at all. Time will tell, but it seems strange that we still cannot be sure of the habitat of a fish which has been known since 1932. As with most livebearers, there is no question which are the males. Broods are quite small even with fully grown fish, and more than thirty young is unusual. The fry are tiny, and must be carefully fed with very fine foods at first, almost like the fry of egglayers. With proper feeding, however, they grow rapidly and in three to four months are ready to have young of their own. These fish do a little picking on algae from the plants, but never extend their appetites to the plants themselves.

Photo by Dr. Herbert R. Axelrod.

RASBORA ARGYROTAENIA (Bleeker) *Silver Rasbora*

Range: Japan, China, Thailand, Malacca, Malaya, Java, Bali and Borneo.
Habits: Peaceful toward other fishes, but likely to be shy if kept alone.
Water Conditions: Soft water, about 5 to 8 DH. Should be kept about 74°, but
drops in temperature down to 65° are tolerated.
Size: Attains a size of 6 inches in natural waters, about 4 inches in captivity.
Food Requirements: Being an active fish, it requires generous feeding. Will accept
dried foods, but these should be supplemented with live foods.
Color Variations: Body silvery, darker on the back and lighter toward the belly.
Golden stripe with black edging below runs the length of the body.

Even though it lacks much of the color which we associate with the *Rasbora*
species, *Rasbora argyrotaenia* lends a great deal of life to the community
aquarium with its ceaseless activity, its gleaming silvery body and the black
edging of its tail fork. Sexes can only be determined with certainty when
mature. At this time the male retains his slim outline, but the female becomes
heavier in the belly. As with any other active fish, a cover should be kept on
the aquarium to prevent them from jumping out. It is not surprising that a
fish with such a wide distribution should have many local varieties, and that
there should be a certain amount of confusion as to proper identification.
For this reason an ichthyologist who is called upon to identify a fish will give
hardly any attention to color, but rather to body characteristics like scale
counts, ray counts, head measurements, etc. These vary only slightly if at all,
but colors may vary greatly depending on location. There have been no
accounts of this fish being bred as yet, which is not to say it has not been
done. One thing can safely be said: it has not been done often!

RASBORA BORAPETENSIS (Smith)/*Redtailed Rasbora*

Range: Thailand (Bung Borapet).
Habits: Peaceful; likes to swim in small schools and does not nibble at plants.
Water Conditions: Soft, acid water. Temperature 75 to 80°.
Size: To 2½ inches.
Food Requirements: Eats anything, but should get live foods occasionally.
Color Variations: Back greenish, belly silvery. Black stripe on side with narrow golden stripe on top of it. Tail bright red.

It would hardly seem appropriate to call this the "Redtailed" Rasbora on the strength of the small amount of color which this picture shows, but this illustrates one of the great but little-known difficulties of fish photography: the fish are in gorgeous color until you get them set up, then they quickly fade when the photographer is about to snap the picture. Normally, in good color, the fish has a great deal of red in its tail and is a real beauty. Besides, the fish are easy to keep, eat anything and live for a long time in the aquarium. Getting them to spawn is far from being a difficult task; the author knows a breeder who has produced them by the thousands. Still, dealers hesitate to stock them because every time they do they cannot move them, even when the price is very reasonable. For breeding they should be given a tank of at least ten gallons capacity with some bushy plants. The water should be soft, about 2 or 3 DH, and the pH acid, 6.5 or 6.6. A ripe pair, where the female is heavy with eggs and the male active and in good color, is put into this tank and the water temperature raised to 80°. Eggs are laid in the plants and hatch in 36 hours.

F-525.00

RASBORA CAUDIMACULATA (Volz)/*Greater Scissortail*

Range: Malaya and Sumatra.
Habits: Peaceful and active, but should not be combined with small fishes.
Water Conditions: Soft, slightly acid water. Temperature 76 to 80°.
Size: To 8 inches.
Food Requirements: Eat just about anything, but should get live foods occasionally.
Color Variations: Body greenish with a violet sheen; faint horizontal stripe. Caudal
fin yellow to reddish with black tips.

This handsome Rasbora has a great resemblance to its smaller cousin *R. trilineata*, the Scissortail, because of the unusual pattern in the tail. Closer examination also shows that the first impression is not so accurate, because the three stripes which are prominent are missing here, and there is only one faint stripe. The fish in this photograph were just shipped and the black spot in the lower caudal lobe had evidently been nipped off. This was no great tragedy, because it quickly grew back. There are as yet no reports of any spawnings, and the probability is that this will require a large tank. In their home waters this fish is said to attain a length of 8 inches. Their aquarium should be firmly covered at all times; the author once lost a good pair because the cover glass was not replaced well enough and both jumped out. It is a pity that we do not see this graceful, beautiful fish more often; perhaps it has suffered the same fate as many other fishes which have the misfortune to look like another better-known species. Young specimens are said to have a black tip on the dorsal fin as well as on the caudal lobes.

F-526.00

RASBORA DUSONENSIS (Bleeker)/ *Yellowtail Rasbora*

Range: Thailand, Malaya, Sumatra, Borneo.
Habits: Peaceful and active. Should have a large tank with a tight cover.
Water Conditions: Soft, somewhat acid water. Temperature 75 to 82°.
Size: 6 inches.
Food Requirements: Not choosy; will eat dried as well as live foods.
Color Variations: Body silvery with violet tinge; black stripe on side, topped with
  gold. Tail lemon yellow with black posterior edge.

The Yellowtail Rasbora is one of the lesser-known beauties of the family,
not because of a lack of good looks or any other disadvantages but because it
is so seldom imported. It is a slender, active fish with a black stripe which
runs from the gill-covers to the caudal base. Above this black stripe is another
golden one. In the picture only the golden stripe shows, and for some reason
or other the black one is practically invisible. A slight idea of the violet
iridescence can also be gotten, but another thing that is not brought out
plainly enough is the lemon-yellow tail with the dark posterior edge. This
Rasbora, and for that matter most of the other Rasboras, are active jumpers
and must be protected from their own exuberance by a tight-fitting cover. *R.
dusonensis* is frequently confused with *R. argyrotaenia*, which is much more
common in the Asiatic collecting areas. The only difference is that the dark
stripe is wider and not as pronounced in *R. dusonensis*. Both are beautiful
and well worth the trouble of keeping them, but it is necessary to let them
have a roomy aquarium which their active nature requires.

Photo by Dr. Herbert R. Axelrod.

RASBORA EINTHOVENI (Bleeker) *Brilliant Rasbora, Einthoven's Rasbora*

Range: Malacca, Malaya, Thailand, Sumatra and Borneo.
Habits: In its native waters it travels in schools. An active swimmer, it should be given adequate quarters, with a good amount of swimming space.
Water Conditions: Not critical, but prefers soft, acid water and temperatures between 75 and 78°. For spawning, about 80°.
Size: Up to 3¼ inches.
Food Requirements: Being an active fish, they should be fed frequently. Dried foods are accepted, but should be supplemented with dried and frozen foods.
Color Variations: Greenish to yellowish, with a dark stripe running from the tip of the snout through the fork of the tail.

With the frequent importation of newer, more colourful *Rasbora* species, many of the ones we used to see frequently have all but disappeared from the picture. This is one of the species we see all too seldom today, which has made room for the more colorful species. It used to be that most well-stocked dealers had some of these around most of the time, but today some of them might not even recognize them if they were to see them. Nevertheless, this is a very attractive little fish, and a number of them swimming actively with the sun reflecting from their shiny scales and turning their dark stripe to deep green is a pleasant sight. This species is often confused with some of the other similar species such as *R. taeniata*, *R. daniconius* and *R. cephalotaenia*, all three of which it resembles very closely. Sexes are difficult to distinguish; the only difference is the heavier body of the females. One might have what is thought to be a pair, and find that it is a ripe and an unripe female. Easily spawned, and the non-adhesive eggs fall to the bottom, which should be covered with pebbles to prevent the parents from eating them.

F-528.00

RASBORA ELEGANS (Volz)/*Two-Spot Rasbora, Elegant Rasbora*

Range: Malaya and the Sunda Islands.
Habits: Peaceful, active. Good community tank fishes.
Water Conditions: Soft, slightly acid water. Temperature 76 to 82°.
Size: To 5 inches.
Food Requirements: Easily fed with live, frozen or dry foods.
Color Variations: Upper part of body brownish, silvery below. There is a light violet shimmer. Rectangular spot on sides, round spot on caudal base.

No chance of confusing the Two-Spot Rasbora with any other species of the genus. Its outstanding characteristic is a rectangular spot on the sides in the middle of its body. The pigmentation in most fishes occurs in the skin, but the skin and flesh of this attractive fish appear to be quite transparent at this point, and the spot is deeper down. The picture shows this to a certain extent: compare the rectangular spot on the sides with the black streak just above the anal fin. Probably the spot is of equal intensity, but being imbedded more deeply we see some of the light violet of the body on it. Males are usually a bit smaller than the females and have deeper colors. A ripe pair will spawn readily in the same manner as the Barbs, with a great deal of driving and hide-and-seek among the bushy plants, coming to a frequent quivering halt among the plants and scattering adhesive eggs. Like the Barbs, the breeders will eat their eggs if they are not removed as soon as spawning is completed. Hatching takes place on the following day; fry are easily fed with hard-boiled egg-yolk squeezed through a cloth, until they are able to handle newly hatched brine shrimp later on.

Photo by Dr. Herbert R. Axelrod.

RASBORA HETEROMORPHA (Duncker) *Rasbora, Harlequin Fish*

Range: Malaya, southern Thailand, Sumatra and Java.

Habits: Peaceful and harmless to even the smallest fishes. Active swimmers which prefer to travel in schools.

Water Conditions: Comes from very soft and acid waters, and this is what it should get. Temperatures 76 to 80°.

Size: 2 inches, usually a little smaller.

Food Requirements: Will accept dried foods, but should get frequent feedings with live and frozen foods besides.

Color Variations: Back and fore part of the body brownish red. After part of the body deep red with a large black triangle.

Almost every picture which depicts a group of tropical aquarium fishes will include Angelfish, Discus and our little friend the *Rasbora heteromorpha*. The little red fish with the black triangle is almost as well known as the ubiquitous Guppy. Its popularity is well deserved: besides being unquestionably decorative, it is always out in front where it can be seen and admired, and never in the least aggressive toward its tankmates. This fish was long a mystery to German breeders. They knew that there was a good profit in breeding *Rasboras*, and some of them were able to breed large numbers of them with very little trouble. These were all in a single district, and other breeders found that the very soft water in this district was the reason for success. As soon as they duplicated the chemical properties of this water, their fish began breeding too. Sexes can usually be distinguished by a fine gold line along the upper part of the triangle in the males, and the heavier, deeper body of the females. Eggs are usually laid on the underside of a wide plant leaf, and afterward ignored by both parents. Fry hatch in 24 to 26 hours, and should be given infusoria feedings at first.

F-530.00

RASBORA LEPTOSOMA (Bleeker)/ *Copper-Striped Rasbora*

Range: Sumatra.
Habits: Peaceful and active; will not bother other fish or plants.
Water Conditions: Soft and neutral to slightly acid. Temperature 75 to 80°.
Size: 4 inches.
Food Requirements: Easily fed with either live, frozen or dried foods.
Color Variations: Back brown, sides yellowish and belly white. From the snout to the caudal rays there is a coppery stripe, black underneath.

Here we do not yet know if we are dealing with a valid species. In his booklet *Rasboras*, Dr. Martin R. Brittan describes *R. leptosoma* as a doubtful species, and says that probably most hobbyists who reported on it did not have this fish but *R. pauciperforata*. Both are very similar in appearance. A comparison of the two shows that the red line of this species is not nearly so pronounced as in *R. pauciperforata*, but color is frequently a geographical thing and an ichthyologist is never swayed by it. Sizes for the two vary as well. 4 inches is given for this one, and only 2½ for *R. pauciperforata*. This does not prove anything either, because here again we are confronted with the fact that a species in one district will grow larger than the same species in another district where conditions are not as favorable. In order to prove his point one way or another, an ichthyologist must make thorough comparisons of the physical measurements and characteristics of the two supposed species before he can prove whether or not the original identifications are still valid. This accounts for the frequent re-shuffling of genera and species, a thing we must put up with.

Photo by H.J. Richter

RASBORA MACULATA (Duncker) *Dwarf Rasbora, Spotted Rasbora*

Range: Parts of India, southern Malaya, Singapore and Sumatra.
Habits: Very peaceful, but because of their tiny size and special water requirements should have a tank of their own, which need not be big.
Water Conditions: These fish are only at their best in water which is quite acid, ph 6.2 to 6.4, very soft, about 2 DH. Temperature 76 to 78°.
Size: ¾ to 1 inch.
Food Requirements: Larger foods like tubiflex or white worms should be chopped before feeding. Dried foods accepted in the finer sizes.
Color Variations: Back red, shading to orange toward the belly. Large round black spot on the side, with others in the dorsal and anal fins.

Not one in a dozen people who have seen this lovely little fish has seen it in its full glory, and glory it is. It demands special treatment, and when it gets it shows its gratitude by displaying an array of colors which rival those of any fish. These colors are difficult to describe; they must be seen to be appreciated. A proper background must be prepared. Their tank should be well planted around the sides and back, with an open space in front. Here is where you will usually see the little beauties. The bottom should be dark; the black gravel which is now available is perfect for the purpose. Sunlight should come into the tank from behind the observer. These fish love sunlight, and will strut around in it like little butterflies. At certain angles the sides will take on a deep violet shimmer. Females are a little bigger than the males, and almost as brightly colored. Spawning takes place in bundles of bushy plants, and the pair should be well fed before being put out to spawn, because the females are very fond of eating their own eggs. Fry hatch in 24 to 36 hours, and are suprisingly easy to raise on finely-ground dried foods.

RASBORA MYERSI (Brittan)/*Myers' Rasbora*

Range: Malaya, Sumatra, Borneo, Thailand.
Habits: Peaceful toward any other fishes which it cannot swallow.
Water Conditions: Soft, neutral to slightly acid water. Temperature 75 to 80°.
  Should have a good-sized tank with ample swimming space.
Size: 6 inches.
Food Requirements: Live, frozen or dried foods taken equally well.
Color Variations: Lead-colored body with a yellowish edge from opercle to the
  caudal base. Caudal rays black.

One look at this *Rasbora* species should serve to convince anyone as to why it is so seldom seen in the collections of fish hobbyists. It just simply does not have any outstanding colors, unless you could call attention to that slight tinge of black in the tail. Doubtless the collectors in the Asiatic waters have the same problems as do the South American collectors: a netful of fish is brought up, and 95 out of 100 are of no value for several reasons: they are or get to be too big for the aquarium, they are undesirable because they are vicious toward other fishes or, most of all, they have no colors to make them decorative and desirable in the aquarium. Our Rasbora would probably miss making the grade on two counts: a fish as large as this costs a lot to ship, and after it reaches the market its lack of beauty does not exactly cause the hobbyists to fall all over each other in a mad scramble to buy it. On the good side of the ledger is the fact that it has a nice, well-proportioned shape and is a graceful, active swimmer. There is no record of this species having ever been bred, probably because nobody ever felt that it was worth the effort.

RASBORA PAUCIPERFORATA (Weber & de Beaufort)
Red-Line Rasbora

Range: Sumatra.
Habits: Peaceful and well-behaved in mixed company.
Water Conditions: Water should be somewhat acid, pH 6.2, and soft, DH 2 or 3. Temperature 75 to 80°.
Size: About 2½ inches.
Food Requirements: Live foods preferred, but all kinds accepted.
Color Variations: Brownish with chocolate stripe, red above.

A well-planted tank with lighting from above and about a dozen Red-Line Rasboras is all that is needed to make a breathtaking display which will attract anyone's attention and admiration. An added touch may be attained by the use of black gravel, which sets off the colors of the fish and plants. Only a few other fishes have a stripe which matches this one in brilliance. One is the Glowlight Tetra. A little experimenting is necessary to get the best lighting for the most effective results. When just right, the fish lights up from tail to snout like a red neon sign. This fish was named by Weber and de Beaufort in 1916, and hobbyists saw their first specimens in 1928. Spawning is similar to the other long-bodied *Rasboras:* bushy plants should be provided, and a generous amount of swimming space. Males drive actively, coming frequently to a stop alongside of a female among the plants and scattering eggs all over, many of them falling to the bottom. Fry hatch in 24 to 36 hours.

F-534.00

RASBORA SOMPHONGSI (Meinken)/*Somphongs' Rasbora*

Range: Thailand.
Habits: Peaceful; a good community fish.
Water Conditions: Soft, acid water desirable. Temperature 73 to 83°F.
Size: About 1¼ inches.
Food Requirements: All types of food accepted, provided that it is small enough to be swallowed.
Color Variations: Body color silvery, shading to yellow. Black line, with a faint golden line above and below, runs from below dorsal to caudal base. Fins more yellow than body, but clear.

Just a little bit bigger than *Rasbora maculata*, the Dwarf or Spotted Rasbora, is *Rasbora somphongsi*, a fish ideally suited to the needs of the hobbyist who has small tanks. Peaceful and hardy, Somphongs' Rasbora is a very good community fish with only one drawback: its preference for strictly soft, acid water. This insistence by the fish of being maintained only in water which is difficult for some hobbyists to duplicate has led to a curtailment of its popularity among hobbyists who can obtain only hard, alkaline water, and *Rasbora somphongsi* finds itself in the same boat as *Rasbora maculata:* it is not seen as often as it deserves, while other less attractive and less accommodating fishes are given preference. For spawning, which is accomplished through the laying of eggs in bunches of plants or synthetic plant fibers, soft and acid water is a necessity. The fry are very tiny, as is to be expected from the size of the parents, and they require plenty of small infusoria for the first few days of their free-swimming life. *Rasbora somphongsi* is not a brilliantly colored fish, but its quiet beauty can be shown off better if it is kept in a well-planted tank having a dark background and bottom.

RASBORA STEINERI (Nichols & Pope)/*Chinese Rasbora*

Range: Southern China, Hainan Province.
Habits: Peaceful and well behaved with other fishes.
Water Conditions: Soft and considerably acid water. Temperature 74 to 78°.
Size: Up to 3 inches.
Food Requirements: Live foods preferred, but all kinds accepted.
Color Variations: Body brownish to light pinkish, belly silvery Black stripe from opercle to caudal base, bordered with gold above. Base of tail reddish.

Most of China is in the Temperate Zone, and there are very few fishes of interest to the fish hobbyist available today from waters which are warm enough to be considered "tropical." *Rasbora steineri*, from the Hainan Province, is one of the exceptions. In appearance it resembles the much better-known *R. borapetensis*, the main differences being that *R. borapetensis* has a shade brighter red in the tail, toward the base. There is as yet no record of any spawning of *R. steineri*. Probably it spawns like the other long-bodied *Rasboras*, but any guess may be far off base. It is a logical point from which to start when making an attempt to spawn it, however. But we already have *Rasboras*, many of them far surpassing this one in beauty and, what is more important, readily available. But the fish hobbyist is an odd proposition; tell him about a fish which is not particularly beautiful but comes from a part of the world which is practically inaccessible and they are willing to pay astronomical prices for it; show them a perfectly beautiful fish which is a perfect candidate for the aquarium but comes from their own country, and they pay it no heed whatsoever.

F-536.00

RASBORA TAENIATA (Ahl) *Black-Striped Rasbora*

Range: Sumatra.
Habits: Peaceful, active swimmers; will mix with other active species in a community aquarium.
Water Conditions: Water should be clean, very soft and with a pH of about 6.6. Temperature 76 to 82°.
Size: About 3 inches.
Food Requirements: Will take dried foods, but live or frozen foods preferred.
Color Variations: Back greenish, belly lighter. Bluish-black stripe runs from behind the head to the caudal base, with a golden stripe underneath.

The specific name *taeniata* means "striped." German hobbyists know this fish as the "Gold-Striped Rasbora," while American hobbyists call it the "Black-Striped Rasbora." Neither description is incorrect, because it has both a black and a golden line running from just behind the head to the caudal base. There is also a very narrow black stripe on the side of the head which runs from the tip of the snout through the eye and across the operculum, and a very narrow one at the base of the anal fin. Females are distinguished by the deeper bodies. For spawning, a tank of not less than 10 gallons should be provided, with several bunches of bushy plants. Spawning is sometimes extended over several days, and the usual practice is to leave the breeders in until the first fry are seen. The youngsters grow slowly in the first few days, and should be given infusoria as well as finely powdered dry food. After two to three weeks the rate of growth increases, and in a half-year the youngsters attain a size of 1½ inches and more. This species is one of the earlier-known *Rasbora,* having been first imported into Germany in 1913.

RASBORA TORNIERI (Ahl) *Yellow-tailed Rasbora*

Range: Central and western Sumatra.
Habits: Peaceful, active swimmers which require a good-sized aquarium with a good amount of open space.
Water Conditions: Acid, soft water required for best results. Temperature 74 to 78°.
Size: 4 inches.
Food Requirements: Being a large, active species feedings should be generous; all foods are accepted.
Color Variations: Back brown, sides silvery with a violet sheen at certain angles. Greenish-black stripe runs from the tip of snout through the tail.

This is one of the larger members of the *Rasbora* family, attaining a length of 4 inches. A very active swimmer, it seems to be always on the move. In sunlight, the sides sometimes shimmer silver, sometimes violet and sometimes green. There is a lateral stripe which runs from the tip of the snout through the middle rays of the tail. Another less distinct stripe runs along the upper half of the body and still another from the gill-plate to the first rays of the anal fin. The tail is a greenish yellow, edged with black. The iris of the eye is a golden yellow. The other fins are colorless. This very attractive species was first brought into Germany in 1929. This shipment died out and the fish was not seen again until 1938, when some young ones, which were mistaken for *Rasbora urophthalma*, were introduced. One account only exists of their spawning, and that one incomplete. Hermann Meinken had a pair spawn for him. The female pursued the male, who finally turned the tables and chased her into some bushy plants. Each trip resulted in the male clasping the female with his dorsal and anal fins, resulting in some eggs being expelled. This took place in a community tank, and the eggs were eaten.

F-538.00

Photo by Dr. Herbert R. Axelrod.

RASBORA TRILINEATA (Steindachner)
Three-Lined or Scissortailed Rasbora

Range: Sumatra and Borneo, where it is common.

Habits: Peaceful; active swimmers who should have plenty of swimming space in their aquarium.

Water Conditions: Soft, acid water with a pH value of about 6.5. Temperature 76 to 78°.

Size: Up to 4 inches.

Food Requirements: Will accept dried foods as well as live foods, but live or frozen foods should be given occasionally.

Color Variations: Sides silvery, with three horizontal stripes. Tail lobes have a large black spot in a white area.

In the last decade or so, the Scissortailed *Rasbora* has become one of the most popular members of the group. This is certainly not due to the presence of any brilliant colors, but the fish has other things to recommend it. For one, it is usually out in front where it can be seen. Another is that it is always on the move. It accepts and thrives on practically any food, and never becomes belligerent toward its neighbors. It spawns quite easily and the young are not difficult to raise. Although it is at its best in acid water, it will also get along in alkaline water but might possibly make known its objection to it by refusing to spawn. All in all, it is a very hardy and adaptable species. Females are a trifle longer than the males, and considerably bigger around. After considerable driving, the male gets the female into some bushy plants, where he wraps his body about hers and 15 to 25 eggs are expelled and fertilized. The eggs have very little adhesive power, and many fall to the bottom. The first of the fry hatch after 24 hours. In 5 days the youngsters begin to swim, at which time they may be fed with very finely grained dry food, followed in a week or so by newly hatched brine shrimp.

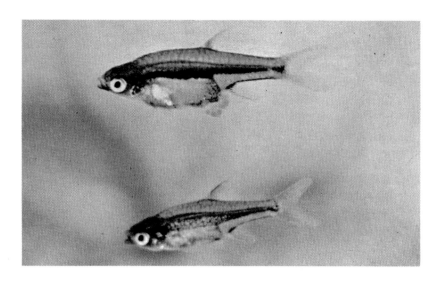

RASBORA UROPHTHALMA (Ahl)
Ocellated Dwarf Rasbora, Exclamation-Point Rasbora

Range: Sumatra.
Habits: Peaceful; because of their diminutive size, they should not be kept with large fishes.
Water Conditions: Soft water, no more than 5 DH, with an acidity of pH 6.5.
Size: 1 to 1¼ inches.
Food Requirements: Smaller live foods preferred, but dried foods also accepted. They are also fond of picking at algae.
Color Variations: Body golden brown, back reddish, belly yellowish. Steel blue horizontal stripe narrows to a point and ends in a spot at the tail base.

This is one of the small *Rasboras*, easily recognized by the horizontal stripe which is at its widest below the beginning of the dorsal fin, and then narrows down to a point toward the tail base. Here there is an ocellated round spot of steel blue, ringed with gold. This fish, and the other small *Rasboras* for that matter, requires a well-planted aquarium or it may turn out to be very shy. Given proper conditions and sunlight shining in on them, it will be seen that the dark line is edged above with a delicate gold. Like the other *Rasboras*, this species is very gregarious, and happy only when kept in a small group of at least six. Then they are active and always playing about in the open spaces. Spawning may be accomplished in a small aquarium of 3 to 5 gallons, which should be planted with one or two broad-leaved plants like the *Cryptocoryne* species, and a bunch of fine-leaved plants like *Myriophyllum*. Temperature should be gradually raised to 80°. Driving is not at all vigorous, almost polite. Eggs are either hung on the underside of the broad leaves, or the fish may decide to spawn in the bushy plants.

RASBORA VATERIFLORIS (Deraniyagala) *Ceylonese Fire Barb*

Range: Ceylon.
Habits: Very peaceful, active fish which should be given adequate swimming space.
Water Conditions: Soft, acid water like the other species. Temperature should not sink below 76°.
Size: Maximum length 1¼ inches.
Food Requirements: Will accept dried foods as well as live or frozen foods.
Color Variations: Basic color orange-purple. Dorsal and anal fins, as well as the lower half of the tail and lower half of the body orange.

The derivation of the scientific name *vaterifloris* for this lovely little *Rasbora* is an interesting one. There is a tree which grows in Ceylon which the natives call "Hal," and the scientific name is *Vateria acuminata*. This tree has a beautiful yellow to red flower, and the color of this *Rasbora* species reminded the great ichthyologist Deraniyagala of the Hal blossoms, therefore the name. Like so many other fishes, this one may be rather pale and uninteresting in a dealer's bare tanks, and the hobbyist who does not know what beautiful color this species is capable of might easily pass it up as too drab for his tanks. Then he might see the same fish in all their glory in a friend's aquarium and rave about their beauty. Females are easily recognizable by their lighter colors and heavier dimensions. Males are active drivers, and pursue the females into plant thickets, where a very rapid spawning act takes place. The eggs have little adhesive power, and most of them fall to the bottom. The pair should come out as soon as the eggs have been laid, or most of them will be eaten. The water level should then be reduced to 6 inches, and the young will hatch in 36 to 40 hours.

F-541.00

RHODEUS SERICEUS (Pallas)/*Bitterling*

Range: Middle Europe.

Habits: Peaceful, but not a good community fish, as it is not a tropical species and cannot take normal aquarium temperatures.

Water Conditions: Water composition not of great importance, as long as extremes are avoided. Temperature 58 to 70°F.

Size: Up to 3 inches.

Food Requirements: Accepts most commercial foods; paste foods especially good.

Color Variations: Outside of breeding season, a plain silvery fish. In breeding season, male becomes suffused with reddish-purple.

Very few American hobbyists have had any experience with this fish, but it is popular in Europe, where there is less stress placed on tropical species and more attention is paid to native fishes. Perhaps the Bitterling is more favored in Europe because of its interesting habits; European hobbyists pay more attention to behavioral characteristics than Americans do. In any event, the Bitterling is fascinating in its breeding pattern. Many fishes go to great lengths to protect their young, but the Bitterling really confounds its enemies: the female uses her extremely long ovipositor to place the eggs within living molluscs, where they are safe from all harm. The hatched fry remain in their living refuge until they become free-swimming. The mollusc, usually a mussel, is not to be considered as a victim, because the young *Rhodeus* are not parasites, and they take nothing from the bivalve. As a matter of fact, the protection afforded the young fish only serves to even up the score between mollusc and fish, for many young bivalves spend their larval stages attached to the skin of fishes, who thus transport them to new homes.

RIVULUS COMPRESSUS (Henn)/*Blue Rivulus*

Range: Amazon tributaries, in the vicinity of Manaos.

Habits: Best kept with its own kind or similar fishes.

Water Conditions: Soft, slightly acid water. Temperature 75 to 80°. Tank should be kept covered at all times.

Size: To 3 inches.

Food Requirements: Living foods preferred; frozen or prepared foods only accepted when very hungry.

Color Variations: Body has a bluish tinge with horizontal rows of red dots. Male's ventral, anal and the bottom of the caudal fin tinged with orange.

There is very little reference to this fish in aquarium literature, even in scientific publications. The pair shown here were collected by the great ethnologist Harald Schultz, whom the aquarium world has to thank for numerous new fish species and enlightening articles on Brazilian fishes and conditions under which he has found them during his travels for the São Paulo Museum in search of Indian tribes and their folklore. Mr. Schultz's work takes him to many out-of-the-way places where he studies the flora and fauna of the region as well as its native humans. Most *Rivulus* species have a muddy body color and no particular beauty to speak of, but this one is quite attractive with its greenish-blue sides adorned with rows of reddish spots. The male (upper fish) is easily distinguished by its larger anal fin and the touch of orange in the ventral and anal fins as well as the lower edge of the tail. There have been no spawnings reported, and probably their breeding procedure is the same as the others. An interesting variation has been observed with another Brazilian species: the eggs hung in a bunch from the female's vent, like the *Oryzias* species.

RIVULUS CYLINDRACEUS (Poey) *Cuban Rivulus*

Range: Cuba, possibly also Florida.
Habits: Fairly peaceful in the community aquarium.
Water Conditions: Soft, slightly acid water preferred, with temperatures 76 to 78°.
Size: Males slightly under 2 inches; females slightly larger.
Food Requirements: Should get live foods only, but will accept dried foods if hungry.
Color Variations: Body dark brown, lighter in the females. Males have a blue edge on the dorsal fin and the upper edge of the tail.

As with the African *Aphyosemion* species, there is little danger of getting the males and females of this attractive fish confused. Even at an early age, females develop the well-known "Rivulus spot." This is an ocellated spot in the upper part of the caudal base. It is totally absent in the males. Besides, the males have much more to offer in the way of color. Both have a lateral stripe, but the male's is a deeper brown and more distinct. The male's dorsal fin has a blue edge, as has the upper part of the tail, and his sides have regular rows of red dots. These fish are very easy to spawn, and a small aquarium suffices. Eggs are laid in bushy plants near the surface, a few each day, and take from 12 to 14 days to hatch. There are several ways to separate the eggs and breeders. One is to pick out the eggs every few days: A simpler method is to leave the breeders in with the eggs, which they seldom eat, for about 10 days and then fish out the parents. Still another is to remove the plants with the eggs every 10 days and place them in similar water to hatch. The fry are free-swimming upon hatching, and may be fed immediately with newly hatched brine shrimp.

F-544.00

RIVULUS HARTI (Boulenger) *Hart's Rivulus, Giant Rivulus*

Range: Trinidad, Venezuela and eastern Colombia.
Habits: Peaceful and likely to remain hidden. Will not harm any fish it cannot swallow.
Water Conditions: Not at all critical, but slightly sensitive to lower temperatures. The temperature should never be allowed to drop below 76°.
Size: 4 inches.
Food Requirements: Should get live food, but will take dry food when very hungry.
Color Variations: Greenish to bluish sides, with rows of dots which are red in the males, brownish in the females.

Some of the *Rivulus* species, of which this is one, have a strange habit which is not mentioned in most of the books: they will often jump out of the water and cling to the glass sides of the aquarium above the surface, or to the cover glass for considerable periods of time. When they feel themselves beginning to become dry, they drop back, sometimes to repeat the procedure soon afterward. What the reason for this behavior might be is something for animal behaviorists to figure out, and the answer, if we ever get it, might be very interesting. Perhaps in their native waters they escape some natural enemies in this manner; then again, maybe they just *like* to do it! In any case, their tank must be kept covered if these jumpers are to remain in it. Sexes are easily distinguished, as with most *Rivulus* species. The males have rows of red dots on the sides, which are only faintly indicated in the females. If the breeders are well fed, the young may be raised with them with no losses. Eggs are deposited every day or two. There is no one breeding period as with Barbs or Characins.

RIVULUS PUNCTATUS (Boulenger)/*Spotted Rivulus*

Range: Paraguay, Bolivia and Western Brazil.
Habits: Generally peaceful but shy with other fishes.
Water Conditions: Soft, slightly acid water. Temperature 75 to 80°. Tank should be always covered to prevent fish from jumping.
Size: To 3 inches.
Food Requirements: All sorts of live foods; dry foods taken only when very hungry.
Color Variations: Back olive, underside silvery white, broad black horizontal stripe. Sides covered with red dots. Unpaired fins yellow.

The Spotted Rivulus is a real rarity which is seldom seen in hobbyist collections today. Another fish, *Rivulus dorni*, has been mistakenly offered as this species by dealers from time to time. The fish pictured here was caught by Harald Schultz in the Mato Grosso Region of Brazil. The V-shaped arrangement of dots in the after part of the body are highly reminiscent of the bars in *R. strigatus*, another very attractive member of the genus. All *Rivulus* species are excellent jumpers and can leap surprisingly high out of the water. A covered tank is therefore a necessity if you do not want to find your precious fish on the floor some morning. To the best of our knowledge this fish has not yet been spawned in captivity, but the task of getting them to spawn should not be a difficult one. A well conditioned pair should be placed in a tank of about 5 gallons capacity, with plenty of bushy plants floating on the surface. Rather than search for eggs every day, keep a close eye on the female to see when she is losing some of her rotundity. Once she has become slimmer it is time to begin the egg-hunt. *Rivulus* eggs take from 10 to 15 days to hatch.

RIVULUS UROPHTHALMUS (Günther)/*Golden Rivulus*

Range: Guianas to the lower Amazon region.
Habits: Prefer to be kept by themselves; large tank not essential. Like to hide in plant thickets. Very active jumpers.
Water Conditions: Soft, slightly acid water is best. Temperatures around 76° are best, but not sensitive to gradual drops.
Size: 2½ inches.
Food Requirements: Live foods are essential, preferably those which remain near the surface like mosquito larvae.
Color Variations: Golden variety has yellow body with rows of horizontal red dots. Females are lighter in color and have smaller fins.

The *Rivulus* genus is one which is not generally noted for its brilliance of colors. Most of the species have a coloration which blends in with their native background, making them a drab lot. *Rivulus urophthalmus* is one of the exceptions, even in the green form which we seldom see. The upper two-thirds of the body is covered with horizontal rows of red dots. This species often has a xanthistic variation, which is the one which most hobbyists are offered. Here the entire body is a golden yellow instead of green, and the red dots are exceptionally brilliant. Probably these yellow fish occur quite frequently in their native waters, but such a fish would seldom attain full growth. Its color would be equivalent to a death warrant, because such a fish would find it next to impossible to hide from its many enemies. However, in the aquarium the golden ones can be separated from the green ones in a batch of fry and raised to maturity without being attacked by enemies, and the results are beautiful. Easily spawned; a few eggs are laid daily among floating vegetation. These are best picked out and allowed to hatch separately, which they do in 12 days. Fry are easily raised.

Photo by Harald Schultz

ROEBOIDES GUATEMALENSIS (Günther)/*Guatemalan Headstander*

Range: Eastern coastal region of Central America from southern Mexico to Panama.
Habits: Active, fairly peaceful if kept with fishes which are not too small.
Water Conditions: Water should be clean, temperatures 76° to 80°. Tank should not be too heavily planted. Water characteristics not important.
Size: To 6 inches, in the aquarium seldom exceeds 3 inches.
Food Requirements: Live foods preferred, but prepared foods also accepted quite readily. An easy fish to feed.
Color Variations: Scales very small; entire body covered with tiny specks. Horizontal stripe ends at the caudal base with a spot.

This fish is seldom offered to aquarium hobbyists, not because it is rare and hard to get, but because the few importations brought in so far have not found great favor. A demand for these would bring in a regular flood of shipments. This is one of the most common fishes in Guatemala, where the natives fry it in oil and eat it, bones and all. *Roeboides guatemalensis* has a few points which would make it interesting to aquarists. Its skin and flesh are very transparent, making its skeletal structure easy to see. Another unique characteristic is their manner of swimming in a downward-tilted position. Closer inspection proves that actually this downward tilt is not as great as it seems: it is the after half of the body that has the tilt, while the forward half is almost level. What Mother Nature's reasons were for constructing a fish in this manner could lead to some fairly wild guesswork. Given a large aquarium and a temperature of about 80°, the male will soon begin to drive the female and spawning will take place in plant thickets. A large number of eggs will result, which will hatch in 25 to 30 hours. The young are easily raised.

F-548.00

These two *Roeboides* species were captured and photographed in the wild by Dr. Herbert R. Axelrod during one of his trips to the Amazon.

ROHTEE ALFREDIANA (Cuvier & Valenciennes)/*Copper Minnow*

Range: India, Burma, Thailand.
Habits: An active fish, fairly peaceful.
Water Conditions: Soft, slightly acid water; tank should be well planted, as the fish likes vegetable matter in its diet. Temperature 70 to 80°F.
Size: Up to 3 inches.
Food Requirements: Typically Barb-like in its food preferences.
Color Variations: Body copper color, sometimes showing gold.

The genus *Rohtee* is very little known to aquarists, as these fishes have never been imported in quantity for the aquarium market, although some of them, or at least some fishes which have been identified as *Rohtee* species, have been seen offered for sale occasionally. There is almost a complete lack of information on how they fit into the aquarium hobby, but, judging by the performance of some of their relatives, it is safe to assume that they make acceptable aquarium specimens. They can certainly be regarded as not much more than curiosities, as they are not strikingly colored and have no outstanding points of interest.

F-550.00

Photo by Harald Schultz.

*SARCODACES ODOE (Bloch)/*African Pike*

Range: Widely distributed all over tropical Africa.

Habits: Vicious, greedy and predatory. Can only be kept with their own kind or larger fishes.

Water Conditions: Not critical, but soft, slightly acid water is best. Temperature 75 to 80°.

Size: To 12 inches.

Food Requirements: Living smaller fishes only; possibly they may be trained to eat strips of raw fish.

Color Variations: Body olive green, belly golden. Young specimens have dark spotted fins.

All over the world Mother Nature has some fishes which serve to keep the waters from becoming overpopulated. These are the predators, the fishes which feed ravenously on smaller living fishes. They have large mouths and appetites to match. The eyes are large and keen, and everything which moves and is small enough to be swallowed is sought out by them. The teeth are designed for holding the struggling prey; they turn inward and a fish impaled on them and managing to get off will only find himself nearer the hungry, greedy throat. The temperate waters of the world have similar counterparts to this fish, namely the Pike, Pickerel and Muskellunge. *Sarcodaces odoe* has been known to science since 1794 and is very rarely imported. It would be no problem for a collector to find them; they occur all over tropical Africa. This specimen was collected and photographed by Pierre Brichard, the well-known collector, in the Stanley Pool region of the Congo River. Although they might make interesting showpieces for public aquariums, only young ones would be of a size small enough for the average hobbyist's tanks, and very few hobbyists would find them interesting enough for theirs.

* Now identified as *Hepsetus odoe.*

Photo by Dr. Herbert R. Axelrod.

SCATOPHAGUS ARGUS (Gmelin)/*Spotted Scat*

Range: Tropical Indo-Pacific Region along the coasts.

Habits: Peaceful toward other fishes, but will graze on aquatic plants right down to the roots.

Water Conditions: Fairly hard, alkaline water with a teaspoonful of salt per gallon added. Temperature 74 to 78°.

Size: To 13 inches in their home waters, about half that in captivity.

Food Requirements: Live foods of all kinds, with the addition of vegetable substances like lettuce or spinach leaves. Will also eat frozen foods.

Color Variations: Variable, depending upon size and origin. Silvery to brown with large black spots. Dorsal, anal and caudal fins have a black base.

Actually the Spotted Scat is an estuarial fish which spends its time in coastal waters. We do not know much of its spawning habits, but it is thought that this takes place in marine water, in the coral reefs. The young ascend the streams and grow through their juvenile stages in fresh or only slightly brackish water. It is at this stage that most of them are collected, and for this reason they can be kept in fairly fresh water with only a little salt added to make them feel at home. A translation of the generic name is "offal-eater," which is given to the fish because it is frequently found near the sewer outlets of coastal cities. The reason may be that they are after what comes out of the pipes, or that they are attracted to the smaller life which feeds on this. Scats are very hardy, long-lived fish if given conditions they like and live for a long time in captivity. Captive specimens of course never attain the more than 12-inch size they would reach in their home waters where they could make their migrations into salt water, and whether or not they will ever be spawned in captivity is a real question. So far we do not even know the sex differences.

Photo by K. Paysan.

SCATOPHAGUS ARGUS (Gmelin) VAR. RUBRIFRONS
Tiger Scat

Range: Tropical Indo-Pacific Region along the coasts.
Habits: Peaceful toward other fishes, but cannot be trusted to leave plants alone.
Water Conditions: Fairly hard, alkaline water with a teaspoonful of salt added per gallon. Temperature 74 to 78°.
Size: To 13 inches in their home waters, about half that in captivity.
Food Requirements: Heavy eater, not fussy. Vegetable substances should be added to their diet.
Color Variations: Like *S. argus*, but there are bright red bars across the forehead and sometimes also along the body.

There are experts who consider this as an entirely different species, but the consensus seems to be that *S. rubrifrons* is merely a color variation of *S. argus*, and for this reason we have given it a variety status, calling it *S. argus var. rubrifons*. There are two other possibilities: since we do not know of any external sex differences, it is possible that the nicely colored red-striped fish is the male, while the plainer-colored ones are females. There is also the possibility that *S. a. rubrifrons* is merely a color phase through which all the fish pass. We are forced merely to speculate until some scientist answers the question once and for all by capturing, killing and opening a large number of specimens. This gives him the opportunity to separate the sexes definitely by looking at the internal organs and then comparing them for other similarities or differences. The Tiger Scat is a very attractive aquarium fish, and if conditions are to its liking the red markings are very bright. Scats become very tame once they have become established in the aquarium.

F-553.00

SCHILBE MARMORATUS (Boulenger)/*African Shoulder-Spot Catfish*

Range: Congo River and its tributaries.
Habits: Peaceful, inclined to be shy.
Water Conditions: Soft, neutral to slightly acid water. Temperature 75 to 80°. Hiding places should be provided.
Size: To 6¼ inches.
Food Requirements: Prefers live foods, but may possibly be trained to accept frozen foods.
Color Variations: Light gray, sprinkled with some brown. Large round black spot on the shoulder.

There are a great many Catfishes which come from African waters. Some are highly interesting in color and habits, and others have a great similarity to our North American Bullheads. *Schilbe marmoratus* has only one feature which makes it a little different: on a drab gray body there is a large round black spot. Another African Catfish with a similar black spot comes to mind, *Mystus tengara*. The difference is that this fish has the spot squarely on the sides, while *Schilbe marmoratus* carries its spot higher on the shoulder. There are no known external sex differences, and no recorded spawnings. One thing which can be said in their favor is that they are not particularly nocturnal in their habits. If kept in a tank which gets too much light, however, they tend to be shy and inclined to hide. As with so many other timid species, the more hiding-places which are provided, the oftener they are seen. Having a place where they can retreat gives them confidence in the safety of their surroundings and gives them the courage to venture forth, which otherwise they would not have. Boulenger named this fish in 1911, and it has been known to the hobby since about 1956.

SELENOTOCA MULTIFASCIATA (Richardson)/*False Scat*

Range: All Australian coastal waters except in the south.
Habits: Peaceful toward other fishes, but cannot be trusted with plants.
Water Conditions: Fairly hard, alkaline water with a teaspoonful of salt added per gallon. Temperature 74 to 78°.
Size: To 4 inches.
Food Requirements: Live foods, with the addition of vegetable substances like lettuce or spinach leaves. Will also eat frozen foods.
Color Variations: Greenish silvery, with a golden tint above. 9 to 15 narrow black bars on the sides, becoming rows of spots below.

Only a highly trained eye can spot the difference between this attractive fish and one of an entirely different genus, *Scatophagus tetracanthus* (Lacepede), the Striped Scat, with which and as which it is frequently shipped. *Selenotoca multifasciata* has a slightly more elongated body, and the soft part of the dorsal and anal fins are smaller than in the Scat. Otherwise they are practically identical, both in appearance and habits. Both fishes have a highly variable number of black bars on the sides, which give way to vertical rows of spots. As with many fishes which have barred markings, the bars in young specimens probably split now and then to become two. Exactly the same attention should be given the *Selenotoca* species as was specified for the Scats, and they are very likely to be just as hardy and long-lived as their better-known cousins. One thing you will not find in the *Selenotoca* species is the red color which appears in *Scatophagus argus var. rubrifrons*, but that would be asking for too much! Living habits for both fish groups are identical and they occur together in many instances, so the same conditions may be provided for both.

F-555.00

Serrasalmo brandti, known as *Pirambeba* to Brazilians, is less dangerous than other Piranhas, as the teeth are smaller and the jaws are weaker than in the other species.

An introduction to an unwelcome visitor: this is the Black Piranha, which gets to be over 5 lbs. in weight in its home waters.

*SERRASALMO HOLLANDI (Eigenmann)/*Holland's Piranha*

Range: Rio Guaporé, Brazil. Probably occurs elsewhere as well.
Habits: Vicious, cannot even be kept with another of its own kind.
Water Conditions: Soft, slightly acid water. Temperature 75 to 80°.
Size: About 5 inches.
Food Requirements: Smaller living fishes preferred; can be trained to take strips of raw fish or beef heart.
Color Variations: Greenish silvery body with black spots. Anal fin red. Inside edge of tail black.

The solons who enacted the law forbidding the import, sale and possession of any species of the genus *Serrasalmo, Rooseveltiella* and *Pygocentrus* passed a bit of legislation which, even if its intentions were good, left the inspectors in a bit of a dilemma as to deciding what was a dangerous fish and what wasn't. There are many fishes which have the almost identical form of a Piranha but which are perfectly harmless. An inspector cannot be expected to open up a carton, open a plastic bag and then stick his hand in; if it comes out without the usual complement of fingers the fish should be confiscated. A little of this and there would soon be a drastic shortage of customs inspectors! Consequently there are now just as many Piranhas offered for sale as there were before July 1, 1961, when the law was passed. The hobbyist who keeps a fish with dental equipment sharp and strong enough to amputate a finger or at the very least to inflict a serious wound should not do so unless he takes some important precautions: 1. Keep the tank where children cannot get at it. 2. Be very careful when netting the fish; don't even put your hand close to it! *The genus *Serrasalmo* is also known as *Serrasalmus*.

F-557.00

SERRASALMO NATTERERI (Kner)
Natterer's Piranha, Red-Bellied Piranha

Range: Widely distributed throughout the Amazon and Orinoco Basins.
Habits: Vicious, must be kept alone in the average-sized tank.
Water Conditions: Soft, slightly acid water. Temperature 75 to 80°.
Size: Up to 12 inches in natural waters; shipped specimens usually much smaller.
Food Requirements: Smaller living fishes, or strips of raw fish or beef heart.
Color Variations: Back steel gray with many tiny shining scales; large black spot on
sides; throat, belly and anal fin bright red.

Authorities differ as to whether the Piranha on this page properly belongs to
the genus *Serrasalmo* or *Rooseveltiella*. Whatever we call him, he is a nasty

F-558.00

customer and can use those razor-sharp teeth and powerful jaws with very telling effect. This is the most widely-distributed and most commonly found of the Piranha group, and probably the most handsome of the lot. There has been a good deal of controversy as to how dangerous the Piranha really is. In the author's opinion a Piranha is not really dangerous until he feels he is trapped and confined, and then he attacks in self-defense. Most Piranha bites are sustained when the fish are being handled. This is not to say that a hungry Piranha is never a dangerous proposition. Usually there is a plenitude of small fish life on which they can forage, but if such is not the case and there is a leg or arm in the water, the temptation to take an experimental nip might prove too great to resist. Once blood is drawn others are attracted to the scene and the bloody shambles that follows has been described all too often and vividly. Natterer's Piranha is frequently seen in public aquariums, and small specimens are often kept by hobbyists.

Serrasalmo rhombeus, known as the White Piranha.

Photo by Harald Schultz.

F-559.00

SORUBIM LIMA (Bloch & Schneider)/*Shovelnose Catfish*

Range: Magdalena and La Plata river systems in South America.

Habits: A lazy, fairly slow-moving fish, but one which is capable of eating smaller fishes.

Water Conditions: Soft, slightly acid water is best, but not of prime importance. Temperature 72 to 82 F.

Size: Up to 1½ feet, although imported specimens are rarely anywhere near this size.

Color Variations: Body olive to gray, lighter in the belly. A dark stripe runs over the back, and another runs along the sides and into the tail.

This South American Pimelodid Catfish has been known to hobbyists for many years. It is usually kept as an oddity, which indeed it is, but it is the type of fish which soon loses the interest of its owner, primarily because it demands certain conditions and makes no repayment for the effort expended on it. It is a nocturnal fish which is not at home in a bright tank, and it should be provided with hiding places. The Shovelnose Catfish is easy to take care of, for it will accept almost any food. In this regard it must be considered to be dangerous to smaller fishes which are small enough, and unwary enough, to be engulfed by the large mouth. The Shovelnose Catfish does not seem to take part in an active chase of small fishes, but it manages to get its share nevertheless, usually at night. For proper growth, the fish should be located in a large tank; in a big tank, also, it has less chance of eating smaller fishes, especially fast-moving species. As with other fishes of the family Pimelodidae, the adipose fin is comparatively large, and the barbels are long.

Photo by Harald Schultz.

This is *Sorubimichthys planiceps* (Agassiz) a nocturnal Catfish which occurs in northern South American waters. The contour of the head, as shown in this dorsal view, is very much different from the head contour of *Sorubim lima*. Whereas *S. lima* has a very long snout, the frontal outline of *S. planiceps* is very rounded. The ventral fins are also placed differently. Hobbyists equate the word "Catfish" with "harmless," but this is a mistake. It is best to keep a sharp eye on any Catfish with a big mouth.

Photo by H.J. Richter.

SPHAERICHTHYS OSPHROMENOIDES (Canestrini)
Chocolate Gourami

Range: Malaya and Sumatra.
Habits: Peaceful and very shy. Better kept by themselves.
Water Conditions: Very soft, slightly acid water. Temperature should never drop below 76°, and should be around 82°.
Size: 2 inches, usually a bit smaller.
Food Requirements: Live foods should be fed at all times. This fish shows little interest in dried or frozen foods.
Color Variations: Sides chocolate brown, with yellowish mottled markings on the sides. Dorsal and anal fins streaked and dotted with dark brown.

This little beauty has always had the reputation of being delicate, but will do very well if the proper conditions are provided. A prime requisite for this species is an adequate supply of heat. They come from a hot climate, where they inhabit slowly-flowing streams and ponds where they do not stray far from the surface, which makes this requirement fairly obvious. There has long been a controversy as to how this fish spawns, and some authorities still claim that it builds a bubble-nest of sorts like most of the other Gouramis, but most are agreed at this time that it is a mouthbreeding species. It was even thought for a time that only males were exported, to make the hobbyist dependent on wild stock for his supply. Sexes are very difficult to distinguish, the males having a deeper anal fin and a little more color. The fact is that these fish have been known to aquarists for 54 years, and in all this time there have been only a few reports of spawnings, and many of these conflicted. One thing we can be sure of is that even if they are spawned successfully, they will not be very prolific, because even in their native waters they are not very common.

F-562.00

STEATOCRANUS CASUARIUS (Poll)/*Lionhead Cichlid*

Range: Stanley Pool, Belgian Congo.
Habits: Fairly peaceful for a Cichlid.
Water Conditions: Should have hard, alkaline water. Temperature 75 to 82°F.
Size: About 4 inches.
Food Requirements: Will rarely accept dry foods, although some frozen foods, particularly frozen adult brine shrimp, are taken.
Color Variations: Dark gray, with darker bands on sides. Eye shows luminescent green.

This fish has one characteristic which makes it noteworthy and without which it would have to be considered as just any drab bottom-dwelling African Cichlid. The characteristic is this: males of the species develop a large bump on the head. This protuberance gives the fish an odd appearance, and hobbyists viewing *Steatocranus* for the first time are likely to believe that it is the victim of a cancerous growth, but such is not the case, for the bump is a normal physical development and causes the male *Steatocranus* neither pain nor difficulty. Other Cichlids develop a cranial protuberance with age, but in no other case is the bump developed to such a prominent degree. The Lionhead Cichlid breeds by laying its adhesive eggs in a cave-like structure, and the male stands guard and takes care of them while they are hatching. After the eggs hatch both parents assume responsibility for their offspring, and they make things a little easier for the fry by providing them with regurgitated foods. When the young venture from their cave to depressions which are dug in the gravel by the male, the female hovers over them in an attitude of vigilance and attacks anything that may venture near. This species grows quickly.

Photo by Dr. Herbert R. Axelrod.

*STERNARCHUS ALBIFRONS (Linneaus)/*Black Ghost*

Range: Amazon River and Surinam.

Habits: A peaceful, friendly fish.

Water Conditions: Soft, slightly acid water best, but this is not too important, as variations in water composition are taken in stride.

Size: Up to 1½ feet.

Food Requirements: Not a fussy eater; will take dry, frozen and live foods. *Tubifex* eagerly accepted.

Color Variations: Body jet black, with white stripe on back between head and dorsal fin, and two white bands at tail end of body.

This is altogether a weird fish, so odd that it has a genus all to itself, and it even shares a whole family with only one other fish, the equally odd *Sternarchella schotti* of central Brazil. Their family, the Sternarchidae, is separated from the other South American Knifefishes in that its members possess both a dorsal and a caudal fin, although the dorsal is just a worm-like extension and the caudal is so small as to be almost indistinguishable. *Sternarchus albifrons* is different from the Knifefishes in another way, too; it is a completely peaceful fish and will not disturb others. What's more, it can be tamed and accustomed to taking food directly from the hand of its owner, like some of the larger Cichlids. In a fish as large as *Sternarchus*, this can be a very impressive sight. This, coupled with the fish's very prepossessing appearance, makes the Black Ghost a distinctive attraction, well worth the high price that is asked for the specimens that are occasionally available. Some of the South American Indians, no doubt themselves impressed with the fish's appearance, have endowed *Sternarchus* with a spiritual quality. They believe that the ghosts of the departed take up residence in *Sternarchus*, and they refuse to molest it.

*The currently acceptable scientific name of this fish is *Apteronotus albifrons*.

STONIELLA LEOPARDUS (Fowler)/*Orange-Trim Sucker Catfish*

Range: British Guiana.
Habits: Peaceful with other species, but sometimes quarrelsome with other plecostomus-type Catfishes.
Water Conditions: Soft, slightly acid water should be used if possible, but the fish can take variations from this if not too great.
Size: Up to 6 inches.
Food Requirements: Will take prepared foods from the bottom, but the biggest part of the diet consists of algae scraped from rocks, leaves, and the sides of the aquarium.
Color Variations: Body blue-black, with large round spots on fins. Upper edge of dorsal and upper and lower lobes of caudal fin edged in orange.

This fish, along with some other Sucker Catfishes, was one of the chief aquarium importations of 1961. The fish were brought into the country by Paramount Aquarium, and even though the firm had come back from its collecting expedition with quite a few specimens of each species, they soon had to make plans to look for more, because all of these Catfish were eagerly snapped up by dealers throughout the country. *Stoniella leopardus* is the best looking Catfish to come into the country in a long time, despite the fact that recent years have seen some really attractive new species introduced. One of the main features of the appearance of this fish, besides the touch of color which is such a welcome relief in a type of fish which usually has no color at all, is the magnificent high dorsal fin. This fin is made even more attractive by the large, irregularly scattered spots. *Stoniella leopardus* has been spawned at least once in this country, but the spawning was accidental. The breeding was not observed, but young fish were raised. It would indeed be a lucky thing for hobbyists if *Stoniella*, which is so far the prettiest of The Sucker Cats, is also easiest to breed.

F-565.00

SYMPHYSODON AEQUIFASCIATA AEQUIFASCIATA (Pellegrin)
Green Discus

Range: Brazil (Lago Teffe).

Habits: Peaceful for a Cichlid.

Water Conditions: Should have soft, slightly acid water. In extremely hard, alkaline water, this species will waste away. Temperature 75 to 83°F.

Size: 6 inches.

Food Requirements: Dry foods not relished; frozen beef heart willingly accepted, as are live foods, but this fish should not be fed on any one food exclusively, as it needs variety.

Color Variations: Body color a dark brownish-green, with nine vertical bars which vary in intensity. Irregular blue streaks on body.

Discus fishes of any species have always been held in high regard by aquarists, because they are beautiful. Also, these fish have an attraction for another reason: Discus specimens always sell for a good price, and many hobbyists have attempted to set up prospective pairs in hopes of getting them to spawn, thus providing themselves with a steady source of income. The trouble is that even those persons who have succeeded in spawning the fish and raising some young have not been able to duplicate their accomplishments on a recurrent basis, and it turns out that their "steady" source of income is not so steady after all. All of the known Discus varieties follow the same breeding pattern.

SYMPHYSODON AEQUIFASCIATA AXELRODI (Schultz)
Brown Discus

Range: Brazil.
Habits: Peaceful for a Cichlid.
Water Conditions: Soft, acid water best.
Size: About 5 inches.
Food Requirements: Takes all live foods and some frozen foods (beef heart, liver, bloodworms); does not accept any dried food except pelletized brine shrimp.
Color Variations: Body color varies from light to dark brown; nine vertical bars cross body and head; fins yellowish.

The Brown Discus, although less colorful than *Symphysodon aequifasciata aequifasciata* and *Symphysodon aequifasciata haraldi*, is still a pretty fish and one much in demand. The Brown Discus differs considerably from *Symphysodon discus*, even though it wasn't classified as a new subspecies until 1960. Like its relatives, *S. a. axelrodi* feeds its young from a thick coating of slime which forms on the body at spawning time.

SYMPHYSODON AEQUIFASCIATA HARALDI (Schultz)
Blue Discus

Range: Rio Negro and its tributaries.
Habits: Very peaceful; requires a large and well-planted aquarium.
Water Conditions: Soft, slightly acid water preferred. Temperature 75 to 85°.
Size: Up to 8 inches; mature at about half that size.
Food Requirements: White worms, mature brine shrimp and chopped beef heart.

Considered by many to be the most beautiful of the *Symphysodon* species, the Blue Discus possesses the additional advantage of being the hardiest fish in this specialized group. It breeds in the same way as its relatives, and the parents get along very well together. One of the things that must be done to maintain any Discus species in good health is to make many partial changes of water. Two of the world's most successful Discus breeders make it an absolutely hard and fast rule to change at least one-third of the water in their Discus tanks each week. This is important, as it stimulates the fish to better feeding and consequently better growth, and it is also important in that it builds up the fish's resistance to some of the more troublesome Discus diseases. Many hobbyists who have kept Discus at one time or another complain that no matter how much care they give their fish the Discus eventually begin to turn black, waste away and die. One of the best preventives to avoid this is to make frequent partial changes of water.

F-568.00

SYMPHYSODON DISCUS (Heckel) / *Red Discus* , *Pompadour*

Range: Brazil.
Habits: Peaceful for a Cichlid.
Water Conditions: Soft, acid water desirable. This species is especially susceptible to abrupt changes in water composition.
Size: About 6 inches.
Food Requirements: Does best on live foods, but worms should not be fed too often.

When the *Pterophyllum scalare,* and later *Pterophyllum eimekei* were introduced, hobbyists were quick to dub them "King of the Aquarium Fishes." This was quickly forgotten when the Discus first made their appearance around 1932, and the title went to these regal newcomers. Their proud bearing, their wonderful colors and their high price made them seem worthy of the title, and they still are. Although they are not exactly a rarity in their native waters, shipping them was quite a problem in the old days. Small ones were not easily found or caught, and the big ones had to have a shipping can all to themselves. Breeders had difficulty in getting them to spawn, and the fish remained very scarce and high-priced. Nowadays air transport has made their shipping faster, and new methods of packing them have cut down the weight problem. In addition, breeders are making more and more tank-raised fish available all the time, and the price has dropped greatly. They breed exactly like the Angelfish, but the young should be left with the parents.

A closeup of the brood pouch of a male *Syngnathus spicifer*; many of the eggs have already hatched.

Four newly hatched Freshwater Pipefish fry. The fry refuse to eat after being released from the pouch. Perhaps they might be carried successfully through the first few days of their free-swimming life if they are fed on the organisms present in green water.

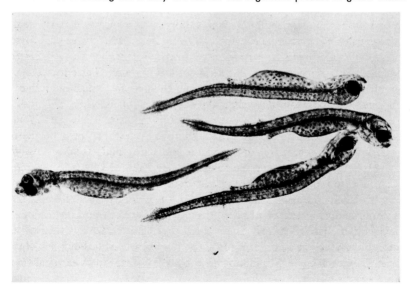

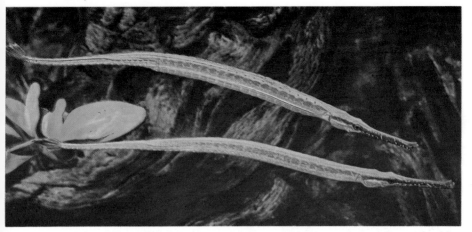

SYNGNATHUS SPICIFER/*Freshwater Pipefish*

Range: Ceylon.

Habits: Peaceful with any fish that cannot be swallowed.

Water Conditions: Should have brackish water, although the salt can vary in concentration from light to heavy. Tank should not be too heavily aerated. Temperature 75 to 85°F.

Size: About 5 inches.

Food Requirements: In the home aquarium, this fish will accept only newborn livebearers.

Color Variations: General body color golden brown. Male shows thin red line along sides.

The Freshwater Pipefish is an extremely interesting novelty which, although difficult to keep, rewards its owners with many hours of fascinating viewing. Like its saltwater relative, the Seahorse, *Syngnathus spicifer* is covered with rows of bony plates which encase the fish in a suit of armor. The odd, trumpet like mouth is very small at its opening, and the fish has difficulty in eating anything that is not small enough to be ingested whole. This complicates matters for the hobbyist who wants to keep this fish, and it has been found that *Syngnathus* specimens kept in aquariums will accept nothing but newborn livebearers, which it is quite expert at stalking and catching, despite their lack of speed. However, even some baby livebearers are too big for *Syngnathus* to swallow. In its reproductive methods the Freshwater Pipefish is very odd, for the female lays her eggs in a pouch formed by folds in the abdomen of the male; at a temperature of about 80°, the eggs hatch in a day and a half to two days. The newly hatched fry are small, and they move through the water in short, jerky motions. Unfortunately, although all sorts of small living foods are offered to the young, they refuse to eat, and they die of starvation.

Photo by Aaron Norman.

SYNODONTIS ANGELICUS (Schilthuis)/*Polka-Dot African Catfish*

Range: Tropical West Africa.
Habits: Peaceful with other fishes, and will not uproot plants.
Water Conditions: Medium-soft, slightly acid to neutral water. Tank should be heavily planted and provided with rock grottoes in which the fish may hide. Temperature 72 to 85°F.
Size: 8 inches.
Food Requirements: Will take prepared and frozen foods; likes algae and worms.
Color Variations: Bluish-black body with many yellowish-white spots on sides. Tail area has five white vertical stripes.

There is a very good reason for the scarcity of this fish on the aquarium market: it is extremely rare in its home waters in the Congo, and fish exporters have a great deal of difficulty in catching them, so the price of the few specimens which are made available remains prohibitively high. It is a nocturnal fish which hides in the mud during the day and comes out to feed only at night, the way many other Mochokid Catfishes do. But *Synodontis angelicus* seems to have a very distinct choice as to the area in which it will do its feeding; for some reason, the fish is attracted to places in which there is a lot of iron. They will congregate around rusty metal submerged in the water, and it almost seems as if they actually graze on the surface of the metal! There are no recorded spawnings of *Synodontis angelicus*, but the fish might spawn like the Upside-Down Catfish, *Synodontis nigriventris*, which lays its eggs in caves or similar shelters and does not bother its young, perhaps even gives them protection. If someone is ever able to breed *S. angelicus* in quantity it will be a noteworthy achievement of definite value to the aquarium hobby in general.

F-572.00

Synodontis decorus, another African Catfish which occasionally swims upside down. This specimen was collected in the Congo by Dr. Herbert R. Axelrod.

A spotted African Catfish. Note the branched lower barbels, which resemble plant roots.

F-573.00

SYNODONTIS NIGRIVENTRIS (David)/*Upside-down Catfish*

Range: Central West Africa, the Congo Basin and tributaries.
Habits: Peaceful, prefers to remain hidden in the darker regions of the aquarium and come out for food after dark.
Water Conditions: Soft, slightly acid water with little or no salt content. Temperatures should range between 76 and 80°.
Size: Females up to 3¾ inches, males a little smaller.
Food Requirements: Enjoys just about all kinds of foods; will come to the surface for dried food and grub in the bottom for worms.
Color Variations: Yellowish brown body with dark marbled markings. Fins have dark spots.

Here we have one of the real oddities of the fish world: a fish which prefers to swim upside-down! Other members of the genus *Synodontis* are seen to do this occasionally, but this fellow does it most of the time. Mother Nature has even seen fit to bow to his whim, and has reversed his coloration. Most fish are darker on the back, and lighter on the belly. This makes their color blend in with the dark bottom when viewed from above by a bird, and when a larger fish or other enemy looks up at them, the light belly blends in with the glare from the surface. This fish has a lighter back and a dark belly, which would give him the benefits of camouflage when swimming upside down. An accidental spawning was reported by a Swedish aquarist. His theory was that *Synodontis nigriventris* made use of their inverted position to facilitate the capture of mosquito larvae at the surface, and fed them great quantities of these. As he was about to move them, he placed them temporarily in a 3-gallon aquarium, in which he inverted a flowerpot with a notch broken out for their refuge. When he found youngsters, the fish had been in this tank for 11 days.

TANICHTHYS ALBONUBES (Lin)
White Clouds or White Cloud Mountain Fish

Range: Small streams in the vicinity of White Cloud Mountain in Canton, China.
Habits: Peaceful in the community tank. Very active, and prefers to swim in schools.
Water Conditions: Not critical. Best kept at relatively low temperatures, 65 to 70°.
Size: 1½ inches.
Food Requirements: Will eat dried as well as live foods. When it is desired to spawn them, live foods should be given.
Color Variations: Back greenish. Greenish gold stripe on the upper half of the sides, with a brown to reddish stripe below. Red spot in tail.

This little fish has the distinction of being one of the easiest aquarium fishes to spawn. A pair placed together in a well-planted aquarium and well fed with live foods, preferably *Daphnia*, will soon produce fry, and if well fed they show little tendency to eat them. When young, the green stripe glows so bright that they are often mistaken for small Neon Tetras. It must be remembered that this is not exactly a tropical species, and comes from comparatively cool mountain streams which are fairly well oxygenated; as a result, they would be very uncomfortable in a warm, crowded community tank. This fish has an interesting history. The first specimens were found by a Chinese scoutmaster named Tan Kam Fei, who gave them to the Director of a fisheries experimental station for identification. This man, Lin Shu-Yen, gave them their name, *Tanichthys* (Tan's fish) *albonubes* (White Cloud). This was in 1932, but aquarists did not get to see the fish until about 1938, at which time it became known as "the poor man's Neon Tetra." Since then the status has reversed itself and so many Neon Tetras have come in that the price is lower than that of the White Clouds.

F-575.00

These are Meteor Minnows, a long-finned development of the common White Cloud, *Tanichthys albonubes*. This strain was developed in Canada by Mr. Edward Sollory from regular White Cloud parents. In order to keep his strain pure after the first long-finned youngsters had shown up in his tanks, Mr. Sollory culled ruthlessly, and he was able to get enough young to stock a number of petshops, but the strain is no longer available today.

TELEOGRAMMA BRICHARDI (Poll)/*Brichard's African Dwarf Cichlid*

Range: Congo.

Habits: Playful, but sometimes quarrelsome with members of its own species.

Water Conditions: Medium-soft, slightly acid water best. Tank should have plenty of rocks and caves to make the fish feel at home. Temperature 70 to 80°F.

Size: About 4 inches.

Food Requirements: Live foods much preferred, although some frozen foods are accepted.

Color Variations: Over-all body color light to dark brown, with specks of blue and green.

Judging by the body shape of *Teleogramma brichardi*, an experienced aquarist will immediately recognize that this is a fish that comes from fairly rapidly flowing waters, for its streamlined contours are designed to make things easy for the fish in its efforts to move from one place to another; a body shape like this is an asset to a fish that has to fight the pull of swift water. Also, the fins are very large in comparison to the mass of the body, and extra propulsive force is thus gained. All of this points to one almost inescapable conclusion on the part of the hobbyist: if it is a fish used to moving water, won't it be uncomfortable in a tank? And, since moving water is usually very high in oxygen, won't it make special demands concerning aeration? Luckily, in the case of *Teleogramma brichardi*, the answer is no, for the species is not extraordinarily difficult to keep. These fish , named after the famous African collector Pierre Brichard, are not highly colorful, but they are interesting. In a tank they prove to be among the most playful of fishes; one of their favorite games a modification of the children's game of "King of the Mountain," whereby one fish, usually a male, lies atop a rock while the others try to knock him off.

Photo by Dr. Herbert R. Axelrod.

TELMATHERINA LADIGESI (Ahl) *Celebes Rainbow Fish*

Range: Celebes.

Habits: Peaceful, may be combined with other fishes with similar requirements.

Water Conditions: Water should have a slight addition of salt, a teaspoonful per gallon. Tank should be sunny, temperature 76° to 80°.

Size: 3 inches.

Food Requirements: Will take dried foods, but should have frequent supplements of living foods.

Color Variations: Body has a glassy iridescence; fins are lemon yellow, first dorsal and anal rays of the males are black.

This beautiful fish has a reputation which it does not fully deserve. Many who have kept and had trouble with it claim it is delicate, but the only thing which should be critized is the fact that they did not give it the proper care. There are two things it does require: a little salt in the water, about a teaspoonful per gallon, and a proper amount of heat. 78° suits them fine. Even before they attain their full size and coloration, males may be distinguished by the more pointed body cavity as seen through the transparent sides with a light behind them. When fully grown, of course, there can be no doubt as to which are the males. One look at the gorgeous yellow dorsal and anal fins with the long filaments and black first rays is sufficient. One other thing this beauty is particularly sensitive to is a great deal of moving around. Once they have adapted themselves to the conditions in a tank, they should then be left alone. They are by nature a bit timid, and a tank where they are kept should have a sufficiency of plant life in which they can hide if any real or imagined danger is present. Eggs are laid in bushy plants and hatch in two days.

Photo by Dr. Herbert R. Axelrod.

TETRAODON CUTCUTIA (Hamilton-Buchanan)/*Malayan Puffer*

Range: Malaya and parts of India, in fresh and brackish waters.
Habits: Quarrelsome toward other fishes and even among themselves. Should have
their own tank.
Water Conditions: Hard, alkaline water with salt added, 1 teaspoonful per gallon.
Temperature 75 to 80°F.
Size: To 6 inches.
Food Requirements: Live foods in the larger sizes, or chopped-up pieces of table
shrimp. Crushed snails are a delicacy.
Color Variations: Back dark green, sides yellowish, tail dirty white. White line
connects the eyes. Dark ocellated spot before dorsal and on each side.

The Puffers are an odd group of fishes which inhabit the fresh, brackish and
even the marine waters in many parts of the world. They have the odd
capability of being able to inflate themselves with water until their bodies
swell up to many times their size, and a fish which takes one into its mouth
often finds that he cannot swallow it. This one comes mostly from brackish
waters and a small amount of salt is advisable (1 teaspoonful per gallon).
Unfortunately they are very quarrelsome even among themselves and should
never be kept with other fishes. They are useful in the aquarium because of
their love for snails, and will depopulate a snail-ridden tank in short order.
Their rabbit-shaped teeth are useful in crushing the shells and biting the
tough flesh. The Puffers soon lose their shyness and come begging for food
to the surface whenever the tank is approached. Spawning the Puffers is not
the easiest thing in the world, but it has been done repeatedly. The females
are easily distinguished by their larger size and lighter colors. Strangely
enough this species has no ventral fins. The Malayan Puffer has been known
to the aquarium hobby since 1903.

F-579.00

Tetraodon schoutedeni is the most peaceful of the Puffers, and may be kept with some of the other fishes without bloodshed. Unfortunately they sometimes nibble plants.

Tetraodon somphongsi, below, can quickly make its colors lighter or darker to fit in with its background.

THAYERIA OBLIQUA (Eigenmann) *Penguin*

Range: Middle Amazon region.

Habits: Peaceful; may be kept in the community aquarium. Active swimmers.

Water Conditions: Water should be soft and slightly acid. Best temperature 76° to 78°.

Size: 3 inches.

Food Requirements: Will take dried foods, but these should be alternated frequently with live foods.

Color Variations: Body brownish to dark green on the back, silvery white below. Dark horizontal stripe extends from the gill-plate to lower tip of tail.

Our British friends seem to have been the first to dub these fish "Penguins," and with the help of a little imagination it can be seen why. First of all there is the sharp black and white contrast between the belly and the dark horizontal stripe, and then there is the way the fish carries itself, with its head erect and sort of "standing on its tail." Although the Penguin has been known to science since specimens were collected in 1865 by the Thayer Expedition (which was led by Louis Agassiz), fish hobbyists did not get to see them until 1935. When the first specimens to be shipped alive reached this country they were really a different species. Sexes are difficult to distinguish, practically impossible in immature fish. When maturity is reached, the heavier bodies of the egg-laden females identify them easily. Spawning takes place in bushy plants, and the eggs are brown in color. A prolific species, there may be as many as 1,000 eggs laid at a single spawning. It has been found advisable, when spawning is over, to draw off part of the water and replace it with fresh water. Hatching takes place in as little as 12 hours, and when they begin to swim, the fry should get very fine foods.

In *Thayeria boehlki*, the black line runs right up to the gill covers.

Photo by Dr. Shih-chieh Shen.

THERAPON JARBUA (Forskal) *Jarbua, Target Fish*

Range: Red Sea, Eastern Coast of Africa, Indian Ocean, Malay Archipelago, North Coast of Australia. Plentiful in the mouth of the Ganges River.

Habits: Peaceful; although it is a salt-water species, it can be acclimated to completely fresh water.

Water Conditions: If kept in fresh water, it should have some salt added, about a teaspoonful to the gallon. Tank should be shaded.

Size: 3 inches. Wild specimens up to 15 inches.

Food Requirements: Prefers live foods of all kinds; a greedy eater which should be fed at least twice daily.

Color Variations: Body yellowish. Three stripes which bend upward, giving the appearance of concentric circles when viewed from above.

Usually the salt-water fish species are not equipped to exist in totally fresh water, but this is one of the exceptions. It is common enough to be an important item of food for the natives where it occurs, and is eaten with rice and curry. This will come as a shock to those aquarists who have had to pay rather high prices for this very pretty fish. This species, once it has accustomed itself to life and conditions in a tank, should be moved as little as possible and when it is moved, care must be taken that the water in its new quarters is of the same characteristics as that from where it came. It is best to give it a well-shaded aquarium, as it will always shun any light coming in. Care must also be taken when handling it; when frightened it spreads out its gill-plates, which carry some sharp spines and can inflict a painful wound. There is a recorded spawning of this fish which took place in Ceylon. Brackish water was used, and the temperature was 86°. The eggs were laid Cichlid-fashion on a rock, and guarded by the male. Hatching took place in 24 hours.

* **THORACOCHARAX MACULATUS** (Steindachner)/*Spotted Hatchetfish*

Range: Panama to Western Colombia.
Habits: Peaceful surface fishes which may be combined with other non-aggressive fishes in the community aquarium.
Water Conditions: Clean, fairly soft water, temperatures 75° to 78°. Tank should be well planted, but the water surface should be mostly clear.
Size: To 3½ inches, mostly smaller.
Food Requirements: Difficult to feed; should get live food which remains at or near the surface.
Color Variations: Sides bluish silvery with rows of vertical dark spots. Females have a deeper body with less distinct colors.

There are quite a few kinds of Hatchetfishes known to science, and they are all very similar in many ways: they are surface fishes, they all have a keeled belly and long, wing-like pectoral fins with which they can skim along the surface with considerable speed, and in the aquarium they often prove a little difficult to keep and very difficult to spawn. Probably the main reason for this is that the aquarist is hard put to duplicate exactly the living conditions of this very attractive fish. Their main article of diet, as can be seen by the shape of the mouth, is insect life which swims at the surface or flies just above it. Mosquitoes are a perfect example of this sort of life. Their larval and pupal stages are spent in the water, where they must make frequent trips to the surface for air. The adult winged form flies close to the water when laying eggs. However, feeding mosquito larvae in the home aquarium has its attendant difficulties, and some hobbyists have used wingless fruit-flies (*Drosophila*) with success, but there are still no records of the Spotted Hatchetfish being spawned in captivity.

*This fish is now known as *Gasteropelecus maculatus*.

F-584.00

Photo by Harald Schultz.

THORACOCHARAX STELLATUS (Kner)/*Silver Hatchetfish*

Range: Amazon, Paraguay, Orinoco Basin to Venezuela.

Habits: An extremely peaceful surface fish. A good jumper, its tanks should be covered.

Water Conditions: Soft, slightly acid water a necessity. This fish dies easily if maintained in hard, alkaline water.

Size: 3 inches.

Food Requirements: Floating foods of all kinds taken, provided they can be swallowed.

Color Variations: A plain silvery fish.

This Hatchetfish is occasionally offered for sale, but it is rarely identified under its proper name, as it is usually sold just as "a Hatchetfish," with no attempt at placing the species. One reason for the lackadaisical attitude shown by both dealers and hobbyists when confronted with the many different Hatchetfishes is that these fishes are almost never bred in captivity; since almost no attempt is made to breed them, no one seems to bother to break up shipments of Hatchetfishes into species, which would of course be necessary if they were to be bred. None of the Hatchetfishes could be considered as a really hardy fish, and they are especially susceptible to some of the more common aquarium diseases, such as Ich. Perhaps this is because they are often neglected when kept in a community tank. Unless precautions are taken to see to it that the Hatchetfishes are fed in accordance with their specific requirements, that is, that food is made available to them at the top of the water, they will soon decline. *Thoracocharax stellatus* should have a large roomy tank for themselves, because they are timid and sometimes hurt by more aggressive tankmates.

Tilapia rendalli, an African mouthbrooder.

The large mouth of *Sarotherodon mossambicus* is adapted for brooding the young. This species was formerly known as *Tilapia mossambica*. Photo by Dr. Herbert R. Axelrod.

Photo by DR. R.J. Goldstein.

TILAPIA THOLLONI (Sauvage)/*Thollon's Tilapia*

Range: Tropical West Africa from Congo to Cameroon.

Habits: Mature pairs should be kept by themselves; even young males are apt to battle fiercely.

Water Conditions: Tank should be provided with many possibilities for the female to hide. Plants are eaten. Temperatures 76° to 80°.

Size: To 7 inches, usually smaller.

Food Requirements: In addition to the usual live foods, lettuce leaves are also relished and should be fed frequently.

Color Variations: Sides green, belly yellow. There are two rows of oblong spots on the sides, which are sometimes connected.

Tilapia tholloni holds a unique position in the *Tilapia* genus, because of its breeding habits. The others are mouthbreeders, but this one breeds like many of the other Cichlids. It also has the distinction of being more handsomely colored than most of the others of the genus. Spawning them is simplicity itself: a well-fed pair is placed in a good-sized tank (20 gallons or more). The male chooses a spawning site, where he digs a hole in the bottom gravel. When things are prepared to his satisfaction, he begins to try luring and coaxing his mate to the hole. She soon gets the idea, and a large number of eggs are laid in the gravel. Both parents take care of the eggs and fry, which hatch in 3 to 5 days. A good first food for the fry is newly-hatched brine shrimp, and they grow rapidly. As they grow the male constantly digs new holes for them, and the appearance of the aquarium is constantly being changed. It will be found that as they approach maturity the males will be more and more inclined to become scrappy. Such males should be separated to prevent bloodshed, and finding room for them all may easily become a problem. This species is seldom imported.

F-587.00

Photo by Dr. Herbert R. Axelrod.

TOXOTES JACULATOR (Pallas)/*Archer Fish*

Range: India, Burma, Malaya, Philippines, East Indies, Thailand.

Habits: Usually peaceful, but individual specimens can be aggressive. Not a good community fish unless kept with other fishes liking slightly brackish water.

Water Conditions: Water should be slightly salty. Tank should be large. Temperature 74 to 85°F.

Size: Over half a foot, but always sold at a much smaller size.

Food Requirements: Best food is live insects which the fish captures for itself, but it will accept meaty substitutes. Some hobbyists claim that it will accept dry food, but this depends on the individual fish.

Color Variations: A silvery fish with yellow shadings. Six heavy black bands on the sides, one running through the eye.

One of the wonders of the aquatic world, the Archer Fish, is always in demand, for the fish's peculiar method of catching food evokes wonder in everyone who is privileged to watch it. *Toxotes* is equipped with a strange mouth structure which enables the fish to expel pellets of water at resting insects which come within range; it sometimes even shoots at flying insects, and it can occasionally be coaxed into shooting at pieces of meat suspended within its range of vision. To do this with any degree of accuracy, of course, the Archer Fish must be able to allow for the refractive property of the water itself, and this it has learned to do. *Toxotes* is decidedly a surface fish which spends little time at the bottom of the aquarium, but it has been noted that specimens that have been maintained in a tank for a long time without ever having been given a chance to use their remarkable skill will spend less time at the surface. The actual force with which the water pellets are expelled is surprising and bears testament to the pressure which is built up in the mouth preparatory to expulsion. It is said that at close range the drops have enough force behind them to cause a stinging sensation to uncovered human skin.

F-588.00

Photo by R. Zukal.

TRICHOGASTER LEERI (Bleeker)
Pearl Gourami, Leeri, Mosaic Gourami

Range: Thailand, Malayan Peninsula, Penang, Sumatra and Borneo.
Habits: Peaceful, may be kept in any community aquarium, if not too small. Inclined to be a bit shy.
Water Conditions: Not critical, but water should be rather warm, about 78°. A full-grown pair should be kept in a good-sized tank, at least 15 gallons.
Size: 4 inches.
Food Requirements: Will eat any kind of dried foods, but should also get live foods occasionally.
Color Variations: Body silvery, covered with reticulated markings. Dark horizontal line from snout to caudal base, male's belly deep yellow to orange.

This is the king of all the Gouramis. Its regal bearing, coupled with the lovely violet sheen of its sides makes it a very desirable fish to see. The males have longer, more pointed dorsal fins, and at mating time the belly color is a deep orange. The only thing that could possibly be said in their disfavor is that they are apt to be shy and timid. This might result in their not getting the full amount of food that they require if kept with a lot of boisterous, greedy tankmates. Their tank should be roomy and well planted, and if possible it should be in a place which is away from slamming doors and street noises. A healthy pair can easily be induced to spawn in such a tank. The driving which takes place before spawning is not as wild as with the other Gouramis; they always seem to maintain themselves with a great deal of dignity. The bubble-nest is apt to be large, and the number of eggs may be very high. At this time especially it is important to avoid frightening them. Usually the female may be left with the male while the eggs are being guarded.

F-589.00

TRICHOGASTER MICROLEPIS (Guenther)/*Moonbeam Gourami*

Range: Thailand.
Habits: A fairly peaceful fish, but large specimens tend to be bullies, at least with others of their species.
Water Conditions: Soft, slightly acid water best, but this is not of great importance. Temperature 75 to 85°F.
Size: Up to 6 inches.
Food Requirements: Takes prepared, frozen, and live foods.
Color Variations: Over-all body color silvery, with bluish sheen. Males have orange ventrals.

The Moonbeam Gourami is a recent import, although it is certainly not new to science. They are very similar in their requirements to the Pearl Gourami, except that they are less subject to the fungus which often plagues *T. leeri*, and they don't have to be as big (comparatively) before they begin to breed. The male builds a large bubblenest which is not very high in form; not much vegetable matter is woven into this nest, and the bubbles are allowed to float rather freely. During spawning, the color of the thread-like ventral fins becomes intensified, changing for a short time from orange to red. For best results in breeding, the water depth in the breeding tank should be low, and floating plants should be present to give the fish a feeling of security. The female should also be provided with a thicket of fine-leaved plants into which she may flee if the male shows too much aggressiveness, but, fortunately for her, the male *T. microlepis* is not a real wife-beater. The fry, which hatch quickly at a temperature of 80°, are very tiny. As with other Anabantid fry, they are very delicate for the first few weeks of their lives.

F-590.00

Photo by Dr. Herbert R. Axelrod

TRICHOGASTER PECTORALIS (Regan)/*Snakeskin Gourami*

Range: South Vietnam, Malayan Peninsula.
Habits: Peaceful and entirely harmless to other fishes, even young ones.
Water Conditions: Soft, slightly acid water. Temperature 75 to 80°F.
Size: To 10 inches in their home waters. Mature at 4 inches.
Food Requirements: Not choosy as to food; dry food accepted as well as frozen and live foods.
Color Variations: Olive green to grayish green sides with a number of diagonal yellow to gold bars. Dark horizontal line from snout to tail.

Even though it grows to a good size, the Snakeskin Gourami cannot be described as anything but peaceful. The colors are very attractive and it is an asset to any group of the larger fishes. It is an easy fish to maintain and will accept any food offered. At 3 to 4 inches maturity is attained and if allowed to spawn, it will be found that both parent fish will get along harmoniously, which is not the case with many other Labyrinth Fishes. The male builds a large bubblenest and if she is of good size the female will be found to be extraordinarily productive. Another thing in their favor is that the parent fish will never eat their young. They cannot even be coaxed to eat the young of other fishes, or snails. This gives the hobbyist the opportunity of raising a family of Snakeskins without ever having to remove their parents, as long as the tank is large enough to accommodate all of them. The youngsters can be raised easily by feeding progressively larger sizes of dried foods, beginning with the finest sizes and as the fish grow giving them coarser sizes. Naturally an occasional feeding with live foods such as newly hatched brine shrimp is a welcome change in the diet.

TRICHOGASTER TRICHOPTERUS
Blue Gourami

Range: Sumatra.
Habits: Peaceful in a community tank with fishes which are not too small.
Water Conditions: Not critical, but slightly acid, soft water is best. Temperature 76 to 82°F.
Size: To 6 inches.
Food Requirements: Takes any food, dried as well as live or frozen.

The Blue Gourami from Sumatra has become so popular that it has backed the Three-Spot Gourami right out of the picture, so much so that only the real "old-timers" still know what a Three-Spot looks like. It is a very attractive fish, and by far the most available. A pair can almost always be counted on to spawn in a tank which is to their liking, that is to say, one which has a fair amount of plants, a good-sized surface and enough heat. About 80° is a good spawning temperature, and one does not need to worry about there being too much depth as one does with the Fighting Fish. A large bubblenest is built, usually in a corner. Here the male coaxes the female until she gets the idea and permits herself to let him wrap his body around hers. Many works insist that the eggs are squeezed from her in this process, but the pressure, if any, is very light. If she is well filled a spawning may be huge, 700 to 800 eggs. Although she is seldom damaged by the male, it is still advisable to remove the female after she has finished with her egg-laying chores. The male takes good care of his babies, but should be taken out when they are free-swimming.

In some cases intensive breeding has resulted in the development of Gouramis which show the spots much less clearly than their forebears.

This is the Cosby Gourami, the most popular of the variations of the original Blue Gourami.

TRIGONECTES STRIGABUNDUS (Myers)/*Brazilian False Panchax*

Range: Rio Tocantins, Brazil.
Habits: Peaceful with fishes it cannot swallow.
Water Conditions: Soft, slightly acid water. Temperature 75 to 80°F.
Size: To 2½ inches.
Food Requirements: Live foods of all kinds; can be trained to take frozen foods.
Color Variations: Bluish green with series of closely-spaced dots forming stripes on the body and fins.

At first glance, if one did not know that the fish came from South America, one would be led to believe that this handsome fish is a species of *Aplocheilus* from the East Indies. The long, pointed dorsal fin and filamentous rays of the male's ventral fins certainly make it look like a "Panchax" of some sort or other, but the fish comes from South America and is closely related to the well-known *Rivulus* species. This fish comes from the Rio Tocantins in Brazil, where it was found by our good friend Harald Schultz. The sexes are unmistakable: note that the female, the upper fish, lacks the black chin sported by the male and has shorter, more rounded fins. When we had several pairs of these fish in our office we were fortunate to have them spawn for us. The female expelled about a dozen eggs which were fertilized by the male and hung from her vent for quite a time by a thread until they were brushed off and hung from a plant. Neither time nor space permitted further observations, but it is a safe bet that the eggs take up to 2 weeks to hatch. We had no trouble keeping the parents in good shape, so the fry should be easy to raise.

TRIPORTHEUS ELONGATUS (Günther) *Elongated Hatchetfish*

Range: Middle and Lower Amazon, Rio Madeira, Rio Negro, Orinoco, and the Guianas.

Habits: Active and peaceful with other fishes of its own size.

Water Conditions: Not critical; tank should be in a sunny location and permit ample swimming space. Temperature about 76°.

Size: Wild specimens attain a size of about 8 inches.

Food Requirements: Not very fond of dried foods, and should be richly fed with living foods such as *Daphnia* or adult brine shrimp.

Color Variations: Body silvery with large scales. Faint horizontal line. Middle rays of tail are black and elongated beyond the caudal lobes.

This fish has no bright colors, but is an active species which will always remain in the open spaces and will not bother the other tank-mates. Its long pectoral fins and keeled belly identify it as a jumper, and a tank with these in it should always be kept covered, or they are very likely to be found on the floor. This species has long been known to science; Günther identified it in 1864 as *Chalcinus elongatus*, but recently the generic name was reclassified as *Triportheus*. There is an interesting peculiarity of structure which this species shares with some of the African Characins: the middle rays of the caudal fin are elongated and black in color, waving like a pennant far behind the tips of the caudal lobes. If the fish were not such an active swimmer, this elongation would make an irresistible target for other fishes and would often get nipped off. What the purpose of such an ornament might be could be the basis for much conjecture, and we will not attempt to make any guesses. One thing we do know, if this tip does get nipped off, it will quickly regenerate itself. So far, there have been no recorded spawnings, and there are no known external sex differences.

Above and below: these photos illustrate the differences between juvenile and adult specimens of *Triportheus pictus*.

F-596.00

TROPHEUS MOOREI (Boulenger)/*Blunt-headed Cichlid*

Range: Lake Tanganyika, Africa.
Habits: Inhabits rocky bottoms in Lake Tanganyika, and should be provided with some rocks in the aquarium.
Water Conditions: Slightly alkaline, temperature 75° to 78°.
Size: Up to 4 inches, sometimes slightly larger.
Food Requirements: Live foods, mostly tubifex or white worms.
Color Variations: Front of body to the beginning of the dorsal fin dark olive, followed by a light shoulder-spot which is red in the dorsal.

To give the reader an idea of the wealth of fishes in Lake Tanganyika, allow us to point out that there are no less than 134 species of Cichlids alone in this big, deep lake. According to paleontologists, this was one of the few lakes which still held water during the great dry periods of the Miocene and Pleistocene Eras, and the fauna here became more or less segregated. This gives the aquarist a whole new world of fishes which are just becoming available. According to the few sporadic accounts from Germany from breeders who have tried to get this and other species from this region to spawn, there has so far been no success with this species, but one day one of these fish when it was netted to be transferred to another tank surprised its captor by spitting out five huge eggs about ¼ inch in diameter. It is therefore assumed that we are dealing with a mouthbreeding species here, which is a small start. Whether it is the male or the female which carries the eggs was not said. One thing is sure: it would not be possible to pack many more eggs as big as this into this fish's mouth! All in all, it promises to be a really fascinating species.

Photo by Harald Schultz.

UARU AMPHIACANTHOIDES (Heckel)/*Triangle Cichlid*

Range: Amazon Basin and the Guianas.
Habits: Should be as undisturbed as possible, in a large shaded tank. May be kept with Angelfish or Discus.
Water Conditions: Clean water with a number of hiding-places should be provided, also high temperatures, about 80°.
Size: 10 inches.
Food Requirements: Larger live foods, such as full-grown brine shrimp, cut-up earthworms, etc.
Color Variations: Greenish sides, with a large black wedge-shaped area covering the lower rear area of the body.

This large Cichlid is seldom available, and is only to be recommended for the aquarist who has a special interest in Cichlids and large facilities for keeping them. As is often the case, young specimens are so different in color that they are sometimes shipped as a "new species." Then they grow and grow, resulting in this interesting Cichlid. Unlike *Astronotus ocellatus* and some of the other large Cichlids, *Uaru amphiacanthoides* is not easy to maintain. Once they have become accustomed to their surroundings, they should be moved as little as possible and should not get light which is too bright. The author recalls the only time he ever saw living specimens of this attractive fish, in the Nürnberger Tierpark in Germany. Two pairs were kept in a very large tank. They had their mature colors and were the pride and joy of the Herr Direktor. According to the few records of their breeding, they spawn like most other Cichlids. The young are said to be very delicate, and pulling them through the first stages of development is supposed to be very difficult. They were first made available to hobbyists in Germany in the year 1913.

F-598.00

Uaru amphiacanthoides. The fully adult female, about 11 inches in total length, has the typical black markings on the upper caudal peduncle, along the sides and at the base of the pectoral fins. The juvenile, below, about 2 inches in total length, has a completely different coloration. The photo on the facing page shows a 5 inch fish with still another coloration. Photo by Dr. Herbert R. Axelrod of fish from the Rio Negro, Brazil.

XENOCARA DOLICHOPTERA (Kner)/*Bushy-Mouthed Catfish*

Range: Northeastern South America.
Habits: Peaceful; will not harm even the smallest fishes.
Water Conditions: Can take a very wide range of water conditions, as long as abrupt changes are not made.
Size: Up to 5 inches.
Food Requirements: Accepts all foods and is especially fond of algae.
Color Variations: Dark bluish-black, with white spots scattered all over the body. Spots fade on older specimens.

This Armored Catfish is one of the few that has ever been bred in home aquariums. They spawn in cave-like shelters, which may be duplicated in the home aquarium by rock caves or tubular shelters; of the latter, perhaps bamboo tubes are best, as these have been used on many occasions with good success in the breeding of this bewhiskered species. The male, which sometimes spawns with more than one female at a time, cleans off a space on which to deposit the adhesive eggs. The male guards the eggs and fans them vigorously all during their 5 to 7 day incubation period; the fry do not become free-swimming until about four days after they have hatched, but as soon as they are able to swim well they hide themselves within the tank. On chopped *Tubifex* worms and dry food they grow fast, reaching a size of about 1½ inches in less than a month and a half. As can be seen from the photo above, the name "Bushy-Mouth" is well deserved, as both male and female have a large growth of whisker-like appendages growing from the frontal area of the head. This is not at all an unusual characteristic in Catfishes of the family Loricariidae, and many species besides *X. dolichoptera* are so adorned.

F-600.00

XIPHOPHORUS HELLERI (Heckel)/*Swordtail*

Range: Southern Mexico to Guatemala.

Habits: This fish is very variable in temperament. Some specimens show very little aggression towards other fish, while others, especially large males, are out and out bullies.

Water Conditions: Slightly alkaline, medium hard water. An addition of salt is sometimes of benefit, but this is not necessary. Temperature 70 to 80°F.

Size: Wild specimens up to 5 inches. Almost always seen much smaller than this.

Food Requirements: Accepts all regular aquarium foods, but there should be variety.

Color Variations: Swordtails come in many different colors, with many different marking patterns. Red, green, black, albino and intermediate forms are available.

The Swordtail is an extremely popular fish, and one of the prettiest. Easy to keep, easy to breed, colorful, fast-growing, always available . . . the list of the fish's good points could stretch on and on. The male Swordtail is a beautiful fish, and his "sword," which is an extension of the caudal fin, is one of the most striking physical characteristics possessed by any aquarium fish. Unfortunately, many Swordtails of today do not have the same majestic tail of the original Swordtail, but they do have color, and this makes up somewhat for their lack of tail development. One of the prime factors which has served to popularize the Swordtail is the fact that the fish is a livebearer, and thus bred with extreme ease. Even beginners in the aquarium hobby have no great difficulty in sexing and breeding this species, although they do often run into the problem of raising good-size young, something that the beginner is not able to do until he has mastered at least the fundamentals of aquarium management. Large females can give birth to more than 150 young at one time at intervals of about a month, so it is easy to see why this is considered a prolific fish.

F-601.00

These magnificent Swordtails are the famous Simpson Hi-Fins.

This is a marigold twinbar lyretail swordtail female. Photo by Edward C. Taylor.

A swordtail very close to the original "green" swordtail that with the platy crosses formed the basis for all the "swordtails" in our hobby today.

All varieties of color and form can be seen in modern swordtails. This tuxedo strain has fairly normal fins plus a well developed "sword" in the male.

XIPHOPHORUS MACULATUS (Günther)/*Platy*

Range: Mexico to Guatemala.
Habits: Peaceful and active. A very good community fish if not kept with soft-water species.
Water Conditions: Water should be slightly alkaline and medium-hard. Tank should be well planted and lighted. Temperature 70 to 80°F.
Size: Females up to 3 inches, males smaller.
Food Requirements: Takes all aquarium foods; also likes to pick algae from plants and aquarium ornaments.
Color Variations: An extreme variety of solid colors and combinations.

The Platy possesses every good point that is enjoyed by other livebearing species, and it is an improvement over many of the others in that it is a peaceful fish which never goes out of its way to make trouble. The Platy is an old scientific standby, for it was used in many experiments valuable in the fields of genetics and medicine. Like the Swordtail, it is a popular fish for beginners, and it is better suited to the beginner than the Swordtail because it is hardier, more peaceful, and smaller. This last factor is important, for it makes it possible to grow large, healthy Platies in less space than is required for Swordtails, and in much less space than is required to grow a good Molly. The dependably prolific Platy produces broods of young on an average of once a month, but this time can be shorter or longer, depending mainly on temperature. Many advanced hobbyists look askance at the Platy, considering it as nothing more than a beginner's fish, but other advanced hobbyists specialize in them after they have mastered many of the rarer and more expensive egglaying species. For sheer bright color, a good Platy can beat almost any other fish.

This is what is called a salt-and-pepper platy. This fish is a prize winner at an FTFFA show.

The pattern at the base of the tail of this type platy has been called a Mickey Mouse pattern.

Photo by Dr. Herbert R. Axelrod.

XIPHOPHORUS MONTEZUMAE (Jordan & Snyder)/*Mexican Swordtail*

Range: Rio Panuco, Mexico.
Habits: Peaceful with other species.
Water Conditions: Neutral to slightly alkaline medium-hard water is best; salt may be added, but is unnecessary. Temperature 68 to 78°F.
Size: Female 2½ inches, male 2 inches.
Food Requirements: Accepts all usual aquarium foods; also browses on algae.
Color Variations: Grayish-brown, with dark zigzag line at center of sides. Dorsal fin spotted.

This little livebearer is still seen occasionally, but it can never rival its Swordtail and Platy cousins in popularity, for it is a most drab fish in comparison to them. However, the wild Platies were not the beautiful fish they are today when first introduced to hobbyists, either, so it is possible that *X. montezumae* might someday blossom into an attractive species if some dedicated livebearer specialist expends on them the same effort and attention to detail that has been spent in making Guppies and Platies the gems they are today. The Mexican Swordtail is not as readily bred as its relatives, and it also has smaller broods, although the gestation period is about the same as in Platies and Swordtails. The species hardly merits the name "Swordtail" at all, as the male's sword is extremely short, shorter even than the stunted swords on many of the current Platy-Swordtail hybrids. *Xiphophorus montezumae* is valuable for its potential as an easily-hybridized species; they cross-breed fairly readily with other *Xiphophorus* species, especially *Xiphophorus variatus*.

XIPHOPHORUS PYGMAEUS (Hubbs & Gordon)/*Pygmy Swordtail*

Range: Rio Axtla, Mexico.
Habits: Peaceful toward other fishes and plants.
Water Conditions: Not critical as long as the water is clear and clean. Temperature
73 to 80°F.
Size: Males 2¼ inches, females slightly larger.
Food Requirements: All foods accepted.
Color Variations: Sides grayish with an indistinct horizontal stripe. Dorsal fin has
black edge.

For those who want to keep an unusual livebearer which demands very little
and is very hardy, we recommend the Pygmy Swordtail. Don't let the name
"Swordtail" fool you; there is no trace of a sword in the tail, even a short one.
The name exists because all of the other members of the genus *Xiphophorus*
have some sort of sword in the caudal fin. Of the three species, the Pygmy
Swordtail is the latest to be introduced as an aquarium fish, making its
appearance in 1939. In their native waters, the Swordtails live in clear,
running waters, and the Pygmy Swordtail has been found in streams which
were quite swift. Strangely enough, *X. pygmaeus* has not been used in
hybridization experiments, and doubtless this fish would lend itself very well
to this sort of thing. Perhaps it is better this way; there has been entirely too
much hybridizing done already, and it is scarcely possible to get pure-bred
livebearers of any kind any more. The Pygmy Swordtail is very undemanding
as an aquarium fish. It accepts any food, does not fight with its tankmates
and has young regularly which are just as hardy and easy to raise.

Photo by Dr. Herbert R. Axelrod.

XIPHOPHORUS VARIATUS (Meek) *Sunset Platy, Platy Variatus*

Range: Mexico.
Habits: Peaceful, active. Excellent for the community aquarium.
Water Conditions: About neutral, fairly hard is best but not essential. Temperature about 76°.
Size: Females about 2½ inches, males a little smaller.
Food Requirements: Will accept any and all foods, whether dry or living. Of course they should get living foods often for best results.
Color Variations: Very variable, no two males alike. Males have yellow to green body with black spots; dorsal yellow and tail red.

This very attractive livebearer has been bred to so many color varieties and hybridized by crossing with the *X. helleri* and *X. maculatus* that at the present time it is just as difficult to find the pure-bred original strain as it is to find a Guppy which has not yet responded to the breeder's touch. This is a very hardy fish, and the females make up for their almost complete lack of color by producing a great number of offspring regularly (some strains have colorful females). The fry are very easily raised, but try their owner's patience because the males do not show any color until after they have reached maturity. However, their beautiful colors are usually worth waiting for. Although they were first identified by Seth Meek in 1904 as *Platypoecilus variatus*, aquarists did not get to see them until 1932, when they scored an immediate hit and became one of the best-liked livebearing species. Today there are many color varieties, thanks to the variability of coloration and the breeder's art, plus the fact that it crosses readily with the other *Xiphophorus* species. A sunny spot and good plant growth is preferred by the Sunset Platy, and like its close relative the Molly it likes to pick algae.

F-608.00

COMPREHENSIVE INDEX

EXOTIC TROPICAL FISHES

covering the basic volume *and* inserts 1 through 257

The index following is a comprehensive index covering all of the four separate books (Aquarium Management, indicated by the prefix letter **M**; Plants, indicated by the prefix letter **P**; Commercial Breeding, indicated by the prefix letter **C**; and Fish, indicated by the prefix letter **F**) that constitute *EXOTIC TROPICAL FISHES.*

In addition, index entries are included for all of the supplement additions to the basic volume that are contained in Supplement Books 1 through 20.

PLEASE NOTE: Because this index combines references to both the original basic volume of *EXOTIC TROPICAL FISHES* and the supplements issued to the basic volume, the appearance of an entry in this index does not mean that the page referenced in the index will be contained in your book; in order to be in possession of all of the pages referenced, you must have available the entire book, including all of the supplements.

Page numbers ending in —.00 are contained in the basic volume; page numbers ending in any other decimal are contained in supplements. The only exception to this is the group of pages numbered F-494.161 through F-494.226.

This Index will be expanded periodically.

T.F.H. PUBLICATIONS, INC. LTD.
P.O. Box 27 • Neptune, N.J. 07753

116.00
Artificial Light, M-20.00-22.00
Arrowhead Tetra, **F-294.10**
Asellus aquaticus, M-54.00, **55.00**
Astronotus ocellatus, C-21.00, **F-90.10**,
  90.13; **F-91.00**, 184.00, 598.00
Astyanax, F-94.00
  bimaculatus, **F-92.00**
  mexicanus, F-38.00, **93.00**
  mutator, **F-94.00**
Atherinidae, F-116.00
Atipa, **F-333.00**
Aufwuchs, F-494.219
Aulonocara nyassae, **F-94.01-94.04**
Aureomycin, M-66.00, 69.00
Australian Pygmy Perch, **F-427.00**
Australian Rainbow, F-116.00, **393.00**
Australian Sleeper Goby, **F-154.00**
Austrofundulus dolichopterus, **F-94.05**,
  94.06
  myersi, **F-94.10**
  transilis, **F-94.07-94.08**
Award Winning Guppies, **F-370.10-**
  370.17
Axelrodia riesei, **F-94.12**, **94.13**
Azolla, P-18.00-21.00
  caroliniana, P-19.00-21.00, 69.00
  filiculoides, **P-19.00-21.00**, 69.00
  mexicana, P-19.00
  nilotica, P-19.00

B
Baby Fishes as Live Food, C-7.00,
  17.00, 20.00, 21.00; F-117.00,
  230.00, 317.00, 415.00, 571.00
Bacopa, P-8.14, **70.00**, 71.00
  amplexicaulis, **P-8.05-8.08**
  caroliniana, P-7.00, **8.00**, 69.00
Bacteria, P-77.00; C-20.00, 40.00;
  M-15.00, 72.00, 74.00, 107.00
Badis, F-95.00
  badis, **F-95.00**, 96.00; M-50.00,
  113.00
  badis burmanicus, **F-96.00**
Bait Fish, C-21.00
Bala Shark, **F-97.00**
Balanced Aquarium, P-3.00, 4.00;
  M-5.00, 6.00, 10.00
Balantiocheilus melanopterus, **F-97.00**
Banana Plant, **P-28.10-28.12**
Banded Barb, **F-109.00**, **150.00**, **516.00**
Banded Characidium, **F-170.00**
Banded Chromide, **F-279.00**
Banded Corydoras, **F-201.00**
Banded Ctenopoma, **F-236.00**

Banded Cynolebias, **F-244.00**
Banded Dwarf Sunfish, **F-265.00**
Banded Knife Fish, **F-303.00**
Banded Leporinus, **F-375.00**, 378.10
Banded Limia, **F-382.00**
Banded Loach, **F-126.00**
Banded Minnow, **F-44.00**
Banded Panchax, **F-273.00**
Banded Pyrrhulina, **F-521.00**
Bandit Catfish, **F-208.00**
Banka Rasbora, **F-524.10**
Barber's Tetra, **F-403.00**
Barbodes, F-100.00, 104.00, 106.00
  anema, F-113.00
  binotatus, **F-98.00**
  callipterus, **F-99.00**
  camptacanthus, **F-100.00**
  chlorotaenia, **F-112.00**
  dorsimaculatus, **F-101.00**
  dunckeri, **F-102.00**
  everetti, **F-103.00**
  fasciatus, **F-104.00**, 108.00
  fasciolatus, **F-105.00**
  hexazona, **F-106.00**, 109.00, 150.00
  holotaenia, **F-107.00**
  kerstenii, **F-108.10**, 108.11
  lateristriga, **F-108.00**
  pentazona, F-106.00, **109.00**, 150.00
  schwanenfeldi, **F-110.00**, 502.00
  unitaeniatus, **F-111.00**
  usumbarae, **F-112.00**
  viviparus, **F-113.00**
Barb(s), F-103.00, 105.00, 106.00,
  108.00, 109.00, 111.00-113.00,
  144.00, 148.00, 153.00, 253.00,
  263.00, 377.00, 502.00, 504.00-
  517.00, 529.00, 545.00; M-8.00,
  80.00
  African, F-105.00, 112.00, 113.00,
  149.00
  Asian, F-105.00, 513.00
Barbus, C-28.00
  bifasciatus, F-149.00
  bimaculatus, F-149.00
  multilineatus, F-100.00
  pobeguini, F-149.00
  sachsi, F-151.00
  schuberti, F-151.00
Barclaya, P-29.00, 72.00
  longifolia, P-29.00
  motleyi, P-29.00
Barilius christyi, **F-114.00**
Barred Hemiodus, **F-328.00**
Barred Loach, **F-128.00**, 439.00
Barred Pencilfish, **F-483.00**
Barred Siamese Catfish, **F-372.00**